**AN INTRODUCTION TO
DATA STRUCTURES
WITH APPLICATIONS**

McGRAW-HILL COMPUTER SCIENCE SERIES

RICHARD W. HAMMING, Bell Telephone Laboratories

EDWARD A. FEIGENBAUM, Stanford University

BELL AND NEWELL: Computer Structures: Readings and Examples
COLE: Introduction to Computing
DONOVAN: Systems Programming
GEAR: Computer Organization and Programming
GIVONE: Introduction to Switching Circuit Theory
HAMMING: Computers and Society
HAMMING: Introduction to Applied Numerical Analysis
HELLERMAN: Digital Computer System Principles
HELLERMAN AND CONROY: Computer System Performance
KAIN: Automata Theory: Machines and Languages
KOHAVI: Switching and Finite Automata Theory
LIU: Introduction to Combinatorial Mathematics
MADNICK AND DONOVAN: Operating Systems
MANNA: Mathematical Theory of Computation
NEWMAN AND SPROULL: Principles of Interactive Computer Graphics
NILSSON: Artificial Intelligence
RALSTON: Introduction to Programming and Computer Science
ROSEN: Programming Systems and Languages
SALTON: Automatic Information Organization and Retrieval
STONE: Introduction to Computer Organization and Data Structures
STONE AND SIEWIOREK: Introduction to Computer Organization and
        Data Structures: PDP-11 Edition
TONGE AND FELDMAN: Computing: An Introduction to Procedures
      and Procedure-Followers
TREMBLAY AND MANOHAR: Discrete Mathematical Structures with
        Applications to Computer Science
TREMBLAY AND SORENSON: An Introduction to Data Structures
       with Applications
WATSON: Timesharing System Design Concepts
WEGNER: Programming Languages, Information Structures, and
   Machine Organization
WINSTON: The Psychology of Computer Vision

McGRAW-HILL
BOOK COMPANY
New York
St. Louis
San Francisco
Auckland
Düsseldorf
Johannesburg
Kuala Lumpur
London
Mexico
Montreal
New Delhi
Panama
Paris
São Paulo
Singapore
Sydney
Tokyo
Toronto

J. P. TREMBLAY
P. G. SORENSON
Department of Computational Science
University of Saskatchewan, Saskatoon

An Introduction to Data Structures with Applications

This book was set in Modern 8A by Monotype Composition Company, Inc.
The editors were Kenneth J. Bowman and Michael Gardner;
the production supervisor was Dennis J. Conroy.
The drawings were done by ANCO Technical Services.
Fairfield Graphics was printer and binder.

Library of Congress Cataloging in Publication Data

Tremblay, Jean-Paul, date
    An introduction to data structures with applications.

    (McGraw-Hill computer science series)
    Includes bibliographies and index.
    1. Data structures (Computer science) 2. Electronic
digital computers—Programming. I. Sorenson, P. G.,
joint author. II. Title.
QA76.9.D35T73   001.6′442   75-34284
ISBN 0-07-065150-7

**AN INTRODUCTION TO
DATA STRUCTURES
WITH APPLICATIONS**

    8 9 0 FGRFGR 8 3 2 1 0

Dédié - Dedicated

À mes parents
Philippe et Anna
TREMBLAY

To my wife Linda,
and our daughter Kimberly
SORENSON

CONTENTS

Computer science is primarily concerned with the study of data (information) structures and their transformation by mechanical means. The importance of data structures is recognized in the ACM's "Curriculum 68" report[1] and the ACM's curriculum-committee reports on computer education for management and information systems [2,3,4] in courses entitled "Data Structures" and "Information Structures," respectively.

The first coherent and comprehensive treatment of data structures is due to Donald E. Knuth.[5] His great contribution to the area of data structures has influenced the organization and notation in Chaps. 3, 4, 5, and 6 of this book.

Most computer-science curricula have at least one course in data structures. However, in many instances such a course is given in the junior or senior year of study. This condition makes it difficult for the student to apply data-structure concepts to material taught in advance courses involving the manipulation of information (e.g., information-

[1] *CACM*, **11**, No. 9, pp. 172–173, 1968
[2] *CACM*, **14**, No. 9, pp. 573–588, 1971
[3] *CACM*, **15**, No. 5, pp. 363–398, 1972
[4] *CACM*, **16**, No. 12, pp. 727–749, 1973.
[5] "The Art of Computer Programming: Fundamental Algorithms," Addison-Wesley, Reading, Mass., 1968.

systems analysis and design, information storage and retrieval, operating systems, compiler construction, computer graphics, and artificial intelligence and heuristic programming). This book is an outgrowth of notes used in a two semester course given in the *second semesters of the first and second* years at the University of Saskatchewan. The reason for its appearance so early in the program is that the course is intended to introduce the student to concepts and terminology used in later courses. A desirable set of goals for a course in data structures is:

1 To introduce the student to those aspects of data structures which are required in subsequent computer science courses.
2 To motivate the student by illustrating the key concepts with various examples in computer science.
3 To increase the student's intuitive understanding of basic concepts.

New concepts should be introduced in a modular manner, i.e., in terms of previously understood concepts and in a way which permits the student to view computer science as a unified discipline. This cohesiveness can be achieved by trying to touch as many advanced courses as possible that require a knowledge of the basic structures introduced. Well-chosen applications can facilitate the realization of this goal and also greatly motivate the student. The course should attempt to introduce the student to terminology used in later courses. This approach will tend to generate a sense of familiarity at the beginning of such courses. We wish to emphasize that concepts and terminology should be introduced well before they are used. Otherwise, a student must invariably struggle with both the basic tools and the subject matter to which the tools are applied.

Although the applications which are discussed are meant to touch on as many areas of computer science as possible, an equally important goal is to emphasize the problem-solving process. Most students are employed by firms that require problem solvers. Many students find it difficult to formulate a problem by examining a particular situation within an organization. Frequently, such students upon finishing their studies are unable to structure a problem; indeed, they expect it to be already formulated.

Chapter 1 contains a discussion of the nature of information. Primitive data structures such as real, integer, character, pointer, etc. are introduced along with a number of storage representations which have been used on different computers. The concepts of number conversion and codes are briefly discussed.

The second chapter deals with the topic of string manipulation. A discussion of two formal systems for string manipulation is given—namely, the Markov formalism and the formal grammar. Using this approach a number of desirable primitive operations for string manipulation and pattern matching can be determined. Their derivations are also motivated by considering certain string-processing applications such as a text-editing system and the KWIC (Key Word In Context) indexing system.

Chapter 3 is concerned with linear data structures such as arrays, stacks, queues, double-ended queues, etc. and the associated operations that can be performed on these structures. A number of possible storage structures, based on sequential allocation, are discussed. The topic of recursion (and its implementation) is dealt with in some detail, since many programming languages permit its use. The concept of recursion is important in its own right because students will encounter throughout their career problems where recursion is unavoidable, because of the recursive nature of the process or because of the recursive structure of the data. The **ALLOCATE** and **FREE** features of PL/I are mentioned. A number of applications in linear data structures such as the compilation of expressions in Polish notation and the simulation of a simple "timesharing" system are given.

Chapter 4 deals with the storage representation of linear data structures based on linked storage allocation. The **POINTER** and **BASED** attributes of PL/I are described. Doubly linked and circular structures are also discussed. Applications such as symbol-table construction and multiple-precision arithmetic are presented.

Chapter 5 gives a comprehensive description of nonlinear structures and their sequential and linked representations in storage. The most important nonlinear structures are trees, and their representations and manipulations are discussed at some length. Furthermore, a number of applications such as dictionary construction and decision tables are included. Multilinked structures are also described. Graph structures and certain relevant applications such as PERT and CPM networks and computer graphics are presented. Finally, the topic of dynamic storage management is introduced.

Chapter 6 describes internal searching and sorting techniques. Searching methods based on binary trees and hashing techniques are introduced. Sorting methods such as the Quicksort, Heapsort, and Mergesort are described in some detail. A comparison of these methods is made, and it is shown that the performance of certain methods can be significantly improved by choosing an appropriate data structure (and an associated storage structure).

Finally, Chap. 7 contains a rather comprehensive description of external files. External storage devices are described, since their characteristics are important in file design and manipulation. A number of file organizations such as sequential, index sequential, and random are introduced. Certain multiple-key file organizations such as multilists and inverted lists are also discussed. A number of applications are introduced for most of the types of files mentioned. Among the applications considered are a small billing system, an on-line banking system, and a student-records retrieval system. Data-base management systems are briefly introduced.

The emphasis of the course is on problem solving, algorithms, and, to a lesser extent, on programming. We have strived to make sure that new concepts are well illustrated by examples and worked-out problems. The approach used in teaching the courses is modular—more complex structures are viewed in terms of simpler structures. The ordering is primitive data structures, linear data structures, trees, multilinked structures, graphs (lists), and files.

The selection of the programming language(s) used to solve the problems in the exercises is an integral part of the problem-solving process. Ideally, the student should select the language which facilitates a "painless" formulation of the solution for a problem. While numerous special-purpose languages exist for particular application areas, it is unrealistic to expect the student to be fluent in all such languages. Special features from a wide variety of languages are discussed in the text; however, all the exercises are completed in a language with which the students are familiar and which contains the following features:

1   Character strings of dynamically varying length.
2   Structure variables, i.e., variables which can contain elements with a mixture of data types.

3 Facilities which allow the programmer to create and destroy instances of variables (including structure variables) dynamically.

4 Recursion.

5 Control structures which promote the proper structuring of programs.

Suitable programming languages are ALGOL W, PL/I, and SNOBOL (although the control structures in SNOBOL are deficient in terms of feature 5). FORTRAN is the antithesis of the language to be used (it fails to have any of the five features). We have chosen PL/I as the main language because it provides the file-accessing facilities required.

Although a number of texts are available on data structures, few texts give a comprehensive treatment of files in terms of simpler structures that have been introduced in the same text. In addition, no text that we have encountered has been written adopting the philosophy and organization we are suggesting.

This book is suitable for course I1, Data Structures, of "Curriculum 68"[6] and for courses UC1 and UC3 in the "Curriculum Recommendations for Undergraduate Programs in Information Systems" report.[7] We do not follow the outlines of these courses exactly but the book is close enough to preserve their spirits. A basic familiarity with PL/I is assumed.

We owe a great deal to John A. Copeck who made many valuable criticisms and suggestions throughout the entire preparation and proofreading of the book. In particular, John A. Copeck assisted in the preparation of Secs. 5-2.2, 5-5.1, and 5-6. We also owe a lot to Richard F. Deutscher who formulated and tested many programs and assisted in the formulation of Secs. 4-3.3, 5-3.1, 5-5.4, 7-1, and 7-3. We appreciate the efforts of Linda Nylander who did many of the figures and assisted in the preparation of Secs. 3-7.1, 3-9, 5-2.4, 5-4.2, and 5-5.2.

We also acknowledge Walter Ridgway's assistance in the preparation of Secs. 2-5.4, 7-5, 7-7, and 7-9. Richard Cooper assisted us in the index-generation application and Lorna Stewart prepared all of the figures in Chap. 7. Allan Listoe proofread most of the manuscript and tested a number of programs. Finally, Robert Kavanagh assisted us in Sec. 5-5.2 and Richard Bunt proofread Secs. 3-9, 7-1, and 7-2. We owe a very special thanks to Dianne Good and Doreen Baker who did such an excellent job of typing the manuscript and to Gail Walker for providing typing support. This work would not have been possible without the support given by the University of Saskatchewan.

In conclusion, we would like to thank Doug Bulbeck, Joe Wald, and Darwin Peachey for assisting us in the preparation of the Teacher's Guide.

J. P. TREMBLAY

P. G. SORENSON

[6] ibid 1
[7] ibid 4

0

INTRODUCTION

We begin this chapter with a discussion outlining the importance of structuring not only the data pertaining to the solution of a problem, but also the programs that operate on the data. The task of formulating a solution to a problem is made simpler if the problem can be analyzed in terms of subproblems. This structuring process in problem solving is usually reflected in the program for the problem—the program tends to be modular. This approach to problem solving and organization has had a profound impact on the design of many programming languages, in particular, the design of "goto-less" languages. Processes, or modules concerned with operations performed on data structures, are frequently represented by subroutines or functions. For the program implementation of any significant problem the organization of a program into suitable modules or subroutines is indispensable. The simple way to write programs is to organize them in such a modular fashion. The algorithms and programs presented in this text are written with this philosophy in mind.

In the second and final section of this chapter, a description of the algorithmic notation adopted throughout the text is introduced and illustrated with examples.

0-1   STRUCTURE AND PROBLEM SOLVING

Problems solved on digital computers have become progressively larger and more complex. The computer programs providing the solutions to such problems have grown larger and more difficult to understand. The programmer(s) responsible for implementing the solutions to these large problems are given volumes of information consisting of problem specifications and flowcharts.

The task of writing a computer program is made simpler if the problem can be analyzed in terms of subproblems. This structuring process in problem solving is usually reflected in the program for the problem with the result being a modular program consisting of a number of small parts.

The concept of modularity in programs is not new. There have been for some years now a number of operating systems which have been constructed in a modular fashion. The computer manufacturer supplies the user with an operating system which consists of many program modules. The user can choose and construct his own particular operating system for his environment by selecting an appropriate set of modules. The selected modules can be tuned to a particular operating environment by assigning system parameters representative of that environment. Also, since the operating system program is in a continual state of change, changes can be made much more easily if the entire program is divided into a number of program modules whose interrelationships are simple and clearly defined.

A complex program usually cannot be written as a set of program modules unless its solution is structured or organized in that way. The programming of large problems usually involves many programmers, and the decisions made by one programmer, such as the choosing of labels and variable names, should not affect other programmers. This can only be accomplished if the description and specifications of each program module and its interfaces are made as clear and simple as possible. Indeed, for certain problems, the tasks of organizing and defining the problems are much more time-consuming and costly than the task of programming them.

The modularity of most systems can be represented by a hierarchical structure (graph) such as that given in Fig. 0-1.1.

The structure has a *single* main module, with which we associate a level number of 1, that gives a brief general description of the system. The main module refers to a number of subordinate modules, with which we associate a level of 2, that give a more detailed description of the system than was done in the main module. The modules at level 2 refer to a further subdivision of modules at level 3, and so on. It is quite possible that modules at higher levels refer to modules at lower levels (this would be indicated by upward pointing arrows in the diagram), although this was not the case in Fig. 0-1.1 and is not the case in general. The concept of hierarchically structuring a problem in this fashion is a fundamental one in problem solving. It is this form of organization or structuring which permits us to understand a system at different levels and allows us to make changes at one level without having to completely understand more detailed descriptions at higher levels. Also important in this hierarchical structuring process is the desirability of being able to understand a module at a certain level independently of all remaining modules at that same level.

Ideally, a program will be structured similar to that described in the previous dia-

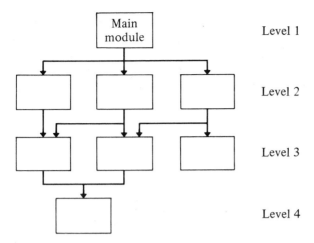

Level 1

Level 2

Level 3

Level 4

FIGURE 0-1.1   Hierarchical structure of a system.

gram. This ideal modular structure does not necessarily imply that there is a direct correspondence between the flow of control in the program and the interconnections between subproblem modules. It is true that in most instances a module corresponds to a subroutine or procedure, but it is entirely possible that a problem module does not have any executable statements associated with it.

The best example of such a module is one which describes the organization of information required for communication between other modules. In such a module we are concerned with structuring the information to facilitate easily understood and efficient methods of information access. Of course, such methods involve the use of appropriate data structures with efficient storage representations. Hence, the hierarchical structuring of program modules and submodules should not only reduce the complexity of the flow of control in program statements, but should also promote the proper structuring of information.

Thus far we have discussed the desirability of organizing the solution to a problem into a number of modules which can be understood independently. The modules in such a structural system correspond to concepts in the programmer's mind when he attempts to understand the problem. Indeed, greater independency between the modules in general implies greater clarity and distinctness in these concepts.

In organizing a solution to a problem which is to be solved with the aid of a computer, we are confronted with at least four interrelated subproblems. The subproblems are:

1   To understand thoroughly the relationships between the data elements that are relevant to the solution of the problem.

2   To decide on the operations that must be performed on the logically related data elements.

3   To devise methods of representing the data elements in the memory of the computer such that (*a*) the logical relationships which do exist between data items can best be retained, and/or (*b*) the operations on the data elements can be accomplished easily and efficiently.

4 To decide on what problem-solving (programming) language can best aid in the solution of the problem by allowing the user to express in a "natural" manner the operations he or she wishes to perform on the data.

Let us examine, more closely, each of these subproblem areas.

To understand the logical relationships between the data items in the problem implies that we must understand the data itself. (Of course, to have a good understanding of the data, we must first of all take great care in the preparation and recording of the data!) Data in a particular problem consist of a set of elementary items or atoms. An atom usually consists of single elements such as integers, bits, characters, or a set of such items. A person solving a particular problem is concerned with establishing paths of accessibility between atoms of data. The choice of atoms of data is a necessary and key step in defining and then solving a problem. The possible ways in which the data items or atoms are logically related define different *data structures*. By choosing a particular structure for the data items, certain items become immediate neighbors, while other sets of items are related in a weaker sense. The interpretation of two items being immediate neighbors is that of adjacency relative to the ordering relation that may be imposed by the structure.

It is important to point out that the class of concepts dealing with data structures has become increasingly important in recent years. Initially, computers were used to solve primarily numerical scientific problems, but this has changed drastically with the emergence of many nonnumerical problems. Associated with the solution of numerical problems were rather primitive data structures such as variables, vectors, and arrays. These structures were, for most cases, adequate for the solution of numerical problems. However, in the solution of nonnumerical problems, these primitive data structures were clearly not sufficiently powerful to specify the more complex structural relationships in the data.

We turn to the second subproblem, that is, to decide on the operations which must be performed on the data structures that are to be used. A number of operations can be performed on data structures—operations to create and to destroy a data structure, operations to insert elements into and delete elements from a data structure, and operations to access elements within a data structure. Of course, these operations vary functionally for different data structures (for example, in Chap. 3 we will discover that the insert operation for a queue differs from the corresponding operation for a stack). The operations associated with a given data structure may be implemented as a set of fairly sophisticated algorithmic processes in a particular language, or these operations may be realized through basic instructions in the programming language that is used. Which situation occurs depends on the data structures being used and the programming languages that are available. For either case, the way in which data are manipulated is dependent on how the data structure is to be represented in memory—the third subproblem.

The representation of a particular data structure in the memory of a computer is called a *storage structure*. The distinction between a data structure and its corresponding storage structure is often confused. It frequently leads to a loss of efficiency and prevents the problem solver from making optimal use of his tools and resources. There are many possible memory configurations or storage structures corresponding to a particular data structure. For example, there are a number of possible storage structures for a data structure such as an array. It is also possible for two data structures to be represented by the same storage structure. In many instances, almost exclusive attention is directed towards the storage structures for certain given data and little attention is given to the data structure per se. In essence, there is significant confusion between the properties that belong to the interpretation and meaning of the data on the one hand and the storage structures that can be selected to represent them in a programming system on the other hand.

In discussing storage structures, we will be concerned with representing data structures in both the main and the auxiliary memory of the computer. A storage structure representation in auxiliary memory is often called a *file structure*.

The fourth subproblem which we posed earlier related to the selection of a programming language to be used in the solution of the problem. If the representation for a data structure does not exist in the programming language being used, then the program for a particular algorithm may be quite complex. For example, in a payroll (data processing) application, a tree-like representation of information for an employee may be required. This structure does not exist in certain programming languages, such as FORTRAN. This does not mean that we cannot program a payroll application in FORTRAN. It could be done by writing programs to construct and manipulate trees; but this would be complex. It would be more suitable to use a data-processing language such as COBOL in this case. Ideally, the programming language chosen for the implementation of an algorithm should possess the particular representations chosen for the data structures in the problem being solved. In practice, the choice of a language may be dictated by what is available at a particular computing center, what language is preferred by some key personnel, etc.

It is clear from the above discussion that data structures, their associated storage structures, and the operations on data structures are all integrally related to problem solving using a computer. These three aspects will be examined in great detail in this text.

A fourth aspect, that of selecting an appropriate language in which to express a programmed solution to a problem, will not be rigorously pursued. However, whenever possible, we will be introducing programming language concepts from a variety of languages, especially as these concepts relate to the expressibility of a data structure and its associated operations.

A number of applications will be discussed in a comprehensive manner throughout the book. The problem-solving aspects of many applications will be examined in three stages, as follows:

1 The selection of an appropriate mathematical model (including data structures)
2 The formulation of algorithms based on the choice made in stage *1*
3 The design of storage structures for the data structures obtained in stage *1*

The next section gives a description of the algorithmic notation which will be used to express the algorithms discussed throughout the book.

0-2 ALGORITHMIC NOTATION

The notation for algorithms used in this book is best described with the aid of examples. Consider the following algorithm for determining the largest algebraic element of a vector.

Algorithm GREATEST.   This algorithm finds the largest algebraic element of vector **A** which contains n elements and places the result in **MAX**. i is used as a subscript to **A**.

1.   [Is the vector empty?]   If n $<$ 1 then print **message** and **Exit.**
2.   [Initialize]   Set MAX $\leftarrow$ A[1], i $\leftarrow$ 2.   (We assume initially that A[1] is the greatest element.)
3.   [All done?]   Repeat steps 4 and 5 while i $\leq$ n.
4.   [Exchange MAX if it is smaller than next element]   If MAX $<$ A[i] then set MAX $\leftarrow$ A[i].
5.   [Get next subscript]   Set i $\leftarrow$ i $+$ 1.
6.   [Finished]   **Exit.**

The algorithm is given an identifying name (**GREATEST**, in this example); this name is followed by a brief description of the tasks the algorithm performs, thus providing an identification for the variables used in the algorithm. This description is followed by the actual algorithm—a sequence of numbered steps.

Every algorithm step begins with a phrase enclosed in square brackets which gives an abbreviated description of that step. Following this phrase is an ordered sequence of statements which describes actions to be executed or tests to be performed. Note that, in general, the statements in each step must be executed from left to right in order. An algorithm step may terminate with a comment enclosed in parentheses that is intended to help the reader better understand the step. The comments specify no action and are included only for clarity.

Step 2 in the example algorithm contains the arrow symbol "$\leftarrow$" which is used to denote the assignment operator. The statement MAX $\leftarrow$ A[1] is taken to mean that the value of the vector element A[1] is to replace the contents of the variable MAX. In this algorithmic notation, the symbol " $=$ " is used as a relational operator and never as an assignment operator. One assignment statement, or a group of several assignment statements separated by commas, is preceded by the word 'set'. The action of incrementing i by one in step 5 is indicated by i $\leftarrow$ i $+$ 1. Many variables can be set to the same value by using multiple assignments. The statements i $\leftarrow$ 0, j $\leftarrow$ 0, and k $\leftarrow$ 0 could be rewritten as the single statement i $\leftarrow$ j $\leftarrow$ k $\leftarrow$ 0. An exchange of the values of two variables (as accomplished by the sequence of statements TEMP $\leftarrow$ AL, AL $\leftarrow$ B, B $\leftarrow$ TEMP) will sometimes, for convenience, be written as AL $\leftrightarrow$ B. Observe that subscripts for arrays are enclosed in square brackets. Thus, A[4] is the fourth element of array A.

The execution of an algorithm begins at step 1 and continues from there in sequential order unless the result of a condition tested or an unconditional transfer (a "go to") specifies otherwise. In the same sample algorithm, step 1 is first executed. If vector A is empty, the algorithm terminates; otherwise, step 2 is performed in which MAX is initialized to the value of A[1] and the subscript variable, i, is set to 2. Step 3 leads to the termination of the algorithm if we have already tested the last element of A. Otherwise, step 4 is taken. In this step, the value of MAX is compared with the value of the next element of the vector. If MAX is less than the next element, then MAX is set to this new value. If the test fails, no reassignment takes place. The completion of step 4 is followed by step 5, where the next subscript value is set; control then returns to the testing step, step 3.

Throughout the text an element of a vector may be denoted either by A_i or by A[i]; in an algorithm, such an array reference would appear as A[i], while in PL/I programs, such a reference would appear as A(I). Variables, in algorithms, are usually written in capital letters (e.g., MAX and A), but single-letter variables used as loop counters, subscripts, or string position indices, etc., appear in the lower case.

Two of the more complicated instructions available for use as statements in algorithm steps are the *if-statement* and the *repeat-statement*. These are now described in more detail.

The if-statement has one of the following forms:

1 If____,then____,____, . . .,____.
2 if____,then____,____, . . . ; otherwise____,____, . . .,____.

Following the "then" is an ordered sequence of statements which are all to be executed if the condition tested is true. Unless a **'go to'** must be followed, control then passes to the first statement after the if-statement. A semi-colon (type *2*) or the period (type *1*) terminates the range of the then-clause. If the tested condition is false, then either the next statement (type *1*) is executed or the ordered sequence of statements following the "otherwise" (type *2*) is executed. In this latter case, when the otherwise-clause has been completed, control goes to the next statement (unless there was a **'go to'** in the otherwise-clause). If-statements can be nested within other if-statements, but in an effort to improve the reader's understanding of algorithms, we try to avoid the excessive nesting of ifs and the nesting of ifs within then-clauses.

To provide for easy control of iteration, a repeat statement has been provided. This statement has one of the following forms:

1 Repeat for index = sequence:____,____, . . .,____.
2 Repeat steps n and n + 1 for index = sequence.
3 Repeat steps n to p for index = sequence.
4 Repeat steps n to p while logical expr.

Type *1* is used to repeat the group of statements immediately following the colon in the same algorithm step. This group is terminated by a period. Type *2* is simply a special case of type *3*. Type *3* is used to repeat, in order, all the steps in the indicated range of steps. **'index'** is simply some variable of the algorithm used as a loop counter, while **'sequence'** is some representation of the sequence of values that **'index'** will successively take. The starting value, the final value, and the increment size must be indicated in some way by the representation chosen. For example, **'repeat for i = 1, 2, ..., 25: ___.'**, **'repeat for TOP = n + k, n + k −1, ..., 0:____.'**, **'repeat steps 5 and 6 for k = 9, 11, ..., 2 ∗ MAX + 1.'** are various examples of valid repeat statements. Type *4* is used to repeat, in order, steps n through p repeatedly until the logical expression is false. The evaluation and testing of the logical expression is performed at the beginning of the loop, and semantically the statement is similar to the while-clause in PL/I. As soon as all the statements in the range of a repeat statement are executed, the index assumes the next value in the sequence of values, and the statements in the range are executed in order once again. We assume testing of an index for completion takes place prior to execution of any statement so that a repeat statement may, in fact, result in the loop being executed zero times. For example, **'repeat for i = −1, −2, ..., 10'** and **'repeat for k = 5, 6, ..., −17'** would not cause any statements to be executed; instead, the repeat statements would be treated as having completed their execution. As soon as a repeat statement has finished its execution, control is transferred to the first statement outside the range of the repeat statement. If, however, a 'go to' is encountered during the execution of a repeat statement and control is transferred out of its range, then the repeat statement is considered to have finished its execution. The control is transferred to the step referenced by the 'go to'.

Note however the following segment:

.

.

.

6. [Initialize counter]   Set COUNT ← 0.
7. [Processing loop]   Repeat steps 8 and 9 for i = 1, 2, ..., n.
8. [Get number]   Read A[i].
9. [Count if negative]   If A[i] < 0, then set COUNT ← COUNT + 1.
10. [Output results]   Print COUNT.

.

.

.

If n has the value 5 and the first numbers in the data stream are 7, 4, −3, −2, 6, −17, 8, ..., then the number 2 will be printed in step 10 because step 8 and 9 will execute five times. The if-statement in step 9 does *not* cause control to go to step 10 when it has finished execution. Instead, control is returned to the repeat-statement where the index is incremented and steps 8 and 9 are executed once again. (You may think of these steps 8 and 9 as including a CONTINUE-like statement immediately after the if-statement.)

Since many of the applications we will be concerned with involve nonnumeric processing (i.e., symbol manipulation rather than "number-crunching"), it was felt advisable to incorporate into the algorithmic notation certain features that facilitate the processing of nonnumeric information. These features are provided as an addition to those standard mathematical functions and operations which one would expect to find useful in most applications. The programs appearing throughout are written in PL/I. Consequently, we pattern the nonnumeric processing features after certain PL/I operations or functions. For example, in Chap. 2 we add the string manipulation functions LENGTH, INDEX, and SUB which are patterned after PL/I's LENGTH, INDEX, and SUBSTR functions, respectively.

In the remaining chapters of the book, we will introduce additional algorithmic notation to represent new operations on data structures. This new notation will be explained and illustrated when it is required.

1

INFORMATION AND ITS
STORAGE REPRESENTATION

To begin a study of data (or information) structures, it is necessary to establish clearly what is meant by information, how information is transmitted, and how (in its most basic form) information is stored in a computer. It is not our intention to delve deeply into questions concerning the nature of information and information transmittal; for us to do so would involve an intensive study in information and communication theory. However, we do wish to discuss information and its transmission and storage from a clear and simplistic viewpoint so that the student of information structures can appreciate what information is and how it is physically handled.

In the latter part of this chapter, we relate the earlier discussion on information concepts to a description of the primitive data structures commonly used to solve problems with a computer. The primitive data structures we introduce are the integers, reals, logical data, character *data, and* pointer data. *In the discussion of each primitive data structure, its storage representation will be emphasized.*

1-1   THE NATURE OF INFORMATION

It can be said that the study of any aspect in computer science involves the storage, retrieval, and manipulation of information. For example, information is stored when a student's record file is updated with term marks. Information is retrieved when a compiler requests, for translation, the next source language instruction from a program source file. And, information is manipulated when two numbers are added together in the arithmetic unit of a computer. Hence, students' marks, program instructions, and numbers are all information. In this context, we can define information as recorded or communicated material that has some meaning associated with its symbolic representation.

Can we measure information? For example, how much information is there in a student's mark? Does program *A* contain more information than program *B*? Because the answer to such questions are very basic to computer science, as well as to other areas of research (e.g., psychology, business management, and communication engineering), a separate field of study called *information theory* has evolved. In this section we introduce basic notions from information theory to provide some understanding of the nature of information.

In an attempt to discover a "yardstick" for measuring information, Hartley [1928], Kolmogoroff [1942], Wiener [1948], and Shannon [1949] have presented formal definitions for information content. In an information theoretic sense, information is viewed as the resolution of uncertainty. Suppose we are given a set of *n* configurations (or data items) of any system in which each configuration has an independent probability of occurrence p_i. Then the *uncertainty* of the set is defined as

$$H = -\sum_{i=1}^{n} p_i \log_2(p_i) \tag{1-1.1}$$

To illustrate how Eq. (1-1.1) is applied, assume we have eight poker chips numbered on one side, 1 through 8. Suppose the chips are placed on a table, numbered-side down, and we select one chip from the set of eight. We might ask: "What is the number on the selected chip?" Or, phrasing the question in terms of the measurement of uncertainty, how much uncertainty is there associated with the identity of the chip before we turned the chip over? We know that with probability $\frac{1}{8}$ the chip is marked with a given number for all numbers between 1 and 8. Therefore, if we apply Eq. (1-1.1), the average uncertainty associated with the nature of the selected chip is

$$H = -\sum_{i=1}^{8} \frac{1}{8} \log_2\left(\frac{1}{8}\right) = -\log_2\left(\frac{1}{8}\right) = \log_2(8) = 3 \text{ bits}$$

Notice that we have assigned a unit of measure, namely *bits*, to the measure of uncertainty of the set. A bit is a measure of uncertainty (or information) which represents the presence of a two-state condition, as exemplified by an on-off condition or a true-false condition. Observe that we have said a bit is both a measure of uncertainty and of information. This association is intentional, since the amount of information gained can be equated with the amount of uncertainty that is removed upon discovering the nature of an information source, such as the number on a chip. If one asks the question: "Is Bill's dog brown?," then the uncertainty involving the color of Bill's dog can be removed by answering correctly yes or no. Because an answer, whether it be yes or no, arises from a

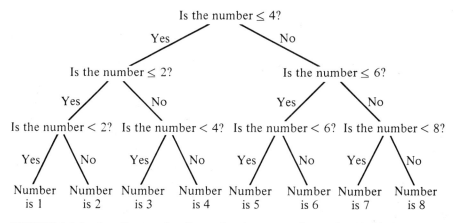

FIGURE 1-1.1 Question tree for discovering the nature of a numbered chip.

two-state condition, the amount of uncertainty removed or information gained by receiving a yes or no is one bit.

For the case of the selected numbered chip, we calculated that three bits of information were necessary to remove the uncertainty of the number on the chip. From our definition of bit, this would imply that if we were allowed to ask three "yes-no questions," the nature of the chip would be uncovered. In fact this is true! The "question tree" in Fig. 1-1.1 illustrates how the number of the chip can be discovered assuming correct yes-no answers are received for the questions.

The three bits of information associated with the discovery of the chip's number can be represented by a message of length three, composed of 0's and 1's (where a 1 represents a "yes" answer and a 0 represents a "no" answer). In Table 1-1.1, message scheme A represents all possible paths in the question tree where the ith bit, $i = 1, 2,$ or 3, in a message represents the ith question asked. Message scheme B illustrates that

Table 1-1.1 Message schemes representing the eight numbered chips.

Chip Number	Message Scheme A	Message Scheme B
1	111	001
2	110	010
3	101	011
4	100	100
5	011	101
6	010	110
7	001	111
8	000	000

scheme A is by no means unique, i.e., many three-bit schemes could be devised to represent the identity of each of the eight chips.

Note that if we had considered nine chips with numbers 1 to 9, a bit message of at least length four would be required. In fact, it has been shown (Reza [1961]) that for any coding scheme representing a set of n elements which are equally probable of being selected, at least one of the codes must have its length greater than or equal to the information measure of the set, that is,

$$H = -\sum_{i=1}^{n} p_i \log_2 p_i$$

Messages consisting of 0's and 1's are very important in the study of information structures. As we will observe in the next section when discussing the transfer of information, messages in a computer are of this form (i.e., strings of 0's and 1's). Our measure of average information content H, which yields a bound on message length, can be helpful in determining a good storage structure for a given data structure. In Chap. 7, for example, we will use this information measure to compute the efficiency of certain storage structures used for record organizations in files.

It would be misleading to imply that all information is measurable. For example, we can ask whether or not the information content on this page is the same for an undergraduate student as it is for a child of six. Obviously, it is not. A main ingredient necessary for information to be transferred is understanding. In communication theory, messages that are received, but not completely understood, are said to contain "noise." It is the problem of deciding what is noise and what is meaningful information that has prevented the application of information theory to everyday situations—situations such as measuring the information content of a lecture or measuring the information flow through a company.

Exercises for Sec. 1-1

1. Consider the probabilities associated with the event of rolling a pair of dice. The probability that a certain number shows is given in Table 1-1.2. Compute the average uncertainty H that is associated with the event of rolling a pair of dice.

Table 1-1.2

Rolled Amount	Probability	Rolled Amount	Probability
2	1/36	8	5/36
3	1/18	9	1/9
4	1/12	10	1/12
5	1/9	11	1/18
6	5/36	12	1/36
7	1/6		

2. Create a fixed-length binary code capable of representing each of the possible rolled amounts in Exercise 1. (By "fixed length," we mean that all codes are of the same length.) Compare the length of this code to the value computed in Exercise 1. Should it be higher or lower?

3. Design a variable-length binary code representing the rolled amounts in Exercise 1. The code should be designed so that if a number of events are recorded using this code, the average length of a code for these events is less than that derived in Exercise 2.

1-2   THE TRANSMISSION OF INFORMATION

Shannon [1949] depicts the process of transmitting information as a five-element system: a *source*, or originator of a message; a *transmitter*, or encoder of the message to be sent; a *channel*, the medium through which the message is conveyed; a *receiver*, or decoder of the message received; and a *destination*, or recipient of the information. These are illustrated in Fig. 1-2.1. An example of a communication system is a human (or human brain) as a source, his mouth, tongue, and other speech organs as a transmitter, air as the channel, the auditory system of another human as a receiver, and the brain of the receiving person as the destination. In a simple batch computer system, a deck of cards can be considered a source, the card reader a transmitter, a transmission line from the card reader to the computer mainframe a channel, a channel selector control unit a receiver, and main memory of the computer the destination.

   While the above discussion illustrates the physical components of an information transmission process, there are three aspects that must be considered to ensure the transfer of information between the source and destination. These are the syntactic, semantic, and pragmatic aspects (Morris [1946]). The *syntactic* aspect concerns the physical *form* of the information transmitted. For example, the syntactic aspect of the information received while reading this sentence is the form or shape of the ink blots of which it is constituted. The ink blots are recognized as letters from the English alphabet which are combined to form words, which in turn are combined to form a sentence. Through a sentence, a concept or concepts are expressed and meaning is associated with the syntactic form of the information. The *semantic* aspect refers to this *meaning*, which is attached to the syntactic representation. The *pragmatic* aspect of information transmission involves the *action* taken

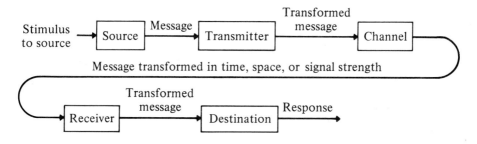

FIGURE 1-2.1   A diagram of a general communication system.

as a result of the interpretation (i.e., attached meaning) of the information. The actions taken as a result of the interpretation of the information often depend heavily on previous conditioning. For example, if we disagree with what is written in a particular book (based on previous experience), we may choose to close the book—possibly permanently.

Successful communication must take all three aspects into consideration. If we were to change the syntactic structure of the English language—as would be the case if "bl anks" were inserted within words—proper communication would be inhibited. Similarly, communication is inhibited if it is impossible to associate any semantics with the words. For example, what is the meaning of "Data evade lowly."? It is a syntactically correct English sentence, but has no accepted meaning. Of course, the pragmatic aspect (i.e., the action taken) depends on the semantic aspect just as the semantic aspect depends on the syntactic aspect. In the case of the sentence "Data evade lowly," the semantics are questionable. Hence, no action can be expected to follow—except possibly to reread the words.

A further example illustrating the relationship between the three aspects of information transfer can be drawn from the area of computer programming. For the successful execution of a PL/I program, the source statements must be syntactically correct. If a comma or semicolon is missing or appears in a wrong place, the statement is syntactically incorrect, and possibly an invalid interpretation may be given to the statement. (Again, the semantics depend on the syntactic form of the information.) Even if a source statement is syntactically correct, the semantic interpretation that the programmer and the compiler attach to the statement may differ. For example, we may write the statement

$$X = A + B * C;$$

wishing X to be assigned the expression $(A + B) * C$; whereas, the compiler may interpret the assigned expression as $A + (B * C)$. Of course, the pragmatic result or action of the compiler is to generate the machine code associated with $X = A + (B * C);$.

In summary, for information to be transferred successfully, it is necessary to have rules which are mutually accepted by the sender and the receiver regarding the syntactic and semantic aspects of the information, plus a set of appropriate actions taken in response to the meaning derived by the receiver.

In introducing the three aspects necessary for information transmission, we assumed that the transmission process should fall into the general class of communication systems as proposed by Shannon [1949] (see Fig. 1-2.1). It is interesting to note, however, that there are, in general, two methods of physically transmitting information: *continuous* and *discrete*.

Information transmitted in a continuous form appears as signals selected from a spectrum of amplitudal values, as illustrated in Fig. 1-2.2. The classical example of continuous-information transmission takes place in verbal communication which relies on the frequency and amplitude of sound waves.

Information transmitted in a discrete form appears as signals which may only assume a finite number of states within a continuum of amplitudal values. For example, the presence and absence of a pulse can represent a discrete form of information, such as a true-false or an on-off condition. This is illustrated in Fig. 1-2.3. Notice a cutoff point exists for determining if the pulse is on or off. Written text provides us with a classical ex-

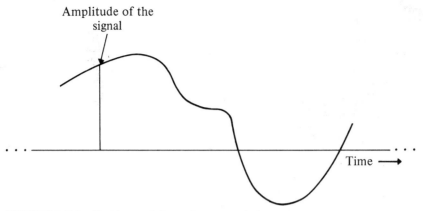

FIGURE 1-2.2   Continuous information transmission.

ample of a method of communication which relies on discrete-information transmission. That is, whether we write "DATA" or "data," we receive the same information. Even though each person has his or her own writing style, we always attempt, when interpreting a piece of written English text, to resolve each symbol to one of twenty-six different letters from the English alphabet. Of course, the twenty-six letters represent the finite number of states that characterize discrete information transmission.

Analog computers are designed to store, retrieve, and manipulate information which is continuous in nature. These types of computers are particularly well suited to the solution of linear, integral, and differential equations as might be required, for example, in controlling a fractionation process where the composition and amount of gas in a fractionation tower is regulated. Based on information representing the correct composition of raw materials entering the tower, plus current temperature and pressure readings, a new temperature setting is calculated via a control law. This control law has been "programmed" (i.e., hardwired) into the integrating and differentiating circuitry of the analog computer. All readings, settings, and calculations are in the form of continuous signals.

An analog computer does not have the speed, computational ability and, above all, the accuracy to handle the processing needs of many of the common computer applications such as payroll accounting. In fact, even in process control applications like the fractionation tower example, the analog computer is not completely satisfactory and is being replaced by the more expensive, yet computationally superior, digital computer or by a combination of digital and analog computers known as *hybrid computers* (see Smith [1970]).

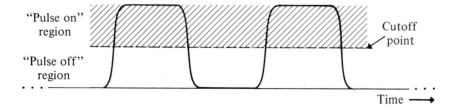

FIGURE 1-2.3   On-off (two-state) discrete information transmission.

In a digital computer, all information is transferred in a discrete form which involves signals representing one of two states. The binary signals are created by the presence or absence of an electrical current, or the presence of a positive or a negative current. Certain research efforts have been made toward the development of nonbinary computers (especially ternary computers); however, such computers are still at a testing stage, as to date they are much less reliable than binary computers.

Throughout the remainder of this text we are interested in the storage, retrieval, and processing of discrete information (more precisely, information represented in a binary encoded form) by digital computers. There are two types of discrete information present in digital computers; namely, machine instructions (or operations) and the data which are to be manipulated by these operations. In our study of data structures, we are primarily concerned with the organization of the data to solve a problem for a particular application. However, associated with a data structure is a particular set of operations needed to properly access information in that structure. Therefore, in discussing how information should be structured, we will also be concerned with the operations for accessing the information. The operations we consider will be presented in a high-level language such as PL/I; however, such high-level operations are translatable to a functionally equivalent set of machine-level operations.

1-3   THE STORAGE OF INFORMATION

In a digital computer there are two types of memory units; namely, operational units and storage units. The name that is commonly associated with an operational unit is a *register*. A register is used for the temporary storage and the manipulation of information.

Some of the most important registers are contained in the central processing unit (CPU) of the computer. The CPU contains registers (sometimes called accumulators) which hold the arguments (i.e., operands) of arithmetic computations. Some very complex integrated circuitry allows the information which is stored in the accumulators to be added, subtracted, multiplied, and divided. In addition, certain bits of the accumulator can be tested to determine if the normal sequence of control in a program should be altered (e.g., the testing of a particular bit in an accumulator designated as the sign bit of a number to see if a branch should be taken based on a negative value). Besides storing operands and the results from arithmetic operations, registers are also used to store temporarily program instructions and control information concerning which instruction is to be executed next. Because of their highly specialized nature, registers have a great deal of combinational logic (i.e., circuitry) associated with them. This makes them expensive relative to storage-type memory units in a computer. Consequently, registers are only used to store information temporarily.

The storage-type memory unit is designed to store information which is more permanent in nature. For example, a particular storage unit or set of storage units are associated with a particular variable in a program. However, to perform arithmetic computations involving a variable, it is required that the value of the variable, as stored in the memory unit, be transferred to a register unit before the computation can be performed. The transfer must take place because memory units do not have the necessary logic associated with them (or between them) to effect arithmetic operations. If the result of a computation is to be assigned to a variable, the resultant value must be transferred from an arithmetic register back to the memory unit associated with the variable.

When a program is executed, its instructions and data generally reside in storage units. The entire set of storage units in the main frame or main part of a computer is often called *main memory*. Later, in Chap. 7, we discover that in some instances programs can also reside in storage units which do not belong to main memory. Examples of such storage-unit devices (often called *secondary storage devices*) are magnetic disks and drums.

In the remainder of this section, we will concentrate on describing how information is stored in main memory, since it is in main memory that the instructions and data are stored for programs in execution. Currently, there are primarily two types of main memory in use: core memory and semiconductor memory. While a number of new technologies are making other kinds of storage-type memory units feasible we focus our discussion on the two types which are popularly used. The discussion to follow is not completely accurate for all core or semiconductor memories; nevertheless, it presents a representative picture.

A magnetic core storage unit uses magnetic cores to store binary information. A magnetic core is a doughnut-shaped toroid of magnetic material. One bit of information is stored in each core, and the nature of a core (i.e., whether it currently represents a zero or a one) is determined by the direction of the magnetic flux within the core.

Cores reside in planes within the computer and three wires are wound through each core, as illustrated in Fig. 1-3.1. A particular core is addressed by the x and y lines which run through it. To read a core, pulses in the form of negative currents are applied to the x and y lines. The combined effect of these pulses can cause the magnetic flux in the core to change direction. If prior to a read the magnetic flux in the core is in the positive direction (the "one" direction), then the negative currents applied to the x and y lines cause the flux to change to the negative or "zero" direction. This change in flux induces a difference in potential (or voltage) in the third line—the sense line. If the magnetic flux in the core is in the negative or zero direction prior to the application of pulses to the x and y lines, then a change in flux does not take place and a current is not produced in the sense line. Therefore, the absence of the current in the sense line shows that the core had a zero value stored, and the presence of a current in the sense line means the core had a one value stored.

The process just described allows core units to be read. Note that the reading process is a destructive process, since all cores which are read are set to zero. Therefore, it is required that a rewrite phase must be undertaken to restore the affected memory units to their previous state. The rewrite is undertaken immediately after the initial read phase.

A combination of two negative pulses or two positive pulses on the x and y lines of any core can shift the direction of magnetization in that core. Hence the write process (and also the rewrite phase of the read process) can be accomplished by applying a set of pulses just once.

The two processes, read and write, are the only processes required of a storage unit. As stated earlier, information read from core is transmitted to registers for processing, and results which are present in registers are written into core if a more permanent record of these results is desired.

The second type of commonly used storage is semiconductor memory. A semiconductor memory unit (see Fig. 1-3.2) is made up of special sequential and combinatorial

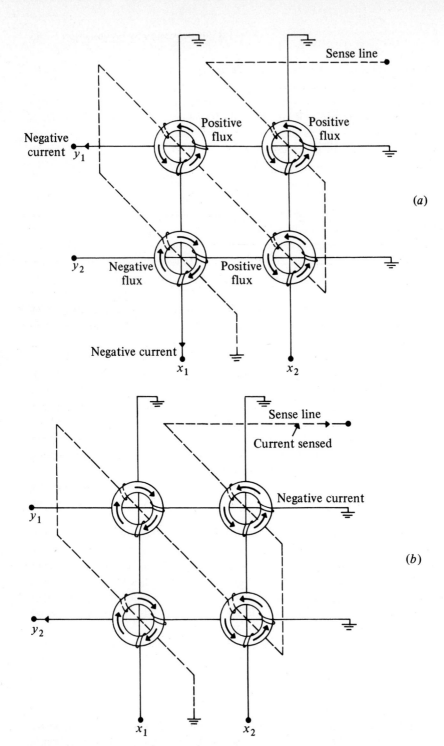

FIGURE 1-3.1 Reading bit (x_1, y_1) from magnetic core. (a) State of core before destructive read; (b) state of core after destructive read.

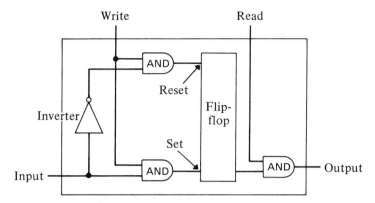

FIGURE 1-3.2 A semiconductor storage unit.

circuitry, and it resides in a small block of material (commonly called a *chip*) along with many other such memory units. As in the case of a core storage unit, a semiconductor unit holds one bit of information. Information is input to a storage unit by the presence of a negative or positive voltage. If a negative voltage represents a zero value, the positive voltage represents a one value, or vice versa. The state of the information associated with a memory unit is stored in a piece of sequential circuitry called a *flip-flop*. A flip-flop is a simple two-state device and, hence, is ideal for storing binary information. A one value is stored in the flip-flop by simultaneously applying positive pulses to the input line and the write line. This activates the line that sets the flip-flop (placing it in a one state). On the other hand, if a negative input pulse is combined with a write pulse, the inverter causes a pulse to appear in the reset line of the flip-flop. This produces a zero state.

A read line is combined with the output line from the flip-flop. When the read line is pulsed, the state of the flip-flop can be determined and, hence, the binary value of the memory unit can be read.

Core memory has been used as a type of storage medium since the 1950s. Of late, semiconductor memory has become more popular, namely due to the tremendous decrease in the price of integrated circuitry. Other considerations favoring semiconductor memory are its physical compactness, its smaller energy demands (i.e., less electrical power is needed to read or write information and to keep the memory units cool), and its quicker response time to read or write commands. No doubt other more compact and functionally superior memory units will be used for the storage of information in the future.

1-4 PRIMITIVE DATA STRUCTURES

In this section we are concerned with the structuring of data at their most primitive level within a computer, that is, the data structures which can be directly operated upon by machine-level instructions. We will present storage representations for these data structures for a variety of machines. The primitive data structures examined in this section form a basis for the discussion and the composition of more sophisticated data structures introduced in the remaining chapters of the book.

Prior to a discussion of data structures, primitive or otherwise, we must be familiar with a number of common operations used to manipulate data structures and their elements.

1-4.1   Operations on Data Structures

An operation frequently used in conjunction with data structures is one which creates a data structure. This operation will be called a **CREATOR** operation. For example, variables in PL/I, FORTRAN, ALGOL, plus many other languages, can be created by using a declaration statement. In PL/I, the declaration statement

    DECLARE N FIXED DECIMAL;

causes space to be created for **N** upon entering, at execution time, the block (i.e., **BEGIN** block or **PROCEDURE** block) in which the declaration for **N** occurs. In contrast, a FORTRAN declaration such as

    INTEGER Z

results in the creation of memory space for **Z** during the compilation of the declaration statement. Storage space for a variable can also be created at execution time when its name is first encountered in the source program. Programming languages such as SNOBOL and APL use this form of data structure creation. As we progress through the text, we will discover still other ways of creating data structures. For now, the key point is that, irrespective of what programming language is used, the data structures present in a program are not manufactured "out of thin air" but are specified, either explicitly or implicitly, with creator statements.

Another operation, providing the complementary effect of a **CREATOR** operation, is one which destroys a data structure. The operation is called a **DESTROYER**. Certain languages, such as FORTRAN, do not allow a programmer to destroy data structures once they have been created, since all creations are performed at compile time and not at execution time. In ALGOL and PL/I, data structures within a block are destroyed when the block is exited during execution. While a **DESTROYER** operation is not a necessary operation, it aids in the efficient use of memory.

Probably the most frequently used operation associated with data structures is one which the programmer uses to access data within a data structure. This type of operation is known as a **SELECTOR**. The form of the **SELECTOR** depends to a significant degree on the type of data structure being accessed. As more complex structures are introduced, we will see that the method of access is one of the most important properties of a structure—especially as this property relates to the decision as to whether or not we should use a particular data structure.

Another operation used in conjunction with data structures is one which changes data in the structure. This operation will be called an **UPDATER**. An assignment operation is a good example of an update operation. Other more complicated forms of update operations exist (e.g., parameter passing operations). We will see that the updating operation is an important property which must be considered in data-structure selection.

The four operations just discussed provide us with all the operations that are normally applied to the primitive data structures that will be discussed in this chapter. In procedure-oriented languages such as PL/I and FORTRAN, a primitive data structure is equated with a simple variable such as a real variable, integer variable, logical variable, etc. A simple variable is assigned a single value such as a real value. The single value associated with a simple variable is referenced through a simple identifier name such as X.

1-4.2 Number Systems

We begin a discussion of primitive data structures by examining integer and real numbers. To provide a proper perspective for a study of data structures which are numeric in nature, it is worthwhile to briefly examine the types of number systems that have arisen.

Numbers are used symbolically to represent quantities of objects. A very simple method of representing a quantity is through the use of tally symbols. In a tally system, a one-to-one correspondence is established between tally marks and the objects being counted. For example, six objects can be represented as ****** or 111111. It should be immediately obvious that this type of system is very inconvenient when attempting to represent large quantities.

Number systems, such as the Roman number system, provide a partial solution to the problem of representing a large number of objects. In the Roman system, additional symbols are available for expressing groups of tally symbols. For example, if I = *, then V = IIIII, X = VV, L = XXXXX, etc. A given quantity is represented by combining symbols according to a set of rules which depend to some degree on the position of the symbols in a number. The disadvantage of a system which relies primarily on grouping one set of symbols to form a new symbol is that in order to represent extremely large quantities (e.g., the number of sand pebbles on a beach) a multitude (i.e., potentially infinite number) of unique symbols is required.

To avoid the problem of having to create and remember a large number of symbols, positional number systems were created. In a positional number system a finite number, say R, of unique symbols is used. R is often referred to as the *radix* of the positional number system. A quantity is represented in a positional number system by the symbols themselves and the positions of the symbols. We can exemplify this point by examining the positional number system we are most familiar with: the *radix ten* or *decimal* number system. To illustrate why the decimal system is a positional system, consider the number 1303. We interpret 1303 to mean

$$1 \times 10^3 + 3 \times 10^2 + 0 \times 10^1 + 3 \times 10^0$$

Note that while two 3's appear in the number, the left-most 3 represents the quantity three hundred, while the other 3 represents the quantity "three." Clearly, the quantity represented by a symbol is position dependent.

Fractional values can also be represented in a positional system. For example, one-quarter is written as .25, which is interpreted as $2 \times 10^{-1} + 5 \times 10^{-2}$.

The rules for discovering the value of a decimal number are based on the position of symbols in the number. These same rules can be applied to other positional number systems such as the *binary number system*. A binary number 11001.101 represents a quantity equivalent to that represented by the decimal number 25.625. We can arrive at this equivalence by expanding the binary number according to its positional representation, that is,

$$1 \times 2^4 + 1 \times 2^3 + 0 \times 2^2 + 0 \times 2^1 + 1 \times 2^0 + 1 \times 2^{-1} + 0 \times 2^{-2} + 1 \times 2^{-3}$$

$$= 16 + 8 + 1 + .5 + .125 = 25.625.$$

The number systems we will be most concerned with have radices of 2, 8, 10, and 16 and are commonly referred to as the binary, octal, decimal, and hexadecimal number systems respectively. Our interest in these number systems arises from the fact that many computers perform their operations in base 2, 8, and 16. We are especially interested in understanding how to convert between the decimal number system and any one of the three other number systems generally available in computers. Table 1-4.1 familiarizes us with the binary, octal, and hexadecimal representations of the integers from 0 to 17.

In the discussion to follow, we will distinguish between numbers in different systems by adding a subscript to the number (unless it is obvious by context in which base the number is represented, such as in Table 1-4.1). When a subscript is not present, the number is assumed to be a decimal number. As an example, we say that $(11011)_2$, $(33)_8$ and $(1B)_{16}$ are all numerically equivalent to the number 27. One further point of notation—since our list of symbols from the decimal system is exhausted, we use the letters A, B, C, D, E, and F to denote 10, 11, 12, 13, 14, and 15, respectively, in the hexadecimal system.

Table 1-4.1 Binary, octal, and hexadecimal numbers between 0 and 17.

Number	Binary	Octal	Hexadecimal
0	0	0	0
1	1	1	1
2	10	2	2
3	11	3	3
4	100	4	4
5	101	5	5
6	110	6	6
7	111	7	7
8	1000	10	8
9	1001	11	9
10	1010	12	A
11	1011	13	B
12	1100	14	C
13	1101	15	D
14	1110	16	E
15	1111	17	F
16	10000	20	10
17	10001	21	11

Exercises for Sec. 1-4.2

1. Write the first 17 integers in base 3.

2. Write the first 17 integers in base 9. Is there any relationship between the numbers written in base 3 and those written in base 9?

1-4.3 Number Conversions

From grade school we have been taught to express numbers in decimal notation. We have become so accustomed to the decimal number system that it is very difficult to get a "true feeling" for a quantity expressed in another number system. For example, if we saw the advertisement "FLY—\$86 TO EUROPE" in a travel bureau window, we would become immediately excited in anticipation of a bargain. If, upon further inquiry, we discover that the \$86 was expressed in radix 21, our excitement would dissipate quickly. In addition to considering a suit for false advertising, we may want to find out if $\$(86)_{21}$ is a bargain rate. The easiest way of finding out is to express $(86)_{21}$ as a decimal number and to compare this result with known fares from other travel bureaus.

The above example, while admittedly far-fetched, points out our dependence on the decimal system for understanding and expressing quantities. However, as mentioned in the previous section, present-day computers are not decimal-number oriented, but are binary-number oriented. Therefore, as computer scientists, we are faced with the problems of understanding the binary system and of being able to convert from the binary system to the decimal system, and vice versa.

We are also interested in the octal- and hexadecimal-number systems. Computer programmers, programming at the machine level, have found that it is easier to express large binary numbers in the more compact octal and hexadecimal notations. In addition, many machine operations are octal or hexadecimal oriented, and very often the encoding schemes for character data (which we will discuss in Sec. 1-4.7) are expressed in an octal or hexadecimal format. Consequently, most of the examples in this section involve conversions among the binary, octal, decimal, and hexadecimal systems.

Six number-conversion methods will be given. We begin with very simple special-purpose procedures and progress to more difficult general-purpose procedures. Unless otherwise stated, we will be considering conversion routines for rational numbers.

1 Conversion of a number in radix R to a decimal number.

Using the method by which we have defined a positional number, we can express a number in radix R as a decimal number D by applying the following formula:

$$D = \sum_{i=-M}^{N} d_i R^i$$
$$= d_{-M}R^{-M} \cdots + d_{-2}R^{-2} + d_{-1}R^{-1} + d_0R^0 + d_1R^1 + \cdots + d_NR^N$$
$$= d_NR^N + \cdots + d_1R + d_0R^0 + d_{-1}R^{-1} + d_{-2}R^{-2} + \cdots + d_{-M}R^{-M} \qquad (1\text{-}4.1)$$

For example,

$$(1101.011)_2 = 1 \times 2^3 + 1 \times 2^2 + 0 \times 2^1 + 1 \times 2^0 + 0 \times 2^{-1} + 1 \times 2^{-2} + 1 \times 2^{-3}$$
$$= 8 + 4 + 1 + .25 + .125 = 13.375$$

Note that we can reduce the amount of computation necessary to evaluate D in Eq. (1-4.1) by using a procedure, called Horner's rule, applied separately to the integer and fractional parts of the number

$$D = ((\cdots((d_N \times R + d_{N-1}) \times R + d_{N-2}) \times R \cdots + d_1) \times R + d_0)$$
$$+ ((\cdots((d_{-M} \times R^{-1} + d_{-M+1}) \times R^{-1} + d_{-M+2})$$
$$\times R^{-1} \cdots + d_{-1}) \times R^{-1}) \quad (1\text{-}4.2)$$

In Eq. (1-4.2), $N + 1$ is the number of digits present in the integer part and M is the number of digits present in the fractional part of the given number. We will now express Eq. (1-4.2) in algorithmic notation.

Algorithm CONVERSION_TO_DECIMAL.   Given a number

$$D_R = (d_N d_{N-1} \cdots d_0 \cdot d_{-1} d_{-2} \cdots d_{-M})_R$$

convert the number to decimal representation. The decimal result for the integer and fractional parts of D_R will be stored in variables IRESULT and FRESULT, respectively. The final answer will appear in the variable RESULT.

1. [Initialize]   Set RESULT ← IRESULT ← FRESULT ← 0.
2. [Loop forming decimal equivalent of integer part]
    Repeat step 3 for i = N, N − 1, ..., 1, 0.
3. [Accumulate integer result]   Set IRESULT ← IRESULT * R + d_i.
4. [Loop forming decimal equivalent of fractional part]
    Repeat step 5 for i = −M, −M + 1, ..., −1.
5. [Accumulate fractional result]
    Set FRESULT ← (FRESULT + d_i)/R.
6. [Evaluate final result]   Set RESULT ← IRESULT + FRESULT, and Exit.

Example 1-1   What is $(1B.C)_{16}$ in decimal notation? Table 1-4.2 gives a trace of the values for the variables IRESULT, FRESULT, RESULT, i and d_i as the above algorithm is executed. Initially N←1, M←1, and R←16.

Table 1-4.2

Step	i	d_i	IRESULT	FRESULT	RESULT
1	undefined	undefined	0	0	0
2	1	1	0	0	0
3	1	1	1	0	0
2	0	$11(B_{16})$	1	0	0
3	0	11	27	0	0
4	−1	$12(C_{16})$	27	0	0
5	−1	12	27	.75	0
6	−1	12	27	.75	27.75

////

2 Conversion of a number in radix R to a number in radix S where $R^k = S$ for some integer $k > 1$.

The decimal equivalent for a number in radix R can be realized by Eq. (1-4.1)

$$D = \sum_{i=-M}^{N} d_i R^i$$

$$= d_N R^N + \cdots + d_1 R^1 + d_0 + d_{-1} R^{-1} + d_{-2} R^{-2} + \cdots + d_{-M} R^{-M}$$

$$= (d_N R^{k-1} + d_{N-1} R^{k-2} + \cdots + d_{N-k+2} R + d_{N-k+1}) R^{N-k+1} + \cdots$$

$$+ (d_{k-1} R^{k-1} + d_{k-2} R^{k-2} + \cdots + d_1 R + d_0)$$

$$+ (d_{-1} R^{k-1} + d_{-2} R^{k-2} + \cdots + d_{-k})/R^k + \cdots$$

$$+ (d_{-M+k-1} R^{k-1} + d_{-M+k-2} R^{k-2} + \cdots + d_{-M})/R^M$$

Note that if we group the polynomial terms into sets of size k moving left and right from the radix point, then each set can be represented by a digit from the number system of radix S where $S = R^k$. That is, if $S = R^k$, then there exists a digit d in base S such that $d = d_{k-1} R^{k-1} + \cdots + d_1 R^1 + d_0$ for any set of digits $[d_{k-1}, \ldots, d_0]$ expressed in radix R.

Example 1-2 What is $(1101.011)_2$ in octal representation?

$$(1101.011)_2 = (001101.011)_2$$

$$= 1 \times 2^3 + 1 \times 2^2 + 0 \times 2^1 + 1 \times 2^0 + 0 \times 2^{-1} + 1 \times 2^{-2} + 1 \times 2^{-3}$$

$$= (0 \times 2^2 + 0 \times 2^1 + 1 \times 2^0) \times (2^3)^1$$

$$+ (1 \times 2^2 + 0 \times 2^1 + 1 \times 2^0) \times (2^3)^0$$

$$+ (0 \times 2^2 + 1 \times 2^1 + 1 \times 2^0) \times (2^3)^{-1}$$

$$= 1 \times 8^1 + 5 \times 8^0 + 3 \times 8^{-1}$$

$$= (15.3)_8$$

We know that $2^3 = 8$. Hence, any group of three binary digits can be represented by a single octal digit. By starting at the radix point and grouping digits three at a time, moving both ways from the radix point, we can effectively transform a binary number into its equivalent octal representation.

Since $2^4 = 16$, we can group binary digits in sets of four, from the radix point, to arrive at an equivalent hexadecimal representation. Therefore, $(1101.011)_2 = (1101.0110)_2 = (D.6)_{16}$.   ////

3 Conversion of a number in radix S to a number in radix R where $R^k = S$ for some integer $k > 1$.

By reversing the grouping-of-digits procedure previously discussed, that is, by expanding digits from a number in radix S into digits with radix R, we can convert numbers in radix S to numbers in radix R. We illustrate how this is accomplished, in general, by manipulating Eq. (1-4.1). The decimal equivalent of a number of radix S is expressed as:

$$D = \sum_{i=-M}^{N} d_i S^i = d_N S^N + \cdots + d_2 S^2 + d_1 S^1 + d_0 S^0 + d_{-1} S^{-1} + \cdots d_{-M} S^{-M}$$

$$= d_N (R^k)^N + \cdots + d_2 (R^k)^2 + d_1 (R^k)^1 + d_0 (R^k)^0 + d_{-1} (R^k)^{-1}$$

$$+ \cdots + d_{-M} (R^k)^{-M} \tag{1-4.3}$$

Note, the d_i's are digits expressed in radix S notation. We can find an equivalent radix R representation for d_i by expanding the digit d_i to k digits in the radix R system. That is,

$$(d_i)_S = d'_{i,k-1} \times R^{k-1} + d'_{i,k-2} \times R^{k-2} + \cdots + d'_{i,1} \times R + d_{i,0}$$

By substituting the above formula for each d_i in Eq. (1-4.3) and multiplying through by the terms $(R^k)^i$, we have the following formula:

$$
\begin{aligned}
D = {} & d'_{N,k-1} \times R^{(N+1)k-1} + d'_{N,k-2} \times R^{(N+1)k-2} + \cdots + d'_{1,k-1} \times R^{2k-1} \\
& + d'_{1,k-2} \times R^{2k-2} + \cdots + d'_{1,0} \times R^k + d'_{0,k-1} \times R^{k-1} + d'_{0,k-2} \times R^{k-2} \\
& + \cdots + d'_{0,0} \times R^0 + d'_{-1,k-1} \times R^{-1} + d'_{-1,k-2} \times R^{-2} + \cdots \\
& + d'_{-1,0} \times R^{-k} + \cdots + d'_{-M,1} \times R^{-Mk+1} + d'_{-M,0} \times R^{-Mk}
\end{aligned}
$$

The coefficients $d'_{i,j}$ are the values of the digits for the radix R representation of the original radix S number. In the following example, we illustrate how we can apply this procedure of expanding digits from a number in radix S to achieve a radix R representation.

Example 1-3   What is $(76.21)_8$ in the binary number system?

$$
\begin{aligned}
D = {} & 7 \times 8^1 + 6 \times 8^0 + 2 \times 8^{-1} + 1 \times 8^{-2} \\
= {} & 7 \times (2^3) + 6 + 2 \times (2^3)^{-1} + 1 \times (2^3)^{-2} \\
= {} & (1 \times 2^2 + 1 \times 2^1 + 1 \times 2^0) \times (2^3) + (1 \times 2^2 + 1 \times 2^1 + 0 \times 2^0) \times (2^3)^0 \\
& + (0 \times 2^2 + 1 \times 2^1 + 0 \times 2^0) \times (2^3)^{-1} + (0 \times 2^2 + 0 \times 2^1 + 1 \times 2^0) \\
& \times (2^3)^{-2} \\
= {} & 1 \times 2^5 + 1 \times 2^4 + 1 \times 2^3 + 1 \times 2^2 + 1 \times 2^1 + 0 \times 2^0 + 0 \times 2^{-1} \\
& + 1 \times 2^{-2} + 0 \times 2^{-3} + 0 \times 2^{-4} + 0 \times 2^{-5} + 1 \times 2^{-6}
\end{aligned}
$$

By collecting the binary coefficients, we obtain $(76.21)_8 = (111110.010001)_2$. Of course, once we become comfortable with the process of expanding a digital value, we should not have to go through the "long-hand" procedure just given. For example, we should be able to expand the digits "in-line" as follows:

$$
\begin{aligned}
(7.A2)_{16} &= ((0111)_2 . (1010)_2 \, (0010)_2) \\
&= (0111.10100010)_2 = (111.1010001)_2 \qquad\qquad \text{////}
\end{aligned}
$$

4   *Conversions between numbers in radix S and numbers in radix T where $S \neq T$ and $S = R^N$ and $T = R^M$.*

A straightforward two-step procedure exists for this type of conversion.

1   Convert the number in radix S to a number in radix R by the expansion given in procedure *3*.

2   Convert the new representation in radix R to a number in radix T by the grouping procedure *2*.

Example 1-4   What is the representation of $(132.6)_8$ in the hexadecimal number system?
   Step 1: Convert $(132.6)_8$ to a binary number.

$$
\begin{aligned}
(132.6)_8 &= ((001)_2 (011)_2 (010)_2 . (110)_2) \\
&= (001011010.110)_2
\end{aligned}
$$

Step 2: Convert $(001011010.110)_2$ to a hexadecimal number.

$$(001011010.110)_2 = ((0101)_2(1010)_2.(1100)_2)$$
$$= (5A.C)_{16} \qquad\qquad ////$$

5 Conversion of decimal integers to integers in radix R where R is not a power of 10.

Conversion of an integer from the decimal system to a system in another radix is best accomplished by using the repeated-division algorithm.

Algorithm REPEATED_DIVISION. Given a decimal integer I, convert I to a number (called RESULT) in a system with radix R. DIV represents a temporary variable used for dividends, REM is a temporary variable used for remainders, and MOD(X,Y) is a function which returns the remainder of X divided by Y.

1. [Initialize]   Set DIV ← I and RESULT ← empty.
2. [Iterate until a zero dividend is achieved]
   Repeat steps 3 to 5 while DIV ≠ 0.
3. [Find remainder]   Set REM ← MOD(DIV, R).
4. [Find a new dividend]   Set DIV ← DIV / R. (/ means integer division)
5. [Form number in radix R]   Set RESULT ← REM ○ RESULT.
6. [Finished]   Exit.

The symbol '○' used in step 5 of the algorithm represents the concatenation operator. For example, if REM is $(0)_{16}$ and RESULT is $(B)_{16}$, then the concatenation of REM and RESULT, i.e., REM ○ RESULT, is $(0B)_{16}$. A more formal treatment of the concatenation operator will be given in Chap. 2.

Example 1-5   What is the integer 267 in hexadecimal notation? Table 1-4.3 gives a trace of the variables when the repeated division algorithm is applied to the integer 267. Note that R = 16 throughout.

Table 1-4.3

Step	DIV	REM	RESULT
1	267	not defined	empty
2 & 3	267	$11 = (B)_{16}$	empty
4	16	$(B)_{16}$	empty
5	16	$(B)_{16}$	$(B)_{16}$
2 & 3	16	$(0)_{16}$	$(B)_{16}$
4	1	$(0)_{16}$	$(B)_{16}$
5	1	$(0)_{16}$	$(0B)_{16}$
2 & 3	1	$(1)_{16}$	$(0B)_{16}$
4	0	$(1)_{16}$	$(0B)_{16}$
5	0	$(1)_{16}$	$(10B)_{16}$
2 & 6	0	$(1)_{16}$	$(10B)_{16}$

$////$

After carefully working through the above example, we can use the repeated-division algorithm to show that $47 = (101111)_2$.

6   Conversion of decimal fractions to fractions in radix R where R is not a power of 10.

To convert decimal fractions to another base, we apply the dual of the repeated-division procedure—namely, the repeated-multiplication procedure.

Algorithm REPEATED_MULTIPLICATION.   Given a decimal fraction F, convert this number to a fraction in radix R. PROD is a temporary variable used for products and L is the number of digits of desired accuracy in the radix R fraction. FRACT(P) is a function returning the fractional part of P and INT(P) is a function returning the integer part of P (e.g., FRACT (3.92) $\equiv$ .92, INT (3.92) $\equiv$ 3). The variable RESULT is used to hold the converted radix R fractional number.

1. [Initialize]   Set RESULT $\leftarrow$ empty.
2. [Iterate until the desired accuracy of L digits is achieved]
   Repeat steps 3 to 5 for i = 1, 2, 3, . . ., L.
3. [Calculate new product]   Set PROD $\leftarrow$ F * R.
4. [Extract new fraction part]   Set F $\leftarrow$ FRACT(PROD).
5. [Form partial result]   Set RESULT $\leftarrow$ RESULT $\bigcirc$ INT(PROD).
6. [Finished]   Set RESULT $\leftarrow$'.' $\bigcirc$ RESULT and Exit.

Example 1-6   What is .961 in octal representation with three digits of accuracy?
   The trace given in Table 1-4.4 illustrates how the repeated multiplication procedure works. Note that L = 3, and R = 8 throughout.
   To test the accuracy of our result, we can convert $(.754)_8$ back to decimal using conversion procedure *1*. If we do so, we get .9609 to four figures of accuracy.

Table 1-4.4

Step	PROD	F	RESULT
1	not defined	.961	empty
2 & 3	7.688	.961	empty
4	7.688	.688	empty
5	7.688	.688	$(7)_8$
2 & 3	5.504	.688	$(7)_8$
4	5.504	.504	$(7)_8$
5	5.504	.504	$(75)_8$
2 & 3	4.032	.504	$(75)_8$
4	4.032	.032	$(75)_8$
5	4.032	.032	$(754)_8$
2 & 6	4.032	.032	$(.754)_8$

////

The conversion procedures described in this subsection provide us with the "tools" needed to understand how numeric information is stored in a computer. However, before examining the representation of numeric information, we discuss integer and real numbers as primitive data structures.

Exercises for Sec. 1-4.3

1. Convert the following numbers to decimal: (a) $(38)_{16}$, (b) $(22.2)_8$, (c) $(1011)_2$, (d) $(1011)_8$, (e) $(1011)_{16}$, (f) $(AD.4)_{16}$, (g) $(.353)_6$, (h) $(92)_{12}$, (i) $(-77)_8$, (j) $(-77)_{16}$.
2. Perform the following conversions: (a) $(1100101)_2$ to base 16, (b) $(10101)_2$ to base 8, (c) $(1.11011)_2$ to base 16, (d) $(1.11)_2$ to base 8, (e) $(2.31)_4$ to base 16.
3. Perform the following conversions: (a) $(AC)_{16}$ to base 2, (b) $(712)_8$ to base 2, (c) $(61.61)_8$ to base 2, (d) $(.D1)_{16}$ to base 2, (e) $(D1)_{16}$ to base 4.
4. Perform the following conversions: (a) $(7621)_8$ to base 16, (b) $(11)_{16}$ to base 8, (c) $(11)_8$ to base 16, (d) $(E.E)_{16}$ to base 8, (e) $(22)_4$ to base 8.
5. Convert the following decimal integers to integers in the desired base: (a) 72 to base 16, (b) 36 to base 8, (c) -24 to base 2, (d) 16 to base 16, (e) 961 to base 2.
6. Convert the following decimal numbers to numbers in the specified base: (a) 7.2 to base 16, (b) .275 to base 8, (c) .5625 to base 2, (d) .5625 to base 16, (e) 23.1 to base 8.

1-4.4 Integers and Their Representation

We are all familiar with the concept of an integer and many of the operations commonly applied to integers (e.g., addition, multiplication, etc.). The set of integers can be defined rigorously (e.g., the set of nonnegative integers can be defined by applying the Peano axioms); however, whether or not the reader has seen a formal definition is not of major importance to the current discussion. It suffices to say that the set of integers, I, is the set

$$\{\ldots -(n + 1), -n, \ldots, -2, -1, 0, 1, 2, \ldots, n, n + 1, \ldots\}$$

The importance of integer data in terms of computation is obvious. A quantity representing objects which are discrete in nature (i.e., the number of objects are countable) can be represented by an integer. The number of dollars in a bank account, the number of passengers on a flight, and the number of pieces on a chess board are all information items expressible as integers.

The uses of integers are many, varied, and obvious; therefore, further motivation for their importance as a data type is unnecessary. However, the method of representing integers as signed numbers is less obvious—especially if we are concerned with performing computations efficiently and inexpensively. In this section, we concentrate on several representations of integers as signed numbers and discover that the representation we are most familiar with is not necessarily the best representation for performing computations on a computer.

The conventional method for writing negative integers is to place a sign symbol in front of a number. This method, often called *the sign and magnitude method*, has been used for the representation of signed numbers in several computers. Generally, the sign is represented as the first or leftmost bit of the binary number representation and the magnitude portion of the number appears in the remainder of the representation. For example, $+7$ and -6 are represented in binary as:

Number	Sign Bit	Magnitude
+7	0	00....0111
−6	1	00....0110

Note that in this example 0 and 1 are used to represent the positive and negative signs, respectively. This sign representation is customary.

While the sign and magnitude representation has the advantage of being familiar and readable to the programmer, it is not the most economical representation. If we want to add or subtract two numbers, a special effort must be made to interpret the sign of each number in order to decide what operation should be performed. For example, the addition of +7 and −6 really involves the subtraction operation, and the subtraction of −6 from +7 really involves the addition operation. Special circuitry is required to examine the sign bit and, in addition, both subtractor and adder units are required when using sign and magnitude representation.

The most economical and popular representation of integers is the *radix complement representation*, in general, and the *2's complement representation* as applied specifically to binary computers. In radix complement representation, all arithmetic operations are performed modulo M, for $M = R^N$, where R is the radix in which the integer is expressed and N is the maximum number of digits required to represent an integer modulo M. We can illustrate what is meant by modulo arithmetic in general with the following discussion. Assume that an operation $*$ is performed on numbers x and y, yielding result z (i.e., $z = x * y$). If the same operation is performed modulo M (we designate this new operation by $*_M$), then the result of $x *_M y$ is $z_M = z \bmod M$. That is, z_M is the remainder or *residue* when dividing z by M.

In modulo M arithmetic, the following relationship holds for addition on an integer x,

$$x = x + M \tag{1-4.4}$$

Employing some very simple algebra, we can find an expression for the "negation of x," namely,

$$-x = M - x \tag{1-4.5}$$

This equation holds providing both sides are computed modulo M (i.e., both sides have the same residue).

Equation (1-4.5) gives an indication as to how both positive and negative integers can be represented in radix complement form. As an example, assume that we are working with 2's complement numbers using modulo $M = 16$ arithmetic (implying the number of binary digits N required to express an integer is 4—i.e., $2^4 = 16$). Table 1-4.5 illustrates how the sixteen numbers representable in a 2's complement modulo 16 system are related to the integers from −8 to +7.

Note that the representation of the negative integers in complement form has been derived by applying Eq. (1-4.5). An alternative method of deriving the complemented form for the negative integers is by performing the complementation using binary arithmetic. For example, the complemented form of −2 is

$$16 - 2 = (10000)_2 - (10)_2 = (1110)_2$$

Table 1-4.5 Two's complement representation for integers expressed in modulo 16.

Integer	Two's Complement Representation	Integer	Two's Complement Representation
0	0000	-1 (16 $-$ 1 = 15)	1111
1	0001	-2 (16 $-$ 2 = 14)	1110
2	0010	-3 (16 $-$ 3 = 13)	1101
3	0011	-4 (16 $-$ 4 = 12)	1100
4	0100	-5 (16 $-$ 5 = 11)	1011
5	0101	-6 (16 $-$ 6 = 10)	1010
6	0110	-7 (16 $-$ 7 = 9)	1001
7	0111	-8 (16 $-$ 8 = 8)	1000

Let us consider another example.

Example 1-7 What is the 2's complement representation for -38 expressed in a modulo 32 system?

First, we must express -38 as a modulo 32 number. We know that -38 mod (32) = -6. To find an equivalent 2's complement representation, we apply Eq. (1-4.5). That is,

$$32 - 6 = 26 = (11010)_2$$

or $\quad (100000)_2 - (110)_2 = (11010)_2$ ////

One of the major advantages of radix complement notation is that we can perform addition and subtraction operations using only addition and complementation. Note that a complementation operation for binary numbers is a very simple operation. It involves

1 Copying the 0's to the right of the rightmost 1
2 Copying the rightmost 1
3 Writing the complement of all bits to the left of the rightmost 1

Hence, the 2's complement of 6 expressed as a five-digit number is 2's COMP(6) = 2's COMP($(00110)_2$) = $(11010)_2$. Thus, 2's COMP can be viewed as a function which accepts an integer expressed in some radix R and converts it to its 2's complement form. The result $(11010)_2$ matches the result in Example 1-7.

The following example illustrates that only a binary addition and 2's complementation are required for the addition and subtraction of integers.

Example 1-8 Evaluate $3 + 4$, $3 - 4$, $-3 + 4$, $7 + 7$, $-7 - 7$ using 2's complement representation and modulo 16 arithmetic.

(*a*) $\quad 3 + 4 = (0011)_2 + (0100)_2 = (0111)_2 = 7$

(*b*) $\quad 3 - 4 = (0011)_2 + $ 2's COMP($(0100)_2$) $= (0011)_2 + (1100)_2$

$\quad\quad\quad = (1111)_2 = -1$

Recall that $(1111)_2$ is equal to -1 in 2's complement form.

(c) $-3 + 4 = 2\text{'s COMP}((0011)_2) + (0100)_2 = (1101)_2 + (0100)_2$

$\qquad\qquad = (0001)_2 = 1$

(d) $7 + 7 = (0111)_2 + (0111)_2 = (1110)_2 = -2$

(e) $-7 - 7 = 2\text{'s COMP}((0111)_2) + 2\text{'s COMP}((0111)_2)$

$\qquad\qquad = (1001)_2 + (1001)_2 = (0010)_2 = 2$ ////

In Example 1-8, parts (d) and (e) yield invalid results. Remember that the range of integers we can represent in 2's complement form assuming a modulo 16 system is -8 to $+7$. Therefore, the evaluation of the expressions $7 + 7$ and $-7 - 7$ result in *overflows*. We will return to consider the problem of overflow after introducing another representation scheme used for integers in computers.

The *diminished radix-complement* form of a digit d of the radix R number system is defined as $R - 1 - d$. Therefore, the binary digits 0 and 1 expressed in diminished radix-complement form are 1 and 0, respectively. An integer I expressed in such a form is found by the following equation

$$\text{DRCOMP}(I) = R^n - 1 - I$$

Note that R^n is expressed in the radix R number system as a 1 followed by n zeros.

The essential difference between the radix complement form and the diminished radix-complement form is that the modulo for complementation (i.e., R^n) is diminished by 1 in the latter case. The diminished radix-complement form for integers expressed in binary is commonly called *1's complement*. The 1's complementation of the integer 6 in a modulo 16 system is $16 - 1 - 6 = 9$ or $(10000)_2 - 1 - (0110)_2 = (1111)_2 - (0110)_2 = (1001)_2$. It is important to note that 1's $\text{COMP}(x)$, where x is a binary number, is found very simply by exchanging all 0's in x with 1's and all 1's in x with 0's. Table 1-4.6 further illustrates this point.

Table 1-4.6   One's complement representation for integers expressed in modulo 16.

Integer	One's Complement Representation	Integer	One's Complement Representation
0	0000	-1 (1's COMP$(0001)_2$)	1110
1	0001	-2 (1's COMP$(0010)_2$)	1101
2	0010	-3 (1's COMP$(0011)_2$)	1100
3	0011	-4 (1's COMP$(0100)_2$)	1011
4	0100	-5 (1's COMP$(0101)_2$)	1010
5	0101	-6 (1's COMP$(0110)_2$)	1001
6	0110	-7 (1's COMP$(0111)_2$)	1000
7	0111	-0 (1's COMP$(0000)_2$)	1111

One disadvantage of the diminished radix-complement system is the presence of both $+0$ and -0. The fact that both are numerically equivalent, yet syntactically different, can create many computational problems. However, with diminished radix-complement notation, we can perform addition and subtraction operations using addition and complementation (as was necessary using radix complement), plus the ability to "add the carry-out." We illustrate in Example 1-9 how addition and subtraction are performed on numbers represented in 1's complement notation.

Example 1-9   Evaluate $3 + 4$, $3 - 4$, $-3 + 4$, $7 + 7$, $-7 - 7$ using 1's complement representation and modulo 16 arithmetic.

(a) $3 + 4 = (0011)_2 + (0100)_2 = (0111)_2 = 7$

(b) $3 - 4 = (0011)_2 + $ 1's $\text{COMP}((0100)_2) = (0011)_2 + (1011)_2$

$\qquad = (1110)_2 = -1$

Recall that $(1110)_2$ in 1's complement form is -1.

(c) $-3 + 4 = $ 1's $\text{COMP}((0011)_2) + (0100)_2 = (1100)_2 + (0100)_2$

$\qquad = (0000)_2 = 0$

Note a carry-out of 1 takes place here.

(d) $7 + 7 = (0111)_2 + (0111)_2 = (1110)_2 = -1$

(e) $-7 - 7 = $ 1's $\text{COMP}((0111)_2) + $ 1's $\text{COMP}((0111)_2)$

$\qquad = (1000)_2 + (1000)_2 = (0000)_2 = 0$ ////

From Example 1-9, we see that part (c) does not yield the correct answer (i.e., $-3 + 4$ should be 1 not 0). Note that if we add the carry-out to the final results of (a), (b), and (c), we obtain the correct answers of 7, -1, and 1, respectively. In 1's complement additions and subtractions, this end-around carry addition must be performed.

In parts (d) and (e) of Example 1-9 we again have overflow, as we did in parts (d) and (e) of Example 1-8. It is important, when performing computations, to detect overflow and, in a computer, an overflow error message is usually posted. To derive conditions for detecting overflow, we must realize:

1   The addition of a positive number and a negative number can never cause overflow.

2   The addition of two positive numbers or two negative numbers does not cause overflow if the resulting sum has the same sign as the two operands.

These rules hold for 1's and 2's complement additions with the exception of a 2's complement addition of two n-bit negative numbers, a and b, such that $|a| + |b| = 2^{n-1}$. To detect an overflow in this case, we must check for the magnitude bits being all zeros and for the carry-out bit value of 1. More detailed discussions concerning 1's complement end-around carry and overflow detection are found in Tremblay and Manohar [1975], Stone [1972], and Dietmeyer [1971].

Of course, these rules are violated when $7 + 7$ and $-7 - 7$ are evaluated using modulo 16 arithmetic.

Overflow can take place when other arithmetic operations, such as multiplication and division, are applied as well. The classical example of an overflow situation arises when a number is divided by zero.

In this section we have intentionally concentrated on introducing two alternative systems of integer representation to the sign and magnitude representation with which we are familiar. In Sec. 1-4.6 we will discuss the storage representation of integer data. It will be shown that because the radix complement and diminished radix-complement are efficient and inexpensive methods of representation, one of these two methods is generally adopted by computer manufacturers. For now let us turn to an examination of another type of primitive numeric data structure—the real numbers.

Exercises for Sec. 1-4.4

1. Express the following integers in 2's complement, assuming a 6-bit representation: (a) -33, (b) -52, (c) $(-33)_8$, (d) $(-E)_{16}$, (e) -241.
2. Evaluate the following expressions using 2's complement and modulo 16 arithmetic: (a) $6 - 1$, (b) $7 - (-2)$, (c) $-3 - 3$.
3. Evaluate the following expressions using 1's complement and modulo 32 arithmetic: (a) $8 + 8$, (b) $6 - 1$, (c) $7 - 11$.

1-4.5   Real Numbers and Their Representation

While not explicitly stating it, in Sec. 1-4.2 we introduced the *fixed-point representation* for a real number A_R in radix system R as

$$A_R = \pm(a_{N-1}\, a_{N-2} \ldots a_1 a_0 . a_{-1} \ldots a_{-(M-1)} a_{-M})_R$$

which has a literal expansion of

$$A = \pm \sum_{i=-M}^{N-1} a_i R^i \tag{1-4.6}$$

Fixed-point notation is sufficient to represent most of the real numbers normally arising when computations are performed on a computer. However, there exist computer applications which involve very large or very small real numbers. One such application area is astronomy. Large distance and mass measurements are used in computations concerned with the gravitational force between celestial bodies. Distances such as 16,800,000,-000,000 kilometers are not abnormal. At an atomic level, on the other hand, calculations for energy emissions in a bubble chamber demand extremely small distance measurements. A typical distance might be .0000000000832 meters.

The cost of a computer is directly affected by the precision of the numbers that can be handled in computations. A major cost factor is in the central processing unit alone. The greater the precision allowed, the larger and more complex is the arithmetic unit. Arithmetic computations, involving both of the real numbers just cited, would require a precision of 27 decimal digits. To obtain an equivalent precision in binary representation, a computer would require approximately ninety binary digits (or bits). Since most computers today provide from 16 to 64 bits of precision, a computer with a word size of ninety would not be economical as a general-purpose machine.

An alternative method of representation which overcomes this difficulty is the *floating-point* or *scientific* notation. In this shorthand notation, the two measurements given earlier would be expressed as $.168 \times 10^{14}$ kilometers and $.832 \times 10^{-10}$ meters.

The general form of a real number in radix R expressed in floating-point notation is

$$f_{-1}f_{-2}\ldots f_{-M} \times R^{E}$$

where $f_{-1}f_{-2}\ldots f_{-M}$ is called the *fractional part* or *mantissa* and E, which is always an integer, is the *exponent*.

It is obvious that considerable effort is saved by expressing numbers in floating-point notation. Because computer designers are very conscious about the amount of "space" (i.e., the number of bits) required to represent a number, floating-point notation has been adopted as a means of representing real numbers. (In the next section, we present a number of storage structures for real numbers expressed in floating-point notation.)

It should be noted that the fractional part of a floating-point number is meant to contain only the most significant digits of a real number. For example, $.168 \times 10^{14}$ kilometers is expressed with a mantissa of three digits in length. It is likely that the distance measurement originally taken was accurate to the first three digits. That is, $.168 \times 10^{14}$ is an approximation of an accurate measurement such as 16,817,210,391,704 kilometers. The difference between the approximate measurement and the accurate measurement is called *round-off error*.

The previous discussion points out that floating-point notation allows for the efficient representation of extremely large and extremely small real numbers which are assumed to contain few significant digits. Computers can store only a finite number of significant digits and, therefore, not all real numbers can be represented. In general, the number of significant digits retained in most computer applications is such that round-off error is negligible. However, if the computer we are using cannot represent all the significant digits of a real number with which we are working, then we are left with three alternatives.

The first alternative is to do our computation on a larger machine. In the next section, we discover that computers exist which provide almost twenty decimal digits of accuracy. However, as indicated earlier, such precision comes at a price, and the computing charge rates may be prohibitively high.

A second alternative is to use a multiple-precision program package. (In Sec. 4-3.3 we will be discussing in detail an example of multiple-precision arithmetic.) In a multiple-precision package, a real number is divided into several segments, each segment usually corresponding to a computer word. Operations such as additions are performed on individual segments, and the programs in the package are responsible for handling "carries" and "borrows" which take place between segment operations. Since each segment operation must be interpreted by the program package, the use of multiple-precision arithmetic can be very expensive as well.

The third alternative, and the one that is most often accepted, is to round the real number to as many significant digits as can be represented in the machine. Rounding is a very simple operation which can be described best by an example.

Example 1-10   What is the real number 21.833652 rounded to five decimal digits of accuracy?

$$21.833652 + .0005 = 21.834152$$

The rounded answer is 21.834.

The procedure we have adopted is simply to add 5 to the sixth decimal digit and then to isolate the five most significant digits for our answer. Of course, in general, to round a decimal number at the nth digit, we add 5 to the $(n + 1)$st digit and retain the leftmost n digits.   ////

1-4.6   Storage Structures for Numeric Data

In the previous sections we identified two types of primitive data structures—integer and real numbers—and considered how they should be represented to best facilitate computations in a computer. In this section we more closely examine integers and reals from the viewpoint of their storage structure in a computer. We do so with the aid of example storage structures from several computer series: IBM 360-370, CDC 6000 and CYBER 70-170, Burroughs B5000 and B6000, Univac 1108, PDP-10, Hewlett-Packard 2100, and PDP-11. We begin by considering the storage representation of integers.

1-4.6.1   Integer storage representation

Integers are most commonly represented as binary numbers in a computer. Typically, one computer word is devoted to the storage representation of an integer. In assembly languages and in some programming languages (such as PL/I), the programmer is able to specify an amount of storage, less than the word size, in which an integer can be stored. The smallest directly addressable unit of memory, often called a *byte*, is the least amount of storage that can be used for integer representation.

Using a storage structure which is less than a word in length has some drawbacks, however. When computations are performed on an integer stored in less than a word of memory, the integer representation is brought into the arithmetic unit, expanded to a full-word representation, and computations are performed on this new representation. To store an integer in less than a word, the reverse procedure must be taken, i.e., the appropriate subfield of the full word is isolated in a register, and this subfield (which is at least as large as a byte) is assigned to a desired set of memory locations.

Negative integers are generally represented in a 2's complement form, as opposed to a 1's complement form, to avoid the $+0$ and -0 controversy. Table 1-4.7 illustrates this fact for a representative sample of machines from the computer industry. The first bit in the binary representation is the sign bit; the remaining portion of the representation is an expression of the magnitude of the number in complemented form. A 32-bit 2's complement representation for the integer 13 is illustrated in Fig. 1-4.1. Examples of integers stored in 16-bit representation are shown in Table 1-4.8.

It is important to know the range of integer values that can be expressed using an n-bit storage representation. The summation formula for $2^0 + 2^1 + 2^2 + \cdots + 2^{n-1}$ is

$$\sum_{i=0}^{n-1} 2^i = 2^n - 1 \qquad\qquad (1\text{-}4.7)$$

In an n-bit 2's complement storage representation, the first bit expresses the sign of the integer. Therefore, we can represent positive integers in the range 0 to $1 \times 2^0 + 1 \times$

Table 1-4.7 Storage structure for integer data from a sample of computers.

Computer	Binary Representation	Decimal Representation
IBM 360-370 Series	2's complement 16- & 32-bit numbers	packed decimal nos. 7 decimal digits per 32-bit word
CDC 6000 and CYBER 70-170 series	1's complement 18- & 60-bit numbers	packed decimal nos. 14 decimal digits per 60-bit word
Burroughs B5000 and B6000 series	sign & magnitude 40-bit numbers (sign and magnitude)	character mode (6 bits/character) 8 decimal digits per 48-bit word
Univac 1108	1's complement 36- & 72-bit numbers	does not exist
PDP-10	2's complement 36-bit numbers	does not exist
Hewlett-Packard series	2's complement 16-bit numbers	does not exist
PDP-11	2's complement 16-bit numbers	does not exist

$2^1 + \cdots + 1 \times 2^{n-2}$ or (by Eq. 1-4.7) 0 to $2^{n-1} - 1$. In 2's complement notation, all other bit configurations are devoted to negative numbers in the range of -2^{n-1} to -1. To summarize, in general, an integer N can be accommodated using an n-bit, 2's complement storage representation if

$$-2^{n-1} \leq N \leq 2^{n-1} - 1$$

Because both $+0$ and -0 can be represented, the range of integers representable in 1's complement is one less than the range representable in 2's complement. Hence, if an n-bit, 1's complement storage representation is used, then N can be in the range

$$-2^{n-1} + 1 \leq N \leq 2^{n-1} - 1$$

We can illustrate the limitations placed on the representation of integers by examining storage representations of length 16 and 32 bits. A 16-bit word machine using 2's complement notation can represent an integer N where $-2^{15} \leq N \leq 2^{15} - 1$ or $-32,768 \leq N \leq 32,767$. A 32-bit word machine using 2's complement notation can represent a much larger range, namely, $-2^{31} \leq N \leq 2^{31} - 1$ or $-2,147,483,648 \leq N \leq 2,147,483,647$.

Sign

0	00000000000000000000000000001101

FIGURE 1-4.1 32-bit 2's complement word-length storage representation of the integer 13.

Table 1-4.8 Example of integers stored in 16-bit one's and two's complement representation.

Decimal Integer	One's Complement Storage Representation	Two's Complement Storage Representation
9613	0010010110001101	0010010110001101
−9613	1101101001110010	1101101001110011
317	0000000100111101	0000000100111101
−317	1111111011000010	1111111011000011
32767	0111111111111111	0111111111111111
−32767	1000000000000000	1000000000000001
−32768	not representable	1000000000000000

In some of the large computers, a decimal form of storage representation is available for integers in addition to a binary form. Associated with the decimal representation are some basic decimal instructions which include at least add, subtract, and compare instructions. The main purpose for decimal instructions and decimal representations is to improve performance when there are few computational steps between source input and output. Conversions between source and a decimal form can be achieved without a conversion to an intermediate form, as is necessary in conversions between a source and binary form. In fact in some systems, the IBM 360-370 systems in particular, the intermediate form necessary for source to binary conversions is the decimal representation.

All of this discussion pertaining to the representation and manipulation of integer data in decimal form appears to be contrary to our earlier premise that information in a computer is stored in binary digits (i.e., bits). Not so! To represent integers in a decimal format, we encode the decimal digits using a 4-bit binary-coded decimal (often called "pure BCD") scheme. In pure BCD, each decimal digit is represented by its 4-bit binary equivalent. For example, the integer 9613 would be encoded as

1001	0110	0001	0011
9	6	1	3

Note that in pure BCD, the 4-bit codes 1010, 1011, 1100, 1101, 1110, and 1111 do not have decimal digit equivalents. Two of these extra codes often are used to represent the sign of the number.

A form of pure BCD representation (called *packed decimal*) is available in the IBM 360-370 series. The general form of a packed-decimal number is given in Fig. 1-4.2. Some examples of integers represented in packed-decimal form are given in Table 1-4.9. Note that 1100 and 1101 are codes representing the plus and minus signs, respectively. Other forms of decimal representation are available; in particular, a 6-bit encoding scheme has been adopted by Burroughs (see Table 1-4.7).

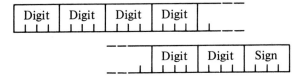

FIGURE 1-4.2.

1-4.6.2 Real-number storage representation

We have already discussed two methods of representing real numbers (a floating-point representation, such as in .2364 × 10², and fixed-point representation, such as in 23.64). Floating-point representation is the most common storage structure used for real data and we will discuss it first in this section. Fixed-point notation will be described later, at which time some of its advantages and pitfalls will be highlighted.

The floating-point format that is generally adopted for the representation of reals consists of one or two fixed-length fields (where a field is a computer word in length). The radix and the number of digit positions representable with a floating-point format vary from one computer to another. Nevertheless, a general format does exist and can be illustrated, as in Fig. 1-4.3.

Usually, the *sign* is the first bit in a floating-point representation, and by convention 0 denotes a positive number and 1 denotes a negative number. The *characteristic* or *biased exponent* is an expression of the exponent in a form of notation called *excess notation*. To illustrate what is meant by excess notation, assume that the characteristic part of the floating-point representation is seven bits in length (as it is in the IBM 360-370 series, RCA Spectra 70, and XDS Sigma 7). In a 7-bit field, we are capable of representing integers in the range of −64 to +63 in 2's complement, for example. However, 2's complement notation is not a particularly good representation for exponents. When adding or subtracting floating-point numbers, left or right shifting is required in the fractional part of the floating-point number to ensure the two operands are aligned. Shifting can be achieved by using a single counter which, when given a positive number, counts down to zero until the desired shifts have occurred. Because of hardware considerations such as these, it is desirable to use an exponent notation in which each exponent is expressed as a

Table 1-4.9 Examples of packed-decimal representations.

Integer	Packed-Decimal Form
0149	00000001010010011100
−0149	00000001010010011101
935	1001001101011100
−6	01101101

Sign	Characteristic	Fraction		

FIGURE 1-4.3.

nonnegative integer. In a seven-digit field, we can express nonnegative integers in the range of 0 to 127. To achieve such a range, and yet be able to express positive and negative exponents, it is necessary to bias the true exponent by 64. Therefore, to derive the characteristic for a floating-point number from its exponent, we add the bias or excess factor, namely 64 in this case. Hence, a floating-point number with an exponent of -48 would have a characteristic of $-48 + 64 = 16$ in what is commonly called *excess-64 notation*.

The third and final component in a floating-point storage representation is the *fractional part* or *mantissa*. A condition, called *normalization*, is often imposed on the storage structure of the fractional part to increase the number of trailing digits after the significant digits and to permit division without overflow. This condition dictates that the fractional part, say F, must lie in the interval $R^{-1} \leq F < 1$, except in the instance of a fractional part which is identically zero. If we choose the radix R of the fractional part to be 2, then a nonzero fractional part of any floating-point storage structure must begin with a (1_2) (that is, $2^{-1} \leq F < 1$). However, of late, octal- and hexadecimal-based floating-point storage representations have become popular. They have two definite advantages over binary-based floating-point representations. For example, in a hexadecimal-based storage structure, a nonzero fractional part F need only lie in the interval $16^{-1} \leq F < 1$ or $(.0001)_2 \leq F < 1$ for the number to be in a normalized form. Eight times as many binary fractions need normalization after computations as do hexadecimal fractions. The second advantage is that for a given number of bit positions in the characteristic, a hexadecimal-based system permits the representation of numbers of much larger magnitude. That is, for a 7-bit characteristic, we can represent numbers as small as 16^{-64} and as large as 16^{+63} in a hexadecimal system; whereas, the comparable magnitudes would be 2^{-64} and 2^{+63} in a binary system.

One advantage of a binary-based floating-point representation is that normalization always generates a fraction in which the first bit position is a $(1)_2$. Therefore, in some machines (in particular the PDP-11), this initial $(1)_2$ is assumed to be present at all times; however, it is never recorded in the fractional part. This extra bit is often referred to as the *hidden bit*.

In some computers the radix point is placed at the *right end* of the mantissa. In such cases, the mantissa is not necessarily treated as a fraction and normalization is not used (for example, in the Burroughs' machines). An advantage of this representation is that reals and integers are represented using the same storage structure. An integer is identified simply by having a zero exponent. In the CDC 6000 series machines, a special instruction is provided for performing normalization (i.e., normalization is not automatically performed). For computations involving integers, normalization is not performed; and for computations involving reals, normalization should be requested explicitly to increase the number of significant digits attainable in the final answer. IBM machines supply two sets of floating-point instructions, one for normalized computations and one for computations which are not normalized.

Figure 1-4.4 illustrates how some real numbers would be stored in a machine using 32-bit floating-point representation, which is composed of a 1-bit sign field, 7-bit characteristic (expressed in excess-64 notation), and a 24-bit fractional part (normalized hexadecimal number).

In most computers (see Table 1-4.10), the entire floating-point representation is contained in a computer word. However, for some scientific applications, the fractional part in a single-word representation is not large enough to yield the precision that is demanded. Consequently, most machines have a double-precision floating-point representation. For example, the double-precision floating-point storage structure for the IBM 360-370 series is given in Fig. 1-4.5.

Before completing our discussion of floating-point storage representation, it should be noted that in some smaller computers (i.e., minicomputers such as the PDP-11 and Nova series computers), floating-point operations may not be an integral part of the computer's instruction repertoire. In such instances, "add-on" hardware boxes may be purchased and attached to the CPU. Alternatively, software packages (i.e., programs) may exist which simulate the action of hardware floating-point instructions. Because the operations are simulated, floating-point computations are extremely slow and should be avoided, if possible.

In addition to a floating-point storage representation of real numbers, a fixed-point storage representation is possible. In general, the machine instructions performed on real numbers stored in a fixed-point format are identical to those involving integer numbers. There is a reason for this: namely, that the storage structure for fixed-point represented real numbers is the same as for integers. In fact in the programming language PL/I, an integer must be declared as a fixed-point number in which the radix point is declared to be on the right-hand end of the fixed-point format.

Real numbers expressed in fixed-point format are very easy to cope with when computations are completed by hand (for example, $3.782 + 93.2 = 96.982$), but this is not the situation in a computer. As already suggested, fixed-point hardware arithmetic operations do not exist, per se, in computers; rather, they are simulated using integer operations. As a hypothetical example, in a "decimal computer," 3.782 and 93.2 would be represented as 00 . . . 03782 and 00 . . . 00932, respectively. Of course, accompanying these storage representations is information kept as to the position of the radix point for each number (i.e., positions 3 and 1 in this example). If a computation such as an addition is performed involving these numbers, then the stored number 00 . . . 00932 must be shifted to the left

Decimal Number	Hexadecimal Number	32-bit Floating-Point Number		
$.0 \times 10^0$	$.(0)_{16} \times 16^0$	0	1000000	000000000000000000000000
$-.17307 \times 10^5$	$-.(439B)_{16} \times 16^4$	1	1000100	010000111001101100000000
$.28692 \times 10^2$	$.(1CB126E9)_{16} \times 16^2$	0	1000010	000111001011000100100110
$-.75 \times 10^0$	$-.(C)_{16} \times 16^0$	1	1000000	110000000000000000000000
$.8317 \times 10^{-3}$	$.(36819C4)_{16} \times 16^{-2}$	0	0111110	001101101000000110011100

FIGURE 1-4.4 Illustration of floating-point storage format.

Table 1-4.10   Storage structures for real data from a sample of computers.

Computer	Exponent	Base of Exponent	Mantissa (excluding sign) Single	Mantissa (excluding sign) Double	Radix Point	Normalization
IBM 360-370 Series	7 bits (excess-64)	16	24 bits	56 bits	left of mantissa	Yes/No
CDC 6000 Series	11 bits (excess-1024)	2	48 bits	—	right of mantissa	by instruction
Burroughs B5500 & B6500	sign + 6 bits	8	39 bits	78 bits (B6500 only)	right of mantissa	No
PDP-10	8 bits*	2	27 bits	—	left of mantissa	Yes
Univac 1108	8 bits (excess-128 for single) 11 bits (excess-1024 for double)	2	27 bits	61 bits	left of mantissa	Yes
PDP-11 (45 model)	8 bits (excess-128)	2	23 bits + hidden	55 bits + hidden	left of mantissa	Yes
Hewlett-Packard 2100 Series	Floating-point representation does not exist in hardware but is available in software package or as a microprogram add on.					

* Excess-128 notation for positive exponent, 1's complement notation for negative exponent.

two positions to make a correct summation possible. After the integer addition is complete, we would have a result of 00 . . . 96982 with an implied radix position of 3. While the previous discussion involves decimal integer operations, it is easy to visualize how comparable operations would be performed on fixed-point binary numbers.

When declaring a variable to be of type FIXED in PL/I, both the precision of the number and the position of the radix point can be specified. Any computations which involve a FIXED variable, whether the variable has a base attribute of DECIMAL (i.e., packed-decimal storage representation) or BINARY, must take into consideration the assumed radix point. While fixed-point operations such as addition, subtraction, and multiplication present few difficulties, FIXED division results in nonintuitive quotients. This is illustrated in Example 1-11.

Sign	Characteristic			Fractional	Part		
1	2	8	9	32	33		64

FIGURE 1-4.5.

Example 1-11   Suppose X and Y are variables in a PL/I program which are declared to have precisions of 6 and 15 decimal digits and scale factors (i.e., radix point positions) of 3 and 0, respectively. If X is assigned the value 432.432 (which is represented as 432Δ432) and Y has the value 2 (which is represented as 00 . . . 02Δ), the result of the operation X/Y is 216Δ216000000000. On the other hand, if Y has a precision of 15 decimal digits, a scale factor of 9 and an assigned value of 2.00001 (which is represented as 000002Δ000010000), then by the rules of FIXED division in PL/I, X/Y yields the result 000000000216Δ216. We conclude that the more significant digits we specify in the operands of the division, the less significant digits are contained in the result.

////

A note on PL/I data types

A major complaint with PL/I as a high-level language is the unfortunate choice of numeric data types. Basically, there are four numeric types (we ignore the COMPLEX data type in this discussion): FIXED BINARY, FIXED DECIMAL, FLOAT BINARY, and FLOAT DECIMAL. The PL/I programmer does not declare numeric items in terms of the familiar primitive data types INTEGER and REAL. Instead, the PL/I programmer must describe numeric information in terms of the storage structures that are available on a particular series of IBM computer. (In fact, the data types in PL/I are not entirely consistent with the storage structures available, since a FLOAT DECIMAL variable is really stored in the standard hexadecimal floating-point format available on the IBM 360-370 series computers.) This unfortunate choice of data types makes PL/I a difficult language to learn because the programmer is forced to learn detailed storage representations before he can program in the language.

In this section we have introduced, as primitive numeric data structures, the integers and reals. We have concentrated on presenting the storage structures commonly used to represent these data structures; we will continue this approach when examining the nonnumeric data structures in the following sections of this chapter.

Exercises for Sec. 1-4.6

1. Express the following integers in 16-bit (i) 1's complement representation, and (ii) 2's complement representation: (a) 27, (b) −256, (c) −7, (d) 7, (e) 44.
2. Express the numbers given in Exercise 1 in a packed-decimal storage representation.
3. Express .250 as a floating-point number stored in (i) the IBM 360-370 series of machines, and (ii) the CDC 6000 series of machines.
4. Express .625 as a floating-point number in the Univac 1108.

1-4.7   Character Information

The first computers were actually sophisticated calculators in the sense that they were only capable of handling numeric data. Even the first computer programs were written in a strictly numeric form, i.e., machine code. It was soon realized that machine-code programming was cumbersome and the programs were difficult to read and correct. To overcome this problem, symbolic codes were developed to represent information items which were "character" rather than numeric in nature (by a character we mean the literal expression of some element selected from an alphabet—therefore, for example, 'A' is a character from the English alphabet). The use of character data led to the formation of mnemonics for operations and addresses, which in turn led to the development of assembly languages and, later, the development of procedure-oriented languages.

A wide variety of character sets (or alphabets) are handled by the most popular computers. Two of the largest and most widely used character sets are those represented by EBCDIC (Extended Binary Coded Decimal Interchange Code) and ASCII (American Standard Code for Information Interchange). EBCDIC is a character coding system used primarily on the IBM 360-370 series of computers. ASCII was developed as a standard coding scheme for the computer industry and is used on many non-IBM machines. The character sets provided by these two coding schemes are as follows.

ASCII character set

1 English alphabet in both small and capital letters, {a,b,c, . . ., z,A,B,C, . . .,Z}
2 Decimal number characters {0,1,2,3,4,5,6,7,8,9}
3 Operation and special characters { +, −,*,/, >, =, <,|,space (SP), !,", #,$,%,&, ',(,),,,,:,;,?,@,[,\,],↑,→,', {,},~}
4 Control characters such as DEL (delete or rub out), STX (start of text), ETX (end of text), ACK (acknowledge), HT (horizontal tab), VT (vertical tab), LF (line feed), CR (carriage return), NAK (negative acknowledge), SYN (synchronous idle for synchronous transmission), ETB (end of transmission block), FS (file separator), GS (group separator), and RS (record separator)

EBCDIC character set

1 through 3 above, plus control characters which, although having different mnemonics and names than those given in 4, perform the same control functions

Let us examine these character sets in terms of the function they commonly perform. English characters, decimal number characters, and special characters can be combined to form English text. Computer applications involving natural-language text are both wide-ranging and numerous. Of course, numbers are most often used in computations. Characters which are operational in nature (for example, +, −,*,/, =) are commonly used in programs to represent operations in the programming language such as addition, subtraction, multiplication, and division. The control characters are the set of characters with which programmers are least familiar. They are signal characters which aid in the transmission or storage of information. For example, the typical format for transmitting a block of data in which several records are included in a block is illustrated in Fig. 1-4.6.

When storing information, control characters such as FS, GS, and RS are required to separate files, groups, and records of information. In Chap. 7, more will be said concerning the importance of control characters in the organization of files. The function of control characters is that of structuring information, and not of providing information relating to the solution of a problem. Therefore, control characters play an integral part in the storage representation of data structures, but not in data structures per se.

Character sets have been created for special-purpose computer applications. Many computer graphic systems use operational-type characters for the manipulation of points

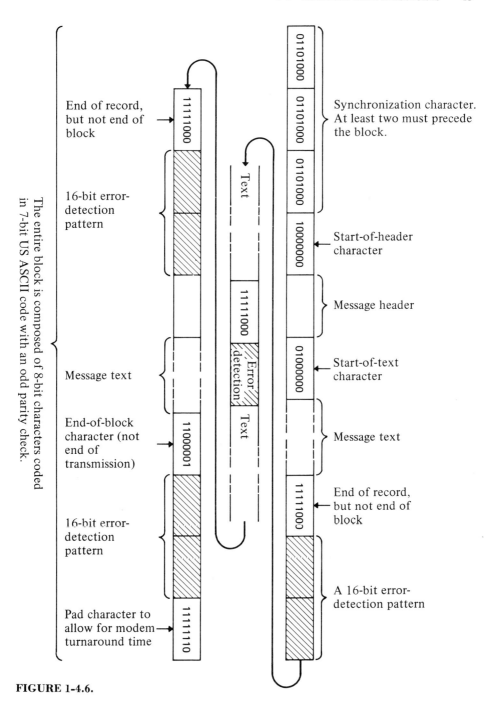

FIGURE 1-4.6.

and lines on a cathode-ray tube. For example, special characters have been used to designate the notation, translation, enlargement, or contraction of pictures on the screen. Another example of a special character set is the character set used in the APL (A Programming Language) programming system. APL, a programming language designed originally
by K. Iverson, is very effective for manipulating arrays. The APL character set includes
the capital letters from the English alphabet, the decimal numerals, the special characters
which are included in the EBCDIC and ASCII character sets, some Greek letters ($\alpha, \Delta, \epsilon,$
ι, ρ, ω) and a number of mathematically oriented characters ($\subset, \supset, \cap, \cup, \Gamma, L, \bot, \top, \downarrow, \rightarrow, \div,$
$\times, \ddot{}, \leq, \geq, \neq, \bigcirc, \square, \circ$). Many other "nonstandard" alphabets exist for special-purpose
applications, but it is beyond the scope of this text to document a number of such cases.

In the earlier discussion in this section, it was pointed out that the introduction of
character data was a necessary step towards the development of high-level languages.
However, it is interesting to note that many of the first languages, such as FORTRAN and
ALGOL 60, accommodate character data only to the limited extent of allowing the programmer to annotate the output with literal text. In languages which were developed
later, such as SNOBOL, PL/I, and ALGOL 68, *character strings* along with instructions to
manipulate string data were provided. A character string is simply a number of literal
characters which are combined under concatenation to form a data structure which is more
complex than a simple-character element (e.g., the four characters **'D'**, **'A'**, **'T'**, and **'A'** when
concatenated form the character string **'DATA'**).

While it is worthwhile to investigate characters as primitive data structures, they
are in many ways too primitive to be useful in expressing much of the nonnumeric information which can be processed by a computer. It was not purely coincidental that the designers of languages such as PL/I chose the character string as the basic data type as opposed to the character. The reasoning behind this design decision will be further illustrated
in Chap. 2.

1-4.8   Storage Structures for Character Data

A character is represented in memory as a sequence of bits, where a distinctive bit sequence
is assigned to each character in the character set. Fixed-length bit sequences can be
handled much more efficiently than variable-length bit sequences. Therefore, it is a generally adopted policy by computer manufacturers that character sets are encoded in
fixed-length bit sequences.

In the discussion in Sec. 1-1, it was demonstrated that a bit sequence of length n
could be used to represent x unique objects, where $\log_2 x = n$. If the objects we are considering are characters, then $x = 2^n$ characters can be represented using bit sequences of
length n. Therefore, with $n = 6$ and 8, we can encode up to 64 and 256 characters, respectively.

In the previous section, we presented a number of character sets which have been
designed for use on computers. Most of these character sets include the decimal numerals,
the letters from a natural-language alphabet, punctuation characters, and arithmetic
operators. Unfortunately, the bit codes for representing identical or nearly identical character sets have not been standardized in spite of a considerable effort towards standardiza-
tion in the computer industry. Some of the more commonly used codes for the FORTRAN
character set are listed in Table 1-4.11. (We have chosen this particular character set since

Table 1-4.11 Character codes in common use for the FORTRAN character set, given in octal.

Character	360 EBCDIC	ASCII	UNIVAC CPU Code	6600 Display Code	External BCD	Hollerith Punch Positions
A	301	101	06	01	61	12-1
B	302	102	07	02	62	12-2
C	303	103	10	03	63	12-3
D	304	104	11	04	64	12-4
E	305	105	12	05	65	12-5
F	306	106	13	06	66	12-6
G	307	107	14	07	67	12-7
H	310	110	15	10	70	12-8
I	311	111	16	11	71	12-9
J	321	112	17	12	41	11-1
K	322	113	20	13	42	11-2
L	323	114	21	14	43	11-3
M	324	115	22	15	44	11-4
N	325	116	23	16	45	11-5
O	326	117	24	17	46	11-6
P	327	120	25	20	47	11-7
Q	330	121	26	21	50	11-8
R	331	122	27	22	51	11-9
S	342	123	30	23	22	0-2
T	343	124	31	24	23	0-3
U	344	125	32	25	24	0-4
V	345	126	33	26	25	0-5
W	346	127	34	27	26	0-6
X	347	130	35	30	27	0-7
Y	350	131	36	31	30	0-8
Z	351	132	37	32	31	0-9
0	360	060	60	33	12	0
1	361	061	61	34	01	1
2	362	062	62	35	02	2
3	363	063	63	36	03	3
4	364	064	64	37	04	4
5	365	065	65	40	05	5
6	366	066	66	41	06	6
7	367	067	67	42	07	7
8	370	070	70	43	10	8
9	371	071	71	44	11	9
+	116	053	42	45	60	12-6-8
−	140	055	41	46	40	11

Table 1-4.11   Character codes in common use for the FORTRAN character set, given in octal. (Continued)

Character	360 EBCDIC	ASCII	UNIVAC CPU Code	6600 Display Code	External BCD	Hollerith Punch Positions
*	134	052	50	47	54	11-8-4
/	141	057	74	50	21	0-1
blank	100	040	05	55	20	space
(	115	050	51	51	34	12-5-8
)	135	051	40	52	74	11-5-8
$	133	044	47	53	53	11-8-3
=	176	075	44	54	13	6-8
,	153	054	56	56	33	0-8-3
.	113	056	75	57	73	12-8-3

the FORTRAN language, and hence its character set, has been standardized and is available on a wide variety of computers.)

The codes adopted by the sample set of computers are listed as follows:

EBCDIC -------------- IBM 360-370 series
ASCII ------------------ Burroughs 5000-6000 series, PDP-10, PDP-11, Hewlett-Packard 2100 series
Univac CPU Code -- Univac 1108
6600 Display Code -- CDC 6600

The External BCD code is a 6-bit code which is used for storing information on magnetic tape. The Hollerith code has become a standard code for representing information on punched cards. Both of these codes can be handled on a wide variety of machines.

The most widely accepted code for internal use (i.e., for character-string information in the main memory of the computer) is the ASCII (American Standard Code for Information Interchange), in spite of IBM's tremendous influence in the computer industry. Most computer manufacturers which have recently entered the industry have adopted ASCII. Established companies, such as IBM, hesitate to change their character codes because their new products will not be compatible with previously developed products.

Earlier in this section, we stated that a bit sequence of length 8 could represent up to 256 characters. While the EBCDIC code is 8 bits in length, the standard character set which is supported by IBM equipment contains only 105 characters (including control characters). Therefore, in most circumstances, the EBCDIC code is only $105/256 \times 100\% = 41\%$ efficient. However, if additional characters are needed for special-purpose applications (e.g., computer graphics applications), they can be readily assigned to the open codes existing in the coding scheme.

The ASCII scheme uses 7 bits, implying that a total of 128 characters are representable. Since each of these codes is assigned to a unique character, ASCII is a very efficient coding scheme. If, however, new characters are required for special-purpose applications, open codes are nonexistent. Undoubtedly, the designers of ASCII felt that the character set was universal enough to be used for any application. Unfortunately, they did not allow for the advent of programming systems such as APL.

One method of extending a character set which is already 100 percent utilized is to use one or two of the existing characters as *escape* (or shift) *characters*. An excellent example of character-set extension can be seen in the 5-bit (32 character) telegraphy code shown in Table 1-4.12. In this case, two characters (a letter shift and a figure shift) extend the range of the character set. Whenever a figure-shift character appears, the characters following are upper-case characters, until a letter-shift character appears in a sequence of characters. Similarly, the characters following a letter shift are letters until a figure shift occurs.

For example, the text

OIL PRODUCTION (MAY 4) 94,247 BPD.

would be encoded as

lsOIL PRODUCTION fs (lsMAY fs4) 94,247 lsBPDfs.

where ls means letter shift and fs means figure shift.

Table 1-4.12   Baudot 5-bit telegraphy code.

Code	Lower Case	Upper Case	Code	Lower Case	Upper Case
11000	A	×	11100	Q	1
10011	B	?	01010	R	4
01110	C	:	10100	S	,
10010	D	$	00001	T	5
10000	E	3	11100	U	7
10110	F	!	01111	V	;
01011	G	&	11001	W	2
00101	H	#	10111	X	/
01100	I	8	10101	Y	6
11010	J	Bell	10001	Z	"
11110	K	(	00000	Blanks	
01001	L	)	11111	Letter shift	
00111	M	.	11011	Figure shift	
00110	N	,	00100	Space	
00011	O	9	00010	Carriage return	
01101	P	0	01000	Line feed	

A simple variation on this same scheme is to use an escape character to represent a change in mode. The appearance of an escape character indicates that all subsequent characters, up to the next appearance of the escape character, are taken from the extended character set. Using this scheme, the previous text would be represented as

OIL PRODUCTION es(esMAY es4) 94,247 esBPDes.

where es means escape character.

Coding schemes involving escape characters are commonly used in the transmission or temporary storage of information. For applications requiring the manipulation of character text, characters are usually transformed into a "complete" code (i.e., a code not involving escape characters, such as ASCII) which can be handled more easily by the processing unit in a computer.

A final topic related to the storage representation of character data is that of conversion between numbers and characters. It is commonplace to find text which contains characters representing numerical information (e.g., the date, an address, or a quantity on order). Even applications which are generally considered to be nonnumeric in nature, such as business data-processing applications, require the manipulation of numeric information using arithmetic operators. To perform such operations, it is necessary to convert the numeric characters into a fixed-point or floating-point internal representation. In some machines (e.g., IBM 360-370 series), hardware instructions are provided to do the conversion. In most instances, however, conversions between character and numeric representation must be implemented by programs.

By examining the character-coding schemes that have been developed, it is obvious that the majority of character codes are designed with conversion in mind. Adjacent numerals (e.g., 6 and 7) are assigned adjacent codes (e.g., $(066)_8$, $(067)_8$ in ASCII, and $(F6)_{16}$, $(F7)_{16}$ in EBCDIC). This adjacency property facilitates conversion in the following manner. By subtracting the character code for zero from the given character code, we arrive at the numeric value of the character. For example, the ASCII representations of the characters '0' and '9' are $(060)_8$ and $(071)_8$, respectively. The result of subtracting the encoded value of '0' (i.e., $(120)_8$) from the encoded value of '9' (i.e., $(131)_8$) is $(11)_8$, which of course is the correct fixed-point representation for 9 in octal.

The following algorithm handles character to fixed-point numeric conversion for any coding scheme which has the adjacency property. To be more precise, the algorithm is generalized so as to handle the conversion of multidigit character strings, such as '4937', to a fixed-point representation.

Algorithm CONVERT_CHARACTER_TO_NUMERIC.   Given a multidigit character string designated as NUMBCHAR, find its equivalent integer representation and store this value in NUMBER. NUMBCHAR[i] denotes the ith character starting from the left in the multidigit string NUMBCHAR. The function DECODE returns the code representation for its character argument (e.g., if the character '0' is encoded in ASCII, then DECODE('0') returns $(120)_8$ or an equivalent numeric representation).

1.   [Initialize the integer value and the constant ZEROREP]   Set NUMBER ← 0 and
     ZEROREP ← DECODE('0').

2. [Establish repeat loop to handle a number of length LENGTH(NUMBCHAR)] Repeat step 3 for i = 1, 2, 3, . . ., LENGTH(NUMBCHAR).
3. [Convert ith character]   Set NUMBER ← 10 × NUMBER + DECODE(NUMBCHAR[i]) − ZEROREP.
4. [End]   Exit.

The problem of converting a positive number to a sequence of numeric characters involves a process which is basically the converse of the previous conversion algorithm. The following algorithm is a solution to this conversion problem in general.

Algorithm CONVERT_NUMERIC_TO_CHARACTER.   Given an integer NUMBER, find its equivalent character-string representation. The function ENCODE returns the character equivalent of the encoded representation of its argument (e.g., ENCODE$((131)_8)$ is '9' in ASCII). MOD is a function which returns the remainder in the division of its first argument by its second argument (e.g., MOD(23, 10) is 3).

1. [Initialization]   Set NUMBCHAR ← empty string.
2. Repeat steps 3 and 4 while NUMBER ≠ 0.
3. [Concatenate new numeric equivalent to the part of the number already formed] Set NUMBCHAR ← ENCODE(DECODE('0') + MOD(NUMBER,10)) ○ NUMBCHAR
4. [Remove least significant decimal digit]   Set NUMBER ← NUMBER / 10.
5. [End]   Exit.

In this section we have concentrated upon the storage representation of character data. We have by no means completed our discussion on character information. In Chap. 2 we will consider the character as part of a more complex data structure—namely, the character string.

Exercises for Sec. 1-4.8

1. Given a single-character argument, the PL/I function UNSPEC returns a string of bits which are representative of the internal storage representation for that character. For example, UNSPEC('1') returns '11110001'B and UNSPEC('*') returns '01011100'B. Write a PL/I program for converting a decimal-digit character to its FIXED representation. That is, the program should convert '4' to 4.
2. Write a PL/I procedure for converting an integer to a decimal digit character (i.e., 4 to '4').

1-4.9   Logical Information

A logical data item is a primitive data structure that can assume the values of either "true" or "false." (In a programming situation, true and false are expressed in many different ways, depending on the programming language used—for example, FORTRAN—.TRUE. and .FALSE., ALGOL—true and false, PL/I—'1'B and '0'B, LISP—T and NIL, etc.) Logical quantities represent constant truth values (e.g., "2 divides exactly into 4" is always true and "2 divides exactly into 5" is always false), or values which change depending on time or circumstance (e.g., "Jim is twenty years old"). Only two logical constants exist: *true* and *false*. Logical situations which are subject to change can be represented by logical variables. However, to properly motivate the need for logical variables, first we should discuss the logical operations that can be applied to logical data.

Just as operations exist for arithmetic data (i.e., operations such as addition, subtraction, multiplication, etc.), operations exist for logical data. The three most common logical operations are "anding", "oring", and "complementing" which are popularly represented by the operators $\wedge$, $\vee$, and $\sim$, respectively. If X and Y depict logical variables, then $\wedge$, $\vee$, and $\sim$ are defined as follows:

$\wedge$ The result of X $\wedge$ Y is true only if X and Y both have the value true; otherwise, the result is false.

$\vee$ The result of X $\vee$ Y is false only if X and Y have the value false; otherwise, the result is true.

$\sim$ The result of $\sim$X (note that $\sim$ is a unary operator, i.e., an operator with one operand) is true if X has the value false, and the result of $\sim$X is false if X has the value true.

Table 1-4.13 defines the results of the three logical operations.

Expressions involving logical operands commonly arise when using the *relational operators:* $<$, $\leq$, $=$, $\neq$, $\geq$, $>$. We are familiar with the application of relational operators to arithmetic operands. The results of relational operations are the logical values "true" and "false," as exemplified in expressions like $(1 + 5) = 6$ (which is true) and $5 < 4$ (which is false). Relational operators can also be used in conjunction with character and pointer data (in a restricted sense), and we will encounter examples of these relational operators later on in the book.

As computer programmers, we continually face problems which involve logical decisions. When formulating an algorithm, our ideas are organized in terms of logical steps that lead to a solution of the problem to be solved. These logical steps are reflected in the control structure of the programs for the algorithms which are formulated. For example, in programming an accounts-payable application, part of the problem statement might be: "If the current balance is negative, then calculate and add the interest charge." The condition "current balance is negative" is a logical one and, as part of a program, it could be written as "CURRENT_BAL < 0".

The value of such a condition may be variable because it is dependent upon the

Table 1-4.13   Tabular definition of the logical operators
$\wedge$, $\vee$, and $\sim$.

X	Y	X $\wedge$ Y	X $\vee$ Y	$\sim$X
T	T	T	T	F
T	F	F	T	F
F	T	F	T	T
F	F	F	F	T

values of the operands, which may change during program execution. Sometimes it is convenient to represent logical conditions which vary during program execution, such as "CURRENT_BAL < 0", by logical variables. Logical variables are used most often to represent the values of complex logical expressions (for example, (A < B & C < D)|(B < A & D < C)), which might needlessly require reevaluation several times during the execution of a program. Also, logical variables are popularly used to represent terminating conditions on loop constructs in which the terminating condition depends on a logical expression (e.g., the DO WHILE group in PL/I).

1-4.10 Storage Structures for Logical Data

The storage representation of logical values is dependent upon the language translator (i.e., compiler or interpreter) that is processing the program and the machine for which the translator is designed. The most obvious storage structure that can be applied to logical data is the single bit. In this scheme it is conventional to represent the value *true* by an "on" bit (i.e., a bit with a value of 1) and the value *false* by an "off" bit (i.e., a bit with a value of 0). The IBM PL/I level-F compiler attempts to use a bit storage structure for logical values whenever possible.

Most machines do not have instructions which allow direct access of a given bit in memory. Therefore, the isolation of the value of a particular logical data item may involve the execution of several machine instructions. Consequently, other storage representations have been adopted.

One of the most inefficient ways (in a storage sense) of representing logical data is to assign an entire word of memory to a logical item. In the WATFIV compiler, for example, the values .TRUE. and .FALSE. are represented by eight 1 bits and eight 0 bits in the leftmost byte of a 32-bit word, respectively. While such full-word representations are extremely wasteful of memory space, they facilitate fast access of logical information. Of course, fast access is achieved because most machine instructions operate on words of data, as opposed to specific bits of information.

Other compilers, such as the PL/C compiler for the IBM 360-370 series computers, utilize the smallest addressable unit of memory (i.e., the 8-bit byte) to represent logical values. This storage representation has the advantage of quick access and relatively small storage requirements.

This section completes a brief description of logical data and their representation. In subsequent chapters, we will return to a discussion of logical data when describing more complex data structures, in particular, logical (or bit) strings and logical arrays.

1-4.11 Pointer Information

A *pointer* (or *link*) is a reference to a data structure. We can illustrate how a pointer might be used by considering a problem which often arises when compiling a program. Suppose a program contains four occurrences of the real constant, 3.1459. During the compilation process, four copies of 3.1459 could be created. However, it is more efficient to use one copy of 3.1459 and three pointers referencing the single copy, since less space is needed to repre-

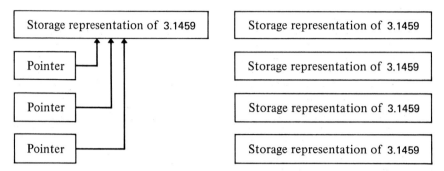

FIGURE 1-4.7   Multiple references to a real number through a pointer versus multiple copies of a real number.

sent a pointer than a real number in floating-point representation (see Fig. 1-4.7). In the next section we will be saying more about the storage representation of pointers.

Probably the most important property of a pointer is that, as a single fixed-size data item, it provides a homogeneous method of referencing any data structure, regardless of the structure's type or complexity. In the previous example, the three pointers could point to an integer constant, a character constant, or a logical constant, and the method of referencing would have been the same, i.e., an address pointing at the required data item.

A final important characteristic of pointers is that, in some instances, they permit faster addition and deletion of elements to and from a data structure. In later chapters, in particular Chaps. 4, 5, and 7, we will see that this restructuring property is an extremely important one.

It is crucial to realize that, with the introduction of a pointer, we are now provided with two methods of accessing a data structure. The method we are most familiar with is commonly called the *computed address method*. In this method, a data structure is accessed directly through an address (either an absolute or relative address). This address is computed by the language translator (i.e., compiler, interpreter, or assembler) which is processing the source program. In the second method, the *pointer* or *link addressing method*, the address of a data object is not computed, but is assigned to a pointer. To access a data-structure element, we first load a pointer value. The pointer value (i.e., address) provides a reference to the data structure of interest. Access to a particular data element within the data structure may require some additional computation, depending upon the complexity of the data structure. We will be more concerned with this aspect as we introduce more complex data structures. The pointer addressing method is, in general, more time consuming than the computed address method, since access to an item is always done via a pointer. However, there are situations in which the flexibility provided by indirectly referencing a data object using a pointer is well worth any time inefficiencies that are generated.

The difference between the two addressing modes is clearly identified by examining a subject which is too often misunderstood by programmers—parameter passing in subroutines (i.e., procedures) and functions. Consider the following program segment:

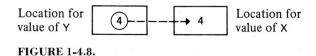

Location for value of Y ... Location for value of X

FIGURE 1-4.8.

```
                                ┌──────formal parameter
      module EXAMPLE(X)◄╯
         .
         .
         .
      end EXAMPLE
         .
         .
         .
      Y ← 4                ┌──────actual parameter
      call EXAMPLE(Y)◄╯
         .
         .
         .
```

In this program, **EXAMPLE** is the name of a module (i.e., subroutine or function), **X** is a *formal parameter*, and **Y** is the *actual parameter* in the call statement. One method of parameter passing which is available in programming languages such as SNOBOL, LISP, and ALGOL W is *call-by-value*. In call-by-value, the value of an actual parameter is assigned (at execution time) to a predetermined location that has been allocated to the corresponding formal parameter (see Fig. 1-4.8).

Whenever access to a formal parameter is required, it is done directly via the predetermined *computed address*. Any assignment to the formal parameter affects only the value of the formal parameter, and *not* the value of the actual parameter. Therefore, in the example program, when execution returns from the module to the statement following the call statement, **Y** retains the same value it had prior to the call.

Two other parameter-passing schemes (*call-by-name* in ALGOL 60 and ALGOL W, and *call-by-reference* in FORTRAN and PL/I) make use of the pointer method for accessing parameter values. Instead of the value of the actual parameter, a pointer to the location of the actual parameter is passed and is assigned to the formal parameter. This association is shown in Fig. 1-4.9. Therefore, when the value of **X** is desired in the module **EXAMPLE**, the value of **Y** is retrieved via the pointer assigned to **X**.

Problems can arise when using parameter-passing methods which involve pointers. If the actual parameter is an expression, such as **Y + 4**, instead of a simple variable, then

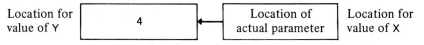

Location for value of Y ... Location of actual parameter ... Location for value of X

FIGURE 1-4.9.

it does not make sense to assign a value to the corresponding formal parameter, since the effect would be to assign a value to the expression Y + 4.

Such meaningless assignments have created problems when using call-by-reference in FORTRAN. For example, if we call the module EXAMPLE with the expression 2 as the actual parameter, then the address of the constant 2 is assigned to the formal parameter X (see Fig. 1-4.10). If X is assigned the value 4, then the effect is to assign 4 to the memory location at which the constant 2 resides, that is, 2 now becomes 4. When a return is made to the statement following the call to EXAMPLE, the statement Y ← 2 + 2 is executed. However, the constant 2 now has the value 4 and Y will take on the value 4 + 4 or 8. Amazing but true! This situation has been eliminated in PL/I by creating a dummy location for the value of the evaluated expression which appears as an actual parameter. Hence, if a formal parameter is assigned a value of 4, the value of the dummy location is changed, not the constant 2.

In call-by-name parameter passing, assignments to formal parameters with expressions as actual parameters are disallowed. A special routine, called a *thunk*, is set up to perform the evaluation of the actual parameter. The address of the thunk is assigned to the location of the formal parameter. Therefore, whenever the value of the formal parameter is required, the thunk is located via the pointer assigned to the formal parameter location and then is evaluated. Hence, while both call-by-reference and call-by-name use a pointer addressing scheme, a basic difference does exist. In call-by-reference, an actual parameter is evaluated only once—before the procedure is called. In call-by-name, an actual parameter is evaluated each time the formal parameter is referenced.

Some of the first programming languages developed, such as COBOL, FORTRAN, and ALGOL 60, did not have a pointer data type. However, the effect of a pointer can be simulated in these languages using an index into an array. (We will discuss this idea in Chap. 4.) Languages which were developed later, such as PL/I, SNOBOL, ALGOL W, and ALGOL 68, have a pointer type which can be controlled explicitly by the programmer. The advantages of a pointer type will become clearer when we consider the algorithms for accessing linked data structures in later chapters.

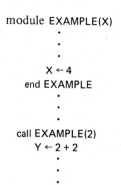

```
module EXAMPLE(X)
        .
        .
        .
      X ← 4
   end EXAMPLE
        .
        .
        .
 call EXAMPLE(2)
      Y ← 2 + 2
        .
        .
        .
```

FIGURE 1-4.10 Program illustrating pitfalls of call-by-reference form of parameter passing that exists in FORTRAN.

1-4.12   Storage Structures for Pointer Information

In the previous section on pointer data, it was indicated that a pointer is an address which references a data structure. In terms of storage representation, addresses are generally assigned a word or half-word of storage in most computers. Of course, the larger the number of addresses (i.e., the address space) in the computer, the larger the amount of storage needed to represent an address.

The address of a pointer may reference a data structure in one of two modes—absolute or relative. Absolute mode implies that the value of the pointer is an absolute memory location, such as 7632, at which the data structure being pointed at may reside. A relative pointer carries as a value an offset into a region of memory relative to some base location for that region. (This base location is often stored in a special register called a *base register*.) Hence, if the value of a pointer is 5 and the base location of the data area for a program is 7627, then the effective absolute address of the pointer is 7627 + 5 = 7632.

In early computers only an absolute mode of addressing was available. Today, however, all but very unsophisticated minicomputers have relative-mode addressing capabilities. Most computer systems allow more than one program to reside in memory at one time. Therefore, if a program is executed twice, there exists a good possibility that it is not allotted the same memory locations. If a relative mode of addressing is used, then programs can be relocated in memory by simply changing the base location rather than all the pointer values, as would be necessary in an absolute mode. Hence, relative-mode addressing is more popular than absolute-mode addressing.

At the machine instruction level, the accessing of a data structure via a pointer is generally accomplished in one of two ways. The first method involves the loading of the pointer's value (i.e., the address of the first element in the data structure) into an accumulator or index register. A machine-level instruction whose operand refers to this index register is then used to provide access to the desired data structure. This use of an index register is illustrated in machine-level instructions as follows:

(LD means "load" and LDI means "load with index")
LD X, R1   —   load the pointer X into register R1
LDI R1, R2—   load the contents of the memory location specified by the pointer (i.e., address) contained in R1 into register R2

The second method involves the use of *indirect addressing*. In this method, the operand of a machine instruction is used to derive directly the address of the information we wish to access. For example, consider a machine-level instruction such as

LD @X, R2

If the contents of memory location X are an address, say Y, then the contents of memory location Y are loaded into the register R2 upon execution of the above instruction. Therefore, the net effect is to load directly into R2 the contents of the memory location pointed to by Y. The one instruction involving an indirect address is equivalent to the two instructions given previously involving an index register.

Indirect addressing provides a quicker single access to a data structure than a method using index registers. However, if accesses are required for a large number of data

Table 1-4.14   Addressing capabilities for the set of sample computers.

	Indirect Addressing (Yes or No)	*Number of Index and Base Registers*	*Addressable Space*
IBM 360-370 Series	No	16 index and base registers	Memory access via index and base registers. Largest offset relative to a base register is 4095 bytes.
CDC 6600	No	3 index, 8 base registers	Access via index and base registers. Largest offset relative to base register is 262,143 bytes.
Burroughs 5500	No	8 base registers	Can access 32,768 words directly; can use base register with maximum offset of 4095 words.
PDP-10	Yes	15 index registers, memory locations 1-15 can be used as index registers also	Access via base registers has maximum offset of 8192 or 16384 words depending on implementation.
Univac 1108	Yes	2 base and 15 index registers	Access via base register, indirect addressing and index registers. Maximum base register offset of 65,535.
PDP-11	Yes	8 index registers, one is used as the program counter	Access via index register and indirect addressing. Range of valid offsets for indexed operation is -32768 to $+32767$ bytes.
Hewlett-Packard 2100 Series	Yes	the program counter is used as a base register	Access via a relative address from the program counter and indirect addressing. Maximum offset is 1024 words.

elements, the index-register method is superior to indirect addressing. The reason for this superiority is that the index register need only be loaded once and, once loaded, the contents of an index register can be changed more quickly to account for the different offsets for a number of data elements than an indirect address. (An indirect address resides in main memory, not in a register.) Table 1-4.14 exhibits some of the addressing capabilities available in the sample set of computers.

Throughout Chaps. 4, 5, and 7, the pointer plays an integral role in the expression of linked and multilinked structures which are presented. In these chapters the flexibility provided by pointers for accessing, deleting, and inserting data-structure elements will become very evident.

BIBLIOGRAPHY

DIETMEYER, D. L.: "Logic Design of Digital Systems," Allyn and Bacon, Inc., Boston, 1971.

FOSTER, C. C.: "Computer Architecture," Van Nostrand Reinhold Co., New York, 1970.

HARTLEY, R. V. L.: "Transmission of Information," *Bell Systems Tech. J.*, **7**, 1928, p. 535.

IVERSON, K. E.: "A Programming Language," John Wiley & Sons, Inc., New York, 1962.

KOLMOGOROFF, A.: "Interpolation und Extrapolation von Stationarem Sufalligen Folgen," *Bull. Acad. Sci. U.S.S.R. ser. math.*, **5**, 1942, pp. 3–14.

MANO, M. M.: "Computer Logic Design," Prentice-Hall, Englewood Cliffs, N.J., 1972.

MORRIS, C. W.: "Signs, Language, and Behavior," Prentice-Hall, Inc., New York, 1946.

REZA, F. M.: "An Introduction to Information Theory," McGraw-Hill Book Company, Toronto, 1961.

SHANNON, C. E. and W. WEAVER: "The Mathematical Theory of Communication," University of Illinois Press, Urbana, 1949.

SMITH, C. L.: "Digital Control of Industrial Processes," *Computing Surveys*, Vol. **2**, No. 3, Sept., 1970, pp. 211–242.

STONE, H. S.: "Introduction to Computer Organization and Data Structures," McGraw-Hill Book Company, New York, 1972.

TREMBLAY, J. P. and R. P. MANOHAR: "Discrete Mathematical Structures with Applications to Computer Science," McGraw-Hill Book Company, New York, 1975.

WIENER, N.: "Cybernetics," The Technology Press of M.I.T. and John Wiley & Sons, Inc., New York, 1948, 2nd ed., M.I.T. Press, Cambridge, Mass., 1961.

THE REPRESENTATION AND MANIPULATION OF STRINGS

In the previous chapter we introduced the character as a primitive data structure. It was pointed out that the character string, and not the basic character element, is the more useful data structure of the two for programs involving nonnumeric applications. In this chapter, we see how the character string can be built from character elements. We consider two formal systems for string processing; namely, the Markov algorithm and the phrase-structure grammar. String manipulation and pattern matching are discussed, especially as they relate to the programming languages PL/I and SNOBOL. A variety of storage representations for strings are examined. Finally, string applications which involve text editing, lexical analysis, KWIC indexing, and information retrieval are discussed.

2-1 DEFINITIONS AND CONCEPTS

In this chapter we are concerned with the type of operations (or manipulations) that can be performed on strings. There are many interesting properties exhibited by string operations, just as there are interesting properties for arithmetic operations over the natural numbers. To refamiliarize ourselves with some of the properties associated with operations, let us consider the operation of addition on the natural numbers. This operation can be represented, in general, by a functional system in two variables:

$$f(x, y) = x + y$$

where x and y are natural numbers. This system is well known to us and it exhibits certain interesting properties. Firstly, the sum of any two numbers is a natural number. This property is called *closure*. Closure is a necessary property for a system (i.e., a set and an operation on that set) to be classified as an algebra or algebraic system. Secondly, $(x + y) + z = x + (y + z) = x + y + z$ when x, y, and z are natural numbers; accordingly the operation of addition is said to be *associative*. Thirdly, there exists a number i such that for every natural number x, $x + i = x$. This number is zero and is called the unit element or *identity* of the additive system. There are many other important properties, such as distributivity and commutativity, which exist when arithmetic operations such as addition and multiplication are applied to the set of natural numbers.

We begin a discussion of strings by formally defining a string. To do so, we must introduce the notion of an alphabet and the operation of concatenation. Simply stated, an *alphabet* V is a finite nonempty set of symbols. The set V = {a, b, c, ..., z} is a familiar example of an alphabet and {α, β, γ, ϵ} is a four-character alphabet (which is a subalphabet of the Greek alphabet).

The *concatenation* of two alphabetic characters, say 'a' and 'b', is said to form a sequence of characters, namely 'ab'. (Note that henceforth when we refer to a character from an alphabet or a sequence of such characters, they are enclosed in single quote marks.) The operation of concatenation also applies to sequences of characters. For example, 'ab' concatenated with 'ab' is 'abab'. We denote the concatenation operator by the special symbol ○. This allows us to write expressions such as 'ab' ○ 'a' which is identical in value to 'aba'.

A *string* over an alphabet V is (1) a letter from the alphabet V, or (2) a sequence of letters derived from the concatenation of characters from the alphabet V. Examples of strings over an alphabet V = {1, 2, 3} are '1', '31', '33321', and '222'.

Let V ○ V = V² designate all strings of length two on V, V ○ V ○ V = V² ○ V = V³ designate all strings of length three on V, and, in general, V ○ V ○ ... ○ V = Vⁿ designate all strings of length n on V. Then the closure of V, denoted as V⁺, is defined as

V⁺ = V ∪ V² ∪ V³ ∪ ...

For completeness, a special string Λ called the empty (or NULL) string is often combined with V⁺ to form the closure set V* of V. That is, V* = Λ ∪ V ∪ V² ∪ V³ ∪ ... = Λ ∪ V⁺. The string Λ has the *identity* property (that is, x ○ Λ = Λ ○ x = x for any string x which is an element of V*) and it is called the identity element in the algebra formed by the set V* and the operation of concatenation. Associativity is another property of this algebra (that is, (x ○ y) ○ z = x ○ (y ○ z) = x ○ y ○ z for x, y, z ∈ V*).

As an example, consider the set of strings $V*$ that can be generated from an alphabet $V = \{a, b\}$. Some subsets of $V*$ are

$V^2 = \{'aa', 'ab', 'ba', 'bb'\}$

$V^3 = \{'aaa', 'aab', 'aba', 'abb', 'baa', 'bab', 'bba', 'bbb'\}$

$V^4 = \{'aaaa', 'aaab', 'aaba', 'aabb', 'abaa', 'abab', 'abba', 'abbb', 'baaa', 'baab',$
$'baba', 'babb', 'bbaa', 'bbab', 'bbba', 'bbbb'\}$

.

.

.

We will, on many occasions, refer to the closure set $V*$ of an alphabet.

As a final example of a string, let us examine the FORTRAN programming language. The FORTRAN alphabet consists of 26 letters, 10 digits, and a set of special characters, such as '(',')', ',', ' =', ' +', etc. It is only these characters that are used in writing a FORTRAN program. Hence, a program can be viewed as the concatenation of characters over an alphabet to yield an arbitrarily long string. In Sec. 2-5.2, we see that the problem of ensuring that only the proper set of characters appears in a program is handled by the scanning phase of a compiler.

2-2   FORMAL SYSTEMS FOR STRING PROCESSING

In this section we describe two systems for representing and manipulating character strings. We do so with two purposes in mind; namely, to reinforce some of the concepts introduced in Sec. 2-1 and, more importantly, to create an understanding of the primitive operations that can be performed on strings. The first model, the Markov algorithm, is based on a substitution-type operation which can be applied to any input string from a given alphabet. The types of manipulations that can be applied to a string using this model are virtually unlimited. In the second model, the grammar, we are less interested in performing manipulations on strings and more interested in generating or recognizing a specific subset of strings from the set of strings generated from an alphabet. Both models can be applied in practical situations, and some such situations are presented in later sections of this chapter.

2-2.1   Markov Algorithms

The first formal system for string manipulation that we examine is the Markov algorithm (due to the Russian mathematician A. A. Markov). While the Markov algorithm appears formal and mathematical in nature, the first string-processing language, COMIT, was based to a significant extent on the Markov formalism. There is a striking similarity between the Markov model and the SNOBOL programming language, which is a widely used successor of COMIT. Later, in Sec. 2-3.3, we introduce some of the string manipulation functions in SNOBOL, and it becomes clear that both the data and control structures of Markov algorithms are modeled very closely in SNOBOL.

The general strategy in a Markov algorithm is to take as input a string x and, through a number of steps (or productions) in the algorithm, transform x to an output string y. This transformation process is commonly performed in computer application areas such as text editing or program compilation. In particular, the compilation process can be thought of as the transformation of strings from a source language (such as PL/I) into strings of object code (such as an assembly language program or machine code).

The single input string x is the only data structure operated on by the algorithm; however, this string is flexible in its capacity to grow or shrink in length as transformations are applied to it. Both x and the transformed output string y contain characters from an alphabet V. Hence, x and y belong to V*.

A *simple* (Markov) *production* is a statement of the form u → w where u and w represent strings in V*, where V does not contain the symbols "→" and ".". In the production, u is called the *antecedent* and w is called the *consequent*. A production with antecedent u and consequent w is *applicable* to a string z∈V* if there is at least one occurrence of u in z; otherwise, the production is not *applicable*. If the production is applicable, then the first (i.e., leftmost) occurrence of u in z is replaced by w. For example, if a production 'ba' → 'c' is applied to the input string 'ababab', then the resulting string is 'acbab'. However, the production 'baa' → 'c' is not applicable to 'ababab'.

A Markov algorithm consists of an ordered set of productions $P_1, P_2, \ldots, P_n$. The flow of control through a Markov algorithm depends on whether or not productions are applicable. Execution starts with the first production. If a production is applicable, execution resumes with the first production. On the other hand, if a production is not applicable (i.e., a substring to be replaced is not found), execution continues to the next production.

A Markov algorithm terminates in one of two ways:

1 The last production is not applicable.
2 A *terminal production* is applicable.

A terminal production is a statement of the form x → y., where x and y represent strings in V* and the symbol "." immediately follows the consequent.

Example 2-1   Consider the Markov algorithm having the productions

P_1:   'ab' → 'b'
P_2:   'ac' → 'c'
P_3:   'aa' → 'a'

on the alphabet V = {a, b, c}. This algorithm deletes all occurrences of 'a' in a string with the exception of an 'a' if it appears as the last character in the subject string. Let us trace through the execution of this algorithm given an input string 'bacaabaa'. The symbol "⇒" is used to indicate the result of a transformation, and the substring being replaced (or matched) is underlined.

'baca͟ab͟aa' ⇒ 'bacabaa'	(by P_1)
'bac͟ab͟aa' ⇒ 'bacbaa'	(by P_1)
'ba͟c͟baa' ⇒ 'bcbaa'	(by P_2)
'bcb͟aa͟' ⇒ 'bcba'	(by P_3)

Since all productions, including the last production (P_3), are not applicable to the string 'bcba', the algorithm terminates.   ////

We are now able to define, more formally, the execution of a Markov algorithm in terms of our algorithmic notation.

Algorithm MARKOV.   We are given a Markov algorithm with a finite sequence P_1, P_2, ..., P_n of productions which are to be applied to an input string $z_0 \in V*$. Variables i and j are indices and z_i denotes the result after the application of the ith transformation to the input string z_0.

1. [Initialize i, the intermediate string index]   Set i $\leftarrow$ 0.
2. [Initialize j, the production index]   Set j $\leftarrow$ 1.
3. [Establish conditions for execution]
    Repeat step 4 while j $\leq$ n.
4. [Check for production applicability and terminal production]
    If P_j is applicable,
    then apply production P_j and set i $\leftarrow$ i $+$ 1 to obtain a new string z_i,
        if P_j is a terminal production,
        then print z_i and Exit;
        otherwise, set j $\leftarrow$ 1;
    otherwise, set j $\leftarrow$ j $+$ 1.
5. [The algorithm is blocked]   Print z_i, and Exit.

In Example 2-1, the productions P_1:   'ab' $\rightarrow$ 'b', P_2:   'ac' $\rightarrow$ 'c', and P_3:   'aa' $\rightarrow$ 'a' can be expressed in a compressed form 'a'x $\rightarrow$ x (x$\in$V) by using a variable x in an algorithm. The variable x in this production assumes a role similar to that of a variable in a program (that is, x can take on any value from a defined range of values, which in this case is the set {a, b, c}). A formal description of the Markov algorithm for deleting all occurrences of 'a', except for one on the end of the string, is simply:

> MA: DELETE_A (x $\in$ V)
> P_1:   'a'x $\rightarrow$ x

Note that we have included an algorithm header, MA (Markov Algorithm) and a declaration for the variable x along with its range set V.

Example 2-2   Let V be a certain alphabet and let y represent a character from this alphabet. We would like to write Markov algorithms to transform any string z $\in$ V* (1) into the string yz, and (2) into the string zy:

> MA: YZ (y $\in$ V)
> P_1: $\wedge \rightarrow$ y.

Given as input a string z, y is inserted on the front of the string and the algorithm YZ is completed.

The second problem is not as trivial. Since the first occurrence of $\wedge$ in z is to the left of the first symbol in z, a production of the form $\wedge \to y.$ will not work. An algorithm consisting of the production $z \to zy.$ is not appropriate because z is an arbitrary string in $V*$ and variables in a Markov algorithm can only assume single-letter values and cannot take on string values. For the algorithm to work for all possible strings z, it would require an infinite number of productions.

A production is always applied to the first occurrence of x (where $x \to y$ is a production) in string z. A problem arises when we desire to apply a production to the second, third, fourth, or last occurrence of x. To overcome this problem, we create a set of *auxiliary symbols* which are used as *markers*. Markers allow us to mark a particular point within a string, thus making possible the application of a production at that point.

Returning to the second part of this example, let V be the alphabet and α be a marker, $\alpha \notin V$. The result of applying the following Markov algorithm to a string z is the string zy.

MA: ZY $(x,y \in V)$
  P_1: $\alpha x \to x\alpha$
  P_2: $\alpha \to y.$
  P_3: $\wedge \to \alpha$

Since the input string z does not initially contain the auxiliary symbol α, production P_3 is applied to z, yielding αz. Production P_1 is used repeatedly to move α to the right of the symbols in z. If z contains m characters, then the result of applying P_1 m times is $z\alpha$. P_1 no longer applies at this stage, but P_2, which is terminal, does apply. Hence, the result of the Markov algorithm is zy.   ////

Let us consider a final example which also involves the use of marker symbols.

Example 2-3   Given a string $z \in V*$ such that $z = z_1z_2z_3 \ldots z_{n-1}z_n$, we want to generate an output string, z', which is the reverse of z (that is, $z' = z_nz_{n-1} \ldots z_3z_2z_1$). We employ α and β as auxiliary characters.

MA: REVERSE $(x, y \in V)$
  P_1: $\alpha\alpha \to \beta$
  P_2: $\beta\alpha \to \beta$
  P_3: $\beta x \to x\beta$
  P_4: $\beta \to \wedge.$
  P_5: $\alpha xy \to y\alpha x$
  P_6: $\wedge \to \alpha$

Initially, α is placed in front of z by the application of P_6. Then P_5 moves the α until the last character of the string z is encountered or until another α is reached. This process (i.e., the application of P_6 and P_5) is continued until the first symbol remains as α. The symbol β is used to delete all occurrences of α. This is accomplished by the application of P_1, P_2, and P_3. After all α's are removed, the β is removed via P_4 and the algorithm terminates.

Given z = 'abc', the sequence of transformations applied to z by the algorithm **REVERSE** is as follows:

'abc'	$\Rightarrow \alpha$'abc'	(by P_6)
	$\Rightarrow$ 'b'α'ac'	(by P_5)
	$\Rightarrow$ 'bc'α'a'	(by P_5)
	$\Rightarrow \alpha$'bc'α'a'	(by P_6)
	$\Rightarrow$ 'c'α'b'α'a'	(by P_5)
	$\Rightarrow \alpha$'c'α'b'α'a'	(by P_6)
	$\Rightarrow \alpha\alpha$'c'α'b'α'a'	(by P_6)
	$\Rightarrow \beta$'c'α'b'α'a'	(by P_1)
	$\Rightarrow$ 'c'$\beta\alpha$'b'α'a'	(by P_3)
	$\Rightarrow$ 'c'β'b'α'a'	(by P_2)
	$\Rightarrow$ 'cb'$\beta\alpha$'a'	(by P_3)
	$\Rightarrow$ 'cb'β'a'	(by P_2)
	$\Rightarrow$ 'cba'β	(by P_3)
	$\Rightarrow$ 'cba'	(by P_4) ////

From the examples in the previous discussion, it should be obvious that the order in which we arrange the productions totally determines the flow of execution in a Markov algorithm. For example, if we had decided to place production P_6 (that is, $\Lambda \rightarrow \alpha$) as P_1 in Example 2-3, then the **REVERSE** algorithm would generate an infinite number of α's in front of the input string and the algorithm would never terminate. Although the control structure for Markov algorithms is simple, it allows virtually no flexibility in the organization of productions.

As an alternative to the Markov model just proposed, we introduce a model which allows the labeling of productions to effect a more flexible transfer of control between productions. Labeling changes the original Markov model in two ways:

1 If a production is applicable and a label is appended to it, then the transfer of control is to the production bearing that label name.
2 If a production is not applicable or if no label is appended to the production, execution continues to the next production if there is a next production, or halts if there is no next production.

Example 2-4   Let us rewrite the **REVERSE** Markov algorithm as presented in Example 2-3 in the form of a labeled Markov algorithm (henceforth referred to as an LMA).

LMA: REVERSE (x, y ϵ V)
P_1: $\alpha xy \rightarrow y\alpha x$ (P_1)
P_2: $\alpha x\beta \rightarrow \beta x$ (P_4)
P_3: $\alpha x \rightarrow \beta x$ (P_6)
P_4: $\alpha\beta \rightarrow \Lambda.$
P_5: $\alpha\alpha \rightarrow \Lambda.$
P_6: $\Lambda \rightarrow \alpha$ (P_1)

An execution trace for this LMA given an input string 'abc' is as follows:

Intermediate String	Production Applicable	Number of Attempted Applications
$\text{'abc'} \Rightarrow \alpha\text{'abc'}$	(by P_6)	6
$\Rightarrow \text{'b'}\alpha\text{'ac'}$	(by P_1)	1
$\Rightarrow \text{'bc'}\alpha\text{'a'}$	(by P_1)	1
$\Rightarrow \text{'bc'}\beta\text{'a'}$	(by P_3)	3
$\Rightarrow \alpha\text{'bc'}\beta\text{'a'}$	(by P_6)	1
$\Rightarrow \text{'c'}\alpha\text{'b'}\beta\text{'a'}$	(by P_1)	1
$\Rightarrow \text{'c'}\beta\text{'ba'}$	(by P_2)	2
$\Rightarrow \alpha\text{'c'}\beta\text{'ba'}$	(by P_6)	3
$\Rightarrow \beta\text{'cba'}$	(by P_2)	2
$\Rightarrow \alpha\beta\text{'cba'}$	(by P_6)	3
$\Rightarrow \text{'cba'}$	(by P_4)	4

$$\text{Total} = 27$$

(Note that production P_5 is only applicable if z is initially Λ.)

For an input of z = 'abc', 27 tests for production applicability are required in the LMA formulation, while 57 such tests are needed for the MA in Example 2-3. (By the number of tests for production applicability, we mean the number of attempted production applications during the execution of the algorithms.) Not only does the addition of labels provide increased flexibility in algorithm design, but it also allows for more efficient algorithm execution. Much more efficient algorithms exist for reversing a string, and one such algorithm is given below.

LMA: REVERSE1 (x, y ϵ V)

P_1:	$\alpha\alpha \to \Lambda$	(P_4)
P_2:	$\alpha xy \to y\alpha x$	(P_2)
P_3:	$\Lambda \to \alpha$	(P_1)
P_4:	$\alpha \to \Lambda$	(P_4)

This algorithm has two fewer productions, one fewer marker symbols, and reverses the input string 'abc' using only 18 tests for production applicability.   ////

Example 2-5   Let us consider one more example of a labeled Markov algorithm. Consider the problem of deleting the first character 'a' from a string along with all other characters to the left of 'a'. If there are characters to the left of 'a', a 'c' is to be concatenated to the front of the resulting string; otherwise, a 'd' is concatenated to the front of the string.

To construct such an algorithm, we need an auxiliary symbol α to mark the location of the first 'a' in the input string. Once the marker is placed, it is a simple matter to remove all previous characters and place the appropriate character 'c' or 'd' in front of the resulting substring. Two algorithms to do this are given in Table 2-2.1:

Table 2-2.1   Algorithms for Example 2-5.

LMA: LEFTSUBSTR1 $(x \in V)$		LMA: LEFTSUBSTR2 $(x \in V)$	
P_1:	$x'a' \to \alpha$		$x'a' \to \alpha$
P_2:	$x\alpha \to \alpha$ (P2)	DELETE:	$x\alpha \to \alpha$ (DELETE)
P_3:	$\alpha \to 'c'.$		$\alpha \to 'c'.$
P_4:	$'a' \to 'd'$		$'a' \to 'd'$

Notice that in the algorithm to the right in Table 2-2.1, we have dropped the convention of labeling every production and have chosen to label only where necessary. Also, we have used more meaningful label names. Hereafter, we adopt this more readable form of expressing LMAs.   ////

One might question if the introduction of labels to Markov algorithms alters the computational power of the Markov model. Galler and Perlis [1970], from whom we have borrowed our labeling technique, have constructively demonstrated that the two models (i.e., the MA model and the LMA model) are equivalent in computational power (i.e., any function computable using an MA is computable using an LMA, and vice versa). By "constructively demonstrated," we mean that they have produced a Markov algorithm which takes as its input string a labeled Markov algorithm and translates this LMA into an equivalent MA. It is obvious that every MA can be converted to an LMA by simply appending the label (P_1) to each production that is not terminal. Hence, labels are a convenience which help us to write more efficient algorithms, but they provide no additional computing power.

Before concluding this section, two additional important topics must be discussed—namely, the concept of a subalgorithm and the formulation of multiple-input parameters. The purpose of a subalgorithm within the Markov model is identical to that of a procedure or subroutine in a high-level programming language—namely, to reduce the number of productions (or instructions) necessary to express an algorithmic process which contains a number of identical subparts. Example 2-6 illustrates this purpose and shows how subalgorithms are invoked in the Markov model.

Example 2-6   An input string $z \in V^*$ is assumed to have an initial character of $'a'$, $'b'$, or $'c'$. If the first character is an $'a'$, a duplicate copy of the string should be the output. If the first character is a $'b'$, a string composed of four copies of z is the result, and if the first character is a $'c'$, a string made up of eight copies of z is produced. z is unchanged if $z = \Lambda$ or if the first character is other than $'a'$, $'b'$, or $'c'$.

It is immediately obvious that a process which would duplicate a given string would be of great benefit. A description of such an LMA and a trace of the LMA for input $'abb'$ are as follows:

LMA: DUPL $(x,y \in V)$
         $\Lambda \to \alpha$
DOUBLE: $\alpha x \to x\beta x\alpha$ (DOUBLE)

POSITION: $\beta xy \rightarrow y\beta x$ (POSITION)
REMOVEβ: $\beta \rightarrow \Lambda$ (REMOVEβ)

$\qquad\qquad \alpha \rightarrow \Lambda$

A trace for 'abb' is as follows:

'abb' $\Rightarrow \alpha$'abb'	(by first production)
$\Rightarrow$ 'a'β'a'α'bb'	(by DOUBLE)
$\Rightarrow$ 'a'β'ab'β'b'α'b'	(by DOUBLE)
$\Rightarrow$ 'a'β'ab'β'bb'β'b'α	(by DOUBLE)
$\Rightarrow$ 'ab'β'a'β'bb'β'b'α	(by POSITION)
$\Rightarrow$ 'ab'β'ab'β'b'β'b'α	(by POSITION)
$\Rightarrow$ 'abb'β'a'β'b'β'b'α	(by POSITION)
$\Rightarrow$ 'abba'β'b'β'b'α	(by REMOVEβ)
$\Rightarrow$ 'abbab'β'b'α	(by REMOVEβ)
$\Rightarrow$ 'abbabb'α	(by REMOVEβ)
$\Rightarrow$ 'abbabb'	(by last production)

Note that two auxiliary symbols are needed in DUPL: α is used to duplicate a character, and β is used to ensure that the proper sequence of characters in the original string is maintained.

The LMA originally desired in this example can now be written.

LMA: EG2_6

$\qquad \Lambda \rightarrow \alpha$

$\qquad \alpha$'a' $\rightarrow$ 'a'   (2TIMES)

$\qquad \alpha$'b' $\rightarrow$ 'b'   (4TIMES)

$\qquad \alpha$'c' $\rightarrow$ 'c'   (8TIMES)

$\qquad \alpha \rightarrow \Lambda.$

8TIMES: $\Lambda \rightarrow \Lambda$ (DUPL)
4TIMES: $\Lambda \rightarrow \Lambda$ (DUPL)
2TIMES: $\Lambda \rightarrow \Lambda$ (DUPL)

Access to an LMA subalgorithm is gained by using the name of the subalgorithm as the object in a labeled transfer of control. Termination of the execution of a subalgorithm causes control to revert back to the calling algorithm at the step following the step which invoked the subalgorithm.   ////

Thus far we have observed that a Markov algorithm operates on a single input or subject string only. What if we wish to create an algorithm which, for example, removes a substring u of a string w, if such a substring exists? In this case we have two input parameters u and w. We can handle this problem by forming a single input string, z, composed of w and u. The string z contains a symbol, say '#', from the input vocabulary V which is not in the strings w or u and which can be used as a delimiter in the concatenation of w and u to form z. Hence, z = w'#'u.

We can find the substring u in w by first using the function DUPL (previously defined in Example 2-6) to yield a subject string of the form zz. The first string z is scanned destructively left to right to isolate the substring u in w. Concurrently, the progress of the scanning in the first w is mapped nondestructively by markers in the second w. Once the substring u is isolated, if such a u exists in w, the corresponding substring can be removed in the second w. By removing the first partially destroyed z and the second u, the correct result is obtained.

To write an LMA description for the substring procedure is a long tedious process. To help reduce the effort and yet leave the power of the Markov algorithm unaltered, another programming feature called a *memory* or *addressable-storage cell* can be introduced. Memory cells can hold strings; however, the strings contained in these cells are used for intermediate calculations only. There remains only one input and output string, namely the main subject string. A finite set of memory cells, which are denoted $[M_1]$, $[M_2]$, ..., $[M_n]$, can be used in a given algorithm. Galler and Perlis [1970] discuss the concept of a memory cell in detail. Again, it can be demonstrated that memory cells aid in the ease with which a Markov algorithm is formulated; however, they offer no additional computational capabilities.

In addition to providing string-processing functions, Markov algorithms can be used with some difficulty to compute arithmetic functions. For example, if we represent a number N by a string of tally symbols, (for example, 111...1), then the LMA for addition can be accomplished by:

LMA: ADD
'+' → Λ

assuming an input string of the form '11 ... 1 + 11 ... 1'. However, the LMA for multiplication (assuming an input string '11 ... 1*1 ... 11') is more difficult.

LMA:	MULT	
ADDγ:	'1*' → '*'γ	(CREATEβ)
REMOVE1:	'*1' → '*'	(REMOVE1)
REPLACEβ:	β → 1	(REPLACEβ)
	* → Λ.	
CREATEβ.	γ'1' → '1'βγ	(CREATEβ)
MOVEβ:	β'1' → '1'β	(MOVEβ)
	γ → Λ	(ADDγ)

In the algorithm, γ marks the number of additions of the multiplicand (i.e., the right-hand set of tally marks—for example, '11' in '111*11') and β represents a digit in the product (i.e., the resulting string). An intermittent trace of the multiplication of '111*11' is as follows:

$$'111*11' \Rightarrow '11*'\gamma'11' \Rightarrow '11*1'\beta\gamma'1' \Rightarrow '11*1'\beta'1'\beta\gamma \Rightarrow '11*11'\beta\beta\gamma$$
$$\Rightarrow '11*11'\beta\beta \Rightarrow '1*'\gamma'11'\beta\beta \Rightarrow \ldots \Rightarrow '*11'\beta\beta\gamma\beta\beta\beta\beta$$
$$\Rightarrow '*11'\beta\beta\beta\beta\beta \Rightarrow '*1'\beta\beta\beta\beta\beta\beta \Rightarrow '*'\beta\beta\beta\beta\beta\beta \Rightarrow \ldots$$
$$\Rightarrow '*11111'\beta \Rightarrow '*111111' \Rightarrow '111111'$$

It is easy to appreciate that the calculation of an arithmetic expression, such as $25 * 26/(31 + 10)$, would be tedious but not impossible using Markov algorithms. While it appears to be very restrictive, the Markov model is powerful enough to enable the computation of any computable function (i.e., any function we would care to compute).

However, the Markov model is awkward, especially for arithmetic computations. Nevertheless, the Markov algorithm helps illustrate string manipulation at a primitive and understandable level; and as we will see in Sec. 2-3.3, it is the basis for the very powerful string manipulation language SNOBOL.

2-2.2 Grammars

In Sec. 2-1 we introduced the notion of the closure set of strings $V*$ in which a string z is an element of $V*$ if every character in z belongs to the alphabet V. For example, '10011' is an element of $V*$ given that $V = \{0, 1\}$.

In many instances we are interested only in a specific subset of the strings in $V*$. For example, we may be concerned with only those strings of $V*$ (given that $V = \{0, 1\}$) which contain one or more character sequences of a form '0' followed by one or more '1''s. A string of one or more '1''s is commonly denoted as '1+'. Hence, the subset of interest contains strings of the form '01+01+ . . . 01+' or ('01+')+. Let us denote this special subset by L. Then '011010111' ϵ L, and '01001' $\notin$ L, because it contains adjacent '0''s.

Typically, the set of strings L can be used in an application involving the transfer of binary-encoded information from a source to a destination. The number of '1''s in a particular subsequence (a subsequence is delimited by zeros) indicates the value of a transmitted number. For example, '011010111' is interpreted as 2 1 3. From our discussion in Chap. 1, we realize that this is not a very efficient coding scheme. However, the example given here is sufficient to illustrate that in some applications we are not interested in all strings generated from a given alphabet, but only a subset of such strings. Such a subset is often called a *language*. More formally, we define a language L to be a set of strings over some finite alphabet V, so that $L \subseteq V*$.

Both a natural language, such as English, and a programming language, such as PL/I, adhere to our definition of a language. In both instances, the language is defined as a specific subset of the strings $V*$ from alphabets such as $V = \{A, B, C, \ldots, Z, 1, 2, \ldots, 9, 0, \$, \notin, !$, and other special symbols}. The strings which form the language are called *sentences*.

The question that immediately comes to the fore is: "How can we represent a language?" We can present a form of verbal description of the strings that are of interest to us—but this is neither an accurate nor a concise representation. A language-description mechanism must be able to represent an infinite set of strings, for some languages have an infinite number of sentences (e.g., the set of strings ('01+')+). Such a mechanism must be able to exhibit the structural relationships (or syntax) that exist between the substring elements which, when properly combined, form sentences of the language. For example, the string

'I DATA STRUCTURES'

is incorrect syntactically because of the absence of a verb, while the sentence

'I LOVE DATA STRUCTURES'

possesses an obvious meaning. Note that in natural languages and programming languages, we must be concerned with two levels of structural interrelationships—namely, the word level (i.e., the substrings which form words from the vocabulary of that language) and the sentence level (i.e., the substring sequences which combine to form sentences of the language). This distinction will be brought up again in this section and in Sec. 2-5.2 during a discussion of *lexical analysis*.

A method of specification which takes into account these syntactic properties of a language is a *grammar*. A grammar consists of a finite set of replacement rules or *productions*. A grammar production and a Markov algorithm production (as discussed in Sec. 2-2.1) are quite similar in function—namely, that of a replacement specifier. However, they differ in purpose, since a grammar production is used to generate strings (i.e., sentences) from languages whereas a Markov production is used in the manipulation of a given subject string.

Before giving a more formal definition of a grammar, we examine a metalanguage for expressing a grammar. A *metalanguage* is a language used to describe another language; for example, English can be considered as a metalanguage when it is used to teach French. In the area of computer science, at least three such metalanguages have been developed for representing the syntax of programming languages—namely, BNF, ALGOL 68 notation, and the Vienna language definition notation. BNF (meaning either Backus Naur Form or Backus Normal Form) was first made popular when it was used to describe the syntax of ALGOL 60 (Naur [60]). It is still commonly used, and we adopt it as the metalanguage used throughout this book.

We begin a description of BNF by citing an example of a BNF rule (or production) for describing a digit:

$$<\text{digit}> :: = 0\,|\,1\,|\,2\,|\,3\,|\,4\,|\,5\,|\,6\,|\,7\,|\,8\,|\,9$$

To avoid confusion between the symbols of the metalanguage and symbols of the language itself, four special metalinguistic symbols ($<$, $>$, $:: =$, $|$) are used which are not part of the language's alphabet. A grammar is written as a set of productions, each of which has a left part, followed by the metasymbol $:: =$, followed by a list of right parts. The left part is a *nonterminal symbol* (e.g., $<\text{digit}>$) which is a variable representing a syntactic class within the grammar. Nonterminals are always parenthesized with the metasymbols $<$ and $>$. The right parts, which are separated by the metasymbol $|$, are strings containing terminal and/or nonterminal symbols. A *terminal symbol* is a character from an alphabet or a string of characters from an alphabet. For example, the numerals 0, 1, 2, . . ., 9 are terminal symbols in the production for $<\text{digit}>$. We interpret the example production to mean that "a digit is composed of a 0, or 1, or 2, or . . ., or 9".

We more formally define a grammar by a 4-tuple $G = (V_N, V_T, S, P)$ where V_N and V_T are disjoint sets of nonterminal and terminal symbols, respectively. S is the distinguished symbol of V_N, and it is commonly called the *goal* or *starting symbol*. P is a finite set of productions. The set $V = V_T \cup V_N$ is called the *vocabulary* of the grammar.

Example 2-7   Let $G_1 = (V_N, V_T, S, P)$ be a grammar representing the syntax for a small subset of the English language. Then,

    $V_N = \{ <\text{sentence}>, <\text{subject}>, <\text{predicate}>, <\text{article}>, <\text{noun}>, <\text{verb}>,$
        $<\text{object}> \},$

    $V_T = \{$a, the, Linus, Charlie, Snoopy, blanket, dog, song, holds, pets, sings$\},$

S = <sentence>,
P = {1.   <sentence> :: = <subject> <predicate>
    2.   <subject> :: = <article> <noun> | <noun>
    3.   <predicate> :: = <verb> <object>
    4.   <article> :: = a | the
    5.   <noun> :: = Linus | Charlie | Snoopy | blanket | dog | song
    6.   <verb> :: = holds | pets | sings
    7.   <object> :: = <article> <noun> | <noun>}

The productions have been numbered from one to seven for future references. ////

The language, say L_1, generated from the grammar G_1, as described in Example 2-7, consists of a number of sentences (in fact, 972 sentences in all). An enumeration of some of these sentences is as follows:

'Charlie pets the dog'
'Linus holds the blanket'
'Snoopy sings a song'
'The blanket holds a dog'

There are two important things to note concerning the generation of strings (i.e., sentences) from a grammar. First, we have neglected (for legibility reasons) to put into the terminal symbols of the grammar the blank characters which normally appear between the words in the sentences. Throughout the book, we assume, unless it is obvious from context of the text, that a blank delimits all terminal symbols.

Second, it should be noted that not all strings composed of terminal symbols form sentences (e.g., 'Linus the a holds' is not syntactically correct). Hence, it is necessary to devise a method of analyzing the various parts of a string to determine whether or not the string is a sentence in the language. Such a process exists and is called *parsing*. For a given sentence, we can construct a parse, and for a string which is not a sentence, we cannot construct a parse. The diagram of a parse displays the syntax of a sentence in a manner similar to a tree and is, therefore, called a *syntax tree*. A parse of the sentence 'Linus holds the blanket' is shown in Fig. 2-2.1.

How do we construct a parse? Or, equivalently, how do we derive a syntax tree? In general, there are two methods of parsing—top-down and bottom-up. Let us examine both of these methods in some detail.

In *top-down parsing*, an attempt to construct a syntax tree is initiated by starting at the root of the tree (i.e., the distinguished symbol) and proceeding downward toward the leaves (i.e., the symbols forming the string). The effect of such a process is to generate sentences systematically from the language until a match can be found with the string in question. Of course, if no match can be found, the string is not a sentence of the language. This generation of sentences can be mapped with the aid of a special relation $\Rightarrow$ in which $x \Rightarrow y$ is interpreted as "string x produces y (or y reduces to x)" during a step of a parse. We illustrate the steps in the generation of the sentence 'Linus holds the blanket' given the grammatical rules for G_1:

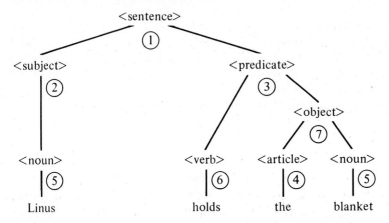

FIGURE 2-2.1   A parse of the sentence 'Linus holds the blanket'.

$$
\begin{aligned}
\text{<sentence>} &\Rightarrow \text{<subject> <predicate>} && \ldots \text{by production 1}\\
&\Rightarrow \text{<noun> <predicate>} && \ldots \text{by production 2}\\
&\Rightarrow \text{Linus <predicate>} && \ldots \text{by production 5}\\
&\Rightarrow \text{Linus <verb> <object>} && \ldots \text{by production 3}\\
&\Rightarrow \text{Linus holds <object>} && \ldots \text{by production 6}\\
&\Rightarrow \text{Linus holds <article> <noun>} && \ldots \text{by production 7}\\
&\Rightarrow \text{Linus holds the <noun>} && \ldots \text{by production 4}\\
&\Rightarrow \text{Linus holds the blanket} && \ldots \text{by production 5}
\end{aligned}
$$

A circled number on the syntax tree in Fig. 2-2.1 represents the production number that is used in that part of the construction of the syntax tree. It is easy to see how the construction of the tree parallels the sentence generation process just given.

In practice, the construction of a syntax tree using a top-down parsing strategy may involve a number of wrong production steps before the correct tree results. For example, the rule <subject> :: = <noun> is used in the second step of the sentence generation. We could have chosen, with the same conviction, to use the production step <subject> :: = <article> <noun>. Of course, to do so leads to the generation of a sentence which is not the input string. This fact can be discovered in the next production step of <article> :: = a or <article> :: = the, since neither 'a' or 'the' are equivalent to 'Linus'. Such errors in production selection can be recovered from relatively easily by simply retracing our steps up the syntax tree and trying an alternative production step. Such an alternative step is the application of <subject> :: = <noun>. We continue in this manner during the entire parse until the correct sentence is generated. More will be said about top-down parsing and backtracking strategies in Sec. 5-2.3.

In the second method of parsing, *bottom-up parsing*, the completion of the syntax tree is attempted by starting at the leaves and moving upward toward the root. Relating this strategy to the grammar G_1 given in Example 2-7, the following series of derivations results in a bottom-up parse of 'Linus holds the blanket' (remember that $x \Rightarrow y$ also means "y reduces to x" and this is the interpretation used in bottom-up parsing):

\<noun\> holds the blanket	$\Rightarrow$ Linus holds the blanket . . . by prod. 5	
\<subject\> holds the blanket	$\Rightarrow$	. . . by prod. 2
\<subject\> \<verb\> the blanket	$\Rightarrow$	. . . by prod. 6
\<subject\> \<verb\> \<article\> blanket	$\Rightarrow$	. . . by prod. 4
\<subject\> \<verb\> \<article\> \<noun\>	$\Rightarrow$	. . . by prod. 5
\<subject\> \<verb\> \<object\>	$\Rightarrow$	. . . by prod. 7
\<subject\> \<predicate\>	$\Rightarrow$	. . . by prod. 3
\<sentence\>	$\Rightarrow$	. . . by prod. 1

Observe that the same syntax tree is constructed (see Fig. 2-2.1), and the same productions are invoked as for the top-down method; however, the production steps take place in a completely different order. In particular, because we parsed the sentence in a left-to-right manner using both methods, the productions are not applied in the reverse order. If our parsing strategy for the top-down method had worked from right-to-left, then the productions would have been applied in the reverse order in which they were applied using the left-to-right bottom-up strategy. Similarly, a bottom-up right-to-left parse applies productions in the reverse order to that of a top-down left-to-right strategy. Because a bottom-up left-to-right parse is so commonly used in compilers for parsing statements from a programming language, it is often called a *canonical parse*.

The basic parsing strategy in a canonical parse begins with the isolation of a special substring in the given input string or the resulting string that has been transformed by a number of production applications to the input string. Such a transformed string is often called a *sentential form*, and the special string which is isolated is commonly called a *handle*. In the bottom-up parse of the sentence 'Linus holds the blanket', the initial string 'Linus holds the blanket', the final derivation ' \<sentence\>', and all intermediate derivations are examples of sentential forms. The handle should be the left-most phrase (a *phrase* is a substring of the sentential form that matches the right-hand side of a production) corresponding to a production that can be applied given the context of the handle in the sentential form. For example, 'Linus' is the handle in the sentential form 'Linus holds the blanket', and ' \<verb\> \<object\>' is the handle in the sentential form ' \<subject\> \<verb\> \<object\>'. In an example given later in this section, we illustrate how an examination of the context of a phrase affects the decision as to whether that phrase is the handle or not.

Once the handle has been isolated, its corresponding left-hand side (in our example, \<noun\>) is substituted at the position of the right-hand side to create a new sentential form (i.e., the sentential form ' \<noun\> holds the blanket', in the case of our example). This process is continued until the goal symbol (' \<sentence\>', in the example) is reached, if possible. If the goal symbol is the only remaining symbol in the transformed string, then the original input string is a sentence from the language described by the grammar; otherwise, it is not.

An important concept in a discussion of grammars and, indeed, in a discussion of many other topics is that of *recursion*. Recursion can be loosely defined as a process by which we define something in terms of itself. An example of a grammar which recursively defines a simple language is as follows:

$G_2 = (V_N, V_T, S, P)$ where
$V_N = \{ <digit>, <no>, <number> \}$
$V_T = \{0, 1, 2, 3, 4, 5, 6, 7, 8, 9\}$
$S = \{ <number> \}$
$P = \{1 \ <number> :: = <no>$
$\qquad 2 \ <no> :: = <digit> \ | \ <no> \ <digit>$
$\qquad 3 \ <digit> :: = 0 \ | \ 1 \ | \ 2 \ | \ 3 \ | \ 4 \ | \ 5 \ | \ 6 \ | \ 7 \ | \ 8 \ | \ 9 \}.$

In production 2, the syntactic phrase $<no>$ can be defined as $<no>$ $<digit>$. This is a recursive definition. To see how it is applied, let us assume we are to generate the string '694' of the language for G_2. We begin with the distinguished symbol $<number>$ and proceed as follows:

$<number> \Rightarrow <no>$
$\qquad\quad \Rightarrow <no> \ <digit>$
$\qquad\quad \Rightarrow <no> \ <digit> \ <digit>$
$\qquad\quad \Rightarrow <digit> \ <digit> \ <digit>$
$\qquad\quad \Rightarrow 6 \ <digit> \ <digit>$
$\qquad\quad \Rightarrow 69 \ <digit>$
$\qquad\quad \Rightarrow 694$

The production step of $<no> :: = <no> \ <digit>$ is a very powerful one, since we are effectively creating a two-digit entity from a one-digit entity. This process of expansion allows us to express any integer we desire, regardless of its value. Of course, for a given integer, this recursive step, and hence the expansion, must cease. This occurs with the application of a nonrecursive production such as $<no> :: = <digit>$. This nonrecursive production step is called the *basis step* in the recursive process.

Recursively defined productions are used in instances in which certain substrings may appear repeatedly in a sentence of a language. For example, in the language which we introduced at the beginning of this subsection (i.e., the language with sentences of the form '01+ ... 01+'), two substrings repeatedly appear; these are '1' and '01+'. These substrings can be defined recursively, as is illustrated in the productions with the syntactic phrases $<ones>$ and $<zero \ ones>$ in the grammar G_3:

$G_3 = (V_T, V_N, S, P)$ where
$V_N = \{ <L>, <zero \ ones>, <ones> \}, \ V_T = \{0, 1\}, \ S = <L>$
$P = \{1 \ <L> :: = <zero \ ones>$
$\qquad 2 \ <zero \ ones> :: = <ones> \ | \ <zero \ ones> \ <ones>$
$\qquad 3 \ <ones> :: = 01 \ | \ <ones> \ 1\}$

The power of recursive productions in a grammar cannot be underplayed, and the following two statements, which can be proved as theorems, illustrate this point:

1 Any grammar containing a recursively defined production describes an infinite language (i.e., a language with an infinite number of sentences).
2 Any grammar containing no recursively defined productions describes a finite language (i.e., a language with a finite number of sentences).

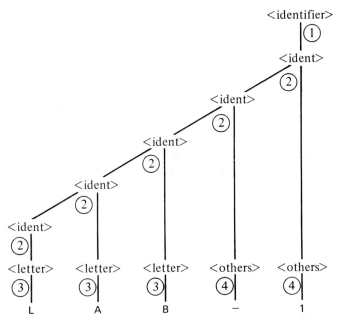

FIGURE 2-2.2 The parse of the string 'LAB_1' using the productions of G_4.

Hence, in this section the languages described by grammars G_2 and G_3 are infinite, while the language described by G_1 is finite.

As another example illustrating the use of recursively defined productions, consider the problem of formulating a grammar for describing an identifier name. An identifier name in many programming languages consists of a single alphabetic character or an alphabetic character followed by a finite number of alphabetic, numeric, and special characters. An example grammar can be given as:

$G_4 = (V_N, V_I, S, P)$ where
$V_N = \{ <identifier>, <ident>, <letter>, <others> \}$
$V_I = \{A, B, \ldots, Z, 0, 1, \ldots, 9, \_, \#, \$\}$
$S = <identifier>$
$P = \{1 \quad <identifier> ::= <ident>$
$\quad\quad 2 \quad <ident> \quad ::= <letter> \mid <ident> <letter> \mid <ident> <others>$
$\quad\quad 3 \quad <letter> \quad ::= A \mid B \mid C \mid \ldots \mid Z \mid \# \mid \$$
$\quad\quad 4 \quad <others> \quad ::= 0 \mid 1 \mid 2 \mid 3 \mid 4 \mid 5 \mid 6 \mid 7 \mid 8 \mid 9 \mid \_ \}$

A syntax tree for the parse of 'LAB_1' is given in Fig. 2-2.2.

In most programming languages, there is a practical limit to the length of an identifier name (e.g., the length of a PL/I identifier name can be at most 31). The grammar G_4 allows for any length of identifier. By a slight modification in the BNF metalanguage, we can accommodate a production which is to be applied iteratively 30 times (at most). Production 2 can be rewritten as:

2 $<$ident$> ::= <$letter$> \mid <$letter$> [<$letter$> \mid <$others$>]^{30}$.

In general, a production of the form $x ::= y[z]^n$ is interpreted as:

$x ::= yz \mid yzz \mid yzzz \mid \ldots \mid \underbrace{yzz \ldots z}_{n \text{ times}}$

Example 2-8   As a final example in this subsection, let us construct a grammar for simple arithmetic expressions in a programming language like PL/I. A simple arithmetic expression can be a simple identifier, a numeric constant (for simplicity, we only allow unsigned integer constants), or an expression involving constants and identifiers as operands of addition $(+)$, subtraction $(-)$, multiplication $(*)$, and division $(/)$ operations. Remember that in PL/I, multiplication and division have precedence over addition and subtraction (that is, $X * 2 - 3/Y + 1$ is interpreted as $(X * 2) - (3/Y) + 1$). We will illustrate how we can account for this precedence in a grammar description.

$G_5 = (V_N, V_T, S, P)$ where
$V_N = \{ <$expr$>, <$term$>, <$form$>, <$primary$> \}$
$V_T = \{+, -, *, /, i, n\}$
  $S = <$expr$>$
  $P = \{1\ <$expr$> ::= <$term$>$
    $2\ <$term$> ::= <$form$> \mid <$term$> + <$form$> \mid <$term$> - <$form$>$
    $3\ <$form$> ::= <$primary$> \mid <$form$> * <$primary$> \mid <$form$> /$
      $<$primary$>$
    $4\ <$primary$> ::= i \mid n\}$

Note that i (equivalent to $<$identifier$>$) and n (equivalent to $<$number$>$) are considered as terminal symbols in this grammar. Both of these terminals have been defined previously as goal symbols in the grammars G_2 and G_4. Therefore, these two grammars can be thought of as subgrammars in G_5, and hence the entire grammar can be defined to the detail of an individual character if so desired.   ////

The breakdown of G_5 into the subgrammars corresponding to $<$number$>$ and $<$identifier$>$ is a conceptual breakdown which most compiler writers must deal with. One module of the compiler, called a *scanner*, handles string recognition at the word (or lexical) level; that is, the character strings forming sentences of the language are analyzed and grouped into word-like constructs such as $<$number$>$s and $<$identifier$>$s.

A second compiler module, the *parser*, takes as input representations or tokens of the word-like constructs which have been resolved by the scanner. The parser is only interested in identifying syntactically correct sentences which are perceived as being composed of words from the language. Therefore, the exact value of a word-like construct (i.e., whether a $<$number$>$ is 26 or 3782) is of no consequence to the parser, since these values are identified by the scanner. It is quite clear that the grammars needed to describe word-like constructs for the scanner are appreciably simpler than grammars for the parser (as illustrated in G_5). If the syntax analysis phase of a compiler is broken into two modules, the scanner and the parser, a great amount of effort can be expended in the production of a very efficient scanner. This efficiency is important because the scanner is called much more often than the parser.

From the previous discussion it should be clear that the grammars G_2 and G_4 are grammars describing syntactic units which are processed by the scanner, while G_5 is a grammar suited to a parser.

Let us perform a canonical (left-to-right bottom-up) parse of the expression $2 + X * Y$. Within the framework of G_5, this expression appears as the string

‘ $<$number$>$ + $<$identifier$>$ * $<$identifier$>$’

Therefore, we can write in shorthand notation (that is, n = $<$number$>$, i = $<$identifier$>$, $<$p$>$ = $<$primary$>$, $<$f$>$ = $<$form$>$, $<$t$>$ = $<$term$>$, and $<$e$>$ = $<$expr$>$) the following trace of the parse.

$<$p$>$ + i * i	$\Rightarrow$ n + i * i	... by production 4
$<$f$>$ + i * i	$\Rightarrow$	... by production 3
$<$t$>$ + i * i	$\Rightarrow$	... by production 2
$<$t$>$ + $<$p$>$ * i $\Rightarrow$		... by production 4
$<$t$>$ + $<$f$>$ * i $\Rightarrow$		... by production 3
$<$t$>$ * i	$\Rightarrow$	... by production 2

Note that the last sentential form begins with the string '$<$t$>$ *'. By examining the productions of G_5, we see that a $<$term$>$ must have either the terminal symbols + or −, or no symbol at all following it. Therefore, the string cannot be resolved to the goal symbol given the current state of the parse.

Consider that point in the parse in which we have the sentential form '$<$t$>$ + $<$f$>$ * i'. By using lookahead, we observe that the symbol '*' follows $<$f$>$ in the string. If we make all the reductions of the substring '$<$f$>$ * i' before combining the result of these reductions with the substring '$<$t$>$ +', we can achieve a parse.

Let us pick up the parse at the sentential form '$<$t$>$ + $<$f$>$ * i' and continue in the manner just proposed.

$<$t$>$ + $<$f$>$ * $<$p$>$ $\Rightarrow$ $<$t$>$ + $<$f$>$ * i		... by production 4
$<$t$>$ + $<$f$>$	$\rightarrow$	... by production 3
$<$t$>$	$\Rightarrow$	... by production 2
$<$e$>$	$\rightarrow$	... by production 1

We have our parse!

The necessity for lookahead within the parsing strategy occurs because certain dependencies exist in the grammar's structure. For example, in G_5 the syntactic form $<$term$>$ is dependent upon $<$form$>$ (i.e., $<$term$>$ :: = $<$form$>$ | $<$term$>$ + $<$form$>$ | $<$term$>$ − $<$form$>$). Hence, all possible reductions that can be made to $<$form$>$ should be made prior to reductions for $<$term$>$. This is the rule we adopted in the parse for '2 + X * Y'. This example clearly indicates the importance of lookahead in the decision as to whether a particular phrase of the sentential form is the handle or not.

The syntax tree shown in Fig. 2-2.3 illustrates that the multiplication operator and its operands are grouped prior to the grouping of the addition operator and its operands. Therefore, the expression is considered to be evaluated as '2 + (X * Y)' and, within the grammar, the precedence of * and / over + and − has been attained.

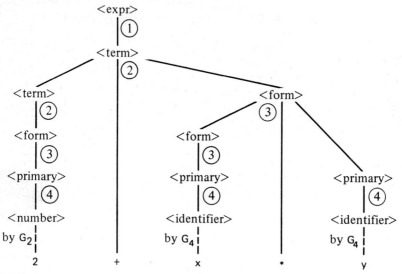

FIGURE 2-2.3   The parse of the expression '2 + X * Y' using the productions of G_5.

As a general rule, the more "complex" a grammar is, the more lookahead is required in the parsing strategy (in fact, some authors have used the amount of lookahead which is required in a parse as a measure of the complexity of a grammar). The grammar G_5 requires a one-symbol lookahead. There are grammars which require k symbols of lookahead for a finite k, and still others which require a potentially infinite amount of lookahead.

Before concluding this subsection, we wish to discuss briefly two additional points—the notions of syntax and semantics and their relationship to grammars, and the relationship between Markov algorithms and grammars. A grammar is only capable of specifying the structure (i.e., syntax) of a sentence. For some languages, it is not always convenient or possible to express exactly that set of strings which form sentences in a language. A good example of this situation is the subset of the English language defined by G_1. Sentences generated by G_1 include:

‘Snoopy sings the blanket’ and
‘The song pets Charlie’

Both of these sentences are syntactically correct, but they have little or no meaning, and from a semantic point of view they are not sentences. It is very often the case that strings which are sentences from a formal grammatical sense are not sentences of a language, and additional checking for semantic correctness must accompany a parse of the sentence. Semantic checking is very often done by compilers when translating a program.

The grammars we have described in this subsection are called *context-free grammars*. A context-free grammar is a grammar in which there is only one nonterminal allowed on the left-hand side of a production. An example of a grammar which is not context free is G_6:

$G_6 = (\{ <S>, <B>, <C> \}, \{a, b, c\}, <S>, P)$ where

$$P = \{ \quad <S> ::= a<S><B><C>$$
$$<S> ::= a<B><C>$$
$$<C><B> ::= <B><C>$$
$$a<B> ::= ab$$
$$b<B> ::= bb$$
$$b<C> ::= bc$$
$$c<C> ::= cc\}$$

G_6 describes the language containing strings of the form $a^n b^n c^n$ for $n \geq 1$ (e.g., for $n = 3$, $a^3 b^3 c^3$ = aaabbbccc). The generation of the string $a^2 b^2 c^2$ is $<S> \Rightarrow a<S><B><C> \Rightarrow$ aa$<B><C><B><C> \Rightarrow$ aa$<B><B><C><C> \Rightarrow$ aab$<B><C><C> \Rightarrow$ aabb$<C><C> \Rightarrow$ aabbc$<C> \Rightarrow$ aabbcc.

It can be shown that any *phrase-structure grammar* is expressible as a Markov algorithm. A phrase-structure grammar is the most general class of grammars in the sense that no restrictions, such as allowing only one symbol on the left-hand side, are placed on the productions. Using Markov algorithms, we can easily write both a generator and a recognizer for strings of the form $a^n b^n c^n$.

```
LMA:   GENERATE
START:  Λ → 'abc'
MOVE:  'ba' → 'ab'    (MOVE)
       'ca' → 'ac'    (MOVE)
       'cb' → 'bc'    (MOVE)
       output string  (START)
```

The command *output string* is introduced to allow for the presentation of each string. Note that the algorithm **GENERATE** produces the set of strings $\{a^n b^n c^n\}$ for every $n \geq 1$.

```
LMA:   RECOGNIZE
       'a' → α'a'
       'b' → β'b'
       'c' → γ'c'
START:   α'a' → α      (DELETEB)
         αβγ → 's'.
         Λ → Λ.
DELETEB:  β'b' → β      (DELETEC)
          Λ → Λ.
DELETEC:  γ'c' → γ      (START)
          Λ → Λ.
```

Upon the termination of **RECOGNIZE**, a string value of 's' indicates that the string is a sentence. Any other value indicates that it is not a sentence.

Markov algorithms and phrase-structure grammars are equivalent with respect to computational power. However, both of these formal models are designed for different purposes. The Markov model exhibits properties which are basic to string handling and rudimentary pattern matching. We expand upon these properties in the next section. The grammar is a model for string recognition and generation, and we investigate these two functions more fully in Sec. 2-5.2.

Exercises for Sec. 2-2

1. Design a Markov algorithm which examines an arbitrary string x on a given alphabet (say V = {a, b, c}) to determine if it is equal to some specified string w (say w = 'abb'). If x equals w, the string x is replaced by a specified string y (say y = 'b'); otherwise, x is replaced by the specified string z (say z = 'c'). Use a marker symbol.

2. Design a Markov algorithm which transforms a string $x_1x_2 \ldots x_n$ where each $x_i \epsilon \{a, b\}$ to the string $x_1x_2 \ldots x_n x_n x_{n-1} \ldots x_1$.

3. In many instances, it is required to know the number of symbols in a particular string. This can be accomplished using the tally notation by replacing every symbol in the string by the tally symbol "1". For example, the algorithm consisting of the production scheme

   $$x \rightarrow 1 \quad (x \epsilon V)$$

   transforms an arbitrary string to a sequence of tally symbols. Since $1 \notin V$, the algorithm terminates when every symbol has been transformed to the tally symbol. Given two strings $x_1x_2 \ldots x_n$ and $y_1y_2 \ldots y_m$, where each x_i and y_i are tally symbols, design a Markov algorithm which transforms the string $x_1x_2 \ldots x_n - y_1y_2 \ldots y_m$ to a string $z_1z_2 \ldots z_{n-m}$, which represents the difference of the tally symbols. For example '111 − 11' is transformed to '1'. Assume $n \geq m$.

4. Design a Markov algorithm (labeled or unlabeled) which recognizes a palindrome. A palindrome is a string of the form $x_1x_2 \ldots x_{n-1}x_nx_nx_{n-1} \ldots x_1$ in which each $x_i \epsilon V$ for some specified alphabet V. If the input string is a palindrome, the output should be the string 'a' where aϵV. If it is not, the output should be 'b' where bϵV.

5. Earlier in the section on grammars, we discussed the simple language

   $$L = \{('01^+')^+ \mid V = \{0,1\}\}$$

   where '01011' and '0110111' are elements of L and '0100' is not. Design a Markov algorithm (labeled or unlabeled) which recognizes only strings from this language. The algorithm should terminate with a '1' if the subject string is an element of L; otherwise, it should terminate with '0'.

6. Write a Markov algorithm which takes an input string z of the form $x_1x_2 \ldots x_n$'#'$y_1y_2 \ldots y_m$ in which x_i, '#', $y_j \epsilon V$ for $1 \leq i \leq n$, $1 \leq j \leq m$. The algorithm should output '#' if x is a substring of y or y is a substring of x; otherwise, the string '##' should be output.

7. Formulate an LMA which performs the integer division of two numbers x and y. The input is in a tally form with the two operands separated by the symbol '/'. Therefore, $5 \div 2$, is represented as '11111/11'. The answer must appear in strict tally notation (that is, '11' for the example given).

8. The Markov formalism discussed in the text does not represent a programming language as such. What additional facilities should be added to the formalism to make it a programming language?

9. Consider the following grammar with the set of symbols {a,b}:

   $$S \rightarrow a, \ S \rightarrow b, \ S \rightarrow Sa, \ S \rightarrow bS$$

   Describe the set of strings generated by this grammar.

10. Write grammars for the following languages.
(*a*) The set of *nonnegative odd integers*
(*b*) The set of *nonnegative even integers* with *no* leading zeros permitted

11. Write grammars for the following languages.
(*a*) {a^{i}ba^i | i ≥ 0}
(*b*) {wbw^R | w∈{0,1}*} where w^R is the reverse of w, i.e., if w = 001, w^R = 100.
(*c*) { <name> | <name> is a FORTRAN name}
(Note that FORTRAN names must have no more than six characters.)

12. Write a grammar (using BNF) which describes a PL/I comment. The set of terminal symbols for the grammar is assumed to be {A, B, C, ..., Z, 0, 1, ..., 9, #, !, *, −, +, /, blank}.
Give a parse of the comment /* INPUT/OUTPUT */ using your grammar.

13. Write a BNF description for a PL/I <procedure head> statement. An example of a procedure head is

Example: PROCEDURE (X, Y, Z) RECURSIVE
RETURNS (CHARACTER (*) VARYING);

Assume that only one of FIXED, FLOAT, BIT(*) VARYING or CHARACTER(*) VARY-ING can appear as a RETURNS argument. You may assume <identifier> to be a terminal in the grammar.

14. The following grammar generates simple arithmetic expressions involving addition (+), subtraction (−), multiplication (*) and division (/). The symbol i represents a variable name.

<factor>   :: = (<expression >) | i
<term>   :: = <factor> | <term> * <factor> | <term> / <factor>
<expression > :: = <term > | <expression > + <term > | <expression > − <term >

Give the derivations for the following expressions:

i + i, i − i/i, i * (i + i), i * i + i.

15. Suppose we want to implement a DDC compiler for the DDC (Decimal Digit Calcu-lator) language which performs arithmetic operations on integer arguments. The BNF grammar description below was written to describe the DDC language syn-tactically. Unfortunately, the grammar is ambiguous. (A grammar for a language is ambiguous if a sentence from the language can be parsed in more than one way.)

<DDC expr> :: = <DDC term>
            | <DDC expr> <op1> <DDC expr>
<DDC term> :: = <decimal arg>
            | <DDC term> <op2> <decimal arg>
<decimal arg> :: = <digit>
            | <decimal arg> <digit>
<digit> :: = 0 | 1 | 2 | 3 | 4 | 5 | 6 | 7 | 8 | 9
<op1> :: = + | −
<op2> :: = * | /

(*a*) Demonstrate that the grammar is, indeed, ambiguous.

(*b*) Correct the grammar so that it is unambiguous.

(*c*) According to your grammar, what is the value of 7 + 6 * 3 / 2?

(*d*) If we change the BNF description of <op1> and <op2> to read

<op1> :: = * | /

<op2> :: = + | −

what is the value of the expression 7 + 6 * 3 / 2 in the language described by your corrected grammar?

16. Write grammars for the following:

(*a*) {a^{n}ba^m} for n, m ≥ 1

(*b*) {a^{n}b^{n}a^n} for n > 1 (*Hint:* You may have to use more than one symbol on the left-hand side of a production.)

2-3 STRING MANIPULATION AND PATTERN MATCHING

The Markov formalism discussed in Sec. 2-2.1 provides us with a good introduction to the concepts relating to string manipulation and pattern matching. Nevertheless, the Markov system is not a practical system from a programming and data manipulation point of view. In this section, we propose a set of primitives and a set of basic string-handling functions which are modeled, in part, on the string-handling capabilities exhibited in the two formal systems presented in Sec. 2-2. Next, string-handling facilities in the general-purpose language PL/I and the string-manipulation language SNOBOL are described and related to the string-handling functions proposed earlier. The section concludes with a discussion of recursive pattern matching.

2-3.1 Primitive Functions

A close analysis of the basic string-handling facilities required of any text creation and editing system (formal or otherwise) should lead to the following list of primitive functions:

1 Create a string of text.

2 Concatenate two strings to form another string.

3 Search and replace (if desired) a given substring within a string.

4 Test for the identity of a string.

5 Compute the length of a string.

In this subsection we discuss the importance of each of these functions in a string-handling system and incorporate into our algorithmic notation operations which effect these functions.

The creation of a string implies not only the ability to construct a representation for a string, but also the ability to retain the value of a string in a variable (or memory-cell location). This feature is inherent in the Markov algorithm model, where one string is created (the subject string), and in the grammar, which is capable of generating a string (in particular, a sentence). The ability to create a string must be present in any string-handling system.

In the algorithmic notation, a string is expressed as any sequence of characters enclosed in single quote marks. To provide a transparent representation for strings, a single quote contained within a string is represented by two single quotes. Therefore, the string "It is John's program." is represented as 'IT IS JOHN''S PROGRAM.'. Variables can be used to retain string values. Therefore, to assign the string 'CAT' to the variable PET, we write

Set PET ← 'CAT'.

The empty (or null) string is denoted by either two single quotes ('') or the symbol Λ.

Concatenation is the most important operation on a string. At the beginning of this chapter, we defined a string to be the concatenation of individual characters. In Markov algorithms and grammars, productions contain right- and left-hand sides made up of strings and/or character elements concatenated together. Concatenation is so important and natural to string manipulation that in many systems (e.g., the SNOBOL programming language), an explicit operator is omitted and concatenation is implied through the juxtapositioning of string arguments. However, in an effort to represent operators in a consistent manner, we use ○ to denote concatenation in our algorithmic notation. Therefore, to concatenate the string 'STRUCTURES' to 'DATA' and assign the result to the variable SUBJECT, we write

Set SUBJECT ← 'DATA' ○ 'STRUCTURES'

String variables as well as string constants can appear as operands (e.g., Set PET ← PET ○ 'DOG').

When searching for a substring within a given string, there must be some method of returning the position of the substring within the string, if the substring is found. This position is often called the *cursor position*, and it is given by an integer value indicating the character position of the leftmost character of the substring being sought. The name of the function used in the algorithmic notation to perform this operation is INDEX. INDEX (SUBJECT,PATTERN) returns (as a value) the cursor position of the leftmost occurrence of the string, PATTERN, in the string SUBJECT. If PATTERN does not occur in SUBJECT, the value 0 is returned. As examples, if SUBJECT = 'BACABABA', then INDEX(SUBJECT, 'ABA') is 4, INDEX(SUBJECT, 'A') is 2, and INDEX(SUBJECT, 'ABC') is 0.

The variable name PATTERN is used as the second argument in the description of INDEX for a definite reason. The string associated with PATTERN is applied to the subject string on a character-by-character basis from the first character of the subject string to the last. This process of applying a pattern string to a subject string is commonly called *pattern matching*. The INDEX function is our first example of a pattern-matching operation. A wide variety of pattern-matching operations exist, and many of these are illustrated in this chapter. However, INDEX provides the most primitive form of pattern matching, and it is a basis upon which more sophisticated pattern-matching operations can be built. Observe that the application of either a Markov or a grammar production relies on a form of pattern matching (e.g., given a subject string 'ABCDE', the application of the Markov production 'CD' → 'E' requires that the pattern 'CD' be found in the subject string before the replacement string 'E' can be assigned).

The ability to extract a substring from a subject string is another important function. In the Markov model, substring designation was provided through the use of marker symbols and character variables. For example, the productions

$$\{\alpha xy \rightarrow y\beta x$$
$$\beta \rightarrow \Lambda.$$
$$\Lambda \rightarrow \alpha\}$$

reverse the first two characters of the subject string. In the algorithmic notation, rather than using special marker symbols, we use the cursor position plus a substring length to isolate a substring. The name given to this function is SUB.

SUB(SUBJECT, i, j) or SUB(SUBJECT, i) returns as a value the substring of SUBJECT that is specified by the parameters i and j, or i and an assumed value of j. The parameter i indicates the starting cursor position of the substring, while j specifies the length of the required substring. If j is not provided, j is assumed to be equal to $k - i + 1$, where k is equal to the length of the argument SUBJECT. To complete a definition of SUB, some additional cases must be handled.

1   If $j \leq 0$ (regardless of i), then the null string is returned.
2   If $i \leq 0$ (regardless of j), then the null string is returned.
3   If $i > k$ (regardless of j), then the null string is returned.
4   If $i + j > k + 1$, then j is assumed to be $k - i + 1$.

Consider the following examples for the function SUB. SUB('ABCDE', 2) and SUB('ABCDE', 2, 7) both return 'BCDE', SUB('ABCDE', 3, 2) returns 'CD', and SUB('ABCDE', 0, 3) and SUB('ABCDE', 6) both return ' '.

The function SUB can also be used on the left-hand side of an assignment (i.e., in a replacement mode of operation). For example, if SUBJECT = 'ABCDE', then Set SUB(SUBJECT, 2, 2) ← 'A. would change the value of SUBJECT to 'AADE'. If SUB(SUBJECT, i, j) appears on the left-hand side of an assignment and $i \leq 0$ or $j \leq 0$, then the assignment is not executed. If $i > k$ or $i + j > k + 1$, then characters are assigned to positions beyond the right-hand end of the subject string. Intermediate character positions which are unassigned are set to blank characters.

The next two primitive functions are not basic operations to the Markov algorithm or formal grammar systems. Nevertheless, they are important in practical applications involving string editing and formatting, and they can be realized as Markov algorithms or grammars.

Testing the identity of a string implies the existence of some form of predicate which returns a *true* or *false* value when a comparison is made between a subject string and a known string. In the algorithmic notation we are supplied with two relations, = and ≠. To illustrate how each is defined, consider the following examples:

'XMAS' = 'XMAS' is *true*, and 'XMAS' ≠ 'CHRISTMAS' is *true*

while

'XMAS' = 'XMAS' is *false* and 'XMAS' ≠ 'XMAS' is *false*

It is easy to expand this comparison feature to include all of the commonly used relational symbols (that is, <, ≤, >, ≥, ≮, and ≯). We do so by defining a character *collating sequence* upon which a lexical (i.e., word) ordering can be made. The collating sequence which is applicable to most card-reader character sets is: blank ¢ . < (+ | & ! $ *) ; - / , % _ > ? : # @ ' = " A through Z, 0 through 9. This sequence is based on the internal representation of the characters, as discussed in Sec. 1-4.7. The lexical ordering on strings is similar to the one found in a dictionary or a telephone directory. Hence, 'XMAS' > 'CHRISTMAS', 'XMAS' ≤ 'XMAS1974', 'XMAS' ≮ 'XMA' are all *true*, while 'XMAS' > 'XMAS', 'Y' ≯ 'XMAS', and 'X' ≥ 'XMAS' are all *false*. From these examples, it is clear that comparisons are made on a character-by-character basis starting from the left-most character of each string in the comparison. The presence of any character (even a blank) is always considered to be greater than the omission of a character (that is, 'X ' > 'X' is *true*).

The length of a string is important in the formatting of character strings for output. This is why formal systems do not bother to include this operation as a basic feature. In the algorithmic notation, the computation of the length of a string is achieved by the function LENGTH. If SUBJECT is a character variable, then LENGTH(SUBJECT) returns as a value the number of symbols in the string represented by SUBJECT. The value 0 is returned if SUBJECT is the empty string. As examples, LENGTH('TOP') is 3, LENGTH(SUBJECT), where SUBJECT is 'ABAB', is 4, and LENGTH(SUB(SUBJECT, 1, 0)) is 0.

2-3.2 Basic Functions

Thus far in this section, we have identified and discussed in detail primitive string-handling functions—primitive in the sense that most string-handling functions can be composed in a modular manner from these functions. We now turn our attention to a discussion of four functions: LEN, MATCH, SPAN, and FIND, which are nonprimitive, yet basic, to string-handling problems. These functions are presented in algorithmic notation and are described in terms of the primitive functions just discussed. We make extensive use of these functions in the application section at the end of this chapter.

Since all the functions are of a pattern-matching nature, we are able to characterize them by using the same set of arguments throughout. Each of the pattern matching algorithms have the following arguments.

1   SUBJECT – the string in which a pattern match is made.

2   PATTERN – the string for which a pattern match is sought within the subject string. (In Algorithm LEN, PATTERN is replaced by NUM, which is the number of characters to be matched.)

3   CURSOR – the character position in SUBJECT at which the pattern matching is to begin. Therefore, from CURSOR to the last character of the SUBJECT is that portion of the subject string which is considered in the pattern-matching operation.

4   MATCH_STR – the variable that is set to the value of the substring which is successfully matched. If the pattern match is unsuccessful, MATCH_STR is left unchanged.

5   REPLACE_STR – the string which replaces the characters which are matched providing REPLACE_FLAG is *true*.

6   REPLACE_FLAG – a flag indicating whether or not a replacement should be made for that portion of the subject string that is matched. If REPLACE_FLAG is *true*, a replacement is made; if *false*, no replacement is made.

The four pattern-matching functions are truth-valued functions (i.e., predicates) in the algorithmic descriptions which follow. In all cases, a value of *true* is returned if a pattern match is achieved; otherwise, a value of *false* is returned.

Algorithm LEN.   Given the six arguments previously described, Algorithm LEN returns *true* if there are NUM characters in SUBJECT following and including the CURSOR character. If there are NUM characters, MATCH_STR is assigned the matched character string which is NUM in length. If REPLACE_FLAG is *true*, then the NUM characters are replaced by REPLACE_STR.

1.   [Check for NUM characters]
     If CURSOR + NUM > LENGTH(SUBJECT) + 1, then set LEN ← false, and Exit.
2.   [Set match and replace if specified]
     Set LEN ← true and MATCH_STR ← SUB(SUBJECT,CURSOR,NUM).
     If REPLACE_FLAG,
     then set SUB(SUBJECT,CURSOR,NUM) ← REPLACE_STR,
          CURSOR ← CURSOR + LENGTH(REPLACE_STR), and Exit.
3.   [No replacement]   Set CURSOR ← CURSOR + NUM, and Exit.

To illustrate how the LEN algorithm works, let us examine its evaluation assuming parameters of SUBJECT = 'TO BE OR NOT TO BE', NUM = 3, CURSOR = 10 MATCH_STR = unknown value, REPLACE_STR = 'NEVER', and REPLACE_FLAG = *true*. Since CURSOR + NUM (equalling 13) is less than or equal to the length of the subject string plus 1 (equalling 19), the test for a possible pattern match is *true* in step 1 of the algorithm. In step 2, LEN is set to *true* and MATCH_STR is set to the substring 'NOT'. Since the RE-PLACE_FLAG is set, that part of the subject string which is matched (i.e., 'NOT') is replaced by the value of REPLACE_STR (i.e., 'NEVER') to yield a new subject string of 'TO BE OR NEVER TO BE'. Finally, CURSOR is updated to a value of 15, which is the cursor position of the character following the last character in the replacement string.

A number of additional examples demonstrating the effect of the LEN function follow. In all examples, the initial value of SUBJECT is 'TO BE OR NOT TO BE'.

LEN(SUBJECT, 1, 19, MATCH_STR, REPLACE_STR, false) returns a value of *false* since the SUBJECT string is only 18 characters in length, and hence cannot contain a substring beginning at position 19.

LEN(SUBJECT, 2, 7, MATCH_STR, REPLACE_STR, false) returns a value of *true* and MATCH_STR is set to 'OR', CURSOR is set to 9, and SUBJECT is left unchanged.

LEN(SUBJECT, 6, 1, MATCH_STR, '', true) returns a value of *true* and MATCH_STR is set to 'TO BE ', CURSOR is set to 1, and SUBJECT becomes 'OR NOT TO BE'.

We now consider the second of our basic pattern-matching functions. MATCH is a function which tests for a pattern match of a given pattern string with a substring of SUBJECT, beginning at the character position indicated by CURSOR.

Algorithm MATCH.   Given the six arguments described previously, Algorithm MATCH returns a value of *true* if the pattern string (PATTERN) is found in the string SUBJECT

starting at the CURSOR position. If the match is successful, MATCH_STR is set to PAT-
TERN, and if REPLACE_FLAG is set, then that portion of the subject string which is
matched is replaced by REPLACE_STR.

1. [Check if PATTERN fits within string bounds]
   If CURSOR + LENGTH(PATTERN) > LENGTH(SUBJECT) + 1,
   then set MATCH ← false, and Exit.
2. [Check for pattern match]
   If SUB(SUBJECT,CURSOR,LENGTH(PATTERN)) ≠ PATTERN,
   then set MATCH ← false, and Exit.
3. [Set MATCH and replace]
   Set MATCH_STR ← PATTERN and MATCH ← true.
   If REPLACE_FLAG,
   then set SUB(SUBJECT,CURSOR,LENGTH(PATTERN)) ← REPLACE_STR,
       CURSOR ← CURSOR + LENGTH(REPLACE_STR), and Exit.
4. [No replacement] Set CURSOR ← CURSOR + LENGTH(PATTERN), and Exit.

As an example of how the MATCH function works, consider the initial parameters of
SUBJECT = 'SHAKESPEAREAN SONNETS ARE IN IAMBIC PENTAMETER', PATTERN =
'SHAKESPEARE', CURSOR = 1, REPLACE_STR = 'ELIZABETH', REPLACE_FLAG = true.
In step 1, CURSOR + LENGTH(PATTERN) (equalling 12) is less than LENGTH(SUB-
JECT) + 1 (equalling 47) and, therefore, a check is made in step 2 to see if the pattern
match is possible. The substring, beginning with cursor position 1 and of length equal to
the length of the pattern string, matches the string represented by PATTERN. In step 3,
MATCH_STR is set to PATTERN and MATCH is set to *true*. Since the REPLACE_FLAG is set,
the SUBJECT is assigned '' ○ 'ELIZABETH' ○ 'AN SONNETS ARE IN IAMBIC PEN
TAMETER', or 'ELIZABETHAN SONNETS ARE IN IAMBIC PENTAMETER', and CURSOR
is set to 10.

Some further examples illustrating how MATCH performs are as follows. In all
cases, SUBJECT is 'SHAKESPEAREAN SONNETS ARE IN IAMBIC PENTAMETER'.

MATCH(SUBJECT, 'ELIZABETH', 2, MATCH_STR, REPLACE_STR, false) does not
result in a match, thus leaving SUBJECT, CURSOR, and MATCH_STR unchanged.

MATCH(SUBJECT, '', 47, MATCH STR, ' AND CONSIST OF THREE QUATRAINS',
true) results in a match with the empty string at the end of subject. Hence, SUBJECT
becomes 'SHAKESPEAREAN SONNETS ARE IN IAMBIC PENTAMETER AND CON
SIST OF THREE QUATRAINS', CURSOR is set to 77 (i.e., one more than the length of
the new subject string), and MATCH_STR is assigned the empty string.

The next basic pattern-matching function we examine allows us to match all characters in the subject string, beginning with the character at the cursor position and ending
at the first character, which is not in the pattern string. This is a particularly useful function in a text-editing application, as will be demonstrated in Sec. 2-5.1.

Algorithm SPAN. Given the six arguments described previously, SPAN returns *true* if
the CURSOR character matches any of the characters in PATTERN. If there is such a

match, MATCH_STR is set to the string of characters, including and following the CURSOR character, all of which match a character in PATTERN. The pattern match ends when a character not in PATTERN is encountered, or when the last character in the subject string is reached. The sequence matched is replaced by REPLACE_STR if REPLACE_FLAG is set to *true*.

1. [Check if the pattern fits in the bounds of the subject string]
    If CURSOR > LENGTH(SUBJECT), then set SPAN ← false, and Exit.
2. [Initialize the subject string index i to CURSOR]   Set i ← CURSOR.
3. [Check to find if character i is in PATTERN]
    Repeat while i ≤ LENGTH(SUBJECT)
    and INDEX(PATTERN, SUB(SUBJECT, i, 1)) ≠ 0:
        Set i ← i + 1.
4. [Character not found in PATTERN]
    If i = CURSOR, then set SPAN ← false, and Exit.
5. [Set match and replace]
    Set SPAN ← true and MATCH_STR ← SUB(SUBJECT, CURSOR, i − CURSOR).
    If REPLACE_FLAG,
    then set SUB(SUBJECT, CURSOR, i − CURSOR) ← REPLACE_STR,
    CURSOR ← CURSOR + LENGTH(REPLACE_STR), and Exit.
6. [No replacement]   Set CURSOR ← i, and Exit.

Consider the subject string of 'HE WALKED.... AND WALKED.... AND WALKED'. Assume we want to edit this string by replacing the first substring of '.'s by a comma. We set PATTERN = '.', CURSOR = 10, REPLACE_STR = ',' and REPLACE_FLAG = true and invoke the algorithm SPAN. Clearly, CURSOR is less than the length of the subject string. The index i is set to the cursor position 10 in step 2. The "while" condition specified in step 3 is true for i = 10, 11, 12, and 13. These positional values correspond to the substring '....', the first such substring in SUBJECT. The while condition is false for i = 14, since SUB(SUB-JECT, 14, 1) is equal to ' ' and this has a zero INDEX in PATTERN. Because i is not equal to CURSOR in step 4, SPAN is set to true and MATCH_STR is set to '....' in step 5. RE-PLACE_FLAG is set and, therefore, SUBJECT is assigned 'HE WALKED, AND WALKED.... AND WALKED'. Finally, CURSOR is set to the value of 11.

Some further examples exhibiting the capabilities and limitations of the SPAN function are as follows. In all cases, SUBJECT is 'HE WALKED.... AND WALKED.... AND WALKED'.

SPAN(SUBJECT, ' ', 1, MATCH_STR, REPLACE_STR, false)
does not result in a pattern match since there is not a blank character at the cursor position of 1.

SPAN(SUBJECT, 'ADEKLW.', 4, MATCH_STR, REPLACE_STR, false)
results in a pattern match with the substring 'WALKED....' and this substring is assigned to MATCH_STR. Since REPLACE_FLAG is not set, no replacement is made and CURSOR becomes the value 14.

SPAN(SUBJECT, 'ADEHKLNW .', 1, MATCH_STR, '', true)
results in a pattern match of the complete subject string, which is assigned to

MATCH_STR. Since REPLACE_FLAG is set, the entire subject string is replaced by the value REPLACE_STR, which is the empty string, and CURSOR has the value of 1.

The final pattern-matching function we discuss is called FIND. FIND matches the first instance of a substring equal to the given pattern lying anywhere between (and including) the initial cursor position and the end of the subject string.

Algorithm FIND. Given the six pattern-matching parameters described previously, Algorithm FIND returns *true* if the string PATTERN is found anywhere in the subject string from the CURSOR character to the end of the subject string. If a match occurs, MATCH_STR is set to the string, beginning with the CURSOR character and including all characters to the left of the first character of the pattern matched. If PATTERN is found starting with the CURSOR character, MATCH_STR is set to the empty string. If RE-PLACE_FLAG is set, then all characters starting from the CURSOR character up to the rightmost character of the matched substring are replaced by REPLACE_STR.

1. [Check if the pattern fits in the bounds of the subject string]
   If CURSOR > LENGTH(SUBJECT) then set FIND ← false, and Exit.
2. [Search for pattern match]
   Set i ← INDEX(SUB(SUBJECT, CURSOR), PATTERN),
   if i = 0, then set FIND ← false, and Exit.
3. [Set FIND and replace]
   Set FIND ← true and MATCH_STR ← SUB(SUBJECT, CURSOR, i − 1).
   If REPLACE_FLAG,
   then set SUB(SUBJECT, CURSOR, LENGTH(PATTERN) + i − 1) ← REPLACE_STR,
   CURSOR ← CURSOR + LENGTH(REPLACE_STR), and Exit.
4. [No replacement]   Set CURSOR ← CURSOR + i + LENGTH(PATTERN) − 1, and Exit.

As an example illustrating the FIND function, consider SUBJECT = 'I MET HER THE SUMMER BEFORE I WAS TO ENTER COLLEGE', PATTERN = 'I', CURSOR = 2, REPLACE_STR = '', and REPLACE_FLAG = true. If FIND is called with these parameters, then execution proceeds in the following manner. CURSOR is less than the length of the subject string, so a search for a pattern match is undertaken in step 2 using the INDEX function. A pattern match is found and the occurrence of the left-most character in the match is at position 29. Since a match is achieved (that is, i = 28), step 3 is executed setting FIND to *true* and MATCH_STR to ' MET HER THE SUMMER BEFORE '. Because the REPLACE_FLAG is set, the substring corresponding to MATCH_STR ○ PATTERN (i.e., ' MET HER THE SUMMER BEFORE I') is replaced by the REPLACE_STR '' to yield a new subject string of 'I WAS TO ENTER COLLEGE'. CURSOR is set to CURSOR plus the length of the replacement string (i.e., CURSOR = 2).

Additional examples using the FIND function and involving the subject string 'I MET HER THE SUMMER BEFORE I WAS TO ENTER COLLEGE' follow:

FIND(SUBJECT, 'ENTERED', 1, MATCH_STR, REPLACE_STR, false)
does not result in a pattern match because the pattern 'ENTERED' is not in the subject string. Hence SUBJECT, MATCH_STR and CURSOR remain unchanged.

FIND(SUBJECT, 'I', 1, MATCH_STR, 'HE', true)

results in a pattern match and replacement. SUBJECT becomes 'HE MET HER THE SUMMER BEFORE I WAS TO ENTER COLLEGE', MATCH_STR is assigned the empty string, and CURSOR is set to 3.

This concludes the subsection on basic string-manipulation functions. In the next two subsections, we examine the string-manipulation facilities available in two programming languages, PL/I and SNOBOL, and we relate these facilities to the primitive and basic functions described thus far in the section.

2-3.3   String Manipulation in PL/I

To provide effective string-manipulation facilities, a programming language must at least contain the primitive facilities and functions (i.e., string variables, string assignments, concatenation, and the SUB, INDEX, LENGTH functions) described in Sec. 2-3.1. While PL/I has all of these facilities, with only minor syntactic differences, there are two major differences at a semantic level.

First, the syntactic differences. The string assignment operator is ' = ' as opposed to '←'. Concatenation is denoted by '||' rather than '○', and the SUB function is referred to as SUBSTR. Hence, "Set X ← SUB(X, 1, 2) ○ 'A' " is written X = SUBSTR(X, 1, 2) || 'A' in PL/I. The INDEX and LENGTH function in PL/I are as described in Sec. 2-3.1.

The first major semantic difference involves the type of character strings that are available in PL/I. All the character strings used thus far were assumed to be variable-length strings. That is, a string, say X, can grow (e.g., Set X ← X ○ 'STRING') or shrink (e.g., Set X ← SUB(X, 1, 1)) as desired. In PL/I, this is not the case.

Two types of character strings are available in PL/I—fixed-length and varying-length strings. A fixed-length string consists of a fixed number of characters. The length of the string is determined from the declaration statement for the string (note that each string in a PL/I program must be declared). For example,

DECLARE S CHARACTER(10);

declares S to be a character-string variable whose length is 10. Fixed-length strings cannot grow or shrink, but remain constant in length. Therefore, if a fixed-length string, say S, is assigned a string longer than its predefined length, the extra characters are chopped from the right-hand end of the assigned string before the assignment is made to S. Hence, if S has the value '0123456789', then

S = S || 'AB'

is interpreted as an attempt to assign '0123456789AB' to S. Since S represents a string of fixed length 10, the value '0123456789AB' is truncated to '0123456789' and then assigned to S.

If a fixed-length string, say S, is assigned a string shorter than its predefined length, additional blanks are added to the right-hand end of the assigned string to form a string of length equal to the predefined length of S. This newly formed string is then assigned to S. For example, if S = '0123456789', then

S = SUBSTR(S, 1, 6)

is viewed as an assignment of '012345' to S. However, S represents a string of fixed length 10 and, therefore, assumes the value '012345bbbb', where b is interpreted as a blank character.

The second type of PL/I string is allowed to vary in length up to and including a declared maximum length. For example, the declaration for a varying-type character-string variable V of maximum length 10 is

DECLARE V CHARACTER(10) VARYING;

Attempts to extend a varying-type string beyond the maximum length results in a right-end truncation procedure identical to that for fixed-length strings. To illustrate the basic difference between a fixed-length string (such as S as declared previously) and a varying-length string (such as V as declared previously) consider the following four PL/I instructions.

S = '0123';   V = '0123';
S = S || S;   V = V || V;

At the conclusion of the execution of these instructions, S has the value '0123bbbbbb' and V has the value '01230123'.

A second important difference between PL/I's string-handling facilities and the string-handling functions described in the previous section is in the selection of a substring. Such a substring selection in PL/I defines a fixed-length substring replacement on either a fixed- or varying-type of character string. To illustrate, let us assume V is declared as a varying-length character string of maximum length 10 and is initialized to '0123456789'. Then the execution of SUBSTR(V, 2, 3) = 'ABCD' results in a new value of '0ABC456789' for V. This result is a consequence of the fact that a fixed-length substring of length 3 has been specified as the replacement pattern and, hence, the extra character 'D' must be dropped from the replacement string before the replacement is invoked. Because of this fixed-length substring replacement rule, SUBSTR(V, 2, 3) = '' changes an initial value of '0123456789' for V to '0bbb456789'. Note that SUB(V, 2, 3) ← 'ABCD' and SUB(V, 2, 3) ← '' result in values of '0ABCD456789' and '0456789' using the SUB function defined in Sec. 2-3.1.

Table 2-3.1 illustrates the equivalent PL/I statements required for a number of substring replacements obtained using the SUB function. The examples help demonstrate the verbosity and the "unnaturalness" of the PL/I SUBSTR function when used in a replacement mode.

Table 2-3.1

Our Model	PL/I equivalent
Set SUB(V, 2, 3) ← 'ABCD'	V = SUBSTR(V, 1, 1) || 'ABCD' || SUBSTR(V, 5)
Set SUB(V, 2, 3) ← 'A'	V = SUBSTR(V, 1, 1) || 'A' || SUBSTR(V, 5)
Set SUB(V, 2, 3) ← ''	V = SUBSTR(V, 1, 1) || SUBSTR(V, 5)

In addition to primitive string-manipulation functions, PL/I contains a number of string-handling functions which may be of some use to the programmer. VERIFY is a function of two arguments, both of which are strings. The result returned by VERIFY is an integer (in FIXED BINARY) indicating the position of the first character in the first argument, which is not a character in the second argument. If all characters in the first argument are in the second argument, the result is 0. For example,

VERIFY ('bbABC', 'b') yields 3

while

VERIFY ('bbABC', 'ABCDb') yields 0,

where 'b' is interpreted as the blank character.

The function REPEAT has two arguments; the first is a string and the second is an integer constant. The result is the value of the first argument concatenated with itself an integer number of times, as given by the second argument. Therefore, REPEAT('ABC', 3) yields the string 'ABCABCABCABC'.

Other PL/I string-handling functions exist which are useful in very special situations. The reader is advised to consult a PL/I language reference manual for descriptions of the functions BIT, BOOL, CHAR, HIGH, LOW, STRING, and TRANSLATE.

The functions LEN, MATCH, SPAN, and FIND can be expressed as PL/I procedures involving string declarations, assignments, concatenation, and the functions LENGTH, INDEX, and SUBSTR. Samples of such procedures are given in Figs. 2-3.1 to 2-3.4. Note that these differ from the algorithms in Sec. 2-3.2, especially with respect to the use of SUBSTR in place of SUB.

These procedures are extremely useful if a PL/I transliteration is needed for some of the algorithms given in the application section at the end of this chapter.

Concepts relating to PL/I bit strings have not been presented in this subsection. In Sec. 2-5.4, PL/I's bit string facilities are discussed in the context of an information retrieval application. We now turn our attention to a language designed specifically for string manipulation.

```
LEN:     PROCEDURE(SUBJECT,NUM,CURSOR,MATCH_STR,REPL_STR,REPL_FLAG)
              RETURNS (BIT(1));
      DECLARE SUBJECT CHARACTER(*) VARYING,
              NUM FIXED BINARY,
              CURSOR FIXED BINARY,
              MATCH_STR CHARACTER(*) VARYING,
              REPL_STR CHARACTER(*) VARYING,
              REPL_FLAG BIT(*);
      IF CURSOR + NUM > LENGTH(SUBJECT) + 1
      THEN RETURN('0'B);
      MATCH_STR = SUBSTR(SUBJECT,CURSOR,NUM);
      IF REPL_FLAG
      THEN DO;
           IF CURSOR + NUM = LENGTH(SUBJECT) + 1
           THEN SUBJECT = SUBSTR(SUBJECT,1,CURSOR-1) || REPL_STR;
           ELSE SUBJECT = SUBSTR(SUBJECT,1,CURSOR-1) || REPL_STR
                      || SUBSTR(SUBJECT,CURSOR+NUM);
           CURSOR = CURSOR + LENGTH(REPL_STR);
      END;
      ELSE CURSOR = CURSOR + NUM;
      RETURN('1'B);
END LEN;
```

FIGURE 2-3.1   PL/I procedure for the LEN function.

```
MATCH: PROCEDURE(SUBJECT,PATTERN,CURSOR,MATCH_STR,REPL_STR,REPL_FLAG)
            RETURNS (BIT(1));
       DECLARE SUBJECT CHARACTER(*) VARYING,
               PATTERN CHARACTER(*) VARYING,
               CURSOR FIXED BINARY,
               MATCH_STR CHARACTER(*) VARYING,
               REPL_STR CHARACTER(*) VARYING,
               REPL_FLAG BIT(*);
       IF CURSOR + LENGTH(PATTERN) > LENGTH(SUBJECT) + 1
       THEN RETURN('0'B);
       IF SUBSTR(SUBJECT,CURSOR,LENGTH(PATTERN)) ¬= PATTERN
       THEN RETURN('0'B);
       MATCH_STR = PATTERN;
       IF REPL_FLAG
       THEN DO;
           IF CURSOR + LENGTH(PATTERN) = LENGTH(SUBJECT) + 1
           THEN SUBJECT = SUBSTR(SUBJECT,1,CURSOR-1) || REPL_STR;
           ELSE SUBJECT = SUBSTR(SUBJECT,1,CURSOR-1) || REPL_STR
                       || SUBSTR(SUBJECT,CURSOR+LENGTH(PATTERN));
           CURSOR = CURSOR + LENGTH(REPL_STR);
       END;
       ELSE CURSOR = CURSOR + LENGTH(PATTERN);
       RETURN('1'B);
END MATCH;
```

FIGURE 2-3.2   PL/I procedure for the MATCH function.

```
SPAN : PROCEDURE(SUBJECT,PATTERN,CURSOR,MATCH_STR,REPL_STR,REPL_FLAG)
            RETURNS (BIT(1));
       DECLARE SUBJECT CHARACTER(*) VARYING,
               PATTERN CHARACTER(*) VARYING,
               CURSOR FIXED BINARY,
               MATCH_STR CHARACTER(*) VARYING,
               REPL_STR CHARACTER(*) VARYING,
               REPL_FLAG BIT(*);
       DECLARE I FIXED BINARY;
       IF CURSOR > LENGTH(SUBJECT)
       THEN RETURN('0'B);
       I = VERIFY(SUBSTR(SUBJECT,CURSOR),PATTERN);
       IF I = 1
       THEN RETURN('0'B);
       IF I = 0
       THEN DO;
           MATCH_STR = SUBSTR(SUBJECT,CURSOR);
           IF REPL_FLAG
           THEN DO;
               SUBJECT = SUBSTR(SUBJECT,1,CURSOR-1) || REPL_STR;
               CURSOR = CURSOR + LENGTH(REPL_STR);
           END;
           ELSE CURSOR = LENGTH(SUBJECT) + 1;
       END;
       ELSE DO;
           MATCH_STR = SUBSTR(SUBJECT,CURSOR,I-1);
           IF REPL_FLAG
           THEN DO;
               SUBJECT = SUBSTR(SUBJECT,1,CURSOR-1) || REPL_STR
                       || SUBSTR(SUBJECT,I+CURSOR-1);
               CURSOR = CURSOR + LENGTH(REPL_STR);
           END;
           ELSE CURSOR = I + CURSOR - 1;
       END;
       RETURN('1'B);
END SPAN;
```

FIGURE 2-3.3   PL/I procedure for the SPAN function.

```
FIND:  PROCEDURE(SUBJECT,PATTERN,CURSOR,MATCH_STR,REPL_STR,REPL_FLAG)
           RETURNS (BIT(1));
   DECLARE SUBJECT CHARACTER(*) VARYING,
           PATTERN CHARACTER(*) VARYING,
           CURSOR FIXED BINARY,
           MATCH_STR CHARACTER(*) VARYING,
           REPL_STR CHARACTER(*) VARYING,
           REPL_FLAG BIT(*);
   DECLARE I FIXED BINARY;
   IF CURSOR > LENGTH(SUBJECT)
   THEN RETURN('0'B);
   I = INDEX(SUBSTR(SUBJECT,CURSOR),PATTERN);
   IF I = 0
   THEN RETURN('0'B);
   MATCH_STR = SUBSTR(SUBJECT,CURSOR,I-1);
   I = I + LENGTH(PATTERN) - 1;
   IF REPL_FLAG
   THEN DO;
       IF CURSOR + I = LENGTH(SUBJECT) + 1
       THEN SUBJECT = SUBSTR(SUBJECT,1,CURSOR-1) || REPL_STR;
       ELSE SUBJECT = SUBSTR(SUBJECT,1,CURSOR-1) || REPL_STR
                    || SUBSTR(SUBJECT,CURSOR + I);
       CURSOR = CURSOR + LENGTH(REPL_STR);
   END;
   ELSE CURSOR = CURSOR + I;
   RETURN('1'B);
END FIND;
```

FIGURE 2-3.4   PL/I procedure for the FIND function.

2-3.4   String Manipulation in SNOBOL

Our discussion of Markov algorithms in Sec. 2-2.1 provides an excellent background for an introduction to the SNOBOL language. SNOBOL was first developed in 1962 at Bell Laboratories specifically to help solve problems involving string manipulation. We examine the fourth major version of SNOBOL, SNOBOL 4. From this examination it will become clear that SNOBOL has string-handling capabilities which are far more powerful than the primitive string-manipulation functions available in PL/I.

A statement in SNOBOL is similar in form and definition to a Markov production. Its general form is:

label subject pattern = replacement branch-label.

The *label* is identical in purpose to the label in a labeled Markov production. It differs in form since it must begin in the first character position of a SNOBOL statement, and it does not have a colon following it. A SNOBOL statement with a blank in the first character position is an unlabeled statement.

The *subject* is a variable or constant which represents the subject string for the pattern-matching operations performed in that statement. This feature allows a program to have as many subject strings as statements. Hence, the flexibility which is achieved by introducing the memory-cell concept to the Markov model is realized here.

The *pattern* plays the role of the "antecedent" in the Markov production. That is, the pattern is a string which is sought in the subject string. A pattern is "matched" if the pattern string is present anywhere in the subject string. An exception arises in a mode of operation, called *anchored mode*, in which the match must start from the first character of the subject string.

The *replacement* represents the string which replaces the matched portion of the subject string, providing a pattern match is successful. Therefore, its role is identical to that of the "consequent" in a Markov production.

The *branch label* differs from the branch label in a Markov production in the sense that a branch can be specified for a pattern-match failure as well as a success. The form of the branch is a colon followed by an F(label), an S(label), a (label), or both F(label) and S(label). F(label) means branch to "label" if the pattern match is a failure, S(label) means branch to "label" if the pattern match is successful, and (label) is interpreted as an unconditional branch (i.e., branch to "label" regardless of whether the pattern match is successful or not). The sequence of control is the same as in the labeled Markov production in the sense that, if a branch does not apply, the next statement in the program is executed.

The following set of SNOBOL statements outputs a string represented by **SUBJECT** which has had all the **'A'**s removed.

```
      SUBJECT = INPUT
AGAIN SUBJECT 'A' = ''   :S(AGAIN)
      OUTPUT = SUBJECT
END
```

Program input is achieved through the pseudovariable **INPUT**, and output is attained by assigning the string intended for output to the pseudovariable **OUTPUT**. In the second statement of the program, the single character string **'A'** is matched with the contents of **SUBJECT**. The left-most **'A'** is matched first and replaced by the empty string. A successful match results in an immediate return to the second statement and a pattern match is again attempted. This process continues until no more **'A'**s are present in the string represented by **SUBJECT**. At this point, the pattern match fails and control transfers to the third statement, where the current value for **SUBJECT** is output. The program halts upon executing the **END** statement.

This program illustrates an important point; namely, that the pattern portion of a statement need not always be present in a SNOBOL statement (as is demonstrated in the first and third statements). Note also that a pattern match always begins from the first character in **SUBJECT**. That is, if **SUBJECT** is initially **'CABBAC'**, then after the first pattern match and replacement, it has the value **'CBBAC'**. The second time the statement labeled **AGAIN** is executed, the pattern-matching cursor is reset to point at the first character **'C'**, and pattern-matching attempts begin here, not at where the last pattern match succeeded (i.e., at the first **'B'**). Hence, some rescanning must be done before achieving the second pattern match. While this may appear to be inefficient, rescanning of the subject string is necessary in some applications. We will examine such an application in Sec. 2-5.1.

SNOBOL is substantially different from PL/I in many ways. One fundamental difference is that variables do not have to be declared in a program. While there are integer, real, and character-string data types in SNOBOL, the exact type of variable at a given point in a program is dictated by the context in which that variable appears. For example, the variable X takes on three different types (namely, integer, real, and character string) in the context of an integer addition, a real multiplication, and a string concatenation, as exhibited in the following three statements:

```
X = X + 2
X = X * 2.0
X = X 'STRING'
```

Notice that because concatenation is performed so frequently, there is no explicit operator for it. Strings to be concatenated are simply written down, one after the other, with one or more blanks separating each of them.

Two very important concepts in SNOBOL are *pattern variables* and *pattern structures*. A pattern variable is assigned a pattern structure. The simplest form of pattern structure is a string. For example, in the statements

```
PAT = 'ERE'
SUBJECT = 'THERE HOME IS OUR HOME'
SUBJECT PAT = 'EIR'
OUTPUT = SUBJECT
```

PAT is a pattern variable which has the pattern structure 'ERE'.

Pattern structures can be made more complex with the introduction of the two pattern operations—alternation and concatenation. The alternation operation (denoted by |) is useful in the formulation of a pattern which allows for the application of a number of patterns to the same subject string in a given pattern-matching situation. For example, if we want to replace all digits in a string by the character ' # ', then the following program can be used. (The variable TEXT holds the string value.)

```
        DIGIT = '0' | '1' | '2' | '3' | '4' | '5' | '6' | '7' | '8' | '9'
        TEXT = INPUT
LOOP    TEXT DIGIT = ' # '   :S(LOOP)
        OUTPUT = TEXT
END
```

We interpret the pattern structure for DIGIT to mean that a match is made if either a '0', or a '1', or a '2', ..., or a '9' is found in the subject string to which it is applied. The match is made to the left-most digit and this digit is replaced by ' # '. Hence, if we trace the value of TEXT through the execution of the program, assuming an initial value of 'May 14, 1942' for TEXT, we have 'May 14, 1942' ... 'May # 4, 1942' ... 'May # #, 1942' ... ... 'May # #, # # # #'.

To illustrate how concatenation can be used, let us assume we wish to construct a program which counts the number of words that end in a vowel in a given string represented by the variable TEXT.

```
        ENDING = 'A ' | 'E ' | 'I ' | 'O ' | 'U '
        TEXT = INPUT
LOOP    TEXT ENDING = ' # '        :F(OTPT)
        COUNT = COUNT + 1          :(LOOP)
OTPT    OUTPUT = 'NUMBER OF WORDS ENDING IN A VOWEL IS ' COUNT
END
```

In the "LOOP" statement, a scan is made of TEXT in an effort to detect a two-character sequence containing a vowel followed by a blank. If such a sequence is found, it is replaced by the string ' # ', and COUNT (which is automatically initialized to the empty string which, in turn, is implicitly converted to the integer zero in the context of the fourth statement) is incremented by 1. A return is made to the "LOOP" statement to attempt another pattern match. This looping process continues until no further pattern matches are successful, and a transfer is made to the statement which outputs the result.

The pattern ENDING can be simplified by using concatenation. We can write ENDING as

ENDING = ('A' | 'E' | 'I' | 'O' | 'U') ' '

in which case, each of the alternatives are concatenated with the blank character. Note that we cannot use

ENDING = 'A' | 'E' | 'I' | 'O' | 'U' ' '

since concatenation has precedence over alternation, and this statement would be interpreted as

ENDING = 'A' | 'E' | 'I' | 'O' | 'U '

Two operations which are extremely helpful and sometimes necessary when using pattern structures involving alternation are the *conditional value assignment* and *immediate value assignment*. In the previous example, we have no way of determining which of the alternative patterns is matched, given that a match takes place. If we desire this information, the conditional-value-assignment operator (denoted by ·) can provide it. If ENDING is expressed as

ENDING = (('A' | 'E' | 'I' | 'O' | 'U') ' ') · RESULT

then the pattern string which is matched from the set of alternatives is assigned to the variable RESULT. A list of all pattern matches can be constructed by placing the statement

LIST = LIST RESULT

between the "LOOP" statement and the statement for updating the COUNT.

If it is desirable to obtain temporary results during a pattern-matching process, then the immediate assignment operator (denoted by $) is used to obtain this information. For example, if a printout of all vowels is desired in the program for detecting words that end in vowels, then the pattern ENDING should be formulated as

ENDING = ('A' | 'E' | 'I' | 'O' | 'U') $ OUTPUT ' '

In this instance, any partial pattern match involving a vowel is assigned to the pseudo-variable OUTPUT, and hence is printed. Therefore, if TEXT = 'THE DOG RAN HOME ' and ENDING is defined as just indicated, then

E

O

A

Ⓞ

E

NUMBER OF WORDS ENDING IN A VOWEL IS 2

would be output from the execution of the last programming example.

A comparison between the MATCH function, which was described algorithmically in Sec. 2-3.2, and the pattern-matching facilities in SNOBOL described thus far reveals that both have the capabilities of matching a pattern string with a substring of the subject string, of replacing the matched pattern with a replacement string (i.e., using the RE-PLACE_STR in MATCH and the assignment operator " =" in SNOBOL), and of assigning the matched string to a string variable (i.e., using MATCH_STR in MATCH and the conditional value assignment operator "." in SNOBOL). The major difference between these two facilities is that the MATCH function must match the pattern string to the substring of the subject string starting at a specified CURSOR position; whereas, in the basic SNOBOL pattern-matching statement, a match is attempted in a left-to-right scan, for all substrings of the subject string.

We are now prepared to describe and to give examples of some of the more powerful pattern-matching functions available in SNOBOL.

> LEN(integer) returns a pattern defined to match any string of a length indicated by the integer-valued argument. Therefore,

> SUBJECT LEN(5) · X =

> matches the first five characters of SUBJECT and assigns these characters, via the conditional-value-assignment operator, to the variable X (providing SUBJECT is of length greater than 4). If a pattern match is achieved, the matched part of the subject string is replaced by the empty string. An empty string assignment can be denoted by an empty right-hand side, as well as by assigning ".
> The statement

> LOOP TEXT (' ' LEN(3) ' ') · WORD = ' '   :S(LOOP)

> results in the match and removal of all three-letter words in TEXT which are not followed by a punctuation mark.

The LEN function described in algorithmic notation in Sec. 2-3.2 and the LEN function in SNOBOL are almost identical in function, differing only in the manner in which the pattern-matching cursor is controlled. In the algorithmic case, the CURSOR value is an explicit parameter, while in the SNOBOL LEN, the cursor always refers to the next character position in the pattern matching scan. Note also that the algorithmic LEN returns *true* or *false,* while the SNOBOL LEN returns a pattern.

SPAN(string) returns a pattern defined to match the longest substring of the subject string, beginning at the current cursor position and containing only characters of the string argument. Therefore,

```
NUMB_STR = SPAN('0123456789')
TEXT NUMB_STR . NUMBER
```

creates the pattern which matches the first string of numbers in the string represented by TEXT. Hence, if TEXT = 'A0932-716', then the substring '0932' is matched and assigned to the variable NUMBER. However, if TEXT = 'ABC-DC', then the pattern match fails. Note that we can always express this and any other pattern-matching function in-line in the SNOBOL statement (e.g., TEXT SPAN('0123456789') · NUMBER); however, the reading of a program is often simplified by separating the formation of the pattern structure from the pattern-matching statement.

The SPAN function in SNOBOL and the SPAN function algorithmically described in Sec. 2-3.2 are identical in purpose; however, they differ in effect. The SNOBOL SPAN function begins spanning at the position of the first character which matches a character in the argument string. The SPAN function which was described algorithmically begins pattern matching from the specified cursor position. Also, the algorithmic SPAN returns *true* or *false*, while the SNOBOL SPAN returns a pattern.

BREAK(string) returns a pattern defined to match the longest substring containing only characters not in the argument string. Hence, it is the converse function of SPAN. The program

```
AGAIN     TEXT BREAK(' ,.!?:;') · WORD =        :F(END)
          OUTPUT = WORD
          TEXT SPAN(' ,.!?:;') =                :(AGAIN)
END
```

can be used to output all of the words in TEXT, excluding surrounding blank characters. Note that the pattern-matching process continues until the entire TEXT is set to the empty string assuming TEXT ends in a punctuation mark. Once this happens, the pattern returned by the BREAK function fails to match TEXT and the program ends.

Observe that the BREAK function is quite similar to the FIND function as described in Sec. 2-3.2. The primary difference is that in the FIND function, the pattern-matching process is concluded when the entire PATTERN string argument is matched, and not just a character from that pattern argument. All characters up to and *including* the pattern portion of the matched string can be replaced by REPLACE_STR in the case of the FIND function.

TAB(integer) returns a pattern defined to match all characters from the current cursor position up to the tab position indicated by the integer argument. TAB can be used to move the cursor to specific positions when handling highly formatted subject strings. For example,

TEXT TAB(10) 'SEX:' LEN(1) · SEXTYPE

produces a successful match if the substring 'SEX:' immediately follows the first ten characters in TEXT. If 'SEX:' is matched, then the character following is matched by the LEN function and assigned to the variable SEXTYPE.

A function RTAB also exists and it matches all characters from the current cursor position up to, but *excluding*, the tab as specified by an integer argument indicating the number of positions from the end of the string. Combining TAB and RTAB, we can write

TEXT TAB(10) RTAB(10) · MIDDLE

to assign to MIDDLE the substring of TEXT which excludes the first and last ten characters of TEXT. Of course, if TEXT is less than twenty characters in length, the pattern match fails.

POS(integer) returns a pattern which matches the empty string, if the cursor is located at the position of the subject string indicated by the integer argument. Therefore,

TEXT 'SEX:' POS(14) LEN(1) · SEXTYPE

produces a successful match if the substring 'SEX:' appears immediately prior to and including the fourteenth character in TEXT. This example and the first example statement for TAB are functionally equivalent. Note, however, that POS is used to test the current position of the cursor, whereas TAB moves the cursor. The statement

TEXT BREAK(' ') POS(5)

results in a successful pattern match only if the first four characters are nonblank and the fifth is a blank.

A function RPOS is also available which matches the empty string at an integral number of positions from the end of the string, as specified by the integer argument.

Before concluding our discussion of string-handling facilities in SNOBOL, we should introduce a number of functions which are not pattern matching in nature, but are, nevertheless, important in string handling.

SIZE(string) returns the length of its string argument. Therefore, if TEXT has the value 'DATA', then SIZE(TEXT) returns the value 4. SIZE is identical to the LENGTH function.

DUPL(string, integer) returns a string of duplications of its argument string. (DUPL is similar but not identical to the PL/I REPEAT function.) Thus, DUPL('ABC', 3) is 'ABCABCABC'.

A predicate function in SNOBOL returns an empty string if the condition tested is *true*; otherwise, the statement containing the condition fails. Besides the arithmetic predicates such as LT, LE, GT, GE, EQ, and NE, there exists a string predicate LGT. The prefix L means "lexically," and the predicate function LGT returns the empty string (i.e., *true*), if its first argument is greater than its second argument according to the lexical ordering determined by the collating sequence of the computer's character set. Therefore, LGT('B', 'A') is *true*, while LGT('A', 'B') is *false*.

Predicates can appear on the right-hand side of assignment statements, thus making the assignment conditional on the value of the predicate. For example,

```
BEGIN    LINE = INPUT                        :F(OUT)
         J = LT(J, 5) J + 1                  :S(BEGIN)
         OUTPUT = 'MORE THAN 5 LINES'        :(END)
OUT      OUTPUT = 'LESS THAN 6 LINES'
END
```

continues reading in cards until six cards (i.e., LINES) have been read or there are no more cards to be read in. The latter case is detected by a failure in the input statement.

As a final example, let us consider the problem of converting an input item of the form

```
CHARLES W. SMITH          9872
```

to an output item of the form

```
SMITH, C. W.              $98.72
```

An input item consists of a name (composed of a first name, an initial, and a surname) followed by an expenditure in cents. No format can be assumed about the input item, except that one input item appears per input card. The end of the input items is designated by a card with an '*' in column 1.

An output item consists of a name (composed of a surname, a comma, and two initials) followed by an appropriately formatted expenditure. An output item begins in column 5, and the formatted expenditure starts in column 50.

The following SNOBOL program accomplishes the desired changes in formatting.

```
* COMMENTS IN SNOBOL ARE DESIGNATED BY USING AN * IN THE FIRST COLUMN.
* CONSTRUCTION OF PATTERNS USED IN THE PROGRAM
     BLANKS = SPAN(' ') | ''
     FIRST_INITIAL_PATTERN = BLANKS LEN(1) · FIRSTINIT BREAK(' ') BLANKS
     SECOND_INITIAL_PATTERN = LEN(1) · SECONDINIT BREAK(' ') BLANKS
     SURNAME_PATTERN = BREAK(' ') · SURNAME
     AMOUNT_PATTERN = BLANKS BREAK(' ') · AMOUNT
* MAIN BODY OF PROGRAM
START CARD = INPUT
     CARD POS(1) '*'                              :S(END)
```

```
      CARD FIRST_INITIAL_PATTERN =
      CARD SECOND_INITIAL_PATTERN =
      CARD SURNAME_PATTERN =
      CARD AMOUNT_PATTERN
* SEPARATE AMOUNT INTO DOLLARS AND CENTS
      AMOUNT RTAB(2) · DOLLARS LEN(2) · CENTS
* CONSTRUCT OUTPUT FORM
      NEWNAME = DUPL(' ', 4) SURNAME ', ' FIRSTINIT '. ' SECONDINIT '.'
      EXPENDITURE = '$' DOLLARS '.' CENTS
      OUTPUT  = NEWNAME DUPL(' ', 49 - LENGTH(NEWNAME)) EXPENDITURE
          :(START)
  END
```

SNOBOL is a very powerful and interesting programming language. The discussion in this subsection provides only a brief introduction to the language with a concentration on some of the more important string-handling capabilities. To acquire a complete knowledge of the language, the interested reader is directed to "A SNOBOL4 Primer" by Griswold and Griswold [1973]. It is not surprising that the primitive and basic string-handling facilities presented in Sec. 2-3.2 are all available in the SNOBOL language; indeed, SNOBOL provides many additional facilities. One other such facility we shall now examine is that of a recursively defined pattern structure.

2-3.5 Recursive Pattern Structures

By this point in the chapter, the importance of pattern matching as a string-manipulation facility should be very clear. In this subsection, we extend the previous discussion on pattern matching by introducing the concept of a *recursive pattern structure*. We have already encountered several examples of recursively defined patterns in Sec. 2-2.2, where the notion of a recursively defined production in a grammar was introduced. Recall that the recursive definition of an unsigned integer is given as

$$\text{<unsigned integer>} ::= \text{<digit>} \mid \text{<unsigned integer>} \text{ <digit>}$$
$$\text{<digit>} ::= 0 \mid 1 \mid 2 \mid 3 \mid 4 \mid 5 \mid 6 \mid 7 \mid 8 \mid 9$$

Hence, an unsigned integer is defined to be a single digit, or an integer consisting of a single digit followed by a digit, or an integer composed of two digits followed by a digit, et cetera. While the productions for an unsigned integer provide a concise definition, they enable the recognition of any member of the infinite set of unsigned integers. Of course, the process of string recognition is a form of pattern matching.

Recursive pattern structures can be defined in SNOBOL with the aid of the *unevaluated-expression operator* *. This operator delays evaluation of its operand until a pattern value is required during pattern matching.

We begin a description of * by illustrating how it is used in defining a nonrecursive pattern structure. In a pattern definition such as

    PAT = TAB(N) LEN(1) · X

the pattern constructed for PAT is determined, in part, by the value of N at the time the assignment statement is executed. In SNOBOL, it is convenient and conventional to define all pattern structures at the beginning of the program, and thus avoid the continual reevaluation which takes place if the patterns are used "in-line." To maintain this convenience and convention, and yet allow a pattern to change based on a parameter such as N, we use the * operator. For example, if PAT is defined as

> PAT = TAB(*N) LEN(1) · X,

then the * operator prevents the evaluation of the assignment statement until PAT is used as a pattern in another SNOBOL statement, such as

> LAB SUBJECT PAT =

However, each time the statement labeled LAB is executed, the pattern assignment is reevaluated, thus allowing a different value of N and, hence, the construction of a different pattern each time PAT is used.

This ability to defer the evaluation of a pattern is necessary in the construction of a recursive pattern structure. For example, the SNOBOL statements

> DIGIT = '0' | '1' | '2' | '3' | '4' | '5' | '6' | '7' | '8' | '9'
> UINTEGER = DIGIT | *UINTEGER DIGIT

define a pattern for an unsigned integer. Therefore, in the statements

> SUBJECT = 'A13982'
> SUBJECT UINTEGER =

the pattern UINTEGER is evaluated initially as the pattern alternative DIGIT, which matches the character '1'. The second numeric character '3' is matched along with '1' by the second alternative for UINTEGER—namely UINTEGER DIGIT. This is possible because UINTEGER evaluates to DIGIT and, hence, the second alternative is the pattern DIGIT DIGIT. In a similar fashion, the string '139' is matched by the alternative *UINTEGER DIGIT, where *UINTEGER now evaluates to DIGIT DIGIT. It is easy to see how this pattern evaluation process is extended recursively to pattern match the entire digit string '13982' and, indeed, any digit string forming an unsigned integer.

Consider, as another example, the recursive pattern structure that might be used to define an identifier.

> LETTER = 'A' | 'B' | 'C' | 'D' | 'E' | 'F' | 'G' | 'H' | 'I' | 'J' | 'K' | 'L' | 'M' | 'N' | 'O' | 'P' |
> 'Q' | 'R' | 'S' | 'T' | 'U' | 'W' | 'V' | 'X' | 'Y' | 'Z'
> DIGIT = '0' | '1' | '2' | '3' | '4' | '5' | '6' | '7' | '8' | '9'
> IDENTIFIER = LETTER | *IDENTIFIER LETTER | *IDENTIFIER DIGIT

These statements describe a pattern structure consisting of a set of strings, each string of which consists of a single letter or a letter followed by an arbitrary number of alphanumeric characters.

There is no operator or function in the list of primitive and basic character-manipulation functions, given in Secs. 2-3.1 and 2-3.2, which performs a role similar to that of the unevaluated expression operator (*) in SNOBOL. Nevertheless, pattern-matching functions can be called recursively to simulate the effect of a recursive pattern structure. For example, an unsigned integer can be scanned for recursively by using two algorithms. The first algorithm, UINTEGER, isolates the initial digit in the subject string. UINTEGER calls the second algorithm, DIGIT_SCAN, which matches the string of digits forming the left-most unsigned integer in the subject string. The matching is achieved by recursive calls to DIGIT_SCAN.

Algorithm UINTEGER.   A given string, SUBJECT, is scanned until the first (i.e., left-most) digit is found. The function DIGIT_SCAN is invoked to isolate the left-most unsigned integer. The six pattern-matching parameters assume the roles defined in Sec. 2-3.2.

1. [Initialize CURSOR]   Set CURSOR ← 1.
2. [Scan for first numeric character]
   Repeat while
   LEN(SUBJECT, 1, CURSOR, MATCH_STR, REPLACE_STR, false)
   and MATCH_STR < '0'. (In the string-comparison operation involving <, it is assumed that the numeric characters 0 through 9 are higher than all other characters in the collating sequence. CURSOR is automatically incremented in the LEN function when the pattern match is successful).
3. [Do we have a numeric character?]
   If MATCH_STR < '0',
   then set UINTEGER ← ' '; (No digits exist in SUBJECT.)
   otherwise set UINTEGER ← DIGIT_SCAN(SUBJECT, CURSOR). (Otherwise, return digit string as unsigned integer.)
4. [Finished]   Exit.

The DIGIT_SCAN algorithm recursively concatenates numerical characters from SUBJECT to form the string of digits making up the unsigned integer.

Algorithm DIGIT_SCAN   Given a string SUBJECT and a cursor value CURSOR, isolate the longest string of numerical characters starting from the cursor character of SUBJECT.

1. [Test for end of digit string]
   If LEN(SUBJECT, 1, CURSOR, MATCH_STR, REPLACE_STR, false)
   and MATCH_STR ≥ '0',
   then set DIGIT_SCAN ← MATCH_STR ○ DIGIT_SCAN(SUBJECT,CURSOR);
   otherwise, set DIGIT_SCAN ← ''. (Return empty string.)
2. [Finished]   Exit.

In the Algorithm DIGIT_SCAN, digits are isolated and concatenated with the results of previous invocations of DIGIT_SCAN. For example, if SUBJECT = 'MAY 1980' and CURSOR initially has the value 5, then a trace of the DIGIT_SCAN algorithm is illustrated in Table 2-3.2.

Table 2-3.2

Step	CURSOR	MATCH_STR	DIGIT_SCAN
1	5	'1'	?
1	6	'9'	?
1	7	'8'	?
1	8	'0'	?
1	8	''	''
return to 1 and exit at 2	8	'0'	'0'
return to 1 and exit at 2	8	'8'	'80'
return to 1 and exit at 2	7	'9'	'980'
return to 1 and exit at 2	6	'1'	'1980'
return to UINTEGER			

Note that four recursive calls of Algorithm DIGIT_SCAN are made during the process of scanning the SUBJECT string. For each such call, a return is made to the point of invocation in step 1 (i.e., DIGIT_SCAN ← MATCH_STR ○ DIGIT_SCAN(SUBJECT, CURSOR)) and the value returned is concatenated with the value MATCH_STR has at that particular invocation of DIGIT_SCAN. It is important that intermediate values be retained for MATCH_STR during the recursive calls of DIGIT_SCAN. A more in-depth discussion of recursive functions is undertaken in Sec. 3-7.1, where it will be explained how these intermediate values are stored from one invocation of a recursive function to the next.

Observe that Algorithm DIGIT_SCAN can be implemented without the use of recursion. An iterative approach, such as the approach used for removing leading non-numerical characters in Algorithm UINTEGER, can be adopted. However, the given version of DIGIT_SCAN illustrates how recursive pattern matching can be achieved using the basic string-handling functions. For many problems, it is easier to formulate a recursive algorithm than an iterative algorithm. We will encounter examples of such problems in Chap. 5 when discussing the traversal of trees.

Exercises for Sec. 2-3

1. In the discussion of primitive string-manipulation functions, we introduced the operation of concatenation and the functions INDEX, SUB, and LENGTH. Can any one of these functions or operations be implemented in terms of the remaining functions? If possible, give the implementation.

2. How does the PL/I function VERIFY differ (a) from the basic string manipulation function SPAN, and (b) from the SNOBOL SPAN function?

3. Design an algorithm for duplicating a given character string. For example, given the argument string 'WAKA', Algorithm DUPL should generate the string 'WAKAWAKA'.

4. Design an algorithm which trims off all the trailing blanks of a character string. For example, given the argument 'HE ENDED IT ALL! bbbbb', Algorithm TRIM returns the string 'HE ENDED IT ALL!'.

5. Construct an algorithm which effects the "break" pattern-matching operation. Given a subject string, a pattern string, an initial cursor position, an initially empty matched string, a replacement string, and a replacement condition (*true* or *false*), the algorithm scans the subject string on a character-by-character basis, starting at the given cursor position and proceeding to the first instance of a character which is also a character in the pattern string. If such a character is found: (a) the algorithm exits with a value of *true*; and (b) the matched string argument is assigned the substring of the subject from the initial cursor position up to, but excluding, the character found; (c) the replacement string replaces the matched string in the subject if the replacement condition is *true*; and (d) after a replacement is completed, the cursor value is updated to point at the break character found. If a pattern character is not found, the algorithm returns *false*, and no changes are made. Therefore, given a subject string (SUBJECT) of ' "THIS", HE SAID, "CANNOT BE SO".', a pattern string (PATTERN) of ' .,;:?!', a cursor position (CURSOR) of 1, and a replacement string (REPLACE_STR) of the empty string '', BREAK(SUBJECT, PATTERN, CURSOR, MATCH_STR, REPLACE_STR, true) sets the subject string to

   ', HE SAID, "CANNOT BE SO".'

the MATCH_STR to ' "THIS" ' and the CURSOR to 1.

6. What will be printed by each of the following PL/I statements?
   (a) I = INDEX ('TESTSTRING','T');
        PUT LIST ('I =', I);
   (b) STRING = 'LIST OF LETTERS';
        SUBSTR(STRING,9,8) = 'NUMBERS';
        PUT LIST ('STRING = ' , STRING);
   (c) NUMBERS = '01234567890';
        PUT LIST ('VERIFICATION OF 35 ', VERIFY(NUMBERS,'35'));

7. Write a PL/I program called DELETE to delete all occurrences of each character contained in one given string from another given string. The two strings are as follows:
   (a) STR, the string from which deletions are to be made
   (b) LIST, the string providing the characters whose occurrences in STR should be deleted
   For example, if STR = 'THEbEZNZZXDX' and LIST = 'XZ', then the required answer is STR = 'THEbEND'.

8. Write (a) a PL/I program or (b) a SNOBOL program to determine whether or not a sentence conforms to a particular pattern. For example, consider the following:

   THE _____ BELONGS TO THE _____.

   Sentences which would match this pattern are:

   THE BOOK BELONGS TO THE LIBRARY.
   THE CAT BELONGS TO THE FORD FAMILY.

9. An interesting problem in linguistics is the analysis of textual material. Let us assume that we are interested in developing an algorithm which is designed to analyze a manuscript to obtain:
   (a) the number of sentences in the manuscript

(b)   the average number of words in a sentence

(c)   the average number of symbols in a word

We will assume that:

(a)   Each sentence within the text is delimited by a period followed by two blanks and embedded periods are not permitted.

(b)   Each word within a sentence is delimited by one blank space.

(c)   Commas, semicolons, periods, and hyphens are not to be counted as characters.

(d)   The last sentence in the manuscript is indicated by a slash in the symbol position following the period-blank-blank sequence.

(e)   Words are not divided from one line to the next and the last word on each line is followed by at least one blank.

(f)   The first word on each line is preceded by blanks only if it is the first word in a paragraph.

Write a PL/I or SNOBOL program to perform the above.

10.   Given expressions of the form

$$\begin{aligned}
\langle \text{expression} \rangle &::= \langle \text{expression} \rangle + \langle \text{term} \rangle \\
&\quad | \langle \text{term} \rangle \\
\langle \text{term} \rangle &::= \langle \text{form} \rangle * \langle \text{term} \rangle \\
&\quad | \langle \text{form} \rangle \\
\langle \text{form} \rangle &::= \mathsf{I}
\end{aligned}$$

Formulate a recursively defined SNOBOL pattern to recognize the strings 'I + I', 'I * I + I' and 'I'. A string, such as 'I + I I', should not be matched by the pattern.

2-4   STORAGE REPRESENTATION OF STRINGS

A string is a sequence of characters and, as such, it is most conveniently represented using a sequence of storage locations in memory. In Sec. 1-4.8, it was pointed out that characters are binary encoded in fields which are typically 6, 7, or 8 bits in length. Therefore, in almost all machines, an integral number of characters, say n, are stored in a computer word, where $n = \lfloor w/f \rfloor$ and w is the word size in bits and f is the field length in bits of the binary encoded character. For the IBM 360/370 series computer w = 32 bits, f = 8 bits (for the EBCDIC code), and hence n = 4 characters per word.

In this chapter, we identified three types of character strings, namely, fixed-length strings (available in PL/I), "varying"-length strings (available in PL/I), and variable-length strings (available in SNOBOL). The idea of using a sequence of memory words or locations to represent a string is applied to the storage representation of all three types of character strings.

The amount of storage required by a fixed-length string is known when the string is created. For example, the PL/I statement

DECLARE S CHARACTER (6) INITIAL('*A1');

declares a field of six binary-encoded characters (which for an IBM 360/370 implementation implies a field of six bytes). An initialization of S to '*A1' implies that S is assigned

Word i				Word i + 1			
*	A	1	Blank	Blank	Blank		
01011100	11000001	11110001	01000000	01000000	01000000	Not used	Not used
X'5C'	X'C1'	X'F1'	X'40'	X'40'	X'40'		

FIGURE 2-4.1 Fixed-length EBCDIC character string representation for '*A1   '.

'*A1bbb'. This assignment is represented in Fig. 2-4.1, where X'5C', X'C1', X'F1', and X'40' are read as "hexadecimal 5C, C1, F1, and 40" (i.e., $(5C)_{16}$ $(C1)_{16}$, $(F1)_{16}$, and $(40)_{16}$), and are the EBCDIC representations of '*', 'A', '1', and blank, respectively. Observe that there are two bytes in word$_{i+1}$ which are not assigned to S. Extra bytes, such as these, may be assigned to another character string if the string storage area is managed efficiently by the compiler or interpreter.

The maximum length of a "varying"-length string is also known at creation time. Enough storage is allocated to accommodate up to this maximum number of characters along with storage for an information field which contains the current length of the string. The execution of the PL/I declaration

DECLARE C CHARACTER(6) VARYING INITIAL ('*A1');

results in an allocation of storage as illustrated in Fig. 2-4.2.

The EBCDIC representation which is adopted in Fig. 2-4.2 allows a string to assume a current length of up to 65535 (that is, $2^{16} - 1$), subject to the restriction that the current length is less than the maximum allowable length. In some implementations, it is necessary to add a second length field which contains the maximum length. This second field is used in checking for a string overflow condition (e.g., the assignment of a string which is larger than the predefined maximum length).

The most dynamic and powerful type of string is the variable-length string. In this case, neither the precise length nor maximum length is known at creation time. The storage structure for this type of string can be handled in many ways, but two popular methods of representation employ *boundary markers* and *string descriptors*. A boundary marker is a character which need not be printable, and which does not appear in the text of a string. For example, the printable character '↑' is used in the ASCII storage representation for the string '*A1', as shown in Fig. 2-4.3. A 7-bit ASCII character representation on a 16-bit word machine, such as the PDP-11, is assumed in Fig. 2-4.3. Note that the first bit of each half-word (i.e., byte) can be either a "zero" or "one" depending on the

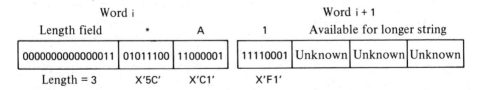

Word i			Word i + 1			
Length field	*	A	1	Available for longer string		
0000000000000011	01011100	11000001	11110001	Unknown	Unknown	Unknown
Length = 3	X'5C'	X'C1'	X'F1'			

FIGURE 2-4.2 Varying-length EBCDIC character-string representation for '*A1'.

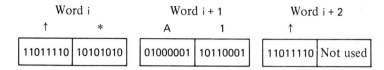

Word i   Word i + 1   Word i + 2

↑   *   A   1   ↑

| 11011110 | 10101010 | | 01000001 | 10110001 | | 11011110 | Not used |

FIGURE 2-4.3 Variable-length ASCII 7-bit character-string representation for '*A1' using boundary markers.

type of parity error checking that is adopted in the computer. If all binary encodings of characters must have *even parity*, as is the case in Fig. 2-4.3, then the number of "ones" in an encoded character must be an even number. If *odd parity* is adopted, then the number of "ones" must be an odd number. Of course, if the parity of an encoded character disagrees with the adopted convention, an error has occurred in the transmission or storage of that character.

A string descriptor is a two-field element which contains a length field and a pointer field. The length field contains the current length of the variable-length string. The pointer field contains the address of the first character of the string in a large data area called *string space*. String space holds the encoded character information for all strings in the program. For example, in Fig. 2-4.4, the string '*A1' is represented using a descriptor. Note that to reference a string, we first must reference the descriptor which, in turn, provides the string address via the pointer field.

To aid in the understanding of the string storage structures presented in this section, it is worthwhile to examine how some of the primitive string-manipulation operations and functions (i.e., assignment, concatenation, LENGTH, SUB, INDEX) are realized using the different storage representations. A string assignment results in the copying of the string or a reference to the string formed by the right-hand side (or subject) of the assignment to the storage location(s) referenced by the left-hand side (or object) of the assignment. Problems do not arise when assigning values to fixed-length and "varying"-length string variables because enough storage is allocated for these variables when they are created. If

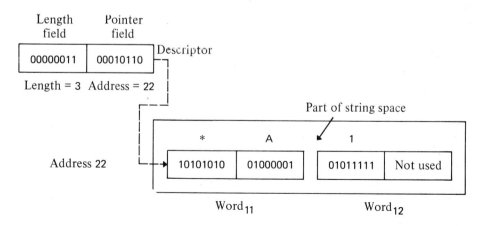

FIGURE 2-4.4 Variable-length ASCII 7-bit character-string representation for '*A1' using descriptors.

the string value to be assigned is longer than the length allotted to the fixed or "varying"-length string variables, then the extra characters are removed from the right-hand end of the string so as to assign a string equal to the maximum length for the variable. When a string value is assigned to a fixed-length string variable, the value must be padded to the right with blanks before assignment (if its length is less than the predetermined fixed length allotted the string variable). The string value is padded until it is equal in length to the fixed length of the variable.

Assignments to variable-length string variables present some storage allocation problems. The space currently allocated to the string variable may be insufficient to store the string value being assigned. To illustrate this fact, suppose the assignments S1 = 'CAT' and S2 = 'ANIMAL' are executed. The resulting effects on the string space, when using the boundary-marker method, are depicted in Fig. 2-4.5a. Figure 2-4.5b illustrates the effects on the string space when using the descriptor method. For brevity and clarity, we have used characters and not a binary-encoded representation of the characters in Fig. 2-4.5 and the remaining figures in this section.

The assignment S1 = 'MOUSE' necessitates the creation of new space in the string area for the variable S1, as is illustrated in Figs. 2-4.6a and 2-4.6b.

Observe in Fig. 2-4.7 that an assignment of the value of one variable to another, such as S1 = S2, does not require the allocation of additional space in the string area. Instead, the assignment can be accomplished by assigning the reference to (in the boundary-marker method) or the description of (in the descriptor method) the subject string S2 to the object string S1.

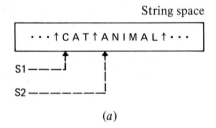

(a)

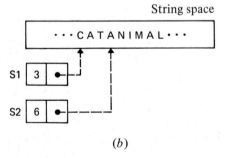

(b)

FIGURE 2-4.5 Assignments of the variable-length strings 'CAT' and 'ANIMAL' to S1 and S2, respectively.

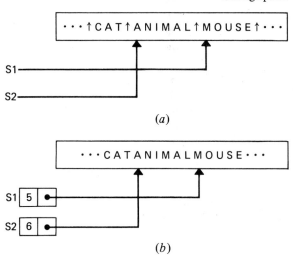

FIGURE 2-4.6   Effect of the variable-length string assignment S1 = 'MOUSE'.

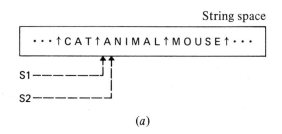

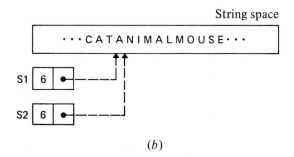

FIGURE 2-4.7   Effect of the variable-length string assignment S1 = S2.

If this policy is adopted for variable-to-variable assignments, new string storage must be allocated in instances involving string-expression and string-constant assignments. Otherwise, if S2, as depicted in Fig. 2-4.7, is assigned 'DOG' as shown in Fig. 2-4.8, then a side effect from this assignment would occur. Assigning 'DOG' to S2 changes the value of S1 to 'DOG' when using boundary markers, and 'DOGMAL' when using descriptors, which are, of course, both erroneous. Therefore, a correct assignment policy is to allocate additional string space for the new value of S2, as shown in Fig. 2-4.9.

The operation of concatenation results in the formation of a new string from two argument strings. Because the argument strings are not necessarily adjacent in memory and may not be stored in the order specified by the concatenation, storage is required to copy the argument strings into adjacent storage locations in order to perform the concatenation. In the case of a fixed-length or "varying"-length string storage structure, this storage may already exist if the concatenated string is being assigned to a variable. For variable-length string concatenations, additional storage must always be allocated—thereby adhering to the policy relating to variable-length string assignments involving string expressions. Given that S1 and S2 are as indicated in Fig. 2-4.9, Fig. 2-4.10 illustrates the effect of executing the statement S1 = S1 ○ 'HORSE'.

The **LENGTH** function is easily computed for fixed-length strings, since the length must be known in order to allocate storage for such strings. The lengths of a "varying"-length string and a variable-length string using the descriptor method are explicitly available through a field in the storage structure for each string type. The entire string must be scanned in order to calculate the length of a variable-length string bracketed with boundary markers.

The **SUB** function, when used to return a substring of a subject string, is implemented in a similar fashion for all string storage structures (i.e., once the sequence of

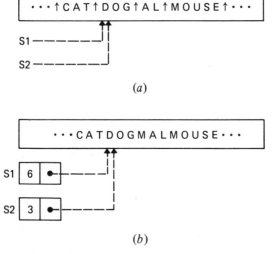

(a)

(b)

FIGURE 2-4.8   Side effects of altering the contents of the storage assigned to S2.

String space

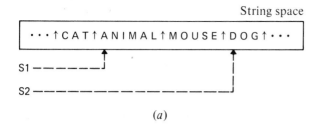

(a)

String space

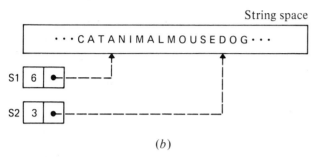

(b)

FIGURE 2-4.9 Effects of allocating additional string space for the variable-length string assignment S2 = 'DOG'.

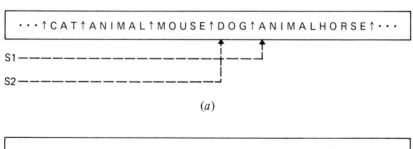

(a)

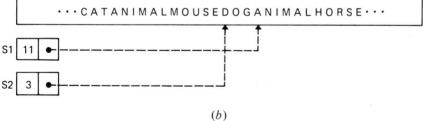

(b)

FIGURE 2-4.10 Effects of executing the variable-length string assignment S1 = S1 ○ 'HORSE'.

storage locations for a string is discovered, it is a simple matter to isolate the appropriate subsequence indicated by the arguments of the SUB function). A check must be made to determine if the index and length, i.e., the second and third arguments of the SUB function, are plausible for the given subject string. A similar check must be made on the arguments of SUB when it is used in a replacement mode such as in SUB(X, 1, 1) = '?'. If the index or length arguments specify a substring beyond the limited length of the fixed-length or "varying"-length string variable, an error occurs. For variable-length string variables, such a check is not necessary on the subject string, since such "SUB" assignments are valid.

As is the case with the SUB function, the INDEX function is implemented in a similar fashion for all string storage structures once the sequence of storage locations for a string is known. It is a simple yet time-consuming process to examine the subject string on a character-by-character left-to-right basis in an effort to match the pattern argument of the INDEX function.

Before concluding this section, it is important to point out that while variable-length strings are extremely flexible, they present some problems from a storage management point of view. For example, in Fig. 2-4.6, the assignment of 'MOUSE' to S1 leaves the string 'CAT' inaccessible, and "garbage" is created in the string area. More and more garbage results after a number of string assignments. Some method of collecting this garbage must be used in order to utilize the string area efficiently. In Sec. 5-6, we will examine some garbage-collection techniques that can be applied to string areas for variable-length strings. In the next section, we look at some of the applications to which character manipulation can be applied.

Exercises for Sec. 2-4

1. Give storage representations for the string S which has the value 'STRING' assuming S is a
    (a) fixed-length string
    (b) "varying"-length string with maximum length of 8
    (c) variable-length string
    Use an EBCDIC internal character representation for (a) and (b), and an ASCII internal character representation for (c). Recall that the EBCDIC and ASCII character codes are given in Chap. 1.

2. In this subsection, the following rule was established for variable-length character strings.
    "... a correct assignment policy is to allocate additional string space for each new value assigned to a character string variable, unless the assignment is variable-to-variable (such as S1 ← S2). In this case S1 can simply be assigned the reference or descriptor of S2"
    (a) Illustrate the effects of variable-to-variable assignments like
        Set S1 ← 'DATA', S2 ← S1.
        using the descriptor method of storing variable-length strings.
    (b) Consider the algorithm statement
        Set S1 ← SUB (S1, 1, 2).
        Can or cannot substring assignments, such as the one above, be handled without requesting new string space when using:

(i) the boundary marker method

(ii) the descriptor method

3. When using variable-length strings, a tremendous amount of "garbage" space accumulates as string variables are assigned new values. One suggestion for collecting this garbage and reusing it appropriately when using the descriptor method is to keep a vector of "old" descriptors which point to sections of available free space. If a request for new string space occurs, then a search is made first of the availability list of descriptors and, if possible, some of the garbage space is reclaimed for use. Elaborate on the feasibility of such a system—specifically, how do you decide what is garbage and how would you set up and manage such a "garbage collection agency"?

2-5 STRING MANIPULATION APPLICATIONS

This section contains four applications illustrating how the concepts and, specifically, the string-handling functions discussed in this chapter can be applied. In the first application, we introduce the text editor **ETEXTE** and describe the text-handling operations that **ETEXTE** provides. It is an excellent application because it involves a wide variety of character string-manipulation problems. The second and third applications deal with lexical analysis and **KWIC** index generation. Both of these applications are interesting and practical. The fourth application is concerned with an information-retrieval problem which is solved using bit strings. Since bit strings were not discussed in detail earlier in the chapter, this fourth application introduces them and their associated operations, as well as showing how such strings can be applied.

2-5.1 Text Editing

Text editing is one of the most common application areas in which string manipulation is used. Newspaper editing and typesetting, book and report editing, and computer program and data editing are all applications involving on-line text-editing facilities. Therefore, rather than storing text on paper and then manually revising it, the text in each of these applications can be stored in a character form on an external storage medium (such as a disk unit) of a computer. Text-editing programs are then used to add to, delete from, or change the text, and to output the text in a desired format.

The particular example of a text editor which we discuss in this section is called **ETEXTE** (*E*lementary *TEXT E*ditor). **ETEXTE** is capable of performing the basic operations required of a text editor and does so by using a list of commands. **ETEXTE** commands start in character position one of a line of input. They begin with the two character sequence $$ so as to clearly distinguish a command from text material (i.e., we assume that a line of text never begins with $$). Each command must appear with its arguments on a separate line of input. Let us examine the **ETEXTE** commands in detail.

$$ADD

The **$$ADD** command specifies that the text to follow is to be inserted, a line at a time, at the end of the body of text that is currently stored. If **ETEXTE** is used in a card input mode, then a card image is considered to be a line of input. To illustrate, suppose we wish to input text explaining how a line of text is stored in ETEXTE.

```
$$ADD
ASSUME THE INPUT TEXT IS ON PUNCHED CARDS. THE TEXT IS
STORED IN CHARACTER POSITIONS 11 THROUGH 91 OF AN
ELEMENT OF A SINGLE DIMENSIONED CHARACTER STRING ARRAY. ONE
ELEMENT OF THE ARRAY CORRESPONDS TO ONE LINE OF INPUT.
CHARACTER POSITIONS ONE TO FIVE OF AN ARRAY ELEMENT
CONTAIN A SEQUENCE NUMBER. FOR ANY BODY OF TEXT
SEQUENCE NUMBERS BEGIN WITH 00010 AND ARE INCREMENTED
BY 00010.
```

Upon recognizing an $$ADD command, ETEXTE reads the next line and invokes a routine for adding all text which follows, up to the next ETEXTE command or to the end of the ETEXTE session. An end of session is indicated by a sign-off command if working with ETEXTE on-line through a terminal, or is signaled by an end-of-file indicator in the case of off-line input such as card input. An algorithmic description demonstrating the effects of the $$ADD command is now formulated.

Algorithm $$ADD.   Given INPUT, the first line of text to be added at the end of the current text body, the input text up to the next ETEXTE command or end-of-session indicator is added to the text body. The index LCNT (meaning line count) is the position in the single-dimension character array LINE at which the current input is stored. The function F_COMMANDS checks for format commands before storing INPUT. F_COMMANDS is discussed later in this section after format codes have been introduced. For now, F_COM-MANDS can be thought of as a "dummy" function (i.e., it returns the parameter INPUT unchanged). L and C are intermediate variables and CONVERTCHAR is a function which converts a numeric argument to a character string, as discussed in Chap. 1.

1. [Repeat until $$ADD is no longer in effect]
    Repeat steps 2 to 5 while (not end of session).
2. [Set line count]   Set SUB(LINE[LCNT], 1, 5) ← '00000',
    C ← CONVERTCHAR(LCNT * 10), L ← LENGTH(C), SUB(LINE[LCNT],6 − L, L) ← C.
3. [Store card image]   Set SUB(LINE[LCNT], 11) ← F_COMMANDS(INPUT).
4. [Increment line counter]   Set LCNT ← LCNT + 1.
5. [Read a new card and check for a new command]   Read INPUT.
    If SUB(INPUT, 1, 2) = '$$', then Exit.
6. [End of session]   Exit.

Given a mode of inputting text to the editor, it is desirable to be able to display what has been stored previously. Such a display allows us to detect errors and aids in the process of correcting these errors. The ETEXTE command which provides this display facility is called $$LIST.

$$LIST/[beginning line number]/[ending line number]/

$$LIST has a parameter list as shown by the general format given. To illustrate three possible forms of the $$LIST command, consider the following examples:

$$LIST/00010/*/

results in a listing of all stored text. In the $$LIST command and all $$ commands to follow the * implies the line number of the last line of the text to be added. For example, if the stored text is the text that was input using the $$ADD command, then $$LIST would result in the following output:

```
00010     ASSUME THE INPUT TEXT IS ON PUNCHED CARDS. THE TEXT IS
00020     STORED IN CHARACTER POSITIONS 11 THROUGH 91 OF AN
00030     ELEMENT OF A SINGLE DIMENSIONED CHARACTER STRING ARRAY. ONE
00040     ELEMENT OF THE ARRAY CORRESPONDS TO ONE LINE OF INPUT.
00050     CHARACTER POSITIONS ONE TO FIVE OF AN ARRAY ELEMENT
00060     CONTAIN A SEQUENCE NUMBER. FOR ANY BODY OF TEXT
00070     SEQUENCE NUMBERS BEGIN WITH 00010 AND ARE INCREMENTED
00080     BY 00010.
```

The command
$$LIST/00020/00040/
results in the following listing.

```
00020     STORED IN CHARACTER POSITIONS 11 THROUGH 91 OF AN
00030     ELEMENT OF A SINGLE DIMENSIONED CHARACTER STRING ARRAY. ONE
00040     ELEMENT OF THE ARRAY CORRESPONDS TO ONE LINE OF INPUT.
```

Therefore, lines with line number between and including 00020 and 00040 are output.
$$LIST/00070/*/
initiates the output

```
00070     SEQUENCE NUMBERS BEGIN WITH 00010 AND ARE INCREMENTED
00080     BY 00010.
```

When the $$LIST command is recognized, a routine is called upon to list the text given the parameters BEGINLINE (meaning beginning line number) and ENDLINE (meaning end line number). If the parameter * appears for either BEGINLINE or ENDLINE, then a value of I CNT − 1 (i.e., the line number of the last text item to be entered) is assumed. This substitution policy for BEGINLINE and ENDLINE parameters is adopted for the remaining $$ commands. An algorithmic description of such a routine is given.

Algorithm $$LIST. Given a single-dimensioned character string array named LINE and parameters BEGINLINE and ENDLINE, the appropriate elements of LINE are output. The index j is used in the output of LINE array elements.

1. [Output specified text]
   Repeat for j = BEGINLINE to ENDLINE:
       if SUB(LINE[j], 11) ≠ ' '   (... if not the empty string),
       then print SUB(LINE[j], 1, 5) ○ 'bbbbb' ○ SUB(LINE[j], 11).
2. [Finished] Exit.

In step 1, the sequence number, 5 blank separator characters, and the text for the line are printed for all lines between and including BEGINLINE and ENDLINE. LINE[j] is not printed verbatim because the character positions 6 through 10 may contain nonblank character information, the nature of which will be described later in this section.

On many occasions it is necessary to change a line of input because of typographical errors, misspellings, or a desire to alter the contents of a line. The CHANGE command, which we now describe, provides this ability.

$$CHANGE/[beginning line number]/[ending line number]/
<text to be replaced>/<replacement text>/

Assume that in line 30 of the example text given previously, we want to change the phrase 'SINGLE DIMENSIONED CHARACTER STRING ARRAY' to the shorter phrase 'CHARACTER STRING VECTOR'. The commands to achieve this are

$$CHANGE/30/30/SINGLE DIMENSIONED//
$$CHANGE/30/30/ARRAY/VECTOR/

In the following algorithmic description for processing the $$CHANGE command, the variables BEGINLINE, ENDLINE, PATTERN, and REPLACEMENT correspond to the values of the four command parameters.

Algorithm $$CHANGE. Given the four parameters BEGINLINE, ENDLINE, PATTERN, and REPLACEMENT, the lines designated by the BEGINLINE to ENDLINE line sequence of the character string array LINE are changed by replacing the text PATTERN by the text REPLACEMENT. The variable j is an index for the array LINE, IND is used as a temporary variable, and CHANGEFLAG indicates if at least one instance of a change takes place.

1. [Establish repeat loop] Set CHANGEFLAG ← false.
   Repeat steps 2 and 3 for j = BEGINLINE to ENDLINE.
2. [Locate text to be changed] Set IND ← INDEX(LINE[j], PATTERN).
3. [Perform substitution if possible]
   If IND ≠ 0,
   then set SUB(LINE[j], IND, LENGTH(PATTERN)) ← REPLACEMENT and
   CHANGEFLAG ← true.
4. [Finished] If ⌐ CHANGEFLAG, then print 'TEXT TO BE CHANGED NOT LOCATED'.
   Exit.

It is obvious from the algorithm description that the $$CHANGE command involves a very simple pattern-matching process. Nevertheless, the applicability of pattern matching to an important application area is illustrated well. Note that $$CHANGE does not match strings across LINE elements. This very important feature must be in a good text editor. We leave, as an exercise at the end of this subsection, the design of a $$CHANGE algorithm which incorporates this facility.

ETEXTE also provides a command for deleting lines of text. The general form of this command is as follows:

$$DELETE/[beginning line number]/[ending line number]/

$$DELETE allows us to delete a single line or all the lines starting from a specified beginning line number. For example, to remove the last line of sample text, we use the command

$$DELETE/00080/00080/

If following this command, a $$LIST command is used to list the stored text, then statement 00080 would be excluded from the printout. The commands

$$CHANGE/00060/00060/ FOR ANY BODY OF TEXT//
$$DELETE/00070/*/

remove the last sentence of the sample text. The second command illustrates how a sequence of statements can be deleted. The command

$$DELETE/00010/00080/

or

$$DELETE/00010/*/

deletes the entire sample text.

An algorithmic description for the line deletion command is now given. In the algorithm, BEGINLINE represents the beginning line number in the deletion sequence and ENDLINE contains the final line number in the sequence.

Algorithm $$DELETE. Given the two parameters BEGINLINE and ENDLINE, the set of lines between and including BEGINLINE and ENDLINE are deleted.

1. [Delete multiple lines]
    Repeat for i = BEGINLINE, . . ., ENDLINE: set LINE[i] ← ' '.
2. [Finished]   Exit.

As is true for the other algorithms given thus far, Algorithm $$DELETE is very simple, and little explanation is required. Note that a line is deleted by setting it to the empty string. Lines which are equal to the empty string are not listed when the $$LIST command is invoked.

The final ETEXTE command we wish to introduce provides us with the capability to output the stored text in a highly stylized format. Such format features as tab setting, titling, right justifying, and line-and-page skipping are available. The ETEXTE command which supplies all of these facilities is called $$PRINT.

$$PRINT/[beginning line number]/[ending line number]/

The $$PRINT command makes substantial use of the basic pattern-matching functions described in Sec. 2-3.2. In the processing of the $$PRINT command, each line of a requested portion of the text is searched for a *format code*. Format codes are inserted in the text to specify when indenting, page titling, and many of the other format features are to be invoked.

There are four groups of format codes: tabbing, titling, skipping, and right-justifying codes. Each code must begin in the eleventh character position of a line and is composed of two special characters followed by an optional parameter list. Format codes are introduced in the text by format commands. Let us examine each of these commands in detail.

Tab command – @@TAB <tab settings>[@|⌐]

An indentation command begins with the characters @@, which are followed by the word **TAB** and a list of tab settings. The symbol @ at the end of the tab setting list is present if the tab setting is to apply not only for the given line, but for all lines up to the next tab code. The symbol ⌐ is used if the tab settings are to apply only to the remainder of the line immediately following the tab command. The tab command, and all format commands to be discussed, are not stored in the form of their input. To economize in terms of memory, the key word (in this case **TAB**/) is removed and the rest of the command is stored. Therefore, @@TAB/6/61/@ is stored as @@6/61/@, starting at character position 11 of the stored line.

Text items which are printed at the tab locations are separated by the character string '/'. For example, assume a text-editing session contains the following input and that no previous text has been stored by the editor:

```
$$ADD
@@TAB/15/30/45/@MILES/MILES//GALLON/COST/
200/19.5/$5.25/250/21.0/$6.85/
195/16.4/$5.20/
$$LIST/00010/*/
$$PRINT/00010/*/
```

The $$LIST command results in the following output:

```
00010       @@15/30/45/@MILES/MILES//GALLON/COST/
00020       200/19.5/$5.25/250/21.0/$6.85/
00030       195/16.4/$5.20/
```

The $$PRINT command yields a formatted output:

MILES	MILES/GALLON	COST
200	19.5	$5.25
250	21.0	$6.85
195	16.4	$5.20

Observe that if the command $$PRINT/00020/00030/ is used instead of $$PRINT, then the output is

200	19.5	$5.25
250	21.0	$6.85
195	16.4	$5.20

Therefore, tabs are still in effect although the tab codes are not in the specified output lines. To create a table with columns that are centered under the headings and are more appropriately spaced, the following set of commands can be used.

```
$$ADD
@@TAB/15/26/43/⌉MILES//MILES//GALLON/COST/
@@TAB/16/30/43/@200/19.95/$5.25/250/
21.0/$6.85/195/16.4/$5.20/
$$PRINT/00010/*/
```

The **$$PRINT** command results in the output:

MILES	MILES/GALLON	COST
200	19.5	$5.25
250	21.0	$6.85
195	16.4	$5.20

If we use **$$PRINT/00020/00020/** in place of **$$PRINT**, then the following is printed:

200	19.5	$5.25
250		

Therefore, tab settings apply to incompletely specified lists of tabbed data items as is the case with item 250.

Indentation is easily accommodated by using a tab code. For example,

```
$$DELETE/00010/*/
$$ADD
@@TAB/5/⌉THIS IS THE BEGINNING OF A PARAGRAPH AND IT WILL BE USED FOR
ILLUSTRATIVE PURPOSES ONLY.
$$PRINT/00010/*/
```

yields the output

THIS IS THE BEGINNING OF A PARAGRAPH AND IT WILL BE USED FOR ILLUSTRATIVE PURPOSES ONLY.

Titling commands – %%TITLE/[C or L][U or N]/

In **ETEXTE** titles can be centered, as indicated by C, or placed at the left margin, as indicated by L. Titles can be underlined, as designated by U, or not underlined, as indicated by N. Assume that we have a 72-character line and no text has been entered in the system as yet. Then the input

```
$$ADD
%%TITLE/CU/ INTRODUCTION TO DATA STRUCTURES WITH APPLICATIONS
%%TITLE/CN/ BY
```

```
%%TITLE/CN/ J.P. TREMBLAY
%%TITLE/CN/ P.G. SORENSON
%%TITLE/LU/ Published by:
%%TITLE/LN/ McGraw-Hill
$$PRINT/00010/*/
```

results in the output

INTRODUCTION TO DATA STRUCTURES WITH APPLICATIONS
BY
J.P. TREMBLAY
P.G. SORENSON

Published by:

McGraw-Hill

Observe that title codes apply to one line and do not remain in effect until the next title code.

Skip commands – ##SKIP/<number of lines>|P/

Skip codes provide both line and page skipping. The general form of a skip code is ##/<number of lines>|P/ where the parameter following the characters ## is a number (meaning number of lines) or the letter P (meaning page). For example, the input commands

```
$$DELETE/0010/*/
$$ADD
##SKIP/P/
%%TITLE/CN/CHAPTER 2
##SKIP/1/
%%TITLE/CN/THE REPRESENTATION AND MANIPULATION OF STRINGS
##SKIP/1/
@@TAB/5/⌐IN THE PREVIOUS CHAPTER WE INTRODUCED THE LITERAL CHARACTER
$$PRINT/00010/*/
```

generate the output displayed in Fig. 2-5.1.

CHAPTER 2

STRING MANIPULATION

IN THE PREVIOUS CHAPTER WE INTRODUCED THE LITERAL CHARACTER

FIGURE 2-5.1   Illustration of the effects of skip codes.

Justification commands – **&&JUSTIFY/[ ]** <right tab >/

By the right justification of text we mean that the printed form of the text is such that the right margin is aligned for all lines in the output. For example, the text on this page is aligned on the right side, and hence is right justified. In text that is typeset, such as this book is, right justification is achieved by first attempting to split words across lines, then by leaving a certain amount of space between words, and finally, if necessary, by expanding the space between letters.

The typesetting of books, magazines, and newspapers has become very automated in the past five to ten years. Computers aid in the editing and formatting of text through facilities similar to those provided by **ETEXTE**. Right justification presents the major problem in the typesetting process. Word splitting can be handled in most instances by storing the syllables of many of the common words plus a number of simple rules governing syllable separations. To split an "uncommon" word may require operator intervention. Once an uncommon word is split by an operator, the system can store the word and its split location. This may enable the system to split the word the next time it overlaps the end of a line which is to be printed.

For text which is printed on a line printer or teletype, spacing between words must be handled in a more primitive fashion. Altering the spacing between letters is impossible, at present, because both printers and teletypes are fixed-print devices (i.e., the amount of space between given adjacent characters cannot be altered). Spacing between words can be handled by allowing more than one blank character between words. An algorithm for right justification is presented based on a procedure which adjusts between-word separations.

Algorithm JUSTIFICATION. Given a character string **PRINTLINE** which contains text beginning and ending in nonblank characters and is of length greater than the right tab position **RMARGIN**, **PRINTLINE** is right justified and any excess text is returned from the algorithm invocation. **BLANKS** is a variable which holds the number of blanks to be inserted and **BFIELD** is a character string of blank characters equal in size to the size of the field of blanks which separates words. Initially, the size of this field is one.

1. [Check to see if text is immediately right justifiable]
   If SUB(PRINTLINE, RMARGIN, 1) ≠ 'b'
   and SUB(PRINTLINE, RMARGIN +1, 1) = 'b',
   then print SUB(PRINTLINE, 1, RMARGIN),
   set JUSTIFICATION ← SUB(PRINTLINE, RMARGIN +1), and Exit.
2. [Check to see if position RMARGIN is a nonblank character]
   Set j ← RMARGIN − 1,
   if SUB(PRINTLINE, RMARGIN, 1) ≠ 'b'
   then
       repeat while SUB(PRINTLINE, j, 1) ≠ 'b': set j ← j − 1.
3. [Look for next nonblank character]   Set j ← j − 1.
   Repeat while SUB(PRINTLINE, j, 1) = 'b': set j ← j − 1.
4. [Establish loop for adding blanks]
   Set BLANKS ← RMARGIN − j, BFIELD ← 'b'.
   Repeat step 5 for k = 1, 2, . . ., BLANKS:

5. [Successively add blanks to the blank field separating the words]
    Repeat while ⌐ MATCH(PRINTLINE, BFIELD, j, '', BFIELD ○ 'b', true):
        set j ← j − 1,
        if j = 0,
        then set j ← RMARGIN − BLANKS + k − 1, BFIELD ← BFIELD ○ 'b'.
    Set j ← j − LENGTH(BFIELD) − 2.   (Reposition counter j)
6. [Output justified text]   Print SUB(PRINTLINE, 1, RMARGIN).
    Set JUSTIFICATION ← SUB(PRINTLINE, RMARGIN + 1) and Exit.

Step 1 of Algorithm JUSTIFICATION handles text which does not need the insertion of blanks to achieve right justification. As a simple example, assume PRINTLINE has the value

'THE BOOK IS AUTHORED BY W. M. FINDLING. HE DISCUSSES DATA
MANAGEMENT...'

and RMARGIN is 20. Then SUB(PRINTLINE, 20, 1) is 'D' and SUB(PRINTLINE, 21, 1) is 'b'. Therefore, by step 1, the string

'THE BOOK IS AUTHORED'

can be printed and the remainder of the string is returned from Algorithm JUSTIFICATION.

If the leading blank is removed from the returned string and this new string is assigned to PRINTLINE and is considered for justification, then SUB(PRINTLINE, 20, 1) is 'b' and, by step 1, immediate justification is not possible. In step 2, j is set to 19 and the nineteenth position of PRINTLINE contains 'b'. Therefore, the repeat loop in step 2 is avoided and we proceed to find the right-most nonblank character. Such a character is found at position 18, as denoted by the value of j. In step 4, BLANKS is set to 20 − 18 or 2, and BFIELD is initialized to 'b'. Step 5 is repeated for k with values 1 and 2. In step 5, the basic pattern-matching function MATCH (as described in Sec. 2-3.2), is invoked. Subfields of PRINTLINE are examined while scanning right to left in an effort to match the current value of BFIELD. For our example, a match succeeds when j is 9, at which point a blank is inserted as indicated by a b. Therefore, PRINTLINE now has the value

'BY W. M. bFINDLING. HE DISCUSSES DATA MANAGEMENT...'

The value of j is tested to see if it is zero, which it is not. Then j is set to 11 − 1 − 2 = 8 and step 5 is repeated for a final time with k = 2. Again a search is initiated for the next right-most blank from the current position represented by j. A blank is found at character position 6 and another blank is inserted making PRINTLINE equal to

'BY W. bM. bFINDLING. HE DISCUSSES DATA MANAGEMENT...'

In step 6, the twenty-character line

'BY W. bM. bFINDLING.'

is printed and the string ' HE DISCUSSES DATA MANAGEMENT...' is returned.

As before, we can remove the preceding blanks of the returned string and assign this new string to PRINTLINE for further right justification. In this case, PRINTLINE is

'HE DISCUSSES DATA MANAGEMENT...'

Upon examining the twentieth character in both steps 1 and 2, we discover that it is the first 'A' in 'MANAGEMENT'. To right justify this text, we look for the first nonblank character to the left of the first field of blanks immediately preceding 'MANAGEMENT'. The second 'A' in data is the character we are searching for, and it is found at character position 17 in PRINTLINE. Steps 2 and 3 of the algorithm accomplish this search. Therefore, it is the string

'HE DISCUSSES DATA'

which must be expanded to 20 characters.

In step 4, j has the value 17, implying that the number of blanks which must be inserted is 3 (i.e., BLANKS = 3). Step 5 is repeated three times. The first two times blanks are inserted between 'DISCUSSES' and 'DATA', and 'HE' and 'DISCUSSES'. The third time through step 5, j is eventually decremented to zero, at which point it is reset to 19 and BFIELD is set to 'bb'. A right-to-left rescan of the text is made while looking for the first occurrence of a field with two blank characters. Such a field is found between the words 'DISCUSSES' and 'DATA'. The two blanks are replaced by a field of three blanks, and the JUSTIFICATION algorithm terminates by printing

'HE bDISCUSSES bbDATA'

and returning a value of ' MANAGEMENT...'.

The justification codes have not as yet been described. The general form is && <number> ⌐ <number> where <number> refers to the RMARGIN setting and ⌐ indicates that the text to follow is not to be right justified. Therefore the command,

&&JUSTIFY/80/

indicates that all text up to the next && code with the exception of text containing title codes is to be right justified at eighty characters per line of print. Text subject to title codes should not be right justified for obvious reasons. The command

&&JUSTIFY/⌐80/

turns off the right-justification process, but leaves the RMARGIN at eighty. This means that if column eighty of PRINTLINE is blank, then the first eighty characters are printed. If column eighty is nonblank, then a search is made for the first blank character to the left of column eighty. All characters to the left of this blank character are then printed. We leave, as an exercise at the end of this subsection, the design of the Algorithm NO_JUSTI-FICATION, which accepts as parameters PRINTLINE and RMARGIN and outputs a line which is not right justified.

An exception arises in the right justification of text if the line of text following a line which is being considered for right justification is a blank line or a line with a skip code, tab code, or a justification code which turns off right justification. In these situations, it is unreasonable to right justify text, since such situations arise when a paragraph of text is terminating. For example, if RMARGIN is set to 60 and PRINTLINE is the text 'END OF PARAGRAPH', then the right justification of this text leads to the following output.

'END bbbbbbbbbbbbbbbbbbbbbbbOF bbbbbbbbbbbbbbbbbbbbbbbPARAGRAPH.'

Such output is not aesthetically appealing! In addition, if an attempt is made to right justify a line in which there is only one character left at the end of a paragraph, it is impossible to insert blanks and the Algorithm JUSTIFICATION would never terminate. Of course, such a situation should be checked for when processing a $$PRINT command and the right-justification routine should not be invoked.

We are now prepared to describe an algorithm for handling the $$PRINT command. Algorithm $$PRINT is invoked when a $$PRINT command is recognized as input to ETEXTE.

Algorithm $$PRINT. Given the stored text in the character array LINE and the line number parameters BEGINLINE and ENDLINE, the text between and including LINE [BEGINLINE] and LINE[ENDLINE] is printed as dictated by the format codes included in the text. TAB_FOUND and JUST_FOUND are logical variables used to indicate when the tab and justification controls are found in a search starting from BEGINLINE and moving backwards until the first line of input. TABFLAG indicates if the current tab control is global, local (i.e., affecting only the next line), or not in effect. Respectively, TABFLAG can have values of 'G', 'L', or 'N'. NO_OF_TABS has as a value the number of tab settings currently in effect, and the tab settings are stored in the array TAB. RJUSTIFY is a logical variable which, when true, indicates the text to follow is to be right justified and, when false, indicates the text to follow is not to be right justified. RMARGIN contains the current right margin setting. Other functions and variables are described after the algorithmic description.

1. [Initialization of search for previous tab and justification codes]
   Set TAB_FOUND ← JUST_FOUND ← false, CURSOR ← 13.
   Repeat steps 2 to 4 for i = BEGINLINE, ..., 2, 1:
2. [Check to see if tab and justification codes have been located]
   If TAB_FOUND and JUST_FOUND, then go to step 5.
3. [Check if LINE[i] contains a tab code]
   If ⌐TAB_FOUND and SUB(LINE[i],11,2) = '@@',
   then set TAB_FOUND ← true,
       DUMMY ← SPAN(LINE[i],'0123456789/',CURSOR,TABLIST,'',false),
       if SUB(LINE[i],CURSOR,1) = '@',   (... global tab setting?)
       then set TABFLAG ← 'G' and call SET_TABS(TABLIST);
       otherwise, set TABFLAG ← 'N'.
4. [Examine LINE[i] for a justification code]
   If ⌐JUST_FOUND and SUB(LINE[i],11,2) = '&&',
   then

       if SUB(LINE[i],13,1) = '⌐',

       then set RJUSTIFY ← false and c ← 14;

       otherwise, set RJUSTIFY ← true and c ← 13.

       RMARGIN ← SUB(LINE[i],c,INDEX(SUB(LINE[i],c),'/') − 1).

       Set i ← BEGINLINE − 1 and PRINTLINE ← "

5. [Initialize print phase]

6. [Begin print phase] Set i ← i + 1. If i > ENDLINE, then print PRINTLINE, and Exit.

7. [Check for skip codes]
   If SUB(LINE[i],11,2) = '##'
   then print PRINTLINE,
       if SUB(LINE[i],13,1) = 'P',
       then skip to a new page;
       otherwise, skip SUB(LINE[i],13,INDEX(SUB(LINE[i],13),'/') − 1) lines.
       Set PRINTLINE ← SUB(LINE[i],14+INDEX(SUB(LINE[i],14),'/')).

8. [Check for title codes]
   If SUB(LINE[i],11,2) = '%%',
   then print PRINTLINE,   (... no output if PRINTLINE is empty)
       if SUB(LINE[i],13,1) = 'C',
       then call CENTER(LINE[i],RMARGIN);
       otherwise,
           print SUB(LINE[i],16), and set PRINTLINE ← "
           if SUB(LINE[i],14,1) = 'U'
           then print underscores.

9. [Check for indentation code]
   If SUB(LINE[i],11,2) = '@@',
   then print PRINTLINE, set CURSOR ← 13,
       set DUMMY ← SPAN(LINE[i],'0123456789/',CURSOR,TABLIST,",false),
       Call SET_TABS(TABLIST),
       if SUB(LINE[i],CURSOR,1) = '@',
       then set TABFLAG ← 'G';
       otherwise set TABFLAG ← 'L'.
       Set PRINTLINE ← SUB(LINE[i],CURSOR + 2),
       if PRINTLINE = ", then go to step 6.

10. [Check for justification code]
    If SUB(LINE[i],11,2) = '&&',
    then
        if SUB(LINE[i],13,1) = '⌐',
        then set RJUSTIFY ← false and
        RMARGIN ← SUB(LINE[i],14,INDEX(SUB(LINE[i],14),'/') − 1);
        otherwise, set RJUSTIFY ← true and
        RMARGIN ← SUB(LINE[i],13,INDEX(SUB(LINE[i],13),'/') − 1).

11. [Handle indentations if applicable]
    If TABFLAG = 'L' or TABFLAG = 'G',
    then

> if NO_OF_TABS > 1,
> then call TABPRINT(PRINTLINE) and go to step 6;
> otherwise, set PRINTLINE ← DUPL('b',TAB[1]) ○ PRINTLINE.

12. [Set up loop for line printing]
> Repeat steps 13 and 14 while LENGTH(PRINTLINE) ≥ RMARGIN:

13. [Handle right justification]
> If RJUSTIFY,
> then set PRINTLINE ← JUSTIFICATION(PRINTLINE,RMARGIN);
> otherwise, set PRINTLINE ← NO_JUSTIFICATION(PRINTLINE,RMARGIN).

14. [Left justify the text in PRINTLINE and establish indentation]
> Set DUMMY ← SPAN(PRINTLINE,'b',1,'','',true).
> (Dummy assignment is made to invoke spanning of initial blanks.)
> If TABFLAG = 'G' then set PRINTLINE ← DUPL('b',TAB[1]) ○ PRINTLINE.

15. [Update TABFLAG]   If TABFLAG = 'L' then set TABFLAG ← 'N'.
> Go to step 6.

It is obvious that Algorithm $$PRINT is long and involved, and consequently it is worthwhile to examine it in some detail. Steps 1 to 4 discover any previous global tab settings and the right-justification controls that apply to the lines between BEGINLINE and ENDLINE. Step 1 initializes variables used in this search and establishes the "decreasing" repeat loop needed for the search. When both the tab and justification codes are found, an exit is made from this first section via step 2. In step 3, a check is made for the tab control characters '@@', if the tab code has not already been located. The argument list associated with the tab code is isolated and assigned to TABLIST by using the basic pattern-matching function SPAN. Note that we are using SPAN in a dummy assignment mode to get the desired pattern-matching effect without using the value returned by SPAN in a logical expression. The Algorithm SET_TABS is invoked to establish the tab settings as given by the tab code, if the tab code is global. (The specification for SET_TABS is left as an assignment at the end of the subsection.) Step 4 checks to see if there is a justification code, and if so, sets RJUSTIFY appropriately.

In step 6, the print phase begins. A key point to realize is that when execution begins at step 7, PRINTLINE is always left justified and less than RMARGIN in length. Step 7 checks for skip codes in LINE[i], and if such a code exists, prints PRINTLINE and handles the correct number of line skips or page skip. Step 8 recognizes title codes. The Algorithm CENTER, which is invoked if the 'C' code is specified, is left as an exercise at the end of this subsection.

Indentation codes are handled in step 9. Again SPAN and SET_TABS are invoked to establish tab settings. TABFLAG is set to 'G' or 'L', depending if the tab settings are to be global or local. Step 10 sets the RJUSTIFY indicator and assigns the new RMARGIN value that is specified.

In step 11, if TABFLAG is 'L' and NO_OF_TABS is less than 2, then blanks are added to the front of PRINTLINE; otherwise, Algorithm TABPRINT is invoked. TABPRINT is responsible for handling printed text with multiple tab settings. A description of TABPRINT follows the discussion of this algorithm.

Steps 12 through 14 involve a loop which results in the continued output of text until **PRINTLINE** is less than the **RMARGIN** setting. The function **DUPL** is borrowed from the SNOBOL language and is used in steps 11 and 14 to create an indentation.

In step 15, **TABFLAG** is set to "not applicable" if the previous tab settings only applied locally.

In Algorithm **TABPRINT**, which is now described, the tab settings, as stored in the vector **TAB**, are applied to the text contained in **PRINTLINE**. Textual items which begin at new tab settings are terminated by the symbol '/'. Note that right justification is ignored when **TABPRINT** is invoked, since it is assumed that text containing multiple tabs should not be right justified.

Algorithm TABPRINT.   Given the parameter **PRINTLINE** and the tab settings as found in the vector **TAB**, the text in **PRINTLINE** is printed in a tabulated form up to and including the last item preceding the separator symbol '/'. **LINEOUT** is a character string which contains the line to be printed in tab form, **NO_OF_TABS** is the current number of tab settings, and i is a loop counter.

1. [Initialization] Set i ← 1, LINEOUT ← '', and CURSOR ← 1.
2. [Loop searching for separator symbol '/']
   Repeat steps 3 to 5,
   while FIND(PRINTLINE,'/',CURSOR,MATCH_STR,'',false):
3. [Check for / in text which is represented as //]
   If SUBSTR(PRINTLINE,CURSOR,1) = '/',
   then set TEMP_STR ← TEMP_STR ○ MATCH_STR ○ '/', CURSOR ← CURSOR + 2,
   and go to step 2;
   otherwise, TEMP_STR ← TEMP_STR ○ MATCH_STR.
4. [Place the TEMP_STR value at the correct tab location in LINEOUT]
   Set SUB(LINEOUT,TAB[i],LENGTH(TEMP_STR)) ← TEMP_STR, and TEMP_STR ← ''.
5. [Update i and check if less than number of tabs]
   Set i ← i + 1.
   If i > NO_OF_TABS,
   then set PRINTLINE ← SUB(PRINTLINE,CURSOR), print LINEOUT, i ← 1 and
   LINEOUT ← ''.
6. [Output tab set line]
   Print LINEOUT and Exit.

The final aspect of **ETEXTE** which we discuss is the command interpreter. The command interpreter receives either card-oriented or teletype input and examines each input for a command. The interpretation of commands involves the insertion of format codes and the invoking of modules to perform the actions specified by the commands. Algorithm **C_INTERPRET** illustrates the functioning of the **ETEXTE** command interpreter.

Algorithm C_INTERPRET.   Given an input string **INPUT**, this string is examined for **ETEXTE** commands. All **ETEXTE** commands are then interpreted by invoking many of the modules discussed earlier in this subsection. **LCNT** is the index in **LINE** associated with the next available line of text and **LMTFIND** is an algorithm which computes **BEGINLINE** and **ENDLINE** for the '$$' commands.

1. [Process input until end of ETEXTE session]
   Repeat steps 2 to 9 while not end of session.
2. [Get next input line and echo]
   Read INPUT and print INPUT.
3. [$$ commands?] If SUBSTR(INPUT,1,2) $\neq$ '$$',
   then print 'ILLEGAL INPUT' and go to step 1.
4. [Process $$ commands beginning with $$ADD]
   If SUBSTR(INPUT,1,5) = '$$ADD', then call $$ADD and go to step 1.
5. [$$LIST?] Set CURSOR $\leftarrow$ 8.
   If SUB(INPUT,1,6) = '$$LIST',
   then call LMTFIND(INPUT,CURSOR) (LMTFIND establishes the values
   for BEGINLINE and ENDLINE), call $$LIST(BEGINLINE,ENDLINE),
   and go to step 1.
6. [$$CHANGE?] Set CURSOR $\leftarrow$ 10.
   If SUB(INPUT,1,8) = '$$CHANGE',
   then call LMTFIND(INPUT,CURSOR),
   call $$CHANGE(BEGINLINE,ENDLINE), and go to step 1.
7. [$$DELETE?] Set CURSOR $\leftarrow$ 10.
   If SUB(INPUT,1,8) = '$$DELETE',
   then call LMTFIND(INPUT,CURSOR),
   call $$DELETE(BEGINLINE,ENDLINE), and go to step 1.
8. [$$PRINT?] Set CURSOR $\leftarrow$ 9.
   If SUB(INPUT,1,7) = '$$PRINT',
   then call LMTFIND(INPUT,CURSOR),
   call $$PRINT(BEGINLINE,ENDLINE), and go to step 1.
9. [Error in INPUT] Print 'ILLEGAL COMMAND', and go to step 1.

The Algorithm C_INTERPRET is composed of one large repeat loop which interprets
$$ commands. The identification of a $$ command is by a simple string comparison for
equality. The function LMTFIND is invoked to store the line count limits in BEGINLINE
and ENDLINE. The algorithms as presented earlier in this subsection are invoked according
to the specified command.

Algorithm LMTFIND, which calculates the BEGINLINE and ENDLINE line number
limits, is formulated as follows.

Algorithm LMTFIND. Given the text string INPUT and the cursor position indicating
the start of the line number argument list for a particular $$ command, the values for
BEGINLINE and ENDLINE are calculated.

1. [Isolate parameter fields for BEGINLINE and ENDLINE]
   If FIND(INPUT,'/',CURSOR,BEGINLINE,'',false),
   then
        if ⌐FIND(INPUT,'1',CURSOR,ENDLINE,'',false),
        then print 'error — endline, parameter missing', and Exit.
   Otherwise print 'error — missing parameters', and Exit.

2. [Check for * and set to last line]
  If BEGINLINE = '*' then set BEGINLINE ← LCNT — 1 and Exit.
  If ENDLINE = '*' then set ENDLINE ← LCNT — 1 and Exit.
  Set BEGINLING ← BEGINLINE/10, ENDLINE ← ENDLINE/10, and Exit.

Figure 2-5.2 is given to help clarify the logical connection between the algorithms presented or left as exercises in this subsection.

The only algorithm left for the ETEXTE system which is not either given already or left as an exercise is F_COMMANDS, which is called from Algorithm $$ADD. We did not describe F_COMMANDS when discussing $$ADD because format codes had not been introduced. Since we are now well versed in format codes, let us consider the description of Algorithm F_COMMANDS.

Algorithm F_COMMANDS. The given string INPUT is scanned for format commands. Once found, the format commands are interpreted and the appropriate format codes are stored.

1. [Check for format commands and replace keywords]
  If MATCH(INPUT,'@@TAB/',1,'','@@',true) then go to step 2.
  If MATCH (INPUT,'%%TITLE/',1,'','%%',true) then go to step 2.
  If MATCH(INPUT,'##SKIP/',1,'','##',true) then go to step 2.
  Set DUMMY ← MATCH(INPUT,'&&JUSTIFY/',1,'','&&',true).
2. [Set return value and exit]   Set F_COMMANDS ← INPUT and Exit.

In the algorithm, format commands are identified using the basic pattern-matching function MATCH, as discussed in Sec. 2-3.2. The keywords TAB, TITLE, SKIP, and JUSTIFY are removed from the codes which are stored in the LINE array.

Let us consider an example which incorporates most of the ETEXTE features that have been presented. A business-machine manufacturing corporation, which sells equipment throughout Canada and the United States, controls sales from its head office, but has salesmen working out of offices in each province and state. The company sends letters annually to prospective buyers informing them that the local sales representative will call on them in the near future. The letters are mass produced, but an effort is made to personalize them by utilizing a computer. The letter is entered into the ETEXTE system in the following general form.

```
$$ADD
&&JUSTIFY/⌐70/
@@TAB/40/@187 MAIN STREET
WINNIPEG 1, MANITOBA
*DATE*
##SKIP/1/
@@TAB/0/@
*X*
*ADDRESS*
*CITY*, *PROVINCE*
```

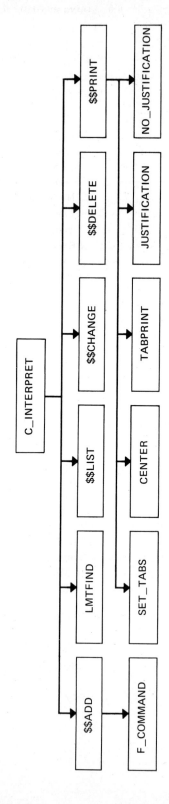

FIGURE 2-5.2 An illustration of the logical connections between modules of which the **ETEXTE** system is comprised.

134

```
##SKIP/1/
DEAR *Z*,
##SKIP/1/
&&JUSTIFY/70/
@@TAB/5/⌐
```

THE BUSINESS WORLD IS RAPIDLY CHANGING AND OUR CORPORATION HAS
BEEN KEEPING PACE WITH THE NEW REQUIREMENTS FORCED UPON OFFICE
MACHINERY. WE ARE GIVING YOU, *Z*, AS A KEY FIGURE IN THE *CITY*
BUSINESS COMMUNITY, AN OPPORTUNITY TO BECOME FAMILIAR WITH THE
LATEST ADVANCEMENTS IN OUR EQUIPMENT. A REPRESENTATIVE OF OUR
CORPORATION IN *PROVINCE* WILL BE SEEING YOU WITHIN *N* WEEKS. HE
WILL TAKE SEVERAL MACHINES TO *CITY* WHICH ARE INDICATIVE OF A
WHOLE NEW LINE OF OFFICE MACHINES WE HAVE RECENTLY DEVELOPED.
@@TAB/5/⌐ OUR SALES REPRESENTATIVE IS LOOKING FORWARD TO HIS
VISIT IN *CITY*. HE KNOWS THAT THE MACHINES HE SELLS COULD BECOME
AN INTEGRAL PART OF YOUR OFFICE ONLY A FEW DAYS AFTER INSTALLATION.

```
##SKIP/1/
&&JUSTIFY/ 70/
@@TAB/40/@
SINCERELY,
##SKIP/1/
ROGER SMITH, MANAGER
OFFICE DEVICES INCORPORATED
##SKIP/P/
```

The general letter is introduced into memory and a copy of the letter is stored in an
auxiliary file for later processing. Next the fields of text which are delineated by *'s are
changed, based on the following specific information:

1   Date (e.g., August 17, 1975)
2   MR. (or MRS., etc.), initial, surname (e.g., Mr. A.L. Strider)
3   Street address (e.g., 2014 Centennial Drive)
4   City, Province(or State) (e.g., Thompson, Manitoba)
5 N, the number of weeks before salesman will visit (e.g., three)

An **ETEXTE** session for creating a personal letter proceeds as follows:

```
$$CHANGE/00010/*/*DATE*/AUGUST 17, 1975/
$$CHANGE/00010/*/*ADDRESS*/2014 CENTENNIAL DRIVE/
$$CHANGE/00010/*/*CITY*/THOMPSON/
$$CHANGE/00010/*/*PROVINCE*/MANITOBA/
$$CHANGE/00010/*/*N*/THREE/
$$CHANGE/00010/*/*X*/MR. A.L. STRIDER/
$$CHANGE/00010/*/*Z*/MR. STRIDER/
$$PRINT/00010/*/
```

The formatted output is then printed:

```
                                   187 MAIN STREET
                                   WINNIPEG 1, MANITOBA
                                   AUGUST 17, 1975



MR. A.L. STRIDER
2014 CENTENNIAL DRIVE
THOMPSON, MANITOBA



DEAR MR. STRIDER,



    THE BUSINESS WORLD IS RAPIDLY CHANGING AND  OUR  CORPORATION  HAS
BEEN KEEPING  PACE  WITH  THE  NEW  REQUIREMENTS  FORCED  UPON  OFFICE
MACHINERY.  WE ARE GIVING YOU, MR. STRIDER, AS A  KEY  FIGURE  IN  THE
THOMPSON BUSINESS COMMUNITY, AN OPPORTUNITY TO  BECOME  FAMILIAR  WITH
THE LATEST ADVANCEMENTS IN OUR EQUIPMENT.  A  REPRESENTATIVE  OF  OUR
CORPORATION IN MANITOBA WILL BE SEEING YOU  WITHIN  THREE  WEEKS.   HE
WILL TAKE SEVERAL MACHINES TO THOMPSON WHICH ARE INDICATIVE OF A WHOLE
NEW LINE OF OFFICE MACHINES WE HAVE RECENTLY DEVELOPED.
    OUR SALES REPRESENTATIVE IS  LOOKING  FORWARD  TO  HIS  VISIT  IN
THOMPSON.  HE KNOWS  THAT  THE  MACHINES  HE  SELLS  COULD  BECOME  AN
INTEGRAL PART OF YOUR OFFICE ONLY A FEW DAYS AFTER INSTALLATION.



                             SINCERELY,



                             ROGER SMITH, MANAGER
                             OFFICE DEVICES CORPORATION
```

Once a specific letter is printed, a new set of **$$CHANGE** commands can be entered or read in corresponding to information about another customer. Of course, with a new set of data, a new copy of the general letter must be read into memory from the auxiliary device which holds the master copy. This process continues for as many customer letters as required.

In this subsection we have examined text editing in detail, mainly because it has provided an excellent opportunity to illustrate the concepts relating to character manipulation as discussed earlier in the chapter. As detailed as we have been, we have not touched upon many important commands that should be in a text editor. In particular, commands for inserting text between lines or for merging large pieces of text have not been presented. To handle such operations requires a particular type of storage representation, a linked list, which we discuss in Chap. 4. The exercises at the end of Chap. 4 include problems relating to the design of insert and merge commands for **ETEXTE**. The exercises to follow require the designing of those algorithms that were introduced in this subsection, but were not formally presented.

Exercises for Sec. 2-5.1

1. The Algorithm $$CHANGE does not match strings across elements of the array LINE which is used to store the text line-by-line. Construct a new $$CHANGE algorithm which has this capability.

2. Given as parameters the character string PRINTLINE and the right margin value RMARGIN, formulate the Algorithm NO_JUSTIFICATION which is invoked when the printed text is not to be right justified.

3. Given the character string TABLIST, which contains the tab settings as indicated by the @@TAB command, write an algorithm for isolating the individual tab settings and assigning these values to the vector TAB. For example, if TABLIST is '/20/40/60/', then the algorithm should set TAB[1] ← 20, TAB[2] ← 40, and TAB[3] ← 60.

4. Given a particular line of text LINE[i] and the current RMARGIN value, construct an algorithm for centering the text of LINE[i] in a line of output assuming the right margin RMARGIN.

2-5.2 Lexical Analysis

In our discussion of grammars in Sec. 2-2.2, we pointed out that often the description of a language must be viewed at two levels—the "word" level and the "sentence" level. For example, in the English language only certain combinations of characters from the English alphabet can be combined under concatenation to form a word. If a string of symbols contains a form which is not an English word, then this string cannot be a sentence from the English language. On the other hand, even if a string of symbols from the English alphabet is made up of English words, the entire string does not necessarily form a sentence from the English language (as illustrated by the string 'The sang the girl.'). Therefore, the decision as to whether a string forms a sentence from a "natural-like" language involves some analysis at the word (or lexical) level to decide if the string is composed of a set of legitimate symbols and words, and then some analysis at the sentence (or syntactic) level to determine if the words in the string combine to form sentences from the language.

In this subsection we are concerned with the lexical analysis of source strings (or statements) from a subset of a hypothetical high-level programming language. Nevertheless, many of the techniques presented are applicable to the lexical analysis of natural language machine translation.

In Sec. 5-2.3, a discussion of the second part of the analysis phase, namely the syntactic analysis, is undertaken. We concentrate on the syntactic analysis of a programming language as performed in a compiler or interpreter.

In a compiler or an interpreter, the module which separates the source input into basic "word-like" constructs, such as identifier names, numeric constants, string constants, keywords or reserved words, operators, etc., is commonly called the *scanner*. In the discussion to follow, we consider the design of a scanner for a simple language which is only composed of arithmetic expressions. The words or lexical components for such a language are identifiers, numeric constants, and the addition, subtraction, multiplication, division, and exponentiation operators, as well as parentheses and the assignment operator. The syntax for each of these primitive lexical classes is given by the grammatical descriptions:

<identifier> :: = <name>
    <name> :: = <letter>
              | <name> <letter>
              | <name> <digit>
    <letter> :: = A | B | C | D | E | F | G | H | I | J | K | L | M | N | O | P | Q | R |
              S | T | U | V | W | X | Y | Z
    <numeric> :: = <digit string>
              | . <digit string>
              | <digit string> . <digit string>
    <digit string> :: = <digit>
              | <digit string> <digit>
    <digit> :: = 0 | 1 | 2 | 3 | 4 | 5 | 6 | 7 | 8 | 9
<add/sub op> :: = + | −
<mult/div op> :: = * | /
<exponent op> :: = **
        <(> :: = (
        <)> :: =)
        <=> :: = =

The terminals of the grammar (that is, A, B, ..., Z, 0, 1, ..., 9, +, −, *, /, **, (,), =)
plus the blank character form the alphabet for our sample language. The nonterminal
symbols which appear in the left part of each rule (i.e., <identifier>, <numeric>,
<add/sub op>, <mult/div op>, <exponent op>, <(>, <)>, <=>, etc.) represent
the lexical classes which the scanner must identify. Once the lexical class of a source form
is identified, the class name (or some token representative of the class name) plus the
source form is passed on to the parser, which is responsible for the syntactic analysis
phase. The class names appear as terminals to the grammar which describes the sentences
of the language. It is this grammar which forms the basis of the syntactic analysis phase.
For our example language, the grammar for the parser might be:

<assign stat> :: = <identifier> <=> <expression>
<expression> :: = <term> | <expression> <add/sub op> <term>
    <term> :: = <form> | <term> <mult/div op> <form>
    <form> :: = <primary> | <form> <exponent op> <primary>
<primary> :: = <identifier> | <numeric> | <(> <expression> <)>

In most instances it is inefficient to pass a lexical class name, such as ' <identifier>',
to the parser. Instead, a unique representation number is associated with each class and it
is this number along with the source form (e.g., the identifier name) which is handed to the
parser. For our example language, we adopt the following representation number assignments: <identifier> is 1, <numeric> is 2, <add/sub op> is 3, <mult/div op> is 4,
<(> is 5, <)> is 6, <=> is 7, and <exponent op> is 8.

A class of symbols called delimiters must be handled by a scanner, and yet their
presence is not passed on to the parser. In our example assignment-statement language,
the blank character is such a delimiter (that is, X = A*Z is syntactically equivalent to
X = A * Z).

We are now prepared to present an algorithm for scanning a source statement from the assignment statement language given earlier.

Algorithm SCAN.   Given a source statement SOURCE, the statement is separated into its constituent lexical classes and the source forms with their corresponding representation numbers are printed. CHAR represents the source string character which is currently being examined. FORM contains the latest source form to be isolated, and REP# holds the representation number for this source form. LETTERS is the character string 'ABCDEFGHIJKL MNOPQRSTUVWXYZ', and DIGITS is the character string '0123456789'. CURSOR represents the current index into the character string SOURCE. DUMMY, S, and F are intermediate variables.

1. [Initialization]   Set CURSOR ← 1, print SOURCE.
2. [Set source scan]   Repeat steps 3 to 9 while CURSOR ≤ LENGTH(SOURCE).
3. [Remove blanks]
    If SPAN(SOURCE,'b',CURSOR,'',false),
    then go to step 2.
4. [Isolate next character]   Set CHAR ← SUB(SOURCE,CURSOR,1).
5. [Check for identifier]
    If INDEX(DIGITS, CHAR) ≠ 0,
    then set DUMMY ← SPAN(SOURCE,LETTERS ○ DIGITS,CURSOR,FORM,'',false),
        REP# ← 1, and go to step 9.
6. [Check for numeric]
    If INDEX(NUMBERS,CHAR) ≠ 0,
    then set DUMMY ← SPAN(SOURCE,DIGITS,CURSOR,FORM,'',false),
        if MATCH(SOURCE,'.',CURSOR,'','',false),
        then if SPAN(SOURCE,DIGITS,CURSOR,F,'',false),
            then set FORM ← FORM ○ '.' ○ F;
            otherwise, set FORM ← FORM ○ '.',
        set REP# ← 2, and go to step 9;
    otherwise,
        if CHAR = '.',
        then set CURSOR ← CURSOR + 1,
            DUMMY ← SPAN(SOURCE,DIGITS,CURSOR,FORM,'',false),
            FORM ← '.' ○ FORM, REP# ← 2, and go to step 9.
7. [Check for exponentiation]
    If MATCH(SOURCE,'**',CURSOR,FORM,'',false),
    then set REP# ← 8 and go to step 9.
8. [Other operators]   Set S ← INDEX(' +*() =',CHAR) and FORM ← CHAR.
    If S > 0,
    then set REP# ← S + 2;
    otherwise, set S ← INDEX(' − /',CHAR),
        if S = 0,
        then print 'illegal character in source string',
            set CURSOR ← CURSOR + 1, and return to step 2;
        otherwise, set REP# ← S + 2.

   Set CURSOR ← CURSOR + 1.
9.   [Print representation number and source form]   Print REP#, FORM.
10. [Finished]   Exit.

If Algorithm SCAN is called with a source statement '   Z1 = 2+Y', then

   Z1 = 2+Y

is printed in step 1. In step 3 the initial two blanks are removed by the SPAN function and a return is made to step 2, where the while condition is tested with the cursor position of 3 and the length of source equal to 10. Since the while condition is *true*, step 3 is again tried. SPAN returns *false* (there is no blank at cursor position 3) and CHAR becomes 'Z' in step 4. In step 5, 'Z' is identified as a letter and a span is made which incorporates both 'Z' and '1'. 'Z1' is assigned to FORM and CURSOR is set to 5. REP# becomes 1 and a transfer of control is made to step 9. At step 9, 1 and 'Z1' are printed and a return is made to the repeat in step 2.

A complete trace of the algorithm for the source statement '   Z1 = 2+Y' yields the following output:

```
Z1 = 2+Y
1     Z1
7     =
2     2
3     +
1     Y
```

Output from the lexical analysis of the source statements 'TAX = RATE *(INCOME − DEDUCTIONS)' and '1 = XY Z + **2' is

```
TAX = RATE *(INCOME − DEDUCTIONS)
1    TAX
7    =
1    RATE
4    *
5    (
1    INCOME
3    −
1    DEDUCTIONS
6    )

1 = XY Z + **2
2    1
7    =
1    XY
1    Z
3    +
8    **
2    2
```

The last example illustrates that the scanner is responsible only for recognizing properly formed lexical units, and not for identifying sentences from the source language. The problem of parsing sentences from a programming language will be discussed in more detail in Sec. 5-2.3.

In some compilers (especially one-pass "student" language compilers), the representation number and source form are passed directly to the parser. The parser uses the class representation number in the parsing routines. The production number corresponding to the reduction made by the parser is passed to a code-generation phase. In this phase, the source form along with the production number are used in the generation of object code which involves specific variable names, constant values, arithmetic operators, etc.

In a multipass compiler, the representation number and source form are often passed to a table-generating routine. This routine generates, in the first pass of the source statements of the program, a number of tables such as an identifier name table, a source statement-number table, a programmer-defined function table, a "macro" or preprocessor table, etc.

Steps 5 through 8 in Algorithm SCAN are language-dependent steps. It is possible to encode the information relevant to the logical decisions involved in these steps into a tabular form. If a new scanner is desired, then the contents of these tables are changed to suit the new language and the general scanning algorithm remains unchanged. These "table-driven" scanners are particularly useful when more than one scanner is needed for a compiler. Such a situation arises when a compiler must handle input from two or more different input devices which have different character sets (e.g., teletype and a card reader).

As a final note on lexical analysis, it should be remarked that we have neglected to discuss two very important functions of a scanner—namely, the removal of comments and the creation of line numbers. Two of the exercises to follow involve these functions.

Exercises for Sec. 2-5.2

1. Write a PL/I program which scans source statements from the assignment language discussed in this subsection. The program should handle PL/I-type comments. Of course, comments should be printed by the scanner along with the assignment statements, but no indication of the presence of comments should be passed to the parser. Therefore,

    X = /*SQUARE OF X*/ X **2.

    should only generate the following strings:

    '1 X', '6 =', '1 X', '8 **', '2 2'.

2. Add the capability of automatically numbering source statements to the scanner in Exercise 1. Therefore, if the first two assignment statements in a program are 'X = Y' and 'Y = Z*4', then they should be output as

    1   X = Y
    2   Y = Z*4

3. As a term project, write a scanner for a subset of the PL/I language which includes string and numeric assignments, procedures, DO loops, DO groups, DO whiles, IF-THEN-ELSE statements, and LIST I/O statements.

4. As an extension to Exercise 3, add automatic paragraphing to the scanner. With automatic paragraphing, the bodies of procedures and **DO** constructs are automatically indented by a certain number of character positions, say four. **IF**, **THEN**, and **ELSE** clauses are automatically aligned vertically. Therefore, if a source statement is entered on one line or a card as

```
'IF X = Y THEN DO; X = Z; Y = 0; END; ELSE X = 0;'
```

it should be printed as

```
IF X = Y
THEN
    DO;
        X = Z; Y = 0;
    END;
ELSE X = 0;
```

by the scanner.

2-5.3 KWIC Indexing

A rapidly growing area in computer science is information retrieval. In information-retrieval applications, a data base, which may contain a wide variety of data structures, is maintained on an on-line basis using large random-access (e.g., disk) files. These files are searched for requested information based on index items generated from a user query. One of the problems associated with information-retrieval systems (and especially automated library systems) is that of creating a good *indexing scheme.*

One method of indexing that is widely used in library systems is the permuted or KWIC (key-word-in-context) indexing scheme. A KWIC index provides the context surrounding each occurrence of each word. In practice, KWIC indexing is most often applied to phrases, especially titles, selected from the documents of interest. While KWIC indexing allows us to determine the role of a word quickly, it is an indexing method which requires a large amount of storage due to the amount of contextual information that must be stored.

To illustrate this point, let us consider an example involving the title of a certain book "An Introduction to Data Structures with Applications." In a KWIC indexing scheme, each item of the phrase (in this case the title) is scanned for keywords and reproduced once in a permuted fashion for each keyword. In our example, the list of permuted indices are:

Introduction to Data Structures with Applications// An
Data Structures with Applications// An Introduction to
Structures with Applications// An Introduction to Data
Applications// An Introduction to Data Structures

We refer to the underscored first word in each index as the *index word.* The set of index words generated from a title form the set of key words for that title (i.e., Introduction, Data, Structures, Applications are the key words in the example). Key words are considered to be those words which impart some meaning as to the nature of the document. Ordinary words such as 'a', 'for', 'to', 'the', 'an', 'and', 'with', 'its', etc. tell little about the subject of a document. In the implementation of a KWIC index generator, keywords are those words which are not the prepositions, conjunctions, pronouns, and, in many instances, the adverbs, adjectives, and verbs which form the ordinary word list.

In the following description of the KWIC index generator, it is assumed that the information necessary to generate the indices is stored in four one-dimensional arrays. The first array, ORD_WORDS, holds an ordered list of ordinary words for the index generating system—one word per array location. In the examples used in the discussion to follow, assume that ORD_WORDS contains 'a', 'an', 'and', 'for', 'its', 'the', 'to', and 'with'. The second array, TITLE, contains complete book titles as input to the generator. A third array, KEYWORD, contains an ordered list of the keywords that are present in the titles currently stored in the system. Associated with these keywords, and stored in a fourth array called TITLE#S, is a list of array indices which refer to titles stored in the TITLE array. If a given keyword is stored at position i in the KEYWORD array, then TITLE#S[i] contains a character string which holds the TITLE array indices for all titles possessing that keyword. The array indices in the character string are separated by blank characters.

To illustrate the relationships between the arrays TITLE, TITLE#S, and KEYWORDS, assume TITLE[1], TITLE[2], ..., TITLE[5] are assigned the five titles:

'AN INTRODUCTION TO DATA STRUCTURES WITH APPLICATIONS//'
'AN INTRODUCTION TO PROGRAMMING//'
'PL/I PROGRAMMING WITH APPLICATIONS//'
'A SNOBOL4 PRIMER//'
'A PRIMER FOR LISP PROGRAMMING//'

Then KEYWORD[i] and TITLE#S[i] hold the information as shown in Table 2-5.1 for i ranging from one to the total number of keywords.

Table 2-5.1

i	KEYWORD	TITLE#S
1	'APPLICATIONS'	'1 3'
2	'DATA'	'1'
3	'INTRODUCTION'	'1 2'
4	'LISP'	'5'
5	'PL/I'	'3'
6	'PRIMER'	'4 5'
7	'PROGRAMMING'	'2 3 5'
8	'SNOBOL4'	'4'
9	'STRUCTURES'	'1'

Therefore, the titles which contain the keyword PROGRAMMING, for example, are TITLE[2], TITLE[3], and TITLE[5].

We now present the Algorithm KWIC_OUT which is capable of generating a KWIC index listing for all titles currently entered in the system.

Algorithm KWIC_OUT.   Given the arrays TITLE, KEYWORD, and TITLE#S, this algorithm generates a KWIC index ordered lexically by index words. KEYSTRING is an intermediate variable used to hold the string of TITLE indices as stored in an element of TITLE#S. IND holds a particular TITLE array index, LAST_KEY is the number of stored keywords, and T is used in the formation of a permuted index.

1. [Establish loop in which keywords are used as index words]
    Repeat steps 2 to 5 for i = 1, . . ., LAST_KEY.
2. [Set KEYSTRING]   Set KEYSTRING ← TITLE#S[i] ○ 'b'.
3. [Repeat until no more TITLE indices in KEYSTRING]
    Repeat steps 4 and 5 while LENGTH(KEYSTRING) > 1.
4. [Get next TITLE index]
    Set IND ← SUB(KEYSTRING,1,INDEX(KEYSTRING,'b')−1),
    KEYSTRING ← SUB(KEYSTRING,INDEX(KEYSTRING,'b')+1).
5. [Set T and output in KWIC format]   Set T ← TITLE[IND], CURSOR ← 1.
    If FIND(T,KEYWORD[i],CURSOR,MATCH_STR,'',true),
    then set T ← KEYWORD[i] ○ SUB(T,CURSOR) ○ 'b' ○ MATCH_STR, and print T;
    otherwise, print 'system error − keyword not found in title'.
6. [Finished]   Exit.

Let us proceed through a partial trace of Algorithm KWIC_OUT using the five titles given previously as data. Step 1 sets up a repeat loop for i running from 1 to 9. The first time step 2 is executed, KEYSTRING has the value '1 3 '. In step 3, a check is made to see if all TITLE indices corresponding to a given keyword have been used. IND is set to 1 and KEYSTRING is reduced to '3 ' in step 4. In step 5, T is temporarily set to

'AN INTRODUCTION TO DATA STRUCTURES WITH APPLICATIONS//'

and then reset, using the FIND function described in 2-3.2, to

'APPLICATIONS// AN INTRODUCTION TO DATA STRUCTURES WITH '

The while condition in the repeat loop in step 3 is reexamined and the loop is repeated with KEYSTRING equal to '3 '. The output after the loop is completed a second time is

'APPLICATIONS// PL/I PROGRAMMING WITH '

If a complete trace were provided, then the next three and last two items to be printed by the KWIC_OUT routine for the given data would be:

'DATA STRUCTURES WITH APPLICATIONS// AN INTRODUCTION TO '
'INTRODUCTION TO DATA STRUCTURES WITH APPLICATIONS// AN '

'INTRODUCTION TO PROGRAMMING// AN '
      .
      .
      .

'SNOBOL4 PRIMER// A '
'STRUCTURES WITH APPLICATIONS// AN INTRODUCTION TO DATA '

Algorithm KWIC_OUT produces a proper KWIC index listing given that the appropriate information is stored in the three arrays TITLE, KEYWORD, and TITLE#S. Algorithm KWIC_FORM, which we now describe, analyzes the input phrases and creates the three arrays needed in Algorithm KWIC_OUT. KEYIND is used as an index into the array KEYWORD.

Algorithm KWIC_FORM.   Given as input a sequence of phrases (e.g., titles) in the form of character strings, the arrays TITLE, KEYWORD, and TITLE#S are formed. PHRASE contains the current input phrase. ORD_SEARCH is an algorithm which searches the ORD_WORDS array to determine if a word is an ordinary word (in which case, the nonzero array index is returned) or is not an ordinary word (in which case a zero value is returned). KEY_SEARCH is an algorithm for searching the KEYWORD array to discover if the keyword has been used previously. If it has, its keyword array index is returned. If it has not appeared previously, the keyword is inserted at the appropriate array element location and the index associated with this location is returned. LAST_TITLE is the index of the latest element to be added to the TITLE array, and WORD is an intermediate variable which contains word forms.

1. [Establish repeat loop]   Repeat steps 2 to 7 while there is input.
2. [Read input phrase]   Read PHRASE.
3. [Remove any leading blanks and concatenate end markers //]
   Set DUMMY ← SPAN(PHRASE,'b',1,'','',true), PHRASE ← PHRASE ○ '//'.
4. [Store in TITLE]   Set LAST_TITLE ← LAST_TITLE + 1,
   TITLE[LAST_TITLE] ← PHRASE.
5. [Handle keywords]   Repeat steps 6 and 7 while SUB(PHRASE,1,2) ≠ '//'.
6. [Remove a word]   Set WORD ← SUB(PHRASE,1,INDEX(PHRASE,'b') −1),
   PHRASE ← SUB(PHRASE,INDEX(PHRASE,'b')+1).
7. [Is word a keyword?]
   If ORD_SEARCH(WORD) = 0,
   then set KEYIND ← KEY_SEARCH(WORD),

   $\qquad$ TITLE#S[KEYIND] ← TITLE#S[KEYIND] ○ 'b' ○ LAST_TITLE.
8. [Finished]   Exit.

If an input phrase is the title 'A SNOBOL4 PRIMER', then in step 2 of the Algorithm KWIC_FORM, this title is assigned to the variable PHRASE. If the input phrase has leading blanks, they are removed by the SPAN function, as defined in Sec. 2-3.2, and the markers '//' are concatenated to the end of the value for PHRASE in step 3. PHRASE is stored in the TITLE array at the next open location in step 4. Steps 6 and 7 are repeated until all word forms in the input phrase are examined as to their identity (i.e., whether they are key-words or not). If the word is not a keyword, as in the case of 'A', then a return is made to the repeat statement in step 5. If the word is a keyword, as in the case of 'SNOBOL4', ORD_SEARCH returns a nonzero value and the keyword is placed at its appropriate position in the KEYWORD array by the Algorithm KEY_SEARCH. (Note that both ORD_SEARCH and KEY_SEARCH are left as exercises to be completed at the end of this sub-section.) Finally, in step 7, the TITLE#S array is updated by concatenating the TITLE array index onto the end of the other TITLE indices for the given keyword.

The algorithms KWIC_OUT and KWIC_FORM allow us to store titles, or any type of descriptive phrase, and to produce a KWIC index listing. The KWIC index generator is a simple yet practical application of character-string manipulation. In an exercise to follow, there is an interesting extension to the basic index generator described in this subsection.

Exercises for Sec. 2-5.3
1. Given as input a word form assigned to the variable WORD, derive Algorithm ORD_SEARCH which searches the ORD_WORDS array looking for the word form. If the word form is present, its index location in ORD_WORDS is returned; otherwise, a value of zero is returned. (There are a number of search procedures which can be used for ORD_SEARCH and these are discussed in Chap. 6. A simple linear search is a sufficient answer to this question.)
2. Given as an input parameter a keyword assigned to the variable WORD, construct Algorithm KEY_SEARCH which searches the KEYWORD array looking for the keyword. If the keyword is present, its index location in KEYWORD is returned; otherwise, the keyword is inserted in the KEYWORD array at the appropriate location as determined by the lexical ordering of keywords. Note that space must also be left at the corre-sponding location in the TITLE#S array to hold the string of TITLE array indexes for the keyword. Again, a simple linear search and linear insertion procedure is ad-equate for this question. Better procedures will be presented in Chap. 6.
3. Algorithm KWIC_OUT does not handle the situation in which a keyword appears more than once in a title. For example, the title

   'TECHNIQUES FOR SYSTEM DESIGN AND SYSTEM IMPLEMENTATION'

   should be printed twice

   'SYSTEM DESIGN AND SYSTEM IMPLEMENTATION// TECHNIQUES FOR '
   'SYSTEM IMPLEMENTATION// TECHNIQUES FOR SYSTEM DESIGN AND '

   Alter KWIC_OUT so that it provides this facility.
4. As more and more documents are added to a KWIC-index-generating system, it be-comes less attractive to receive a KWIC index printout for the complete list of docu-ments. Instead, it is more desirable to receive a KWIC-index listing for those docu-ments which contain in their title (or some other representable phrase) certain select index words. For example, we might pose a command of the form

   LIST KWIC FOR <index word expression>

   where <index word expression> is defined to be:

<index word expression > :: = index

| (<index word expression > <oper > index)

| (index <oper > <index word expression >)

<oper > :: = OR | AND

The terminal "index" can be any index word we choose to search on. Therefore, example commands are

LIST KWIC FOR PRIMER

LIST KWIC FOR (APPLICATIONS AND PROGRAMMING)

LIST KWIC FOR ((DATA AND STRUCTURES) OR PL/I)

Write a PL/I program which interprets the "LIST KWIC" commands and outputs only the KWIC index terms as specified in the index-term expression for the command.

2-5.4 The Use of Bit Strings in an Information-Retrieval Application

Thus far in the chapter we have concentrated on discussing character strings, their operations and storage representations. A special type of string that is provided in PL/I and ALGOL W is the bit string (in ALGOL W the bit string data type is referred to as **BITS**). A bit string is a string which only contains characters from the alphabet {0, 1}. Examples of PL/I bit string constants are '00010'B and '1'B. The B is placed at the end of the string of zeros and ones to signify the difference between a character string (for example, '010') and a bit string (for example, '010'B).

Generally, bit strings are stored using one computer bit per string element. Therefore, in the IBM 370, a bit string of length 32 can be stored in one computer word. By encoding values in the binary format that is implied when using bit strings, a very compact storage representation for information can be obtained.

In PL/I, bit strings can be fixed or varying in length. The technique for handling varying-length bit strings is similar to that described for varying-length character strings. The operations available to bit strings are the same as those available to character strings (i.e., concatenation, **SUBSTR**, **INDEX**, **LENGTH**, **VERIFY**, etc.). In addition, bit strings can be "ANDed" (using the logical operator &) and "ORed" (using the logical operator |). We illustrate these two operations in the discussion of the information-retrieval application which we now present.

A problem which frequently arises in computer applications is that of extracting particular information from a large data base (i.e., a large pool of information encompassing many aspects of a particular application). For example, in an airline reservation system, which contains a massive data base, it is necessary to extract specific information about the flights between two cities, such as the number of seats which are available for each flight. Such a problem is an example of a problem in information retrieval.

In this subsection we consider an information-retrieval design problem which is not nearly as complicated as the problem relating to the design of an airline reservation system. Nevertheless, the problem is interesting, nontrivial, and it provides us with an opportunity to exhibit a solution which makes use of bit strings. Not all information-retrieval problems lend themselves to solutions involving bit strings. Even for those that do, such a solution may not be the best solution. In Chap. 7 we introduce many other methods of information organization which are alternatives to the use of bit strings.

The problem we will examine deals with the computerization of payroll and accounting procedures for a certain transportation company operating in Alberta's mountain national parks. After some initial planning and problem analysis, it is decided that an employee file should be created which contains the following information:

1   Employee's social insurance number (SIN) – a nine-digit field.
2   Employee's name (NAME) – a twenty-five character field.
3   Employee's sex (SEX) – a one-character field coded as 'M' for male and 'F' for female.
4   Employee's type of work (TYPE) – encoded as a one-character field with 'A' meaning agent, 'D' meaning driver, 'H' meaning driver's helper, and 'P' meaning payroll.
5   Employee's wage (WAGE) – encoded as a one-digit field where '1' means $3.00/hr., '2' means $3.80/hr., '3' means $5.00/hr., and '4' means $7.00/hr.
6   Employee's location (LOCATION) – encoded as a one-character field where 'B' means Banff, 'J' means Jasper, and 'L' means Lake Louise.

In the descriptions just given, the names in parentheses will be used as field reference names for an employee record in the discussion to follow. The values which these fields can assume are also given.

The following list of employee records will be used throughout the discussion in this subsection. For clarity, blanks have been inserted between the fields and titles have been added.

SOCIAL INSURANCE	NAME		SEX	TYPE	WAGE	LOCATION
693121053	PATRICIA L	FOX	F	D	2	J
686725001	LARRY R	BROWN	M	D	2	B
591146235	LINDA L	GARDNER	F	H	1	B
661301964	ROY B	ANDERSON	M	A	3	J
529270792	DAVID N	PARKER	M	P	2	B
637263675	SUSAN C	FROST	F	P	3	J

When computing the bimonthly paychecks, the company feels it is desirable to extract specific information from this file. For example, they may want a listing of all employees earning $5.00 per hour, a listing of all drivers in Lake Louise, a listing of all female employees in Jasper, etc.

To solve this information-retrieval problem, we make use of 13 bit strings. The length of each string is equal to the total number of employees currently in the file (here, we use the term file generically; in Chap. 7 we provide a precise definition). For example, one string represents male employees; another, female employees; a third, employees working in Jasper, etc. The 13-bit strings correspond to the thirteen values which are possible for SEX (2 values), TYPE (4 values), WAGE (4 values), and LOCATION (3 values). A '1' in the ith position of the bit string for Jasper employees indicates that the ith employee works in Jasper. A '0' in the ith position of the bit string for drivers designates that the ith employee is not a driver.

For our sample file of six records, the bits strings would be as follows:

KEYWORD	BIT STRING	KEYWORD	BIT STRING
MALE	'010110'B	WAGE_TYPE3	'000101'B
FEMALE	'101001'B	WAGE_TYPE2	'110010'B
AGENT	'000100'B	WAGE_TYPE1	'001000'B
DRIVER	'110000'B	BANFF	'011010'B
HELPER	'001000'B	JASPER	'100101'B
PAYROLL	'000011'B	LAKE_LOUISE	'000000'B
WAGE_TYPE4	'000000'B		

To provide an easy mode of system interaction for payroll personnel (many of whom must convert from manual procedures), it is desirable to create a nonprocedural command language which is quite English-like in nature. A command has the format

LIST EMPLOYEES [specifications]

The specifications field consists of a logical combination of the keywords which are representative of the subset of employee records desired. For example, to request a listing of all employees who are drivers in Banff, we use

LIST EMPLOYEES DRIVER & BANFF.

In response to this command, the following action takes place in the retrieval system, assuming we have in storage the sample set of records given earlier:

1 After the command is analyzed, the bit strings corresponding to the keywords **DRIVER** and **BANFF** are retrieved ('110000'B and '011010'B, respectively).
2 The logical conjunction, as indicated by the operator **&**, is found ('110000'B & '011010'B = '010000'B).
3 The corresponding record(s) are retrieved and listed under appropriate headings.

SOCIAL INSURANCE	NAME	SEX	TYPE	WAGE	LOCATION
686725001	LARRY R. BROWN	M	D	2	B

Hence our general strategy for interpreting commands is to isolate the command keywords, retrieve the corresponding bit strings, and perform the specified logical operations on these bit strings to arrive at a final bit string. We then take this bit string, and wherever there is a 1, we output the corresponding record from the file. Note that when interpreting commands we should check for input errors, and if there are errors, we should print an error message and ignore the erroneous command.

The logical operators which may be used with the specifications of the command are

| | (logical disjunction – OR)
  & (logical conjunction – AND)
  ⌐ (logical negation – NOT)

The ⌐ operator has precedence over the & operator, which in turn has precedence over the | operator. This precedence can be altered by the use of parenthesis. Therefore, the commands

LIST EMPLOYEES MALE | FEMALE & ⌐BANFF.

and

LIST EMPLOYEES MALE | (FEMALE & (⌐BANFF)).

are equivalent.

To process the commands, it is necessary to have an algorithm which isolates the next command element, whether it be an operator or a keyword. The Algorithm NEXTSYM performs this command analysis.

Algorithm NEXTSYM.   Given a string S consisting of operator and keyword command elements, find the leftmost element, delete it from S, and exit with this element assigned to NEXTSYM. X is used as an intermediate variable.

1. [Initialization]   Set NEXTSYM ← '', CURSOR ← 1.
2. [Remove leading blanks]   Set DUMMY ← SPAN(S,'b',CURSOR,'','',true).
3. [Determine if next character is an operator]   Set X ← SUB(S,CURSOR,1).
   If INDEX('|&⌐.',X) ≠ 0, then set NEXTSYM ← X, S ← SUB(S,2) and Exit.
4. [Isolate word]
   If BREAK(S, 'b|&⌐.',CURSOR,NEXTSYM,'',true),
   then set S ← SUB(S,CURSOR), and Exit;
   otherwise, print 'command syntactically incorrect', set S ← '', and Exit.

In step 2 of Algorithm NEXTSYM, we use the SPAN pattern-matching function, as described in Sec. 2-3.2, to remove all preceding blanks. The remainder of the algorithm is simple to understand and involves a straightforward application of the character-handling functions discussed previously, with the exception of the BREAK function. The BREAK function is described in Exercises for Sec. 2-3, and it is very similar to the BREAK pattern-matching function in SNOBOL. In the context of this example, the BREAK function is used to find the end of a keyword by locating either the next operator, a blank between symbols, or the end of the command.

If NEXTSYM is invoked with S = ' & BANFF.', '&' is returned and S is set to ' BANFF.'. If called again, NEXTSYM returns 'BANFF' and S is set to '.'.

The evaluation resulting from an interpretation of a command is outlined in the Algorithm EVALUATE. The algorithm assumes that the command operators and their keyword operands have been transformed to a postfix form. In Sec. 3-7.2 we describe in detail a method for translating expressions in which the operator is between its operands (i.e., infix expressions) to expressions in which the operator follows its operands (i.e., postfix expressions). The following examples illustrate the postfix form of a given infix expression:

FEMALES | MALES & ⌐JASPER has the postfix form FEMALES MALES JASPER ⌐& |

and

(PAYROLL | AGENT) & BANFF has the postfix form PAYROLL AGENT | BANFF &.

Postfix expressions have two advantages over infix expressions; namely, the expression can be evaluated in a single left-to-right scan without backing up and parentheses are eliminated from postfix expressions. The evaluation of a postfix expression is a process of finding the leftmost operator and applying its operands. The result from this operation may then be used as an operand for the next leftmost operator. Therefore, in FEMALE MALES JASPER ⌐ & |, JASPER ⌐ is evaluated first. Its value, say R1, is used as an operand in the evaluation of MALES R1 &. The result of this expression, say R2, can again be used in the evaluation of the final expression FEMALE R2 |.

Assuming a basic understanding of postfix expressions, we can now present Algorithm EVALUATE.

Algorithm EVALUATE.   Given the input string REQUEST, evaluate the command expression in REQUEST in terms of the corresponding bit-string arguments and exit with a final bit string which indicates the records that satisfy the given command. BITS is an array used to store intermediate results and i is an index for BITS. SYM holds command elements and KEYS is a character string containing the concatenation of all keyword operands. POSTFIX is a function which returns the Polish postfix form of an infix command expression. COMMAND holds the postfix form of the command. REFERENCE is a function which, given a keyword, returns the bit string corresponding to the keyword.

1. [Initialization]   Set $i \leftarrow 0$, COMMAND $\leftarrow$ POSTFIX(REQUEST).
2. [Evaluation loop]   Repeat steps 3 to 5 while LENGTH(COMMAND) > 1.
3. [Get next element]   Set SYM $\leftarrow$ NEXTSYM(COMMAND).
4. [Check for keyword and place corresponding bit string in BITS]
   If INDEX(KEYS,SYM) $\neq 0$, then set $i \leftarrow i + 1$, BITS[i] $\leftarrow$ REFERENCE(SYM),
      and go to step 2.
5. [Check for operator and perform the operation indicated]
   If SYM $=$ '|', then set BITS[i -1] $\leftarrow$ BITS[i] | BITS[i -1], $i \leftarrow i - 1$,
      and go to step 2.
   If SYM $=$ '&', then set BITS[i -1] $\leftarrow$ BITS[i] & BITS[i -1], $i \leftarrow i - 1$,
      and go to step 2.
   If SYM $=$ '⌐', then set BITS[i] $\leftarrow$ ⌐BITS[i] and go to step 2.
   If SYM $\neq$ '.', then print 'error', set EVALUATE $\leftarrow$ '0'B, and Exit.
6. [Return]   If $i = 1$, then set EVALUATE $\leftarrow$ BITS[i], and Exit;
      otherwise, print 'error', set EVALUATE $\leftarrow$ '0'B, and Exit.

In the algorithm the operators |, &, and ⌐ are the logical operators OR, AND, and NOT, respectively, as applied to bit-string arguments on a bit-by-bit basis. That is, '0100'B | '1101'B is '1101'B, '0100'B &'1101'B is '0100'B, and ⌐'1101'B is '0010'B. PL/I function procedures for EVALUATE and REFERENCE are given in Fig. 2-5.3. In the program given, a number of variables are declared and set globally. L holds the total number of records in the employee file. S is an index into the BITS array which holds the Polish postfix form that is examined in the EVALUATE procedure. The thirteen-bit-string variables MALE, FEMALE, JASPER, etc., each of length thirteen, hold unique bit-string values. That is, MALE = '1000000000000'B, FEMALE = '0100000000000'B, etc. These variables are used to encode query operands.

```
        EVALUATE: PROCEDURE (REQUEST);

/* THIS PROCEDURE IS USED TO EVALUATE THE INPUT COMMAND AND RETURN   */
/* IN A BIT STRING THE RESULTS OF THE EVALUATION.                    */
/* TO EVALUATE THE COMMAND, THE INPUT FROM IS CONVERTED TO A POLISH  */
/* POSTFIX FORM AND THEN THIS FORM IS EVALUATED WITH THE HELP OF     */
/* THE REFERENCE PROCEDURE.                                          */

/* THE KEY VARIABLES ARE:                                            */
/*      REQUEST:  HOLDS THE INPUT COMMAND                            */
/*      BITS:     AN ARRAY USED TO EVALUATE THE POLISH POSTFIX FORM. */
/*      S:        A POINTER INTO BITS.                               */
/*      COMMAND:  A STRING USED TO TEMPORARILY HOLD THE POSTFIX FORM */
            DECLARE REQUEST CHARACTER(*) VARYING,
                    BITS(10) BIT(L),
                    SYMBOL CHARACTER(11) VARYING,
                    CPERATORS CHARACTER(5),
                    KEYWORDS CHARACTER(108) INITIAL('MALE FEMALE JASPER '
                    || 'BANFF LAKE_LOUISE PAYROLL DRIVER HELPER AGENT '
                    || 'WAGE_TYPE1 WAGE_TYPE2 WAGE_TYPE3 WAGE_TYPE4');
                    POLISH CHARACTER(120) VARYING INITIAL(''),
                    S FIXED BINARY INITIAL(1),
                    I FIXED BINARY;

        REFERENCE: PROCEDURE (K);
/* THIS PROCEDURE IS USED TO SIMULATE A CASE STATEMENT TO INSERT     */
/* THE DESIRED BITSTRING INTO THE BITS ARRAY DURING EVALUATION OF THE*/
/* POSTFIX FORM OF THE COMMAND.                                      */
/*      K:        THE INPUT NUMBER WHICH DETERMINES WHICH CASE.      */
                DECLARE K FIXED BINARY,
                        LAB(84) LABEL;
              GO TC LAB(K);
        LAB(1):    BITS(S) = MALE;
                   RETURN;
        LAB(6):    BITS(S) = FEMALE;
                   RETURN;
        LAB(13):   BITS(S) = JASPER;
                   RETURN;
        LAB(20):   BITS(S) = BANFF;
                   RETURN;
        LAB(26):   BITS(S) = LAKE_LOUISE;
                   RETURN;
        LAB(38):   BITS(S) = PAYROLL;
                   RETURN;
        LAB(46):   BITS(S) = DRIVER;
                   RETURN;
        LAB(53):   BITS(S) = HELPER;
                   RETURN;
        LAB(60):   BITS(S) = AGENT;
                   RETURN;
        LAB(66):   BITS(S) = WAGE_TYPE1;
                   RETURN;
        LAB(77):   BITS(S) = WAGE_TYPE2;
                   RETURN;
        LAB(88):   BITS(S) = WAGE_TYPE3;
                   RETURN;
        LAB(99):   BITS(S) = WAGE_TYPE4;
                   RETURN;
        END REFERENCE;
```

FIGURE 2-5.3   Procedure for Algorithm EVALUATE.

As an example which illustrates how EVALUATE works, consider the REQUEST

LIST EMPLOYEES DRIVER & BANFF.

In step 1, the function POSTFIX returns the command form 'DRIVER BANFF &'. Steps 3 and 4 are executed twice placing the bit string for DRIVER and BANFF in the BITS array at

```
/* THIS PORTION OF EVALUATE EVALUATES THE POLISH POSTFIX FORM.       */
         S = 0;
         COMMAND = POSTFIX(REQUEST);
         DO WHILE (LENGTH(COMMAND) > 1);
             SYMBOL = NEXTSYM(COMMAND);
             IF INDEX(KEYWORDS,SYMBOL) ¬= 0
             THEN DO;
                 S = S + 1;
                 /* STORE APPROPRIATE BIT STRING */
                 CALL REFERENCE(INDEX(KEYWORDS,SYMBOL));
             END;
             ELSE DO;
                 I = INDEX(OPERATORS,SYMBOL);
                 IF I = 1
                 THEN DO;
                     BITS(S-1) = BITS(S) | BITS(S-1);
                     S = S - 1;
                 END;
                 ELSE IF I = 2
                     THEN DO;
                         BITS(S-1) = BITS(S) & BITS(S-1);
                         S = S - 1;
                     END;
                     ELSE IF I = 3
                         THEN BITS(S) = ¬BITS(S);
                         ELSE DO;
                             CALL ERROR;
                             RETURN('0'B);
                         END;
             END;
         END; /* OF DO WHILE */
         IF S = 1
         THEN RETURN(BITS(S));
         ELSE DO;
             CALL ERROR;
             RETURN('0'B);
         END;
     END EVALUATE;
```

FIGURE 2-5.3 (Continued)

positions one and two. Step 3 is executed a third time placing '&' in **SYM**. Step 5 performs the conjunction of the **DRIVER** and **BANFF** bit strings and places the result at position one of **BITS**. The algorithm concludes by exiting with the first element of **BITS** as the return value.

We now present the main algorithm for accomplishing a retrieval of the information specified in a command. Implied in the initialization step of the Algorithm **RETRIEVE** is the creation and initialization of the employee file and the 13-bit strings. In an actual application, this file would be present and stored on auxiliary storage (e.g., a disk).

Algorithm RETRIEVE. Given a set of employee records, print the records which satisfy the input request as found in the string **REQUEST**. RECORD is a bit string which is used to determine which records to print. It is given a value by the process **EVALUATE** which evaluates the input command.

1. [Initialization] Set RECORD ← '0'B.
2. [Get REQUEST, delete trailing blanks, and check validity] Read REQUEST.
   Repeat while SUB(REQUEST,LENGTH(REQUEST),1) = 'b':
       set REQUEST ← SUB(REQUEST,1,LENGTH(REQUEST) −1).
   If ¬MATCH(REQUEST,'LIST EMPLOYEES' ,1,'','',true),
   then print ERROR and go to step 5.

3. [If no command list, print all records; otherwise, evaluate]
   If LENGTH(REQUEST) ≤ 1, then set RECORD ← '1111...1'B;   (to all 1's)
        otherwise, set RECORD ← EVALUATE(REQUEST).
4. [Print headings and records]   Print Headings,
   Repeat while INDEX(RECORD,'1'B) ≠ 0:
        set i ← INDEX(RECORD,'1'B), print ith record, and
        set SUB(RECORD,i,1) ← '0'B.
5. [End of requests]   If end of requests then stop; otherwise, go to step 2.

In this subsection we have presented a solution to a particular problem in information retrieval. In Chap. 7 we introduce a number of file and record structures which can be used in the design of an information-retrieval system. One such record structure involves bit strings which are used in a manner similar to that used here.

Exercises for Sec. 2-5.4

1. Given the sample file of six records as presented in this subsection, what is the output for the following commands:

   (a)   LIST EMPLOYEES BANFF | JASPER.
   (b)   LIST EMPLOYEES PAYROLL & ⌐FEMALE | MALE.
   (c)   LIST EMPLOYEES DRIVER & LAKE_LOUISE & WAGE_TYPE1.

2. Give the Polish postfix expressions for the command expressions given in question 1.
3. What are the printed results for the following PL/I statements?

   DECLARE (X, Y, Z) BIT(5) VARYING;
   X = '0010'B, Y = '1'B; Z = '10010'B:
   PUT LIST('X|Y =', X|Y, 'Z&X =', Z&X, '⌐Y =', ⌐Y);

4. In the information-retrieval problem discussed in this subsection, we assumed a set of four fixed-wage classifications. More realistically, we should allow for a spectrum of wages of the form $X.YZ/hour (e.g., $3.52/hour). To handle such a change in system specification would imply that the specific hourly wages for each employee must be stored in the employee record along with the employee's name and social insurance number. We can still use a bit field of the bit string to answer queries such as

   LIST EMPLOYEES WAGE > $4.75.

   What is required is the encoding of wage brackets where, for example, '1' means less than $3.50/hour, '2' means $3.50/hour to $4.49/hour, '3' means $4.50/hour to $5.49/hour, '4' means $5.50/hour and greater. To answer the question regarding wages greater than $4.75/hour, it is required that a search be made of all records for personnel in wage bracket '3' and that these records be included with the records for personnel in wage bracket '4'. Devise an algorithm for handling queries such as the one just given, which uses bit strings devoted to the expression of wage brackets (as opposed to exact hourly wages).

BIBLIOGRAPHY

GALLER, B. A., and A. J. PERLIS: "A View of Programming Languages," Addison-Wesley, Reading, Mass., 1970.

GRIES, D.: "Compiler Construction for Digital Computers," John Wiley & Sons, Inc., Toronto, 1971.

GRISWOLD, R. E. and M. T. GRISWOLD: "A SNOBOL Primer," Prentice-Hall, Englewood Cliffs, N.J., 1973.

HARRISON, M. C.: "Data Structures and Programming," Scott, Foresman and Co., Glenview, Ill., 1972.

"IBM System/360 Operating System PL/I(F) Language Reference Manual," File No. S360-29, Order No. GC28-6594.

MARKOV, A. A.: "The Theory of Algorithms" (tr. from Russian), U.S. Dept. of Commerce, Office of Technical Services, No. OTS 60-51085.

NAUR, P. (ed.), "Revised Report on the Algorithm Language ALGOL 60," *Communications of the ACM*, vol. 6, no. 1, Jan., 1963, pp. 1–17.

LINEAR DATA STRUCTURES AND
THEIR SEQUENTIAL STORAGE REPRESENTATION

The previous chapters have dealt with primitive data structures such as integers, reals, and strings. In this chapter we will be concerned with nonprimitive data structures which are linear. A number of possible storage representations for these linear structures will be given. All such representations are based on sequential allocation.

The first part of the chapter will discuss the concepts and terminology associated with nonprimitive data structures. These structures are classified into batches, arrays, and lists. A number of associated operations on certain linear structures will be described. The storage representations of arrays in row-major and column-major order are given in Sec. 3-5.

An important linear structure, the stack, is discussed in Sec. 3-6. The programming aspects of stacks in PL/I using controlled storage and the associated **ALLOCATE** *and* **FREE** *statements are introduced.*

Section 3-7 describes certain classical applications of stacks such as recursion, the compilation of arithmetic expressions, and stack machines. Recursion is available in many programming languages such as ALGOL 60 and PL/I. The compilation of infix expressions into Polish notation and their subsequent conversion into some object language is an important application in the area of compiler writing. A number of computers such as the PDP-11 and the Burroughs 5000 have stack memories, and some of their properties are described in this section.

Another important data structure known as a queue is introduced in Sec. 3-9. Certain variations of a basic queue are also mentioned. A simple application of queues is given in Sec. 3-9. It is concerned with the simulation of a time-sharing computer system and is followed by a discussion of priority queues.

3-1   CONCEPTS AND TERMINOLOGY FOR NONPRIMITIVE DATA STRUCTURES

A brief discussion of the importance of structure in problem solving was given in Sec. 0-1. The often confused distinction between a data structure and a storage structure was also mentioned. Chapter 1 was concerned with the description of primitive data structures such as integers, real numbers, characters, and pointers and their corresponding storage representations. In Chap. 2, we saw how characters can be combined under concatenation to form a string—a data structure basic to most programming applications. We now proceed to extend our discussion to more complex data structures.

Nonprimitive data structures can be classified as *batches*, *arrays*, and *lists*. A batch is an unordered set of objects which can be of fixed or variable size. The size of a structure here is defined to be its number of data items. Batches are frequently used in the solution of data-processing problems. Batches will be discussed in Chap. 7. An array is an ordered set which consists of a fixed number of objects. No deletion or addition operations are performed on arrays. At best, elements can be changed to a value which represents an element to be ignored. The setting of an element in an array to zero to delete it is an example. A list, on the other hand, is an ordered set consisting of a variable number of elements to which additions and deletions can be made.

A list which displays the relationship of adjacency between elements is said to be *linear*. Any other list is said to be *nonlinear*. In the remainder of this chapter we are concerned with linear lists.

3-2   OPERATIONS IN NONPRIMITIVE DATA STRUCTURES

Operations performed on lists include those which are performed on arrays. However, there is one important difference in that the size of a list may be changed by updating. Indeed, updating may add or delete elements, as well as change existing elements. The addition and deletion of elements in a list is specified by position. For example, we may want to delete the ith element of a list or add a new element before or after the ith existing element. Frequently, it may be required to add or delete an element whose position in a list is based on the values of the other elements in the list (as in sorting). It may be required to add or delete a given element to or from a list, respectively. Such an element may precede or follow an element having a specified value or satisfying a particular relationship.

There are other important operations besides insertion and deletion that are commonly performed on lists. Each element in a list is composed of one or more *fields*. A field can be considered to be the smallest piece of information that can be referenced in a programming language. A number of these operations include the following:

1   Combine two or more lists to form another list.
2   Split a list into a number of other lists.
3   Copy a list.
4   Determine the number of elements in a list.

5   Sort the elements of a list into ascending or descending order, depending on certain values of one or more fields within an element.

6   Search a list for an element which contains a field having a certain value.

These operations will be discussed for various structures throughout the text.

3-3   SEQUENTIAL STORAGE STRUCTURES

In discussing sequential storage structures, we will be primarily concerned with the main memory of the conventional digital computer. Main memory is organized into an ordered sequence of words. As was pointed out in Chap. 1, each word contains from 8 to 64 bits and its contents can be referenced by using an address. For efficiency reasons, it is desirable to arrange data in a manner in which a particular element of the data can be referenced by computing its address rather than searching for it.

In Chap. 1 we discussed two possible ways that could be used to obtain an address of an element. The first method of obtaining an address was by using the description of the data being sought. This type of address is known as a computed address. Such a method of obtaining an address is used very extensively in many programming languages to compute the address of an element of an array and in the acquisition of the next instruction to be executed in the object program. The second method of obtaining an address was to store it somewhere in the memory of the computer. This type of address is referred to as a link or pointer address. In FORTRAN the addresses of the actual arguments of a subroutine are stored in the computer memory. The return address which is used by a subroutine to return to the calling program is also stored, and not computed. Certain structures require a combination of computed and link addresses.

In this chapter storage structures based on the computed-address principle will be discussed. The next chapter deals with storage structures based on the link-address technique. In discussing files in Chap. 7, we will be concerned primarily with storage structures on disk and magnetic-tape storage devices.

There are many data structures which can be represented so as to permit the referencing of any element by knowing its position in the structure. The selector associated with such a structure is said to possess an *addressing function*. An *addressing function* for a data structure consisting of n elements is a function which maps the ith element of the data structure onto an integer between one and n. In the case of a vector, the addressing function f maps the ith element onto the integer i, that is,

$$f(i) = i$$

which is a *linear addressing function*. We are particularly interested in data structures having linear addressing functions that are computationally simple. Addressing functions are discussed further in a later section of this chapter. A very important class of data structures which has a linear addressing function is discussed in Chap. 5. Another associated class of functions, known as *hashing* functions, is discussed in detail in Chap. 6, and to a lesser extent in Sec. 4-3.2.

We now proceed to the next section, which deals with the description, representation, and manipulation of the most trivial nonprimitive data structure—a complex number.

3-4 SIMPLE PROGRAMMER-DEFINED DATA STRUCTURES

A detailed discussion of certain primitive data structures such as the integer, real number, and the character was given in Chap. 1. A number of possible representations of these primitive structures in the main memory of a typical digital computer (i.e., possible storage structures) were also described. We will now turn to the representation in storage of more complex data structures. Actually, a complex (nonprimitive) data structure can be considered to consist of a structured set of primitive data structures. For example, a vector may consist of an ordered set of integers.

Recall that we have called integers, real numbers, and character elements primitive because the instruction repertoire of a computer has instructions which will manipulate these primitive structures. We can perform the common arithmetic operations on numbers. A word which contains a number of characters can be modified by using a number of machine language instructions.

Let us concern ourselves with a nonprimitive, yet very simple data structure—a complex number. A complex number is not considered to be a primitive since very few computers, if any, have machine-language instructions which add, subtract, multiply, and divide complex numbers. Many higher-level languages, however, such as PL/I and FORTRAN, permit the handling of complex numbers. Before commenting on the programming aspects of complex arithmetic in such languages, the definitions of the four complex operations are given.

Let $U = x + yi$ and $V = m + ni$ be two complex numbers where $i = \sqrt{-1}$ and x, y, m, and n denote real numbers. Then the complex arithmetic operations which can be performed on these numbers are defined as follows:

$$U \oplus V = (x + m) + (y + n)i$$

$$U \ominus V = (x - m) + (y - n)i$$

$$U \circledast V = (x*m - y*n) + (x*n + y*m)i$$

$$U \oslash V = (x*m + y*n)/(m*n + n*n) + (y*m - x*n)/(m*m + n*n)i$$

where the operators $\oplus$, $\ominus$, $\circledast$, and $\oslash$ denote complex addition, subtraction, multiplication, and division, respectively. From this it is clear that complex numbers can be used in complex arithmetic operations using the ordinary arithmetic operators. Note, however, that the multiplication of two complex numbers, for example, consists of a sequence of many (six) machine-language instructions, while in the case of real numbers, it consists of only one such instruction. The same applies for the remaining arithmetic operators. Also, a complex number is considered to consist of an ordered pair of real numbers. Each number in this ordered pair is treated differently.

A complex variable Z in PL/I is created by using a declaration statement such as

    DECLARE Z COMPLEX;

and the assignment of $Z = 1.5 + 3.2i$ can be accomplished by the statement

    Z = 1.5 + 3.2I;

The real and imaginary parts of any complex number can be individually referenced by using the built-in functions **REAL** and **IMAG**, respectively. For example, the real part of **Z** can be denoted by **REAL(Z)** and its imaginary part by **IMAG(Z)**. So **REAL** and **IMAG** act as selectors for the two parts of a complex number.

The storage structure for a single-precision complex number consists of an allocation of two consecutive words in memory, the first containing the value of the real part of the number, and the second the imaginary part. The statement

    A = B * C

will generate a different machine-language code, depending on the type of the variables **A**, **B**, and **C**. If **A**, **B**, and **C** are real numbers, one set of instructions is produced, while if they represent complex numbers, a much different set of instructions results.

The trend in certain modern programming languages is to make available to the programmer a number of primitive operators and data structures. The programmer then uses these primitives to define additional more powerful operators and data structures. Among the languages which possess this facility are ALGOL 68 and MAD-1.

PL/I does not permit the programmer to define additional operations in terms of primitive operators, but it does permit the definition of data structures in terms of primitive data structures. PL/I contains certain basic data structures such as strings, integers, real numbers, arrays, and nonhomogeneous data aggregates called structures. Certain aspects of programmer-defined data structures will be discussed throughout the book and in Sec. 3-6.2 of this chapter. In the remaining pages of this section, we are going to simulate complex arithmetic by using PL/I structures. Such structures can be extended to an array of structures.

The declaration statement

    DECLARE 01   Z,
             02 REAL FLOAT BINARY,
             02 IMAG FLOAT BINARY;

creates a structure which consists of the two real variables **REAL** and **IMAG**. Now the structure **Z** can be interpreted as a complex number where the variables **REAL** and **IMAG** represent the real and imaginary parts of a complex number, respectively. For example, **Z** can be set to a value of **1.5 + 3.2i** by the following sequence of assignment statements:

    REAL = 1.5; IMAG = 3.2;

Suppose that we declare two additional complex numbers called **X** and **Y** by executing the statement

    DECLARE 01   X,
             02 REAL FLOAT BINARY,
             02 IMAG FLOAT BINARY,
         01 Y,
             02 REAL FLOAT BINARY,
             02 IMAG FLOAT BINARY;

Now assume that it is required to refer to the variable REAL in structure X. How can this be accomplished? If we simply refer to REAL, there is an ambiguity since REAL is an element of the three structures X, Y, and Z. In order to make the reference unambiguous or unique, the term X.REAL is used where X is used to qualify that REAL of structure X is required. The period is used to separate the qualifier from the variable being qualified. This name-qualification property avoids the necessity of having to create variable names for essentially the same class of items, each item of which may be associated with a different but similar structure.

It is an interesting exercise to formulate a procedure for simulating the addition of two complex numbers. Let us assume that the procedure is to have three structure variables, as previously described, called A, B, and C. The following procedure simulates the desired addition:

```
CADD:  PROCEDURE (A,B,C);
          DECLARE 01  A,
                       02 R FLOAT BINARY,
                       02 I FLOAT BINARY,
                  01  B,
                       02 R FLOAT BINARY,
                       02 I FLOAT BINARY,
                  01  C,
                       02 R FLOAT BINARY,
                       02 I FLOAT BINARY;
          C.R = A.R + B.R;
          C.I = A.I + B.I;
       END CADD:
```

The mainline statement

```
CALL CADD(X,Y,Z);
```

invokes the procedure and the desired result is placed in the REAL and IMAG parts of the structure Z. Similar procedures can be written to simulate the other complex operations.

The structures described in this example each have two variables which are of the same type. This is not always the case. As an example, the following statement creates a simplified structure for an employee.

```
DECLARE 01  EMPLOYEE,
            02  NAME CHARACTER(20),
            02  ADDRESS CHARACTER (50),
            02  RATE_OF_PAY FIXED BINARY,
            02  DEPENDENTS FIXED DECIMAL;
```

This structure contains the four elementary variables NAME, ADDRESS, RATE_OF_PAY, and DEPENDENTS. Note that the first two variables denote strings, while the last two represent numbers of different types. In certain respects, a structure is like an array, except for one very important point—unlike an array, a structure does not require all its constituent parts to be of the same type.

PL/I also allows arrays of structures. For example, the declaration

```
DECLARE 01   EMPLOYEE(50),
             02 NAME CHARACTER(20),
             02 ADDRESS CHARACTER(50),
             02 RATE_OF_PAY FIXED BINARY,
             02 DEPENDENTS FIXED DECIMAL;
```

creates an array of fifty elements, each of which consists of four variables. The variable NAME in the ith element of this array can be referenced as NAME(I), or more completely, as EMPLOYEE(I).NAME or EMPLOYEE.NAME(I) in the case of a possible ambiguous reference.

The basic description of structures given here will be used and generalized in a number of applications throughout the book. We next proceed to discuss the representation of arrays within the memory of the computer.

3-5   STORAGE STRUCTURES FOR ARRAYS

The simplest data structure which makes use of computed addresses to locate its elements is the one-dimensional array we have called a vector. Normally, a number of (contiguous) memory locations are sequentially allocated to the vector. Assuming that each element requires one word of memory, an n element vector will occupy n consecutive words in memory. A vector size is fixed and, therefore, requires a fixed number of memory locations. In general, a vector A with a subscript lower bound of "one" can be represented pictorially as in Fig. 3-5.1, where L_0 is the address of the first word allocated to the first element of A, and c represents the number of words allocated to each element. The address of A_i is given by the following equations:

$$loc(A_i) = L_0 + c * (i - 1)$$

Let us consider the more general case of representing a vector A whose lower bound for its subscript is given by some variable b. The location of A_i is then given by

$$loc(A_i) = L_0 + c * (i - b)$$

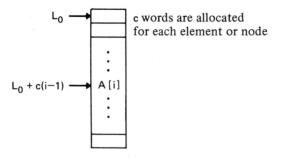

FIGURE 3-5.1.

In FORTRAN, memory allocation is performed at *compile time* where the size of the vector obtained in the DIMENSION statement is saved along with the starting address L_0. The size of a vector cannot be defined in FORTRAN during execution, as can be done in ALGOL and PL/I. A programming language which can read a value for n from a card at run time and declare a vector of n elements during the execution of the program is said to be able to allocate memory *dynamically*.

A multidimensional array can be represented by an equivalent one-dimensional array. For example in FORTRAN, a two-dimensional array consisting of two rows and four columns is stored sequentially by columns as

A[1,1] A[2,1] A[1,2] A[2,2] A[1,3] A[2,3] A[1,4] A[2,4]
↑
L_0

The address of element A[i,j] can be obtained by evaluating the expression

$$L_0 + (j - 1) * 2 + i - 1$$

For element A[2,3], the address is given as $L_0 + 5$. In general, for a two-dimensional array consisting of n rows and m columns (which is stored by column), the address of element A[i,j] is given by the linear expression

$$L_0 + (j - 1) * n + (i - 1)$$

In many programming languages, a two-dimensional array will be stored row by row (sometimes referred to as *row major order*) instead of column by column (*column major order*). An array (with subscripts having a lower bound of "one") consisting of n rows and m columns will be stored sequentially as

A[1,1] A[1,2] ... A[1,m] A[2,1] A[2,2] ... A[2,m] ... A[n,1] A[n,2] ... A[n,m]

The address of matrix element A[i,j] is given by the expression

$$L_0 + (i - 1) * m + (j - 1)$$

Now the representation of a two-dimensional array can be generalized to arbitrary lower and upper bounds on its subscripts. Assume that $b_1 \leq i \leq u_1$ and $b_2 \leq j \leq u_2$. The location of element A_{ij} is given by

$$loc(A_{ij}) = L_0 + (i - b_1) * (u_2 - b_2 + 1) + (j - b_2)$$

where each row of A contains $u_2 - b_2 + 1$ elements. For example, the location of A_{03}, when $b_1 = -2$, $b_2 = 2$, and $u_2 = 3$ is given as

$$loc(A_{03}) = L_0 + (0 - (-2)) * (3 - 2 + 1) + (3 - 2)$$
$$= L_0 + 5$$

A similar type of formula can be obtained for the representation of a two-dimensional array in column major order.

Consider the storing of a three-dimensional array B whose typical element is denoted by B[i,j,k] and whose subscript limits are given by $1 \leq i \leq 2$, $1 \leq j \leq 3$, and $1 \leq k \leq 4$. The row-major-order storage representation of this matrix will be:

B[1,1,1] B[1,1,2] B[1,1,3] B[1,1,4] B[1,2,1] B[1,2,2] B[1,2,3] B[1,2,4]
B[1,3,1] B[1,3,2] B[1,3,3] B[1,3,4] B[2,1,1] B[2,1,2] B[2,1,3] B[2,1,4]
B[2,2,1] B[2,2,2] B[2,2,3] B[2,2,4] B[2,3,1] B[2,3,2] B[2,3,3] B[2,3,4]

This array is pictorially represented in Fig. 3-5.2 as a cube consisting of two planes with each plane having 12 points. Ignoring the base address L_0, the addressing function for the element B[i,j,k] of the array is given as

$$f(i,j,k) = (i - 1) * 12 + (j - 1) * 4 + k - 1$$

which is linear in i, j, and k. The lower limits on subscripts i, j, and k above could have been all made zero and, for the same upper limits, the new addressing function would now be

$$f(i,j,k) = 20 * i + 5 * j + k$$

Consider the generalization of the above to an n-dimensional array whose typical element is denoted by $A[s_1, s_2, \ldots, s_n]$ and subscript limits given by $1 \le s_1 \le u_1$, $1 \le s_2 \le u_2$, ..., and $1 \le s_n \le u_n$. The storage representation of this array in row major order will be of the form

$A[1,1,\ldots,1,1]$ $A[1,1,\ldots,1,2]$ ... $A[1,1,\ldots,1,u_n]$
$A[1,1,\ldots,2,1]$ $A[1,1,\ldots,2,2]$ ... $A[1,1,\ldots,2,u_n]$
. . . .
$A[u_1,u_2,\ldots,u_{n-1},1]$ $A[u_1,u_2,\ldots,u_{n-1},2]$ ... $A[u_1,u_2,\ldots,u_{n-1},u_n]$

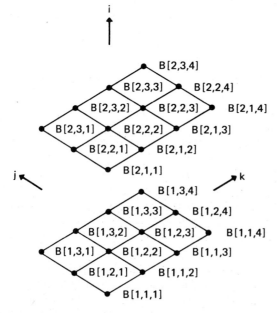

FIGURE 3-5.2 Pictorial representation of the three-dimensional array B[i, j, k] for $1 \le i \le 2$, $1 \le j \le 3$, and $1 \le k \le 4$.

The addressing function for the element $A[s_1, s_2, \ldots, s_n]$ is given as

$$f(s_1, s_2, \ldots, s_n) = u_2 u_3 \ldots u_n (s_1 - 1) + u_3 u_4 \ldots u_n (s_2 - 1) + \cdots +$$

$$u_n (s_{n-1} - 1) + (s_n - 1)$$

The function can be rewritten in the more convenient form

$$f(s_1, s_2, \ldots, s_n) = \sum_{1 \le i \le n} p_i (s_i - 1)$$

where $p_i = \prod_{i < r \le n} u_r$ and is a constant, $\sum$ and $\prod$ are symbols which represent mathematical summation and product, respectively. Again, the addressing function is linear. In general form, the row major addressing function is given by

$$f(s_1, s_2, \ldots, s_n) = \sum_{1 \le i \le n} p_i (s_i - b_i)$$

where

$$p_i = \prod_{i < j \le n} (u_j - b_j + 1) \qquad \text{for} \qquad b_i \le s_i \le u_i.$$

Of course, the same approach could have been used to obtain the addressing function of the n-dimensional array if it had been stored in column major order instead. Some compilers allocate storage in a sequentially decreasing fashion from the "high" end of memory. Here, we have assumed that memory is allocated in an increasing address sequence. Both methods are equivalent, with the exception that the value of the addressing function f is subtracted from the base location L_0.

Although many applications exist where arrays can be used to represent the structural relationships present in the data, there are an increasing number of applications where arrays are just not suitable. We shall briefly discuss such an unsuitable application. Consider the familiar symbol-manipulation problem of performing various operations on polynomials such as addition, subtraction, multiplication, division, differentiation, etc. Let us direct our attention, in particular, to the manipulation of polynomials in two variables. It may be required, for example, to write a program which subtracts polynomial $x^2 + 3xy + y^2 + y - x$ from polynomial $2x^2 + 5xy + y^2$ to give a result of $x^2 + 2xy - y + x$.

We are interested in finding a suitable representation for polynomials so that the operations mentioned above can be performed in a reasonably efficient manner. If we are to manipulate polynomials, it is clear that individual terms must be selected. In particular, we must distinguish between variables, coefficients, and exponents within each term.

It is possible to represent a polynomial as a character string and solve the problem by searching for individual terms and then searching for the various parts of a term. This approach tends to be complex, especially if one tries to program this approach in FORTRAN or PL/I.

A two-dimensional array can be used to represent a polynomial in two variables. In a programming language that permits subscripts to have zero values, the coefficient of the term $x^i y^j$ would be stored in the element identified by row i and column j of the array. If we restrict the size of an array to a maximum of 5 rows and 5 columns, then the powers of x and y in any term of the polynomial must not exceed a value of 4. The array representing polynomial $2x^2 + 5xy + y^2$ is given as:

```
0 0 1 0 0
0 5 0 0 0
2 0 0 0 0
0 0 0 0 0
0 0 0 0 0
```

and the array for $x^2 + 3xy + y^2 + y - x$ is

```
  0  1 1 0 0
 -1  3 0 0 0
  1  0 0 0 0
  0  0 0 0 0
  0  0 0 0 0
```

Once we have an algorithm for converting the input data to an array representing a polynomial and another for converting an array to an appropriate output form, then addition and subtraction of polynomials reduce to the adding and subtracting of corresponding elements in the two arrays, respectively.

A number of disadvantages are evident in using this representation. In the first case, the array tends to be sparsely filled with nonzero elements. Secondly, the exponents within each polynomial term are restricted in size. In the next chapter, a more efficient representation of such polynomials will be given. This can be accomplished by using a type of storage allocation other than sequential allocation.

In a number of applications involving matrices, there are instances where (because of certain properties) only a part of each matrix need be stored. An example of such an application will now be discussed. Suppose that the solution to the specialized system of equations which follows is sought:

$$A_{11}X_1 \qquad\qquad\qquad\qquad\qquad = b_1$$

$$A_{21}X_1 + A_{22}X_2 \qquad\qquad\qquad = b_2$$

$$A_{31}X_1 + A_{32}X_2 + A_{33}X_3 \qquad = b_3$$

$$\cdots\cdots\cdots\cdots\cdots\cdots\cdots\cdots\cdots\cdots\cdots\cdots$$

$$A_{n1}X_1 + A_{n2}X_2 + A_{n3}X_3 + \cdots + A_{nn}X_n = b_n$$

This problem can be solved by the usual methods of setting up a two-dimensional array of n^2 coefficient elements in storage. In so doing, however, nearly half of the matrix coefficients are not used. We could solve a larger system of equations if we could represent this "triangular" array by an equivalent one-dimensional array. In the given system, there are $[n(n + 1)]/2$ coefficient elements. Therefore, a vector representation must contain at least an equivalent number of elements.

The elements of the triangular array can be stored as a vector in the order

$$A_{11}A_{21}A_{22}A_{31}A_{32}A_{33}, \ldots, A_{nn}$$

i.e., row by row. It is easily verified that the addressing function for element A_{ij} is given by (assuming A_{11} is at location 1)

$$\frac{(i - 1) * i}{2} + j$$

For example, the addressing function yields $[(3 - 1)(3)]/2 + 1 = 4$ for the element A_{31}. The addressing function is not linear, but quadratic. It is still a simple addressing function. Symmetric arrays which have every $A_{ij} = A_{ji}$ can also be represented in the same manner.

Using this representation for a triangular matrix, we can formulate an algorithm which solves the system of equations.

Algorithm TRIANGULAR. Given a system of n equations whose coefficient matrix A is triangular and is stored in a vector R and the right-hand side vector B, it is required to obtain the solution vector X. SUM is a temporary variable.

1. [Compute and print X[1]] Set X[1] ← B[1] / R[1] and print X[1].
2. [Repetition with row index of triangular matrix]
   Repeat steps 3 and 4 for i = 2, 3, ..., n, and Exit.
3. [Initialize SUM and repeat using column index] Set SUM ← 0.
   Repeat for m = 1, ..., i − 1:
     set SUM ← SUM + R[i * (i − 1) / 2 + m] * X[m].
4. [Calculate and print X[i]] Set X[i] ← (B[i] − SUM) / R[i * (i + 1) / 2]
   and print X[i].

The algorithm is easy to follow. X_1 is first computed from the first equation and then substituted in the second to obtain X_2, and so on.

Another common application is one in which most (greater than 95 percent) of the elements of a large matrix are zeros. In such a case, only the nonzero elements need be stored along with their row and column subscripts. A representation of a matrix based on this idea will be given in Sec. 5-3.1.

3-6 STACKS

One of the most important linear structures of variable size is the stack. The first subsection introduces the concepts associated with this structure. Next, the associated insertion and deletion algorithms for a stack are given. The vector representation of a stack is described. The programming aspects of stacks in PL/I using **CONTROLLED** storage and the **ALLOCATE** and **FREE** statements are introduced.

3-6.1 Definitions and Concepts

In the most general form of a linear list, we are allowed to delete an element from and add an element to any position in the list. An important subclass of lists permits the addition or deletion of an element to occur only at one end. A linear list belonging to this subclass is called a *stack*. The addition operation is referred to as "push," and the deletion operation as "pop." The most and least accessible elements in a stack are known as the *top* and *bottom* of the stack, respectively. Since insertion and deletion operations are performed at the end of a stack, the elements can only be removed in the opposite order from that in which they were added to the stack. This phenomenon will be observed in conjunction with recursive functions in Sec. 3-7.1, and such a linear list is frequently referred to as a LIFO (Last-In, First-Out) list.

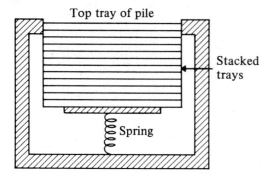

FIGURE 3-6.1   A cafeteria-tray holder.

A common example of a stack phenomenon, which permits the selection of only its end element, is a pile of trays in a cafeteria. These are supported by some kind of spring action in such a manner that a person desiring a tray finds that only one is available to him at the surface of the tray counter. The removal of the top tray causes the load on the spring to be lighter, and the next tray to appear at the surface of the counter. A tray which is placed on the pile causes the entire pile to be pushed down and that tray to appear above the tray counter. Such an arrangement of trays is shown in Fig. 3-6.1.

Another familiar example of a stack is a railway system for shunting cars, as shown in Fig. 3-6.2. In this system, the last railway car to be placed on the stack is the first to leave. Using the insertion and deletion operations repeatedly permits the cars to be arranged on the output railway line in various orders.

The update operation associated with a stack may be restricted to the examination of the top element of a stack with a view to altering (not inserting or deleting) it. This operation is sometimes extended to other elements of the structure (in addition to the top element of a stack).

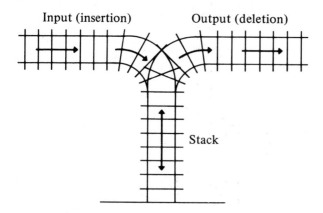

FIGURE 3-6.2   A railway shunting system representation of a stack.

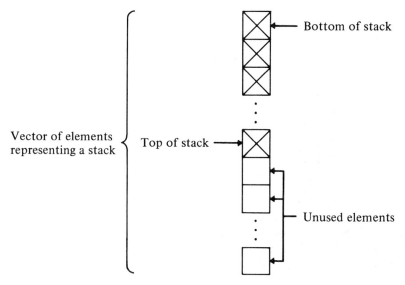

FIGURE 3-6.3 Representation of a stack by a vector.

3-6.2 Operations On Stacks

Initially, the operations on a stack are simulated by using a vector consisting of some large number of elements which should be sufficient in number to handle all possible insertions likely to be made to the stack. A representation of such an allocation scheme is given in Fig. 3-6.3.

A pointer TOP keeps track of the top element in the stack. Initially, when the stack is empty, TOP has a value of zero and when the stack contains a single element, TOP has a value of "one," and so on. Each time a new element is inserted in the stack, the pointer is incremented by "one" before the element is placed on the stack. The pointer is decremented by "one" each time a deletion is made from the stack.

An alternate, and for our purposes, a more suitable representation of a stack is given in Fig. 3-6.4. The rightmost occupied element of the stack represents its top element. The leftmost element of the stack represents its bottom element.

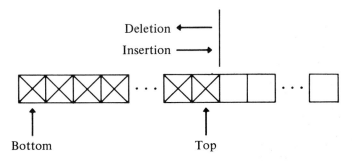

FIGURE 3-6.4 Alternate representation of a stack.

The algorithm for inserting an element in a stack follows.

Algorithm PUSH. Given a vector S (consisting of n elements) representing a sequentially allocated stack, and a pointer TOP denoting the top element in the stack, it is required to insert an element X in the stack.

1. [Overflow?] If TOP $\geq$ n, then print overflow message, and Exit.
2. [Increment TOP] Set TOP $\leftarrow$ TOP $+ 1$.
3. [Insert element] Set S[TOP] $\leftarrow$ X, and Exit.

The first step of this algorithm checks for an overflow condition. If such a condition exists, then the insertion cannot be performed and an appropriate error message results.

The algorithm for deleting an element from a stack is given as follows.

Algorithm POP. Given a vector S consisting of n elements representing a sequentially allocated stack, and a pointer TOP denoting the top element of the stack, it is required to store the top element in the stack in the variable POP.

1. [Underflow?] If TOP $\leq$ 0, then print underflow message, and Exit.
2. [Unstack element] Set POP $\leftarrow$ S[TOP].
3. [Decrement pointer] Set TOP $\leftarrow$ TOP $- 1$, and Exit.

An underflow condition is checked for in the first step of the algorithm. If there is an underflow, then some appropriate action should take place. In many applications involving stacks, an underflow may occur repeatedly and is checked for as elements are inserted on and deleted from the stack.

Another algorithm commonly used is one to obtain the value of the ith element from the top of a stack without deleting it.

Algorithm PEEP. Given a vector S consisting of n elements representing a sequentially allocated stack, and pointer TOP denoting the top element of the stack, it is required to obtain the ith element of the stack without deleting it.

1. [Underflow?] If TOP $- i + 1 \leq$ 0, then print underflow message, and Exit.
2. [Obtain ith element of stack] Set PEEP $\leftarrow$ S[TOP $- i + 1$], and Exit.

Note that the first step of the algorithm checks for a possible underflow due to some improper value of i.

A fourth algorithm which changes the contents of the ith element from the top of a stack is also useful.

Algorithm CHANGE. Given a vector S consisting of n elements representing a sequentially allocated stack, and a pointer TOP denoting the top element of the stack, it is required to change the value of the ith element of the stack to that contained in X.

1. [Underflow?] If TOP $- i + 1 \leq$ 0, then print underflow message, and Exit.
2. [Change ith element of stack] Set S[TOP $- i + 1$] $\leftarrow$ X, and Exit.

Let us now consider a simple example which involves the use of a stack. The set

$$L = \{wcw^R | w \in \{a,b\}*\}$$

(where w^R is the reverse of w) defines a language which contains an infinite set of strings. For example, if w = ab, then w^R = ba. A grammar which generates the above language is

$$G = (V_N, V_T, S, P)$$

where

$$V_N = \{S\}$$
$$V_T = \{a,b,c\}$$
$$P = \{S \rightarrow aSa, S \rightarrow bSb, S \rightarrow c\}$$

Some of the strings generated by the grammar are c,aca,bcb,abcba,bacab,abbcbba, abacaba,aabcbaa, etc. It is required to formulate an algorithm which, given an input string on the alphabet {a,b,c}, will determine whether or not this string is in the language L. This algorithm requires a stack in order to accomplish the task. We assume that the input string is padded on the right end with a blank (denoted by ∅). For example, the string aabcbaa is given as aabcbaa∅.

Algorithm RECOGNIZE. Given an input string named STRING on the alphabet {a,b,c} which contains a blank in its rightmost character position and a function NEXTCHAR which returns the next symbol in STRING, it is required to determine whether or not the contents of STRING belong to the above language. The vector S represents the stack and TOP is a pointer to the top element of the stack.

1. [Initialize stack] Set TOP ← 1 and S[TOP] ← 'c'. (A symbol 'c' is placed on the stack.)
2. [Get and stack symbols until 'c' or blank is encountered]
   Set NEXT ← NEXTCHAR(STRING).
   Repeat while NEXT ≠ 'c':
       if NEXT = ' '
       then print 'invalid string', and Exit;
       otherwise, call PUSH(S,TOP,NEXT) and set NEXT ← NEXTCHAR(STRING).
3. [Scan characters following 'c'; compare them to characters on stack]
   Repeat while S[TOP] ≠ 'c':
       set NEXT ← NEXTCHAR(STRING) and X ← POP(S,TOP),
       if NEXT ≠ X, then print 'invalid string', and Exit.
4. [Is next symbol a blank?]
   If NEXT = ' '
   then print 'valid string';
   otherwise, print 'invalid string'.
   Exit.

The algorithm operates in the following way. Initially, the symbol 'c' is placed on the stack. Until a 'c' is encountered in the input string, all symbols are placed on the stack. When 'c' is encountered in the input, a transfer to step 3 occurs. At this point, the remaining input symbols are compared with the stack by removing an 'a' from the top of the stack each time the input symbol is 'a', and a 'b' each time the input symbol is a 'b'. Should the top element of the stack not match the input symbol, the algorithm terminates and no further processing of the input string is performed. If all symbols match the inputs, the symbol 'c' at the bottom of the stack will become the top element of the stack. All symbols can be removed from the stack only for the case where the string read in after the symbol 'c' is the reverse of the input string processed before the 'c'.

The tracing of the contents of the stack for a number of input strings is given in Table 3-6.1.

In the section thus far we have illustrated the operations on a stack by using a vector representation. Now we are going to examine an alternative method of stack representation.

Table 3-6.1   Trace of contents of stack for Algorithm **RECOGNIZE**.

Input String	Character Scanned	Contents of Stack (top element of stack is the rightmost character)
abcba̸	none	c
	a	ca
	b	cab
	c	cab
	b	ca
	a	c
	̸	c
	valid string	
aabcaab̸	none	c
	a	ca
	a	caa
	b	caab
	c	caab
	a	caa
invalid string since a ≠ b		
aabcbaaa̸	none	c
	a	ca
	a	caa
	b	caab
	c	⟍ caab
	b	caa
	a	ca
	a	c
	a	c
invalid string since c is top element of stack and **NEXT** ≠ ' '.		

In some programming languages, such as PL/I and ALGOL W, we are allowed explicit control (i.e., control through instructions) of when and how much storage is to be allocated for certain variables in the program. Storage which can be controlled in this manner is called **CONTROLLED** storage in PL/I. Whenever additional storage is required for a new copy of some **CONTROLLED** variable or set of variables, this storage can be obtained by using an **ALLOCATE** statement. When the storage for the latest copy of a variable is no longer needed, it can be released by the execution of a **FREE** statement. Let us consider an example which illustrates how these programming constructs work.

Suppose we declare in a PL/I program a variable named **IDENTIFICATION** which consist of two subentities, a student's name and a student's ID number. If it is desired that the storage allocation for **IDENTIFICATION** be under direct programmer control, the following declaration should be used:

```
DECLARE 1  IDENTIFICATION CONTROLLED,
         2   NAME CHARACTER(30),
         2   IDNO FIXED DECIMAL(6);
```

To obtain storage for a new copy of **IDENTIFICATION**, we use the instruction

```
ALLOCATE IDENTIFICATION;
```

Note that the **ALLOCATE** statement only provides storage and that the subentities **NAME** and **IDNO** do not have values assigned to them. Assignment of values can be achieved through the execution of assignment statements such as:

```
NAME = 'RICK BUNT';    ID = 673129;
```

Consider what happens if, following the above assignment statements, another allocate statement plus two more assignment statements are executed. For example, statements such as:

```
ALLOCATE IDENTIFICATION;
NAME = 'ROBT. KAVANAGH';    IDNO = 641785;
```

After the execution of these statements, any reference to **NAME** or **IDNO** would bring forward values assigned to the latest storage to be allocated (i.e., the value **'ROBT. KAVANAGH'** and 641785). Note that the storage for the identification of **'RICK BUNT'** is not lost; however, it is at this point inaccessible. To access this identification record requires that the latest storage for **IDENTIFICATION** be released. We achieve this through execution of the statement

```
FREE IDENTIFICATION;
```

Now a reference to **NAME** would have the value **'RICK BUNT'**. If a second **FREE IDENTIFICATION** statement is executed, then storage would not exist for **IDENTIFICATION**, and any reference to **NAME** or **IDNO** would result in an error.

It should be evident that the allocating and freeing of **CONTROLLED** storage is performed in a "last-in, first-out" manner. Elements are inserted and deleted from a stack in this same manner and, consequently, it is easy to effect the operations of a stack using the **ALLOCATE** and **FREE** instructions. To **PUSH** an element onto a stack **S** (which should be declared to be of storage-type **CONTROLLED**) involves the following sequence of PL/I statements:

```
/* PUSH(S,X) — PUSH ELEMENT X ONTO STACK S */
ALLOCATE S;
S = X;
```

To **POP** an element involves the instruction:

```
/* POP(S) — REMOVE TOP ELEMENT OF S */
FREE S;
```

Note that there are some major differences between representing a stack with **CONTROLLED** storage as opposed to a vector representation. The notion of a stack as a possible multiple-element data structure is less apparent when using controlled allocation. The declaration of a "stack-like" structure involves the declaration of a prototype element which is used in allocating and freeing **CONTROLLED** storage for each instance of the declared variable. Not only can elements be added or deleted just from the top of the stack, but only the top element can be referenced in a **CONTROLLED** storage representation (i.e., the Algorithms **PEEP** and **CHANGE** are not applicable in the **CONTROLLED** storage case).

The location of the top element in a stack represented in **CONTROLLED** storage is handled implicitly by the PL/I compiler. Hence, as we saw earlier, the operations of **PUSH** and **POP** do not require knowledge of the index **TOP** when the implementation involves **CONTROLLED** storage. While in the remainder of this chapter we use the algorithm **PUSH** and **POP** as described for the vector representation, it should be remembered that a **CONTROLLED** storage representation provides the same insertion and deletion capabilities without the necessity of updating the index **TOP**. In Sec. 3-7.1, we give an example illustrating how a stack can be represented using **CONTROLLED** storage and the **ALLOCATE** and **FREE** instructions.

Quite often a program contains more than one stack. In such a situation, it can happen that one stack has encountered an overflow condition, while others are far from being full. Instead of imposing a maximum size on each stack, it would be preferable to allocate a common pool or maximum block of memory which all stacks can use.

The particular case of two stacks leads to a simple memory layout which permits them to exist together, as shown in Fig. 3-6.5.

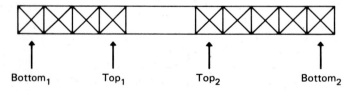

FIGURE 3-6.5   A sequential allocation scheme for two stacks.

The first stack grows to the right, while the second stack grows to the left. With this arrangement it is possible for one stack to occupy more than half of the memory allocated to both stacks. An overflow will occur only if the total size of the two stacks exceeds the allocated memory space.

It is not possible to have more than two stacks sharing a common block of memory and still preserve the overflow property of the above configuration and the property of each stack having a fixed bottom element. If the overflow property is to be maintained, then the fixed-bottom property must be sacrificed. The amount of bookkeeping involved in keeping track of the bottom and top elements of a number of sequentially allocated stacks sharing a common block of memory is very significant. At certain times, entire stacks must be moved in order to preserve the sequential allocation property. A more convenient storage-allocation scheme for such a situation will be discussed in the next chapter.

3-7 APPLICATIONS OF STACKS

This section contains three applications in which stacks are used. The first application deals with *recursion*. Recursion is an important facility in many programming languages such as ALGOL 60 and PL/I. There are many problems whose algorithmic description is best described in a recursive manner. Such instances are given throughout the text and occur frequently in Chap. 5. The second application of a stack is classical; it deals with the compilation of infix expressions into object code. This application of stacks is perhaps one of the earliest examples given. The section ends with a brief discussion of stack machines. Certain computers perform stack operations at the hardware or machine level, and these operations enable insertions to and deletions from a stack to be made very rapidly.

3-7.1 Recursion

Often in mathematics, a property or a set P can be specified by an inductive definition. An inductive definition of a set can be realized by using a given finite set of elements A and the following three clauses:

1 Basis clause – the elements of A are in P.
2 Inductive clause – the elements of B, all of which are constructed from elements in A, are in P.
3 Extremal clause – the elements constructed as in cases *1* and *2* are the only elements in P.

The inductive definition of the natural numbers which uses the operation of successor $S(x) = x + 1$ to produce new integers can be written as

1 0 is an integer (basis clause).
2 If x is an integer, so is the successor of x (inductive clause).
3 The natural numbers are the only elements constructed from cases *1* and *2*.

The natural numbers have been defined *recursively* through the process of *induction*.

Recursion is the name given to the technique of defining a set or a process in terms of itself.

The factorial function, whose domain is the natural numbers, can be recursively defined as

$$\text{FACTORIAL(N)} = \begin{cases} 1, \text{ if } N = 0 \\ N * \text{FACTORIAL(N} - 1), \text{ otherwise} \end{cases}$$

Here FACTORIAL(N) is defined in terms of FACTORIAL(N − 1), which in turn is defined in terms of FACTORIAL(N − 2), etc., until finally FACTORIAL(0) is reached, whose value is given as "one." A recursive definition of a set or process must contain an explicit definition for particular value(s) of the argument(s); otherwise, the definition would never converge. The basic idea is to define a function for all its argument values in a constructive manner by using induction. The value of a function for a particular argument value can be computed in a finite number of steps using the recursive definition, where at each step of recursion we get nearer to the solution.

An important facility available to the programmer is the *procedure* (function or subroutine). Procedures in programming languages are a convenience to the programmer since they enable him to express just once an algorithm which is required in many places in a program. Corresponding to a recursive step in the definition of a function, we have in certain programming languages, such as ALGOL, PL/I, and SNOBOL4 (but not FOR-TRAN), the opportunity to use a procedure which may contain a procedure call to any procedure (including itself). A procedure that contains a procedure call to itself, or a procedure call to a second procedure which eventually causes the first procedure to be called, is known as a *recursive* procedure.

There are two important conditions that must be satisfied by any recursive procedure. First, each time a procedure calls itself (either directly or indirectly), it must be "nearer," in some sense, to a solution. In the case of the factorial function, each time that the function calls itself, its argument is decremented by "one," so the argument of the function is getting smaller. Second, there must be a decision criterion for stopping the process or computation. In the case of the factorial function, the value of n must be zero.

There are essentially two types of recursion. The first type concerns *recursively defined functions* (or primitive recursive functions); an example of this kind is the *factorial* function. The second type of recursion is the *recursive use of a procedure* (nonprimitive recursive). A typical example of this kind of recursion is Ackermann's function, which is defined as

$$A(M,N) = \begin{cases} N + 1, \text{ if } M = 0 \\ A(M - 1, 1), \text{ if } N = 0 \\ A(M - 1, A(M, N - 1)), \text{ otherwise} \end{cases}$$

The recursion in Ackermann's function arises because the function A appears as an argument for a call of A; and this is typical of this type of recursion.

Many people believe that recursion is an unnecessary luxury in a programming language. This is based on the fact that any primitive recursive function, and therefore any function we would normally care to compute, can be solved iteratively.

An iterative process can be illustrated with the aid of the flowchart given in Fig.

3-7.1. There are four parts in the process; initialization, decision, computation, and update. The functions of the four parts are as follows:

1 *Initialization.* The parameters of the function and a decision parameter in this part are set to their initial values. The decision parameter is used to determine when to exit from the loop.

2 *Decision.* The decision parameter is to determine whether or not to remain in the loop.

3 *Computation.* The required computation is performed in this part.

4 *Update.* The decision parameter is updated and a transfer to the next iteration results.

It is possible to transform mechanically any primitive recursive function into an equivalent iterative process. However, this is not the case for nonprimitive recursive functions. Although there does exist an iterative solution for Ackermann's function, in general there are many problems of that form for which iterative solutions either do not exist or are not easily found. Certain inherently recursive processes can be solved in programming languages which do not permit recursion only by essentially setting up a recursive framework. We will have occasion to return to this topic later. Recursion is becoming increasingly important in symbol manipulation and nonnumeric applications.

Throughout the text we will encounter problems where recursion is unavoidable because of the recursive nature of the process or because of the recursive structure of the data which has to be processed. Even for cases where there is no inherent recursive structure, the recursive solution may be much simpler (though sometimes more time consuming) than its iterative counterpart.

There are special problems associated with a recursive procedure that do not exist for a nonrecursive procedure. A recursive procedure can be called from within or outside itself, and to ensure its proper functioning, it has to save in some order the return addresses so that a return to the proper location will result when return to a calling statement is made. The procedure must also save the formal parameters, local variables, etc., upon entry and restore these parameters and variables at completion.

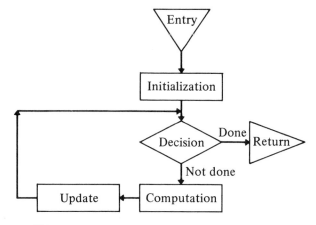

FIGURE 3-7.1.

The general algorithm model for any recursive procedure contains the following steps:

1. [Prologue]   Save the parameters, local variables, and return address.
2. [Body]   If the base criterion has been reached, then perform the final computation and go to step 3; otherwise, perform the partial computation and go to step 1 (initiate a recursive call).
3. [Epilogue]   Restore the most recently saved parameters, local variables, and return address. Go to this return address.

A flowchart model for this algorithm is given in Fig. 3-7.2. The model consists of a prologue, a body, and an epilogue. The purpose of the prologue is to save the formal parameters, local variables, and return address, and that of the epilogue is to restore them. Note that the parameters, local variables, and return address that are restored are those which were most recently saved, i.e., the last saved are the first to be restored (last-in, first-out). The body of the procedure contains a procedure call to itself; in fact, there may be more than one call to itself in certain procedures.

It is rather difficult to understand a recursive procedure from its flowchart, and the best we can hope for is an intuitive understanding of the procedure. The key box contained in the body of the procedure is the one which invokes a call to itself. The dotted-line exit from this box indicates that a call to itself is being initiated within the same procedure. Each time a procedure call to itself is executed, the prologue of the procedure saves all necessary information required for its proper functioning.

The procedure body contains two computation boxes—namely, the partial and final computation boxes. Frequently, the partial-computation box is combined with the procedure call box. (This is the case for the computation of the factorial function.) The final-computation box gives the explicit definition of the process for some value or values of the argument(s). The test box determines whether or not the argument value(s) is that for which an explicit definition of the process is given.

Associated with each call to (or entry into) a recursive procedure is a *level number*. The entry into the procedure due to the initial call from the main program is given the level number "one," as the main program is assumed to have level number "zero." Each subsequent entry into the procedure has an associated level number "one" higher than the level number of the procedure from which the call was made. Another characteristic of recursive procedures is the *depth* of recursion, which is the number of times the procedure is called recursively in the process of evaluating a given argument or arguments. Usually, this quantity is not obvious, except in the case of extremely simple recursive functions, such as FACTORIAL(N), for which the depth is N.

The last-in and first-out characteristic of a recursive procedure suggests that a stack is the most obvious data structure to use to implement steps 1 and 3 of this procedure. At each procedure call (or level of recursion), the stack is pushed to save the necessary values; upon exit from that level, the stack is "popped" to restore the saved values of the preceding (or calling) level.

The recursive mechanism is best described by an example. Consider an algorithm to calculate FACTORIAL(N) recursively which explicitly shows the recursive framework. (The recursive definition of FACTORIAL is given at the beginning of Sec. 3-7.1.)

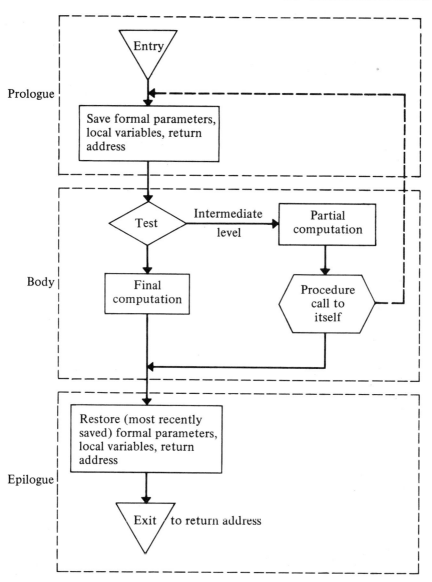

FIGURE 3-7.2.

Algorithm FACTORIAL.   Given an integer N, the algorithm evaluates N!. The stack A is used to store records of activation for each recursive call of FACTORIAL. An activation record contains two elements—the current value of N and the current return address RET_ADDR. TEMP_REC is a two-element temporary variable (consisting of PARM and ADDR) which is needed to simulate the proper transfer of control from one activation of the procedure FACTORIAL to the next. Whenever a TEMP_REC is pushed onto stack A, copies of **PARM** and **ADDR** are pushed onto **A** and assigned to **N** and **RET_ADDR**, respectively. **TOP** points to the top element of **A** and is initially zero. At the beginning the return address is set to the main calling address (that is, **ADDR ← main address**) and **PARM** is assumed to have the initial value of **N**.

1. [Save N and return address]   Call PUSH(A, TOP, TEMP_REC).
2. [Is the base criterion found?]
   If N = 0,
   then set FACTORIAL ←1 and go to step 4;
   otherwise, set PARM ← N − 1, ADDR ← step 3, and go to step 1.
3. [Calculate N!]   Set FACTORIAL ← N ∗ FACTORIAL (the factorial of N − 1).
4. [Restore previous N and return address]   Set TEMP_REC ← POP(A, TOP)
   (that is, PARM ← N, ADDR ← RET_ADDR, then pop stack) and go to ADDR.

Steps 1 and 4 are the prologue and epilogue of this algorithm, respectively. Steps 2 and 3 make up the body; the test and final computation are in step 2. Step 3 contains the partial computations and the recursive call. A trace of Algorithm **FACTORIAL** with N = 2 is given in Fig. 3-7.3.

A recursive PL/I formulation of the factorial function together with a main procedure to test the function is given in Fig. 3-7.4. Note that all variables used in the program are given the characteristics binary and fixed with precision of (31, 0). This was necessary for proper execution of the procedure. Since the identifier **FACTORIAL** defaults to float decimal, the **RETURNS** attribute must be used in both a declaration of the function in the invoking procedure and in the **PROCEDURE** statement. This procedure, as well as all procedures which reactivate themselves, must be declared to have the **RECURSIVE** attribute.

Let us now consider a more complex recursion example. A well-known algorithm for finding the greatest common divisor of two integers is Euclid's algorithm. The greatest common divisor function is defined by the following:

$$GCD(m, n) = \begin{cases} GCD(n, m), & \text{if } n > m \\ m, & \text{if } n = 0 \\ GCD(n, MOD(m, n)), & \text{otherwise} \end{cases}$$

Here, MOD(m, n) is m modulo n—the remainder on dividing m by n. The first part of the definition interchanges the order of the arguments if n > m. If the second argument is zero, then the greatest common divisor is equal to the first argument. (This defines the base values of the function.) Finally, the GCD is defined in terms of itself. Note that the process must terminate since MOD(m, n) will decrease to a value of zero in a finite number of steps. As an example, the GCD(20, 6) is obtained from the following computation:

$$20 = 6 * 3 + 2$$

By the euclidean algorithm, the GCD(20, 6) is the same as the GCD(6, 2). Therefore,

$$6 = 2 * 3 + 0$$

and the GCD(6, 2) is the same as the GCD(2, 0), which is 2. If we were required to find the GCD(6, 20), this could be solved by finding a solution to the GCD(20, 6) instead.

Level Number	Description	Stack 'A' Contents

| Enter level 1 (main call) | Step 1: PUSH(A,0,(2,main address)) Step 2: N ≠ 0 PARM ← 1, ADDR ← Step 3 | 2 / Main address — TOP |

Enter
level 1
(main call)

Step 1: PUSH(A,0,(2,main address))

Step 2: N ≠ 0
PARM ← 1, ADDR ← Step 3

2		
Main address		

↑
TOP

Enter
level 2
(first recursive
call)

Step 1: PUSH(A,1,(1,Step 3))

Step 2: N ≠ 0
PARM ← 0, ADDR ← Step 3

2	1	
Main address	Step 3	

↑
TOP

Enter
level 3
(second recursive
call)

Step 1: PUSH(A,2,(0,Step 3))

Step 2: N = 0
FACTORIAL ← 1

2	1	0
Main address	Step 3	Step 3

↑
TOP

Step 4: POP(A,3),
go to Step 3

2	1	
Main address	Step 3	

↑
TOP

Return to
level 2

Step 3: FACTORIAL ← 1 * 1

Step 4: POP(A,2),
go to Step 3

2		
Main address		

↑
TOP

Return to
level 1

Step 3: FACTORIAL ← 2 * 1

Step 4: POP(A,1),
go to main address

↑
TOP

FIGURE 3-7.3.

```
RUNFACT:
    PROCEDURE OPTICNS(MAIN);
    /* TEST THE RECURSIVE FACTORIAL FUNCTION */
    DECLARE
        FACTORIAL RETURNS(BINARY FIXED(31)),
        (I,K) BINARY FIXED(31);
    DO I = 3 TO 7 BY 2;
        PUT SKIP(2) EDIT('FACTORIAL(',I,') IS ',FACTORIAL(I))
            (A(10),F(1),A(5),F(5));
    END;

FACTORIAL:
    PROCEDURE (N) RECURSIVE RETURNS(BINARY FIXED(31));
    DECLARE
        N BINARY FIXED(31);
    IF N = 0
    THEN RETURN(1);
    ELSE RETURN(N * FACTORIAL(N - 1));
END FACTORIAL;

END RUNFACT;


FACTORIAL(3) IS      6

FACTORIAL(5) IS    120

FACTORIAL(7) IS   5040
```

FIGURE 3-7.4   Recursive formulation of the factorial function.

The PL/I program for the **GCD** function is given in Fig. 3-7.5. The same comments for the **FACTORIAL** procedure apply to the **GCD** procedure. Note also the use of the **ON ENDFILE(SYSIN)** statement which specifies the action required on exhaustion of the input card file. PL/I also has a **MOD** function which is a convenience in programming the **GCD** procedure.

Another complex recursive problem is that of the Tower of Hanoi, which has an historical basis in the ritual of the ancient Tower of Brahma. The problem is as follows:

Given N discs of decreasing size stacked on one needle and two empty needles, it is required to stack all the discs onto a second needle in decreasing order of size. The third needle may be used as temporary storage. The movement of the discs is restricted by the following rules:

1   Only one disc may be moved at a time.
2   A disc may be moved from any needle to any other.
3   At no time may a larger disc rest upon a smaller disc.

A pictorial representation of the problem is given in Fig. 3-7.6.

The solution to this problem is most clearly seen with the aid of induction. To move one disc, merely move it from needle A to needle C. To move two discs, move the first disc to needle B, move the second from needle A to needle C, then move the disc from needle B to needle C. In general, the solution of the problem of moving N discs from needle A to needle C has three steps:

1   Move $N - 1$ discs from A to B.
2   Move disc N from A to C.
3   Move $N - 1$ discs from B to C.

```
RUN_GCD:
      PROCEDURE OPTICNS(MAIN);
      /* TEST THE EUCLIDEAN ALGORITHM */
      DECLARE
            (I,J) BINARY FIXED(31),
            GCD RETURNS(BINARY FIXED(31));
      ON ENDFILE(SYSIN) GO TO END;
READ:  /* GET SCME VALUES TO TEST THE GCD FUNCTION */
      GET SKIP LIST(I,J);
      PUT SKIP(2) EDIT('THE GREATEST COMMON DIVISOR OF ',I,' AND ',J,
         ' IS ',GCD(I,J))(A(31),F(5),A(5),F(5),A(4),F(5));
      GO TO READ;

GCD:
         PROCEDURE (M,N) RECURSIVE RETURNS(BINARY FIXED(31));
         DECLARE
            (M,N) BINARY FIXED(31);
         IF N > M /* REVERSE THE CALL */
         THEN RETURN(GCD(N,M));
         IF N = 0 /* M IS THE GREATEST COMMON DIVISOR */
         THEN RETURN(M);
         RETURN(GCD(N,MOD(M,N))); /* EQUIVALENT VALUE */
      END GCD;

      END: END RUN_GCD;
```

```
THE GREATEST CCMMON DIVISOR OF    84 ANC   246 IS    6

THE GREATEST CCMMON DIVISOR OF     6 AND    20 IS    2

THE GREATEST COMMON DIVISOR OF   121 AND    33 IS   11
```

FIGURE 3-7.5 Recursive formulation of the GCD function.

A close examination of the first and third steps will reveal that these are recursive in nature; i.e., the first step is the implementation of the solution using needles A and B in place of needles A and C and $N-1$ discs in place of N, while the third step is the implementation of the solution using needles B and C in place of needles A and C and $N-1$ discs in place of N. Therefore, a recursive procedure can be formulated to solve the Tower of Hanoi problem. A PL/I recursive procedure which implements this solution, along with a mainline program to test it with three discs, is given in Fig. 3-7.7. The program should be self-explanatory; statements 10, 11, and 12 correspond to the three steps of the general solution described previously.

The labels H_ADDR1, H_ADDR2, and MAIN_ADDR are not necessary; they are included to enable the reader to more readily comprehend the correspondence between the

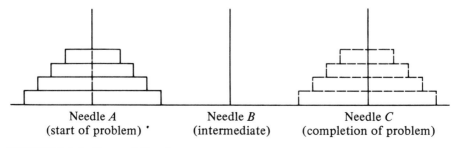

Needle A Needle B Needle C
(start of problem)   (intermediate)   (completion of problem)

FIGURE 3-7.6 Tower of Hanoi.

```
1          HAN2:   PROCEDURE OPTIONS(MAIN);
           /*  RECURSIVE PROCEDURE SOLUTION OF TOWERS OF HANOI PROBLEM         */

2              DECLARE N FIXED BINARY(31),
                       HANOI ENTRY (FIXED BINARY(31),CHARACTER(1),
                                    CHARACTER(1),CHARACTER(1));

               /*  INPUT NUMBER OF DISCS ON STARTING NEEDLE                     */
3              GET LIST(M);

               /*  INITIATE CALL TO HANOI                                      */
4              PUT EDIT('TOWERS OF HANOI PROBLEM WITH ',M,' DISCS')
                       (SKIP,A,F(2),A);
5              CALL HANOI(M,'A','B','C');

6              HANOI:   PROCEDURE(N,SN,IN,DN) RECURSIVE;

               /*  PROCEDURE 'HANOI' MOVES 'N' DISCS FROM NEEDLE 'SN' TO        */
               /*           NEEDLE 'DN' USING NEEDLE 'IN' AS AN INTERMEDIATE    */

7                  DECLARE N FIXED BINARY(31),
                           (SN,IN,DN) CHARACTER(1);
8                  IF N = 0
9                  THEN RETURN;
                   /*  MOVE N-1 DISCS FROM START TO INTERMEDIATE NEEDLE         */
10                 ELSE CALL HANOI(N-1,SN,DN,IN);

11             H_ADDR1:
                   /*  MOVE DISC N FROM START TO DESTINATION NEEDLE; MOVE N-1 */
                   /*       DISCS FROM INTERMEDIATE TO DESTINATION NEEDLE      */
                   PUT EDIT('MOVE DISC ',N,' FROM ',SN,' TO ',DN)
                           (SKIP,A,F(2),A,A(1),A,A(1));
12                 CALL HANCI(N-1,IN,SN,DN);
13             H_ADDR2:
                   END HANOI;

14         MAIN_ADDR:
           END HAN2;


TOWERS OF HANOI PROBLEM WITH  3 DISCS
   MOVE DISC  1 FROM A TO C
   MOVE DISC  2 FROM A TO B
   MOVE DISC  1 FROM C TO B
   MOVE DISC  3 FROM A TO C
   MOVE DISC  1 FROM B TO A
   MOVE DISC  2 FROM B TO C
   MOVE DISC  1 FROM A TO C
```

FIGURE 3-7.7   Recursive formulation of Tower of Hanoi problem.

recursive-procedure solution, as in Fig. 3-7.7, and the recursive-procedure simulation solution to be discussed now.

To show more clearly the recursive path of the solution to the Tower of Hanoi problem, an algorithm (and program) which simulates the recursive-procedure solution is described. This solution explicitly constructs the recursive framework using a stack mechanism.

Algorithm HANOI.   Given N_VALUE, the number of discs to be moved; SN_VALUE, the starting needle; IN_VALUE, the intermediate needle; and DN_VALUE, the destination needle, Algorithm HANOI performs the steps necessary to move N_VALUE discs from needle SN_VALUE to needle DN_VALUE, according to the rules of the Tower of Hanoi problem.

The stack ST is used to implement the recursive framework; each element of ST has

5 fields, N, SN, IN, DN, and RET_ADDR, which are used to store the values of N_VALUE SN_VALUE, IN_VALUE, DN_VALUE and the return address, respectively. TEMPREC is a five-element temporary variable consisting of N_VALUE, SN_VALUE, IN_VALUE, DN_VALUE, and ADDRESS, which is needed to simulate the proper transfer of control from one activation of HANOI to the next. TOP points to the top element of ST. The Algorithms PUSH and POP, previously described, are used to manipulate the stack ST. ADDRESS is initially set to the main algorithm calling address; TOP is initially set to zero.

1. [Save parameters and return address]
   Call PUSH(ST, TOP, TEMPREC).
   (The effect of the PUSH operation is as follows:
   TOP ← TOP + 1, N[TOP] ← N_VALUE, SN[TOP] ← SN_VALUE,
   IN[TOP] ← IN_VALUE, DN[TOP] ← DN_VALUE,
   RET_ADDR[TOP] ← ADDRESS)
2. [Test for stopping value of N; if not stopping value, move N − 1 discs from starting needle to intermediate needle]
   If N = 0,
   then go to RET_ADDR;
   otherwise, set N_VALUE ← N − 1, SN_VALUE ← SN, IN_VALUE ← DN,
   DN_VALUE ← IN, ADDRESS ← step 3, and go to step 1.
3. [Move Nth disc from start to destination needle; move N − 1 discs from intermediate needle to destination needle]
   Set TEMPREC ← POP(ST,TOP), print 'MOVE DISC' N 'FROM NEEDLE' SN
   'TO NEEDLE' DN, set N_VALUE ← N − 1, SN_VALUE ← IN, IN_VALUE ← SN,
   DN_VALUE ← DN, ADDRESS ← step 4, and go to step 1.
4. [Return to previous level]
   Set TEMPREC ← POP(ST,TOP) and go to RET_ADDR.

The algorithm compares N[TOP] to zero. If N[TOP] is not zero, a recursive call to move N[TOP] − 1 discs from SN[TOP] to IN[TOP] is simulated. Having completed that, the N[TOP] disc is moved from needle SN[TOP] to DN[TOP]. Finally, a recursive call to move N[TOP] − 1 discs from IN[TOP] to DN[TOP] is simulated. Assuming that Algorithm HANOI is called with N = 2, SN = 'A', IN = 'B', DN = 'C', and ADDRESS = MAIN, Fig. 3-7.8 is a trace of the execution of Algorithm HANOI(2, 'A', 'B', 'C'). Figure 3-7.9 is a PL/I program which implements Algorithm HANOI. This program uses the implicit stacking mechanism provided by the PL/I ALLOCATE − FREE feature rather than a stack simulation like the one used in the algorithm. The statements ALLOCATE ACTIVATION_ RECORD and FREE ACTIVATION_RECORD are used to effect the PUSH and POP operations of the algorithm.

The correspondence between the programs in Figs. 3-7.7 and 3-7.9 should be clear from the comments and statement labels. The variables N_VALUE, SN_VALUE, IN_VALUE, and DN_VALUE in Fig. 3-7.9 take the place of the passed parameters in the CALL HANOI statements in Fig. 3-7.7. The application of a stack in this section has been concerned with the storage of values for parameters and local variables in the evaluation of recursive functions. Stacks, however, can be used to control the allocation of storage in many block-structured languages (see Sec. 5-6).

Step Executed	Description		Stack Contents		
1	PUSH(ST,0,(2,A,B,C,Main))	N	2		
2	N ≠ 0, perform equivalent of call HANOI(1,A,C,B) with ADDRESS = Step 3	SN	A		
		IN	B		
		DN	C		
		RET_ ADDR	Main		
			↑ TOP		
1	PUSH(ST,1,(1,A,C,B,3))		2	1	
2	N ≠ 0, perform equivalent of call HANOI(0,A,B,C,) with ADDRESS = Step 3		A	A	
			B	C	
			C	B	
			Main	3	
				↑ TOP	
1	PUSH(ST,2,(0,A,B,C,3))		2	1	0
2	N = 0, go to step 3		A	A	A
			B	C	B
			C	B	C
			Main	3	3
					↑ TOP
3	POP(ST,3), move disk 1 from A to B, perform equivalent of call HANOI(0,C,A,B) with ADDRESS = Step 4		2	1	
			A	A	
			B	C	
			C	B	
			Main	3	
				↑ TOP	
1	PUSH(ST,2,(0,C,A,B,4))		2	1	0
2	N = 0, go to step 4		A	A	C
			B	C	A
			C	B	B
			Main	3	4
					↑ TOP

FIGURE 3-7.8.

Step Executed	Description	Stack Contents		
4	POP(ST,3), go to Step 3	2	1	
		A	A	
		B	C	
		C	B	
		Main	3	
			↑ TOP	
3	POP(ST,2), move disk 2 from A to C, perform equivalent of call HANOI(1,B,A,C) with ADDRESS = Step 4	2		
		A		
		B		
		C		
		Main		
		↑ TOP		
1 2	PUSH(ST,1,(1,B,A,C,4)) N ≠ 0, perform equivalent of call HANOI(1,B,C,A) with ADDRESS = Step 3	2	1	
		A	B	
		B	A	
		C	C	
		Main	4	
			↑ TOP	
1 2	PUSH(ST,2,(0,B,C,A,3)) N = 0, go to Step 3	2	1	0
		A	B	B
		B	A	C
		C	C	A
		Main	1	3
				↑ TOP
3	POP(ST,3), move disc 1 from B to C, perform equivalent of call HANOI(0,A,B,C) with ADDRESS = Step 4	2	1	
		A	B	
		B	A	
		C	C	
		Main	4	
			↑ TOP	

FIGURE 3-7.8 (Continued)

Step Executed	Description	Stack Contents

| 1 | PUSH(ST,2,(0,A,B,C,4)) | |
| 2 | N = 0, go to Step 4 | |

2	1	0
A	B	A
B	A	B
C	C	C
Main	4	4

↑
TOP

| 4 | POP(ST,3), go to Step 4 | |

2	1	
A	B	
B	A	
C	C	
Main	4	

↑
TOP

| 4 | POP(ST,2), go to main call | |

2		
A		
B		
C		
Main		

↑
TOP

FIGURE 3-7.8 (Continued)

Exercises for Sec. 3-7.1

1. The usual method used in evaluating a polynomial of the form

$$p_n(x) = a_0x^n + a_1x^{n-1} + a_2x^{n-2} + \cdots + a_{n-1}x + a_n$$

is by using the technique known as nesting or Horner's rule. This is an iterative method which can be described as follows:

$$b_0 = a_0$$

$$b_{i+1} = x \cdot b_i + a_{i+1}; i = 0, 1, \ldots, n - 1$$

from which one can obtain $b_n = p_n(x)$.

An alternate solution to the problem is to write

$$p_n(x) = x \cdot p_{n-1}(x) + a_n$$

where

$$p_{n-1}(x) = a_0 x^{n-1} + a_1 x^{n-2} + \cdots + a_{n-2} x + a_{n-1}$$

which is a recursive formulation of the problem. Write a recursive-function program to evaluate such a polynomial. Use as data

$$n = 3, \ a_0 = 1, \ a_1 = 3, \ a_2 = 3, \ a_3 = 1, \text{ and } x = 2$$

2. Consider the set of all valid, completely parenthesized, infix arithmetic expressions consisting of single-letter variable names, nonnegative integers, and the four operators $+$, $-$, $*$, and $/$. The following recursive definition gives all such valid expressions:

   1 Any single-letter variable (A $-$ Z) or a nonnegative integer is a valid infix expression.

   2 If α and β are valid infix expressions, then $(\alpha + \beta)$, $(\alpha - \beta)$, $(\alpha * \beta)$, and (α / β) are valid infix expressions.

   3 The only valid infix expressions are those defined by steps *1* and *2*.

   Write a recursive-function program that will have as input some string of symbols and which is to output "VALID EXPRESSION" if the input string is a valid infix expression and "INVALID EXPRESSION" otherwise. Write a main program to read the input data and invoke this function.

3. Write a recursive-function program to compute the square root of a number. Read in triples of numbers N, A, and E, where N is the number for which the square root is to be found, A is an approximation of the square root, and E is the allowable error in the result. Use as your function

$$\text{ROOT(N,A,E)} = \begin{cases} \text{A, if } |A^2 - N| < E \\ \text{ROOT}\left(N, \dfrac{A^2 + N}{2A}, E \right), \text{ otherwise} \end{cases}$$

   Use the following triples as test data:

2	1.0	.001
3	1.5	.001
8	2.5	.001
225	14.2	.001

4. Another common application for recursion is the problem of generating all possible permutations of a set of symbols. For the set consisting of symbols A, B, and C, there exists six permutations—namely, ABC, ACB, BAC, BCA, CBA, and CAB. The set of permutations of N symbols is generated by taking each symbol in turn and prefixing it to all the permutations which result from the remaining N -1 symbols. It is therefore possible to specify the permutations of a set of symbols in terms of permutations of a smaller set of symbols. Write a recursive-function program for generating all possible permutations of a set of symbols.

5. In many applications it is required to know the number of different partitions of a given integer N; that is, how many different ways can N be expressed as a sum of

```
HAN1:   PROCEDURE OPTIONS(MAIN);
/*   EXAMPLE 3.7.1                                                    */
/*   RECURSIVE PROCEDURE SIMULATION SOLUTION OF TOWER OF HANOI        */
/*        PROBLEM                                                     */

      DECLARE M FIXED BINARY(31),
              1 ACTIVATION_RECORD CONTROLLED,
                2 RET_ADDR LABEL,
                2 N FIXED BINARY(31),
                2 SN CHARACTER (1),
                2 IN CHARACTER (1),
                2 DN CHARACTER (1),

                N_VALUE FIXED BINARY(31),
                (SN_VALUE,IN_VALUE,DN_VALUE) CHARACTER (1),
                ADDRESS LABEL;

      /*   READ IN NUMBER OF DISCS ON NEEDLE                          */
      GET LIST(M);

      /*   INITIATE CALL TO HANOI - INITIALIZE CALL PARAMETERS        */
      /*        MOVE 'N_VALUE' DISCS FROM NEEDLE 'SN_VALUE' TO NEEDLE  */
      /*        'DN_VALUE' USING NEEDLE 'IN_VALUE' AS AN INTERMEDIATE  */

      PUT EDIT ('TOWERS OF HANOI PROBLEM WITH ',M,' DISCS')
               (SKIP,A,F(2),A);
      N_VALUE = M;
      SN_VALUE = 'A';
      IN_VALUE = 'B';
      DN_VALUE = 'C';
      ADDRESS = MAIN_ADDR;
      GO TO HANOI_CALL;

MAIN_ADDR:    STOP;

HANOI_CALL:
      ALLOCATE ACTIVATION_RECORD;
      N = N_VALUE;
      SN = SN_VALUE;
      IN = IN_VALUE;
      DN = DN_VALUE;
      RET_ADDR = ADDRESS;
      IF N = 0
      THEN GO TO RET_ADDR;
      ELSE DO;

          /*   MOVE N-1 DISCS FROM START NEEDLE TO INTERMEDIATE NEEDLE*/
          N_VALUE = N - 1;
          SN_VALUE = SN;
          IN_VALUE = DN;
          DN_VALUE = IN;
          ADDRESS = H_ADDR1;
          GO TO HANOI_CALL;
      END;
```

FIGURE 3-7.9   PL/I implementation of Algorithm HANOI.

integer summands. If we denote by Q_{MN} the number of ways in which an integer M can be expressed as a sum, each summand of which is no larger than N, then the number of partitions of N is given by Q_{NN}. The function Q_{MN} is defined recursively as

$$Q_{MN} = \begin{cases} 1, & \text{if } M = 1 \text{ and for all } N \\ 1, & \text{if } N = 1 \text{ and for all } M \\ Q_{MM}, & \text{if } M < N \\ 1 + Q_{M,M-1}, & \text{if } M = N \\ Q_{M,N-1} + Q_{M-N,N}, & \text{if } M > N \end{cases}$$

Write a recursive-function program and use values of N = 3, 4, 5, and 6 as data.

```
H_ADDR1:
    FREE ACTIVATION_RECORD;

    /*  MOVE DISC N FROM START TO DESTINATION NEEDLE           */
    /*      MOVE N-1 DISCS FROM INTERMEDIATE TO DESTINATION NEEDLE */
    PUT EDIT('MOVE DISK ',N,' FROM ',SN,' TO ',DN)
             (SKIP,A,F(2),A,A(1),A,A(1));
    N_VALUE = N - 1;
    SN_VALUE = IN;
    IN_VALUE = SN;
    DN_VALUE = DN;
    ADDRESS = H_ADDR2;
    GO TO HANOI_CALL;

H_ADDR2:
    FREE ACTIVATION_RECORD;
    GO TO RET_ADDR;

END HAN1;
```

```
TOWERS OF HANOI PROBLEM WITH  3 DISCS
MOVE DISK  1 FROM A TO C
MOVE DISK  2 FROM A TO B
MOVE DISK  1 FROM C TO B
MOVE DISK  3 FROM A TO C
MOVE DISK  1 FROM B TO A
MOVE DISK  2 FROM B TO C
MOVE DISK  1 FROM A TO C
```

FIGURE 3-7.9   (Continued)

3-7.2   Polish Expressions and Their Compilation

In this section we are primarily concerned with the mechanical evaluation or compilation of infix expressions. We shall find it to be more efficient to evaluate an infix logical expression by first converting it to a suffix expression and then evaluating the latter. This approach will eliminate the repeated scanning of an infix expression in order to obtain its value. We shall use examples of expressions found in scientific programming languages in this section, although the theory developed applies to any type of expression.

It was seen in Sec. 2-2 that a language consisting of the set of all valid infix expressions can be precisely described by a grammar. The same can be done for the corresponding set of all valid Polish expressions (suffix or prefix). When we convert a sentence in a language, say L_1, to a sentence in another language L_2 by some mapping, it is required that L_2 have many of the properties possessed by L_1. Properties such as "well-formed expression," associativity, and commutativity of operators in the conversion of expressions from one type to another must be preserved by the mapping.

Initially, a theorem which permits us to determine whether or not a Polish expression is well-formed (and consequently its corresponding infix counterpart) will be given. The translation of infix expressions to Polish notation is examined in detail and represents one of the classical applications of a stack. Finally, the generation of assembly-language instructions for Polish expressions is discussed at some length. The properties of the operators can be used in achieving some degree of code optimization (normally, a program consisting of fewer instructions than an unoptimized one).

3-7.2.1   Polish notation

In this subsection we introduce the notation for Polish expressions. This notation offers certain computational advantages over the traditional infix notation. Initially, an inductive definition of the set of valid suffix Polish expressions is given. A simple theorem which can be used to determine the validity of Polish expressions is then discussed. Also, the evaluation of Polish expressions is briefly introduced.

Consider the set of all valid, completely parenthesized arithmetic expressions consisting of single-letter variable names, nonnegative integers, and the four operators $+$, $-$, $*$, and $/$. The following recursive definition gives all such valid expressions:

1   Any single letter variable (a $-$ z) or a nonnegative integer is a valid infix expression.
2   If α and β are valid infix expressions, then $(\alpha + \beta)$, $(\alpha - \beta)$, $(\alpha * \beta)$, and (α / β) are valid infix expressions.
3   The only valid infix expressions are those defined by steps 1 and 2.

This is an inductive definition where expressions such as (a $+$ b), ((a $+$ b) $-$ 5), and (10 $+$ ((b $*$ c) $/$ d)) are considered valid (according to the definition), while expressions like a $+$ 5, (a $+$ b $*$ c), etc. are considered to be invalid.

In writing a valid expression, complete parenthesization must be used. Such a requirement is somewhat severe and, in order that the number of parentheses does not become excessively large, certain conventions have been developed. An obvious convention is one in which the outermost parentheses of an expression are dropped so that (p $+$ q) $*$ r can be taken to be a valid formula instead of ((p $+$ q) $*$ r), as required by the original definition.

One method of reducing the number of parentheses further is to prescribe an order of precedence for the connectives. Once this is done, further reductions can be made by requiring that for any two binary operators appearing in a formula having the same precedence, the left one is evaluated first. The same requirement can be stated by saying that the binary operators are left-associative. Such a convention is commonly used in arithmetic; for example, $4 + 6 \times 3 - 7$ stands for $(4 + (6 \times 3)) - 7$. If an evaluation of such an expression is to be done mechanically, it is important that the number of parentheses be reduced so that an excessive number of scannings of the expression is avoided.

Let us consider, initially, the mechanical evaluation of unparenthesized arithmetic expressions consisting of single-letter variables, nonnegative integers, and the four operators $+$, $-$, $*$, and $/$. The precedence of the operators $*$ and $/$ are considered to be equal and of higher value than that of $+$ and $-$. An example of such an unparenthesized arithmetic expression is

a $+$ b $*$ c $+$ d $*$ e

      1   2

  3

    4

According to our convention, the above expression stands for (a $+$ (b $*$ c)) $+$ (d $*$ e). For the evaluation of this expression, we must scan from left to right repeatedly. The numbers below the subexpressions indicate the steps of such an evaluation. This process of evaluation is inefficient because of the repeated scanning that must be done.

If there are parentheses in an expression, then the order of precedence is altered by the parentheses. For example, in (a + b) * c we first evaluate a + b and then (a + b) * c. In fact it is possible to write expressions which make the order of evaluation of subexpressions independent of the precedence of the operators. This is accomplished by parenthesizing subexpressions in such a way that, corresponding to each operator, there is a pair of parentheses. This pair encloses the operator and its operands. We now define the parenthetical level of an operator as the total number of pairs of parentheses that surround it. A pair of parentheses has the same parenthetical level as that of the operator to which it corresponds, i.e., of the operator which is immediately enclosed by this pair. Such an expression is called a *fully parenthesized expression*. For example, in the fully parenthesized expression

$$(a + ((b * c) * (d + e)))$$
$$1 \quad\; 3 \quad 2 \quad\; 3$$

the integers below the operators specify the parenthetical level of each operator. When evaluating such an expression, the subexpression containing the operator with the higher parenthetical level is evaluated first. In the case of more than one operator having the highest parenthetical level (as in the above example), we evaluate them one after the other from left to right. Once the subexpressions containing operators at the highest parenthetical level have been evaluated, the subexpressions containing the operators at the next highest level are evaluated in the same way. Thus in the above example, the subexpressions are evaluated in the following order:

$$(b * c), \; (d + e), \; ((b * c) * (d + e)), \; (a + ((b * c) * (d + e)))$$

As mentioned earlier, for a fully parenthesized expression no convention regarding the order of precedence of an operator is needed.

In the case when the order of precedence of the operators is prescribed and the expressions are partly parenthesized, or in the other case when the expressions are fully parenthesized, a repeated scanning from left to right is still needed in order to evaluate an expression. The reason is that the operators appear along with the operands inside the expression. The notation used so far is to write the operator between the operands, for example, a * b. Such a notation is called an *infix notation*. Repeated scanning is avoided if the infix expression is converted first to an equivalent parenthesis-free *suffix* or *prefix* expression in which the subexpressions have the form

	operand	operand	operator
or	operator	operand	operand

in place of an infix form where we have

	operand	operator	operand

This type of notation is known as Łukasiewiczian notation (due to the Polish logician Jan Łukasiewicz), or "reverse Polish" and "Polish" notation, respectively. For example, the expressions given in each row of Table 3-7.1 are equivalent.

Table 3-7.1

Infix	Suffix (Reverse Polish)	Prefix (Polish)
a	a	a
a + b	ab +	+ab
a + b + c	ab + c +	+ +abc
a + (b + c)	abc + +	+a +bc
a + b * c	abc* +	+a*bc
a * (b + c)	abc + *	*a +bc
a * b * c	ab*c*	**abc

Note that in both the suffix and prefix equivalents of an infix expression, the variables are in the same relative position. The expressions in suffix or prefix form are parenthesis free, and the operators are rearranged according to the rules of precedence for the operators.

A fully parenthesized infix expression can be directly translated to suffix notation by beginning with the conversion of the inner parenthesized subexpression and then proceeding towards the outside of the expression. In the case of the fully parenthesized expression

(a + ((b * c) * d))

    1   3   2

the innermost parenthesized subexpression of level 3 is

(b * c)

and is converted to bc*. This suffix subexpression becomes the first operand of the operator * at level 2. Therefore, the subexpression bc* * d of level 2 is converted to the suffix equivalent of bc*d*, and finally at level 1, the term a + bc*d* is converted to the final suffix form of abc*d* +.

Programmers, of course, do not program expressions in fully parenthesized form. Certain FORTRAN (and other) compilers initially convert partially parenthesized expressions to a fully parenthesized form before conversion to a suffix form is performed. (Suffix form seems to be most convenient for compilers.)

Let us consider the problem of mechanically converting a parenthesis-free expression (containing +, −, *, and /) into suffix form. As was mentioned previously, only the operators are rearranged in order to obtain the suffix Polish equivalent. Scanning left to right, the leftmost operator having the highest precedence will be the first operator to be encountered in the suffix string. The next-highest-precedence operator will be the second operator to be encountered in the expression. Note that for infix expressions, if we do not specify that a leftmost operator has precedence over other operators of equal precedence, then the suffix equivalent is not unique. For example, the expression a + b + c would be converted to ab +c + or abc + + if no mention was made that the leftmost operator + in the infix string has precedence over the remaining operator. From this it is clear that when we scan a suffix expression from left to right, we encounter the operators in the same order in which we would have evaluated them by following the precedence convention for operators in the infix expression. For example, the suffix equivalent of a + b * c, abc* +, where the operator * is encountered before + in a left-to-right scan, indicates that the multiplication is to be evaluated before addition.

In practice it is often necessary to evaluate expressions, i.e., to determine their value for a given set of values assigned to the variables appearing in the expressions. This can be done more easily by using a suffix representation of the expression, because scanning of the expression is required in only one direction, viz. from left to right, and only once, whereas for the infix expression the scanning has to be done several times and in both directions. For example, to evaluate the suffix expression abc* +, we scan this string from left to right until we encounter *. The two operands, viz. b and c, which appear immediately to the left of this operator are its operands, and the expression bc* is replaced by its value. Let us assume that this value is denoted by T_1. This reduces the original suffix string to aT_1 +. Continuing the scanning beyond T_1, the next operator encountered is + whose operands are a and T_1, and the evaluation results in a value which we will denote by T_2.

This method of evaluating suffix expressions can be summarized by the following four rules, which are repeatedly applied until all operators have been processed:

1 Find the leftmost operator in the expression.
2 Select the two operands immediately to the left of the operator found.
3 Perform the indicated operation.
4 Replace the operator and operands with the result.

As a further example, the suffix expression abc/d* + corresponding to the infix expression a + (b / c) * d is evaluated below for values of a = 5, b = 4, c = 2, and d = 2:

Suffix Form	*Current Operator*	*Current Operands*
abc/d* +	/	b, c
aT_1d* +	*	T_1, d
aT_2 +	+	a, T_2
T_3		

Note that in this example T_1 = 2, T_2 = 4, and T_3 = 9.

As previously mentioned, there are a number of compilers that convert infix arithmetic expressions into Polish notation. In such compilers invalid Polish expressions, and consequently their invalid infix-expression counterparts, must be detected in the compiling phase of translation. The remaining pages of this section will be concerned with the description of a method that can be used to detect such invalid expressions. We will restrict ourselves to suffix Polish expressions, although an analogous method can also be developed for prefix Polish expressions. Let us first describe by induction the set of valid suffix Polish expressions.

Suppose S is a set of symbols s_1, s_2, . . ., s_q (typically, variable names and literals) and the set o_1, o_2, . . ., o_m consists of operators for constructing expressions using elements of S. The *degree* of an operator is the number of operands which that operator has; e.g., the degree of the multiplication operator is two. A suffix expression is defined by the following:

1   A single symbol s_i is an expression.

2   If x_1, x_2, . . ., x_n are expressions and o_i is of degree n, then $x_1 x_2 \cdots x_n o_i$ is an expression.

3   The only valid expressions are those obtained by steps *1* and *2*.

To determine whether or not an expression is valid, we next associate a *rank* with each expression, which is determined as follows:

4   The rank of a symbol s_i is "one."

5   The rank of an operator o_j is 1 − n, where n is the degree of o_j.

6   The rank of an arbitrary sequence of symbols and operators is the sum of the ranks of the individual symbols and operators.

For example, let the sets of symbols and connectives consist of single-letter variables (a − z) and the four arithmetic operators, respectively. The rank function, which is denoted by r, is given as:

$$r(s_j) = 1, \text{ for } 1 \leq j \leq 26$$

$$r(+) = r(-) = -1, r(*) = r(/) = -1$$

The rank of the formula ab+cd−* is obtained from the computation

$$r(a) + r(b) + r(+) + r(c) + r(d) + r(-) + r(*) = 1$$

A theorem to follow is very important since it can be used to determine whether or not a given expression is valid. Before stating the theorem, some mention of the terminology required is in order. If $z = x \bigcirc y$ is a string, then x is a *head* of z. Finally, x is a proper head if y is not empty (y is not $\wedge$).

3-7.2.2   Conversion of infix expressions to Polish notation

We shall first develop an algorithm for translating unparenthesized infix expressions to suffix Polish. This algorithm will be subsequently modified to handle parenthesized expressions. Note that one can also have completely parenthesized infix expressions which do not require any rules of precedence except the usual rule for parentheses. Such expressions are inconvenient to use because of the large number of parentheses which are required.

The evaluation of an infix expression as well as a suffix Polish expression was discussed in the previous section. Recall that in an unparenthesized infix expression, the evaluation is performed in such a manner that the operator with the highest precedence is evaluated before the others. If more than one operator has the same precedence in the expression, then the leftmost operator (for left-associative operators) or rightmost operator (for right-associative operators such as exponentiation and negation) with that precedence is evaluated first. Of course, in such an evaluation process, we need to scan the expression repeatedly, thereby making the process inefficient. The same idea can be applied to partially parenthesized infix expressions. The subexpression that is evaluated first is located by scanning up to the first right parenthesis and moving left until a left parenthesis is detected. The subexpression can then be evaluated using the rule of precedence.

Theorem. A Polish suffix (prefix) formula is well formed if and only if the rank of the formula is "one" and the rank of any proper head of a Polish formula is greater than (less than) or equal to "one." ////

This theorem is very important in the compilation of infix expressions since it permits us to detect an invalid Polish expression (and, consequently, a corresponding invalid infix expression). Table 3-7.2 contains a number of valid and invalid expressions.

We shall next consider the mechanical conversion of infix expressions to Polish notation.

Let us now define in BNF the infix expression containing single-letter variables, natural number constants, and the four binary arithmetic operators $+$, $-$, $*$, and $/$:

$<$identifier$> ::= a|b|c \dots |z$
$<$digit$> ::= 0|1|2 \dots |9$
$<$digit string$> ::= <$digit string$> <$digit$> | <$digit$>$
$<$primary$> ::= <$identifier$> | <$digit string$> |(<$infix expression$>)$
$<$term$> ::= <$primary$> | <$term$> * <$primary$> | <$term$> / <$primary$>$
$<$infix expression$> ::= <$term$> | <$infix expression$> + <$term$> |$
$<$infix expression$> - <$term$>$

The above grammar inherently specifies that the operators $*$ and $/$ have equal precedence which is greater than the precedence of $+$ and $-$.

On the other hand, in a parenthesis-free suffix expression, the subexpressions have the form

$<$operand 1$> <$operand 2$> <$operator$>$

Table 3-7.2

Infix	Suffix Polish	Rank	Valid or Invalid
a + *b	ab*+	0	invalid
a − b * c	abc*−	1	valid
a b + c	abc+	2	invalid
(a + b) * (c − d)	ab+cd−*	1	valid
a + b / d −	abd/+−	0	invalid

and a suffix Polish expression can be specified by the following rules:

$$<\text{reverse Polish}> ::= <\text{reverse Polish}> <\text{reverse Polish}> <\text{operator}>|$$
$$<\text{identifier}>|<\text{digit string}>$$
$$<\text{operator}> ::= +|-|*|/$$

For example, the following expressions are equivalent:

Infix	Reverse Polish
b	b
a + b	ab+
a + b + c	ab+c+
a + b * c	abc*+
a * (b + c)	abc+*
a / b * c	ab/c*

It is an easy matter to devise an algorithm which will convert an infix expression without parentheses into Polish. This conversion is based on the precedence of the operators and requires the use of a stack. The Polish expression will be stored in some output string which will be used later in the generation of object code. Recall that all variables and constants are not reordered in any way when the infix expression is converted to Polish. The operators, however, are reordered in the output string, depending on their relative precedence, and it is for this reason that a stack is required.

Let us initially assign precedence values to the four arithmetic operators displayed in Table 3-7.3. The precedence associated with multiplication and division is greater than the precedence of addition and subtraction. Also included in the table is a precedence value for variables (which are restricted to a single letter for simplicity) and the rank function. The reason for this will be explained shortly.

Assume that the stack contents have been initialized to some symbol ($\vdash$ in Table 3-7.3) which has a precedence value less than all other precedence values given in Table 3-7.3.

Algorithm BASIC. Given an input string **INFIX** containing an infix expression whose symbols have precedence values and ranks given in Table 3-7.3, a vector **S** which is used as

Table 3-7.3

Symbol	Precedence f	Rank r
+, −	1	−1
*, /	2	−1
a, b, c, . . .	3	1
$\vdash$	0	—

a stack, and a function NEXTCHAR which when invoked returns the next character of the input string, it is required to convert the string INFIX to reverse Polish and store it in a vector called POLISH. The variable RANK is used to compute the ranks of the Polish string. A special symbol shown as '⊢' is added to the end of string INFIX.

1. [Initialize stack] Set TOP ← 1, and S[TOP] ← '⊢'.
2. [Initialize output string pointer and RANK] Set RANK ← i ← 0.
3. [Get first input symbol] Set NEXT ← NEXTCHAR(INFIX).
4. [Scan the infix expression]
    Repeat steps 5 and 6 while NEXT ≠ '⊢'.
5. [Remove symbols with greater or equal precedence from the stack]
    Repeat while f(NEXT) ≤ f(S[TOP]):
        set i ← i + 1, TEMP ← POP(S, TOP) (this assigns the top element to TEMP),
        POLISH[i] ← TEMP, RANK ← RANK + r(TEMP), if RANK < 1 then print 'invalid' and Exit.
6. [Push NEXT on stack and get next input symbol]
    Call PUSH(S, TOP, NEXT) and set NEXT ← NEXTCHAR(INFIX).
7. [Remove remaining elements from stack]
    Repeat while S[TOP] ≠ '⊢':
        set i ← i + 1, TEMP ← POP(S, TOP), POLISH[i] ← TEMP, and
        RANK ← RANK + r(TEMP),
        if RANK < 1, then print 'invalid', and Exit.
8. [Is the expression valid?]
    If RANK = 1 then print 'valid'; otherwise, print 'invalid'.
    Exit.

The algorithm operates in a straightforward manner. Initially, a special symbol '⊢' is placed on the stack. The purpose of this symbol is to ensure that, upon the detection of '⊢' at the end of the string INFIX, the remaining elements of the stack (except '⊢') are put in POLISH. The main portion of the algorithm is concerned with the precedence value comparison of the incoming symbol NEXT and the top element of the stack. If the precedence value of NEXT is greater than that of the top element of the stack, then the symbol NEXT is inserted on the stack and the next input symbol is scanned. If, on the other hand, the precedence value of NEXT is less than or equal to that of the top element of the stack, then the latter element is removed from the stack and placed in string POLISH, after which the precedence values for NEXT and the new top element of the stack are compared, etc. The rank of the Polish string is updated each time a symbol is written in POLISH.

Note that since a variable has the highest precedence, it will be placed on the top of the stack. On scanning the very next input symbol, the variable will be deleted from the stack and copied into POLISH (since in a valid infix expression, no two consecutive variables are permitted). Actually, it is a very easy matter to alter the algorithm so that the precedence value of NEXT is tested for a value of three. If this test succeeds, then NEXT is a variable and it can be written out directly into POLISH without being placed on the stack. We do not do this, however, for reasons of generality which become important as the infix expression is permitted to be more complex than those which we are presently considering.

An incoming symbol with a precedence value greater than that of the top element of the stack will result in the operator (or variable) being inserted in the stack. This is understandable since the operation corresponding to this incoming operator should be performed before any other operations corresponding to the other operators on the stack. This will be reflected by the last operator to be placed on the stack being the first to be deleted from the stack and placed in string POLISH. Notice that when the precedence of an incoming operator is equal to the precedence of the operator on the top of the stack, then the latter is placed in the string POLISH. This preserves the property that in an expression containing operators with the same precedence, the leftmost operator is executed first. Therefore, the above algorithm will convert a + b + c to ab +c+ and not to abc + +. The Polish string ab +c+ corresponds to the infix (a + b) + c and abc + + corresponds to a + (b + c). A trace of the stack contents and the Polish string POLISH for the infix expression a + b * c − d / e *h is given in Table 3-7.4.

Let us now consider the problem of converting an infix expression containing parenthesized subexpressions. When a programmer writes an expression containing parentheses, he does not normally write it in a completely parenthesized form. Intuitively, when a left parenthesis is encountered in the infix expression, it should be placed on the stack regardless of its present contents. However, when it is in the stack, it should only be removed and discarded when a right parenthesis is encountered in the infix expression, at which time the right parenthesis is also ignored. A left parenthesis can be forced on the stack by assigning to it a precedence value greater than that of any other operator. Once on the stack, the left parenthesis should have another precedence value (called its *stack precedence*) which is smaller than that of any other operator. We can get rid of the left parenthesis on the stack by checking for an incoming right parenthesis in the infix expression. The right parenthesis

Table 3-7.4 Translation of infix string a + b * c − d / e *h to Polish.

Character Scanned	Contents of Stack (rightmost symbol is top of stack)	Reverse-Polish Expression	Rank
	⊢		
a	⊢a		
+	⊢ +	a	1
b	⊢ +b	a	1
*	⊢ +*	ab	2
c	⊢ +*c	ab	2
−	⊢ −	abc*+	1
d	⊢ −d	abc*+	1
/	⊢ −/	abc*+d	2
e	⊢ −/e	abc*+d	2
*	⊢ − *	abc*+de/	2
h	⊢ − *h	abc*+de/	2
⊢	⊢	abc*+de/h* −	1

is never inserted on the stack. Actually, we can modify the previous algorithm in such a manner that the left and right parentheses can perform the same function as the special symbol '⊢' used earlier. The original table of precedence values (Table 3-7.3) can be revised to have both an input- and stack-precedence value for each operator and operand. This is done, in addition to getting rid of the symbol '⊢', in order to make the algorithm more general in the sense that the algorithm does not grow significantly in complexity when we add other operators such as relational, logical, unary, and ternary operators. Table 3-7.5 is a revised table which includes parentheses. Each symbol has both input-symbol and stack-symbol precedence, except for a right parenthesis which does not possess a stack precedence since it is never placed on the stack. Table 3-7.5 also contains the exponentiation operator denoted here by the symbol ↑. All arithmetic operators except exponentiation have an input precedence which is lower in value than their stack precedence. This preserves the left to right processing of operators of equal precedence in an expression. The exponentiation operator in mathematics is right-associative. The expression a ↑ b ↑ c is equivalent to the parenthesized expression a ↑ (b ↑ c) and not to the expression (a ↑ b) ↑ c.

The conversion of an infix expression into reverse Polish operates in much the same way as the previous algorithm. A left parenthesis is initially placed on the stack and the infix expression is padded on the right with a right parenthesis. The new algorithm is formulated as follows.

Algorithm REVPOL.   Given an input string INFIX containing an infix expression which has been padded on the right with ')' and whose symbols have precedence values given by Table 3-7.5, a vector S, used as a stack, and a function NEXTCHAR, which when invoked returns the next character of its argument, it is required to convert the string INFIX to reverse Polish and store it in a vector called POLISH. The variable RANK is used to compute the rank of the Polish string.

1. [Initialize stack]   Set TOP ← 1 and S[TOP] ←'('.
2. [Initialize output string pointer and RANK]   Set RANK ← i ← 0.

Table 3-7.5

	Precedence		
Symbol	Input Precedence Function f	Stack Precedence Function g	Rank Function r
+, −	1	2	−1
*,/	3	4	−1
↑	6	5	−1
variables	7	8	1
(	9	0	−
)	0	−	−

3. [Get first input symbol] Set NEXT ← NEXTCHAR(INFIX).
4. [Scan the infix expression]
    Repeat steps 5 to 7 while NEXT ≠ empty string.
5. [Remove symbols with greater or equal precedence from the stack]
    Repeat while f(NEXT) ≤ g(S[TOP]):
        set TEMP ← POP(S, TOP),
        if f(NEXT) < g(TEMP),
        then
                set i ← i + 1, POLISH[i] ← TEMP, RANK ← RANK + r(TEMP), and
                if RANK < 1, then print 'invalid', and Exit;
            otherwise, go to step 7 (NEXT is a right parenthesis).
6. [Push NEXT on stack] Call PUSH(S, TOP, NEXT).
7. [Get next input symbol] Set NEXT ← NEXTCHAR(INFIX).
8. [Is the expression valid?]
    If TOP ≠ 0 or RANK ≠ 1, then print 'invalid'; otherwise, print 'valid'.
    Exit.

A trace of the stack contents and the Polish string POLISH for the infix expression

$$(a + b \uparrow c \uparrow d) * (e + f / d)$$

is given in Table 3-7.6. The reader is encouraged to trace the algorithm for the not well-formed expression (a * + b) + c)).

It is possible to extend precedence functions to handle relational operators, conditional statements, unconditional transfers (go to), subscripted variables, and many other features found in present programming languages. Some exercises at the end of this section will deal with these extensions.

We have been concerned until now with the conversion of an infix expression to reverse Polish. The motivation behind this conversion is that reverse Polish can be converted into object code by linearly scanning the Polish string once. The next section deals with the problem of generating code from the Polish string.

The problem of converting infix expressions to prefix Polish will not be discussed in this section. A simple algorithm based on the scanning of an infix expression from right to left can be easily formulated. In many cases the entire infix string is not available, but it is obtained one symbol at a time in a left-to-right manner (because this is the way we write programs). Therefore, a practical algorithm for converting infix to prefix must be based on a left-to-right scan of the infix string. To facilitate such an algorithm, however, two stacks instead of the usual one can be used. This is left as an exercise.

3-7.2.3   Conversion of Polish expressions to code

It will be assumed throughout this discussion that the object code desired is assembly-language instructions. Without getting deeply involved in a description of a hypothetical machine, assume that the object computer which will execute the object code produced by the compiling process is a single-address single-accumulator machine having core memory which is sequentially organized into words. The instructions in a program are

Table 3-7.6 Translation of infix string (a + b ↑ c ↑ d) * (e + f / d) to Polish.

Character Scanned	Contents of Stack (rightmost symbol is top of stack)	Reverse-Polish Expression	Rank
	(		
(	((		
a	((a		
+	((+	a	1
b	((+b	a	1
↑	((+↑	ab	2
c	((+↑c	ab	2
↑	((+↑↑	abc	3
d	((+↑↑d	abc	3
)	(	abcd↑↑+	1
*	(*	abcd↑↑+	1
(	(*(	abcd↑↑+	1
e	(*(e	abcd↑↑+	1
+	(*(+	abcd↑↑+e	2
f	(*(+f	abcd↑↑+e	2
/	(*(+/	abcd↑↑+ef	3
d	(*(+/d	abcd↑↑+ef	3
)	(*	abcd↑↑+efd/+	2
)		abcd↑↑+efd/+*	1

executed in a sequential manner unless a transfer instruction is encountered. The following are some of the assembler instructions which are available in the assembly language:

LOD a — Loads the value of variable a in the accumulator and leaves the contents of a unchanged.

STO a — Stores the value of the accumulator in a word of memory denoted by a. The accumulator contents remain unchanged.

ADD a — Adds the value of variable a to the value of the accumulator and leaves the result in the accumulator. The contents of a remain unchanged.

SUB a — The value of variable a is subtracted from the value of the accumulator and the result is stored in the accumulator. The contents of a remain unchanged.

MUL a — The value of variable a is multiplied by the value of the accumulator and the result is stored in the accumulator. The contents of a remain unchanged.

DIV a — The value of the accumulator is divided by the value of variable a and the result is placed in the accumulator. The contents of a remain unaltered.

JMP b — This is an unconditional branching instruction. The next instruction to be executed is located at a location (word) denoted by label b

BRN b   – This is a conditional branching instruction. The location of the next instruction to be performed is given by the label b if the accumulator content is negative; otherwise, the instruction following the BRN instruction is next.

The above instructions are sufficient for our purpose. A simple example of evaluating a Polish string was given in the previous section. Consider, initially, a "brute-force" algorithm for converting a Polish expression consisting of the four basic arithmetic operators and single-letter variables to assembly language. Assume that the following code will be generated for the basic arithmetic operators:

x + y (xy +)	LOD x
	ADD y
	STO T_i
x − y (xy −)	LOD x
	SUB y
	STO T_i
x * y (xy*)	LOD x
	MUL y
	STO T_i
x / y (xy/)	LOD x
	DIV y
	STO T_i

Each operator generates three assembly-language instructions. The third instruction in the group has the form of STO T_i where T_i represents an address of a location (word) in memory that is to contain the value of an intermediate result. These addresses are created by the Polish-to-assembly-language algorithm which is now given.

Algorithm CODE. Given a vector POLISH consisting of n symbols representing a reverse-Polish expression (which contains the four basic arithmetic operators and single-letter variables) equivalent to some well-formed infix expression, it is required to translate the string POLISH to assembly-language instructions as previously specified. The algorithm uses a stack S as usual. The variable j is an index to a symbol in string POLISH.

1. [Initialize]   Set TOP ← i ← 0 and j ← 1.
2. [Get the next Polish symbol]   Set NEXT ← POLISH[j].
3. [Is NEXT an addition operator?]
    If NEXT = '+', then set OPCODE ← 'ADDø' and go to step 10.
4. [Is NEXT a subtraction operator?]
    If NEXT = '−', then set OPCODE ← 'SUBø' and go to step 10.
5. [Is NEXT a multiplication operator?]
    If NEXT = '*', then set OPCODE ← 'MULø' and go to step 10.
6. [Is NEXT a division operator?]
    If NEXT = '/', then set OPCODE ← 'DIVø' and go to step 10.
7. [Stack variable NEXT]   Call PUSH(S,TOP,NEXT).
8. [Increment j]   Set j ← j + 1.

9. [All done?] If j ≤ n, then go to step 2; otherwise, Exit.
10. [Are there two operands in stack?]
    If TOP < 2, then print 'invalid expression', and Exit.
11. [Unstack two operands]
    Set RIGHT ← POP(S, TOP) and LEFT ← POP(S, TOP).
12. [Output load instruction]   Print 'LODø' ○ LEFT.
13. [Output arithmetic instruction]   Print OPCODE ○ RIGHT.
14. [Obtain temporary storage index] Set i ← i + 1 and TEMP ← 'T' ○ i.
15. [Output temporary store instruction]   Print 'STOø' ○ TEMP.
16. [Stack intermediate result]   Call PUSH(S,TOP,TEMP), go to step 8.

One very important point should be noted. In general, variables and constants (and indeed operators) can be more than one character in length. Instead of storing the variable names, values of constants, etc. in the string **POLISH**, integer pointers (giving the index of a variable or constant or operator) to a vector containing these names and constants are used. In this way, each item in **POLISH** is of the same length. The symbol '○' in steps 12 to 15 denotes the operation of concatenation. The label T_i, in practice, would be a pointer to a vector containing all created variable names in storing temporary results.

The algorithm performs one linear scan on the string **POLISH** looking for an operator. Once one is found, it unstacks two symbols from the stack, outputs the indicated operation, and stores the intermediate result on the stack. This process is repeated until no operators are left in **POLISH**. If, at any operation processing step, the stack does not contain two operands, an error message is printed.

The trace of the translation for the reverse Polish string abc*+de/h*− is given in Table 3-7.7. The assembly language generated by the process is given in the rightmost column of the figure. There are a number of obvious inefficiencies in the code generated. First, there exist redundant pairs of instructions such as

    STO T₃
    LOD T₃

in the sequence of output instructions. A second point is that no advantage is taken of the commutative property of the addition and multiplication operators. The result of this is contained in the code generated for the subexpression a + b * c; namely, the sequence

    LOD b
    MUL c
    STO T₁
    LOD a
    ADD T₁
    STO T₂

which could obviously be replaced by the equivalent sequence

    LOD b
    MUL c
    ADD a
    STO T₁

Table 3-7.7   Sample code generated by Algorithm CODE for the
Polish string abc*+de/h*−.

Character Scanned	Contents of Stack (rightmost symbol is top of stack)	Left Operand	Right Operand	Code Generated
a	a			
b	ab			
c	abc			
*	aT_1	b	c	LOD b MUL c STO T_1
+	T_2	a	T_1	LOD a ADD T_1 STO T_2
d	T_2d			
e	T_2de			
/	T_2T_3	d	e	LOD d DIV e STO T_3
h	T_2T_3h			
*	T_2T_4	T_3	h	LOD T_3 MUL h STO T_4
−	T_5	T_2	T_4	LOD T_2 SUB T_4 STO T_5

since the right operand is already in the accumulator and the values of $a + b * c$ and $b * c + a$ are equal. This last sequence takes advantage of the commutative property of addition. Finally, there is no effort made to economize the number of temporary locations required to store intermediate results. Indeed, if m such results are evaluated, the same number of temporary variables are created. The sequence of instructions

```
LOD b
MUL c
STO T₁
LOD a
ADD T₁
STO T₂
```

can obviously be replaced by the equivalent sequence where all instructions are the same, except the last which becomes STO T_1.

The number of temporary variables required can easily be reduced by performing the following simple test. Before generating instructions for the arithmetic operators, a test is performed on the contents of the left (LEFT) and right (RIGHT) operands associated with the operator in question. For each operand (LEFT, RIGHT) corresponding to a created (T_i) variable, the temporary variable counter i is decremented by "one."

The redundant pairs of store and load instructions and the unnecessary temporary storing and subsequent reloading of a right operand for commutative operators can be eliminated by the following technique. Instead of always storing a partial result in temporary storage, as is done in step 15 of Algorithm CODE, one can delay the generation of such an instruction until it is deemed absolutely necessary. Step 15 of the previous algorithm is altered so as to place an intermediate result marker, '@', on the stack instead of always generating a store instruction. If this marker is never pushed down in the stack deeper than the next to the top position, then an intermediate result need not be saved by the generation of a store instruction. An algorithm based on these comments is left as an exercise.

Exercises for Sec. 3-7.2

1. Write a recursive routine which will recognize if a particular expression is well-formed reverse Polish. Assume that the expression consists of single-letter variable names and the four basic arithmetic operators.

2. Thus far, we have only been concerned with the binary subtraction operator. In mathematics there are three usages of the minus sign, namely, to indicate the binary subtraction operator, the unary minus operator (such as $-x$) and to indicate the sign of a constant (such as $x + (-5)$). Obtain a precedence table capable of handling assignment statements containing the unary minus (denoted by $-$) and the assignment operator (denoted by $\leftarrow$).

   (*Hint:* It is an easy matter to distinguish the different occurrences of minus. A minus symbol will denote a binary operator if it does not occur either at the beginning of an expression or immediately after a left parenthesis. A minus symbol at the beginning of an expression or immediately after a left parenthesis will be a unary operator unless it is followed by a digit or decimal point.)

3. Consider expressions which can contain relational and logical operators. Formulate the precedence functions required to convert such expressions to reverse Polish.

4. As mentioned in the text, for certain applications the scanning of the infix expression is restricted to a left-to-right one-character-at-a-time scan. In an infix to prefix conversion, two stacks instead of one (as for infix to suffix conversion) are required, namely, an operator stack and an operand stack (to store temporarily the intermediate operands). Recall from Sec. 3-7.2.1 that all variables and constants retain their relative order when an infix expression is converted to prefix form. The operators, however, are reordered according to their relative precedence, and the operator stack is used in this reordering. The operand stack is used for temporary storage of intermediate operands so that, when finally the operator which connects them is found to be applicable, it can be placed in front of the concatenated operands. Formulate an algorithm to perform the translation assuming infix expressions consisting of single-letter variables and the four arithmetic operators.

5. Program Algorithm CODE in the text and use suitable data to verify it.

6. Based on the discussion following Algorithm CODE in the text, formulate an algorithm which will generate a more efficient code based on the commutativity of the operators * and +.

7. Program the algorithm obtained in Prob. 6 and use suitable data to verify it.

8. Modify the algorithm obtained in Prob. 6 so as to incorporate the assignment operator.

9. Modify the algorithm obtained in Prob. 8 to generate code for the six relational operators.

10. Modify and program the algorithm obtained in Prob. 6 so that it will also handle the unary minus operator.

11. Describe how conditional and unconditional statements might be implemented in the reverse-Polish framework.

3-7.3 Stack Machines

In the previous section, we discussed code generation for reverse-Polish expressions using fast register-type machines. One of the main problems with using machines which have a very limited number of registers is how to handle the storage of intermediate results. In particular, we must be very cognizant of the generation of wasted store/load instruction sequences. In this subsection, we illustrate how the presence of the simple stack operations of POP and PUSH can enhance the process of generating code from a reverse-Polish string.

Many of the machines which are appearing on the market include in their architecture hardware stacks or stack mechanisms. Two such machines are the PDP-11 and the Burroughs 5000. Both machines are particularly well suited for the stacking of local variables and parameters that arise in procedure calls of block-nested languages, as discussed in Sec. 3-7.1 on recursion. The B5000 and its successors have zero address instructions which make it very attractive when generating code from a suffix-Polish expression. Rather than describing a particular machine, we present a simple hypothetical stack machine which is sufficient to illustrate the important concepts related to the code generation for reverse-Polish strings of arithmetic expressions. The instructions available for this machine are given in mnemonic form as follows:

1 PUSH <name> – Load from memory onto stack. This instruction loads an operand from the memory location named <name> and places the contents of <name> on the stack.

2 POP <name> – Store top of stack in memory. The contents of the top of the stack are removed and stored in the memory location referenced by <name>.

3 ADD, SUB, MUL, DIV – Arithmetic operation.

The indicated operation is applied to the top two values on the stack and the result is left at the second-from-the-top stack location. The top element of the stack is then popped off. Therefore,

ADD means set $S[TOP-1] \leftarrow S[TOP-1] + S[TOP]$, and $TOP \leftarrow TOP - 1$.
SUB means set $S[TOP-1] \leftarrow S[TOP-1] - S[TOP]$, and $TOP \leftarrow TOP - 1$.
MUL means set $S[TOP-1] \leftarrow S[TOP-1] * S[TOP]$, and $TOP \leftarrow TOP - 1$.
DIV means set $S[TOP-1] \leftarrow S[TOP-1] / S[TOP]$, and $TOP \leftarrow TOP - 1$.

As an example, consider the stack machine instructions generated for the PL/I source statement:

A = B * C + A

This can be transformed to the reverse-Polish expression:

'ABC*A + ='

For 'ABC*A + =', the set of stack-machine instructions (left side) and the set of register-machine instructions as produced using Algorithm CODE of Sec. 3-7.2 (right side) are as follows:

PUSH B	LOD B
PUSH C	MUL C
MUL	STO T1
PUSH A	LOD T1
ADD	ADD A
POP A	STO T2
	STO A

Figure 3-7.10 illustrates the effects of the execution of the given sequence of stack-machine instructions.

The set of register-machine instructions can be reduced to

LOD B
MUL C
ADD A
STO A

if we eliminate the store/load sequence for T1 and the needless store in T2. However, the algorithm to generate such a sequence of code for a register machine is quite complex when compared to the algorithm for generating stack-machine code. Let us examine the stack-machine code generation algorithm.

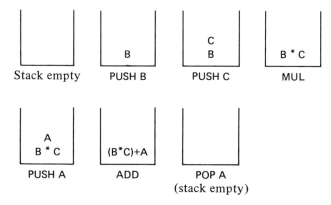

FIGURE 3-7.10 Effects of executing the stack-machine code generated from 'ABC*A + ='.

Algorithm STACK_CODE.   Given a string POLISH consisting of symbols representing a reverse-Polish expression which is composed of the four basic arithmetic operators and single-letter variables, it is required to translate the string POLISH into assembly-language stack-machine instructions. OPERATION is a four-element vector with elements 'ADD', 'SUB', 'MUL', 'DIV' in sequence for index values of 1 to 4. LETTERS is the character string 'ABCDEFGHIJKLMNOPQRSTUVWXYZ'. IND and i are intermediate variables.

1. [Initialize]   Set POP_SYMB ← SUB(POLISH,1,1) and i ← 2.
2. [Scan through string]   Repeat steps 3 to 5 while i ≤ LENGTH(POLISH).
3. [Get the next Polish symbol]   Set NEXT ← SUB(POLISH,i,1).
4. [Is NEXT an operator?]   Set IND ← INDEX('+ − */',NEXT)
    If IND ≠ 0, then print OPERATION[IND], set i ← i + 1 and go to step 2.
5. [Is NEXT an operand?]
    If INDEX(LETTERS, NEXT) ≠ 0,
    then print 'PUSH' ○ NEXT and set i ← i + 1;
    otherwise,
        if NEXT = ' = ' and INDEX(LETTERS,POP_SYMB) ≠ 0,
        then print 'POP' ○ POP_SYMB, set i ← i + 1;
        otherwise, print 'illegal character', and Exit.
6. [Finished]   Exit.

In Algorithm STACK_CODE, the reverse-Polish form is represented as a character string instead of a vector, as is used in Algorithm CODE of Sec. 3-7.2. The difference in the data structure for POLISH results in two algorithms which differ significantly in the operations that are applied. Either approach may be valid, depending on the type of programming language used to implement the algorithm (e.g., whether FORTRAN or PL/I is used).

In step 1 of Algorithm STACK_CODE, the first symbol is saved under the assumption that it contains the variable name to which the arithmetic expression is assigned. If this name is not saved, but instead its value is pushed onto the stack (as in the case for all other variable names), then the generated PUSH instruction is a wasted instruction. Step 3 establishes the next character to be examined from the string POLISH. In step 4, the appropriate arithmetic instruction is emitted if NEXT is an arithmetic operator. If NEXT is a variable name, then the name is emitted as the operand of a PUSH instruction. Finally, if NEXT is an assignment operator, the first symbol of the POLISH expression is emitted as the operand of a POP instruction.

The important point to observe is that, as simple as Algorithm STACK_CODE is, no wasted instructions are generated (such as store/load sequences for temporaries). By tracing through Algorithm STACK_CODE, it becomes clear that the stack operations PUSH and POP fit perfectly into the process of generating object code from a reverse-Polish form.

3-8   QUEUES

Another important subclass of lists permit deletions to be performed at one end of a list and additions at the other. The information in such a list is processed in the same order as it was received, that is, on a first-in, first-out (FIFO) or a first-come, first-served

(FCFS) basis. This type of list is frequently referred to as a *queue*. Figure 3-8.1 is a representation of a queue illustrating how an addition is made to the right of the rightmost element in the queue, and a deletion consists of deleting the leftmost position in the queue. In the case of a queue, the updating operation may be restricted to the examination of the last or end element. If no such restriction is made, any element in the list can be selected. The familiar and traditional example of a queue is a checkout line at a supermarket cash register. The first person in line is (usually) the first to be checked out.

Another perhaps more relevant example of a queue can be found in a time-sharing computer system where many users share the system simultaneously. Since such a system typically has a single central processing unit (called the *processor*) and one main memory, these resources must be shared by allowing one user's program to execute for a short time, followed by the execution of another user's program, etc., until there is a return to the execution of the initial user's program. The user programs which are waiting to be processed form a waiting queue. This queue may not operate on a strictly first-in, first-out basis, but on some complex priority scheme based on such factors as what compiler is being used, the execution time required, the number of print lines desired, etc. The resulting queue is sometimes called a priority queue and is the topic of discussion in Sec. 3-9.

A final example of a queue is the line of cars waiting to proceed in some fixed direction at an intersection of streets. The deletion of a car corresponds to the first car in the line passing through the intersection, while an insertion to the queue consists of a car joining the end of the line of existing cars waiting to proceed through the intersection. This particular example is discussed in an exercise at the end of Sec. 3-9.

We now wish to formulate algorithms for the insertion of an element to and the deletion of an element from a queue. The vector is assumed to consist of a large number of elements, enough to be sufficient to handle the variable-length property of a queue. In Sec. 4-3.1 another representation of a queue will be given which will be truly variable in size. The vector representation of a queue requires pointers f and r which denote the positions of its front and rear elements, respectively. An illustration of such an allocation scheme is given in Fig. 3-8.2. An algorithm for inserting an element in a queue is given as follows.

Algorithm QINSERT.   Given values for pointers f and r which denote the front and rear elements of a queue, respectively, a vector Q consisting of n elements, and an element y, it is required to insert y at the rear of the queue. Initially the pointers f and r have been initialized to a value of zero.

1. [Overflow?]   If $r \geq n$, then output overflow message and Exit.
2. [Increment rear pointer]   Set $r \leftarrow r + 1$.

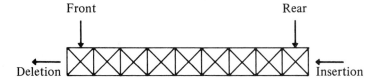

FIGURE 3-8.1   Representation of a queue.

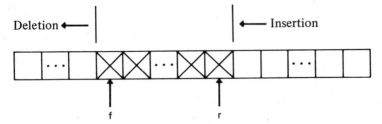

FIGURE 3-8.2   Representation of a queue by a vector.

3.   [Insert element]   Set Q[r] ← y.
4.   [Is front pointer properly set?]   If f = 0, then set f ← 1. Exit.

The following algorithm deletes an element from a queue.

Algorithm QDELETE.   The details given are the same as those for Algorithm QINSERT, except that the deleted element is to be placed in variable y.

1.   [Underflow?]   If f = 0, then output underflow message, and Exit.
2.   [Delete element]   Set y ← Q[f].
3.   [Queue empty?]   If f = r, then set f ← r ← 0, and Exit.
4.   [Increment front pointer]   Set f ← f + 1, and Exit.

This pair of algorithms can be very wasteful of storage if the front pointer f never manages to catch up to the rear pointer. Actually, an arbitrarily large amount of memory would be required to accommodate the elements. This method of performing operations on a queue should only be used when the queue is emptied at certain intervals.

Consider an example where the size of the queue is four elements. Initially, the queue is empty. It is required to insert symbols 'A', 'B', and 'C', delete 'A' and 'B', and insert 'D' and 'E'. A trace of the contents of the queue is given in Fig. 3-8.3. Note that an overflow occurs on trying to insert symbol 'E', even though the first two locations are not being used.

An alternate representation of a queue which circumvents these difficulties will now be discussed.

A more suitable method of representing a queue, which prevents an excessive use of memory, is to arrange the elements Q[1], Q[2], ..., Q[n] in a circular fashion with Q[1] following Q[n]. Pictorially, this can be represented as in Fig. 3-8.4. The insertion and deletion algorithms for a circular queue can now be formulated.

Algorithm CQINSERT.   Given values for pointers f and r which denote the front and rear elements of a queue, respectively, a vector Q consisting of n elements which are considered to be arranged in a circular manner, as described earlier, and an element y, it is required to insert y at the rear of the queue. The queue initially has its pointers set to zero.

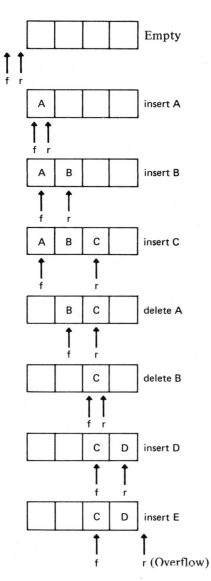

FIGURE 3-8.3 Trace of operations on a simple queue.

1. [Reset rear pointer?] If r = n, then set r ← 1; otherwise, set r ← r + 1.
'2. [Overflow?] If f = r, then output overflow message, and Exit.
3. [Insert element] Set Q[r] ← y.
4. [Is front pointer properly set?] If f = 0, then set f ← 1. Exit.

Algorithm CQDELETE. The details given are the same as that for the insertion Algorithm CQINSERT, except that the deleted element is to be placed in variable y.

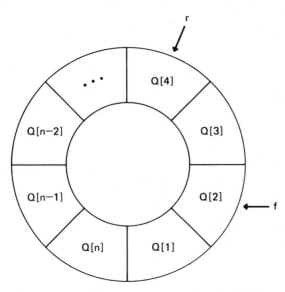

FIGURE 3-8.4   A vector representation of a circular queue.

1. [Underflow?]   If f = 0, then output underflow message, and Exit.
2. [Delete element]   Set y ← Q[f].
3. [Queue empty?]   If f = r, then set f ← r ← 0, and Exit.
4. [Increment front pointer]   If f = n, then set f ← 1; otherwise, set f ← f + 1. Exit.

Consider an example of a circular queue that contains a maximum of four elements. It is required to perform a number of addition and deletion operations on an initially empty queue. A trace of the queue contents, which is not shown as circular for convenience, is given in Fig. 3-8.5.

A single queue has been described as behaving in a first-in, first-out manner in the sense that each deletion removes the oldest remaining item in the structure. A *deque* (double-ended queue) is a linear list in which insertions and deletions are made to or from either end of the structure. Such a structure can be represented by Fig. 3-8.6. It is clear that a deque is more general than a stack or a queue. There are two variations of a deque, namely, the input-restricted deque and the output-restricted deque. The input-restricted deque allows insertions at only one end, while an output-restricted deque permits deletions from only one end.

Exercises for Sec. 3-8
1. Formulate an algorithm for performing an insertion into an input-restricted deque.
2. Formulate an algorithm for performing a deletion from an input-restricted deque.
3. Repeat Probs. 1 and 2 for an output-restricted deque.
4. Saskatchewan Grocerteria (**SASKGROC**) is considering the addition of a new service counter in one of its stores. Currently, the store has three checkouts, but customer

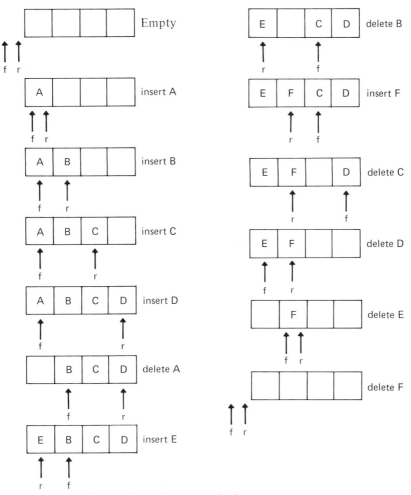

FIGURE 3-8.5 Trace of operations on a circular queue.

volume has increased to the point where a new counter is warranted. To determine if the new counter should be a regular counter or an express counter (i.e., eight items or less), a simulation of customer flow through the checkout area is required.

Our initial simulation is of a checkout area consisting of one express counter and three regular checkouts. All customers with eight or fewer items are assumed to pro-

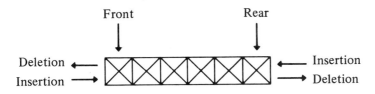

FIGURE 3-8.6 A deque.

ceed to an express counter. Customers with more than eight items go to the standard checkout with the shortest waiting line.

Customers enter the checkout area based on a next-arrival-time figure which we will derive by selecting a random number in the range [0, 360] seconds. (0 is interpreted as a simultaneous arrival of two customers.) The number of items bought by each customer can also be approximated by selecting a random number in the range 1 to 40. The time taken for a customer to proceed through a checkout once the cashier begins "ringing up" his or her groceries can be calculated by using an average rate of 30 seconds per item (ringing plus wrapping time).

In setting up the simulation we should realize that prior to bringing a new customer into the checkout area, we must ensure that all customers who have had their groceries processed are removed from the waiting lines. Assume that no more than 10 customers are waiting in line at any one time for a regular checkout, and no more than 15 are waiting in line at any one time for an express checkout.

You are to formulate an algorithm which simulates the checkout service just described. The desired output should contain the number of customers going through each checkout per hour, the total number of customers handled per hour, the average waiting time at each checkout, the overall average waiting time in minutes, the number of items processed at each checkout per hour, and the total number of items processed per hour. The waiting time is the time a customer spends in the checkout area.

Output having the following format is desirable:

	1	2	3	Express	Total
No. customers/hr	10	11	14	20	55
Avge. waiting time	2.80	3.01	2.96	0.22	1.94
Items processed/hr	192	261	210	65	728

Simulate the situation in which there are four standard checkouts, using the same method of generating arrival times and number of items purchased. Your second algorithm should be designed so that the second simulation can be performed with very few changes in the first algorithm. Implement your algorithms in PL/I.

You are to use the following procedure **RANGE** to generate a number between 0 and **VALUE** -1. RANDOM returns a floating-point number in the interval (0, 1).

```
RANGE:   PROCEDURE (VALUE);
DCL      SEED FIXED BINARY (31, 0) STATIC INITIAL (51771);
DCL      VALUE FIXED DEC;
DCL      RANDOM ENTRY (FIXED BINARY (31, 0)) RETURNS (FLOAT DEC);
DCL      NUM FIXED DEC(3, 0);
RANDOM:  PROCEDURE (IX) RETURNS (FLOAT DEC);
         DCL (IX, IY) FIXED BINARY (31, 0),
         YFL FLOAT DEC;
         (NOFIXEDOVERFLOW):
         IY = IX * 65539;
         IF IY < 0
```

```
          THEN IY = IY + 2147483647 + 1;
          YFL = IY;
          YFL = YFL * .4656613E-9;
          IX = IY;
          RETURN(YFL);
     END RANDOM;
     NUM = RANDOM(SEED) * VALUE;
     RETURN(NUM);
     END RANGE;
```

Can you make any conclusions from the results of the two simulations? Are there any assumptions which were made that may make the simulation model invalid?

3-9 SIMULATION OF A TIME-SHARING SYSTEM

One of the classical areas to which queues can be applied is that of simulation. This section discusses an application from this area which describes the simulation of a time-sharing computer system. Most students have been exposed to some variation of such a system in their undergraduate courses. A brief discussion of priority queues is presented at the end of this section. Since the early 1960s, increasingly more computing is being done through on-line terminals which are connected to time-shared computer systems. A typical configuration for such a computer system is shown in Fig. 3-9.1.

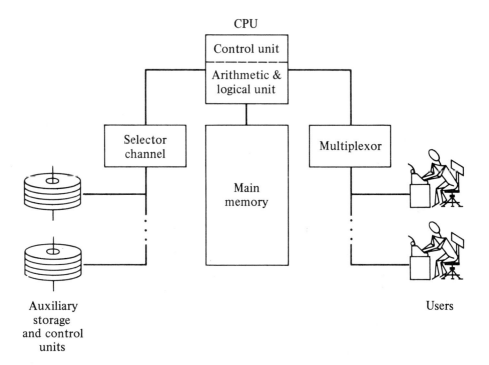

FIGURE 3-9.1   A typical time-shared computer system.

The important thing to note from the diagram is that a number of computer users are sharing the computer simultaneously. Since we have but one CPU (processor) and one main memory, we have to share these resources among our n users. We can share the processor by allowing one user's program to execute for a short time, then allow another user's program to execute, and another, etc., until there is a return to the execution of the initial user's program. This cycle is continued repeatedly on all active user programs. This method of sharing the CPU among many users is often referred to as *time-sharing*. Of course, we can also share memory among the user programs simply by dividing memory into regions and allowing each user program to execute in its own region when it receives CPU control. (There are more sophisticated ways of sharing both the CPU and main memory, but we need not discuss them here.)

In a system such as this, each user is unaware of the presence of the other users. In fact, each terminal appears like a separate computer to the user.

Let us look at a simple example of how a time-sharing system might work. Suppose three users, Tremblay, Sorenson, and Bunt, sit down at their terminals and begin an on-line session with the computer. The following statistics are gathered concerning their session:

Relative Session Starting Time	*Program ID*	*Requested CPU Time Periods*
0	TREMBLAY	4,8,3
1	SORENSON	2,1,2,2
2	BUNT	4,6,1

We interpret these figures in the following manner. After logging on the system at time 0 (the first number given in the statistics is the relative time, in seconds, at which each user begins his session), Tremblay initially is allotted 4 seconds of CPU time before he receives a typed response at his terminal. After examining the response, he then thinks momentarily and types in a new input to his program in memory. A further 8 seconds of CPU time is required before another response can be printed at Tremblay's terminal. Again there is a period of head scratching and of typing in a new input to his program. (We will refer to this total period of thinking then typing as the *user delay period*.) Finally, Tremblay's program uses 3 additional seconds of CPU time and then Tremblay logs off, terminating his session.

What we ignored in the above discussion is the fact that Sorenson and Bunt logged on at times 1 and 2, respectively, and their programs also require immediate CPU attention. Because we have only one CPU, Sorenson's program and Bunt's program will be made to wait until Tremblay's program has finished its first requested CPU time period of 4 seconds. We can indicate the fact that the Sorenson and Bunt programs are waiting for the processor by placing the program ID's (say, **SORENSON** and **BUNT**) in a queue behind Tremblay's program ID (i.e., **TREMBLAY**). Hence the queue at time 2 would appear as in Fig. 3-9.2.

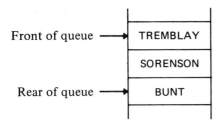

FIGURE 3-9.2 Processor queue at time 2.

When Tremblay's program has completed its first requested CPU time period, a reasonable scheduling strategy would be to allocate the CPU to Sorenson's program while Tremblay is scratching his head during a user delay period. Of course, when Sorenson's program has finished its CPU time period, Bunt's program should be allowed to execute a CPU time period. This type of scheduling strategy is often called a "first-come, first-serve" (FCFS) scheduling strategy. The rules for the FCFS strategy in this application are as follows:

1 When a program requests CPU time, it is placed at the back of the processor queue.

2 The program at the head of the processor queue is the program that is currently being executed. It remains at the head of the queue for its entire current CPU time period.

3 When an executing program completes its current requested CPU time period, it is removed from the processor queue and is not placed back into the queue until a further request is made (i.e., rule *1*).

Following the above rules, the three user programs would behave in the manner graphically described in Fig. 3-9.3. Note that we have allowed a 5-second user delay period throughout.

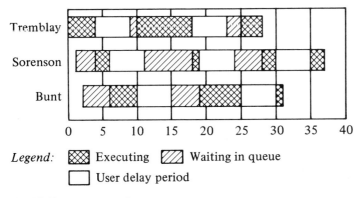

FIGURE 3-9.3.

The problem facing us is to simulate the activity of such a time-sharing system, given data relevant to user starting time and CPU time-period requests. The simulation must place users in the processor queue according to rule *1* and remove them as in rule *3*.

The purpose of such a simulation is to gain information about the efficiency of the time-sharing system. To this end, data are collected for the calculation of the following statistics:

1   CPU utilization $= \dfrac{\text{total CPU time}}{\text{total session time}} \times 100$
(for each user)

2   Total user waiting time = total time − total CPU time
(for each user)   − total user delay

3   Total user delay = 5 * (number of CPU requests − 1)
(for each user)

In order to simulate a system, we must thoroughly investigate the actions which take place within the system. These actions must be imitated in some manner such that certain characteristics of the simulated model are the same as in the real system. For example, users should begin execution in the model at the same time as they would in the real time-sharing system.

The primary actions which occur in this system, and the manner in which the simulation imitates the actions, are:

1   *User requests service.*   In the real system this request would be a teletype signal which would alert the processor. In the model we use a variable set to the time at which the user will require service. When the simulation time reaches or passes this time, the user is added to the processor queue.

2   *User program in execution.*   To imitate this action, we update the simulation time by the length of time requested by the user.

3   *User completes current executing period requested.*   At this point the user is removed from the queue for the delay or "thinking and typing" period. We will assume a delay period of five time units for all users. At this point the variable used to signal service requests, described in action *1*, is updated to indicate that the user is in the delay period.

If, at any point of time in the simulation, all users are in the delay phase and no users are in the processor queue, the simulation time is updated to the earliest service request time.

We now discuss in detail the algorithm that incorporates these ideas.

Algorithm TIME_SHARE.   This algorithm simulates a simple time-sharing system which uses a FCFS scheduling strategy. The following arrays of user-request data and statistical information are used (those marked * are assumed initialized prior to the algorithm's execution):

ID*	− User name.
START_TIME*	− Time user enters system.
END_TIME	− Time user exits system.
NEXT_TIME*	− Time at which user will next require CPU time (at the start of the algorithm NEXT_TIME = START_TIME).

CPU_TIME* — An accumulated total of CPU time requests (initialized to zero).

TIME_SLICE* — A queue which contains the lengths of the CPU time-slices requested by the user.

FRONT*, REAR* — Pointers to the front and rear elements of the TIME_SLICE queue, respectively.

DONE_FLAG* — Flag to indicate whether a user has completed all requests (initially set to zero to indicate not completed).

READY_FLAG* — Flag to indicate whether a user is ready to enter PROCQUEUE. The flag is initially set to zero to indicate a not-ready status.

The algorithm uses the CQINSERT and CQDELETE algorithms for circular queues, described in Sec. 3-8, to manipulate the processor queue PROCQUEUE. The elements of PROCQUEUE are subscripts to the data-array elements corresponding to the user that the processor queue represents, i.e., if the front element of PROCQUEUE = 2, then the user currently controlling the processor is ID[2]. F and R are the front and rear pointers to PROCQUEUE, respectively.

CLOCK is the simulation time; USERS is the number of users in the system and is assumed initialized prior to the TIME_SHARE algorithm. NOT_DONE is a flag to indicate when all user requests have been satisfied. EXEC_CLOCK is the requested time period of the user at the front of the queue. MIN is the minimum value of NEXT_TIME for all users ready to enter the processor queue; MINWAIT is the minimum value of NEXT_TIME for all users.

Note that if NEXT_TIME is set to -1, it indicates that the user is already in the processor queue.

1. [Initialize; set up loop control]
   Set NOT_DONE $\leftarrow 1$ and F $\leftarrow$ R $\leftarrow$ CLOCK $\leftarrow 0$.
   Repeat steps 2 to 11 while NOT_DONE = 1.
   Print statistics and Exit.

2. [Set flag to halt loop if all users are finished; loop through users]
   Set NOT_DONE $\leftarrow 0$ and MINWAIT $\leftarrow 9999$.
   Repeat steps 3 and 4 for i = 1, 2, ..., USERS.

3. [If user not finished, reset loop flag and check if waiting for CPU]
   If DONE_FLAG[i] = 0,
   then
       set NOT_DONE $\leftarrow 1$,
       if NEXT_TIME[i] $\leq$ CLOCK and NEXT_TIME[i] > -1,
       then set READY_FLAG[i] $\leftarrow 1$.

4. [Compare MINWAIT and user reentry time]
   If DONE_FLAG[i] = 0 and NEXT_TIME[i] $<$ MINWAIT,
   then set MINWAIT $\leftarrow$ NEXT_TIME[i].

5. [Add users waiting for CPU to PROCQUEUE in order of increasing value of NEXT_TIME]   Set MIN $\leftarrow 0$.
   Repeat steps 6 to 8 while MIN $<$ 9999.

6. [Search for minimum user reentry time]   Set MIN $\leftarrow 9999$.
   Repeat step 7 for i = 1, 2, ..., USERS.

7. [Compare MIN and user reentry time]

If NEXT_TIME[i] < MIN and READY_FLAG[i] = 1,
then set MIN ← NEXT_TIME[i] and k ← i.

8. [Add user to processor queue]
   If MIN < 9999,
   then call CQINSERT(PROCQUEUE, F, R, k, USERS), set READY_FLAG[k] ← 0,
   and NEXT_TIME[k] ← −1.

9. [No user in processor queue, then increment time and repeat]
   If F = 0, then set CLOCK ← MINWAIT and go to step 2.

10. [User at front of queue gains control of CPU. Delete front element of queue, and
    update statistics and NEXT_TIME]
    Set j ← CQDELETE(PROCQUEUE, F, R, USERS),
    EXEC_CLOCK ← TIME_SLICE[j, FRONT[j]],
    CPU_TIME[j] ← CPU_TIME[j] + EXEC_CLOCK, CLOCK ← CLOCK + EXEC_CLOCK,
    and NEXT_TIME[j] ← CLOCK + 5 (each user is assumed to require a delay of 5 time
    units).

11. [Change TIME_SLICE queue pointers; if user finished, set DONE_FLAG to indicate this]
    If FRONT[j] < REAR[j],
    then set FRONT[j] ← FRONT[j] + 1;
    otherwise, set END_TIME[j] ← CLOCK and DONE_FLAG[j] ← 1.

In step 3, all users ready to enter the processor queue are marked, i.e., READY_FLAG is set to 1. These marked users are added to the queue in order of increasing NEXT_TIME (time at which they were ready to enter the queue) in steps 5 to 8. Step 9 checks for an empty queue. If the queue is not empty, the front user is processed as having executed the requested length of time on the CPU. If the queue is empty, the time is updated to the earliest time at which a user can reenter the system and the loop is repeated.

Figure 3-9.4 is a PL/I program which implements Algorithms TIME_SHARE, CQINSERT, and CQDELETE to simulate the small time-sharing system. The main program has three sections:

1   Statements 46–74:   Read in data and initialize user data arrays.
2   Statements 76–119:   Main simulation loop as in Algorithm TIME_SHARE.
3   Statements 120–130:   Calculate and print statistics.

The procedures and variable names used in the PL/I program correspond to those used in Algorithm TIME_SHARE, with the exception of the main procedure name which is shortened to TIM_SHR because of the PL/I length restriction on main procedure names.

In the discussion of our queueing example, we have concentrated on a model for simulating a simple time-sharing system. It should be evident, however, that in the actual operation of such a system a queue of user ID's must be maintained for processor scheduling, just as we have had to maintain the PROCQUEUE in our simulation. A queue is one of the most commonly used data structures in an operating system which accommodates multiple simultaneous users. The reason for this is that each of the user programs is competing for and sharing system resources (for example, CPU, memory, and input/output devices). When a user program or programs request a facility already held by another user program or programs, the requesting program or programs must be delayed until the request can be satisfied. A reasonable method of scheduling the waiting programs is in a first-come, first-serve manner. The strategy is implemented best through the use of a queue.

Some computer systems provide service for a wide class of user applications. Take, for example, a system which handles real-time monitoring, on-line time-sharing through terminals, and background job processing. The tasks or jobs for each of these classes are all competing for the CPU. A realistic CPU scheduling strategy that is adopted in many such computer systems is to service all real-time tasks first, then on-line programs (if there are no outstanding real-time tasks), and finally batch jobs if there are no real-time or on-line requests for processing. Figure 3-9.5a illustrates a processor queue which might be associated with such a scheduling discipline. When a new real-time task (denoted by R_i) becomes active, it is not inserted at the end of the queue but is inserted at the end of the list of real-time tasks in the queue. Similarly, new on-line requests (denoted by 0_i) are

```
1     TIM_SHR:  PROCEDURE OPTIONS(MAIN);

      /*  APPLICATION 3.9.1                                            */
      /*  SIMULATION OF A SIMPLE TIME-SHARING COMPUTER SYSTEM          */

2         DECLARE 1 USER(10),
                    /*  ARRAY TO HOLD USER REQUEST AND STATISTICAL INFO   */
                  2 ID CHARACTER(16),
                  2 TIME_SLICE(10) FIXED DECIMAL,
                    /*  USER NAME                                         */
                    /*  TIME_SLICE QUEUE HOLDS USER CPU TIME REQUESTS     */
                  2 FRONT FIXED BINARY(8,0),
                  2 REAR  FIXED BINARY(8,0),
                    /*  TIME_SLICE QUEUE FRONT & REAR POINTERS            */
                  2 START_TIME FIXED DECIMAL,
                    /*  CLOCK TIME WHEN USER ENTERED SYSTEM               */
                  2 END_TIME   FIXED DECIMAL,
                    /*  CLOCK TIME WHEN USER EXITTED SYSTEM               */
                  2 NEXT_TIME  FIXED DECIMAL,
                    /*  CLOCK TIME AT WHICH USER WILL NEXT REQUEST CPU TIME*/
                  2 CPU_TIME        FIXED DECIMAL,
                    /*  HOLDS CUMULATIVE SUM OF CPU TIME REQUESTS          */
                  2 READY_FLAG BIT(1),
                    /*  USED TO ADD USERS TO WAITQUEUE IN PROPER ORDER     */
                    /*     READY_FLAG = 1 INDICATES USER TO BE ADDED       */
                  2 DONE_FLAG BIT(1);
                    /*  DONE_FLAG = 1 INDICATES ALL USER REQUESTS SATISFIED*/

3         DECLARE CQDELETE ENTRY((*) FIXED BINARY(8,0), FIXED BINARY(8,0),
                                FIXED BINARY(8,0),FIXED BINARY(8,0))
                                RETURNS (FIXED BINARY(8,0)),
                  CQINSERT ENTRY((*) FIXED BINARY(8,0), FIXED BINARY(8,0),
                                FIXED BINARY(8,0),FIXED BINARY(8,0),
                                FIXED BINARY(8,0));

4         DECLARE PROC_QUEUE (10) FIXED BINARY(8,0),
                    /* PROC_QUEUE IS A CIRCULAR QUEUE WHICH CONTAINS SUBSCRIPTS*/
                    /*    TO THE USER ARRAY FOR THOSE USERS READY TO USE THE  */
                    /*    CPU                                                 */
                  CLOCK       FIXED BINARY(8,0) INITIAL(0),
                    /*  PRESENT TIME IN SYSTEM                             */
                  EXEC_CLOCK  FIXED BINARY(8,0) INITIAL(0),
                  MIN FIXED DECIMAL,
                  (USERNUM,NUM,NEXTDIGITS) FIXED DECIMAL,
                  (EOF,OFF) BIT(1) INITIAL('0'B),
                  ONN         BIT(1) INITIAL('1'B),
                  (I,J,K,USERS,F,R) FIXED BINARY(8,0)INITIAL(0),
                  NOT_DONE BIT(1)  INITIAL('1'B),
                  (TDELAY,TTIME,UTIME,UTIL) FIXED DECIMAL;
```

FIGURE 3-9.4   PL/I program for Algorithm TIME_SHARE.

```
5        QPRINT: PROCEDURE;
         /* PROCEDURE 'QPRINT' PRINTS THE ID OF THE USERS IN PROC_QUEUE       */

6           DECLARE J FIXED BINARY(8,0);
7           PUT EDIT ('PROCESSOR QUEUE AT TIME',CLOCK)
                   (SKIP,A,F(3));
8           PUT SKIP;
9           IF R < F
10          THEN DO;
11             DO J = F TO USERS;
12                PUT EDIT(ID(PROC_QUEUE(J)))(SKIP,X(4),A);
13             END;
14             DO J = 1 TO R;
15                PUT EDIT(ID(PROC_QUEUE(J)))(SKIP,X(4),A);
16             END;
17          END;
18          ELSE DO J = F TO R;
19                PUT EDIT(ID(PROC_QUEUE(J))) (SKIP,X(4),A);
20          END;
21          PUT SKIP(2);
22       END QPRINT;

23       CQINSERT:  PROCEDURE(QUEUE,F,R,I,LAST);
         /*  PROCEDURE 'CQINSERT' INSERTS THE VALUE I AT THE REAR OF 'QUEUE'  */
         /*      QUEUE - ARRAY USED AS CIRCULAR QUEUE, BOUNDS 1 TO LAST       */
         /*      F     - FRONT OF QUEUE                                       */
         /*      R     - REAR OF QUEUE                                        */
         /*      I     - FIXED VALUE TO BE INSERTED IN QUEUE                  */
         /*      LAST  - UPPER BOUND FOR QUEUE ARRAY                          */

24          DECLARE (I,LAST,R,F) FIXED BINARY(8,0),
                    QUEUE(*) FIXED BINARY(8,0);
25          IF R = LAST
26             THEN R = 1;
27             ELSE R = R + 1;
28          IF R = F
29             THEN RETURN;
30          QUEUE(R) = I;
31          IF F=0 THEN F = 1;
33       END CQINSERT;

34       CQDELETE:  PROCEDURE (QUEUE,F,R,LAST) RETURNS (FIXED BINARY (8,0));
         /* PROCEDURE 'CQDELETE' REMOVES THE FRONT ELEMENT FROM 'QUEUE' AND   */
         /*      RETURNS THE VALUE OF THE FRONT ELEMENT                       */
         /*      QUEUE - ARRAY USED AS CIRCULAR QUEUE, BOUNDS 1 TO LAST       */
         /*      F     - FRONT OF QUEUE                                       */
         /*      R     - REAR OF QUEUE                                        */
         /*      LAST  - UPPER BOUND FOR QUEUE ARRAY                          */

35          DECLARE (LAST,F,R,KEEP) FIXED BINARY (8,0),
                    QUEUE(*) FIXED BINARY (8,0);
36          IF F = 0 THEN RETURN (0);
38          KEEP = QUEUE(F);
39          IF F= R THEN F,R = 0;
41                ELSE IF F = LAST
42                        THEN F = 1;
43                        ELSE F = F + 1;
44          RETURN (KEEP);
45       END CQDELETE;
```

FIGURE 3-9.4   (Continued)

placed at the end of other on-line requests. Only with batch processing are new jobs inserted at the end of the queue.

A queue in which we are able to insert items into or remove items from any position based on some property (such as the priority of the task to be processed) is often referred to as a *priority queue*. In Fig. 3-9.5a we have attached priorities of 1, 2, and 3 to the real-time, on-line, and batch job types. Therefore, if a job is initiated with priority i, it is inserted

```
            /* * * * * * * * * * * * * MAIN LINE * * * * * * * * * * * * * **/

            /*  READ IN USER REQUEST DATA AND INITIALIZE USER ARRAY ELEMENTS     */
46          ON ENDFILE(SYSIN)  EOF='1'B;
48          I = 1;
49          GET LIST(NUM,NEXTDIGITS);
50          DO WHILE(¬EOF);
51             NEXT_TIME(I) = NEXTDIGITS;
52             START_TIME(I) = NEXTDIGITS;
53             GET LIST(ID(I));
54             PUT SKIP;
55             PUT EDIT('USER NAME','SESSION START TIME')(SKIP,A(9),X(9),A(18));
56             PUT EDIT(ID(I),NEXTDIGITS)(SKIP,A(16),X(10),F(2));
57             PUT EDIT('CPU TIME REQUESTS:')(SKIP(2),A(18));
58             USER_NUM = NUM;
59             J = 1;
60             GET LIST(NUM,NEXTDIGITS);
61             DO WHILE(USER_NUM=NUM & ¬EOF);
62                PUT EDIT(NEXTDIGITS)(SKIP,X(20),F(2));
63                TIME_SLICE(I,J) = NEXTDIGITS;
64                J=J+1;
65                GET LIST(NUM,NEXTDIGITS);
66             END;
67             REAR(I) = J-1;
68             FRONT(I) = 1;
69             CPU_TIME(I) = 0;
70             DONE_FLAG(I)= OFF ;
71             READY_FLAG = OFF;
72             I = I + 1;
73          END;
74          USERS = I - 1;
75          PUT SKIP(2);

            /*  MAIN SIMULATION LOOP                                          */

76          DO WHILE (NOT_DONE);
77             NOT_DONE = OFF;
               /*  CHECK EACH USER TO FIND IF WAITING FOR SERVICE            */
               /*    IF WAITING, SET READY_FLAG = ONN TO SIGNAL WAITING      */
               /*    NEXT_TIME = -1 INDICATES USER IN PROC_QUEUE.  IF ALL    */
               /*    USERS DONE (DONE_FLAG = ONN) THEN SET FLAG TO HALT      */
               /*    MAIN LOOP                                               */
78             DO I = 1 TO USERS;
79                IF ¬DONE_FLAG(I)
80                THEN DO;
81                   NOT_DONE = ONN;
82                   IF NEXT_TIME(I) <= CLOCK & NEXT_TIME(I) > -1
83                   THEN READY_FLAG(I) = ONN;
84                END;
85             END;

               /*  INSERT USERS WITH READY_FLAG = ONN INTO PROC_QUEUE IN     */
               /*    ORDER OF INCREASING VALUE OF NEXT_TIME                  */
86             MIN = 0;
87             DO WHILE (MIN < 9999);
88                MIN = 9999;
```

FIGURE 3-9.4 (Continued)

immediately at the end of the list of other jobs with priority i, for i = 1, 2, or 3. In this example, jobs are always removed from the front of the queue. (In general, this is not a necessary restriction on a priority queue.)

A priority queue can be conceptualized as a series of queues in instances in which it is known a priori what priorities are associated with queue items. Figure 3-9.5*b* shows how the single-priority queue can be visualized as three separate queues, each exhibiting a

```
 89                     DO I = 1 TO USERS;
 90                         IF NEXT_TIME(I) < MIN & READY_FLAG(I)
 91                         THEN DO;
 92                             MIN = NEXT_TIME(I);
 93                             K = I;
 94                         END;
 95                     END;
 96                     IF MIN ¬= 9999
 97                     THEN DO;
 98                         CALL CQINSERT(PROC_QUEUE,F,R,K,USERS);
 99                         READY_FLAG(K) = OFF;
100                         NEXT_TIME(K) = -1;
101                     END;
102                 END;

103                 IF F  ¬= 0
104                 THEN DO;
                    /*  IF THERE IS A USER IN PROC_QUEUE, PRINT PROC_QUEUE       */
                    /*      DELETE USER AND UPDATE CLOCK AND NEXT_TIME OF USER TO */
                    /*      INDICATE USER RECEIVED TIME REQUESTED.               */
105                     CALL QPRINT;
106                     J = CQDELETE (PROC_QUEUE,F,R,USERS);
107                     EXEC_CLOCK = TIME_SLICE(J,FRONT(J));
108                     CPU_TIME(J) = CPU_TIME(J) + EXEC_CLOCK;
109                     CLOCK = CLOCK + EXEC_CLOCK;
110                     NEXT_TIME(J) = CLOCK + 5;
111                     IF FRONT(J) < REAR(J)
112                     THEN FRONT(J) = FRONT(J) + 1;
113                     ELSE DO;
114                         END_TIME(J) = CLOCK;
115                         DONE_FLAG(J) = ONN;
116                     END;
117                 END;
                    /* NO USER THEN INCREMENT CLOCK AND REPEAT LOOP              */
118                 ELSE CLOCK = CLOCK + 1;
119             END;

        /*  CALCULATE AND PRINT STATISTICS                                      */
120         PUT SKIP(2);
121         PUT EDIT('USER NAME','TOTAL CPU','TOTAL USER','TOTAL WATING',
                    'TOTAL SESSION','CPU')
                    (SKIP,A(9),X(10),A(9),X(6),A(10),X(4),A(13),X(4),A(13),X(8),
                    A(3));
122         PUT EDIT('TIME REQUIRED','DELAY TIME','TIME IN QUEUE','TIME',
                    'UTILIZATION')
                    (SKIP,X(17),A(13),X(4),A(10),X(4),A(13),X(8),A(4),X(9),A(11));
123         PUT SKIP;
124         DO J=1 TO USERS;
125             TDELAY = 5*(REAR(J)-1);
126             TTIME =  END_TIME(J) - START_TIME(J);
127             WTIME = TTIME - TDELAY - CPU_TIME(J);
128             UTIL = CPU_TIME(J) * 100 / TTIME;
129             PUT EDIT(ID(J),CPU_TIME(J),TDELAY,WTIME,TTIME,UTIL,'%')
                        (SKIP,A(16),X(6),F(3),X(13),F(3),X(13),F(3),X(14),F(3),
                        X(13),F(3),A(1));
130         END;
131     END TIM_SHR;
```

FIGURE 3-9.4 (Continued)

strictly FIFO behavior. Elements in the second queue are removed only when the first queue is empty, and elements from the third queue are removed only when the first and second queues are empty. This separation of a single-priority queue into a series of queues also suggests an efficient storage representation of a priority queue. When elements are inserted, they are always added at the end of one of the queues as determined by the priority. Alternatively, if a single sequential storage structure is used for the priority queue, then

```
USER NAME            SESSION START TIME
TREMBLAY                      0

CPU TIME REQUESTS:
                        4
                        8
                        3

USER NAME            SESSION START TIME
SORENSON                      1

CPU TIME REQUESTS:
                        2
                        1
                        2
                        2

USER NAME            SESSION START TIME
BUNT                          2

CPU TIME REQUESTS:
                        4
                        6
                        1


PROCESSOR QUEUE AT TIME   0

    TREMBLAY


PROCESSOR QUEUE AT TIME   4

    SORENSON
    BUNT


PROCESSOR QUEUE AT TIME   6

    BUNT


PROCESSOR QUEUE AT TIME  10

    TREMBLAY


PROCESSOR QUEUE AT TIME  18

    SORENSON
    BUNT


PROCESSOR QUEUE AT TIME  19

    BUNT
```

FIGURE 3-9.4   (Continued)

insertion may mean that the new element must be placed in the middle of the structure. This can require the movements of several items. It is better to split the priority queue into several queues, each having its own storage structure.

In Chap. 7 we encounter another example involving queues of buffers as used by the data-management facilities in most operating systems. In the next chapter, we examine another form of storage representation for list structures such as the queue.

```
PROCESSOR QUEUE AT TIME 25

    TREMBLAY
    SORENSON


PROCESSOR QUEUE AT TIME 28

    SORENSON


PROCESSOR QUEUE AT TIME 30

    BUNT


PROCESSOR QUEUE AT TIME 35

    SORENSON
```

USER NAME	TOTAL CPU TIME REQUIRED	TOTAL USER DELAY TIME	TOTAL WATING TIME IN QUEUE	TOTAL SESSION TIME	CPU UTILIZATION
TREMBLAY	15	10	3	28	53%
SORENSON	7	15	14	36	19%
BUNT	11	10	8	29	37%

FIGURE 3-9.4 (Continued)

Exercises for Sec. 3-9

1. Change the TIME_SHARE algorithm to accommodate a different delay time for each user. Redraw Fig. 3-9.3 using the following delay times:

   Bunt – 2

   Sorenson – 6

   Tremblay – 9

2. A tool frequently used by transportation and city planners is the computer simulation of traffic systems. The systems modeled range from the traffic network of a nation, a city, or area of a city right down to the traffic flow in one bridge or intersection. The models are used to pinpoint present or future bottlenecks and to suggest and test proposed changes or new systems.

   A light-controlled intersection is one example of a traffic system for which the simulation model is relatively simple. Such a model would be used to evaluate inter-section performance. The primary quantity measured would be the length of time motorists were stopped at the intersection. The performance of the intersection would be indicated by the average and maximum waiting times experienced by the motorists.

   The specific model we will consider consists of an intersection of two two-lane streets, each lane being controlled by a three-color traffic light. The street and lane codes used throughout this section are shown in Fig. 3-9.6.

   To simplify the model, we make some assumptions about traffic flow and driver behavior. First, we assume that all traffic entering the intersection proceeds straight ahead; no right or left turns are allowed. Second, we assume that the car and driver

Task identification

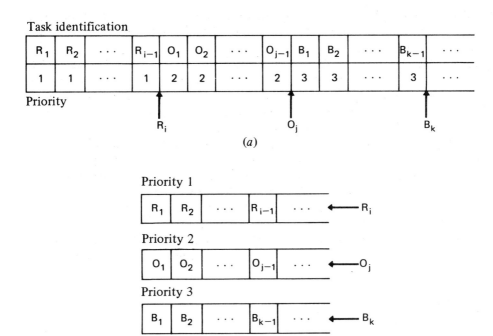

R_1	R_2	$\cdots$	R_{i-1}	O_1	O_2	$\cdots$	O_{j-1}	B_1	B_2	$\cdots$	B_{k-1}	$\cdots$
1	1	$\cdots$	1	2	2	$\cdots$	2	3	3	$\cdots$	3	$\cdots$

Priority

R_i $\qquad$ O_j $\qquad$ B_k

(*a*)

Priority 1

| R_1 | R_2 | $\cdots$ | R_{i-1} | $\cdots$ | $\longleftarrow R_i$ |

Priority 2

| O_1 | O_2 | $\cdots$ | O_{j-1} | $\cdots$ | $\longleftarrow O_j$ |

Priority 3

| B_1 | B_2 | $\cdots$ | B_{k-1} | $\cdots$ | $\longleftarrow B_k$ |

(*b*)

FIGURE 3-9.5   A priority queue (*a*) viewed as a single queue with insertions allowed at any position, and (*b*) viewed as a set of queues.

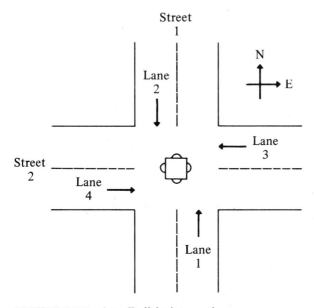

FIGURE 3-9.6   A traffic-light intersection.

response times are the same for all vehicles, i.e., given that the path is clear, it takes the same length of time for each car to respond and enter the intersection. The possibilities of stalling cars and accidents are ignored. We assume that all drivers are extremely law-abiding and, thus, stop for both red and amber lights.

At this point we acknowledge the reader's comment that no such intersection exists. That is true; however, for the sake of clarity of description, such a simplistic intersection will be our subject.

The traffic lights are assumed to have the following characteristics:

1   The traffic lights for the two lanes on each street have identical signal timing and are viewed as a set.
2   The light cycle times for both sets of lights are equal.
3   There are no right- or left-turn arrows and no four-way walk signal.
4   There is a short length of time, known as the *delay time*, between one set of lights turning red and the other set turning green.
5   The red-light period on each set of lights is longer than the combined periods of the green light, amber light, and delay of the other set of lights.

We now consider the problem in greater detail and introduce some ideas from the field of computerized simulation.

One step in the creation of a simulation model is to subdivide the system under consideration into its component parts or entities. In the intersection system we are studying, the primary entities are the traffic lights and the cars. Each entity has attributes associated with it. For example, the light color is a property of the traffic lights; the important attributes of the cars could be the lane in which the car is traveling and the time at which it arrives at the intersection. Other attributes that could be considered for a car would be the speed at which it is traveling, its color, etc., but these are not relevant to the model we have described.

In an accurate computer simulation, the modeled entities should resemble their real counterparts as closely as possible, within the limits of computational efficiency. The methods by which this goal is achieved in the system under consideration are discussed next.

In this model, the intersection lights must change in the same time sequence as the real light signals. Given the initial configuration and the light-timing patterns (i.e., the length of time for each color of light), the configuration of the lights at any time can be determined. For example, if a street light initially turned red at time zero, and the red light period was 60 seconds, then at time 61 we know the light would be green.

The pattern of the cars in the model must closely resemble that of cars at an actual intersection with respect to frequency of arrival and direction of approach. If we have statistical data about an intersection, such as the number of cars entering from each direction and the average time between arrivals, a procedure can be used to introduce into the simulation cars with attributes statistically similar to those of the real traffic. This procedure is termed Monte Carlo sampling, and it determines outcomes at random at decision points in the simulation process.

The first decision regarding a car is the direction in which it is traveling toward the intersection. There are four possible results to this decision, say E_1, E_2, E_3, and E_4 representing north, south, west, and east, respectively. If we know the probabilities

p_1, p_2, p_3, and p_4 ($p_1 + p_2 + p_3 + p_4 = 1$) associated with each result, then a random number can be used to determine which result is chosen by the following procedure. A random number R is obtained using a random-number generator that yields numbers uniformly distributed between 0 and 1. Then the result of the decision is

E_1 if $R < p_1$
E_2 if $p_1 \leq R < p_1 + p_2$
E_3 if $p_1 + p_2 \leq R < p_1 + p_2 + p_3$
E_4 if $p_1 + p_2 + p_3 \leq R$

If we assume that certain characteristics hold true for the traffic flowing through the intersection, then we can also assume that the time between consecutive arrivals (the interarrival time) is exponentially distributed. This means that the function

$$F(x) = 1 - e^{-\alpha x}$$

is the probability that the interarrival time is less than or equal to x. α is equal to 1/ATI where ATI is the average time interval between arrivals. We can generate a random value for x, the interarrival time, from this function by generating a random number R to represent a probability and by using the formula

$$x = -\text{ATI} \log R$$

A more detailed discussion of exponential distributions and associated characteristics can be found in Naylor, Balinty, Chu, and Burdick [1968].

Having discussed the manner in which the light signals and car arrivals will be handled, we now turn our attention to that segment of the model which applies to the relationship between the lights and the cars. It is this segment which is most directly related to the data structures discussed in Sec. 3-8.

This controlling segment of the model will either move cars through a green light (i.e., remove them from the model) or simulate the car stopping at an amber or red light. It is not difficult to realize that a queue is the obvious representation for the cars stopped at the red light. Our model will use four queues to represent the traffic buildup in the four directions. A car is added to the queue when it is stopped; it is deleted from the queue when it passes through the intersection. A queue overflow signals a traffic jam.

The general simulation model has the following steps:

1   Introduce a car into the model.
2   Update the lights and traffic flow to the arrival time of the car.
3   Dispose of the car as indicated by the light signal at the car's arrival time, i.e., move the car through the intersection or add the car to a waiting queue.
4   Go to step 1.

This general solution is graphically represented by the flowchart in Fig. 3-9.7. Three branches emanate from the first event box (labeled A). The branch chosen depends on the color of the lights (at the present simulation time) on the street on which the car approaching the intersection is traveling. Note also the flow of control from the red-to-green-to-amber segments indicated by the broken line. This looping halts only when the light sequences that would occur between the present time and time Y

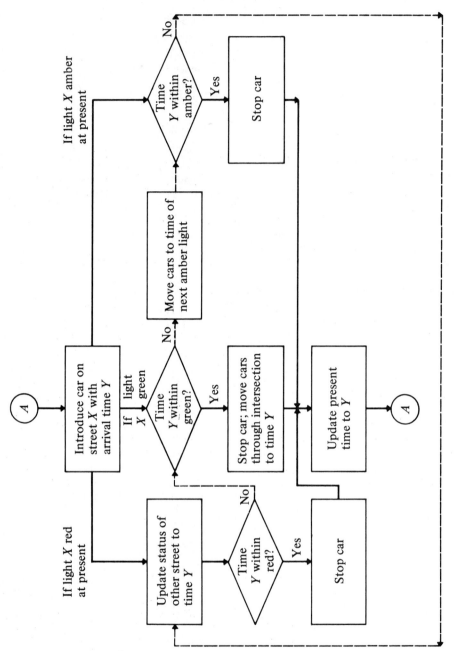

FIGURE 3-9.7   Event flowchart for traffic-light intersection.

have been simulated. The problem is to devise algorithms which implement the simulation of the intersection described, and to program and test these algorithms. The output of the model should include the maximum and average waiting time in each direction and the maximum and average queue length in each direction.

3. Alter the algorithms and program in Exercise 2 to simulate an intersection in which vehicles make both right and left turns, as well as proceeding straight through. Use the following rule to decide right-of-way: A vehicle turning left may leave the wait queue only if there are no vehicles in the approaching queue, or if the front vehicle of the approaching queue is also turning left. Note that an additional value, the direction of turn, must be saved for each car in the wait queues. The same type of sampling method as that used to determine the vehicle's lane of travel can be used to determine the direction in which the vehicle will proceed.

BIBLIOGRAPHY

COHEN, D. J., and P. C. BRILLINGER: "Introduction to Nonnumeric Computation," Prentice-Hall, Englewood Cliffs, N.J., 1970.

FORSYTHE, A. I., T. A. KEENAN, E. I. ORGANICK, and W. STENBERG: "Computer Science: A First Course," John Wiley & Sons, Inc., New York, 1969.

GRIES, D.: "Compiler Construction for Digital Computers," John Wiley & Sons, Inc., New York, 1971.

HARRISON, M. C.: "Data-Structures and Programming," Scott, Foresman and Company, Glenview, Ill., 1973.

D'IMPERIO, M. E.: Data Structures and Their Representation in Storage, *Annual Review in Automatic Programming, vol. 5, pp.* 1–75, Pergamon Press, Oxford, 1969.

KNUTH, D. E.: "The Art of Computer Programming," vol. 1, "Fundamental Algorithms," Addison-Wesley Publishing Company, Inc., Reading, Mass., 1968.

LEE, J. A. N.: "The Anatomy of a Compiler," Reinhold, New York, 1967.

MARTIN, F. J.: "Computer Modelling and Simulation," John Wiley & Sons, Inc., New York, 1968.

MCKEEMAN, W. M., J. J. HORNING, and D. B. WORTMAN: "A Compiler Generator," Prentice-Hall, Englewood Cliffs, N.J., 1970.

NAYLOR, T. H., J. L. BALINTY, K. CHU, and D. E. BURDICK: "Computer Simulation Techniques," John Wiley & Sons, Inc., New York, 1968.

TREMBLAY, J. P., and R. M. MANOHAR: "Discrete Mathematical Structures with Applications to Computer Science," McGraw-Hill Book Company, New York, 1975.

WALKER, T. M., and W. W. COTTERMAN: "An Introduction to Computer Science and Algorithmic Processes," Allyn and Bacon, Inc., Boston, Mass., 1970.

4

LINEAR DATA STRUCTURES AND THEIR LINKED STORAGE REPRESENTATION

The previous chapter described the representation of linear data structures by using the sequential-allocation method of storage. Although this method of allocation is suitable for certain applications, there are many other applications where the sequential-allocation method is unacceptable. The latter class of applications usually has the following characteristics:

1. *Unpredictable storage requirements. The exact amount of data storage required by a program in these areas often depends on the particular data being processed and, consequently, this requirement cannot be easily determined at the time the program is written.*

2. *Extensive manipulation of the stored data is required. Programs in these areas typically require that operations such as insertions and deletions be performed frequently on the data.*

The linked-allocation method of storage can result in both the efficient use of computer storage and computer time. Therefore, in this chapter the concepts of linked allocation, as applied to linear data structures, are introduced.

The first section describes the basic notions of pointers and linked allocation by using a simple polynomial-manipulation application.

In the next section, a number of algorithms associated with linked linear structures are given. The programming aspects of certain commonly performed operations on these linked structures are initially discussed by using arrays. The reasons for this approach are twofold: First, certain programming languages such as ALGOL 60, FORTRAN, and BASIC do not allow linked structures per se, and arrays can be used to simulate them. Second, by using low-level structures such as arrays to simulate linked structures, insight into the manipulation of such structures can be gained. A number of operations are also programmed by using the PL/I ALLOCATE *and* FREE *statements. These statements permit the programmer to control the allocation and definition of his own structures.*

Finally, a number of applications involving linked linear structures such as symbol-table construction and multiple-precision arithmetic are described.

4-1   POINTERS AND LINKED ALLOCATION

The previous chapter discussed at some length how the address of an element in a data structure could be obtained by direct computation. The data structures discussed were linearly ordered, and this ordering relation was preserved in the corresponding storage structures by using sequential allocation. There was no need for an element to specify where the next element would be found.

Consider a list consisting of elements which vary individually in size. The task of directly computing the address of a particular element becomes much more difficult. An obvious method of obtaining the address of a node (element) is to store this address in the computer memory. In Chap. 1 we referred to this addressing mode as pointer or link addressing. If the list in question has n nodes, we can store the address of each node in a vector consisting of n elements. The first element of the vector contains the address of the first node of the list, the second element the address of the second node, and so on.

There are many applications which, by their very nature, have data which is continually being updated (additions, deletions, etc.). Each time a change occurs, significant manipulation of the data is required. In some instances, the representation of the data by sequentially allocated lists results in an inefficient use of memory, wasted computational time, and indeed, for certain problems this method of allocation is totally unacceptable. The representation of polynomials by arrays discussed previously (see Sec. 3-5) had a number of obvious drawbacks. The arrays contained only a few nonzero elements and this was far from being a compact representation of polynomials. Furthermore, the memory requirements associated with certain operations were not always predictable (as in the case of polynomial division), so one was faced with the situation of not knowing in advance how much memory to reserve for the polynomial generated by such an operation.

Recall from Secs. 1-4.11 and 1-4.12 that the interpretation of a pointer as an address is a natural one. Most computers use addresses to find the next instruction to be executed and its operand(s). In many hardware configurations, special registers are used to store such addresses. Pointers are always of the same length (usually no longer than a half word) and this property enables the manipulation of pointers to be performed in a uniform manner using simple allocation techniques, regardless of the configurations of the structures to which they may point.

In the sequential-allocation method one is able to compute an address of an element provided that the storage structure is organized in some uniform manner. Pointers permit the referencing of structures in a uniform way, regardless of the organization of the structure being referenced. Pointers are capable of representing a much more complex relationship between elements of a structure than a linear order.

The use of pointers or links to refer to elements of a data structure (which is linearly ordered) implies that elements which are adjacent (because of the linear ordering) need not be physically adjacent in memory. This type of allocation scheme is called *linked allocation*. We now turn to the problem of representing structures by this type of allocation.

A list has been defined to consist of an ordered set of elements which may vary in number. A simple way to represent a linear list is to expand each node to contain a link or pointer to the next node. This representation is called a *one-way chain* or *singly linked linear list*, and it can be displayed as in Fig. 4-1.1*a*. In that figure, the variable FIRST con-

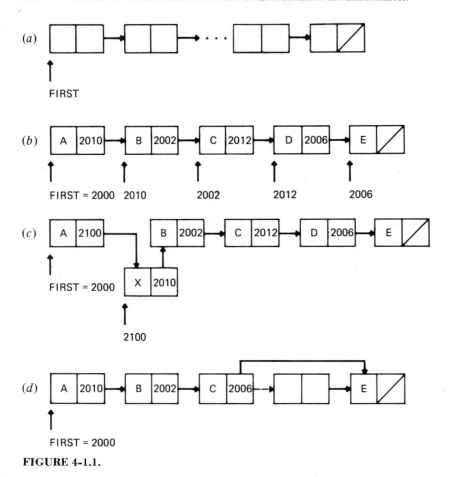

FIGURE 4-1.1.

tains an address or pointer which gives the location of the first node of the list. Each node is divided into two parts. The first part represents the information of the element and the second part contains the address of the next node. The last node of the list does not have a successor node and, consequently, no actual address is stored in the pointer field. In such a case, a null value is stored as the address. The arrow emanating from the link field of a particular node indicates its successor node in the structure. For example, the linked list in Fig. 4-1.1b represents a five-node list whose elements are located in memory locations 2000, 2010, 2002, 2012, and 2006, respectively. We again emphasize that the only purpose of the links is to specify which node is next in the linear ordering. The link address of NULL (indicated by the slash) in the last node signals the end of the list. NULL is not an address of any possible node, but is a special value which cannot be mistaken for an address. For this reason, NULL is used as a special list delimiter. It is possible for a list to have no nodes at all. Such a list is called an empty list, and this is denoted by assigning a value of NULL to FIRST in the current example.

Let us compare the operations commonly performed on sequentially allocated and linked lists. Consider the operations of *insertion* and *deletion* in the case of a sequentially allocated list. If we have an n-element list and it is required to insert a new element between the first and second elements, then the last n −1 elements of the list must be moved so as to make room for the new element. For a list that contains many nodes, this is a rather inefficient way of performing an insertion—especially if many insertions are to be performed. The same principle applies in the case of a deletion, where all elements after the element being deleted must be moved up so as to take up the vacant space caused by the element being removed from the list.

In the case of linked allocation, an addition is performed in a straightforward manner. If a new element is to be inserted following the first element, this can be accomplished by merely interchanging pointers. This is illustrated in Fig. 4-1.1c for a five-element list. The deletion of the fourth element from the original list can be performed by using the pointer change as shown in Fig. 4-1.1d. It is clear that the insertion and deletion operations are more efficient when performed on linked lists than on sequentially allocated lists.

There are a number of other comparisons we can make between the linked and sequentially allocated storage schemes for lists. If a particular node in a linked list is required, it is necessary to follow the links from the first node onwards until the desired node is found. This is clearly inferior to the computed-address technique associated with sequential allocation. In some applications, however, it is required to examine every node in the list. In such a situation, it is only slightly more time consuming to go through a linked list than a sequential list.

It is easier to join or split two linked lists than it is in the case of sequential allocation. This can be accomplished merely by changing pointers and does not require the movement of nodes.

The pointers or links consume additional memory, but if only part of a memory word is being used, then a pointer can be stored in the remaining part. It is possible to group nodes so as to require only one link per several nodes. These two factors make the cost of storing pointers not too expensive in many cases.

The memory address in the link field has been used for illustration purposes in the present discussion. However, in practice, this address may be of no concern (and indeed unknown) to the programmer. Therefore, in much of the discussion to follow, the arrow symbol is used to denote a successor node.

We mentioned the use of pointers in this section only to specify the linear ordering (adjacency) among elements, but pointers can be used to specify more complex relations between nodes, such as that of a *tree* or a *directed graph*. This is difficult and indeed, for certain graphs, impossible to specify by using sequential allocation. These more complex structures can be specified by placing in the nodes a number of pointers. It is possible for a particular node to belong to several structures using this technique. A greatly expanded discussion of this will be given in Chap. 5.

From this discussion and some of the applications which follow, it will become clear that for certain operations, linked allocation is more efficient than sequential allocation; and yet, for other operations the opposite is true. In many applications, both types of allocations are used.

A *pool* or list of *free* nodes, which we refer to as the *availability list*, is maintained in conjunction with linked allocation. Whenever a node is to be inserted in a list, a free node is taken from the availability list and linked to the former list as required. On the other hand, the deletion of a node from a list causes its return to the availability list, where it can be used for insertion purposes at a later time. The advantage of this scheme of memory management is obvious. At any particular time, the only space which is used is what is really required.

The management of available storage in the case of a singly linked list is simple. For structures whose nodes can contain several pointers, this simplicity vanishes. A particular node can belong to many lists, and the deletion of this node from one list does not mean that it can be returned to the available storage list. The algorithm for managing memory, which is often called the *garbage collector*, tends to be nontrivial. This topic will be discussed in detail in Sec. 5-6. We are now prepared to examine some of the operations performed on linear linked lists.

Consider the familiar symbol-manipulation problem of performing various operations on polynomials such as addition, subtraction, multiplication, division, differentiation, etc. Let us direct our attention, in particular, to the manipulation of polynomials in three variables. It may be required, for example, to formulate an algorithm which subtracts polynomial $x^2 + 3xy - x + y^2 + 2z^3$ from polynomial $2x^2 + 5xy + y^2 + yz$ to give a result of $x^2 + 2xy + x + yz - 2z^3$. We are interested in finding a suitable representation for polynomials so that the operations mentioned above can be performed in a reasonably efficient manner. If we are to manipulate polynomials, it is clear that individual terms must be selected. In particular, we must distinguish between variables, coefficients, and exponents within each term.

It is possible to represent a polynomial by a three-dimensional array through an extension of the discussion of Sec. 3-5. From the discussion at the beginning of this section, it follows that this method of representation is unsatisfactory, and hence linked allocation should be used in this case. Before describing how it can be used, we consider the different classes of operations we can perform on linked linear lists.

Data in any type of application is required to be manipulated according to certain operations. If this processing is to be performed by the use of a computer, the first task to be accomplished is the adequate representation of the data in the computer memory. The difficulty and complexity of this task depend to a large extent on the particular programming language that is used to program the algorithms associated with an application. Certain languages have been specifically designed for manipulating linked lists. One such prominent language is LISP 1.5. In other cases, common procedures or functions to be performed on linked lists have been written as subprograms in a simple "host" language. An example of such a case is the list-processing language SLIP, which consists of a number of subprograms which are written in the FORTRAN language. We make use of the PL/I language to represent certain common operations performed on lists.

There are a number of classes of operations which are associated with linked lists. The first class contains those operations which are independent of the data contained in the nodes of a list. These operations include the creation, insertion, deletion, and selection of nodes. Programming languages which possess list-processing capabilities usually have these operations built-in.

Another class of operations associated with list structures is the one containing the operation which converts the raw data from a human readable form to a corresponding machine form. The inverse operation of converting an internal structure to a suitable human readable form is also required. These operations are clearly data dependent, and attention must be given to the interpretation that is associated with the structures. List-processing languages have some standard basic routines for such operations, but any additional routines must be programmed.

Finally, there are operations that must be programmed to manipulate the data according to what is required in a particular application at hand. In the case of polynomial manipulation, for example, such operations would include the addition, subtraction, multiplication, division, differentiation, and integration of polynomials. Once a programmer has access to all the routines for the three classes mentioned above, his task of programming an algorithm is much simpler.

Let us consider the problem of describing singly linked linear-list representations and operations in an algorithmic notation. A node consists of a number of fields, each of which can represent an integer, a real number, etc., except for one field (usually the last for purposes of illustration), called a *pointer*, which contains the location of the next node in the list.

Consider the example of representing a term of a polynomial in the variables x, y, and z. A typical node is represented as in Fig. 4-1.2*a*, which consists of four sequentially allocated fields that we collectively refer to as TERM. The first three fields represent the power of the variables x, y, and z, respectively. The fourth and fifth fields represent the coefficient of the term in the polynomial and the address of the next term in the polynomial, respectively. For example, the term 3xy would be represented as in Fig. 4-1.2*b*.

The selection of a particular field within a node for our polynomial example is an easy matter. Our algorithmic notation allows the referencing of any field of a node given the pointer P to that node. COEFF(P) denotes the coefficient field of a node pointed to by P. Similarly, the exponents of x, y, and z are given by POWER_X(P), POWER_Y(P), and POWER_Z(P), respectively, and the pointer to the next node is given by LINK(P).

Consider as an example the representation of the polynomial

$$2x^2 + 5xy + y^2 + yz$$

as a linked list. Assume that the nodes in the list are to be stored so that a term pointed to by P precedes another term indicated by Q if POWER_X(P) is greater than POWER_X(Q);

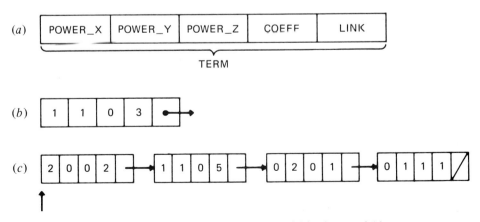

FIGURE 4-1.2 Linked list representation of a polynomial in three variables.

or, if they are equal, then POWER_Y(P) must be greater than POWER_Y(Q); or, if they are equal, then POWER_Z(P) must be greater than POWER_Z(Q). For our example, the list is represented by Fig. 4-1.2c.

Let us now consider the more difficult problem of inserting a node into a linked list. There are a number of steps necessary to accomplish this. First, the values for the various fields of the new node must be obtained either from an input operation or as the result of a computation. Second, we must somehow obtain a node from available storage. Finally, the values of the fields obtained in the first step are copied in the appropriate field positions of the new node, which is then placed in the linked list. The linking of the new node to its successor in the existing list is accomplished by setting the pointer field of the former to a value giving the location of the latter.

In the algorithms to be discussed in this section, assume that we have an available area of storage and that we can request a node from this area. In the polynomial example, the special assignment statement

> Set P $\Leftarrow$ TERM

creates a new node consisting of the five fields previously described, with the location of the first of these being copied in the pointer variable P. At creation, the fields POWER_X(P), POWER_Y(P), POWER_Z(P), COEFF(P), and LINK(P) have undefined values. When a node is no longer required, we can return it to available storage. This we specify by stating, "Restore node P to the availability area." After taking this action, the node is assumed to be inaccessible and P is undefined. We will discuss in more detail the request of nodes from and the return of nodes to the availability area of storage in the next subsection.

We can now formulate an algorithm which inserts a term of a polynomial into a linked list.

Algorithm POLYFRONT.   Given the definition of the node structure TERM and an availability area from which we can obtain such nodes, it is required to insert a node in the linked list so that it immediately precedes the node whose address is designated by the pointer FIRST. The fields of the new term are denoted by NX, NY, NZ, and NCOEFF, which correspond to the exponents for x, y, and z, and the coefficient value of the term, respectively. P is an auxiliary pointer variable.

1. [Obtain a node from available storage]   Set P $\Leftarrow$ TERM.
2. [Initialize numeric fields]   Set POWER_X(P) $\leftarrow$ NX, POWER_Y(P) $\leftarrow$ NY, POWER_Z(P) $\leftarrow$ NZ, and COEFF(P) $\leftarrow$ NCOEFF.
3. [Set link to the list]   Set LINK(P) $\leftarrow$ FIRST, POLYFRONT $\leftarrow$ P, and Exit.

Algorithm POLYFRONT performs all its insertions at one end of the linked list. In general, it is also possible to perform insertions at the other end or in the middle of the list. The zero polynomial (polynomial with no terms) is represented by the null pointer. Before any term of a polynomial has been added to a list, its first node pointer, which we call POLY, has a value of NULL. Note that it is quite possible to get cancellation of terms in adding and subtracting polynomials, and this can result in a zero polynomial.

The algorithm is invoked as a function whose name is POLYFRONT. The address of the created node is assigned to POLYFRONT immediately prior to the Exit and it is this value that replaces the function call.

Given that it is possible to invoke the procedure POLYFRONT, the construction of a linked list for a polynomial is achieved by having a zero polynomial initially and by repeatedly invoking Algorithm POLYFRONT until all terms of the polynomial are processed. For the polynomial $2x^2 + 5xy + y^2 + yz$, this must be done four times. Since we want the first element of the list to be $2x^2$, we start by inserting the term yz followed by the insertion of y^2, etc. If the pointer to the first node of the list is POLY, then a trace of the invoking procedure POLYFRONT is given by Fig. 4-1.3.

Let us now consider an algorithm which performs an insertion at the end of a linked list.

Algorithm POLYEND (Insert a node at the end of a linked list). Given the definition of the node structure TERM and an availability area from which we can obtain nodes, it is required to insert a node at the end of the linked linear list whose address is designated by the pointer FIRST. The fields of the new term are denoted by NX, NY, NZ, and NCOEFF, which correspond to the exponents for x, y, and z and the coefficient value of the term, respectively. NEW is a pointer variable which contains the address of the new node.

1. [Obtain a node from available storage] Set NEW ⇐ TERM.
2. [Initialize fields] Set POWER_X(NEW) ← NX, POWER_Y(NEW) ← NY,
   POWER_Z(NEW) ← NZ, COEFF(NEW) ← NCOEFF, and LINK(NEW) ← NULL.
3. [Is the list empty?] If FIRST = NULL then set POLYEND ← NEW and Exit.
4. [Initiate search for the last node] Set SAVE ← FIRST.
5. [Search for end of list]
   Repeat while LINK(SAVE) ≠ NULL: Set SAVE ← LINK(SAVE).
6. [Set LINK field of last node to NEW] Set LINK(SAVE) ← NEW.
7. [Return first node pointer] Set POLYEND ← FIRST and Exit.

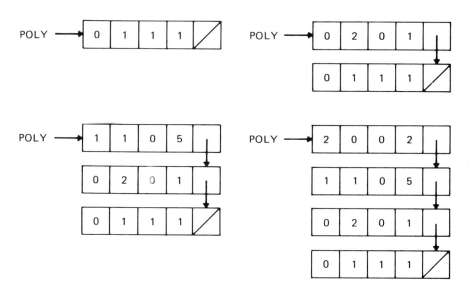

FIGURE 4-1.3 Trace of the construction of polynomial $2x^2 + 5xy + y^2 + yz$ using Algorithm POLYFRONT.

The POLYEND algorithm must deal with two situations when inserting a new node at the end of a list whose pointer address is given by the variable FIRST. In the first case, the value of FIRST is NULL (there are no nodes in the list). A new node is created and its address is assigned to the variable NEW. The information contents of the node are copied in the appropriate fields. The LINK field of the new node is set to NULL. In the second case, the value of FIRST is not NULL, and in order to insert the new node at the end of the list, the end node of the original list must be found. This is accomplished by chaining through the list until a node with a LINK field of NULL is found. The chaining is performed with the help of the temporary variable SAVE, which is successively assigned the value of the LINK field of each node. Eventually, the value of the LINK field of the node pointed to by SAVE is NULL. The LINK field of this node is now assigned a value which points to the new node. Note that in the first case, the pointer variable FIRST is assigned a value which points to the new node while, in the second case, the first node of the list after the insertion remains the same as that before the insertion.

By repeatedly invoking Algorithm POLYEND, a linked-list representation of a given polynomial can be easily achieved. This process is very similar to the one described previously using Algorithm POLYFRONT. Note, however, that the terms of the polynomial need not be reversed in order to obtain the desired list. A trace of building a linked list for polynomial $2x^2 + 5xy + y^2 + yz$ is given in Fig. 4-1.4, where POLY is a pointer to the first node in the list.

Note that Algorithm POLYEND becomes inefficient when the number of nodes in the list is large. In such a case, the entire list must be traversed in order to perform an insertion. This problem can be easily corrected by keeping the address of the last node that was inserted in the list. The next insertion can be performed without chaining through the entire list. The link field of the previously inserted node need only be changed to the ad-

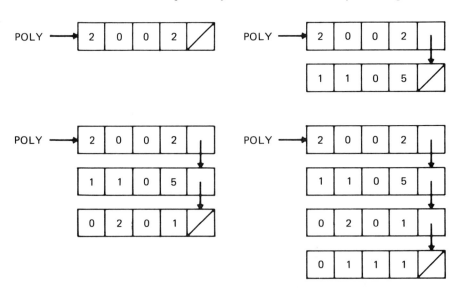

FIGURE 4-1.4 Trace of the construction of polynomial $2x^2 + 5xy + y^2 + yz$ using Algorithm POLYEND.

dress of the new node to be inserted. This obvious modification of Algorithm POLYEND is implemented in the following algorithm.

Algorithm POLYLAST. Given the definition of the node structure TERM and an availability area from which we can obtain nodes, it is required to insert a node at the end of the linked list whose address is designated by the pointer FIRST. The pointer variable LAST denotes the address of the last node in the list. The fields of the new term are denoted NX, NY, NZ, and NCOEFF, which correspond to the exponents for x, y, and z and the coefficient value of the term, respectively. NEW is a pointer variable which contains the address of the new node.

1. [Obtain a node from available storage] Set NEW ⇐ TERM.
2. [Initialize fields] Set POWER_X(NEW) ← NX, POWER_Y(NEW) ← NY,
   POWER_Z(NEW) ← NZ, COEFF(NEW) ← NCOEFF, and LINK(NEW) ← NULL.
3. [Is the list empty?]
   If FIRST = NULL, then set LAST ← POLYLAST ← NEW and Exit.
4. [Insert node in nonempty list] Set LINK(LAST) ← NEW, LAST ← NEW,
   POLYLAST ← FIRST, and Exit.

In this section we have introduced the basic concepts of linked allocation. As a motivating example, these concepts were applied to the representation of polynomials so as to facilitate their symbolic manipulation. A further discussion of this application is given in Sec. 4-3.1.

The next section is concerned with the description of certain storage structures for linear lists and their associated algorithms. Furthermore, the programming aspects of linked structures are discussed in some detail.

4-2 LINKED LINEAR LISTS

The basic notions of linked allocation as applied to the storage representation of linear lists were briefly discussed in the previous section. In this section linked allocation is dealt with in greater detail.

The first subsection is concerned with the formulation of algorithms such as insertion, deletion, traversal, and copying that are associated with linear lists. The programming aspects of these operations are also discussed in detail. In particular, the simulation of linked allocation by using arrays is introduced. This discussion is followed by describing the programmer-defined data-type facility which is available in PL/I for the linked representation of linear lists. The second subsection deals with the circularly linked representation of linear lists.

Since the traversal of a linked linear list is performed in one direction, the deletion operation in such a structure can be inefficient. Moreover, there are a number of applications which require the traversal of a linear list in both directions. For these reasons the "doubly" linked representation of a linear list along with its associated operations is introduced in the last subsection. The programming details of doubly linked linear lists are considered.

4-2.1   Operations on Linear Lists Using Singly Linked Storage Structures

This subsection describes in detail the representation of linear lists using linked allocation. Algorithms, such as the insertion of nodes into and the deletion of nodes from a
linked linear list are given. The request for nodes from and the return of nodes to the
available area of storage are described more fully than in Sec. 4-1.

      The programming aspects of linked allocation are discussed both from the simula-
tion point of view, using arrays, and from the programmer-defined data-type facility
available in PL/I. The first approach is the one which is usually taken in programming
linked represented structures in languages that do not have pointer or link facilities, such
as FORTRAN, ALGOL 60, and BASIC, while the second approach is used in languages
that do have pointer facilities, such as PL/I, SNOBOL, ALGOL 68, ALGOL W, and
LISP 1.5.

      Unless otherwise stated, we assume that a typical element or node consists of two
fields, namely, an information field called INFO and a pointer field denoted by LINK. The
name of a typical element is denoted by NODE. Pictorially, the node structure is given as
follows:

NODE

| INFO | LINK |

It is further assumed that an available area of storage for this node structure consists of a
linked stack of available nodes, as shown in Fig. 4-2.1a, where the pointer variable AVAIL
contains the address of the top node in the stack.

      The task of obtaining a node from the availability stack can now be formulated.
Assume that the address of the next available node is to be stored in the variable NEW.
For practical reasons the availability stack contains only a finite number of nodes; therefore, it must be checked for an underflow condition. This condition is signaled by the value
of AVAIL being NULL. If a node is available, then the new top-most element of the stack is
denoted by LINK(AVAIL). The fields of the node corresponding to the pointer value of NEW
can now be filled in and the field LINK(NEW) is set to a value which designates the successor node of this new node. The availability stack before and after a free node has been
obtained is given in Fig. 4-2.1.

      A similar procedure can be formulated for the return of a discarded node to the avail-
ability stack. If the address of this discarded node is given by the variable FREE, then the
link field of this node is set to the present value of AVAIL and the value of FREE becomes
the new value of AVAIL. This process is shown in Fig. 4-2.2.

      We can now formulate an algorithm which inserts a node into a linked linear list in a
stack-like manner.

Algorithm INSERT.   Given a linked linear list whose typical node contains an INFO and
LINK field, as previously described, and a pointer AVAIL which specifies the top element of
the availability stack, it is required to insert a node in the linked list which immediately
precedes the node whose address is designated by the pointer FIRST. The information of

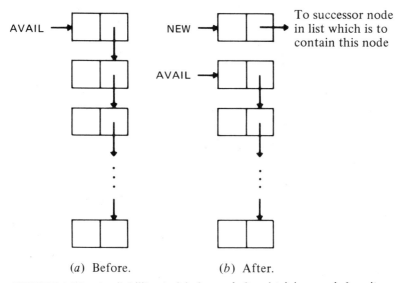

(a) Before.   (b) After.

FIGURE 4-2.1   Availability stack before and after obtaining a node from it.

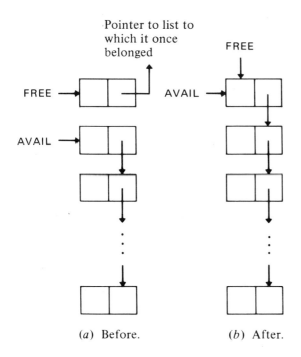

(a) Before.   (b) After.

FIGURE 4-2.2   Availability stack before and after
a free node has been returned.

the new term is to be initialized to a value given by the variable X. NEW is a pointer variable.

1. [Underflow?]
   If AVAIL = NULL, then write 'availability stack underflow', and Exit.
2. [Obtain address of next free node]   Set NEW ← AVAIL.
3. [Remove free node from availability stack]   Set AVAIL ← LINK(AVAIL).
4. [Initialize fields of new node and its link to the list]
   Set INFO(NEW) ← X and LINK(NEW) ← FIRST.
5. [Return address of new node]   Set INSERT ← NEW, and Exit.

INSERT is called as a function which returns a pointer value to the variable FIRST (i.e., FIRST ← INSERT(X, FIRST)). Algorithm INSERT is very similar to Algorithm POLY-FRONT in Sec. 4-1, except for the additional detail of handling a request for a new node from the availability area of storage.

   We now give an algorithm which performs an insertion at the end of a linked linear list. Again, except for the detail of requesting a free node from the availability area, this algorithm is almost identical to Algorithm POLYEND of Sec. 4-1.

Algorithm INSEND (Insert a node at the end of a linked linear list).   Given a linked linear list whose typical node contains an INFO and link field, and a pointer AVAIL which specifies the top element of the availability stack, it is required to insert a node at the end of a list whose first node is denoted by the pointer FIRST. The information field of the new node is to be initialized to a value given by the variable X. NEW and SAVE are pointer variables.

1. [Underflow?]
   If AVAIL = NULL, then write 'availability stack underflow', and Exit.
2. [Obtain location of next free node]   Set NEW ← AVAIL.
3. [Remove node from the availability stack]   Set AVAIL ← LINK(AVAIL).
4. [Copy information into new node]
   Set INFO(NEW) ← X and LINK(NEW) ← NULL.
5. [Is list empty?]   If FIRST = NULL, then set INSEND ← NEW, and Exit.
6. [Initialize for last node search]   Set SAVE ← FIRST.
7. [Search for end node of list]
   Repeat while LINK(SAVE) ≠ NULL: set SAVE ← LINK(SAVE).
8. [Set LINK field of last node to point to the new one]
   Set LINK(SAVE) ← NEW.
9. [Return first node pointer]   Set INSEND ← FIRST, and Exit.

   There are many applications where it is desirable to maintain an ordered linear list. The ordering is in increasing or decreasing order on the INFO field. Such an ordering often results in more efficient processing. For example, in the polynomial example discussed in the previous section, the number of operations required to add two polynomials each of degree n is reduced from order n^2 to order n if the terms of each polynomial are kept in some decreasing order that depends on the powers of x, y, and z.

The following algorithm performs an insertion in a list according to the ordering that all terms are kept in increasing order of their INFO field.

Algorithm INSORD. Given a linked linear list whose typical node contains an INFO and LINK field and whose first node is denoted by FIRST, and a pointer AVAIL which specifies the top element of the availability stack, it is required to insert a node which preserves the ordering of the terms in increasing order of their INFO field. The information field of the new node is to be initialized to the value given by the variable X. NEW and SAVE are pointer variables.

1. [Underflow?]
   If AVAIL = NULL, then write 'availability stack underflow', and Exit.
2. [Obtain location of next free node]   Set NEW ← AVAIL.
3. [Remove node from availability stack]   Set AVAIL ← LINK(AVAIL).
4. [Copy information contents into new node]   Set INFO(NEW) ← X.
5. [If list is empty set LINK field of new node to NULL, and Exit]
   If FIRST = NULL, then set LINK(NEW) ← NULL, INSORD ← NEW, and Exit.
6. [If new node precedes first node then insert at top of list]
   If INFO(FIRST) ≥ INFO(NEW), then set LINK(NEW) ← FIRST, INSORD ← NEW and Exit.
7. [Initialize temporary pointer]   Set SAVE ← FIRST.
8. [Search for predecessor of new node]
   Repeat while LINK(SAVE) ≠ NULL and INFO(LINK(SAVE)) ≤ INFO(NEW):
      Set SAVE ← LINK(SAVE).
9. [Set LINK fields of new node and its predecessor]
   Set LINK(NEW) ← LINK(SAVE) and LINK(SAVE) ← NEW.
10. [Return first node pointer]   Set INSORD ← FIRST, and Exit.

The algorithm considers the case of a null or empty list first of all and its presence causes the LINK field of the new node to be set to NULL. In the second case, the new node is to precede the first node in the original list. This results in the new node becoming the first node in the updated list, and the LINK field of the new node is assigned a pointer value which corresponds to the location of the first node of the original list. In the third and final case, the pointer value of FIRST is not NULL and the INFO value of the node designated by FIRST is less than the INFO value of the new node to be inserted in the list. The value of the variable FIRST is assigned to temporary pointer variable SAVE. The temporary variable is assigned the LINK field values of successive nodes until the value of INFO(LINK (SAVE)) is greater than the value of the INFO field for the new node, or the LINK field of the node designated by the temporary variable value is NULL. In either case, the LINK field of the new node is assigned the address of the node indicated by the old LINK field of the temporary variable. The address of the new node is then assigned to the LINK field of the node indicated by the temporary variable.

By repeatedly invoking Algorithm INSORD, an ordered linked linear list can easily be obtained. For example, the following sequence of statements:

FRONT ← NULL
FRONT ← INSORD(29, FRONT)
FRONT ← INSORD(10, FRONT)
FRONT ← INSORD(25, FRONT)
FRONT ← INSORD(40, FRONT)
FRONT ← INSORD(37, FRONT)

creates a five-element list. A trace of this construction is given in Fig. 4-2.3.

Now that a number of insertion algorithms have been discussed, let us look at another equally important algorithm—that of deleting a node from a linked linear list.

Algorithm DELETE (Deleting a node from a linked linear list). Given a variable FIRST whose value denotes the address of the first node in the linked linear list, a variable X whose value denotes the address of the node to be deleted, and a variable NEXT whose value gives the address of the next node in the list, it is required to delete the node whose address is given by variable X.

1. [Empty list?] If FIRST = NULL, then write 'underflow', and Exit.
2. [Delete first node?]
   If X = FIRST, then set FIRST ← LINK(FIRST) and go to step 9.
3. [Initiate search for predecessor of X] Set NEXT ← FIRST.
4. [Update PRED] Set PRED ← NEXT.

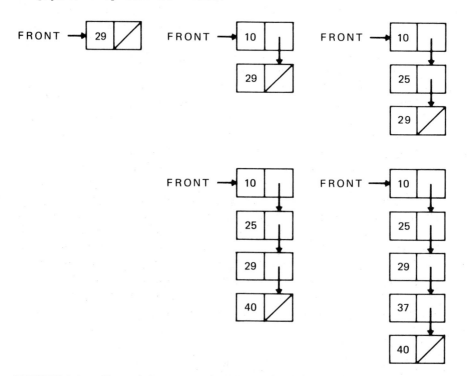

FIGURE 4-2.3 Trace of the construction of an ordered linked linear list using Algorithm INSORD.

5. [Get next node] Set NEXT ← LINK(NEXT).
6. [End of list?] If NEXT = NULL, then write 'node not found', and Exit.
7. [Is this node X?] If NEXT ≠ X, then go to step 4.
8. [Delete X] Set LINK(PRED) ← LINK(X)
9. [Return node to availability area] Set LINK(X) ← AVAIL, AVAIL ← X, and Exit.

The first step in the algorithm checks for an underflow. The second step determines whether or not the node to be deleted is the first node of the list, and if it is, then the second node of the list becomes the new first node. In the case of a list containing a single node, the pointer variable FIRST assumes the NULL value as a result of the deletion.

If X is not the first node in the list, then a search to find the immediate predecessor of X (PRED in the algorithm) is launched. This is accomplished by chaining through the list and storing the address of the next node in variable NEXT until X is found. A value of NULL for NEXT indicates that the node to be deleted has not been found in the list and an error has been made. When variables NEXT and X contain the same value, we are in a position to change the link field of the predecessor node of X to point to its successor node (LINK(X)). This is accomplished in step 8 of the algorithm. The deleted node is returned to the availability area in the final step of the algorithm.

Algorithm DELETE assumes that the address of the node to be deleted is known initially. Such, however, is not always the case. A node to be deleted is very often specified by giving its INFO value. A search is then made for the node with this value. The previous algorithm can be easily modified to accommodate this change.

As a final example, we formulate an algorithm which copies a linked linear list.

Algorithm COPY. Given a linked linear list whose typical node consists of an information (INFO) field and a pointer (LINK) field, and a variable FIRST that denotes the address of the first node in this list, it is required to devise an algorithm that copies this list. The new list is to contain nodes whose information and pointer fields are denoted by FIELD and PTR, respectively. The address of the first node in the newly created list is to be placed in BEGIN. NEW, SAVE, and PRED are pointer variables.

1. [Empty list?] If FIRST = NULL, then set BEGIN ← NULL, and Exit.
2. [Copy first node]
   If AVAIL = NULL,
   then write 'availability stack underflow', and Exit;
   otherwise, set NEW ← AVAIL, AVAIL ← LINK(AVAIL),
   FIELD(NEW) ← INFO(FIRST) and BEGIN ← NEW.
3. [Initialize traversal] Set SAVE ← FIRST.
4. [Move to next node?] Repeat steps 5 and 6 while LINK(SAVE) ≠ NULL.
5. [Update predecessor and save pointers] Set PRED ← NEW and
   SAVE ← LINK(SAVE).
6. [Copy node]
   If AVAIL = NULL,
   then write 'availability stack underflow', and Exit;
   otherwise, set NEW ← AVAIL, AVAIL ← LINK(AVAIL),
   FIELD(NEW) ← INFO(SAVE), and PTR(PRED) ← NEW.
7. [LINK(SAVE) = NULL] Set PTR(NEW) ← NULL, and Exit.

The first step of the algorithm checks for the empty case. In the second step, the first node of the original list is copied. The remaining steps of the algorithm traverse the remaining nodes in the original list. Note that as each new node is created, its address must be placed in the PTR field of the predecessor of this node.

We now turn to the programming aspects of linked structures. These structures are first programmed or simulated by using only arrays. This discussion is followed by a description of the programmer-defined data-type facility which is available in PL/I for the linked representation of linear lists.

Let us consider the problem of implementing linked linear lists using arrays. As mentioned previously, linked structures cannot be programmer-defined in a number of programming languages, such as FORTRAN, ALGOL 60, and BASIC, since there are no pointer-type variables in these languages. Although the PL/I language has pointer facilities, we nevertheless use it throughout the discussion on linked allocation with arrays. The concepts presented are directly applicable to languages without pointer data types.

In an array implementation, a node consists of a number of fields, each of which can represent an integer, a real number, a character string, etc., except for one field (usually the last field) which represents a pointer to the next node in the linear list. This pointer is an index (or subscript) of the array. This index points to the next node (i.e., array element) in the linear list. It is easy to see how an index, together with a field name, allows us to select a field from a particular node.

Consider the example of representing a term in a polynomial of the variables x, y, and z, which was discussed in Sec. 4-1.

Assuming that any polynomial has at most 25 terms, we can declare five vectors: POWER_X, POWER_Y, POWER_Z, COEFF, and LINK, each representing a subscript giving the location of the next node in the list. Let us examine the representation of the polynomial

$$2x^2 + 5xy + y^2 + yz$$

as a linked linear list.

Suppose that the representation of this ordered polynomial is represented in terms of the five vectors as follows:

POWER_X(2) = 2   POWER_Y(2) = 0   POWER_Z(2) = 0   COEFF(2) = 2   LINK(2) = 10
POWER_X(5) = 0   POWER_Y(5) = 1   POWER_Z(5) = 1   COEFF(5) = 1   LINK(5) = 0
POWER_X(10) = 1   POWER_Y(10) = 1   POWER_Z(10) = 0   COEFF 10) = 5   LINK(10) = 21
POWER_X(21) = 0   POWER_Y(21) = 2   POWER_Z(21) = 0   COEFF(21) = 1   LINK(21) = 5

The first node of the list is specified by storing the index value of 2 in a variable called FIRST. The value of LINK(2) gives the index value of the element of the second node in the polynomial. Knowing that LINK(2) has a value of 10 permits us to access the fields of the second node by writing COEFF(LINK(2)), etc. The index of the third node in the list is given by LINK(10) which has a value of 21. Once the index value of the first node is known, it is an easy matter to follow the link pointers to obtain all the nodes in the list. The last node in the list has an index value of 5, and its link value is zero. Note that when using arrays, the NULL link is represented by the number zero.

Another point needs clarification here. By definition, the fields within a node are sequentially allocated. This is not the case in the above representation of linked lists. The field represented by POWER_X(2) is not adjacent in memory to the field denoted by POWER_Y(2). The reason for this is the sequential allocation of vectors in the memory.

An alternate representation of linked lists is accomplished by using a double subscripted array. Let us declare a table called NODE consisting of 25 rows and 5 columns. Each occupied row of the matrix represents a node and, in particular, each element in a row designates a field of that node. The representation of our example polynomial is:

NODE(2,1) = 2	NODE(2,2) = 0	NODE(2,3) = 0	NODE(2,4) = 2	NODE(2,5) = 10
NODE(5,1) = 0	NODE(5,2) = 1	NODE(5,3) = 1	NODE(5,4) = 1	NODE(5.5) = 0
NODE(10,1) = 1	NODE(10,2) = 1	NODE(10,3) = 0	NODE(10,4) = 5	NODE(10,5) = 21
NODE(21,1) = 0	NODE(21,2) = 2	NODE(21,3) = 0	NODE(21,4) = 1	NODE(21,5) = 5

where NODE(I,1), NODE(I,2), NODE(I,3), NODE(I,4), and NODE(I,5) correspond to the fields POWER_X, POWER_Y, POWER_Z, COEFF, and LINK of some node, respectively. The above representation does make the five fields represented by a row of the matrix adjacent in memory because arrays are stored in row-major order in PL/I. The advantage of this approach is debatable, however, since the running time of the program is increased because of the use of double subscripting, and the programming effort is not diminished by this alternate representation.

An obvious representation which has the property that each node is sequentially allocated uses a vector consisting of 125 elements. A group of five consecutive elements of the vector represents a node whose subscript value is a multiple of five. If the vector is denoted by POLY, and I represents the subscript value of the first field in a node, then the following correspondence holds with respect to the original formulation:

POLY(I) $\leftrightarrow$ POWER_X
POLY(I+1)$\leftrightarrow$POWER_Y
POLY(I+2)$\leftrightarrow$POWER_Z
POLY(I+3)$\leftrightarrow$COEFF
POLY(I+4)$\leftrightarrow$LINK

This method of representing a linked linear list for a polynomial is nearly as efficient as the case where five vectors were used.

The selection of a particular field within a node for our polynomial example is an easy matter. Using the representation of the five vectors POWER_X, POWER_Y, POWER_Z, COEFF, and LINK, we can select any field of a node given the index P to that node. The coefficient of the term pointed to by P is denoted by COEFF(P), the exponent of X is given by POWER_X(P), and the pointer to the next node is given by LINK(P). The selector for any field of a node is complete; that is, POWER_X(P), COEFF(P), or LINK(P), etc. can be used as either a left or right operand in an assignment statement.

Using arrays, let us now consider the programming of some of the algorithms discussed earlier in this chapter. Each of these algorithms obtained a node of available storage from the area of available storage. When using arrays to program linked linear lists, the programmer must control the list of available storage, which is usually maintained as a

```
ALIST:
    PROCEDURE;
/*  PROCEDURE TO CONSTRUCT A LINKED STACK OF AVAILABLE NODES FOR A
    POLYNOMIAL IN THREE VARIABLES.  */

    DECLARE I FIXED DECIMAL;

    /* SET THE LINK FIELD OF EACH NODE TO POINT TO ITS SUCCESSOR */

    DO I = 1 TO 99;
       LINK(I) = I + 1;
    END;

    LINK(100) = 0; /* SET POINTER FIELD OF LAST NODE TO EMPTY */

    AVAIL = 1; /* SET TOP OF STACK POINTER 'AVAIL' TO ONE */
    RETURN;
END ALIST;
```

FIGURE 4-2.4   Procedure for constructing a linked stack of available nodes.

linked stack. When a free node is required, the top node of the availability list is deleted from the stack and is used as a new node. The availability list in the case of the polynomial example can be constructed by the PL/I procedure ALIST given in Fig. 4-2.4. This initialization program creates a linked linear list of one hundred nodes. Initially, the values of the LINK fields are ordered in the sense that LINK(I) > I, where I is the subscript or address of the ith node. This, however, changes as nodes are removed from and returned to the availability list. The pointer AVAIL, which is initially set to "one," gives the subscript corresponding to the top node in the stack. The vector LINK is assumed to be global to the procedure, as is the pointer AVAIL.

The task of obtaining a node from the availability list can now be formulated. It is assumed that the address of the next available node is to be stored in the variable NEW. Recall that for practical reasons, the availability list contains only a finite number of nodes (one hundred in this case), so an underflow test must be made. The program to obtain a free node from the availability stack is given as follows:

```
/* PROGRAM TO OBTAIN A FREE NODE FROM THE AVAILABILITY STACK */
/* CHECK FOR UNDERFLOW */
    IF (AVAIL = 0) THEN GO TO _;
/* OBTAIN POINTER VALUE FOR A NEW NODE AND STORE IT IN NEW */
    NEW = AVAIL;
/* OBTAIN ADDRESS OF NEW TOP OF STACK NODE */
    AVAIL = LINK(AVAIL);
```

The stack underflow label in the program has been omitted. This destination will depend on what sort of corrective action (if any) is to be taken when the availability stack underflows. The fields of the node corresponding to the pointer value of NEW can now be filled in, and the field LINK(NEW) is set to a value which designates the successor node of this new node.

A similar program can be written which returns a node to the availability stack. If the pointer to this discarded node is given by the variable FREE, then the link field of this node is set to the present value of AVAIL, and the value of FREE becomes the new value of AVAIL. The program for this operation follows:

```
/* PROGRAM TO RETURN A DISCARDED NODE TO AVAILABILITY STACK */
/* CHANGE THE LINK FIELD OF THE DISCARDED NODE TO POINT TO
   THE PREVIOUS TOP ELEMENT IN STACK */
   LINK(FREE) = AVAIL;
/* THE DISCARDED NODE BECOMES THE NEW TOP ELEMENT OF STACK */
   AVAIL = FREE;
```

The previous programming techniques can be incorporated in a procedure for Algorithm POLYFRONT of Sec. 4-1. In the PL/I procedure given in Fig. 4-2.5, it is assumed that the five vectors POWER_X, POWER_Y, POWER_Z, COEFF, and LINK and the variable AVAIL are global to the procedure.

Now that it is possible to invoke the function POLYFRONT, all that is required to build a linked linear list for a polynomial is to start with a zero polynomial and repeatedly invoke the insertion function until all terms of the polynomial are processed. For the polynomial $2x^2 + 5xy + y^2 + yz$, we must invoke the insertion function four times. Since we want the first element of the list to be $2x^2$, we start by inserting the term yz followed by the insertion of y^2, etc.

If the pointer to the first node of the list is POLY, then the following program steps will construct this polynomial:

```
/* INITIALIZE LIST POINTER TO NULL */
   DECLARE POLY FIXED DECIMAL INITIAL(0);
/* INSERT THE LAST TERM OF POLYNOMIAL */
   POLY = POLYFRONT(0,1,1,1,POLY);
/* INSERT THE THIRD TERM OF POLYNOMIAL */
   POLY = POLYFRONT(0,2,0,1,POLY);
```

```
POLYFRONT:
    PROCEDURE(NX,NY,NZ,NCOEFF,FIRST) RETURNS(FIXED DECIMAL);
/*  A PROCEDURE THAT INSERTS A TERM OF A THREE VARIABLE POLYNOMIAL
    AT THE FRONT OF A LINKED LINEAR LIST.              */

    DECLARE
        (NX,NY,NZ,NCOEFF,FIRST,P) FIXED DECIMAL;

    IF (AVAIL <= 0)  /* CHECK FOR AVAILABILITY STACK UNDERFLOW  */
    THEN
        DO;
            PUT SKIP EDIT('AVAILABILITY STACK UNDERFLOW') (A);
            STOP;
        END;

    P = AVAIL;  /* OBTAIN A NODE FROM AVAILABLE STORAGE  */
    AVAIL = LINK(AVAIL);

/*  INITIALIZE NUMERIC FIELDS  */

    POWER_X(P) = NX;
    POWER_Y(P) = NY;
    POWER_Z(P) = NZ;
    COEFF(P) = NCOEFF;
    LINK(P) = FIRST;  /*  FIRST NODE POINTER  */
    RETURN(P);
END POLYFRONT;
```

FIGURE 4-2.5 Procedure for Algorithm POLYFRONT.

```
/* INSERT SECOND TERM OF POLYNOMIAL */
   POLY = POLYFRONT(1,1,0,5,POLY);
/* INSERT FIRST TERM OF POLYNOMIAL */
   POLY = POLYFRONT(2,0,0,2,POLY);
```

In an analogous manner, a PL/I procedure for Algorithm **POLYEND** can be formulated as shown in Fig. 4-2.6. Again, it is assumed that the five vectors and the variable **AVAIL** are global to the procedure.

A program segment to construct the polynomial $2x^2 + 5xy + y^2 + yz$ follows:

```
/* INITIALIZE LIST POINTER TO NULL */
   DECLARE POLY FIXED DECIMAL INITIAL(0);
/* INSERT FIRST TERM OF POLYNOMIAL */
   POLY = POLYEND(2,0,0,2,POLY);
/* INSERT SECOND TERM OF POLYNOMIAL */
   POLY = POLYEND(1 1,0,5,POLY);
```

```
POLYEND:
    PROCEDURE(NX,NY,NZ,NCOEFF,FIRST) RETURNS(FIXED DECIMAL);
/*  A PROCEDURE THAT INSERTS A TERM OF A THREE VARIABLE POLYNOMIAL
    AT THE END OF A LINKED LINEAR LIST.      */

    DECLARE
        (NX,NY,NZ,NCOEFF,FIRST,NEW,SAVE) FIXED DECIMAL;

    IF (AVAIL <= 0)  /*  CHECK FOR AVAILABILITY STACK UNDERFLOW  */
    THEN
        DO;
            PUT SKIP EDIT('AVAILABILITY STACK UNDERFLOW') (A);
            STOP;
        END;

    NEW = AVAIL;  /*  OBTAIN A NODE FROM AVAILABLE STORAGE  */
    AVAIL = LINK(AVAIL);

    /* INITIALIZE FIELDS */
    POWER_X(NEW) = NX;
    POWER_Y(NEW) = NY;
    POWER_Z(NEW) = NZ;
    COEFF(NEW) = NCOEFF;
    LINK(NEW) = 0;

    /* IS LIST EMPTY? */
    IF (FIRST = 0) THEN RETURN(NEW);

    /* INITIATE SEARCH FOR LAST NODE */
    SAVE = FIRST;

    /* SEARCH FOR END OF LIST */
    DO WHILE(LINK(SAVE) ¬= 0);
        SAVE = LINK(SAVE);
    END;

    LINK(SAVE) = NEW;  /*  SET LINK FIELD OF LAST NODE TO NEW  */

    RETURN(FIRST);  /*  RETURN FIRST NODE POINTER  */
END POLYEND;
```

FIGURE 4-2.6 Procedure for Algorithm POLYEND.

```
/* INSERT THIRD TERM OF POLYNOMIAL */
    POLY = POLYEND(0,2,0,1,POLY);
/* INSERT LAST TERM OF POLYNOMIAL */
    POLY = POLYEND(0,1,1,1,POLY);
```

A PL/I procedure based on Algorithm DELETE is given in Fig. 4-2.7. It is assumed that the two vectors INFO and LINK and the pointer variable AVAIL are defined outside the procedure and are global to it.

The previous procedures are included in a main program whose label is TEST in the program segment of Fig. 4-2.8. As mentioned earlier, the five vectors and the variable AVAIL are global to the procedures ALIST, POLYFRONT, POLYEND, and DELETE.

The representation of linked linear lists by vectors has been discussed at some length to give some insight into their construction and manipulation. The programming of linked lists in PL/I using programmer-defined structures is the topic of the remainder of this subsection.

```
DELETE:
    PROCEDURE(X,FIRST);
/*  A PROCEDURE FOR DELETING A NODE FROM A LINKED LINEAR LIST WHOSE
    NODES CONTAIN TWO FIELDS NAMED INFO AND LINK.  THE DISCARDED
    NODE IS RETURNED TO THE AVAILABILITY AREA.  */

    DECLARE
        (X,FIRST,PRED,NEXT) FIXED DECIMAL;

    IF (FIRST = 0)  /*  CHECK FOR EMPTY LIST  */
    THEN
        DO;
            PUT SKIP EDIT('UNDERFLOW') (A);
            RETURN;
        END;

    IF (X = FIRST)  /*  DELETE FIRST NODE?  */
    THEN
        DO;
            FIRST = LINK(FIRST);
            GO TO RETNODE;
        END;

    NEXT = FIRST; /* INITIATE SEARCH FOR PREDECESSOR OF X */

UPDATE: /* UPDATE PREDECESSOR VARIABLE */
    PRED = NEXT;

    NEXT = LINK(NEXT);  /* GET NEXT NODE  */
    IF (NEXT = 0)  /* END OF LIST? */
    THEN
        DO;
            PUT SKIP EDIT('NODE NOT FOUND') (A);
            RETURN;
        END;

    IF (NEXT ¬= X) THEN GO TO UPDATE;  /* IS THIS NODE X?  */

    LINK(PRED) = LINK(X);  /* DELETE NODE X  */
RETNODE: /* RETURN NODE TO AVAILABILITY AREA */
    LINK(X) = AVAIL;
    AVAIL = X;
END DELETE;
```

FIGURE 4-2.7 Procedure for Algorithm DELETE.

```
TEST:
    PROCEDURE OPTICNS(MAIN);

/* DECLARE FIVE VECTCRS REPRESENTING TYPICAL NODES */
    DECLARE
        (POWER_X(100),POWER_Y(100),POWER_Z(100),COEFF(100),LINK(100),
            AVAIL) FIXED DECIMAL;

    ALIST:   PROCEDURE;

    END ALIST;

    POLYFRONT:   PRCCEDURE(NX,NY,NZ,NCOEFF,FIRST)
                        RETURNS(FIXED DECIMAL);

    END POLYFRONT;

    POLYEND:   PROCEDURE(NX,NY,NZ,NCOEFF,FIRST) RETURNS(FIXED DECIMAL);

    END POLYEND;

    DELETE:   PROCEDURE(X,FIRST);

    END DELETE;

    CALL ALIST;   /*  CONSTRUCT AVAILABILITY STACK  */

END TEST;
```

FIGURE 4-2.8 Main procedure containing procedures **ALIST**, **POLYFRONT**, **POLYEND**, and **DELETE**.

Thus far, we have been primarily concerned with data elements, such as simple variables, and array elements. The facility which allows the programmer to define his own classes of data objects was mentioned briefly in Chap. 3. This idea is pursued further in this section and in particular is applied to the representation of linked linear lists.

The problem of data representation in many applications is often complex. Arrays are not well suited for easily expressing the relationships that exist among elements. A tree, for example, which is discussed in detail in the next chapter, is difficult to represent using arrays.

Consider an application concerning student registration at a university. Each student can be considered, in a tructural sense, as an entity or record. Associated with each entity is a set of properties such as student number, student name, year of study, and many other items. For a particular student, each property has a certain value. A student can have a student name of **'JOHN BROWN'**, a student number of **'89107'** and a year of study of **'1975'**. Conceptually, all of the properties or fields in an entity belong together, thus reflecting their relationship to one another. One could use arrays to represent such a system, where an array element could represent the value of each property. A more desirable situation would be the representation of the entity by a single structure containing a number of fields, each field representing a property.

In PL/I, each programmer can create a template for a desired data entity by declaring a structure to be of the **BASED** storage class. This facility permits the programmer to specify what fields are to be grouped together and in what order. This declaration also gives a name to the grouping.

For example, the statement

```
DECLARE
    1   STUDENT BASED(P),
        2 NUMBER FIXED DECIMAL,
        2 NAME CHARACTER(20),
        2 YEAR FIXED DECIMAL;
```

declares a group or class with a name of **STUDENT** which consists of the fields **NUMBER**, **NAME**, and **YEAR**. Such a declaration results in the definition of a class or a data structure consisting of an ordered sequence of fields. In the above example, the data structure name or class name is **STUDENT**. The class declaration does not allocate storage for the fields named. The declaration merely indicates the makeup of the structure. As many elements of the data structure or class as required can be created elsewhere in the program by using **ALLOCATE** statements. If a specific element of a data structure is desired, the programmer must use the name of the structure in an **ALLOCATE** statement. For example, the execution of the statement

```
ALLOCATE STUDENT;
```

would create a storage area which allocates space for three fields, namely, **NUMBER**, **NAME**, and **YEAR**. Since many copies of the **BASED** structure can be created in this way, a field name such as **NUMBER** is not enough for unambiguously specifying a certain field. We must be able to reference, by the use of an address or pointer, an instance of a field within a particular structure. This reference designator is a variable which has as its value the address of the created entity. The variable P, following **BASED**, in the declaration for **STUDENT** is implicitly defined as a pointer variable, and the address of the most recently created node is automatically assigned to P.

The referencing of a particular node of a **BASED** structure or of a field within this node is accomplished by using pointer qualification. For example, P − >**STUDENT** denotes the node generated by the latest **ALLOCATE** statement. The fields can be referenced as P − >**NUMBER**, P − >**NAME**, or P − >**YEAR**. (The imitation arrow is a minus sign followed immediately by a greater-than sign.)

The sequence of assignment statements

```
P − >NUMBER = 89107;
P − >NAME = 'JOHN BROWN';
P − >YEAR = 1975;
```

initializes **NUMBER**, **NAME**, and **YEAR** of the created node to values of 89107, 'JOHN BROWN', and 1975, respectively. This process can be represented by Fig. 4-2.9. The

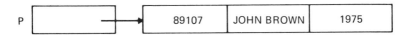

FIGURE 4-2.9.

address of the created element is stored in the pointer variable P and is represented in the figure by the arrow from P to the element.

Having created a node as in the previous **ALLOCATE** statement and placed its address in a reference variable, the programmer is now in a position to use or change the values of the fields of the node. This is illustrated in the simple PL/I program of Fig. 4-2.10 which creates a node, assigns values to the three fields **NUMBER**, **NAME**, and **YEAR**, and outputs the results.

PL/I not only allows the allocation of based structures, it also permits the freeing of such structures to available storage. This is accomplished by the statement

FREE P − >STUDENT;

when the node indicated by pointer P is to be restored to the availability area.

It was mentioned that pointer variables usually specify an address. An exception is that they may be assigned the value returned by PL/I's builtin **NULL** function. This value cannot be related to any address and, therefore, cannot be interpreted as a pointer to a node. **NULL** returns the same value on each invocation and, therefore, it can be used as an end-of-list delimiter. The comparisons "equal" and "not equal" can be made between **NULL** and a pointer variable, as well as between two pointer variables.

As another example consider the following problem. It is required that we write a program which reads in N sets of data consisting of employee number, employee name, hourly wage, and hours worked. A node is created for each set of data consisting of an input set and an additional field denoting gross pay. The addresses of the created nodes are to be stored in a reference array which is indexed by the employee number. Assume that the employee numbers are unique and that their values are between one and fifty. A program which performs the above task is given in Fig. 4-2.11.

The first **DECLARE** statement of the program declares a data structure class with the name **EMPLOYEE** whose typical node consists of four fields having names of **NAME**, **RATE**, **HOURS**, and **PAY**.

```
SAMPLE:  PROCEDURE OPTIONS(MAIN);
/*  PROGRAM TO CREATE A NODE AND OUTPUT ITS CONTENTS  */
    DECLARE
        1 STUDENT BASED(P),
            2 NUMBER FIXED DECIMAL,
            2 NAME CHARACTER(20),
            2 YEAR FIXED DECIMAL;

    ALLOCATE STUDENT;
    P->NUMBER = 2100;
    P->NAME = 'MIKE PEARSON';
    P->YEAR = 1923;
    PUT SKIP EDIT('NUMBER IS ',P->NUMBER) (A,F(4));
    PUT SKIP EDIT('NAME IS ',P->NAME) (A,A);
    PUT SKIP EDIT('YEAR IS ',P->YEAR) (A,F(4));
END SAMPLE;
```

```
NUMBER IS 2100
NAME IS MIKE PEARSON
YEAR IS 1923
```

FIGURE 4-2.10   Creation of a node using PL/I.

```
PAYROLL:
    PROCEDURE OPTICNS(MAIN);
/* SAMPLE PAYROLL PROGRAM */

    DECLARE
        01  EMPLOYEE BASED(P), /* REQUIRED DATA STRUCTURE CLASS */
            02  NAME CHARACTER(20),
            02  RATE FLOAT DECIMAL,
            02  HOURS FLOAT DECIMAL,
            02  PAY FLOAT DECIMAL,
        MEMBER(50) POINTER, /* REFERENCE ARRAY FOR THE EMPLOYEES */
        (I,NUMBER) FIXED DECIMAL;

    GET LIST(N);  /*  READ IN THE VALUE OF N  */

    DO I = 1 TO N;  /*  READ LOOP  */
        ALLOCATE EMPLOYEE;  /*  CREATE A NODE  */

        /* READ AN EMPLOYEE CARD */
        GET LIST(NUMBER,P->NAME,P->RATE,P->HOURS);

        /* PLACE ADDRESS OF CREATED NODE IN THE ELEMENT OF ARRAY
        MEMBER WITH A SUBSCRIPT GIVEN BY THE EMPLOYEE NUMBER
        OBTAINED FROM THE CARD.  */

        MEMBER(NUMBER) = P;
        P->PAY = HOURS * RATE;  /*  COMPUTE GROSS PAY  */
    END;
END PAYROLL;
```

FIGURE 4-2.11 Payroll program.

The second **DECLARE** statement creates a 50-element reference array named **MEMBER** whose associated subscripts can be any employee number.

The **ALLOCATE** statement creates a node and stores its address in the pointer variable P. This address is then used to assign values to the four fields of the newly created node. The subscript of the array element is given by the employee number read from the employee card. For example, the three cards read in which contain the information

    2 'JOHN DOE' 2.50 40
    11 'SAM SMITH' 3.00 45
    20 'TOM BROWN' 3.50 44

result in the creation of three nodes whose addresses are stored in array elements MEM-BER(2), MEMBER(11), and MEMBER(20). Pictorially, this can be described by Fig. 4-2.12.

Let us now discuss the representation of linked linear lists. This can be accomplished by having a reference field in a certain node contain the address of another node. The

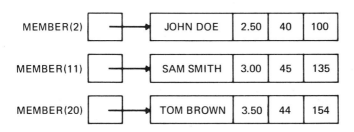

FIGURE 4-2.12.

programming of linked lists using arrays required the management of available space. When programmer-defined data types are used, all available space is allocated by the compiler. Similarly, the return of an unused node from a linked list to the availability list is handled by the compiler. We are therefore not concerned with available storage in the discussion to follow.

Returning to the polynomial example, the declaration statement

```
DECLARE
    1 TERM BASED (P),
      2 POWER_X BINARY FIXED,
      2 POWER_Y BINARY FIXED,
      2 POWER_Z BINARY FIXED,
      2 COEFF BINARY FLOAT,
      2 LINK POINTER;
```

defines the structure of a polynomial term. The node **TERM**, at level 1, collectively represents the five fields at level 2. The fields **POWER_X**, **POWER_Y**, **POWER_Z**, and **COEFF** are capable of containing the required numeric data. **LINK** is given the **POINTER** attribute which specifies that the value of **LINK** will usually denote the address of a **BASED** data type such as **TERM**. The variable P, following **BASED**, is implicitly defined as a pointer variable and its purpose is discussed shortly.

The execution of the statement

```
ALLOCATE TERM;
```

creates a node and automatically assigns the address of the new node to P. Note that many **TERM** nodes may be in use at one time, but each one must be generated by the execution of an **ALLOCATE** statement.

As before, the referencing of a node or a particular field is accomplished by using pointer qualification. For example, P − >**TERM** would denote the node generated by the preceding **ALLOCATE** statement. Each field could also be referenced as Q − >POWER_X, Q − >POWER_Y, Q − >POWER_Z, Q − >COEFF, or Q − >LINK where Q is assumed to be a pointer variable. As an example, we can add the coefficients of two polynomial terms, indicated by P and Q, using the statement:

```
X = Q − >COEFF + P − >COEFF;
```

These PL/I programming concepts should provide an adequate background for the list-processing programs in this and other sections. A procedure for Algorithm **POLYFRONT** is given in Fig. 4-2.13. In procedure **POLYFRONT** and also the subprogram of Fig. 4-2.15 (DELETE), the structure **TERM** is not declared. It is assumed that these procedures are nested within an invoking routine in which the necessary declarations are made.

If the pointer to the first node of the list is **POLY**, then the program in Fig. 4-2.14 will construct the polynomial $2x^2 + 5xy + y^2 + yz$.

A procedure for Algorithm **DELETE** is given in Fig. 4-2.15.

```
POLYFRONT:
      PROCEDURE(NX,NY,NZ,NCOEFF,FIRST) RETURNS(POINTER);
/*INSERT A NODE IN THE LINKED LIST WHICH WILL IMMEDIATELY PRECEDE THE
  NODE WHOSE ADDRESS IS DESIGNATED BY THE POINTER FIRST.  INITIALIZE
  THE NODE'S FIELDS TO NX, NY, AND NCOEF.  RETURN THE POINTER TO THE
  NEW NODE.                                                       */
      DECLARE
           (NX,NY,NZ) BINARY FIXED,
            NCOEFF BINARY FLOAT,
            FIRST POINTER;
      ALLOCATE TERM;
      P->POWER_X = NX;
      P->POWER_Y = NY;
      P->POWER_Z = NZ;
      P->COEFF = NCOEFF;
      P->LINK = FIRST;
      RETURN(P);
END POLYFRONT;
```

FIGURE 4-2.13   Procedure for Algorithm POLYFRONT using based storage.

Exercises for Sec. 4-2.1

1. Given a linked list whose typical node consists of an INFO and LINK field, formulate an algorithm which will count the number of nodes in the list.

2. Formulate an algorithm that will change the INFO field of the kth node to the value given by Y.

3. Formulate an algorithm which will perform an insertion to the immediate left of the kth node in the list.

4. Formulate an algorithm which appends (concatenates) a linear list to another linear list.

5. Given a simple linked list whose first node is denoted by the pointer variable FIRST, it is required to deconcatenate (or split) this list into two simply linked lists. The


```
POLYST:
     PROCEDURE OPTICNS(MAIN);
/*CONSTRUCT A LINKED LIST REPRESENTATION OF A POLYNOMIAL USING
  THE INSERT PROCEDURE. */
     DECLARE
          1 TERM BASED(P),
            2 POWER_X BINARY FIXED,
            2 POWER_Y BINARY FIXED,
            2 POWER_Z BINARY FIXED,
            2 COEFF BINARY FLOAT,
            2 LINK PCINTER,
          Q POINTER,
          POLY POINTER,
          POLYFRONT ENTRY(BIN FIXED,BIN FIXED,BIN FIXED,BIN FLOAT,PTR)
               RETURNS(PTR);

     POLY = NULL; /* INITIALIZE */

     POLY = POLYFRONT(0,1,1,1,POLY); /* INSERT LAST TERM OF POLYNOMIAL*/

     POLY = POLYFRCNT(0,2,0,1,POLY); /*INSERT THIRD TERM OF POLYNCMIAL*/

     POLY = POLYFRONT(1,1,0,5,POLY);/*INSERT SECOND TERM OF POLYNCMIAL*/

     POLY = POLYFRONT(2,0,0,2,POLY); /*INSERT FIRST TERM OF POLYNOMIAL*/

END POLYST;
```

FIGURE 4-2.14   Construction of polynomial $2x^2 + 5xy + y^2 + yz$.

```
DELETE:
        PROCEDURE(X,FIRST);
/*FIND AND DELETE NODE X FROM THE
  POLYNOMIAL LIST PCINTED TO BY FIRST.  */
        DECLARE
            (X,FIRST,NEXT,PRED) POINTER;
        IF FIRST = NULL
        THEN
            DO;/* INDICATE THAT LIST IS EMPTY */
                PUT SKIP LIST('LIST UNDERFLOW');
                RETURN;
            END;
        IF X = FIRST
        THEN
            DO; /* DELETE THE FIRST NODE */
                FIRST = FIRST->LINK;
                GO TO FREE_NODE;
            END;
        NEXT = FIRST; /*INITIATE SEARCH */
LOOP:   PRED = NEXT; /* UPDATE NEXT AND PRED */
        NEXT = NEXT->LINK;
        IF NEXT = NULL
        THEN
            DO; /*INDICATE NODE WAS NOT FOUND */
                PUT SKIP LIST('NODE NOT FOUND');
                RETURN;
            END;
        IF NEXT ¬= X
        THEN GO TO LOOP;
        PRED->LINK = X->LINK; /* DELETE X */
FREE_NODE:
        FREE X->TERM; /* RESTORE NODE X TO THE AVAILABILITY AREA */
        RETURN;
END DELETE;
```

FIGURE 4-2.15   Procedure for Algorithm DELETE using based storage.

node denoted by the pointer variable SPLIT is to be the first element in the second
linked list. Formulate a step-by-step algorithm to perform this task.

6. Suppose that you are given a simply linked list whose first node is denoted by the
pointer variable FIRST and whose typical node is represented by Fig. 4-2.16a, where
the variables KEY and LINK represent the information and link fields of the node,
respectively. The list is ordered on the field KEY so that the first and last nodes
contain the smallest and largest values of the field. It is desired to delete a number of
consecutive nodes whose KEY values are greater than or equal to KMIN and less than
KMAX. For example, an initial list with KMIN and KMAX having values of 25 and 40,
respectively, could look like Fig. 4-2.16b. After deleting the designated nodes, the
updated list would reduce to Fig. 4-2.16c. In this example, we dropped the nodes
whose KEY field values are 25, 29, and 37. Formulate an algorithm and write a program which will accomplish the deletion operation for an arbitrary linked list.

7. An unknown number of cards are punched, each of which contains a student record
with the following information: student number, name, college, sex, and year of
study. Each field is separated by at least one blank, and the fields are in the order
listed above. The sex is punched as M (male) or F (female). A trailer card with student number of 999999 and "dummy" information in the other four fields is placed at
the end of this deck of cards.

The college and year of study of a student may change. A series of update cards
follows the initial deck. Update cards contain students who made changes. The
update deck is also followed by a trailer card having a student number of 999999 and

(a)

(b)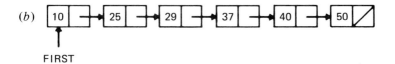

FIRST

(c)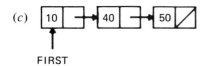

FIRST

FIGURE 4-2.16.

random information in the other two fields. The update deck is then followed by a series of cards on which a college name is punched.

Design an algorithm to create a linked list of the student records which is ordered by student numbers (smallest to largest). Then read the update cards and update this list. Once all update cards have been read in, read the college names and output a well organized report of all students in that college in alphabetical order. Do this for each college name read in. List the student number, name, sex, and year of study for each of these students.

Note that neither the original file cards nor the update cards are ordered, and it is possible that there may be an update card for a student who is not in the original file, in which case, an appropriate error message is to be printed.

8. In the discussion of the text editor **ETEXTE** in Sec. 2-5.1, no facility is provided to insert lines between lines of text which already are stored in the system. The **ETEXTE** command

$$INSERT/ <beginning line number >/

will insert any text between this command and the next $$ command, starting at the beginning line number specified. For example, assume the text for line numbers 320 and 330 is stored as

```
00320    THESE ARE LINES OF EXAMPLE TEXT WHICH HELP
00330    THIS IS THE LINE TO FOLLOW THE INSERTED TEXT
```

and the input is

```
$$INSERT/00322/
ILLUSTRATE HOW THE $$INSERT FUNCTION BEHAVES
WHEN GIVEN A NUMBER OF LINES TO BE PLACED BETWEEN
TWO LINES WHICH ARE ALREADY IN THE ETEXTE SYSTEM
```

The effect of the **$$INSERT** command is to establish a link in positions 6-10 of the stored text which points to a **FREE_TEXT** character array. The inserted text is placed in the open locations at the end of the FREE_TEXT array and line number increments of "one" are assigned. Therefore, if the next FREE_TEXT location which is open is 24, then the $$INSERT command alters the stored text in line 320 to

0032000024THESE ARE LINES OF EXAMPLE TEXT WHICH HELP

and stores the inserted text in the FREE_TEXT array as follows:

00322   ILLUSTRATE HOW THE $$INSERT FUNCTION BEHAVES
00323   WHEN GIVEN A NUMBER OF LINES TO BE PLACED BETWEEN
00324   TWO LINES WHICH ARE ALREADY IN THE ETEXTE SYSTEM

When the text is listed using the $$LIST command, the line numbers are output in the sequence ..., 320, 322, 323, 324, 330, ... Of course, both the $$LIST and $$PRINT commands as given in Sec. 2-5.1 must be altered to handle text inserts.

Devise the Algorithm $$INSERT which is capable of processing text insertions. Your algorithm should check to ensure that a line number associated with an inserted line of text does not equal a line number already in use.

9. Construct Algorithm $$RENUMB which renumbers the entire stored text so that line number increments of "ten" are restored. (Algorithm $$RENUMB is invoked by the ETEXTE command $$RENUMB). For example, if a line sequence is ..., 320, 322, 323, 324, 330, ... due to insertion, then the new line sequence is ..., 320, 330, 340, 350, 360, ..., and the line of text previously numbered 340 is now numbered as 370, etc. Note that Algorithm $$RENUMB should physically move all inserted text stored in FREE_TEXT back to the main text array called LINE and FREE_TEXT should be empty after the execution of the $$RENUMB command.

4-2.2   Circularly Linked Linear Lists

The previous sections have been concerned exclusively with linked linear lists in which the last node of such lists contained the null pointer. We now wish to discuss a slight modification of this representation which results in a further improvement in processing. This is accomplished by replacing the null pointer in the last node of a list with the address of its first node. Such a list is called a *circularly linked linear list* or simply a *circular list*. Figure 4-2.17 illustrates the structure of a circular list.

Circular lists have certain advantages over singly linked lists. The first of these is concerned with the accessibility of a node. In a circular list every node is accessible from a given node. That is, from this given node, all nodes can be reached by merely chaining through the list.

A second advantage concerns the deletion operation. Recall from Algorithm

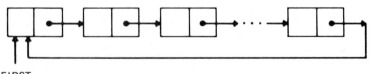

FIRST

FIGURE 4-2.17   A circularly linked linear list.

DELETE of Sec. 4-2.1 that in addition to the address X of the node to be deleted from a simply linked list, it is also necessary to give the address of the first node of the list. This necessity results from the fact that in order to delete X, the predecessor of this node has to be found. To find the predecessor requires that a search be carried out by chaining through the nodes from the first node of the list. It is obvious that such a requirement does not exist for a circular list, since the search for the predecessor of node X can be initiated from X itself.

Finally, certain operations on circular lists, such as concatenation and splitting (see Probs. 4 and 5 in Exercises for Sec. 4-2.1), become more efficient.

There is, however, a disadvantage in using circular lists; namely, that without some care in processing, it is possible to get into an infinite loop! In processing a circular list, it is important that we are able to detect the end of the list. We can help guarantee the detection of the end by placing a special node which can be easily identified in the circular list. This special node is often called the *list head* of the circular list. This technique has an advantage of its own—the list can never be empty. Recalling from Secs. 4-1 and 4-2.1 that most algorithms require the testing of a list as to whether it is empty, this advantage is certainly important. The representation of a circular list with a list head is given in Fig. 4-2.18, where the variable HEAD denotes the address of the list head. Note that the INFO field in the list head node is not used, which is illustrated by shading the field. An empty list is represented by having LINK(HEAD) = HEAD.

The algorithm for inserting a node at the head of a circular list with a list head consists of the following steps:

> Set NEW ⇐ NODE, INFO(NEW) ← Y,LINK(NEW) ← LINK(HEAD), and
> LINK(HEAD) ← NEW.

Circular lists will be used in a number of applications throughout the remainder of the text.

Exercises for Sec. 4-2.2

1. Formulate a deletion algorithm for a circular list with a head node.
2. Formulate an algorithm to concatenate two circular lists. (See Prob. 4 in Exercises for Sec. 4-2.1.)
3. Design an algorithm to split a circular list into two circular lists. (See Prob. 5 in Exercises for Sec. 4-2.1.)
4. Formulate insertion and deletion algorithms for a queue which is represented by a circular list.
5. Obtain an algorithm for the return of a circular list to the availability area of storage.

HEAD

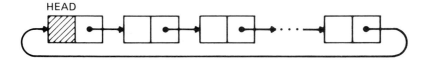

FIGURE 4-2.18 A circularly linked linear list with a head node.

4-2.3   Doubly Linked Linear Lists

Thus far, we have been restricted to traversing linked linear lists in only one direction. In certain applications, it is very desirable and sometimes indispensable that a list be traversed in either a forward or reverse manner. This property of a linked linear list implies that each node must contain two link fields instead of the usual one. The links are used to denote the predecessor and successor of a node. The link denoting the predecessor of a node is called the *left* link and that denoting the successor its *right* link. A list containing this type of node is called a *doubly linked linear list* or a *two-way chain*. Pictorially, such a linear list can be represented by Fig. 4-2.19, where L and R are pointer variables denoting the leftmost and rightmost nodes in the list, respectively. The left link of the leftmost node and the right link of the rightmost node are both NULL, indicating the end of the list for each direction. The left and right links of a node are denoted by the variables LPTR and RPTR, respectively.

Consider the problem of inserting a node into a doubly linked linear list to the *left* of a specified node whose address is given by variable M. A number of cases are possible. First of all, the list could be empty. This is denoted by setting both R and L to NULL. An insertion into an empty list is easily handled by setting the L and R pointers to the address of the new node and by assigning a NULL value to the left and right links of the node being entered.

A second possibility is an insertion in the middle of the list. The list before and after such an insertion can be represented by Fig. 4-2.20, where NEW is the address of the new node being inserted.

Finally, the insertion can be made to the left of the leftmost node in the list, thereby requiring the pointer L to be changed. The list before and after such an insertion is shown in Fig. 4-2.21. The insertion algorithm can now be precisely formulated.

Algorithm DOUBINS (Inserting a node in a doubly linked linear list).   Given a doubly linked linear list whose leftmost and rightmost node addresses are given by the pointer variables L and R, respectively, it is required to insert a node whose address is given by the pointer variable NEW. The left and right links of a node are denoted by LPTR and RPTR, respectively. The information field of a node is denoted by the variable INFO. The name of an element of the doubly linked linear list is NODE. The insertion is to be performed to the left of a specified node with an address given by the pointer variable M. The information to be entered in the node is contained in X.

1.   [Obtain new node from availability stack]   Set NEW ⇐ NODE.
2.   [Copy information field]   Set INFO(NEW) ← X.
3.   [Insertion in an empty list?]
     If R = NULL,
     then set L ← R ← NEW, LPTR(NEW) ← RPTR(NEW) ← NULL, and Exit.
4.   [Leftmost insertion?]
     If M = L,
     then set LPTR(NEW) ← NULL, L ← NEW, RPTR(NEW) ← M, LPTR(M) ← NEW,
     and Exit.
5.   [Insert in middle]   Set LPTR(NEW) ← LPTR(M), RPTR(NEW) ← M,
     RPTR(LPTR(M)) ← NEW, LPTR(M) ← NEW, and Exit.

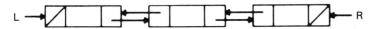

FIGURE 4-2.19 A doubly linked linear list.

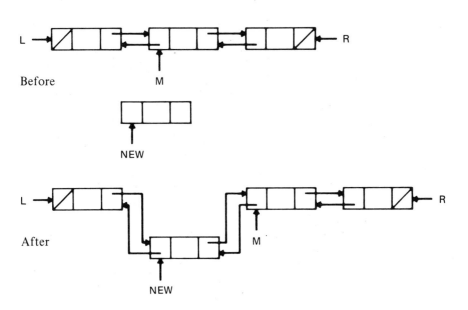

Before

NEW

After

NEW

FIGURE 4-2.20 Insertion in the middle of a double linked linear list.

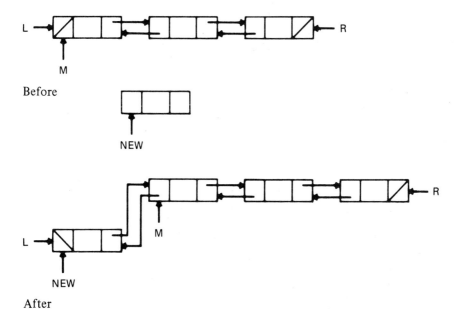

Before

NEW

M

After

NEW

FIGURE 4-2.21 A leftmost insertion in a doubly linked linear list.

We now examine the problem of deleting a node from a doubly linked list. You may recall that the deletion of a node in a singly linked list entailed finding the predecessor of the discarded node. The search was performed by chaining through successive nodes. This search was necessary in order to change the link of the predecessor node to a value that would point to the successor of the node being deleted. Such a search could be very time consuming, depending on the number of deletions and the number of nodes in the list. In a doubly linked list, no such search is required. Given the address of the node which is to be deleted, the predecessor and successor nodes are immediately known. Doubly linked lists are much more efficient with respect to deletions than simple linked lists.

A number of possibilities arise. If the list contains a single node, then a deletion results in an empty list with the leftmost and rightmost pointers being set to NULL. The node being deleted could be the leftmost node of the list. In this case the pointer variable L must be changed. An analogous situation can arise at the rightmost node of the list. Finally, the deletion can occur in the middle of the list.

Algorithm DOUBDEL (Deletion of a node in a doubly linked linear list).   We are given a doubly linked list with the addresses of the leftmost and rightmost nodes given by the pointer variables L and R, respectively, and whose nodes contain a left link and right link with names LPTR and RPTR, respectively. The address of the node to be deleted is contained in the variable OLD.

1. [Underflow?]   If R = NULL, then write 'underflow', and Exit.
2. [Single node in list?]   If L = R, then set L ← R ← NULL and go to step 6.
3. [Is leftmost node being deleted?]
    If L = OLD, then set L ← RPTR(L), LPTR(L) ← NULL, and go to step 6.
4. [Is rightmost node being deleted?]
    If R = OLD, then set R ← LPTR(R), RPTR(R) ← NULL, and go to step 6.
5. [Delete in middle]   Set RPTR(LPTR(OLD)) ← RPTR(OLD) and
    LPTR(RPTR(OLD)) ← LPTR(OLD).
6. [Return deleted node]   Return OLD to the availability list, and Exit.

The PL/I procedure given in Fig. 4-2.22 performs an insertion in a doubly linked linear list according to Algorithm DOUBINS. The declaration

```
DECLARE
    1 NODE BASED(NEW),
        2 LPTR POINTER,
        2 INFO CHARACTER(20),
        2 RPTR POINTER;
```

is assumed to be global to the procedure. A similar procedure can be written for Algorithm DOUBDEL and is left as an exercise.

Doubly linked linear lists can be easily used to represent a queue whose number of elements is very volatile. Such a representation is given in Fig. 4-2.23a, where R and F are pointer variables which denote the rear and front of the queue, respectively. The insertion

```
DOUBINS:
    PROCEDURE(L,R,M,X);
/*  PROCEDURE FOR INSERTING A NODE IN A DOUBLY LINKED LINEAR LIST */
    DECLARE
        (L,R,M) PCINTER,
        X CHARACTER(*),
        PREDM PCINTER;
    ALLOCATE NODE;
    NEW->INFO = X;
    IF (R = NULL)
    THEN
        DO; /* INSERTICN IN EMPTY LIST */
            L = NEW;
            R = NEW;
            NEW->LPTR = NULL;
            NEW->RPTR = NULL;
            RETURN;
        END;
    IF (M = L)
    THEN
        DO; /* LEFTMOST INSERTION */
            NEW->LPTR = NULL;
            L = NEW;
            NEW->RPTR = M;
            M->LPTR = NEW;
        END;
    ELSE
        DO; /* INSERT IN MIDDLE */
            NEW->LPTR = M->LPTR;
            NEW->RPTR = M;
            PREDM = M->LPTR;
            PREDM->RPTR = NEW;
            M->LPTR = NEW;
        END;

END DOUBINS;
```

FIGURE 4-2.22 Procedure for Algorithm DOUBINS.

of a node whose address is NEW at the rear of the queue is shown in Fig. 4-2.23b, where R′ denotes the address of the rear of the queue after the update. The following sequence of steps accomplishes such an insertion:

$$RPTR(R) \leftarrow NEW$$
$$RPTR(NEW) \leftarrow NULL$$
$$LPTR(NEW) \leftarrow R$$
$$R \leftarrow NEW$$

Similarly, a deletion from a doubly linked queue can be represented by Fig. 4-2.23c, where F′ denotes the address of the front node of the updated queue. The deletion from the front of the queue is achieved by the following algorithm steps:

$$F \leftarrow RPTR(F)$$
$$LPTR(F) \leftarrow NULL$$

Let us consider the possibility of simplifying the insertion and deletion algorithms associated with doubly linked linear lists. The case of an empty list can be dispensed with by never permitting a list to be empty. This can be accomplished by using a special node that always remains in the list. Hence, it is the only node in an empty list. The special node

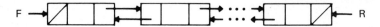

(*a*) Doubly linked representation of a queue.

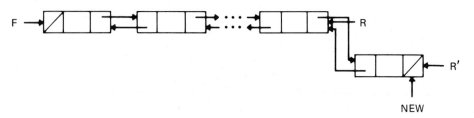

(*b*) Insertion in a doubly linked queue.

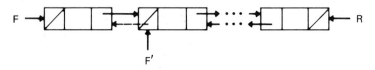

(*c*) Deletion in a doubly linked queue.

FIGURE 4-2.23   Representation of and operations on a doubly linked queue.

is called the *head node* of the list and was described in the previous subsection. By using the head node, we can realize a certain degree of symmetry in the structure by making the list circular, as shown in Fig. 4-2.24. Note that the right link of the rightmost node contains the address of the head node and the left link of the head node points to the rightmost node. The empty list is represented as in Fig. 4-2.25, where both left and right links of the head node point to itself. The algorithm for inserting a node to the left of a specified node M now reduces to the following sequence of steps:

RPTR(NEW) ← M
LPTR(NEW) ← LPTR(M)
RPTR(LPTR(M)) ← NEW
LPTR(M) ← NEW

The insertion of a node into an empty list can be represented before and after the insertion by Figs. 4-2.26*a* and *b*, respectively.

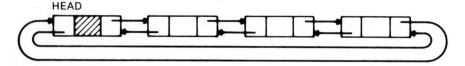

FIGURE 4-2.24   A doubly linked circular list with a head node.

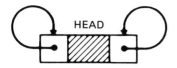

FIGURE 4-2.25 An empty doubly linked circular list with a head node.

In a similar manner, the corresponding deletion algorithms for a node with an address given by the variable OLD consists of the following steps:

RPTR(LPTR(OLD)) ← RPTR(OLD)
LPTR(RPTR(OLD)) ← LPTR(OLD)

The doubly linked method of allocating storage will be used extensively throughout the remainder of the book. In particular, it will be used repeatedly in Sec. 5-1.2 to represent trees, in Sec. 5-5.2 to represent graphs in computer graphics, in Sec. 5-6 to represent the availability area in dynamic-storage management techniques, in Chap. 6 in certain algorithms for searching and sorting, and in Chap. 7 to represent overflow areas for file structures.

Exercises for Sec. 4-2.3
1. Design insertion and deletion algorithms for a deque which is represented by a doubly linked linear list.
2. Repeat Prob. 1 for an input-restricted deque.
3. Repeat Prob. 1 for an output-restricted deque.

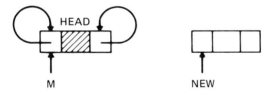

(*a*) Before.

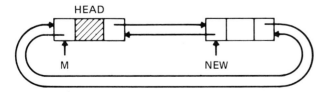

(*b*) After.

FIGURE 4-2.26 Insertion into an empty doubly linked circular list.

4-3   APPLICATIONS OF LINKED LINEAR LISTS

This section will be concerned with a number of applications of linear linked lists. Many examples could be given, but only a few will be described in this section.

We have in our discussion of linked lists used as a typical node a term of a polynomial. A more thorough discussion of polynomials is the first application to be discussed. The need to automate polynomial manipulation has led to the design of special-purpose languages to satisfy the need. Common operations performed on polynomials are addition, subtraction, multiplication, division, integration, and differentiation. Of these operations, addition and subtraction are much easier to implement than the others. The implementation of polynomial addition is the only operation that will be discussed in this chapter. We will discuss algorithms to perform other operations in Secs. 5-2.1 and 5-5.3.

The second subsection describes the organizations and associated algorithms for maintaining a dictionary of names. This problem occurs in many application areas such as in compiler construction and information organization and retrieval.

Another application, which is closely related to polynomial evaluation, is performing arithmetic operations to some arbitrary precision. In certain problems (such as the matrix inversion of ill-conditioned matrices), we may be required to carry a large number of digits in the computation in order to obtain a modest number of significant digits. The number of significant digits required may be specified at program run time, and from this can be computed the number of digits which must be carried. This problem is the last to be discussed in this section.

4-3.1   Polynomial Manipulation

We have in our discussion of linked lists often used, as a typical node, a term of a polynomial. A more thorough discussion of polynomials is now given. The implementation of polynomial addition is the only operation that is discussed in this subsection. Multiplication of polynomials can be obtained by performing repeated additions.

In order to achieve greater efficiency in processing, each polynomial can be stored in decreasing order by term according to the criterion briefly described in Sec. 4-1. Recall that a polynomial term $D_1 x^{A_1} y^{B_1} z^{C_1}$ will precede the term $D_2 x^{A_2} y^{B_2} z^{C_2}$ if $A_1 > A_2$; or, if they are equal, then $B_1 > B_2$; or if they are equal, then $C_1 > C_2$.

This ordering of polynomials makes the addition of polynomials easy. In fact, two polynomials can be added by scanning each of their terms only once. The previous comparison method can easily be used to add corresponding terms in two polynomials. If $A_1 = A_2$, $B_1 = B_2$, and $C_1 = C_2$, then the coefficient of the sum term can be obtained directly as $D_1 + D_2$.

The ordering just described will be used in Algorithm **POLY_ADD**. This algorithm has as input two ordered linked linear lists which represent the two polynomials to be added. Given these inputs, **POLY_ADD** performs the required addition. Each ordered list is constructed by Algorithm **PINSERT**, which is very similar to Algorithm **INSORD** given in Sec. 4-2.1. Algorithm **POLY_ADD** is responsible for creating the polynomial sum. Since the two polynomials to be added are ordered, the resultant polynomial can be constructed by using an algorithm which is essentially identical (except for the handling of the availability area) to Algorithm **POLYLAST** of Sec. 4-1. Algorithm **POLY_ADD** does not alter its two input polynomials, and the address of the sum polynomial is returned to the main algorithm which invoked the algorithm. We now formulate the algorithm which adds two polynomials.

Algorithm POLY_ADD (Addition of polynomials).   Given two polynomials whose first terms are referenced by pointer variables P and Q, respectively, and an insertion algorithm as described in Algorithm POLYLAST of Sec. 4-1, it is required to add these polynomials and store their sum in a third polynomial which is referenced by the pointer variable R. The original polynomials are to remain unchanged. PSAVE and QSAVE are pointer variables. A_1, A_2, B_1, B_2, C_1, C_2, D_1, and D_2 are temporary variables.

1. [Initialize]   Set R ← NULL, PSAVE ← P, and QSAVE ← Q.
2. [End of any polynomial?]
    Repeat steps 3 and 4 while P ≠ NULL and Q ≠ NULL.
3. [Compute values for each term]   Set A_1 ← POWER_X(P), A_2 ← POWER_X(Q),
    B_1 ← POWER_Y(P), B_2 ← POWER_Y(Q), C_1 ← POWER_Z(P), C_2 ← POWER_Z(Q),
    D_1 ← COEFF(P), and D_2 ← COEFF(Q).
4. [Compare terms]
    If (A_1 = A_2) and (B_1 = B_2) and (C_1 = C_2),
    then
        if COEFF(P) + COEFF(Q) ≠ 0,
        then set R ← POLYLAST(A_1, B_1, C_1, D_1 + D_2, R), P ← LINK(P),
        and Q ← LINK(Q);
        otherwise, set P ← LINK(P) and Q ← LINK(Q);
    otherwise,
        if (A_1 > A_2) or ((A_1 = A_2) and (B_1 > B_2)) or
        ((A_1 = A_2) and (B_1 = B_2) and C_1 > C_2)),
        then set R ← POLYLAST(A_1, B_1, C_1, D_1, R) and P ← LINK(P);
        otherwise, set R ← POLYLAST(A_2, B_2, C_2, D_2, R) and Q ← LINK(Q).
5. [Is polynomial P done?]
    If P ≠ NULL,
    then set LINK(LAST) ← P;
    otherwise, if Q ≠ NULL, then, set LINK(LAST) ← Q.
6. [Restore initial pointer values for P and Q]   Set P ← PSAVE,
    Q ← QSAVE, and Exit.

The first step of the algorithm initializes the pointer variable associated with the polynomial to NULL and saves the pointer variable values of polynomials P and Q in PSAVE and QSAVE, respectively.

The second step determines whether or not there are terms remaining in both polynomials which remain to be processed. If both polynomials have not been completely processed, then the third and fourth steps of the algorithm are executed.

The third step computes the values for A_1, A_2, B_1, B_2, C_1, C_2, D_1, and D_2. Step four is concerned with comparing a term of polynomial P with a term of polynomial Q. If the powers associated with two terms (that is, (A_1 = A_2), (B_1 = B_2), and (C_1 = C_2)) are equal, then the sum term is inserted in polynomial R, provided that the original terms do not cancel. This insertion is performed by invoking Algorithm POLYLAST. Note that in order to avoid chaining to the end of the linked list for each insertion, the pointer variable LAST has been used to denote the address of the last node inserted. This technique was described in Sec. 4-1. If the computed powers of the P term are greater than those of the Q term, then the former term is inserted at the end of polynomial R. The remaining possibility causes the term of polynomial Q to be inserted into the sum polynomial. The last step of the algorithm restores the pointer variables of polynomials P and Q to their original values.

We now give the algorithm which is used to build an ordered linked representation of a polynomial.

Algorithm PINSERT.   Given an ordered linked linear list whose typical node contains the information fields POWER_X, POWER_Y, POWER_Z, and COEFF and a pointer field LINK, as previously described in this chapter, it is required to insert a node in the linked list which preserves its order. The fields of the new term are denoted by NX, NY, NZ, and NCOEFF, which correspond to the exponents for x, y, and z and the coefficient value of the term, respectively. The address of the first term in the list is given by the pointer variable FIRST. NEW and SAVE are pointer variables. A, B, and C are auxiliary variables.

1. [Create a new node]   Set NEW ⇐ TERM.
2. [Copy information contents into new node]   Set POWER_X(NEW) ← NX,
   POWER_Y(NEW) ← NY, POWER__Z(NEW) ← NZ, and COEFF(NEW) ← NCOEFF.
3. [If list is empty, set link field of new node to NULL, and Exit]
   If FIRST = NULL, then set LINK(NEW) ← NULL, PINSERT ← NEW, and Exit.
4. [Does new node precede first node of list?]
   Set A ← POWER_X(FIRST), B ← POWER_Y(FIRST), and C ← POWER_Z(FIRST).
   If (A < NX) or ((A = NX) and (B < NY))
   or ((A = NX) and (B = NX) and (C < NZ)),
   then set LINK(NEW) ← FIRST, PINSERT ← NEW, and Exit.
5. [Initialize temporary pointer]   Set SAVE ← FIRST.
6. [Search for predecessor and successor of new node]
   Repeat while LINK(SAVE) ≠ NULL:
       Set A ← POWER_X(LINK(SAVE)), B ← POWER_Y(LINK(SAVE)),
       and C ← POWER_Z(LINK(SAVE)).
       If (A > NX) or ((A = NX) and (B > NY))
       or ((A = NX) and (B = NY) and (C > NZ)),
       then set SAVE ← LINK(SAVE);
       otherwise, go to step 7.
7. [Set LINK fields of new node and its predecessor]
   Set LINK(NEW) ← LINK(SAVE), and LINK(SAVE) ← NEW.
8. [Reset first node pointer]   Set PINSERT ← FIRST, and Exit.

This algorithm is very similar to Algorithm INSORD of Sec. 4-2.1 and no further explanation should be required.

The last algorithm to be discussed reads in the two polynomials and repeatedly invokes Algorithm PINSERT in order to construct the linked representations of these polynomials. Each term of a given polynomial is assumed to be on a separate card which contains four values. The first three values correspond to the powers of x, y, and z, respectively, for a given term. The fourth value represents the coefficient of this term. The end of a polynomial in the data cards is signaled by a dummy card which contains a coefficient value of 0.

Algorithm POLYNOMIAL.   Given Algorithms POLY_ADD, PINSERT, and POLYLAST, as previously described, it is required to read two polynomials from cards and obtain their sum. POLY1, POLY2, and POLY3 are pointer variables associated with the three polynomials. The variables X, Y, Z, and C are used to denote the powers of x, y, z, and the coefficient value of a term read from a card.

1. [Initialize]   Set POLY1 ← POLY2 ← NULL.
2. [Read a card]   Read X, Y, Z, and C from a card.
3. [Is it a delimiter card?]   If C = 0, then go to step 5.
4. [Insert the term in POLY1]   Set POLY1 ← PINSERT(X, Y, Z, C, POLY1), and go to step 2.
5. [Read a card]   Read X, Y, Z, and C from a card.
6. [Is it a delimiter card?]   If C = 0, then go to step 8.
7. [Insert term in POLY2]   Set POLY2 ← PINSERT(X, Y, Z, C, POLY2) and go to step 5.
8. [Add polynomials]   Call POLY_ADD(POLY1, POLY2, POLY3).
9. [Print polynomials, and Exit.]

We note in terminating this section that a circular linked representation of a polynomial could have been used throughout the associated algorithms. In certain cases this representation would have resulted in somewhat simpler algorithms.

Exercises for Sec. 4-3.1
1. Assuming that a polynomial in three variables is represented by a linked linear list as discussed in this section, formulate an algorithm which traverses the linked list and evaluates the polynomial for given values of x, y, and z.
2. Formulate an algorithm to subtract two polynomials in three variables.
3. Formulate an algorithm to create an ordered linear list with no duplicate terms. The input is a polynomial in three variables that is unordered and may have repeated terms.
4. Formulate an algorithm to produce a copy of a polynomial in three variables.
5. Formulate an algorithm to multiply two polynomials in three variables. (*Hint:* This can be achieved by repeated additions.)
6. Formulate an algorithm to divide polynomial P by polynomial Q. The quotient polynomial is to be placed in a linked list whose first term is given by the pointer variable QUOTIENT, while the remainder polynomial is to be stored in a linked list whose first node address is given by the pointer variable REMAINDER.
7. Formulate an algorithm to integrate a polynomial in three variables with respect to one of these variables. Create a linked list for the result.
8. Repeat Prob. 7 for the differentiation of the polynomial with respect to a given variable.
9. Formulate an algorithm to print the polynomials of step 9 in Algorithm POLYNOMIAL.

4-3.2 Linked Dictionary

An important part of any compiler is the construction and maintenance of a dictionary containing names and their associated values. Such a dictionary is also called a *symbol table*. In a typical compiler there may be several symbol tables corresponding to variable names, labels, literals, etc.

The constraints which must be considered in the design of symbol tables are processing time and memory space. Usually, there exists some inverse relationship between the speed of a symbol-table algorithm and the memory space it requires.

There are a number of phases associated with the construction of symbol tables. The principal phases that we discuss at this time are *building* and *referencing*. The building phase involves the insertion of symbols and their associated values (if known) into a table, while referencing is the fetching or accessing of values from a table. We will deal in much more detail with these topics in Chap. 6.

The ratio of the expected number of insertions to references is very important. In many symbol-table systems, insertion time and access time are closely related, but in the absence of such a relationship and in the case where the expected number of references or accesses is high with respect to insertions, it may be advantageous to allocate more time and space to the insertion function in order to improve the referencing function.

It is an easy matter to construct a very fast symbol-table system, provided that a large section of memory is available. In such a case, a unique memory address is assigned to each name, where the address is obtained from the arithmetic value of the characters making up the name. If names were restricted to the set of valid FORTRAN names consisting of, at most, six characters, then some two billion words of storage would have to be allocated to such a dictionary system—a totally unacceptable situation.

The most straightforward method of accessing a symbol table is by using the *linear search* technique. This method involves arranging the symbols sequentially in memory via a vector or by using a simple linear linked list. An insertion is easily handled by adding the new element to the end of the list. When it is desired to access a particular symbol, the table is searched sequentially from its beginning until it is found. It will take, on the average, $N/2$ comparisons to find a particular symbol in a table containing N entries. The insertion mechanism is very fast, but the referencing is extremely slow. In the case where few references are made, this method would be efficient. If many references to symbols in the table are required, then some other method should be used. For example, for a table containing 1,000 entries, it would take, on the average, some 500 comparisons to locate a specified element.

Another relatively simple method of accessing a symbol table is the *binary search* method. The entries in the table are stored in alphabetical or numerically increasing order. A search for a particular item resembles the search for a name in a telephone directory. The middle entry of the table is located and its value is examined. If its value is too high, then the middle entry of the first half of the table is examined and the procedure is repeated on the first half until the required item is found. If the value is too low, then the middle entry of the second half of the table is tried and the procedure is repeated on the second half. An average of $\log_2 N$ comparisons is required in order to locate an entry. This is considerably better than the search time for the linear search method.

The binary search technique has certain undesirable properties. First, it appears that the number of memory words allocated to the table is a function of the number of items which is to be stored in the table, namely, the smallest power of two which is greater than or equal to the number of entries that are to be stored in the table. This can be quite wasteful of memory. The basic method, however, can be changed to get around this restriction. Second, an insertion of an entry requires that a search be done in order to locate the position or address in the table where the entry will be stored. The ratio of insertion time to access time is quite high for this method. This method would be suitable if few insertions are to be made. A rather detailed discussion of the binary search method and other search methods is given in Chap. 6.

Since a fast symbol-table method is not possible by associating a unique memory address that is computed from the arithmetic value of the characters making up the name, let us look at an obvious modification. Suppose that we have a function which maps a name into an integer. This type of function will be called a *hashing function*. Let us consider the set of FORTRAN names that can be used in a computer program and a hashing function, H, which maps each name into an integer between 0 and 9. Such a function can be obtained by dividing the internal representation of the name (binary coded decimal) by the number 10. The remainder of this division must be less than 10. This function obviously maps many names into the same number, and so the mapping is many-to-one. The hashing function partitions all names into a set of classes. Two names are in the same class if, and only if, they are mapped into the same number, i.e., they have the same remainder upon division by 10. A name cannot be in two distinct classes, since it can only be mapped into one number. The partition that is induced by a function is called an *equivalence relation* and the classes formed in this way are called *equivalence classes*.

An efficient symbol-table method is to represent each equivalence class in memory as a simple linked linear list. The insertion algorithm consists of mapping the name into a number. This number determines which equivalence class or linked list the name should be in. If the name is not already in that linked list, it is appended to the end of the list. The search for a name can be performed in a similar manner. The name is mapped into a number which is used to locate the linked list in which this name must belong. A sequential search of this list yields the desired entry.

As an example, let us assume the following:

the names NODE, BRAND, OPERATIONS, and PARAMETERS are all mapped into the number 0
the name STORAGE is mapped into the number 1
the names AN and ADD are mapped into the number 2
the names FUNCTION and B are mapped into the number 8

Let us use a one-dimensional array called EQUIV consisting of 10 elements. Each element of EQUIV contains the address of the first node of the linked list representing a particular equivalence class. If there are no names in a certain equivalence class, then the corresponding element in the array EQUIV has a value of NULL. Figure 4-3.1a shows the structure for the equivalence class consisting of the names NODE, BRAND, OPERATIONS, and PARAMETERS which are mapped into zero. A similar representation is given in Fig. 4-3.1b for the remaining equivalence classes.

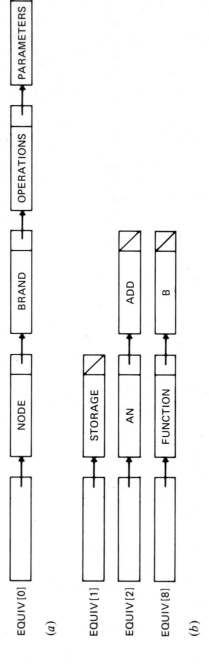

FIGURE 4-3.1.

278

The importance of a suitable hashing function cannot be overemphasized. Ideally, it would be desirable to have a function which results in all equivalence classes having the *same* number of symbols. The worst possible case is one where all names would be mapped into the same number (one equivalence class), thereby causing the insertion and fetching algorithms to be no more efficient than those in a linear search method. It is a nontrivial matter to obtain the "proper" hashing function, since the size of the equivalence classes which it induces depends on the names being used (i.e., on the domain of the hashing function). A more complete discussion of the class of hashing functions will be given in Chap. 6.

Another important factor in attaining a reasonable efficiency is keeping the size of each equivalence class relatively small. For example, if it is known that, on the average, a dictionary will have 125 entries at any given time, then one would want approximately 100 classes. In such a case, the average number of comparisons for accessing an entry is slightly greater than "one" and a similar figure also holds for insertions. These average figures are based on the assumption that all names are mapped into the 100 classes in a uniform manner.

The hashing functions to be used should not be too complex since the time taken to evaluate the function for a particular argument must be added to the insertion and fetch times. It is usually possible to live within this constraint because of the great speed of a computer in doing arithmetic computations.

We now turn to the formulation of an insertion algorithm for the symbol-table system.

Algorithm ENTER (Enters a new name in a symbol table). Given a one-dimensional reference array, each element of which contains a pointer to an equivalence class and a hashing function HASH, which maps a name into an integer, it is required to append the entry denoted by NAME to the end of the appropriate equivalence class (if it is not already there). The typical node in the list representing an equivalence class consists of an information field and a link field denoted by SYMBOL and LINK, respectively. This node structure is referred to as RECORD.

1. [Compute the hash number]   Set RANDOM ← HASH(NAME).
2. [If the equivalence class is empty, enter name in new class]
    If EQUIV[RANDOM] = NULL,
    then set NEW ⇐ RECORD, EQUIV[RANDOM] ← NEW,
    SYMBOL(NEW) ← NAME, LINK(NEW) ← NULL, and Exit.
3. [Initiate search for NAME]   Set POINTER ← EQUIV[RANDOM].
4. [Search]   If SYMBOL(POINTER) = NAME, then Exit.
5. [End of equivalence class?]
    If LINK(POINTER) = NULL,
    then set NEW ⇐ RECORD, SYMBOL(NEW) ← NAME, LINK(POINTER) ← NEW,
    LINK(NEW) ← NULL, and Exit;
    otherwise, set POINTER ← LINK(POINTER) and go to step 4.

The above algorithm is reasonably simple and requires no further comment.

The PL/I program in Fig. 4-3.2 constructs a symbol table. It consists of a hashing

```
HASHING:
     PROCEDURE OPTICNS(MAIN);
/*THIS PROGRAM BUILDS A DICTIONARY OF NAMES CONSISTING OF 1 TO 12
   ALPHANUMERIC CHARACTERS.  EACH NAME IS HASHED INTO AN INTEGER
   WHICH IS BETWEEN 0 AND N-1 INCLUSIVE AND DENOTES TO WHICH OF N
   POSSIBLE EQUIVALENCE CLASSES NAME BELCNGS.  PROCEDURE ENTER PUTS
   NAME IN THE SYMBCL FIELD OF A NODE WHICH IS PLACED AT THE END OF
   ONE OF THE LISTS POINTED TO BY AN ELEMENT OF THE POINTER ARRAY
   EQUIV.                                                      */
     DECLARE
          1 RECORD BASED(NEW),
                2 SYMBCL CHARACTER(12),
                2 LINK POINTER,
           NAME CHARACTER(12) VARYING,
           (I,N) BINARY FIXED,
           PTR POINTER;
     GET LIST(N); /* READ NUMBER OF EQUIVALENCE CLASSES */
BEGIN; /* AUTOMATIC STORAGE ALLOCATION */
     DECLARE
          HASH RETURNS(BINARY FIXED),
          EQUIV(0:N - 1) POINTER;
     ON ENDFILE(SYSIN) GO TO OUTPUT;
     DO I = 0 TO N - 1;
          EQUIV(I) = NULL;
     END;
     PUT EDIT('NAME','HASHED INTO')(X(30),A(20),A(11));
READ:  /* GET NEXT NAME FOR DICTIONARY*/
     GET LIST(NAME);
     CALL ENTER; /* INSERT NAME IN DICTICNARY*/
     GO TO READ;
OUTPUT: /* OUTPUT CONTENTS OF EACH EQUIVALENCE CLASS */
     DO I = 0 TO N - 1;
          PUT SKIP(2) EDIT('EQUIVALENCE CLASS NUMBER ',I)(X(30),A(25),
                                                          F(2));
          PTR = EQUIV(I); /* SCAN LIST */
          DO WHILE (PTR ¬= NULL);
               PUT SKIP EDIT(PTR->SYMBOL)(X(41),A(12));
               PTR = PTR->LINK;
          END;
     END;
END;
```

FIGURE 4-3.2   Program for symbol-table algorithm.

function, a procedure based on the preceding algorithm, and a mainline program. The hashing function finds the remainder on dividing the bit representation (obtained by using UNSPEC) of NAME by N. The MOD function is used to find the remainder when NUMBER is divided by N.

The UNSPEC function is of the form UNSPEC(s) where s is any expression. The result of this function is a bit string containing the internal representation of s. The length of the bit string depends on the attributes of s. For example, if s is a string variable containing n characters, then a bit string of length 8n is returned.

The hashing function used in the procedure HASH takes the first and last characters in the name to be hashed and converts these two characters to a bit string of 16 bits. (For a name containing a single character, the last character is a duplicate of the first.) This bit string is then multiplied by the length of the name. Examples of this process are given in Table 4-3.1.

The main program is written so that up to 10 equivalence classes can be handled in the symbol table. Each name to be inserted is on one input card. On an end-of-file, control transfers to the statement labeled OUTPUT. At this point, each simple linked linear list representing an equivalence class is scanned, and each name in it is printed.

```
ENTER:
          PROCEDURE;
/*EACH ELEMENT OF ARRAY EQUIV IS A POINTER TO A LIST OF NAMES WHICH
   HAVE BEEN MAPPED INTO THE EQUIVALENCE CLASS REFERENCED BY THE
   SUBSCRIPT OF THE ELEMENT.  THIS PROCEDURE PUTS NAME IN A NODE AT THE
   END OF THE LIST WHICH BELONGS TO THE EQUIVALENCE CLASS DENOTED
   BY THE INTEGER RANDOM.*/
          DECLARE
               POINTER POINTER,
          RANDOM BINARY FIXED;
          RANDOM = HASH(NAME); /*COMPUTE THE HASH NUMBER*/
          PUT SKIP EDIT(NAME,RANDOM)(X(30),A(25),F(2));
          IF EQUIV(RANDOM) = NULL
          THEN /* EQUIVALENCE CLASS IS EMPTY */
               DO;
                    ALLOCATE RECORD;
                    EQUIV(RANDOM) = NEW;
                    NEW->SYMBOL = NAME;
                    NEW->LINK = NULL;
                    RETURN;
               END;
          POINTER = EQUIV(RANDOM); /* INITIATE SEARCH FOR NAME */
SEARCH: /* OF LIST FOR AN OCCURRENCE OF NAME */
          IF POINTER->SYMBOL = NAME THEN RETURN;
          IF POINTER->LINK = NULL
          THEN /* INSERT A NEW NODE */
               DO;
                    ALLOCATE RECORD;
                    NEW->SYMBOL = NAME;
                    POINTER->LINK = NEW;
                    NEW->LINK = NULL;
                    RETURN;
               END;
          POINTER = POINTER->LINK; /* CONTINUE SEARCH */
          GO TO SEARCH;
END ENTER;

HASH: /* MAP NAME TO A NUMBER BETWEEN 0 AND N-1 */
          PROCEDURE(NAME) RETURNS(BINARY FIXED);
     DECLARE
          NAME CHARACTER(12) VARYING,
          PART CHARACTER(2),
          BITNAME BIT(16),
          NUMBER BINARY FIXED(31);
/*   GET FIRST AND LAST CHARACTERS OF NAME   */
          PART = SUBSTR(NAME,1,1) || SUBSTR(NAME,LENGTH(NAME),1);
          BITNAME = UNSPEC(PART); /* OBTAIN BIT REPRESENTATION OF PART */
          NUMBER = BITNAME * LENGTH(NAME); /* MULTIPLY BY LENGTH OF NAME */
          RETURN(MOD(NUMBER,N));
END HASH;

END; /* OF BEGIN BLOCK */

END HASHING;
```

FIGURE 4-3.2 (Continued)

Table 4-3.1

Name	Part	UNSPEC(*Part*)	HASH *Number*
B	BB	'1100001011000010'B $* 1 =$ 49858 modulo 10 = 8	
AN	AN	'1100000111010101'B $* 2 =$ 99242 modulo 10 = 2	
LINK	LK	'1101001111010010'B $* 4 =$ 216904 modulo 10 = 4	

```
NAME                    HASHED INTO
AN                          2
B                           8
LINK                        4
NODE                        0
ADD                         2
BRAND                       0
OPERATIONS                  0
STORAGE                     1
PARAMETERS                  0
FUNCTION                    8

EQUIVALENCE CLASS NUMBER    0
           NODE
           BRAND
           OPERATIONS
           PARAMETERS

EQUIVALENCE CLASS NUMBER    1
           STORAGE

EQUIVALENCE CLASS NUMBER    2
           AN
           ADD

EQUIVALENCE CLASS NUMBER    3

EQUIVALENCE CLASS NUMBER    4
           LINK

EQUIVALENCE CLASS NUMBER    5

EQUIVALENCE CLASS NUMBER    6

EQUIVALENCE CLASS NUMBER    7

EQUIVALENCE CLASS NUMBER    8
           B
           FUNCTION

EQUIVALENCE CLASS NUMBER    9
```

FIGURE 4-3.2   (Continued)

Exercises for Sec. 4-3.2

1. The midsquare hashing method follows:
    (a) Square part of the key, or the whole key if possible.
    (b) Either (i) extract n digits from the middle of the result to give $h(\text{key}) \in \{0, 1, \ldots, 10^n - 1\}$, or (ii) extract n bits from the middle of the result to give $h(\text{key}) \in \{0, 1, \ldots, 2^n - 1\}$.

    Write a program which uses this procedure to hash a set of variable names. The midsquare method frequently gives satisfactory results, but in many cases the keys are unevenly distributed over the required range.

2. A hashing method often implemented, called *folding*, is performed by dividing the key into several parts and adding the parts to form a number in the required range. For example, if we have eight-digit keys and wish to obtain a three-digit address, we may do the following:

    $$h(97434658) = 974 + 346 + 58 = 378$$
    $$h(31269857) = 312 + 698 + 57 = 67$$

    (Note that the final carry is ignored.) Implement this method in a computer program.

3. Compare the results of applying the division, midsquare, and folding hashing functions to a fixed set of keys. Make sure the range is the same or almost the same in each case. Which method distributes the keys most evenly over the elements of the range?

4-3.3 Multiple-Precision Arithmetic

There are a number of applications in which a particular accuracy in the results must be obtained. This accuracy, however, depends on the data that are manipulated. For example, a certain accuracy may be required in the solution of a set of simultaneous equations. The program to solve this problem can be run on a computer using single- or double-precision numbers, but this technique may not be accurate enough. In many cases, the desired accuracy can be obtained only through the use of routines which perform multiple-precision operations. The number of digits used in such routines can depend on the number of equations being solved and the ill-conditioned matrix of the floating-point coefficients. The same problem presents itself in obtaining the inverse of an ill-conditioned matrix.

In this section we wish to formulate algorithms for performing multiple-precision arithmetic on the integers. Although this construction is done only for the operations of addition and subtraction, these techniques can be easily extended to the operations of multiplication and division.

Let us consider the problem of performing multiple-precision integer arithmetic. Most digital computers have a certain maximum number or bits of digits for the representation of an integer. The number of bits or digits varies from a minimum of 8 to a maximum of 64, the upper bound representing an integer of approximately 20 decimal digits. In certain applications, the size of the integers used may be considerably greater than this upper bound. If we want to manipulate these integers, we must find a new way to express them.

Let $m - 1$ be the largest integer that can be stored in a particular computer. Then it is possible to express any integer, say A, using a polynomial expansion of the form

$$A = \sum_{i=0}^{k} a_i m^i \qquad \text{where } 0 \le |a_i| < m \text{ for every } i$$

For example, assume that the largest integer that can be stored in a particular computer is 999. An integer A having a value of 12,345,678 can be represented, in the above form, as follows:

$$A = 678 \times 1,000^0 + 345 \times 1,000^1 + 12 \times 1,000^2$$
$$= 678 + 345,000 + 12,000,000$$
$$= 12,345,678$$

In this example, $k = 2$, $a_0 = 678$, $a_1 = 345$, and $a_2 = 12$. If A is a negative integer, then each nonzero a_i will be negative. For example, if A is $-2,000,342$, then it can be represented as

$$A = (-342 \times 1,000^0) + (0 \times 1,000^1) + (-2 \times 1,000^2)$$

Arbitrarily large integers are of little use unless we are able to perform operations on them. In this section we consider the operation of addition and present an algorithm for the addition of signed multiple-precision integers. For the algorithm, we require that the above polynomials be represented as linear linked lists. Before describing the lists used, we consider the different cases that occur in adding two polynomials representing integers.

Given integers

$$A = \sum_{i=0}^{k} a_i m^i \qquad \text{and} \qquad B = \sum_{i=0}^{k} b_i m^i$$

it is required to obtain a polynomial representing the sum

$$S = \sum_{i=0}^{k+1} s_i m^i = A + B$$

Note that k is the exponent of the highest-degree term in either polynomial A or B that is nonzero; that is, $a_k \neq 0$ or $b_k \neq 0$. The maximum degree possible for polynomial S is $k + 1$. Some of the coefficients s_i of S may be zero. As an extreme example, if A is equal to $-B$, then all coefficients of the polynomial are zero.

We now list the five distinct cases which may arise in adding these multiple-precision integers. In all examples given, m is chosen to be $1,000$ for the purpose of illustration.

Case 1: $A = 0$ or $B = 0$. If one of A or B is zero, then S is set equal to the number which is nonzero. If $A = B = 0$, then $S = 0$.

Case 2: $A > 0$ and $B > 0$. In this case, we have

$$s_i = (a_i + b_i + c_{i-1}) \bmod m \qquad \text{for } 0 \leq i \leq k$$

and

$$s_{k+1} = c_k$$

Here, c_i is a "carry value" propagated at the ith stage. c_{-1} is equal to zero in this and all cases in which it is used. If $a_i + b_i + c_{i-1} \geq m$, then c_i is assigned a value of 1; otherwise, c_i is assigned a value of 0. We may formulate this statement as

$$c_i = \lfloor (a_i + b_i + c_{i-1}) / m \rfloor \qquad \text{for } 0 \leq i \leq k$$

since

$$0 \leq a_i + b_i + c_{i-1} \leq (m - 1) + (m - 1) + 1 = 2m - 1 < 2m$$

where the notation $\lfloor P \rfloor$ = largest integer $\leq P$.

As a first example, let $A = 12,345$ and $B = 6,890$. To get $S = A + B$, we write

$$A = a_0 m^0 + a_1 m^1 = 345 \times 1,000^0 + 12 \times 1,000^1$$

$$B = b_0 m^0 + b_1 m^1 = 890 \times 1,000^0 + 6 \times 1,000^1$$

The calculations proceed as follows:

$$c_{-1} = 0$$

$$s_0 = (a_0 + b_0 + c_{-1}) \bmod m$$

$$= (345 + 890) \bmod 1,000 = 235$$

$$c_0 = \lfloor (a_0 + b_0 + c_{-1}) / m \rfloor = \lfloor 1,235 / 1,000 \rfloor = 1$$

$$s_1 = (a_1 + b_1 + c_0) \bmod m$$

$$= (12 + 6 + 1) \bmod 1{,}000 = 19$$

$$s_2 = c_1 = \lfloor (a_1 + b_1 + c_0) / m \rfloor = \lfloor 19 / 1{,}000 \rfloor = 0$$

Thus,

$$S = \sum_{i=0}^{1} s_i m^i = 235 \times 1{,}000^0 + 19 \times 1{,}000^1 = 19{,}235$$

As a second example, let $A = 650{,}125$ and $B = 425{,}975$. The calculations are

$$c_{-1} = 0$$

$$s_0 = (125 + 975 + 0) \bmod 1{,}000 = 100$$

$$c_0 = \lfloor 1{,}100 / 1{,}000 \rfloor = 1$$

$$s_1 = (650 + 425 + 1) \bmod 1{,}000 = 76$$

$$c_1 = \lfloor 1{,}076 / 1{,}000 \rfloor = 1$$

$$s_2 = c_1 = 1$$

and

$$S = 100 \times 1{,}000^0 + 76 \times 1{,}000^1 + 1 \times 1{,}000^2 = 1{,}076{,}100$$

Case 3: $A < 0$ and $B < 0$. We calculate

$$s_i = -(|a_i + b_i + c_{i-1}| \bmod m) \qquad \text{for } 0 \le i \le k \text{ and } s_{k+1} = c_k$$

In this case, c_i must be a carry of 0 or -1, so

$$c_{-1} = 0 \qquad c_i = -\lfloor |a_i + b_i + c_{i-1}| / m \rfloor \qquad \text{for } 0 \le i \le k$$

Consider the example which has $A = -96$ and $B = -99{,}934$. We find S as follows:

$$c_{-1} = 0$$

$$s_0 = -(|-96 - 934 + 0| \bmod 1{,}000) = -30$$

$$c_0 = -\lfloor |-96 - 934 + 0| / 1{,}000 \rfloor = -1$$

$$s_1 = -(|0 - 99 - 1| \bmod 1{,}000) = -100$$

$$s_2 = c_1 = -\lfloor |0 - 99 - 1| / 1{,}000 \rfloor = 0$$

We have

$$S = -100{,}030$$

Case 4: $A < 0$, $B > 0$, $B \ge |A|$; or $B < 0$, $A > 0$, and $A \ge |B|$. In this case, we add integers of opposite sign to obtain a nonnegative result. The calculations are the same as in *case 2*, that is,

$$s_i = (a_i + b_i + c_{i-1}) \bmod m \qquad \text{for } 0 \le i \ge k$$

$$s_{k+1} = c_k$$

$$c_{-1} = 0 \qquad c_i = \lfloor (a_i + b_i + c_{i-1}) / m \rfloor \qquad \text{for } 0 \le i \le k$$

In this case, c_i is not a "carry" but is a "borrow" since we are actually subtracting a positive number from a greater or equal positive number. Since either a_i or b_i is negative, c_i will have a value 0 or -1.

As an example, consider $A = -10,700$ and $B = 12,300$. Then

$$c_{-1} = 0$$

$$s_0 = (-700 + 300 + 0) \bmod 1,000$$

$$= -400 \bmod 1,000 = 600$$

$$c_0 = \lfloor -400 / 1,000 \rfloor = -1$$

$$s_1 = (-10 + 12 - 1) \bmod 1,000 = 1$$

$$s_2 = c_1 = \lfloor 1 / 1,000 \rfloor = 0$$

Thus $S = 1,600$. The final borrow is always zero when the positive number is greater than or equal to the absolute value of the negative number.

Case 5: $A < 0$, $B > 0$, and $B < |A|$; or $B < 0$, $A > 0$, and $A < |B|$. We initially proceed as in *case 4*. Again, the c_i's are borrows. For example, given $A = -789,300$ and $B = 400,700$, we calculate

$$c_{-1} = 0$$

$$s_0 = (-300 + 700 + 0) \bmod 1,000 = 400$$

$$c_0 = \lfloor 400 / 1,000 \rfloor = 0$$

$$s_1 = (-789 + 400 + 0) \bmod 1,000$$

$$= -389 \bmod 1,000 = 611$$

$$c_1 = \lfloor -389 / 1,000 \rfloor = -1$$

At this point we have a borrow, but there is nothing that it can be borrowed from. This serves as an indication that our procedure is incomplete.

Our result is in the form of

$$-1,000,000 + 611,400$$

One way to obtain the answer is to use the same procedure again to add 0 and $-611,400$. This procedure will result in

$$-1,000,000 + 388,600$$

and neglect the "borrow" of -1 and negate the number 388,600 to get the right value of $-388,600$. Thus, $S = -388,600$.

This concludes the discussion of the different cases which arise in adding two integers. All cases except the first use the formulas (or variations of them) given in *case 2*. Care must be taken to ensure that the correct signs are used, and the significance of a final borrow of -1 should be noted. Before devising a formal algorithm, we must consider a representation of multiple-precision integers suitable for computer implementation.

Given the integer A, we can form a singly linked list representing its polynomial expansion. Each node in the list consists of a coefficient a_i and a pointer to the next node in the list. This value field and pointer field are denoted as **COEF** and **LINK**, respectively.

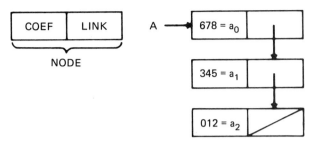

FIGURE 4-3.3   List representation of a multiple-precision integer.

A list representing the number $A = 12{,}345{,}678$ is given in Fig. 4-3.3. The number $-1{,}280{,}000{,}129$ can be represented by the list of Fig. 4-3.4. Note that for this integer, all the nonzero coefficients are negative. Such will always be the case for negative integers. Zero will be represented by a null list.

Several subalgorithms are required in Algorithm **ADDITION**. We will refer to the first as **INSERT**. It is similar to the algorithm of the same name in Sec. 4-2.1, but it allocates the node structure just described. **INSERT** places a node at the front of a list and fills in the **COEF** field. As an example of its use,

$$R \leftarrow \text{INSERT(N, R)}$$

will cause a node to be allocated, place the value of **N** in the **COEF** field, set the **LINK** field to **R**'s pointer value, and assign the address of the new node to **R**.

A second subalgorithm we require is **SIGN**. Given that **R** points to a list representing an integer,

$$N \leftarrow \text{SIGN(R)}$$

will assign -1 to **N** if the integer is negative; otherwise (if the integer is nonnegative), 1 is assigned to **N**. These two algorithms are given as PL/I procedures at the end of this section.

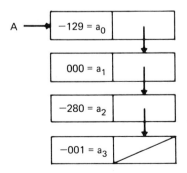

FIGURE 4-3.4.

Given two lists pointed to by P and Q, which represent the integers A and B, respectively, it is required to construct a list pointed to by SUM and representing A + B. Algorithm ADDITION will construct the reverse of list SUM and then employ Subalgorithm REVERSE to reverse the order of the nodes. REVERSE also negates each coefficient value if requested, as will be necessary for additions of the type given in *case 5*. (This will be made clear when Algorithm ADDITION is presented.) A third function performed by it is to delete any nodes having a zero COEF value when they are representative of leftmost zeros in a number, such as 000,125,789. We will first formulate this subalgorithm.

Algorithm REVERSE.   Given a pointer R to the first node in a list, it is required to reverse the order of the nodes in list R. Each node has a COEF and a LINK field. The variable NEGATE has the value "true" when each field must be negated. Any nodes containing a zero coefficient field and situated at the beginning of the list will be deleted. Auxiliary pointer variables S and Q are used, as well as a flag denoted by SIGNIFICANT.

1. [Initialize]   Set SIGNIFICANT ← false and S ← NULL.
2. [End of list?]   If R = NULL, then set REVERSE ← S, and Exit.
3. [Negate a coefficient]   If NEGATE, then set COEF(R) ← −COEF(R).
4. [Reverse the next node]   Set Q ← S, S ← R, R ← LINK(S), and LINK(S) ← Q.
5. [Delete leading zeros]   If SIGNIFICANT, then go to step 2.
   If COEF(S) = 0,
   then restore node S to the availability list and set S ← NULL;
   otherwise, set SIGNIFICANT ← true.
   Go to step 2.

In step 1, SIGNIFICANT is given the value "false" and remains unchanged until a node with nonzero COEF field is encountered in step 5. Any nodes with zero COEF fields encountered before SIGNIFICANT is given the value "true" are deleted. Step 2 checks for the end of list R and exits if the test is successful. Step 3 negates all COEF fields if necessary. In Step 4, R is moved down the original list, and S points to the node previously indicated by R. LINK(S) now has the value NULL or points to the node which follows S in the new order. Algorithm REVERSE may be invoked as

SUM ← REVERSE(SUM, true)

if the COEF fields must be negated. Otherwise,

SUM ← REVERSE(SUM, false)

is used. The variable NEGATE is assigned true or false.

Given the preceding subalgorithms, we can formulate an algorithm for the addition of multiple-precision signed integers.

Algorithm ADDITION.   Given pointers P and Q to lists representing multiple-precision integers, it is required to construct a list pointed to by SUM which represents the sum of the integers. Variable MAX has a value such that $0 \le |COEF(R)| < MAX$ for all nodes R. Variable C represents a carry or borrow value, and SUMCF is used to contain the sum of corresponding COEF fields and C. NEG has value 1 when at least one integer is nonnegative, or −1 when both are negative. SECOND_PASS is a flag used in handling additions of the type given in *case 5*.

1. [Trivial case]   If P = NULL, then set ADDITION ← Q, and Exit.
   If Q = NULL, then set ADDITION ← P, and Exit.
2. [Initialize]
   If SIGN(P) = −1 and SIGN(Q) = −1,
   then set NEG ← −1;
   otherwise, set NEG ← 1.
   Set SUM ← NULL, C ← 0, and SECOND_PASS ← false.
3. [End of list(s)?]   If P = NULL, then go to step 6.
   If Q = NULL, then set Q ← P and go to step 6.
4. [Calculate value for and insert next node]
   Set SUMCF ← NEG * (COEF(P) + COEF(Q) + C), C ← NEG * ⌊SUMCF / MAX⌋,
   and SUM ← INSERT(NEG * (SUMCF mod MAX), SUM).
5. [Obtain addresses of next terms]   Set P ← LINK(P), Q ← LINK(Q), and go to step 3.
6. [Scan remainder of list Q]
   If Q = NULL,
   then go to step 7;
   otherwise, set SUMCF ← NEG * (COEF(Q) + C), C ← NEG * ⌊SUMCF / MAX⌋,
   SUM ← INSERT(NEG * (SUMCF mod MAX), SUM), Q ← LINK(Q),
   and repeat this step.
7. [Second pass required?]
   If C = −1 and NEG = 1,
   then
       if SECOND_PASS,
       then set C ← 0;
       otherwise, set SECOND_PASS ← true, Q ← REVERSE(SUM, true),
       SUM ← NULL, C ← 0, and go to step 6.
8. [Final carry?]   If C ≠ 0, then set SUM ← INSERT(C, SUM).
9. [Reverse the resulting list]
   If SECOND_PASS
   then set ADDITION ← REVERSE(SUM, true);
   otherwise, set ADDITION ← REVERSE(SUM, false).
   Exit.

On termination of this algorithm, P and Q have the value NULL. It is assumed that their original values have been saved for future reference.

Step 1 handles the trivial case when one or both lists are null (one or both integers are zero). In certain cases, it may be desirable to copy the nonzero list and return its pointer instead of making the pointer SUM equivalent to P or Q. In the latter case, a change in list SUM will result in a change of list P or Q.

In step 2, the variables required are initialized. If both integers to be added are negative, then NEG is set to −1; otherwise, it is set to 1. NEG is used to modify the calculations in steps 4 and 6, so that they include *case 3*, as well as the other previously described cases.

In general, lists P and Q may not have the same length. Step 3 detects the end of either list and ensures that Q points to the remainder of the longer list, unless lists P and Q have equal length. Step 4 performs the calculations for *cases 2 to 5* inclusive. Note how NEG is used, particularly when it has value −1. This step adds a new node with the required value to the front of list SUM. In step 5, the pointers P and Q are moved down the list, and control transfers to recheck their values in step 3.

In step 6, the remainder of list Q is scanned. All calculations are the same as in step 4, except COEF(P) has been eliminated. When list Q is finished, control transfers to step 7. This step detects an addition as described in *case 5*—the borrow is −1 when both lists have been scanned and NEG is 1. When these conditions are satisfied, the flag SECOND_PASS is set to true, the list SUM is reversed, and each COEF field is negated. Q points to the inverted list and SUM and C are reinitialized. Control transfers to step 6 which essentially adds the negative integer, represented by list Q, to zero. The next time step 7 is executed, SECOND_PASS has value true, and the borrow C is set from −1 to 0.

In step 8, the final carry, if any, from the addition of integers possessing the same signs is put in the list SUM. Step 9 reverses this list, negating each COEF field if SECOND_PASS has value true (otherwise, we would have the absolute value of the correct answer).

It is instructive to trace this algorithm using several pairs of integers and a low value for MAX. The reader should carefully study the following examples.

Example 4-1   Let P and Q represent integers −99,012 and −915,995, respectively. A list representation of these numbers is given in Fig. 4-3.5. Figure 4-3.6 traces the execution of important steps in Algorithm ADDITION. We have MAX equal to 1,000 and NEG equal to −1. The final list represents the integer −1,015,007.   ////

Example 4-2   Let P and Q represent integers 75,198 and −1,079,239, respectively, with a list representation given in Fig. 4-3.7. Again, MAX is 1,000, but in this case NEG will be 1. A trace of the algorithm is given in Fig. 4-3.8. This final list represents the sum −1,004,041.   ////

Figure 4-3.9 is a PL/I program which implements these algorithms to perform multiple-precision addition.

Exercises for Sec. 4-3.3
1.   Give the list representations of 75,198 and −1,079,238 with MAX equal to 128.
2.   Trace Algorithm ADDITION as in Figs. 4-3.6 and 4-3.8 by using the lists constructed in Prob. 1. Convert the list SUM to its base 10 equivalent in order to check your result.
3.   Devise an algorithm for multiplying two list-represented integers.

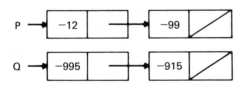

FIGURE 4-3.5.

Step	COEF(P)	COEF(Q)	C	SUMCF	SECOND _PASS	SUM
2	−12	−995	0		F	NULL
4			−1	1007		−7
5	−99	−915				
4			−1	1015		−15 → −7
5	P = NULL	Q = NULL				
8						−1 → −15 → −7
9						−7 → −15 → −1

FIGURE 4-3.6   Trace of Algorithm **ADDITION** with operands −99,012 and −915,995.

4-4   ASSOCIATIVE LISTS

In this subsection the notion of an associative list (or structure) is introduced and a comparison is made between such a data structure and the linear list which we have discussed in Chap. 3 and thus far in Chap. 4. Some examples are presented and the storage representation of associative lists is examined.

An associative list can be thought of as a special form of linear list. It is special in the sense that a particular element of the list is generally not referred to as "the first element of the list" or "the last element of the list" (as in the case of a stack or queue) or "the nth element of the list" (as is commonly done for a general linear list). Instead, a particular element is referenced via an associated name.

As an example of an associative structure, consider the problem of analyzing text and counting the number of occurrences of each word in the text. If we use the last sentence for our example text, the words and their associated counts can be tabulated as shown in Table 4-4.1.

An associative list can be viewed as a linear list in which each element or node of the list contains two or more information items. One of the items in a list node, usually the first item, is unique over all nodes of the associative list. We will refer to this special item as the *associative item*. The remaining item or items of a node will be called the *list item* or *list items*.

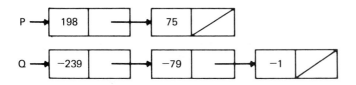

FIGURE 4-3.7.

Step	COEF(P)	COEF(Q)	C	SUMCF	SECOND_PASS	SUM
2	198	−239	0		F	NULL
4			−1	−41		[959]
5	.75	−79				[995]→[959]
4			−1	−5		[998]→[995]→[959]
5	P = NULL					
6		Q = NULL	−1	−2	T	NULL
7		−959	0			[41]
6		−995	−1	−959		[4]→[41]
6		−998	−1	−996		[1]→[4]→[41]
6		Q = NULL	−1	−999		[−41]→[−4]→[−1]
7			0			
9						

FIGURE 4-3.8 Trace of Algorithm ADDITION with operands 75,198 and −1,079,239.

292

```
MULPREC:
    PROCEDURE OPTICNS(MAIN);
/*    M A I N   P R C G R A M
    THIS PROGRAM PERFORMS MULTIPLE PRECISION ADDITION OF SIGNED INTEGERS.
    CHARACTER STRING INTEGERS ARE INPUT AND CONVERTED TO LIST FORM USING
    PROCEDURE SETUP.   THE FUNCTION ADDITION ADDS THE TWO LISTS, FCRMING
    A THIRD WHICH REPRESENTS THE SUM.   THE LIST FORM OF AN INTEGER IS
    CONVERTED TO A CHARACTER STRING USING PROCEDURE LIST_TO_STRING.
    PROCEDURES NOT DIRECTLY INVOKED INCLUDE REVERSE, SIGN, AND INSERT.
    THROUGHOUT THE PROGRAM ARGUMENTS TO PROCEDURES ADDITION, SIGN, AND
    LIST_TO_STRING SHCULD BE PASSED BY VALUE.
NODE:   STRUCTURE CCNTAINING COEF AND LINK FIELDS.
MAX:   IS SUCH THAT 0 <= |COEF| < MAX.   I.E. MAX IS THE MODULUS CF COEF.
EXP:   THE EXPONENT OF THE POWER OF TEN WHICH EQUALS MAX.
ZEROES,BLANKS:   FOR PADDING CHARACTER STRINGS.
L1,L2:   POINT TO LIST REPRESENTED INTEGERS WHICH ARE TO BE ADDED.
SUM:   POINTS TO SUM OF L1 AND L2.
I1,I2,I3:   CHARACTER REPRESENTATIONS OF INTEGERS.                        */
    DECLARE
        ADDITION RETURNS(POINTER),
        SIGN RETURNS(BINARY FIXED),
        INSERT ENTRY(BINARY FIXED(31),PCINTER) RETURNS(POINTER),
        SETUP RETURNS(POINTER),
        LIST_TC_STRING RETURNS(CHARACTER(80) VARYING),
        REVERSE ENTRY(POINTER,BIT(1)) RETURNS(POINTER),
        1 NODE BASED(NEW),
            2 CCEF BINARY FIXED(31),
            2 LINK POINTER,
        MAX BINARY FIXED(31),
        EXP BINARY FIXED,
        ZEROES CHARACTER(10) INITIAL((10)'0'),
        BLANKS CHARACTER(80) INITIAL((80)' '),
        (L1,SUM,L2) POINTER,
        (I1,I2,I3) CHARACTER(80) VARYING;
    ON ENDFILE(SYSIN) GO TO STOP;
    GET LIST(MAX,EXP); /* INPUT MODULUS AND ITS POWER OF TEN */
    DO WHILE('1'B); /* INPUT AND ADD TWC INTEGERS */
        GET LIST(I1,I2);
        L1 = SETUP((I1)); /* CONVERT I1 AND I2 TO LIST REPRESENTATION*/
        L2 = SETUP((I2));
        SUM = ADDITION((L1),(L2)); /* ADD THE NUMBERS */
        /*CUNVERT EACH INTEGER TO APPROPRIATE OUTPUT REPRESENTATION*/
        I1 = SUBSTR(BLANKS,1,80 - LENGTH(I1)) || I1;
        PUT SKIP(2) LIST(I1);
        I2 = SUBSTR(BLANKS,1,80 - LENGTH(I2)) || I2;
        PUT SKIP LIST(I2);
        PUT SKIP LIST(REPEAT('-',80));
        I3 = LIST_TO_STRING((SUM));
        PUT SKIP LIST(I3);
    END;
```

FIGURE 4-3.9 Program for multiple-precision addition.

Table 4-4.1

Word	Count	Word	Count
as	1	text	2
an	2	and	1
example	1	counting	1
of	4	number	1
associative	1	occurrences	1
structure	1	each	1
consider	1	word	1
the	3	in	1
problem	1	analyzing	1

```
SETUP:
          PROCEDURE(I) RETURNS(POINTER);
  /*    S E T U P                              CONVERT THE INTEGER GIVEN BY
    CHARACTER STRING I TO A LIST REPRESENTED INTEGER.
  NEG:  INDICATES THE SIGN OF I.
  J,NUMBER:  AUXILLIARY VARIABLES.
  R:   POINTS TO RESULTING LIST.                 */
          DECLARE
              I CHARACTER(80) VARYING,
              NUMBER BINARY FIXED(31),
              (NEG,J) BINARY FIXED,
              R POINTER;
          R = NULL;
          IF SUBSTR(I,1,1) = '-' /* FIND SIGN OF I */
          THEN
              DO;
                  I = SUBSTR(I,2);
                  NEG = - 1;
              END;
          ELSE NEG = 1;
          /*PAD I WITH ZEROES SO NUMBER OF DIGITS IS MULTIPLE OF EXP. */
          J = EXP - MOD(LENGTH(I),EXP);
          IF J ¬= EXP
          THEN I = SUBSTR(ZEROES,1,J) || I;
          DO J = 1 TO LENGTH(I) BY EXP; /* OBTAIN NUMBERS FOR NODES */
              NUMBER = SUBSTR(I,J,EXP);
              IF J = 1 & NUMBER = 0 /* IS I EQUAL TO ZERO? */
              THEN RETURN(NULL);
              R = INSERT(NEG * NUMBER,R);
          END;
          RETURN(R);
  END SETUP;

  SIGN:
          PROCEDURE(R) RETURNS(BINARY FIXED);
  /*    S I G N
    DETERMINE IF THE INTEGER REPRESENTED BY LIST R IS NONNEGATIVE
    OR NEGATIVE AND RETURN 1 OR -1 RESPECTIVELY.              */
          DECLARE
              R POINTER;
          DO WHILE(R ¬= NULL);
              IF R -> COEF < 0
              THEN RETURN(-1);
              IF R->COEF > 0
              THEN RETURN(1);
              R = R->LINK;
          END;
          RETURN(1);
  END SIGN;
```

FIGURE 4-3.9   (Continued)

As an example, consider the list composed of the words of text and their associated word count as presented previously. In a parenthesis form of list notation, which will be used more extensively in Chap. 5, we can represent this list as ((as, 1)(an, 2)(example, 1) ... (word, 1)(in, 1)). The words, 'as', 'an', 'example', etc., are the set of associative items for this list.

Because of the manner in which elements of associative lists are generally accessed, we consider such a list as a special case of a linear list. In the example given previously, the word count is accessed via its associated word. It is this form of access that is primarily used in an associative list.

In the algorithmic notation, a particular element of an associative list, say the list WORDCNT, is accessed using the form WORDCNT <WORD>, where WORD is a variable

```
INSERT:
        PROCEDURE(NUMBER,R) RETURNS(POINTER);
/*    I N S E R T
  ALLOCATE A NODE STRUCTURE AND PUT THE VALUES OF NUMBER AND R IN THE
  COEF AND LINK FIELDS RESPECTIVELY.  RETURN THE ADDRESS OF THE NODE.*/
        DECLARE
            NUMBER BINARY FIXED(31),
            R POINTER;
        ALLOCATE NODE;
        NEW->COEF = NUMBER;
        NEW->LINK = R;
        RETURN(NEW);
END INSERT;

REVERSE:
        PROCEDURE(R,NEGATE) RETURNS(POINTER);
/*    R E V E R S E
  REVERSE THE ORDER OF THE NODES IN LIST R, PLACING THE LAST NODE FIRST
  ETC.  NEGATE EACH COEF FIELD IF NEGATE HAS VALUE '1'B.  NODES WHICH
  REPRESENT UNNECESSARY LEFTMOST ZEROES IN THE INTEGER ARE DELETED.  */
        DECLARE
            (R,S,T) POINTER,
            NEGATE BIT(1),
            SIGNIFICANT BIT(1);
        SIGNIFICANT = '0'B; /* INITIALIZE */
        S = NULL;
        DO WHILE(R ¬= NULL); /* REVERSE THE LIST */
        IF NEGATE
        THEN R->COEF = -R->COEF;
            T = S;
            S = R;
            R = S->LINK;
            S->LINK = T;
            IF ¬SIGNIFICANT
            THEN
                IF S->COEF = 0
                THEN
                    DO; /* DELETE A NODE */
                        FREE S->NODE;
                        S = NULL;
                    END;
                ELSE SIGNIFICANT = '1'B;
        END;
        RETURN(S);
END REVERSE;


ADDITION:
        PROCEDURE(P,Q) RETURNS(POINTER);
/*    A D D I T I O N
  THIS PROCEDURE ADDS THE INTEGERS REPRESENTED BY LISTS P AND Q,
  FORMING A THIRD LIST POINTED TO BY SUM WHICH CONTAINS THE RESULT.
NEG:  HAS VALUE -1 WHEN P AND Q ARE NEGATIVE; OTHERWISE NEG IS 1.
C:  INDICATES THE VALUE OF A CARRY OR BORROW.
SECOND_PASS:  WHEN EQUAL TO '1'B INDICATES THE DO WHILE BLOCK BEGINNING
              AT LABEL SCAN MUST BE EXECUTED TO COMPLEMENT THE FIRST
              ADDITION RESULT.
SUMCF:  CONTAINS SUM OF CORRESPONDING COEF FIELDS.  */
```

FIGURE 4-3.9 (Continued)

containing an associative item (in this case a word). The braces $<>$ are used to denote the associative item and differentiate clearly an associative-list form of element specification from an array element specification. Therefore, as an example taken from Table 4-4.1,

Set X ← WORDCNT <'AS'>.

assigns the list element 1 to X and

```
/*  A D D I T I C N  */
    DECLARE
        (P,Q,SUM) POINTER,
        SUMCF BINARY FIXED(31),
        (NEG,C) BINARY FIXED,
        SECOND_PASS BIT(1);
    IF P = NULL /* TRIVIAL CASE */
    THEN RETURN(Q);
    IF Q = NULL
    THEN RETURN(P);
    IF SIGN((P)) = -1 & SIGN((Q)) = -1   /* INITIALIZE */
    THEN NEG = -1; /* ADD TWO NEGATIVE NUMBERS */
    ELSE NEG = 1;  /* ADD TWO NONNEGATIVE OR OPPOSITE NUMBERS */
    SUM = NULL;
    C = 0;
    SECOND_PASS = '0'B;
    DO WHILE(¬(P = NULL | Q = NULL)); /* ADD COEFFICIENTS */
        SUMCF = NEG * (P->COEF + Q->COEF + C);
        IF SUMCF < 0
        THEN C = -1;
        ELSE C = NEG * (SUMCF / MAX);
        SUM = INSERT(NEG * MOD(SUMCF,MAX),SUM);
        P = P->LINK; Q = Q->LINK; /* NEXT NODES */
    END;
    IF Q = NULL
    THEN Q = P;
SCAN: /* SCAN REMAINDER OF LIST Q */
    DO WHILE(Q ¬= NULL);
        SUMCF = NEG * (Q->COEF + C);
        IF SUMCF < 0
        THEN C = -1;
        ELSE C = NEG * (SUMCF / MAX);
        SUM = INSERT(NEG * MOD(SUMCF,MAX),SUM);
        Q = Q->LINK;
    END;
    IF C = -1 & NEG = 1
    THEN /* COMPLEMENT OF SUM IS REQUIRED */
        IF SECCND_PASS
        THEN C = 0; /* SECOND PASS COMPLETED */
        ELSE /* PREPARE FOR SECOND PASS */
            DO;
                SECCND_PASS = '1'B;
                Q = REVERSE(SUM,'1'B);
                SUM = NULL;
                C = 0;
                GO TO SCAN;
            END;
    IF C ¬= 0 /* FINAL CARRY */
    THEN SUM = INSERT(C,SUM);
    IF SECOND_PASS
    THEN SUM = REVERSE(SUM,'1'B);
    ELSE SUM = REVERSE(SUM,'0'B);
    RETURN(SUM);
END ADDITION;
```

FIGURE 4-3.9   (Continued)

Set X ← WORDCNT <'OF'>.

assigns the list element 4 to X.

As noted in Chap. 3, an important property of a list is its capacity to grow or to shrink by the removal or addition of elements to the list. In an associative list, this property is available as well. In our algorithmic notation, a new list element is created by an assignment statement. For example,

Set WORD <'NEW'> ← 3

```
LIST_TO_STRING:
        PROCEDURE(R) RETURNS(CHARACTER(80) VARYING);
/*    L I S T _ T O _ S T R I N G
   CONVERT THE INTEGER REPRESENTED BY LIST R TO A STRING FORM.
R:   PASSED BY VALUE
TYPE:   GIVES SIGN FOR CHARACTER REPRESENTATION.
NUMBER:   CONTAINS THE CHARACTER REPRESENTATION OF A NUMBER FROM A NODE.
STRING:   CHARACTER REPRESENTATION OF THE INTEGER                        */
        DECLARE
            R POINTER,
            TYPE CHARACTER(1),
            NUMBER CHARACTER(14) VARYING,
            STRING CHARACTER(80) VARYING;
        IF SIGN((R)) = 1
        THEN TYPE = ' ';
        ELSE TYPE = '-';
        IF R = NULL
        THEN STRING = '0';
        ELSE STRING = '';
        DO WHILE(R ¬= NULL);
            NUMBER = ABS(R->COEF);
            NUMBER = SUBSTR(NUMBER,15 - EXP);
            STRING = TRANSLATE(NUMBER,'0',' ') || STRING;
            R = R->LINK;
        END;
        DO WHILE(INDEX(STRING,'0') = 1 & LENGTH(STRING) > 1);
            STRING = SUBSTR(STRING,2); /* DELETE LEADING ZERO */
        END;
        STRING = TYPE || STRING;
        STRING = SUBSTR(BLANKS,1,80 - LENGTH(STRING)) || STRING;
        RETURN(STRING);
END LIST_TO_STRING;

STOP:
END MULPREC;
```

FIGURE 4-3.9   (Continued)

establishes the new element with a value of 3 and associates the character string **'NEW'**
with it.

   To alter an element also involves an assignment. Again, using the word count
example,

> Set WORDCNT <'AN' > ← WORDCNT <'AN'> + 1

assigns a new value to the list item of an element of WORDCNT.

   If we attempt to reference a list item or items by using a name which is not associated with any element in the list, then either a zero or the empty string is the value returned from the reference. This convention is consistent with the convention adopted in
the programming language SNOBOL, which has an associative data structure. For example, if 'DATA' is a name which is not associated with an element of WORDCNT, then

> Set X ← WORDCNT <'DATA'> + 1.

assigns the value 1 to X, while

> Set X ← 'THE WORD COUNT OF NEW IS' ○ WORDCNT <'DATA'>.

assigns the string 'THE WORD COUNT OF NEW IS' to X.

```
                                                    321045672
                                                            0
--------------------------------------------------------------
                                                    321045672

                                                     12345650
                                                      6890123
--------------------------------------------------------------
                                                     19235773

                                                   650125789654
                                                   425579624759
--------------------------------------------------------------
                                                  1075705414413

                                                        -1096
                                                        -9934
--------------------------------------------------------------
                                                       -11030

                                                 -2789300579624
                                                  1300800555601
--------------------------------------------------------------
                                                 -1488500024023

                                                       -10800
                                                        12300
--------------------------------------------------------------
                                                         1500

                                                        -1403
                                                         1399
--------------------------------------------------------------
                                                           -4

                                                          403
                                                         -399
--------------------------------------------------------------
                                                            4
```

FIGURE 4-3.9   (Continued)

The following algorithm performs a word-frequency analysis on a given piece of text. The words present in the text, plus the associated word counts, are printed at the end of the analysis.

Algorithm WORD_ANALYSIS.   Given the input text TEXT, a word-frequency analysis is made by placing in the associative structure, WORDCNT, the word counts of all words in the text. ALPHABET is the character string 'ABCDEFGHIJKLMNOPQRSTUVWXYZ'.

1.   [Initialize]   Set CURSOR ← 1.
2.   [Find next alphabetic character]
     Repeat while INDEX(ALPHABET,SUB(TEXT,CURSOR,1)) = 0:
          set CURSOR ← CURSOR + 1,
          if CURSOR > LENGTH(TEXT), then print words and associated word
          counts, and Exit.
3.   [Isolate word]   Set DUMMY ← SPAN(TEXT,ALPHABET,CURSOR,WORD,'',false).
     Set WORDCNT <WORD> ← WORDCNT <WORD> + 1, and go to step 2.

After the cursor used for the scanning of TEXT is initialized to 1, the first alphabetic character (i.e., the first letter of a word) is located in step 2. In step 3, the alphabetic field which follows is pattern-matched using the SPAN function, as described in Sec. 2-3.2, and this character-string field is assigned to the variable WORD. The WORD element of the associative list WORDCNT is then updated by 1. Note that the first time a word appears, a value of zero is created for it in the associative list. The algorithm terminates in step 2 when the value of CURSOR becomes greater than the length of the given text. Just prior to termination, the words and the associated word counts are printed. The manner in which both the words and word counts are output depends on the programming system in use. Since SNOBOL has an associative-type of data structure, let us examine how the output might be accomplished.

In SNOBOL the term that is used for describing an associative structure is a TABLE. To illustrate how TABLEs are created and used, let us consider the following SNOBOL program which handles the text-analysis problem as described previously in this subsection.

```
                LETTER = 'ABCDEFGHIJKLMNOPQRSTUVWXYZ'
                PAT = BREAK(LETTER) SPAN(LETTER) · WORD
                WORDCNT = TABLE(5, 4)
READIN          TEXT = TEXT INPUT                             :F(BEGINOUT)
NEXTWORD        TEXT PAT =                                    :F(READIN)
                WORDCNT <WORD> = WORDCNT <WORD> + 1 :(NEXTWORD)
BEGINOUT        OUTFORM = CONVERT(WORDCNT, 'ARRAY')
                I = 1
PRINT           OUTPUT = OUTFORM <I, 1> ' ' OUTFORM <I,2> :F(END)
                I = I + 1                                     :(PRINT)
END
```

In the SNOBOL program, WORDCNT is initialized as a TABLE by the assignment statement WORDCNT = TABLE(5,4). (The significance of the parameters 5 and 4 will be described shortly.) The text is input to the variable TEXT. The pattern PAT is then applied to TEXT. PAT locates the first letter and then spans the substring of alphabetic characters which follows. This substring is assigned to the variable WORD. The TABLE element associated with the word is then updated.

The text analysis continues until all the text is processed. The CONVERT instruction in SNOBOL automatically converts a table to a two-dimensional array. (We shall see in the discussion dealing with the storage structure of associative lists that this type of conversion is relatively easy to accomplish.) The converted table is then output and the SNOBOL program ends.

A discussion of the storage representation of associative lists is now presented. Two representations are considered; the first is a method for representing tables in SNOBOL (the method is similar to that given by Griswold [1972]), and the second involves the application of a hashing function in a manner similar to that described for the linked dictionary in Sec. 4-3.2. Both methods involve a linked form of storage representation.

In SNOBOL, tables can be implemented as blocks of storage cell pairs. Each storage cell pair holds a descriptor or value of the associative item and the table (or list) item of the list. As elements are inserted into the table, a block of storage cells may become full. When a block becomes full, a new block is allocated and is linked on to the end of the previous most recently allocated block. As an example, consider the representation of the first nine elements in the list of word frequencies as derived from the example given earlier in this subsection. Assume the initial block is of size (2 × M) + 1 for M equal to 5, and any extended block is of size (2 × N) + 1 for N equal to 4. In the SNOBOL program presented earlier, we declared the initial size of the table plus the size of extent using the statement

```
WORDCNT = TABLE(5,4).
```

Figure 4-4.1 shows the storage representation for part of the word count list.

In Fig. 4-4.1, the first cell in each block contains the block size less 1 and a pointer to the next block if a next block has been allocated. The first field of all other storage cells represents the type of the item associated with that cell (for example, "S" means string and "I" means integer). The second field contains a string descriptor or a numeric value, depending on the type of the item.

The locating of a list item involves a linear search of the associative items which are located in the first cells of the cell pairs. If the search name does not match an associative item in the first block, a search is made of subsequent blocks via the link field in the first cell of a block.

A second method of representing an associative list is to apply a hashing function to the associative items of the list elements. In Sec. 4-3.2, we illustrated how hashing functions can be used to build a linked dictionary. Let us use the hashing function discussed in that section and show how an associative list can be represented. The hashing function involves the product of the length of a name and a number derived from the internal representations of the first and last characters of a name. This product is divided by the table size, which was chosen to be 10. The remainder from this division is used as the hash value. The hashing process is illustrated in Table 4-3.1. Figure 4-4.2 depicts how our example associative list of word counts can be stored using the hashing function just described and assuming a primary table size of 10. Again, the storage of only the first nine elements of the list is shown.

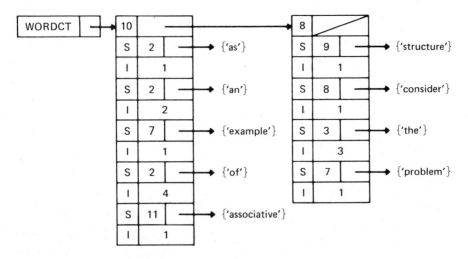

FIGURE 4-4.1   Block representation of an associative list.

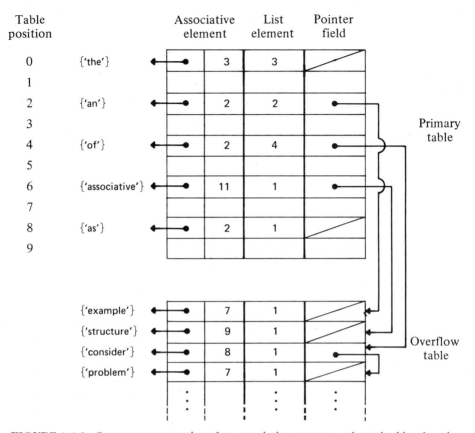

FIGURE 4-4.2 Storage representation of an associative structure using a hashing function.

After a word is scanned and isolated, it is hashed into the primary table as shown in Fig. 4-4.2. If the hash table entry corresponding to the hash value is empty, then the word is placed at that location and the list item entry is initialized to zero. If the hash value location is occupied, a check is made to determine if the associative item stored at this location is the same as the isolated word. If it is, the value of the list item associated with the word is returned. If the associative item is not the word, then a check of the pointer field is made to determine if it is null or a pointer to the overflow table. If the pointer field is null, then the word is placed in the associative item field of the first open location in the overflow table, and the pointer field at the primary table location is updated. If the pointer field contains an address in the overflow table, then the associative item in the overflow table location is examined in a manner identical to that in which the primary table location was examined. The linked list of colliding associative items is followed until either the word is found as an associative item or the word is inserted at the end of the linked list of colliding elements. In the example illustrated in Fig. 4-4.2, 'the' has a hash value of 0; 'an' and 'example' have hash values of 2; 'of', 'consider', and 'problem' have hash values of 4; 'associative' and 'structure' have hash values of 6; and 'as' has a hash value of 8.

In this subsection the associative list involving word counts of a piece of text has been used throughout as a motivating example. Associative structures are applicable to any problem which involves the association of a particular item (such as a word count) or items (such as in a student record) with a uniquely identifying associative item (such as a word or a student name). In Chap. 7 we discuss a particular file organization called *index sequential* which also utilizes the property of list associativity.

Exercises for Sec. 4-4

1.   Design an algorithm (which should contain a number of subalgorithms) to handle the processing of class records using an associative list called **STUDENT**. The associative item is the student's name (initial plus surname). The ID number (**ID**), the college (**COLLEGE**), marks for up to ten assignments (**MARK[I]** for I = 1, 2, . . ., 10), and the grade-to-date (**GRADE**) form the list items of a record. To refer to a particular list item, such as John Brown's mark on the sixth assignment, use the notation

MARK[6] OF STUDENT <'J. BROWN'>

The class records system should handle four input commands:

(*a*)   An insert command of the form
INSERT <student's name> <ID number> <college>
which inserts the ID number and college into the student's record.

(*b*)   A delete command of the form
DELETE <student's name>
which deletes a student record.

(*c*)   An update command of the form
UPDATE <student's name> <assignment number> <mark>
which updates the student's record with the given mark for the given assignment.

(*d*)   An output command of the form
OUTPUT <student's name> or the form OUTPUT ALL
which prints either a particular student's record or all students' records.

2.   Program in PL/I the class record system as described in Exercise 1. Since associative lists do not exist in PL/I, you must simulate their effect by using based storage and a procedure named **STUDENT**. The procedure call

CALL STUDENT('J. BROWN', ID #, COL, MKS, GR);

allows the referencing of the list items of the record corresponding to John Brown by returning his ID number in ID #, his college in **COL**, his marks in the array **MKS**, and his grade-to-date in **GR**. Use either the block method or the hashing method in simulating the storage structure of the associative list.

BIBLIOGRAPHY

BERZTISS, A. T.: "Data Structures: Theory and Practice," Academic Press, Inc., New York, 1971.

BRILLINGER, P. C., and D. J. COHEN: "Introduction to Data Structures and Nonnumeric Computations," Prentice-Hall, Inc., Englewood Cliffs, N.J., 1972.

D'IMPERIO, M. E.: "Data Structures and Their Representation in Storage," *Annual Review in Automatic Programming*, vol. 5, pp. 1–75, Pergamon Press, Oxford, 1969.

GRISWOLD, R. E.: "The Macro Implementation of SNOBOL4: A Case Study of Machine-Independent Software Development," W. H. Freeman and Company, San Francisco, 1972.

HARRISON, M. C.: "Data Structures and Programming," Scott, Foresman and Company, Glenview, Ill., 1973.

KNUTH, D. E.: "The Art of Computer Programming, vol. 1, Fundamental Algorithms," 2d ed., Addison-Wesley Publishing Co., Inc., Reading, Mass., 1973.

KNUTH, D. E.: "The Art of Computer Programming, vol. 2, Seminumerical Algorithms," Addison-Wesley Publishing Co., Inc., Reading, Mass., 1969.

WALKER, T. M. and W. W. COTTERMAN: "An Introduction to Computer Science and Algorithmic Processes," Allyn and Bacon, Inc., Boston, Mass., 1970.

5

NONLINEAR DATA STRUCTURES

Thus far we have been concerned with linear lists. The relationships that can be expressed by such data structures are essentially one dimensional. In this chapter we will introduce data structures which are nonlinear and are, therefore, capable of expressing more complex relationships than that of physical adjacency. The most important nonlinear data structure is probably a tree. Trees are used to represent the relationships among data elements in so many applications that a substantial portion of this chapter is concerned with their manipulations, representations, and associated applications.

The chapter begins with a detailed description of trees from basic concepts to their representations and manipulations. Section 5-2 contains a number of important applications to which trees have been frequently applied. Multilinked structures and their applications are dealt with in Sec. 5-3. More general data structures (graphs) which can contain loops or closed paths are the topics of Sec. 5-4. This section is concerned with the manipulation and storage of graphs by bit matrices and list structures. Section 5-5 contains a number of applications to which graphs can be applied. These complex data structures require sophisticated storage-management techniques, and a number of such techniques are described in Sec. 5-6.

5-1 TREES

The section deals with a very important data structure, the *tree*. The first subsection introduces the basic notions of graph theory which are used throughout the chapter. In particular, trees are discussed in detail. A number of associated operations on trees, such as their traversals and equivalence, are introduced in Sec. 5-1.2. Various storage representations for trees based on sequential allocation and linked allocation are described. Iterative and recursive algorithms are given throughout the second subsection.

5-1.1 Definitions and Concepts

We first consider the definition of a general graph and its associated terminology. A tree can be viewed as a restricted graph. The restriction imposed on a graph to define a tree yields a general tree. For a number of reasons, however, it is convenient to define and manipulate binary trees instead of general trees. Each general tree can be represented by an equivalent binary tree.

Consider the diagrams shown in Fig. 5-1.1. For our purpose here, these diagrams represent graphs. Notice that every diagram consists of a set of points which are shown by dots or circles and are sometimes labeled $v_1, v_2, \ldots,$ or 1, 2, ... Also in every diagram, certain pairs of such points are connected by lines or arcs. The other details, such as the geometry of the arcs, their lengths, the position of the points, etc., are of no importance at present. Notice that every arc starts at one point and ends at another point. A definition of the graph, which is essentially a mathematical system, will now be given. Such a mathematical system is an abstraction of the graphs given in Fig. 5-1.1.

A *graph* G consists of a nonempty set V called the set of *nodes* (*points, vertices*) of the graph, a set E which is the set of edges of the graph, and a mapping ϕ from the set of edges E to a set of pairs of elements of V.

We shall assume throughout that both the sets V and E of a graph are finite. It is also convenient to write a graph as G = (V,E). Notice that the definition of a graph implies that to every edge of the graph G, we can associate a pair of nodes of the graph. If an edge x ∈ E is thus associated with a pair of nodes (u, v) where u, v ∈ V, then we say that the edge x connects or joins the nodes u and v. Any two nodes which are connected by an edge in a graph are called *adjacent* nodes.

In a graph G = (V, E), an edge which is directed from one node to another is called a *directed edge*, while an edge which has no specific direction is called an *undirected edge*. A graph in which every edge is directed is called a *directed graph*, or a *digraph*. A graph in which every edge is undirected is called an *undirected graph*. If some edges are directed and some are undirected in a graph, then the graph is a *mixed graph*.

In the diagrams the directed edges are shown by means of arrows which also show the directions. The graphs given in Figs. 5-1.1b, e, and g are directed graphs. Those given in Figs. 5-1.1c and f are undirected, while the one given in Fig. 5-1.1d is mixed. The graph given in Fig. 5-1.1a could be considered as either directed or undirected. In Fig. 5-1.1f, the nodes 1 and 2, 2 and 3, 3 and 1, 2 and 4, and 3 and 4 are adjacent.

A city map showing only the one-way streets is an example of a directed graph in which the nodes are the intersections and the edges are the streets. A map showing only the two-way streets is an example of an undirected graph, while a map showing all the one-way and two-way streets is an example of a mixed graph.

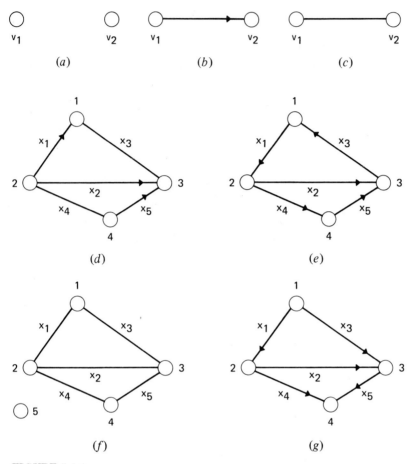

FIGURE 5-1.1.

Let (V, E) be a graph and let x ε E be a directed edge associated with the ordered pair of nodes (u, v). Then the edge x is said to be *initiating* or *originating* in the node u and *terminating* or *ending* in the node v. The nodes u and v are also called the *initial* and *terminal* nodes of the edge x. An edge x ε E which joins the nodes u and v, whether it be directed or undirected, is said to be *incident* to the nodes u and v.

An edge of a graph which joins a node to itself is called a *loop* (*sling*) (not to be confused with a loop in a program). The direction of a loop is of no significance; hence, it can be considered either a directed or an undirected edge.

The graphs given in Fig. 5-1.1 have no more than one edge between any pair of nodes. In the case of directed edges, the two possible edges between a pair of nodes which are opposite in direction are considered distinct. In some directed as well as undirected graphs, we may have certain pairs of nodes joined by more than one edge, as shown in Figs. 5-1.2a and b. Such edges are called *parallel*. In Fig. 5-1.2a, there are two parallel edges joining the nodes 1 and 2, three parallel edges joining the nodes 2 and 3, while there are two parallel loops at 2.

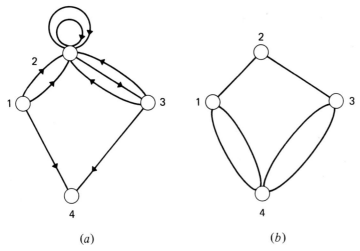

FIGURE 5-1.2.

Any graph which contains some parallel edges is called a *multigraph*. On the other hand, if there is no more than one edge between a pair of nodes (no more than one directed edge in the case of a directed graph), then such a graph is called a *simple graph*. The graphs given in Fig. 5-1.1 are all simple graphs.

The graphs in Figs. 5-1.2a and b may be represented by the diagrams given in Figs. 5-1.3a and b in which the number on any edge shows the multiplicity of the edge. We may also consider the multiplicity as a weight assigned to an edge. This interpretation allows us to generalize the concept of weight to numbers which are not necessarily integers. A graph in which weights are assigned to every edge is called a *weighted graph*.

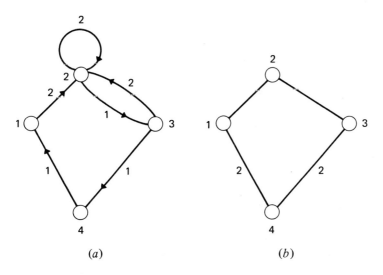

FIGURE 5-1.3.

A graph representing a system of pipelines in which the weights assigned indicate the amount of some commodity transferred through the pipe is an example of a weighted graph. Similarly, a graph of city streets may be assigned weights according to the traffic density on each street.

In a graph, a node which is not adjacent to any other node is called an *isolated node*. A graph containing only isolated nodes is called a *null graph*. In other words, the set of edges in a null graph is empty. The graph in Fig. 5-1.1*a* is a null graph, while that in Fig. 5-1.1*f* has an isolated node. In practice, an isolated node in a graph has very little importance.

The definition of graph contains no reference to the length or the shape and positioning of the arc joining any pair of nodes, nor does it prescribe any ordering of positions of the nodes. Therefore, for a given graph, there is no unique diagram which represents the graph. We can obtain a variety of diagrams by locating the nodes in an arbitrary number of different positions and also by showing the edges by arcs or lines of different shapes. Because of this arbitrariness, it can happen that two diagrams which look entirely different from one another may represent the same graph, as in Figs. 5-1.4*a* and *a'*.

In a directed graph, for any node v the number of edges which have v as their initial node is called the *outdegree* of the node v. The number of edges which have v as their terminal node is called the *indegree* of v, and the sum of the outdegree and the indegree of a node v is called its *total degree*. In case of an undirected graph, the *total degree* or the *degree* of a node v is equal to the number of edges incident with v. The total degree of a loop is 2 and that of an isolated node is 0. We now introduce some additional terminology associated with a simple digraph.

Let $G = (V, E)$ be a simple digraph. Consider a sequence of edges of G such that the terminal node of any edge in the sequence is the initial node of the next edge, if any, in the sequence. An example of such a sequence is

$$((v_{i_1}, v_{i_2}), (v_{i_2}, v_{i_3}), \ldots, (v_{i_{k-2}}, v_{i_{k-1}}), (v_{i_{k-1}}, v_{i_k}))$$

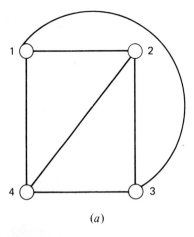

(a)

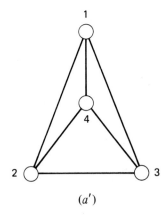

(a')

FIGURE 5-1.4.

where it is assumed that all the nodes and edges appearing in the sequence are in **V** and **E**, respectively. It is customary to write such a sequence as

$$(v_{i_1}, v_{i_2}, \ldots, v_{i_{k-1}}, v_{i_k})$$

Note that not all edges and nodes appearing in a sequence need be distinct. Also, for a given graph, any arbitrary set of nodes written in any order do not give a sequence as required. In fact, each node appearing in the sequence must be adjacent to the nodes appearing just before and after it in the sequence, except in the case of the first and last nodes.

Any sequence of edges of a digraph such that the terminal node of any edge in the sequence is the initial node of the edge, if any, appearing next in the sequence defines a *path* of the graph. A path is said to *traverse* through the nodes appearing in the sequence, *originating* in the initial node of the first edge and *ending* in the terminal node of the last edge in the sequence. The number of edges appearing in the sequence of a path is called the *length* of the path.

Consider the simple digraph given in Fig. 5-1.5. Some of the paths originating in node 2 and ending in node 4 are

$$P_1 = ((2, 4))$$
$$P_2 = ((2, 3), (3, 4))$$
$$P_3 = ((2, 1), (1, 4))$$
$$P_4 = ((2, 3), (3, 1), (1, 4))$$
$$P_5 = ((2, 3), (3, 2), (2, 4))$$
$$P_6 = ((2, 2), (2, 4))$$

A path in a digraph in which the edges are all distinct is called a *simple path (edge simple)*. A path in which all the nodes through which it traverses are distinct is called an *elementary path (node simple)*.

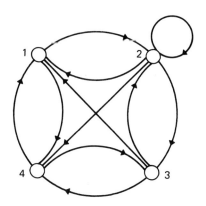

FIGURE 5-1.5.

Naturally, every elementary path of a digraph is also simple. The paths P_1, P_2, P_3, and P_4 of the digraph in Fig. 5-1.5 are elementary, while paths P_5 and P_6 are simple, but not elementary. We shall show here that if there exists a path from a node, say u, to another node v, then there must also be an elementary path from u to v.

A path which originates and ends in the same node is called a *cycle* (*circuit*). A *cycle* is called *simple* if its path is simple, i.e., no edge in the cycle appears more than once in the path. A *cycle* is called *elementary* if it does not traverse through any node more than once.

Note that in a cycle, the initial node appears at least twice if it is an elementary cycle. The following are some of the cycles in the graph of Fig. 5-1.5:

$$C_1 = ((2, 2))$$

$$C_2 = ((1, 2), (2, 1))$$

$$C_3 = ((2, 3), (3, 1), (1, 2))$$

$$C_4 = ((2, 1), (1, 4), (4, 3), (3, 2))$$

Observe that any path which is not elementary contains cycles traversing through those nodes which appear more than once in the path. By deleting such cycles, one can obtain elementary paths. For example, in the path P_5, if we delete the cycle $((2, 3), (3, 2))$, we obtain the path P_1, which also originates at 2 and ends in 4 and is an elementary path. Similarly, if in the path P_6, we delete the cycle $((2,2))$, we get the elementary path P_1. Likewise, it is possible to obtain elementary cycles at any node from a cycle at that node. Because of this property, some authors use the term "path" to mean only the elementary paths, and they likewise apply the notion of the length of a path to only elementary paths.

A simple digraph which does not have any cycles is called *acyclic*. Naturally, such graphs cannot have any loops. We now consider a class of diagrams which are acyclic.

An important class of digraphs called directed trees and their associated terminology will be discussed in the remainder of this section. Trees are useful in describing any structures which involve hierarchy. Familiar examples of such structures are family trees, the decimal classification of books in a library, the hierarchy of positions in an organization, an algebraic expression involving operations for which certain rules of precedence are prescribed, the structure of this chapter as given in Fig. 5-1.6, etc. We shall here describe how trees can be represented by diagrams and other means. Representation of trees in a computer is discussed in Sec. 5-1.2. Applications of trees are given in Sec. 5-1.3.

A *directed tree* is an acyclic digraph which has one node called its *root*, with indegree 0, while all other nodes have indegree 1. Note that every directed tree must have at least one node. An isolated node is also a directed tree.

In a directed tree, any node which has outdegree 0 is called a *terminal node* or a *leaf*; all other nodes are called *branch nodes*. The *level* of any node is the length of its path from the root. The level of the root of a directed tree is 0, while the level of any node is equal to its distance from the root. Observe that all the paths in a directed tree are elementary and that the length of a path from any node to another node, if such a path exists, is the distance between the nodes, because a directed tree is acyclic.

Figure 5-1.7 shows three different diagrams of a directed tree. Several other diagrams of the same tree can be drawn by choosing different relative positions of the nodes with respect to its root. The directed tree of our example has two nodes at level 1, five nodes at

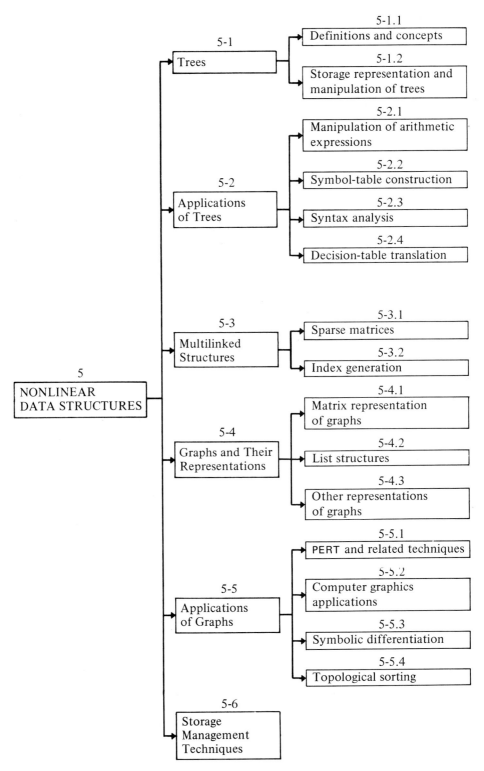

5
NONLINEAR
DATA STRUCTURES

5-1 Trees
  5-1.1 Definitions and concepts
  5-1.2 Storage representation and manipulation of trees

5-2 Applications of Trees
  5-2.1 Manipulation of arithmetic expressions
  5-2.2 Symbol-table construction
  5-2.3 Syntax analysis
  5-2.4 Decision-table translation

5-3 Multilinked Structures
  5-3.1 Sparse matrices
  5-3.2 Index generation

5-4 Graphs and Their Representations
  5-4.1 Matrix representation of graphs
  5-4.2 List structures
  5-4.3 Other representations of graphs

5-5 Applications of Graphs
  5-5.1 PERT and related techniques
  5-5.2 Computer graphics applications
  5-5.3 Symbolic differentiation
  5-5.4 Topological sorting

5-6 Storage Management Techniques

FIGURE 5-1.6.

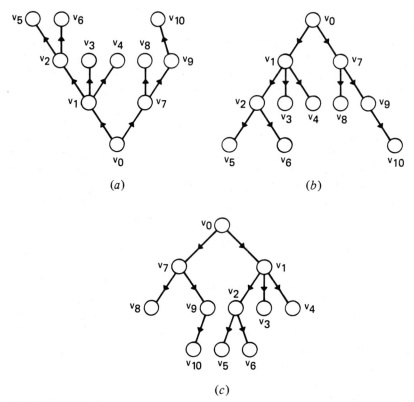

FIGURE 5-1.7.

level 2, and three nodes at level 3. Figure 5-1.7a shows a natural way of representation, namely, the way a tree grows from its root up and ending in leaves at different levels. Figure 5-1.7b shows the same tree drawn upside down. This is a convenient way of drawing a directed tree and is commonly used in the literature. Figure 5-1.7c differs from Fig. 5-1.7b in the order in which the nodes appear at any level from left to right. According to our definition of a directed tree, such an order is of no significance. We shall, however, consider certain modifications so that an ordering of the nodes becomes relevant in a tree.

In many applications the relative order of the sons of a node assumes some significance. In a computer representation such an order, even if it is arbitrary, is automatically implied. It is easy to impose an order on the sons of a node by referring to a particular son as the first son, to another son as the second, and so on. In the diagrams the ordering may be done from left to right. Instead of ordering the nodes, we may prescribe an order on the edges. If, in a directed tree, an ordering of the nodes at each level is prescribed, then such a tree is called an *ordered tree*. According to this definition, the diagrams given in Figs. 5-1.7b and c represent the same directed tree, but different ordered trees. Note that ordered trees as such are no longer directed graphs because the concept of order does not exist in a directed graph. We are mostly concerned with ordered trees in this section and, therefore, we use the term "tree" to mean ordered tree unless otherwise stated.

In both directed and ordered trees, it is important to decide whether the root is shown on top or at the bottom because the terminology used to describe the relative positions of the nodes as above or below may assume different meanings according to the choice made for locating the root. In our discussion we shall assume that the root is at the top and that all other nodes are below the root.

From the structure of the directed tree, it is clear that every node of a tree is the root of some subtrees contained in the original tree. In fact, if we delete the root and the edges connecting the root to the nodes at level 1, we get subtrees with roots which are the nodes at level 1. For the tree in Fig. 5-1.7, the node v_7 is the root of the subtree $\{v_7, v_8, v_9, v_{10}\}$, v_1 is the root of $\{v_1, v_2, v_3, v_4, v_5, v_6\}$, v_2 is the root of $\{v_2, v_5, v_6\}$, v_5 is the root of $\{v_5\}$, and v_9 is the root of $\{v_9, v_{10}\}$, etc. The number of subtrees of a node is called the *degree* of the node. Naturally, the degree of a terminal node is 0. The degree of v_2 is 2 because $\{v_5\}$ and $\{v_6\}$ are its subtrees, while the degree of v_1 is 3 because $\{v_2, v_5, v_6\}$, $\{v_3\}$, and $\{v_4\}$ are its subtrees.

If we delete the root and the edges connecting the nodes at level 1, we obtain a set of disjoint trees. A set of disjoint trees is called a *forest*. We have also seen that any node of a directed tree is a root of some subtree. Therefore, subtrees immediately below a node form a forest.

At this stage we shall give another definition of directed trees which is recursive. According to this definition, a tree contains one or more nodes such that one of the nodes is called the root while all other nodes are partitioned into a finite number of trees called subtrees. This definition permits the formulation of algorithms associated with trees to be simpler. This will be shown in Sec. 5-1.2.

Here, a tree with n nodes has been defined in terms of trees with less than n nodes. For the tree in Fig. 5-1.7, the tree $\{v_0, \ldots, v_{10}\}$ is defined in terms of trees $\{v_1, \ldots, v_5, v_6\}$ and $\{v_7, \ldots, v_{10}\}$, while the tree $\{v_1, \ldots, v_5, v_6\}$ can be defined in terms of $\{v_2, v_5, v_6\}$, $\{v_3\}$, $\{v_4\}$, and so on. Finally, we get trees with one node each, which are its terminal nodes.

There are several other ways in which a directed tree can be represented graphically. These methods of representation for the directed tree of Fig. 5-1.7 are given in Figs. 5-1.8a, b, c, and d. The first method uses the familiar technique of Venn diagrams to show subtrees; the second uses the convention of nesting parentheses; and the third method is the one used in the table of contents for a book. The last method, which is based on a level-number format, is similar to those techniques used in PL/I and COBOL. Using this format, each node is assigned a number. The root of the tree has the smallest number. The number associated with a given node must be less than the numbers associated with the root nodes of its subtrees. Note that all the root nodes of the subtrees of a given node must have the same number.

The method of representation given in Fig. 5-1.8b immediately shows how any completely parenthesized algebraic expression can be represented by a tree structure. Naturally, it is not necessary to have a completely parenthesized expression if we prescribe a set of precedence rules, as discussed in Sec. 3-7.2. As an example, consider the expression

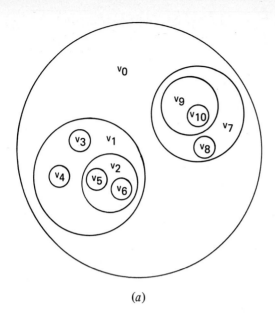

(a)

$$(v_0(v_1(v_2(v_5)(v_6))(v_3)(v_4))(v_7(v_8)(v_9(v_{10}))))$$

(b)

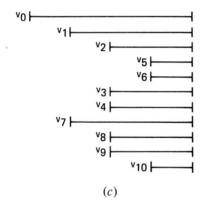

(c)

1 v_0
  2 v_1
    3 v_2
      4 v_5
      4 v_6
    3 v_3
    3 v_4
  2 v_7
    3 v_8
    3 v_9
      4 v_{10}

(d)

FIGURE 5-1.8 Different representations of trees.

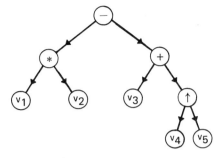

FIGURE 5-1.9.

$$v_1 * v_2 - (v_3 + v_4 \uparrow v_5)$$

The tree corresponding to this expression is shown in Fig. 5-1.9.

In the diagrams representing trees, we have chosen to show the roots on top and the edges pointing downward. All the nodes at any particular level are shown on a horizontal line. In the case of an ordered tree, the nodes at any particular level are ordered from left to right. This ordering distinguishes an ordered tree from other directed trees. It is sometimes convenient to borrow some terminology from a family tree. Accordingly, every node that is reachable from a node, say u, is called a *descendant* of u. Also, the nodes which are reachable from u through a single edge are called the *sons* of u.

So far we have not placed any restriction on the outdegrees of any node in a directed or an ordered tree. If, in a directed tree, the outdegree of every node is less than or equal to m, then the tree is called an *m-ary tree*. If the outdegree of every node is exactly equal to m or 0, then the tree is called a *full* or *complete m-ary tree*. For $m = 2$, the trees are called *binary* and *full binary trees*. We shall now consider m-ary trees in which the m (or fewer) sons of any node are assumed to have m distinct positions. If such positions are taken into account, then the tree is called a *positional m-ary tree*.

Figure 5-1.10a shows a binary tree, Fig. 5-1.10b shows a full binary tree, and Fig. 5-1.10c shows all four possible arrangements of sons of a node in a binary tree. The binary trees shown in Figs. 5-1.10a and d are distinct positional trees, although they are not distinct ordered trees. In a positional binary tree, every node is uniquely represented by a string over the alphabet {0, 1}, the root being represented by an empty string. Any son of node u has a string which is prefixed by the string of u. The string of any terminal node is not prefixed to the string of any other node. The set of strings which correspond to terminal nodes form a *prefix* code. Thus, the prefix code of the binary tree in Fig. 5-1.10b is {00, 010, 011, 10, 11}. A similar representation of nodes of a positional m-ary tree by means of strings over an alphabet {0, 1, ..., $m - 1$} is possible.

The string representation of the nodes of a positional binary tree immediately suggests a natural method of representing a binary tree in a computer. It is sufficient for our purpose at this stage simply to recognize that such a natural representation exists.

Binary trees are useful in several applications. We shall now show that every tree can be uniquely represented by a binary tree so that for the computer representation of a tree, it is possible to consider the representation of its corresponding binary tree. Furthermore, a forest can also be represented by a binary tree.

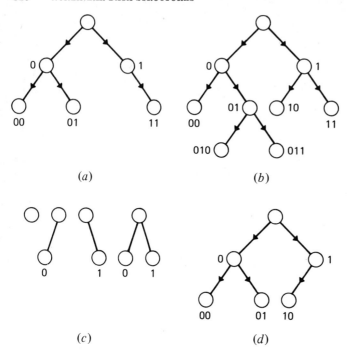

FIGURE 5-1.10   Examples of binary trees and full binary trees.

In Fig. 5-1.11 we show in two stages how one can obtain a binary tree which repre-sents a given ordered tree. As a first step, we delete all the branches originating in every node except the leftmost branch. Also, we draw edges from a node to the node on the right, if any, which is situated at the same level. (This is done only for nodes which were formerly brothers—sons of the same root node.) Once this is done, then for any particular node we choose its left and right sons in the following manner. The left son is the node which is immediately below the given node and the right son is the node to the immediate right of the given node on the same horizontal line. Such a binary tree will not have a right subtree.

The above method of representing any ordered tree by a unique binary tree can be extended to an ordered forest, as shown in Fig. 5-1.12. Both these representations can be defined by algorithms. This correspondence is called the natural correspondence between ordered trees and positional binary trees, and also between ordered forests and positional binary trees. An algorithm which will convert a general tree into an equivalent binary tree will be given in Sec. 5-1.2.

Exercises for Sec. 5-1.1

1. Show that the sum of indegrees of all the nodes of a simple digraph is equal to the sum of outdegrees of all its nodes and that this sum is equal to the number of edges of the graph.

2. Draw all possible digraphs having three nodes. Show that there is only one digraph

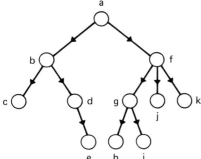

Given directed tree

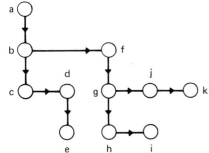

Stage 1

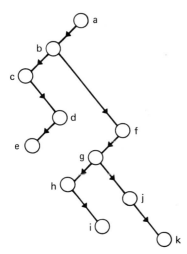

FIGURE 5-1.11 A binary tree representation of a tree.

with no edges, one with one edge, four with two edges, four with three edges, four with four edges, one with five edges, and one with six edges. Assume that there are no loops.

3. Give three different elementary paths from v_1 to v_3 for the digraph given in Fig. 5-1.13. What is the shortest distance between v_1 and v_3? Is there any cycle in the graph?

4. Find all the indegrees and outdegrees of the nodes of the graph given in Fig. 5-1.14.

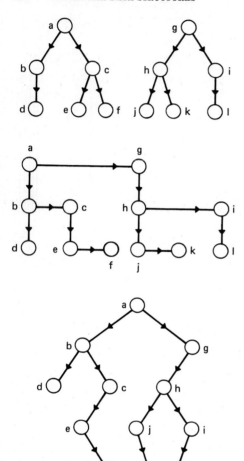

FIGURE 5-1.12   Binary tree representation of a forest.

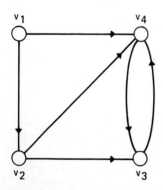

FIGURE 5-1.13.

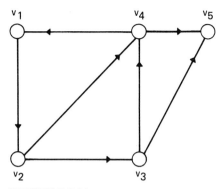

FIGURE 5-1.14.

Give all the elementary cycles of this graph. Obtain an acyclic digraph by deleting one edge of the given digraph. List all the nodes which are reachable from another node of the digraph.

5. Show by means of an example that a simple digraph in which exactly one node has indegree 0 and every other node has indegree 1 is not necessarily a directed tree.

6. How many different directed trees are there with three nodes? How many different ordered trees are there with three nodes?

7. Give a directed tree representation of the following formula: $(a + b) * (c + d) \uparrow e$.

8. Show that in a complete binary tree, the total number of edges is given by $2(n_t - 1)$, where n_t is the number of terminal nodes.

9. Obtain the binary trees corresponding to the directed tree and forest given in Figs. 5-1.15 and 5-1.16, respectively.

5-1.2 Storage Representation and Manipulation of Trees

Throughout the previous chapters the computer representation of certain elementary data structures such as linear lists and arrays was discussed. We now wish to extend these concepts to more complex structures such as trees and graphs. Since trees are probably the

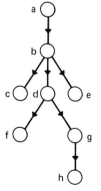

FIGURE 5-1.15.

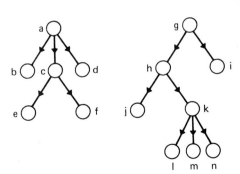

FIGURE 5-1.16.

most important nonlinear structure, their representations and manipulation will be emphasized in this section.

The tree structures will be represented by using sequential and linked allocation. The advantages and disadvantages in the use of linked allocation as opposed to sequential allocation in the representation of simple structures were discussed in Sec. 4-1. Although there are ways of representing trees based on sequential-allocation techniques, we will not emphasize these methods as much as those based on linked allocation. The latter computer representation seems to be more popular because of the ease with which nodes can be inserted in and deleted from a tree, and because tree structures can grow to an arbitrary size—a size which is often unpredictable.

We will restrict our discussions to binary trees since they are easily represented and manipulated. A general tree can be readily converted into an equivalent binary tree by using the natural correspondence algorithm. Such an algorithm will be formulated in this subsection.

The concept of "threading" a binary tree is introduced. This concept is important because the representation of a tree based on this concept is efficient from both time and space considerations. A number of possible traversals which can be performed on binary trees are also described.

We now turn to the task of using linked-allocation techniques to represent binary trees. Recall that a binary tree has one root node with no descendants or else a left, or a right, or a left and right subtree descendant. Each subtree descendant is also a binary tree, and we do make the distinction between its left and right branches. A convenient way of representing binary trees is to use linked-allocation techniques involving nodes with structure

LPTR	DATA	RPTR

where LPTR or RPTR contain a pointer to the left subtree or right subtree, respectively, of the node in question. DATA contains the information which is to be associated with this particular node. Each pointer can have a value of NULL.

An example of a binary tree as a graph and its corresponding linked representation in memory are given in Figs. 5-1.17a and b, respectively. Observe the very close similarity between the figures as drawn. Such a similarity illustrates that the linked-storage representation of a tree is close to the logical structuring of the data involved. This property can be useful in designing algorithms which process tree structures.

Let us now examine a number of operations which are performed on trees. One of the most common operations performed on tree structures is that of traversal. This is a procedure by which each node is processed exactly once in some systematic manner. Using the terminology popularized by Knuth, we can traverse a binary tree in three ways—namely, in preorder, in inorder, and in postorder. The following are recursive definitions for these traversals:

Preorder traversal
    Process the root node.
    Traverse the left subtree in preorder.
    Traverse the right subtree in preorder.

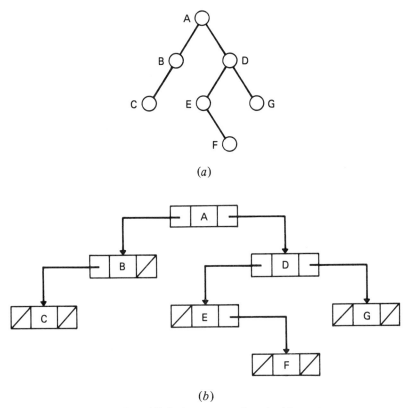

(a)

(b)

FIGURE 5-1.17   Graph and linked representation of a binary tree.

Inorder traversal
> Traverse the left subtree in inorder.
> Process the root node.
> Traverse the right subtree in inorder.

Postorder traversal
> Traverse the left subtree in postorder.
> Traverse the right subtree in postorder.
> Process the root node.

If a particular subtree is empty (i.e., when a node has no left or right descendant), the traversal is performed by doing nothing. In other words, a null subtree is considered to be fully traversed when it is encountered.

If the words "left" and "right" are interchanged in the preceding definitions, then we have three new traversal methods which are called *converse preorder*, *converse inorder*, and *converse postorder*, respectively.

The preorder, inorder, and postorder traversals of the tree given in Fig. 5-1.17 will process the nodes in the following order:

ABCDEFG   (preorder)
CBAEFDG   (inorder)
CBFEGDA   (postorder)

(The respective converse traversals would be ADGEFBC, GDFEABC, and GFEDCBA.)

Although recursive algorithms would probably be the simplest to write for the traversals of binary trees, we will formulate algorithms which are both recursive and nonrecursive.

Let us initially consider recursive programs for traversing binary trees. Such a PL/I program for the inorder traversal of a binary tree is given in Fig. 5-1.18. The node structure is assumed to be global to the procedure and is defined in the main program by the statement

```
DECLARE 01   NODE BASED (P),
             02 LPTR POINTER,
             02 DATA CHARACTER(1),
             02 RPTR POINTER;
```

The procedure in Fig. 5-1.18 has one parameter which receives the address of the root node of the tree. If this pointer variable T is NULL, then the tree is considered to be invalid. The remainder of the procedure follows the recursive definition of inorder traversal given earlier.

A similar program for the preorder traversal of a binary tree is given in Fig. 5-1.19.

Let us next consider the traversal of binary trees by iteration. Since in traversing a tree it is required to descend and subsequently ascend parts of the tree, pointer informa-

```
RINORDER:
    PROCEDURE(T) RECURSIVE;

/*  RECURSIVE PROCEDURE FOR PRINTING THE DATA CONTENT OF EACH NODE
    IN A BINARY TREE WHICH IS TRAVERSED IN INORDER.   */

    DECLARE /* FORMAL PARAMETER */
        T POINTER;

    IF (T = NULL) /* CHECK FOR INVALID TREE */
    THEN DO;
        PUT SKIP LIST('INVALID TREE');
        RETURN;
    END;

    /* PRINT THE LEFT BRANCH OF NODE T IF ONE EXISTS. */

    IF (T->LPTR ¬= NULL)
    THEN CALL RINORDER(T->LPTR);

    /* PRINT THE DATA CONTENT OF NODE T */

    PUT LIST(T->DATA);

    /* PRINT THE RIGHT BRANCH OF NODE T IF ONE EXISTS.  */

    IF (T->RPTR ¬= NULL)
    THEN CALL RINOFDER(T->RPTR);

END RINORDER;
```

FIGURE 5-1.18   Recursive procedure for the inorder traversal of a binary tree.

```
RPREORDER:
    PROCEDURE(T) RECURSIVE;

/*  RECURSIVE PROCEDURE FOR PRINTING DATA CONTENT OF EACH NODE
    IN A BINARY TREE WHICH IS TRAVERSED IN PREORDER.  */

    DECLARE /* FORMAL PARAMETER */
       T POINTER;

    IF (T = NULL) /* CHECK FOR INVALID TREE */
    THEN DO;
        PUT SKIP LIST('INVALID TREE');
        RETURN;
    END;

    /* PRINT THE DATA CONTENT OF NODE T */

    PUT SKIP LIST(T->DATA);

    /* PRINT THE LEFT BRANCH OF NODE T IF ONE EXISTS */

    IF (T->LPTR ¬= NULL)
    THEN CALL RPRECRDER(T->LPTR);

    /* PRINT THE RIGHT BRANCH OF NODE T IF ONE EXISTS */

    IF (T->RPTR ¬= NULL)
    THEN CALL RPRECRDER(T->RPTR);

END RPREORDER;
```

FIGURE 5-1.19 Recursive procedure for the preorder traversal of a binary tree.

tion which will permit movement up the tree must be temporarily stored. Observe that the structural information that is already present in the tree permits downward movement from the root of the tree. Because movement up the tree must be made in a reverse manner from that taken in descending the tree, a stack is required to save pointer values as the tree is traversed. We will now give an algorithm for traversing a tree in preorder.

Algorithm PREORDER. Given a binary tree whose root node address is given by a variable T and whose node structure is the same as previously described, this algorithm traverses the tree in preorder. An auxiliary stack S is used, and TOP is the index of the top element of S. P is a temporary variable which denotes where we are in the tree.

1. [Initialize]
   If T = NULL,
   then Exit; (the tree has no root so it is not a proper binary tree)
   otherwise, set TOP ← 1, and S[TOP] ← T.
2. [Process each stacked branch address]
   Repeat step 3 while TOP > 0.
3. [Get address and descend left chain]
   Set P ← S[TOP] and TOP ← TOP − 1.
   Repeat while P ≠ NULL:
       process node P,
       if RPTR(P) ≠ NULL, then set TOP ← TOP + 1 and S[TOP] ← RPTR(P).
       Set P ← LPTR(P).
4. Exit.

In the third step of the algorithm, we visit and process a node. The address of the right branch of such a node, if it exists, is stacked and a chain of left branches is followed until this chain ends. At this point, we reenter step 3 and delete from the stack the address of the root node of the most recently encountered right subtree and process it according to step 3. A trace of the algorithm for the binary tree given in Fig. 5-1.17 appears in Table 5-1.1, where the rightmost element in the stack is considered to be its top element and the notation "NE," for example, denotes the address of node E. The visit of a node in this case merely involves the output of the label for that node.

A PL/I procedure for Algorithm **PREORDER** is given in Fig. 5-1.20. Note that in this procedure we have used an actual stack instead of the vector representation of it in the algorithm. This is easily accomplished in PL/I by using controlled allocations, as previously discussed in Sec. 3-6 of Chap. 3. The condition of an empty stack in step 2 of the algorithm is determined by using the PL/I function **ALLOCATION**. This function returns a value of false when the stack is empty.

The next algorithm traverses a tree in postorder.

Algorithm POSTORDER. The same node structure described previously is assumed, and T is again a variable which contains the address of the root of the tree. A stack S with its top element pointer is also required, but in this case, each node will be stacked twice—namely, once when its left subtree is traversed, and once when its right subtree is traversed. On completion of these two traversals, the particular node being considered is processed. Hence, we must be able to distinguish two types of stack entries. The first type of entry indicates that a left subtree is being traversed, while the second indicates the traversal of a right subtree. For convenience, we will use negative pointer values for the second type of entry. This, of course, assumes that valid pointer data are always nonzero and positive.

Table 5-1.1 Trace of algorithm preorder for Fig. 5-1.17.

Stack Contents	P	Visit P	Output String
NA			
	NA	A	A
ND	NB	B	AB
ND	NC	C	ABC
ND	NULL		
	ND	D	ABCD
NG	NE	E	ABCDE
NG NF	NULL		
NG	NF	F	ABCDEF
NG	NULL		
	NG	G	ABCDEFG
	NULL		

```
PREORDER:
    PROCEDURE(T);
/* ITERATIVE PROCEDURE FOR THE PREORDER TRAVERSAL OF A BINARY TREE */

    DECLARE
        T POINTER, /* FORMAL PARAMETER - TREE ROOT */
        P POINTER, /* CURRENT NODE DURING TRAVERSAL */
        S POINTER CONTROLLED; /* STACK FOR BRANCH ADDRESSES */

    /* CHECK FOR VALID TREE AND INITIALIZE  */

    IF T = NULL
    THEN DO;
        PUT SKIP FILE(SYSPRINT) LIST('INVALID TREE');
        RETURN;
    END;

    ELSE DO;
        ALLOCATE S;
        S = T;
    END;

    /* PROCESS EACH STACKED BRANCH ADDRESS  */

    DO WHILE(ALLOCATION(S));

        P = S;          /* UNSTACK ADDRESS  */
        FREE S;

        DO WHILE(P¬= NULL); /* PROCESS WHILE DESCENDING LEFT CHAIN */
            PUT SKIP FILE(SYSPRINT) LIST(P->DATA);
            IF P->RPTR ¬= NULL
            THEN DO;
                ALLOCATE S;
                S = P->RPTR;
            END;
            P = P->LPTR;
        END; /* OF LEFT CHAIN DESCENT LOOP */

    END; /* OF TREE TRAVERSAL LOOP */

END PREORDER;
```

FIGURE 5-1.20   Procedure for Algorithm PREORDER.

1. [Initialize]
    If T = NULL,
    then Exit; (with no root, the tree is not a binary tree)
    otherwise, set P ← T and TOP ← 0.
2. [Stack addresses along a left chain]
    Repeat while P ≠ NULL:
        set TOP ← TOP + 1, S[TOP] ← P, and P ← LPTR(P).
3. [Ascend tree, processing right branches]
    Repeat while TOP > 0:
        set P ← S[TOP] and TOP ← TOP − 1;
        If P > 0,
        then set TOP ← TOP + 1, S[TOP] ← −P, (a new right branch is under process)
        P ← RPTR(P), and go to step 2;
        otherwise, set P ← −P (a right branch has been finished) and **process node P.**
4. Exit.

In the second step, a chain of left branches is followed and the address of each node which is encountered is stacked. At the end of such a chain, the stack entry for the last node encountered is checked against zero. If it is positive, the negative address of that node is restacked and the right branch of this node is taken and processed according to step 2. If the stack value is negative, however, we have finished traversing the right subtree of that node. The node is then processed and the next entry is subsequently checked.

If the terms 'RPTR' and 'LPTR' are interchanged in the previous algorithms, the algorithms for converse-preorder and converse-postorder traversals result.

On examining the previously chosen representation for binary trees, it is apparent that there are many NULL links. In fact, it is not difficult to show, by induction, that there are n + 1 NULL links for a binary tree containing n nodes. This wasted space can be used in the reformulation of the previous representations for binary trees. More specifically, the empty links will be replaced by *threads* which are pointers to higher nodes in the tree. A tree is threaded with a particular traversal order in mind. For example, if the LPTR field of some node P is normally NULL, then this field is replaced by an address which points to the predecessor of P with respect to the traversal order for which the tree is being threaded. Similarly, if the RPTR field is normally empty, this field will be made to point to the successor of P with respect to the traversal order. Because the LPTR and RPTR fields can be either a structural link or a thread, it now becomes necessary to distinguish between them. If we use the previous assumption that valid pointer data are positive and nonzero, then structural links can be represented (as usual) by positive addresses, while threads will be represented by negative addresses. Moreover, it is convenient when creating and traversing a tree to have a tree with a head node as discussed in Sec. 4-2.3. This head node is simply another node which serves as the predecessor and successor of the first and last tree nodes with respect to inorder traversal. (This, in effect, imposes a circular structure in addition to the tree structure.) Prior to tree creation, the head node is defined as

HEAD

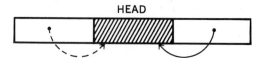

where the dashed arrow denotes a thread link. The tree is attached to the left branch of the head node making the pointer to the root of the tree LPTR(HEAD). The threading of the binary tree for inorder traversal is given in Fig. 5-1.21.

Given a threaded tree for a particular order of traversal, it is a relatively simple task to develop algorithms to obtain the predecessor or successor nodes of some particular node P. These algorithms are given here for inorder traversal.

Algorithm INS.   Given X, the address of a node in a threaded binary tree as formerly described, this algorithm will return the address of the inorder successor of X.

1. [A thread?]   Set INS ← |RPTR(X)|. If RPTR(X) < 0, then Exit.
2. [Branch left?]
    If LPTR(INS) < 0,
    then Exit;
    otherwise, set INS ← LPTR(INS) and repeat this step.

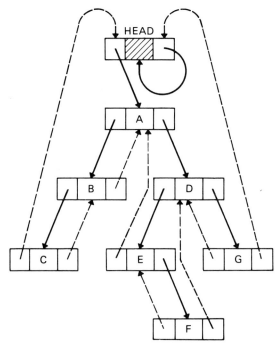

FIGURE 5-1.21 Inorder threading of a binary tree.

Algorithm INP. This algorithm is similar to the previous algorithm except that it returns the address of the inorder predecessor of node X.

1. [A thread?] Set INP ← |LPTR(X)|. If LPTR(X) < 0, then Exit.
2. [Branch right?]
    If RPTR(INP) < 0,
    then Exit;
    otherwise, set INP ← RPTR(INP) and repeat this step.

The main advantage in using threads is twofold. First, a threaded tree traversal is somewhat faster than its unthreaded counterpart because a stack is not required in the former. The tree is traversed by starting at the head node and generating, in order, all the successors, processing them as they are generated. Algorithm INS is used in this operation. The second advantage is more subtle. With a threaded tree representation, we can efficiently determine the predecessor and successor nodes under any traversal order for any node P. In the case of an unthreaded tree representation, however, this task is more difficult. A stack is required to provide upward-pointing information in the tree, which threading provides. Thus, with a threaded tree representation, it is possible to generate the successor or predecessor of any arbitrarily selected node without having to incur the overhead of using a stack mechanism.

Naturally, a price must be paid for these advantages. Threaded trees are unable to share common subtrees, as can unthreaded trees. Furthermore, it takes more time to

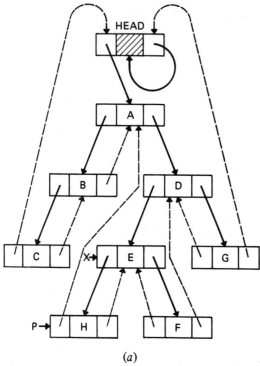

(a)

FIGURE 5-1.22   Insertion of a node to the left of
a given node.

insert nodes into a threaded tree, because the thread links must be maintained as well as
the structural links.

The next algorithm inserts a node in a threaded binary tree to the left of some
designated node.

Algorithm LEFT.   The algorithm inserts node P as the left subtree of a given node X, if
node X has no left subtree. Otherwise, the node is inserted between node X and node
LPTR(X). The proper thread structure with respect to inorder traversal is maintained
when performing the operation. Note that Algorithm INP is used to find a predecessor.

1. [Adjust pointer fields]   Set LPTR(P) ← LPTR(X), LPTR(X) ← P,
   and RPTR(P) ← − X.
2. [Reset predecessor thread, if required]
   If LPTR(P) > 0, then set RPTR(INP(P)) ← − P, and Exit.

An insertion of node H to the left of node E (whose left subtree is null) is shown in Fig.
5-1.22a. Figure 5-1.22b gives an example of the remaining case in which node I is inserted
to the left of node A.

We next turn to the formulation of an algorithm for converting a forest of trees into
an equivalent binary tree. Before discussing this algorithm, however, the specification of
the input format is given.

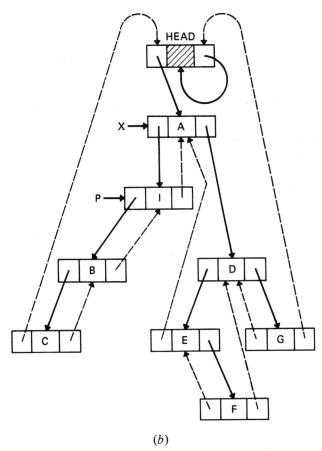

(b)

FIGURE 5-1.22 (Continued)

One of the most convenient and natural ways to specify a general tree (or forest) is to use a formulation similar to that used in writing structures in PL/I. As an example, the two trees of Fig. 5-1.23*a* can be specified in the following manner:

```
01     A
          02 B
          02 C
          02 D
                    03 E
01     F
          02 G
                    03 I
                    03 J
          02 H
```

The equivalent binary tree for this forest is given in Fig. 5-1.23*b*.

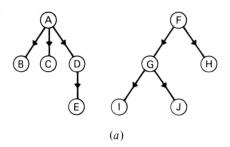

(a)

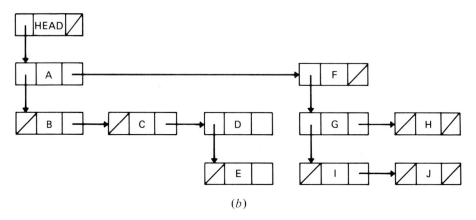

(b)

FIGURE 5-1.23 *(a)* A forest of two trees; *(b)* binary tree representation of a forest.

The input to the algorithm is a sequence of nodes in preorder. For each node, its first and second elements represent the level number and name associated with that node, respectively. A stack is required in this algorithm. Each element of the stack consists of two fields. The first field is the level number associated with a given node and the second field denotes its address.

Algorithm CONVERT. Given a forest whose input format is in the form previously described, it is required to convert this forest into an equivalent binary tree. A stack whose typical element consists of two fields is used. The stack with its associated variable TOP is represented by a pair of vectors. The vector elements of L and ADD are used to denote the level number and address associated with a particular node, respectively. The binary tree which is constructed has a list head whose address is denoted by T. The variables LEVEL and NAME are used to denote the level number and name of a node, respectively. The variable X is a temporary pointer variable. PRED_LEVEL and P give the level number and address of a node, respectively, which has been previously encountered.

1. [Initialize]   Set T ⇐ NODE, LPTR(T) ← RPTR(T) ← NULL, INFO(T) ←'HEAD',
   L[1] ← 0, ADD[1] ← T, and TOP ← 1.
2. [Input a node]   Read LEVEL and NAME from input and, if the end of the data occurs,
   then Exit.
   Set X ⇐ NODE, LPTR(X) ← RPTR(X) ← NULL, and INFO(X) ← NAME.

3. [Compare levels]   Set PRED_LEVEL ← L[TOP], P ← ADD[TOP].
    If LEVEL > PRED_LEVEL, then set LPTR(P) ← X and go to step 5.
4. [Remove top level from stack]
    Repeat while PRED_LEVEL > LEVEL:
        set TOP ← TOP − 1, PRED_LEVEL ← L[TOP], and P ← ADD[TOP].
    If PRED_LEVEL < LEVEL, then print 'mixed level numbers', and Exit.
    Set RPTR(P) ← X and TOP ← TOP − 1.
5. [Push a new node on the stack]   Set TOP ← TOP + 1, L[TOP] ← LEVEL,
    ADD[TOP] ← X, and go to step 2.

The first step of the algorithm creates a list head and places the level number and address of this node on the stack. Step 2 reads in a pair of values associated with a node in the structure. The algorithm terminates in step 2 when the end of the data is detected. The third step copies the level number and address of the topmost element in the stack into the variables PRED_LEVEL and P, respectively. If the level number of the current node is greater than the level number of the node on the top of the stack, then the left link of the latter is set to the address of the former. This is followed by a transfer of control to step 5. In the fourth step, elements are removed from the stack until the level number of the topmost element in the stack is less than or equal to the level number of the current node. If the comparison gives a "less than" result, then an error exists in the numbering of the tree structures; otherwise, in case of equality, the right link of the stack node is set to X and it is removed from the stack. The final step of the algorithm places the level number and address of the current node on the stack and returns to step 2.

A trace of the algorithm using the forest of Fig. 5-1.23a is given in Table 5-1.2,

Table 5-1.2

Current Input	Stack	Level	X	PRED_ LEVEL	P	LPTR(P)	RPTR(P)
	ONT					NULL	NULL
1,A	ONT 1NA	1	NA	0	NT	NA	NULL
2,B	ONT 1NA 2NB	2	NB	1	NA	NB	NULL
2,C	ONT 1NA 2NC	2	NC	2	NB	NULL	NC
2,D	ONT 1NA 2ND	2	ND	2	NC	NULL	ND
3,E	ONT 1NA 2ND 3NE	3	NE	2	ND	NE	NULL
1,F		1	NF	3	NE		
				2	ND		
	ONT 1NF			1	NA		NF
2,G	ONT 1NF 2NG	2	NG	1	NF	NG	NULL
3,I	ONT 1NF 2NG 3NI	3	NI	2	NG	NI	NULL
3,J	ONT 1NF 2NG 3NJ	3	NJ	3	NI	NULL	NJ
2,H		2	NH	3	NJ		
	ONT 1NG 2NH			2	NG		NG

where NA denotes the address of a node with name A, NB denotes the address of a node with name B, etc. A stack entry written as, for example, 1NA means that we have placed on the stack the level number (1) and the address (NA) of some node with name A. The stack top is to the right. Note that if a forest happens to have several nodes with the same name, say B, then each of these nodes will have a different address, even though our notation will refer to each address as NB. The table shows only changes which have occurred since the previous steps.

We next consider the representations of trees using sequential-allocation techniques. Such representations are convenient and efficient, providing that the tree structure does not change drastically (as to insertions, deletions, etc.) during its existence. The choice of representation also depends on the other types of operations which are to be performed on the structure. An example of a static tree structure will be discussed in Chap. 6 in conjunction with the heapsort method of sorting.

Our first example of a straightforward method for the sequential representation of a tree consists of having a vector which contains the father of each node in the tree. For example, the representation for the tree given in Fig. 5-1.24a is given as follows:

i	1 2 3 4 5 6 7 8 9 10
FATHER[i]	0 1 1 1 2 3 3 7 4 4

where the branches in the tree are given by

$$\{(\text{FATHER}[i], i)\} \text{ for } i = 2, 3, \ldots, 10$$

Numeric data fields have been used for the nodes to simplify the representation. Note that the root node (1) has no father, and a value of zero for its father is used. In general, if T denotes the index of the root node of a tree, then FATHER[T] = 0.

This method of representation can be used to represent a forest. An obvious disadvantage of the method is that it does not include certain orderings of the nodes. For example, if nodes 9 and 10 are interchanged, both sequential representations are the same.

Another common method for the sequential representation of trees involves using the physical adjacency relationship of the computer's memory to replace one of the LPTR or RPTR fields of the linked representation method of representing binary trees discussed earlier. Let us consider the omission of the LPTR field from the usual doubly linked representation and examine how a tree can be represented. One possibility is to represent the tree sequentially so that its nodes appear in preorder. Using this approach, the tree given in Fig. 5-1.24b can be described as shown in Fig. 5-1.25a, where RPTR, DATA, and TAG are vectors. Note that in this representation the LPTR pointer is not required, since if it was not null, it would point to the node to its immediate right. The TAG vector is a bit vector with a bit value of "one" denoting a leaf node in the original tree. There is a significant waste of space in this representation, since over one-half of the RPTR pointers are null. This wasted space can be used by making the RPTR of each current node point to the node which immediately follows the subtree below this current node. The field RPTR is renamed RANGE in such a representation, as shown in Fig. 5-1.25b. Note that the TAG field is no longer required, since a leaf node is detected when RANGE(P) = P + 1.

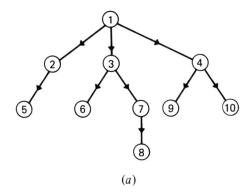

(a)

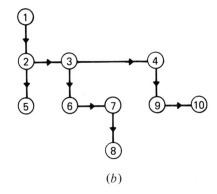

(b)

FIGURE 5-1.24.

A third and final method of sequential representation is to represent a general tree based on its postorder traversal. The representation consists of one vector which represents the nodes of the tree in postorder and a second vector which denotes the outdegree of the nodes. An example of a tree with such a representation is given in Fig. 5-1.26. Recall that this postorder method of representation is useful for evaluating functions which are

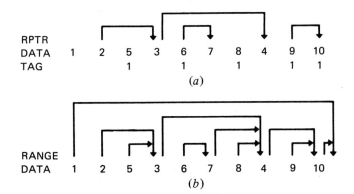

RPTR
DATA   1   2   5   3   6   7   8   4   9   10
TAG   1   1   1   1   1

(a)

RANGE
DATA   1   2   5   3   6   7   8   4   9   10

(b)

FIGURE 5-1.25 Some preorder sequential representations of a tree.

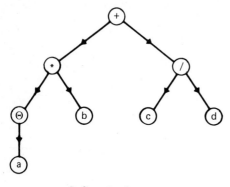

$$\text{Infix} \quad \ominus a * b + c / d$$
$$\text{Degree} \quad 0\,1\,0\,2\,0\,0\,2\,2$$
$$\text{Data} \quad a \ominus b * c\,d / +$$

FIGURE 5-1.26 The postorder sequential representation of a tree.

defined on certain nodes of the tree. An example of such a function was given in Sec. 3-7.2.3 for the generation of object code from the reverse Polish representation of an expression.

In terminating this subsection, let us consider an important concept about binary trees—namely, their similarity and equivalence. Two trees are said to be *similar* if they have the same structure or shape. Two trees are *equivalent* if they are similar and, furthermore, if corresponding nodes contain the same information. An application of similar trees is given in Sec. 5-2.1.

In the preceding pages we have been concerned with the representations and manipulations of trees. In the next section we will discuss certain applications in which trees are used.

Exercises for Sec. 5-1.2

1. Prove that a binary tree with n nodes has exactly n + 1 null branches.
2. Trace through Algorithm **POSTORDER**, using the binary tree of Fig. 5-1.17, and construct a table similar to Table 5-1.1.
3. Formulate an iterative algorithm for the inorder traversal of a binary tree.
4. Given the binary tree in Fig. 5-1.27, determine the order in which the nodes will be visited if the tree is traversed in inorder, in postorder, and in preorder. Repeat this exercise for the converse traversals.
5. In the presentation of inorder threaded binary trees, algorithms were developed for producing the inorder predecessor and successor of an arbitrary node P. Develop similar algorithms for producing the preorder predecessor and successor and the postorder predecessor and successor of an arbitrary node P in an inorder threaded binary tree with list head node as presented.
6. Formulate an algorithm similar to Algorithm **LEFT** called **RIGHT** which inserts a node to the right of a designated node P.

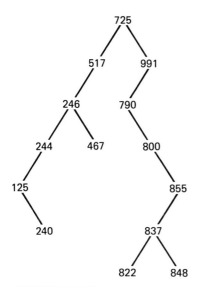

FIGURE 5-1.27.

7. Formulate algorithms similar to Algorithms INP and INS for preorder and postorder threading of trees.
8. Devise an algorithm which will copy a given tree.
9. Obtain a recursive algorithm which will convert a forest into an equivalent binary tree.
10. Formulate an algorithm based on the sequential representation of a tree using the FATHER vector which finds the path between node x and node y.
11. Devise an algorithm for determining whether or not two trees A and B are similar, based on the traversal methods discussed in this section.

5-2 APPLICATIONS OF TREES

The present section contains four applications of trees. The first describes methods for the mechanical manipulation of arithmetic expressions. An interesting application of trees concerning the construction and maintenance of a dictionary of symbol names is discussed in Sec. 5-2.2. The tree also plays an important role in the area of syntax analysis, where it is used to display the structure of a sentence in the language and is used in defining unambiguous grammars. Such topics are dealt with in Sec. 5-2.3, along with a description of top-down parsing by using recursive descent. Finally, the translation of decision tables from some source language to object code can be realized by using a tree structure, as explained in Sec. 5-2.4.

5-2.1 The Manipulation of Arithmetic Expressions

In this subsection we will first discuss the relationship between binary trees and formulas in prefix or suffix notation. Next, we will describe the mechanical manipulation of expressions that are represented by binary trees. Recall that in Sec. 4-3.1, we discussed the formal manipulation of polynomials. In the remainder of this subsection we will extend this previous discussion of manipulating expressions. The discussion here, however, is based on the tree representation of expressions. Therefore, certain operations and properties of such expressions will be described in terms of their tree representation. A number of programmed examples are included.

In Sec. 3-7.2 we observed that formulas in reverse Polish notation are very useful in the compilation process. There is a close relationship between binary trees and formulas in prefix or suffix notation. Let us write an infix formula as a binary tree, where a node has an operator as a value and where the left and right subtrees are the left and right operands of that operator. The leaves of the tree are the variables and constants in the expression. Let $\ominus$ represent the unary minus. There are rules given in Exercises for Sec. 3-7.2 that can distinguish a unary minus from a binary minus and the negative sign of a constant. The operand of $\ominus$ is considered to be a right subtree. The binary tree in Fig. 5-2.1 represents the formula a*$\ominus$b +c/d. If we traverse this tree in preorder, we visit the nodes in the order +*a$\ominus$b/cd, and this is merely the prefix form of the infix formula. On the other hand, if we traverse the tree in postorder, then we visit the nodes in the order ab$\ominus$*cd/+, which is the formula written in suffix notation. Observe that if we had represented the formula as a general tree, as in Fig. 5-2.2a, and then applied the natural correspondence algorithm of Sec. 5-1.2 to convert this tree into an equivalent binary tree, we would have the structure shown in Fig. 5-2.2b. The prefix form of the formula is obtained by traversing the binary tree in preorder, while the suffix form is generated by an inorder traversal of the binary tree (not a postorder traversal!).

In the remainder of this subsection we shall discuss the mechanical manipulation of expressions which are represented as binary trees. Since we have already introduced this topic in Chap. 4, it should be obvious that the expressions themselves are to be manipulated (symbolically) and not their values. We may want to symbolically add, subtract, multiply, divide, differentiate, integrate, compare for equivalence, etc., such

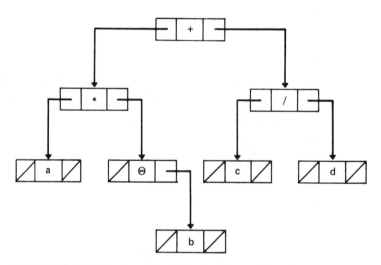

FIGURE 5-2.1   The formula a * $\ominus$b + c/d as a binary tree.

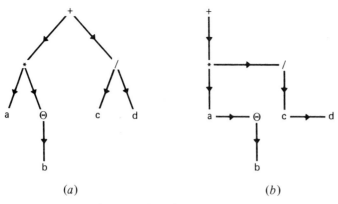

FIGURE 5-2.2 The general and binary tree representations of a $* \ominus b + c/d$. (a) General tree; (b) binary tree.

expressions. Some of these operations are discussed in this subsection, while others such as differentiation and integration are described in Sec. 5-5.3.

There are a number of programming languages which permit the declaration of expressions. For example, an expanded version of ALGOL 60, called FORMULA ALGOL, is such a language where a new data type called FORM was added to basic ALGOL. Expressions in this language are stored as trees, and a number of related operations are available in the language. SNOBOL4 is another language which permits "unevaluated expressions" to be used in a program. These unevaluated expressions can represent a pattern or an expression, and these can be evaluated later in the program. If the unevaluated expression represents a pattern, then this pattern is only evaluated at pattern-matching time (see Sec. 2-3.4) or by using the function **EVAL**. If the unevaluated expression does not represent a pattern, but some arithmetic or string expression, then the reference **EVAL (EXPR)**, where EXPR denotes the expression string, returns the value of **EXPR**.

Let us now describe a binary tree representation for symbolic expressions. Such a representation is given for the expression $a * \ominus b + c \uparrow 2$ in Fig. 5-2.3, where $\ominus$ and $\uparrow$ represent the unary minus and exponentiation operations, respectively. In this figure, **E** is a pointer variable which denotes the root of the tree, each node of which consists of a left pointer **(LPTR)**, a right pointer **(RPTR)**, and an information field **(TYPE)**. The **TYPE** field indicates, in the case of a non-leaf node, the arithmetic operation which is associated with that node. The values of **TYPE** associated with the operators $+$, $-$, $*$, $/$, $\uparrow$, and $\ominus$ are 1, 2, 3, 4, 5, and 6, respectively. For a leaf node, however, **TYPE** denotes a variable or a constant (by having a value of 0). In such a case, the right pointer of the leaf gives the address in the symbol table which corresponds to that variable or constant. Note that the type of the operator (and not the operator itself) is stored in the tree. This choice makes the processing of such trees simple. The symbol table used contains the name of the variable **(SYMBOL)** or constant and its value **(VALUE)**.

Initially, let us consider the evaluation of an expression which is represented by a binary tree. That is, we want to obtain the value of this expression. The simplest way of accomplishing this is to formulate a recursive solution. Such a solution is given in the recur-

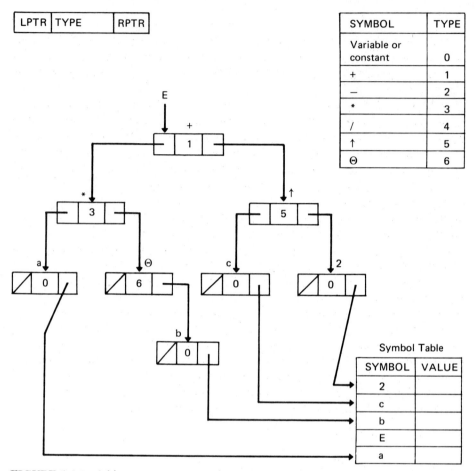

FIGURE 5-2.3   A binary tree representation of an expression.

sive PL/I procedure **EVAL** of Fig. 5-2.4, where it is invoked as a function. The structures defined by the statements

```
DECLARE    01    NODE BASED(P),
           02      LPTR POINTER,
           02      TYPE FIXED DECIMAL (1),
           02      RPTR POINTER;
```

and

```
DECLARE    01    RECORD BASED(Q),
           02      SYMBOL CHARACTER(20),
           02      VALUE FIXED BINARY;
```

are assumed to have been declared in the main program so that they are considered to be global to the procedure.

The procedure given in Fig. 5-2.4 is simple. A label array consisting of seven elements is created and initialized to the desired labels. This array is referenced in the next statement, where the label generated depends on the value of TYPE for the root node. The result of the go to statement is a transfer of control to the appropriately labeled statement. If the node is a leaf, then the value of the variable or constant denoted by this node is returned. This is accomplished by using the right pointer of that node to reference the associated entry in the symbol table. For a non-leaf node, however, the recursive evaluation of the subtree(s) of this node which represent the operand(s) of the current operator is initiated. This is achieved by invoking the EVAL function with the left and right pointers of that operator node as arguments in the case of a binary node; otherwise, only the right pointer is used in the case of the unary minus operator. This process continues until a leaf node is encountered. For a given leaf node, a value from the associated entry in the symbol table is located.

Now that we are able to evaluate an expression which is represented by a binary tree, let us next consider the operation of symbolically adding two such expressions. For example, assume that it is required to add the expressions EXPR1 and EXPR2. Let E1 and E2 be the pointer variables which denote the roots of the binary trees for EXPR1 and EXPR2, respectively. The required addition is easily achieved by creating a root node for the sum expression and using the values of E1 and E2 as the left and right pointer values, respectively, for this new node. The type field of the new root node is also set to 1. The PL/I statements to accomplish this construction are

```
ALLOCATE NODE;
P — > LPTR = E1;
P — > RPTR = E2;
P — > TYPE = 1;
```

```
EVAL:
     PROCEDURE(E) RECURSIVE RETURNS(FIXED BINARY);

     DECLARE
         (F,E) POINTER,
         STAT(0:6) LABEL INITIAL(VC,PLUS,MINUS,MULT,DIV,EXP,UNARY);

     GO TO STAT(F->TYPE);

VC:     F = E->RPTR;      RETURN(F->VALUE);

PLUS:   RETURN(EVAL(E->LPTR) + EVAL(E->RPTR));

MINUS:  RETURN(EVAL(E->LPTR) - EVAL(E->RPTR));

MULT:   RETURN(EVAL(E->LPTR) * EVAL(E->RPTR));

DIV:    RETURN(EVAL(E->LPTR) / EVAL(E->RPTR));

EXP:    RETURN(EVAL(E->LPTR) ** EVAL(E->RPTR));

UNARY:  RETURN(-EVAL(E->LPTR));

END EVAL;
```

FIGURE 5-2.4 Procedure for the EVAL function.

with P containing the address of the root node for the expression **EXPR1** + **EXPR2**. The algorithm is trivial when it is compared with the algorithm developed in Sec. 4-3.1 for essentially the same application.

In practice, however, we would like the addition function to perform certain obvious simplifications. For example, if the expressions being added are constants, then we should create a new constant node representing this constant sum. Moreover, if one of the expressions being added is zero, then no new root node is required. Similar rules can be devised for the other arithmetic operators and are left as exercises.

As a final example, let us consider the problem of determining whether or not two expressions (which are represented by binary trees) are similar. Two binary trees associated with such expressions are said to be similar if they are *identical* for all node types except for those which represent the commutative operators + and *. In this latter case, we can accept the case where the left subtree of the first tree is identical to the right subtree of the second tree and the right subtree of the first tree is identical to the left subtree of the second tree. A PL/I procedure for accomplishing the similarity check is given in Fig. 5-2.5, where the node structure and binary tree representation of Fig. 5-2.3 has been assumed. Note that the operators are divided into three categories—namely, the binary commutative operators, the binary noncommutative operators, and the unary operator.

```
SIMILAR:
    PROCEDURE(A, B) RECURSIVE RETURNS(BIT(1));

    DECLARE
        (A, B) POINTER,
        STAT(0:6) LABEL INITIAL(LEAF,COMMUT,IDENT,COMMUT,IDENT,IDENT,
            UNARY);

    /* CHECK THE ROOT NODES */

    IF A->TYPE ¬= B->TYPE
    THEN RETURN('0'B);

    GO TO STAT(A->TYPE);

    /* COMPARE LEAF NODES */

LEAF:
    IF A->RPTR ¬= B->RPTR
    THEN RETURN('0'B);
    ELSE RETURN('1'B);

COMMUT: /* CHECK FOR COMMUTATIVITY OF + AND *     */

    RETURN(SIMILAR(A->LPTR,B->RPTR) & SIMILAR(A->RPTR,B->LPTR)
        | SIMILAR(A->LPTR,B->LPTR) & SIMILAR(A->RPTR,B->RPTR));

IDENT: /* CHECK FOR IDENTICAL BINARY SUBTREES */

    RETURN(SIMILAR(A->LPTR,B->LPTR) & SIMILAR(A->RPTR,B->RPTR));

UNARY: /* CHECK FOR IDENTICAL UNARY SUBTREE */

    RETURN(SIMILAR(A->LPTR,B->LPTR));

END SIMILAR;
```

FIGURE 5-2.5   Procedure for the similarity check.

Exercises for Sec. 5-2.1

1. Formulate simplification rules, similar to those developed for addition in the text, for the other arithmetic operations.

2. Design an algorithm, based on the binary tree representation of an expression, which will symbolically differentiate a given expression. The expression is assumed to contain variables, constants, and the usual arithmetic operators.

3. Obtain an algorithm, based on the binary tree representation of an expression, which will symbolically integrate a given expression containing variables, constants, and the ordinary arithmetic operators.

5-2.2 Symbol-Table Construction

As an application of binary trees, we will formulate an algorithm that will maintain a tree-structured symbol table. (See Sec. 4-3.2.) One of the criteria that a symbol-table routine must meet is that table searching be performed efficiently. This requirement originates in the compilation phase where many references to the entries of a symbol table are made. The two required operations that must be performed on a symbol table are insertion and look-up, each of which involves searching. A binary tree structure is chosen for two reasons. The first reason is that if the symbol entries as encountered are uniformly distributed according to lexicographic order, then table searching becomes approximately equivalent to a binary search, as long as the tree is maintained in lexicographic order. Second, a binary tree structure is easily maintained in lexicographic order in the sense that only a few pointers need be changed.

For simplicity we assume the use of a relatively sophisticated system which allows variable-length character strings. Very little effort is required on the part of the programmer to handle such strings. We further assume that the symbol-table routine is used to create trees for variables which are local to a block of program code. This implies that an attempt to insert a duplicate entry is an error. In a global context, duplicate entries are permitted as long as they are at different block levels. In a sense, the symbol table is a set of trees—one for each block level.

A binary tree is constructed with typical node of the form

LPTR	SYMBOLS	INFO	RPTR

where LPTR and RPTR are pointer fields, SYMBOLS is the field for the character string which is the identifier or variable name (note that string descriptors might well be used here to allow fixed-length nodes, but it is assumed that this use is transparent to the user), and INFO is some set of fields containing additional information about the identifier, such as its type. A node is created by the execution of the statement P ⇐ NODE, where the address of the new node is stored in P.

Finally, it is assumed that prior to any use of the symbol-table routine at a particular block level, the appropriate tree head node is created with the SYMBOLS field set to a value that is greater lexicographically than any valid identifier. HEAD[n] points to this node where n designates the nth block level. Hence, when a block is entered, a call is made to a main routine which administers to the creation of tree heads. Similarly, when a block is exited, a routine which deletes tree heads is invoked.

Because both the insertion and look-up operations involve many of the same actions (e.g., searching), we will actually produce only one routine, TABLE, and distinguish between insertion and look-up by the value of a global logical variable, FLAG. On invoking Algorithm TABLE, if FLAG is true, then the requested operation is insertion; NAME and DATA contain the identifier name and additional information, respectively. If the insertion is successful, then FLAG retains its original value; otherwise, FLAG's value is negated to indicate an error (because the identifier is already present in the table at that level) and an exit from the algorithm is made. On the other hand, if the algorithm is invoked with FLAG set to false, then the requested operation is look-up. In this case, NAME contains the identifier name to be searched for and DATA is irrelevant. On a successful search, DATA is set to the INFO fields of the matching SYMBOLS entry, FLAG retains its value, and a return is made to the invoking program. An unsuccessful search during a look-up operation causes the value of FLAG to be negated and an exit to be made. In this latter case, it is the responsibility of the invoking main routine to try the look-up procedure at lower block levels (trees headed by HEAD[n −1], HEAD[n −2], etc.).

Algorithm TABLE.   Given n, a global variable indicating the block level of current interest, and FLAG, a global variable which indicates the required operation, this algorithm performs the requested operation on the tree-structured symbol table local to level n. The parameters DATA and NAME are used for data communications between the algorithm and the invoking routine. FLAG is used as a success or failure indicator in the algorithm.

1. [Initialize]   Set T ← HEAD[n].
2. [Compare]
    If NAME < SYMBOLS(T),
    then if LPTR(T) ≠ NULL,
        then set T ← LPTR(T) and go to step 2;
        otherwise,
            if ⌐ FLAG,
            then set FLAG ← ⌐ FLAG, and Exit;
            otherwise, set P ⇐ NODE, SYMBOLS(P) ← NAME, INFO(P) ← DATA,
                LPTR(P) ← RPTR(P) ← NULL, LPTR(T) ← P, and Exit.
    If NAME > SYMBOLS(T),
    then if RPTR(T) ≠ NULL,
        then set T ← RPTR(T) and go to step 2;
        otherwise,
            if ⌐ FLAG,
            then set FLAG ← ⌐ FLAG, and Exit;
            otherwise, set P ⇐ NODE, SYMBOLS(P) ← NAME, INFO(P) ← DATA
                RPTR(P) ← LPTR(P) ← NULL, RPTR(T) ← P, and Exit.
3. [A match]   If FLAG, then set FLAG ← ⌐ FLAG; otherwise, set DATA ← INFO(T).
4. [Finished]   Exit.

The algorithm is simple to understand. In step 2 we compare NAME against a symbol-table entry. If they match, we have either found the required entry or we have attempted to enter a duplicate name. In either case, we exit after step 3. If no match is found, then, depending on whether NAME is less than or greater than the symbol-table entry being examined, we prepare to take the left or right node descendant and return to step 2 for further comparison. However, since a tree ordered in this manner is such that every node in a left subtree or right subtree precedes or follows lexicographically the root node, respectively, we know that whenever an attempt is made to go down an empty subtree, then no match is found. Thus, we have determined where the entry should be. In such a case, an error is reported if the requested operation was a look-up; otherwise, a new node is created, pertinent information is copied into it, and it is inserted either to the left or right of the current node being examined in the existing tree structure.

Exercises for Sec. 5-2.2

1. Trace Algorithm TABLE using as data the following set of names: do, else, get, put, then, declare, fixed, float, binary, character, based, and pointer.
2. Write a PL/I procedure for Algorithm TABLE and use the data of Exercise 1 to verify your procedure.

5-2.3 Syntax Analysis

In Sec. 2-2.2 the notions of a grammar as a mathematical system for defining languages and as a device for giving some useful structure to sentences of a language were discussed. Also, the problem of obtaining a parse for a particular sentence of a language was introduced. Recall that a parse consisted of finding a sequence of productions which would generate a given sentence from the starting symbol of the grammar. The concept of a syntax tree and its relationship to the parse of a sentence of a language were mentioned briefly. The syntax tree (or derivation) corresponding to a sentence of a language could be found in a top-down or bottom-up manner.

This section deals with the use of grammars in syntax analysis or parsing. We will therefore be concerned with the syntax-recognition phase of a compiler. The discrete structure which is central to syntax analysis is the syntax tree. From such a tree and semantics can be derived the meaning of a sentence. Furthermore, a syntax tree is a convenient representation which can be used in the derivation of many important relations for certain classes of grammars.

Initially, the important concept of syntactic ambiguity and its relationship to the parsing problem are mentioned. Next, the top-down method of parsing introduced earlier is discussed in more detail. The approach that is used is informal and very general, but also very slow because of all the backtracking or backup that must be performed. Certain improvements are suggested which can reduce, for certain grammars, the amount of backtracking that is required. Finally, the top-down method of parsing is implemented using recursive procedures.

As previously discussed in Sec. 2-2.2, syntax trees are an important aid to understanding the syntax of a sentence. A syntax tree for a sentence of some language has a distinguished node called its *root* which is labeled by the starting symbol of the grammar.

The leaf nodes of the syntax tree represent the terminal symbols in the sentence being diagrammed. All nonleaf nodes correspond to nonterminal symbols. Each nonterminal node has a number of branches emanating downward, each of which represents a symbol in the right side of the production being applied at that point in the syntax tree.

More generally, any sentential form can have a syntax tree. The leaf nodes in such a tree can designate terminal and nonterminal symbols. Let A be the root of a subtree for a sentential form $\sigma = \phi_1\beta\phi_2$, where β forms the string of leaf nodes emanating from that subtree. Then, β is the phrase for A of the sentential form σ. β is a simple phrase if the subtree whose root is A consists of the application of the single production $A \rightarrow \beta$.

Consider the example grammar

$$G_1 = \{ <expr>, <factor>, <term> \}, \{i, +, *, (,)\}, <expr>, \Phi\}$$

where Φ consists of the productions

$$<factor> ::= i \mid (<expr>)$$
$$<term> ::= <factor> \mid <term> * <factor>$$
$$<expr> ::= <term> \mid <expr> + <term>$$

and i stands for an identifier or variable name. The syntax tree for the sentential form $<expr> + <term> * <factor>$ is given in Fig. 5-2.6, where $<expr> + <term> * <factor>$ and $<term> * <factor>$ are its phrases, while $<term> * <factor>$ is a simple phrase.

An important question which arises in formal languages is whether a sentential form has a unique syntax tree. Consider the simple grammar G_2 which has the following productions:

$$S ::= S * S$$
$$S ::= a$$

where a is a terminal symbol. Let us find a derivation for the sentence $a * a * a$. One such derivation is

$$S \Rightarrow S * S \Rightarrow S * S * S \Rightarrow a * S * S \Rightarrow a * a * S \Rightarrow a * a * a$$

where the leftmost S in the second step has been rewritten as $S * S$. Another possibility, of course, is that the rightmost S in the same step is rewritten as $S * S$. Both possibilities are

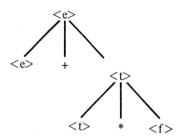

FIGURE 5-2.6 Syntax tree for $<expr> + <term> * <factor>$ in G_1.

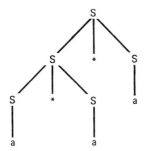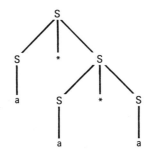

FIGURE 5-2.7 Two distinct syntax trees for the sentence a * a * a in G_2.

diagrammed in Fig. 5-2.7. It is clear that the two syntax trees are different. That is, we have two different parses for the same sentence. The existence of more than one parse for some sentence in a language can cause a compiler to generate a different set of instructions (object code) for different parses. Usually, this phenomenon is intolerable. If a compiler is to perform valid translations of sentences in a language, then that language must be unambiguously defined. This concept leads us to the following definition.

A sentence generated by a grammar is *ambiguous* if there exists more than one syntax tree for it. A grammar is ambiguous if it generates at least one ambiguous sentence; otherwise, it is *unambiguous*.

It should be noted that we called the *grammar* ambiguous, and not the language which it generates. There are many grammars which can generate the same language; some are ambiguous and some are not. However, there are certain languages for which no unambiguous grammars can be found. Such languages are said to be *inherently ambiguous*. For example, the language $\{x^i y^j z^k \mid i = j \text{ or } j = k\}$ is an inherently ambiguous context-free language.

The question which naturally arises at this point is: Does there exist an algorithm which can accept any context-free grammar and determine, in some finite time, whether it is ambiguous? The answer is no! A simple set of sufficient conditions can be developed such that when they are applied to a grammar and are found to hold, then the grammar is guaranteed to be unambiguous. We wish to point out that these conditions are sufficient but not necessary. In other words, even if a grammar does not satisfy the conditions, it may still be unambiguous.

Let us examine another example of an ambiguous grammar. In particular, consider the grammar G_3 for arithmetic expressions consisting of the operators $+$ and $*$ with single-letter variables:

<expr> ::= i | <expr> + <expr> | <expr> * <expr> | (<expr>)

Assume that the sentence i + i * i is to be diagrammed. Two possible derivations are as follows:

<expr> ⇒ <expr> + <expr>
    ⇒ <expr> + <expr> * <expr>
    ⇒ i + <expr> * <expr>

$$\Rightarrow i + i * <expr>$$
$$\Rightarrow i + i * i$$
$$<expr> \Rightarrow <expr> * <expr>$$
$$\Rightarrow <expr> + <expr> * <expr>$$
$$\Rightarrow i + <expr> * <expr>$$
$$\Rightarrow i + i * <expr>$$
$$\Rightarrow i + i * i$$

Their corresponding syntax trees are given in Fig. 5-2.8. Since there exist two distinct syntax trees for the sentence i + i * i, the grammar is ambiguous. Intuitively, this grammar is ambiguous because it is not known whether to evaluate * before + or conversely. The grammar can be rewritten in such a manner that the multiplication will have precedence over addition. This revision is accomplished in the following grammar G_4:

$$<expr> ::= <term> \mid <expr> + <term>$$
$$<term> ::= <factor> \mid <term> * <factor>$$
$$<factor> ::= i \mid (<expr>)$$

Recall from Sec. 2-2.2 the two methods discussed for constructing a parse tree for a sentence generated by a grammar—namely, bottom-up parsing and top-down parsing. The remaining pages of this section are concerned with giving a more detailed discussion of the top-down method of parsing. The term top-down parsing is derived from the idea that an attempt is made to construct a parse tree for some given input string by starting from the root of the tree and working down to the symbols in the sentence. This task is accom-

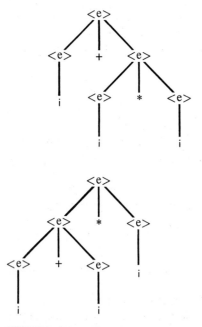

FIGURE 5-2.8 Two syntax trees for i + i * i in G_3.

plished by initially numbering in some fashion the different right-hand sides (or alternates) associated with each metavariable in the grammar. For example, if S :: = $\alpha_1 \mid \alpha_2 \mid \ldots \mid \alpha_n$ are the productions that have the common left-hand side S in the grammar, then we assign some ordering to the alternates of S (the α's).

As an example, consider the grammar

```
<e> :: = <t> + <e> | <t>
<t> :: = <f> * <t> | <f>
<f> :: = ( <e> ) | i
```

and let us order them as shown. That is, $<t> + <e>$ is the first alternate for $<e>$ and $<t>$ is the second; $<f> * <t>$ is the first alternate for $<t>$ and $<f>$ is the second, etc. In the informal discussion of the top-down parsing method which follows, an input pointer which initially points to the leftmost symbol of the input string is used.

Recall that a top-down parser tries to construct a syntax tree for the input string in the following manner. Initially, the tree consists of a node labeled S which is called the initial active node of the tree. The following steps are then performed recursively:

1 If the active node denotes a variable A, then we choose its first alternate, say $X_1 X_2 \ldots X_r$, for A and extend the tree by creating r direct descendants for A labeled $X_1 X_2 \ldots X_r$. The symbol X_1 is then considered to be the new active node.

2 If the active node denotes a terminal symbol, say a, then it is compared with the current input symbol. If they match, then the node to the immediate right of a is considered to be the new active node and the input pointer is moved one symbol to the right. Otherwise, a return is made to the node where the previous rule was applied, the input pointer is changed when required, and the next alternate is tried. If no such alternate exists, a return to the next previous node is made, etc.

During the parsing process, the leaves of the part of syntax tree which has been generated so far always match that part of the input string which has been processed.

Let us trace through this algorithm using our example grammar and the sample input string i + i. The parse begins with the tree having one node labeled $<e>$. We next apply the first alternate of $<e>$ extending the tree to Fig. 5-2.9a. Since the active node now becomes $<t>$, we then apply the first alternate of $<t>$, extending the tree to Fig. 5-2.9b. The active node at this point is $<f>$ and we discard its first alternate since (does not match i in the input string. We next try the second alternate of $<f>$ (that is, i) and find that it matches the symbol i in the input string. The input cursor is advanced to the second character in the input string and the symbol * then becomes the new active node which fails to match the second input character, as shown in Fig. 5-2.9c. The cursor is then reset to a value of 1. The node $<t>$ again becomes the active node and its second alternate (that is, $<f>$) is tried and yields Fig. 5-2.9d. Now $<f>$ becomes the new active node with its first alternate failing. Therefore, the second alternate of this node (that is, i) is chosen and it matches the first symbol in the input string. The cursor is again advanced to the next position and the symbol + now becomes the new active node (which also matches the second input character), as shown in Fig. 5-2.9e. The node $<e>$ then becomes active and its first alternate is chosen to yield Fig. 5-2.9f. This process is continued until the final parse tree of Fig. 5.2-9g is obtained.

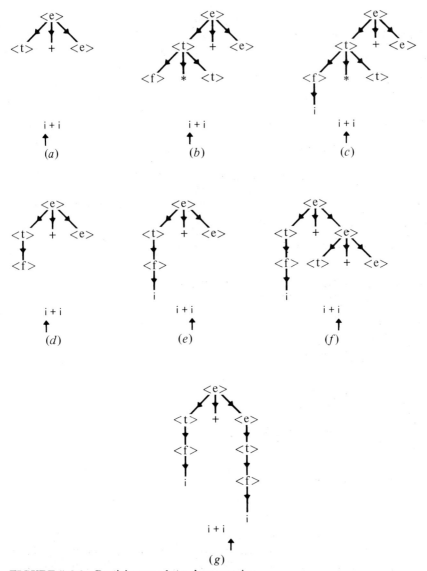

FIGURE 5-2.9 Partial trace of top-down parsing.

The remainder of this subsection deals with a program implementation of the top-down parsing technique that has been just discussed. The parser that is given contains one recursive procedure for each metavariable **A**, which parses phrases for **A**. The procedure is told where to begin its search for a phrase of **A**. Such an approach is goal oriented. The procedure looks for a phrase by comparing the input string beginning at a specified point with the alternates of **A** and invoking other procedures to recognize the subgoals when required.

The parse tree is constructed during the parse in the same way as was described earlier. As an example, the procedures for the variables of our simple grammar are formulated. These are given in Fig. 5-2.10, where it is assumed that we are parsing without backup. This is easily accomplished by using one context symbol following the part of the phrase which has already been passed. The context symbol in question can be either a '+' or a '*'. Note that there are four procedures; namely, SCAN, EXPR, FACTOR, and TERM. All procedures except SCAN are recursive. The following points are made concerning the program:

1 The variable NEXT is global and contains the next symbol of the input string which is being processed. When a procedure to find a new goal is called, the first symbol to be examined is already in NEXT. Similarly, before returning from a procedure after a successful match, the symbol following the substring found by the procedure is put into NEXT.

```
RECDSNT:
    PROCEDURE OPTICNS(MAIN);

DECLARE
        (I, CURSCR) BINARY FIXED,
        INPUT CHARACTER(80) VARYING,
        (NEXT, STRING(80)) CHARACTER(1),
        FACTOR RETURNS(BIT(1)),
        TERM RETURNS(BIT(1)),
        EXPR RETURNS(BIT(1));
    ON ENDFILE(SYSIN) GO TO FIN;

READ:
    GET LIST(INPUT);
    DO I = 1 TO LENGTH(INPUT);
        STRING(I) = SUBSTR(INPUT, I, 1);
    END;
    CURSOR = 1;
    CALL SCAN;
    IF EXPR & NEXT = '#'
    THEN PUT SKIP EDIT(INPUT, 'VALID') (A, X(10), A);
    ELSE PUT SKIP EDIT(INPUT, 'INVALID') (A, X(10), A);
    GO TO READ;

EXPR:
    PROCEDURE RECURSIVE RETURNS(BIT(1));
    IF ¬TERM
    THEN RETURN('0'B);
    IF NEXT = '+'
    THEN
        DO;
            CALL SCAN;
            IF NEXT = '#' THEN RETURN('0'B);
            IF ¬EXPR
            THEN RETURN('0'B);
            ELSE RETURN('1'B);
        END;
    ELSE RETURN('1'B);
END EXPR;

SCAN:
    PROCEDURE;
    NEXT = STRING(CURSOR);
    CURSOR = CURSOR + 1;
END SCAN;
```

FIGURE 5-2.10 Procedures for parsing an expression.

```
TERM:
    PROCEDURE RECURSIVE RETURNS(BIT(1));
    IF ¬FACTOR
    THEN RETURN('0'B);
    IF NEXT = '*'
    THEN
        DO;
            CALL SCAN;
            IF NEXT = '#' THEN RETURN('0'B);
            IF ¬TERM
            THEN RETURN('0'B);
            ELSE RETURN('1'B);
        END;
    ELSE RETURN('1'B);
END TERM;

FACTOR:
    PROCEDURE RECURSIVE RETURNS(BIT(1));
    IF NEXT = '#' THEN RETURN('0'B);
    IF NEXT = '('
    THEN
        DO;
            CALL SCAN;
            IF NEXT = '#' THEN RETURN('0'B);
            IF ¬EXPR
            THEN RETURN('0'B);
            IF NEXT ¬= ')'
            THEN RETURN('0'B);
            ELSE
                DO;
                    CALL SCAN;
                    RETURN('1'B);
                END;
        END;
    IF NEXT ¬= 'I'
    THEN RETURN('0'B);
    ELSE
        DO;
            CALL SCAN;
            RETURN('1'B);
        END;
END FACTOR;

FIN:
END RECDSNT;
```

```
I*I+I#              VALID
(I+I)*(I+I)#             VALID
I+I#              VALID
((I+I*I#              INVALID
(I+I+I*((I+I)+I)))#             INVALID
I*I+I+#             INVALID
```

FIGURE 5-2.10   (Continued)

2   The procedure **SCAN** obtains the next input symbol and places it into **NEXT**.

3   To begin parsing, the main program invokes the procedure **SCAN**, which in turn places the leftmost symbol in the input string into **NEXT**.

4   The variable **CURSOR** is also global to all procedures and denotes the present character position in the input string.

Note that the example grammar used in this subsection has contained right-recursive rules instead of the more popular and natural left-recursive rules used in grammars earlier in the text for the same language. A grammar which contains left-recursive rules causes infinite loops to occur when a top-down method of parsing technique, like the one introduced in this subsection, is used. For example, a left-recursive production such as $<e> ::= <e> + <t>$ will cause the parser to try for an $<e>$, which in turn will cause the parser to try for another $<e>$, etc., resulting in an infinite loop. Such pitfalls can be avoided, but we will not go into the remedies in this subsection.

Exercises for Sec. 5-2.3

1. Show that the grammar consisting of the rules

$$<e> ::= (<e>) \mid <e> + <e> \mid <e> - <e> \mid <e> * <e> \mid <e> / <e> \mid i$$

   is ambiguous by constructing all possible trees for the sentences $i + i + i$ and $i + i * i$.

2. Execute the program of Fig. 5-2.10 by hand in order to parse the string (a) $i + i * i$, (b) $i + (i + i)$, and (c) $i * (i + i)$.

3. Formulate a grammar for generating the set of parenthesized arithmetic expressions consisting of the binary operators $+$, $-$, $*$, $/$, and $\uparrow$ (exponentiation), the unary minus operator θ, and the single letter variable i. Write a top-down parser based on recursive descent.

5-2.4 Decision-Table Translation

It is generally accepted that problem analysis is the most important and the most difficult phase in the process of developing a successful computer system. Computer science students are usually introduced to the flowchart as a tool to be used in program design. This tool is, however, primarily useful for simple problems for which the flowchart is relatively uncluttered. As most real computer applications do not fall into the "simple" category, the flowchart is often not used because the graphic complexity necessary to illustrate the solution destroys the clarity and understandability of the tool.

An alternative analysis tool is the *decision table*, which has a format more suited to indicating complex relationships and solutions. The decision table explicitly shows, in a compact format, the manner in which conditions and actions are related. An example of a decision table is shown in Fig. 5-2.11. A decision table is a rectangular table divided into

CHOOSING OUTERWEAR								
Is it raining outside?	Y	Y	Y	Y	N	N	N	N
Is rain forecast?	Y	Y	N	N	Y	Y	N	N
Is temperature warm?	Y	N	Y	N	Y	N	Y	N
Wear a raincoat.	X	X	X	X				
Carry an umbrella.	X	X	X	X	X	X		
Wear a light jacket.					X		X	
Wear a heavy jacket.		X		X		X		X

FIGURE 5-2.11.

four sectors by the intersection of a vertical and a horizontal double line. The table is divided into rows by horizontal single lines; the rows above the double line are *condition rows*, those below are *action rows*. The right two sectors are divided into columns by vertical lines; each column is a *rule*.

The upper-left sector is the *condition stub;* the entries in the condition stub are *conditions* or questions which must be satisfied to solve the problem (e.g., "Is it raining outside?"). The lower-left sector is the *action stub;* it contains the *actions* or events that are within the scope of the problem (e.g., "Wear a raincoat.").

The upper-right sector of a decision table contains *condition entries* which represent condition-answer combinations. Such a condition entry is indicated by "Y", "N", or "–" (a don't care entry), which denote that a condition is true, false, or irrelevant, respectively. Similarly, the lower-right sector of a decision table contains *action entries* which represent action combinations. An "X" indicates the action is to be performed; a blank signifies no action. The action combination specified in a rule is performed only if the corresponding condition combination in the rule is satisfied.

Each decision table rule can be understood as an "if" statement in English (or a programming language with such statements). For example, rule 1 of Fig. 5-2.11 represents the following: "If it is raining outside and rain is forecast and the temperature is warm, then wear a raincoat and carry an umbrella."

Note that the decision table in Fig. 5-2.11 has a header identification name (i.e., CHOOSING OUTERWEAR). This name is used to distinguish this decision table from other tables if a problem solution is defined by more than one decision table. For example, an action in another table might be "GO TO CHOOSING OUTERWEAR."

A decision table should show the actions corresponding to every possible set of condition values. Thus, in a table limited to "Y" and "N" entries, n conditions would require 2^n rules to completely specify the table. One quickly realizes that decision tables of this type could easily become prohibitively large, even for simple problems. (Note that in Fig. 5-2.11 we have $2^3 = 8$ rules for three conditions.)

Referring again to Fig. 5-2.11, notice that the first and third rules belong to one *action set*, that is, the same actions are marked "X" in each rule. Also, note that the condition entries in the rules are the same except for the entry for condition 2. This indicates that the answer to condition 2 is not important if conditions 1 and 3 are both answered "Y." This can be shown by combining these rules and using a "–" (dash) as the entry for condition 2. The "–" indicates a "don't care" or irrelevant answer.

In general, any two rules which belong to one action set and whose condition entries vary in only one row with no "–" entry in the varying row may be combined to form one rule in which the varying row is replaced by a "–" entry. The rules which do not contain a "–" entry are called *simple* rules, while those which do are called *composite* rules. The decision table which results from applying this rule to Fig. 5-2.11 is shown in Fig. 5-2.12.

Another feature designed to reduce the size of this type of decision table is the *ELSE rule*. All rules not explicitly stated in the condition entry are assumed to have the actions specified by the ELSE rule. This feature is most useful when many rules have the same action set.

The introduction of the "don't care" entry and the ELSE rule produces some problems for decision-table manipulation. Rather than stating all possible combinations of

CHOOSING OUTERWEAR						
Is it raining outside?	Y	Y	N	N	N	N
Is rain forecast?	–	–	Y	Y	N	N
Is temperature warm?	Y	N	Y	N	Y	N
Wear a raincoat.	X	X				
Carry an umbrella.	X	X	X	X		
Wear a light jacket.			X		X	
Wear a heavy jacket.		X		X		X

FIGURE 5-2.12.

conditions and then condensing the table, many decision-table designers attempt to create the condensed version of the table in an ad hoc manner. This approach often results in an ambiguous decision table which contains either (1) redundant or overlapping rules, or (2) intrarule inconsistency.

A redundant or overlapping rule occurs when a composite rule can be expanded to produce a rule which already exists in the table, either as a simple rule or the expansion of a different composite rule. If the duplicated rule, referred to as the *overlap rule*, is identical to a rule already in the table, then that rule is *redundant* and can be discarded. If it is not, then one of the composite rules must be changed so that the overlap disappears. If two overlapping rules belong to different action sets, then there is a contradiction in the table which must be corrected. An example of a table with overlapping rules is shown in Fig. 5-2.13.

SAMPLE TABLE					
Condition 1	Y	Y	N	N	N
Condition 2	–	Y	N	Y	–
Condition 3	N	–	Y	Y	N
Action 1	X	X	X		X
Action 2		X		X	X

FIGURE 5-2.13.

Rules 1 and 2 can be expanded to produce the rules Y   Y and Y   Y respectively.

$$
\begin{array}{cc} Y\ N & Y\ Y \\ N\ N & N\ Y \end{array}
$$

Y

Note that the rule Y is present in both cases, and is thus an overlapping rule.

N

Intrarule inconsistency occurs when a rule contains a combination of conditions that is logically impossible. For example, in rule 1 of Fig. 5-2.14 it is impossible for AGE > 65 and AGE < 40 to both be true.

The problem of intrarule inconsistency is best solved by careful planning on the part of the decision-table creator. In a table where such combinations of conditions are desired, those rules which are logically impossible should be specified and error action should be cited if such a rule is satisfied.

The decision tables shown in Figs. 5-2.11 and 5-2.12, in which the condition entries were limited to "Y", "N", or "–", are called *limited-entry* decision tables. Other types of tables in use are called *extended-entry* and *mixed-entry* decision tables. The extended-entry table allows general answers to the condition queries and action specifications. A mixed-entry table combines the features of the other two. Figure 5-2.15 is the decision table in Fig. 5-2.12 changed to an extended-entry table.

In practice, the extended- or mixed-entry table is preferred, as generally any problem can be defined with a shorter (i.e., fewer conditions, actions, and rules) table of these types than with the limited-entry type. However, any mixed- or extended-entry decision table can be translated into an equivalent limited-entry table. Therefore, most literature and theoretical discussion centers on the limited-entry table. Our discussion is restricted to limited-entry tables with composite rules, but no *ELSE* rule. (The interested reader is referred to Montalbano [1974] for a detailed discussion of all further aspects of decision tables.)

An important characteristic of decision tables is that their format is readily suited to mechanical translation. If the decision table accurately and completely specifies the

INSURANCE					
Age < 40	Y	N	N	N	N
Sex = male	–	Y	Y	N	N
Age > 65	–	Y	N	Y	N
Life insurance	X		X		X
Car insurance	X	X	X		

FIGURE 5-2.14.

CHOOSING OUTERWEAR						
Weather outside	Rain	Rain	Clear	Clear	Clear	Clear
Weather forecast	–	–	Rain	Rain	Clear	Clear
Temperature	Warm	Cool	Warm	Cool	Warm	Cool
Top wear	Raincoat	Raincoat				
Carry	Umbrella	Umbrella	Umbrella	Umbrella		
Jacket to wear		Heavy	Light	Heavy	Light	Heavy

FIGURE 5-2.15.

problem, it can be systematically translated into a computer program which successfully solves the problem. The mechanical translation of decision tables is a desirable and efficient step, as the unique thought processes necessary to understand and analyze the problem have already been accomplished.

There are two general methods of decision-table translation—the rule-mask technique, and the flowchart or decision-tree technique. The rule-mask technique uses a binary coding scheme to encode each rule in two vectors. One vector indicates whether an entry requires testing (denoted by a one) or is a "don't care condition" (denoted by a zero). The second vector indicates, for each entry to be tested, whether a "yes" or "no" is required. The translated program evaluates all conditions and constructs a data vector indicating the "yes" and "no" answers. This vector is systematically compared to the rule vectors until a match is found. This method can, however, produce programs which are inefficient with respect to running time, as all conditions must be evaluated even though some conditions may have no bearing on the result.

The flowchart or decision-tree technique tests one condition at a time until sufficient tests have been made to determine which rule satisfies the data. At each condition test, a branch is made to either test the next condition or perform the correct action set, depending on whether the condition is true or false. This process can be represented by a flowchart (or binary-tree structure). It is this second method which is of particular interest to us in this chapter and it is described in detail.

The general technique of flowchart decision-table translation involves the following steps:

1 Select a condition.
2 Generate two subtables from the original table in which the selected condition is deleted. One subtable contains those rules for which the selected condition is *true;* the other contains those for which the condition is *false.* Don't care or "–" entries are added to both subtables.
3 Repeat steps *1* and *2* for each subtable until the table remaining has only one row.

The condition selected in step *1* is represented by a decision box in a flowchart (i.e., a node in a binary tree representation of the flowchart). If the condition tested is *true*, the right branch of the flowchart (i.e., the right link of the binary tree) is followed. If the condition tested is *false*, the left link is traversed. Terminal nodes or leaves represent the action set which corresponds to the condition path.

A first attack would be to select the conditions as they appear in the table. Using this approach the decision tree generated from Fig. 5-2.12 is shown in Fig. 5-2.16.

Figure 5-2.17 shows the flowchart generated by choosing the conditions 1, 3, and 2 in order.

There are two noticeable differences between the flowcharts in Figs. 5-2.16 and 5-2.17. The first difference is that in Fig. 5-2.16 there are seven decision boxes, while in Fig. 5-2.17 there are only five decision boxes. The second difference is that three decisions must be made before any action is reached in Fig. 5-2.16, while only two decisions are necessary to reach rules 1 and 2 in Fig. 5-2.17. Even this simple decision-table example illustrates that the order in which the conditions are chosen can have an important effect on the structure of the flowchart.

There are two possible criteria for decision-table translation:

1. *Processing time:* time necessary to perform tests before an action node is reached.
2. *Program storage requirement:* storage required to hold code which performs the condition tests.

An optimally translated decision-table program is minimized with respect to *either* of these criteria, as it is usually impossible to minimize with respect to both criteria. This discussion only considers optimization of the first criterion. With the cost of storage steadily decreasing in many computer systems, processing time is the more important factor to consider in an optimization strategy.

The usual measure of the processing time associated with a translated decision table is the expected or average processing time. Given a time required for each condition test, a processing time for any path in the decision tree is the sum of the times associated with the conditions encountered in reaching an action node. Given a probability for each path, the expected or average processing time is the weighted sum of the path times, where the weights used are the path probabilities.

The straightforward approach to finding the decision tree with minimum expected processing time would be to calculate the time for all possible trees equivalent to the decision table and to select the one with minimum processing time. This approach is discussed by Reinwald and Soland [1966], who present an algorithm which assures optimality. Unfortunately, this algorithm (although it assures optimality) is less useful in a practical sense, since it is time-consuming and requires that the input limited-entry decision table contains all possible simple rules. We, therefore, consider a less rigorous algorithm by Verhelst [1972] which is less time-consuming and easier to understand, but which provides an algorithm that still approaches the optimum average processing time.

The Verhelst algorithm assumes that no logical relationships exist between the conditions of the table which are not indicated by the "–", "Y", and "N" entries in the condition entry. With this assumption, it can be shown that the maximum test time occurs when all *don't care*'s must be tested. If the probability of occurrence of rule j is denoted by

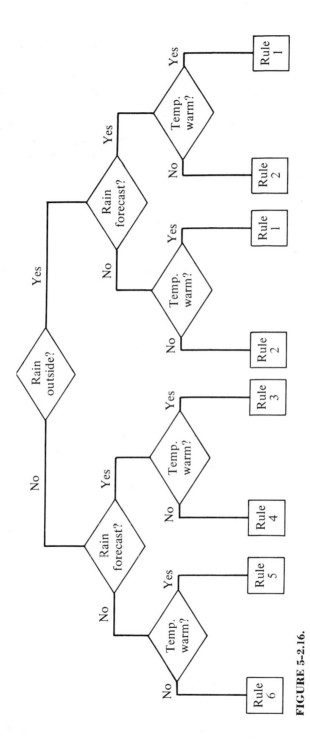

FIGURE 5-2.16.

357

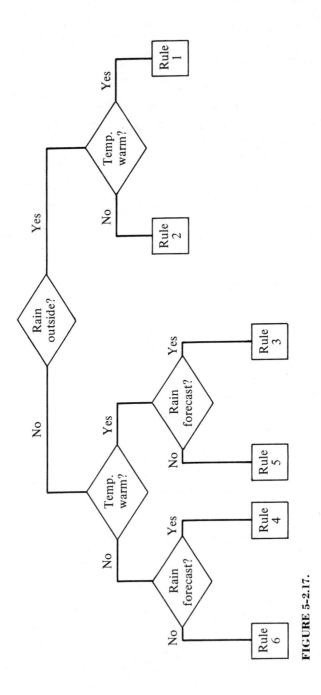

FIGURE 5-2.17.

358

P_j $(j = 1, \ldots, n)$ and the decision time of condition i is denoted by t_i $(i = 1, \ldots, m)$, then the lower bound S of the average decision time can be calculated as follows:

$$S = \sum_{i=1}^{m} [t_i \sum_{j} P_j]$$

for all j in which the answer to condition i is not dashed.

Consider the table in Fig. 5-2.12. If we assign decision times of 1, 3, and 2 to conditions 1, 2, and 3, respectively, and probabilities of .3, .3, .1, .1, .1, .1 to the rules 1 to 6, respectively, then we can calculate S as follows:

$$S = 1(.3 + .3 + .1 + .1 + .1 + .1) + 3(.1 + .1 + .1 + .1)$$

$$+ 2(.3 + .3 + .1 + .1 + .1 + .1)$$

$$= 1 + 1.2 + 2$$

$$= 4.2$$

Hence, the average decision time to test the table is never less than 4.2.

For example, refer to Fig. 5-2.17, which is a flowchart derived from the table in Fig. 5-2.12. The average decision time associated with this flowchart is $.1(6) + .1(6) + .1(6) + .1(6) + .3(3) + .3(3) = 4.2$. Referring to Fig. 5-2.16, if we assume that the frequency of 0.3 for rules 1 and 2 is evenly divided between the "Yes" and "No" answer to condition 2, then the average decision time associated with that flowchart is

$$.1(6) + .1(6) + .1(6) + .1(6) + .15(6) + .15(6) + .15(6) + .15(6)$$

$$= 2.4 + 3.6$$

$$= 6.0$$

The algorithm of Verhelst calculates, for each condition C_i in the table, the quantity

$$T_i = t_i \sum_{j} P_j$$

where t_i is the time necessary to evaluate condition C_i and P_j is the probability associated with rule j. This evaluation is performed for all j in which the condition entry for condition C_i of rule j is a "–" entry. If there is more than one condition with T_i equal to the minimum value of T, the condition with the minimum number of dashes is chosen; otherwise, the condition with minimum T_i is chosen. If both the minimum value of T and number of dashes are equal, then a minimum condition is selected arbitrarily.

The T_i values are calculated from the entire decision table in order to find the root of the decision tree (i.e., the first condition to be tested). Each subsequent node is selected by calculating the T_i values from the appropriate subtable.

As an example, consider again the decision table in Fig. 5-2.12. Using the frequencies and test times previously described, the quantity T_i for each condition would be as follows:

$$T_1 = 0 \qquad \ldots \text{(no "–" entries)}$$

$$T_2 = 3 \,(.3 + .3) = 1.8$$

$$T_3 = 0 \qquad \ldots \text{(no "–" entries)}$$

The number of dashes in condition 1 and 3 are equal. We choose condition 1 to test first because the decision time of condition 1 is less than that of condition 3. This divides the original table into subtables, as shown in Fig. 5-2.18. Note that the condition and action stubs and the action entry have been omitted for graphic simplicity. We now consider the two subtables labeled ① and ② in Fig. 5-2.18. For subtable 1, the T values are as follows:

$$T_2' = 3(.3 + .3) = 1.8$$

$$T_3' = 0$$

The value of T_3' is the lowest; therefore, we choose to test condition 3 next, resulting in the subtables 3 and 4. For subtable 2, the T values are both zero; therefore, we can choose to test either condition 2 or 3. The subtables resulting from choosing condition 3 are shown.

The flowchart which is determined by the preceding process is shown in Fig. 5-2.19. Note that no further tests need to be made when the subtable contains one rule that is all dash entries. This flowchart has an average test time of 4.2, which is equal to the lower bound calculated previously. Thus the Verhelst algorithm has, for this simple example, produced the optimum flowchart. For a more complex table, this algorithm would generally create a flowchart for which the average test time approached the lower bound.

To summarize this method, those conditions with the smallest number of "don't care" entries are generally chosen first, thus minimizing the size of the subtables and resulting subtrees at each step. If there is a tie at a particular point in the construction process, then the condition which has the lowest decision time is chosen, thus delaying the testing of those conditions which require more time for evaluation.

The algorithm just discussed produces a decision tree for which the expected processing time approaches the minimum, given a limited-entry decision table with no ELSE rule, no ambiguities, and with the number of rules minimized by the introduction of "don't care" entries.

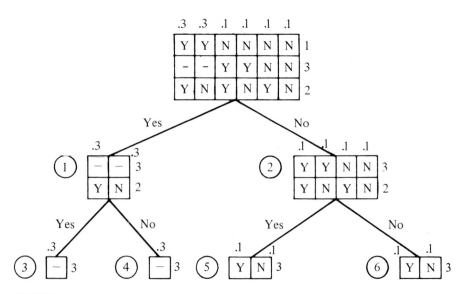

FIGURE 5-2.18.

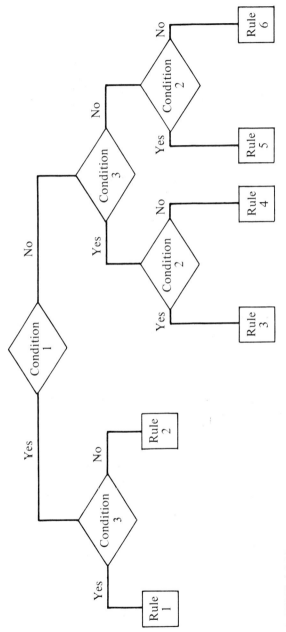

FIGURE 5-2.19.

361

In the remainder of this section, we develop a formal algorithm for constructing a binary decision tree for a given decision table based on the method of Dial [1970], with the exception that the condition-selection subalgorithm is the Verhelst method previously discussed. For simplicity, we assume that one action satisfies each rule; that is, identical action groups are combined so that they can be referenced by one action.

The solution which performs the translation of the limited-entry decision table into an optimum-approaching decision tree consists of the main algorithm DT_TRAN and the three subalgorithms SELECT_COND, SPLIT_TABLE, and SHIFT. SELECT_COND chooses the condition that satisfies the previously discussed criteria, SPLIT_TABLE builds the decision tree, and SHIFT creates the subtables. This decision tree can be traversed to generate a program in any language, providing changes are made to account for the input-character representation of the conditions and actions in the target programming language.

The decision table is stored in two arrays. The two-dimensional array D_TAB contains the condition entry of the table; the (i, j) element of D_TAB is a 'Y', 'N' or '–' corresponding to the entry for condition i in rule j. RULE is a vector which contains integer elements representing the action set corresponding to a particular rule. The value of an element of RULE is used to subscript a vector containing the character representation of each action set.

Two other vectors are necessary in the algorithm; namely, TIME[i] is the time necessary to evaluate condition i and P[j] is the relative frequency of occurrence of rule j. The values of P are estimated by the decision-table creator who is familiar with the problem and can approximate what percentage of the cases satisfy each rule.

It is excessively storage- and time-consuming to recopy parts of the D_TAB array in order to create the subtables. To avoid this, two vectors, ROW and COL, are used to indicate the table under present consideration. The first LROW elements of ROW are subscripts to the conditions in D_TAB in the present table; the FCOL to LCOL elements of COL are subscripts to the rules in D_TAB in the present table.

The example decision table, shown in Fig. 5-2.12, is represented by the following values of the described vectors and arrays:

```
D_TAB     Y  Y  N  N  N  N
          –  –  Y  Y  N  N
          Y  N  Y  N  Y  N
RULE      1  2  3  4  5  6
```

(*Note:* Each rule element contains a different number, since there is a different group of actions corresponding to each rule:)

```
TIME    1
        3
        2
P      .3 .3 .1 .1 .1 .1
```

The initial values of the ROW and COL vectors are

```
ROW    1 2 3                LROW = 3
COL    1 2 3 4 5 6          FCOL = 1    LCOL = 6
```

We now present the algorithm which selects the conditions to be tested according to the previous criterion.

Algorithm SELECT_COND. Given LROW (the maximum subscript to the ROW vector), and FCOL and LCOL (subscripts to the COL vector), Algorithm SELECT_COND returns a subscript to an element of ROW. This element of ROW indexes the condition which satisfies the selection criterion. SUM1 and SUM2 calculate $T_i = t_i \sum_j P_j$ and the dash count, respectively. MIN is the value of the minimum T_i and LOC is a subscript to ROW such that $T_{ROW[LOC]}$ = MIN. DASH_CT is a vector for the number of dashes in each row; i and j are subscript variables.

1. [Initialize] Set MIN ← 999999, LOC ← 0, and i ← 0.
2. [Establish row examination] Set i ← i + 1.
   If i > LROW, then go to step 6.
3. [Calculate dash count and $\sum_j P_j$] Set SUM1 ← SUM2 ← 0,

   repeat for j = FCOL, FCOL + 1, ..., LCOL:
      if D_TAB[ROW[i], COL[j]] = '—'
      then set SUM1 ← SUM1 + P[COL[j]], SUM2 ← SUM2 + 1.
4. [Finish calculation; compare with minimum]
   Set SUM1 ← SUM1 * TIME[ROW[i]], DASH_CT[i] ← SUM2.
   If SUM1 < MIN, then set MIN ← SUM1, LOC ← i, and go to step 2.
5. [Compare dash count if SUM1 = MIN]
   If SUM1 = MIN,
   then if DASH_CT[i] < DASH_CT[LOC], then set LOC ← i.
   Go to step 2.
6. [Check if row contains all don't care elements]
   Set SELECT_COND ← LOC,
   if LOC > 0,
   then if DASH_CT[LOC] = LCOL − FCOL + 1, then set SELECT_COND ← 0.
   Exit.

In step 1 the subscripts are initialized; MIN is set to 999999 on the assumption that no T value will be greater than 999999. In step 2 the ROW subscript i is incremented and a range check is performed. In step 3 the working variables SUM1 and SUM2 are initialized. A loop is made through each column of the ith row; SUM1 is incremented by the P value for the column and SUM2 is incremented by 1, for each dash element in the row. In step 4 the T calculation is completed and the number of dashes is saved in the DASH_CT vector. The calculated T value is compared to the minimum at this point and the minimum pointers are updated if necessary. If the calculated T value is equal to the minimum, the row with the lower number of dashes is chosen; this is performed in step 5. Step 6 sets the value of the algorithm and checks for a row of all dashes, returning a value of zero in that case.

The next algorithm, SHIFT, creates the subtables for each selected condition row by rearranging the elements of COL. The first (FDASH − 1) entries of COL contain subscripts to those rules which contain an "N" in the selected row. The elements from FDASH to

(FYES − 1) contain subscripts to rules with "−" entries, and the remaining elements reference the "Y" entries. The algorithm recursively calls itself to arrange the "−" entries.

As an example, consider condition 2 of Fig. 5-2.12 as the selected condition. It has the following configuration:

Rule:	1	2	3	4	5	6
Value:	−	−	Y	Y	N	N

and the corresponding COL vector has the following value:

COL	1	2	3	4	5	6

After executing the SHIFT algorithm, the COL vector would be the following:

COL	6	5	1	2	4	3

Algorithm SHIFT.   Given ROW (the condition upon which the subtables are to be created), FIRST and LAST (the boundaries on the elements COL[FIRST], ..., COL[LAST] which indicate the rules of the table), FDASH and FYES (variables whose values are set to indicate the position in COL of the element representing the first "−" entry and the first "Y" entry, respectively), and KEY (the entry character "N", "−", or "Y" which indicates which rules are to be shifted leftmost in the rule), Algorithm SHIFT rearranges the elements of COL and sets the values of FDASH and FYES. In the previous example, FDASH and FYES are initially set to 3 and 5, respectively.

1. [Initialize]   Set i ← FIRST and j ← LAST.
2. [Skip leftmost entries equal to KEY]
   Repeat while D_TAB[ROW, COL[i]] = KEY and i ≤ j:
       set i ← i + 1.
3. [Find rightmost KEY entry]
   Repeat while D_TAB[ROW, COL[j]] ≠ KEY and j > i:
       set j ← j − 1.
4. [Interchange]   If i < j, then set COL[i] ↔ COL[j], j ← j − 1 and go to step 2.
5. [Set boundary marker and recall if necessary]
   Set FDASH ← i.
   If KEY ≠ '−', then call SHIFT(ROW, i, LAST, FYES, FDASH, '−').
   Exit.

In step 1, the subscripts to the COL vector are initialized; i will traverse COL from the bottom or left and j from the top or right. In step 2 the leftmost entries of COL that subscript KEY elements of D_TAB are skipped by incrementing i. When an entry not equal to KEY is encountered, step 3 is performed and j is decremented until it subscripts the rightmost element of COL indexing a KEY entry of D_TAB. Then, in step 4, the ith element and the jth element of COL are interchanged, thus moving the KEY subscripting element to the left in the vector. Note that if no pointers to KEY elements exist to the right of the ith element, the test in step 4 would fail and no switch would be made. Step 5 is performed when all elements of COL have been checked. FDASH is set to i to point to the first non-

"KEY" subscript. If KEY is not '–' then the algorithm is called recursively to shift the '–' element subscripts to the immediate right of the KEY element subscripts.

Figure 5-2.20 shows a sequence of steps resulting from the application of Algorithm SHIFT to a condition with the following configuration:

```
index    1  2  3  4  5  6
D_TAB    –  Y  –  Y  N  N
COL      1  2  3  4  5  6
```

The figure shows the execution of the algorithm on the above configuration with parameters at the initial call being

```
FIRST = 1
LAST  = 6
KEY   = 'N'
```

The next algorithm makes use of the two previously discussed algorithms to create the decision tree. A condition is chosen and a corresponding node created; the subtrees are established, and the subtrees corresponding to each condition are created recursively.

Each node of the tree has the following format:

LPTR	NODE_VAL	RPTR

NODE_VAL may contain a subscript to either a condition or action phrase, or may contain zero to indicate no corresponding action rule was input (an error situation). LPTR and RPTR are the links to the "N" and "Y" subtrees, respectively. RPTR = LPTR = NULL indicates a terminal or action node.

Algorithm SPLIT_TABLE.   Given LROW (subscript to ROW) and FCOL and LCOL (subscripts to COL), Algorithm SPLIT_TABLE recursively creates the decision tree corresponding to the table defined by the ROW and COL vectors. The algorithm returns the pointer to the root of the tree created. SUB is the subscript to the selected element of ROW; COND is the selected condition, that is, COND = ROW[SUB]. SAVE is a vector to save the values of the P vector in which those elements corresponding to "–" entries are divided in half for the subtables. PTR is a pointer to the node most recently retrieved from the AVAIL stack; FIRSTDASH and FIRSTYES are subscripts to elements of COL representing the first "–" and "Y" entries, respectively.

1. [Select condition]   Set SUB ← SELECT_COND(LROW, FCOL, LCOL),
   if SUB ≠ 0,
   then set PTR ⇐ NODE, COND ← NODE_VAL(PTR) ← ROW[SUB], ROW[SUB] ←
   ROW[LROW];
   otherwise, go to step 5.
2. [Create subtables and save probability vector]
   Call SHIFT(COND, FCOL, LCOL, FIRSTDASH, FIRSTYES, 'N').
   Repeat for i = FCOL, FCOL + 1, ..., LCOL: SAVE[COL[i]] = P[COL[i]].

3. [Divide frequency for dashed entries in half; create subtree corresponding to 'N' subtable.]

Repeat for i = FIRSTDASH, FIRSTDASH + 1 ..., FIRSTYES − 1:

    P[COL[i]] = P[COL[i]]/2.

Set LPTR(PTR) ← SPLIT_TABLE(LROW − 1, FCOL, FIRSTYES − 1).

4. [Reset COL entries rearranged in recursion; create the subtree corresponding to 'Y' subtable, and restore probability vector].

Call SHIFT(COND,FCOL, FIRSTYES − 1, FIRSTDASH, FIRSTYES, 'N').

Set RPTR(PTR) ← SPLIT_TABLE(LROW − 1, FIRSTDASH, LCOL),

SPLIT_TABLE ← PTR, and ROW[SUB] ← COND.

Repeat for i = FCOL, FCOL + 1, ..., LCOL:

    P[COL[i]] = SAVE[COL[i]].

Exit.

5. [Create a terminal (action) node]. Set PTR ⇐ NODE,

SPLIT_TABLE ← PTR, and LPTR(PTR) ← RPTR(PTR) ← NULL.

If FCOL > LCOL,

then set NODE_VAL(PTR) ← 0;

otherwise, set NODE_VAL(PTR) ← COL[FCOL].

Exit

In step 1 of this algorithm, SELECT_COND is called to determine which condition of the decision table should be tested next. If the condition selected does not contain all 'don't care' entries, a node is created to represent that condition being tested. The value of the node is the subscript to the row. The chosen element in the ROW vector is replaced by the last element in the vector in order to compact the ROW vector. (If the condition selected in step 1 does contain all 'don't care' entries, a terminal node is created in step 5.)

In step 2 Algorithm SHIFT is called to rearrange the elements of the COL vector to group effectively the 'N', '−', and 'Y' elements of the chosen condition. The probability vector P is copied into the vector SAVE.

In step 3 the P values for the '−' elements are halved; then Algorithm SPLIT_TABLE is called recursively to create a subtree corresponding to those rules of the decision table which contained an 'N' or '−' element in the condition chosen in step 1. The LPTR of the node created in step 1 points to this subtree.

After the subtree is complete, step 4 is performed. In this step Algorithm SHIFT is called to rearrange the COL vector which was disturbed during the recursive creation of the 'N' subtree. Then the algorithm is called recursively to create the subtree corresponding to the '−' and 'Y' elements. Upon completion of the 'Y' subtree, the value of the algorithm is set to the node created in step 1, and the chosen element of ROW is reset to its original value. The cleanup continues with the P vector restored to its original values, and then the algorithm halts.

In step 5 a terminal node of the tree is created, indicating a row containing all '−' entries or the absence of any rows at all (i.e., all rows exhausted implies that all conditions are satisfied). A zero value in the terminal node indicates that there is no action which corresponds to the sequence of condition replies that leads to this node. A nonzero value is the index to the column in the original decision table which corresponds to the sequence of condition replies indicated by the path from the start to this terminal node.

Initial call: SHIFT(ROW, 1, 6, X, Y, 'N')
D_TAB[ROW] = − Y − Y N N
COL   = 1 2 3 4 5 6

Step	Description		Vector COL					

Step   Description   *Vector* COL

1. i ← 1, j ← 6   1   2   3   4   5   6
2. D_TAB[ROW, COL[1]] ≠ 'N', go to step 3   ↑   ↑
3. D_TAB[ROW, COL[6]] = 'N', go to step 4   i   j
4. exchange COL[1] and COL[6], j ← 5, go to step 2   6   2   3   4   5   1
                                                                 ↑   ↑

                                                                 i   j
2. D_TAB[ROW, COL[1]] = 'N', i ← 2   6   2   3   4   5   1
    D_TAB[ROW, COL[2]] ≠ 'N', go to step 3   ↑   ↑
3. D_TAB[ROW, COL[5]] = 'N', go to step 4   i   j
4. exchange COL[2] and COL[5], j ← 4, go to step 2   6   5   3   4   2   1
                                                                     ↑   ↑

                                                                     i   j
2. D_TAB[ROW, COL[2]] = 'N', i ← 3   6   5   3   4   2   1
    D_TAB[ROW, COL[3]] ≠ 'N', go to step 3   ↑   ↑
                                                                         i   j

3. D_TAB[ROW, COL[4]] ≠ 'N', j ← 3   6   5   3   4   2   1
    i = j, go to step 4   ↑
4. i = j, go to step 5   i,j
5. X ← 3, KEY ≠ '-',
    call SHIFT(ROW, 3, 6, Y, X, '-'), return.

Second call: SHIFT(ROW, 3, 6, Y, X, '-')

1. i ← 3, j ← 6   6   5   3   4   2   1
                                                                         ↑   ↑

                                                                         i   j
2. D_TAB[ROW, COL[3]] = '-', i ← 4   6   5   3   4   2   1
    D_TAB[ROW, COL[4]] ≠ '-', go to step 3   ↑   ↑
3. D_TAB[ROW, COL[6]] = '-', go to step 4   i   j
4. exchange COL[4] and COL[6], j ← 5, go to step 2   6   5   3   1   2   4
                                                                             ↑   ↑

                                                                             i   j
2. D_TAB[ROW, COL[4]] = '-', i ← 5   6   5   3   1   2   4
    D_TAB[ROW, COL[5]] ≠ '-', go to step 3   ↑
3. i = j, go to step 4   i,j
4. i = j, go to step 5
5. Y ← 5, KEY = '-', return.

FIGURE 5-2.20   Sample trace of Algorithm SHIFT.

Algorithm DT_TRAN inputs the decision table and calls the Algorithm SPLIT_TABLE, to create the tree structure corresponding to the decision table.

Algorithm DT_TRAN.   This algorithm inputs a decision table and creates an equivalent decision tree with an expected processing time which approaches the optimum. HEAD points to the root of the decision tree; ACTION # is the number of action sets. COND_ PHRASE and ACT_PHRASE are vectors containing the character representation of the condition stub entries and action phrases, respectively. The values of these vectors depend upon the computer language to which the table is to be translated. In this implementation, the input to COND_PHRASE must be valid relational expressions (for example, X > Y, NAME = 'BOB', NAME = 'JIM'); the input to ACT_PHRASE must be valid PL/I statements (e.g., 'GO TO STOP_ACT', 'CALL MAKE_NEW', 'Q = 3*Y').

1. [Input size of condition table.]
   Read LROW, LCOL, ACTION #, and set FCOL ← 1.
2. [Input table row by row].
   Repeat for i = 1, 2, ..., LROW:
       repeat for j = 1, 2, ..., LCOL:
           read D_TAB[i, j].
3. [Input conditions and actions].
   Repeat for i = 1, 2, ..., LROW: read COND_PHRASE[i].
   Repeat for i = 1, 2, ..., LCOL: read ACT_PHRASE[i].
4. [Input times and frequencies].
   Repeat for i = 1, 2, ..., LROW: read TIME[i].
   Repeat for i = 1, 2, ..., LCOL: read P[i].
5. [Initialize ROW and COL].
   Repeat for i = 1, 2, ..., LROW: set ROW[i] ← i,
   repeat for i = 1, 2, ..., LCOL: set COL[i] ← i.
6. [Build tree.]   Set HEAD ← SPLIT_TABLE(LROW, FCOL, LCOL) and Exit.

Once the tree has been created it can be traversed by various routines to translate it into the equivalent code of different programming languages. Such a routine is shown in Fig. 5-2.21. The procedure INTERPRET recursively traverses the tree to create a PL/I IF statement which corresponds to a branch in the tree. The parameter I is used to maintain proper indentation of the code.

The program implementation of the other algorithms in this section is not shown since the programs closely resemble the algorithms given.

5-3   MULTILINKED STRUCTURES

The data structures that we have discussed to this point in the text have contained one or two pointer fields. Except for the tree structures, the structures which contained two pointer fields specified the relation of physical adjacency.

In this section we generalize the structures in the sense that more than two pointer fields can be used in the node structure. The first application is concerned with the representation and manipulation of sparse matrices. Section 5-3.2 discusses the problem of generating an index of terms for a book.

```
INTERPRET: PROCEDURE(ROOT,I) RECURSIVE;

/*  PROCEDURE INTERPRET RECURSIVELY TRAVERSES THE BINARY TREE WITH */
/*     ROOT NODE 'ROOT' AND CREATES PL/1 CODE WHICH IS EQUIVALENT */
/*     TO THE FLOWCHART THE TREE REPRESENTS.                      */

    DECLARE ROOT POINTER,
            I FIXED BINARY,
            CLAUSE CHARACTER(36) VARYING;

    IF ROOT->RPTR ¬= NULL
    THEN DO;
        CLAUSE = COND_PHRASE(ROOT->NODE_VAL);
        PUT SKIP EDIT ('IF',CLAUSE) (COLUMN(I),A(3),A);
        PUT SKIP EDIT ('THEN') (COLUMN(I),A);
        CALL INTERPRET(ROOT->RPTR, I + 5);
        PUT SKIP EDIT ('ELSE') (COLUMN(I),A);
        CALL INTERPRET(ROOT->LPTR, I + 5);
    END;
    ELSE DO;
        IF ROOT->NODE_VAL = 0
        THEN PUT EDIT(';') (A(1));
        ELSE PUT EDIT(ACT_PHRASE(RULE(ROOT->NODE_VAL)),';')
                     (COLUMN(I),A,A(1));
    END;
END INTERPRET;
```

FIGURE 5-2.21. PL/I procedure for decision-table generator.

5-3.1 Sparse Matrices

A useful application of linear lists is the representation of matrices that contain a preponderance of zero elements. These matrices are called *sparse* matrices. They are commonly used in scientific applications and contain hundreds or even thousands of rows and columns. The representation of such large matrices is wasteful of storage, and operations with these matrices are inefficient if the sequential allocation methods of Chap. 3 are used for their storage. In this section we describe a representation of sparse matrices using linked allocation and formulate an input algorithm and a multiplication algorithm for matrices in this form. First, however, a different type of sequential allocation scheme for representing sparse matrices is discussed.

Consider the matrix

$$A = \begin{bmatrix} 0 & 0 & 6 & 0 & 9 & 0 & 0 \\ 2 & 0 & 0 & 7 & 8 & 0 & 4 \\ 10 & 0 & 0 & 0 & 0 & 0 & 0 \\ 0 & 0 & 12 & 0 & 0 & 0 & 0 \\ 0 & 0 & 0 & 0 & 0 & 0 & 0 \\ 0 & 0 & 0 & 3 & 0 & 0 & 5 \end{bmatrix}$$

Of the 42 elements in this 6×7 matrix, only 10 are nonzero. These are

$$A[1, 3] = 6, \ A[1, 5] = 9, \ A[2, 1] = 2, \ A[2, 4] = 7, \ A[2, 5] = 8,$$

$$A[2, 7] = 4, \ A[3, 1] = 10, \ A[4, 3] = 12, \ A[6, 4] = 3, \text{ and } A[6, 7] = 5.$$

One of the basic methods for storing such a sparse matrix is to store nonzero elements in a one-dimensional array and to identify each array element with row and column indices, as shown in Fig. 5-3.1a.

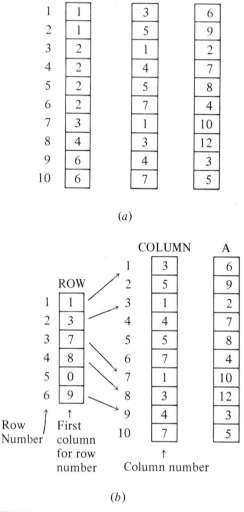

(a)

(b)

FIGURE 5-3.1   Sequential representation of sparse matrices.

The ith element of vector **A** is the matrix element with row and column indices ROW[i] and COLUMN[i]. Note that the matrix elements are stored in row-major order with zero elements removed. A more efficient representation in terms of storage requirements and access time to the rows of the matrix is shown in Fig. 5-3.1b. The ROW vector is changed so that its ith element is the index to the first of the column indices for the elements in row i of the matrix.

We assume that the ROW and COLUMN vectors consist of half words. The representations of matrix A in Fig. 5-3.1 have cut storage requirements by more than one half.

For large matrices the conservation of storage is very significant. This sequential-allocation scheme for sparse matrices is also of value in that matrix operations can be executed faster than possible with a conventional two-dimensional array representation, particularly when matrices are large. The following algorithm adds two matrices that are represented as in Fig. 5-3.1b.

Algorithm MATRIX_ADDITION. Given sparse matrices A and B represented by vectors A and B with row and column indices AROW and ACOL and BROW and BCOL, respectively, it is required to form the matrix sum C = A + B. C must be represented in the same manner as A and B, so indices CROW and CCOL are formed. A and B have the same dimensions, m × n, and contain r and s nonzero elements, respectively. The number of nonzero elements in C on completion of the algorithm is t. Auxiliary variable i is used to index the rows of the matrices, and j and k index the matrix elements in vectors A and B, respectively. Variables SUM and COLUMN are used to contain each new element for matrix C and its column position.

1. [Initialize] Set $i \leftarrow 1$ and $t \leftarrow 0$.
2. [Scan each row] Repeat steps 3 to 10 while $i \leq m$. Exit.
3. [Obtain row indices and starting positions of next rows]
   Set $j \leftarrow$ AROW[i], $k \leftarrow$ BROW[i], and CROW[i] $\leftarrow t + 1$.
   Set AMAX $\leftarrow$ BMAX $\leftarrow 0$.
   If $i < m$,
   then
   　　repeat for $p = i + 1, i + 2, \ldots, m$ while AMAX $= 0$:
   　　　　if AROW[p] $\neq 0$, then set AMAX $\leftarrow$ AROW[p],
   　　repeat for $p = i + 1, i + 2, \ldots, m$ while BMAX $= 0$:
   　　　　if BROW[p] $\neq 0$, then set BMAX $\leftarrow$ BROW[p].
   If AMAX $= 0$, then set AMAX $\leftarrow r + 1$.
   If BMAX $= 0$, then set BMAX $\leftarrow s + 1$.
4. [Scan columns of this row]
   Repeat steps 5 to 9 while $j \neq 0$ or $k \neq 0$.
5. [End of either row?]
   If $j = 0$,
   then set SUM $\leftarrow$ B[k], COLUMN $\leftarrow$ BCOL[k], $k \leftarrow k + 1$, and go to step 8.
   If $k = 0$,
   then set SUM $\leftarrow$ A[j], COLUMN $\leftarrow$ ACOL[j], $j \leftarrow j + 1$, and go to step 8.
6. [Elements in same columns?]
   If ACOL[j] $=$ BCOL[k],
   then set SUM $\leftarrow$ A[j] $+$ B[k], COLUMN $\leftarrow$ ACOL[j], $j \leftarrow j + 1$, $k \leftarrow k + 1$,
   and go to step 8.
7. [Does A column precede B column?]
   If ACOL[j] $<$ BCOL[k],
   then set SUM $\leftarrow$ A[j], COLUMN $\leftarrow$ ACOL[j], and $j \leftarrow j + 1$;
   otherwise, set SUM $\leftarrow$ B[k], COLUMN $\leftarrow$ BCOL[k], and $k \leftarrow k + 1$.
8. [Add new element to sum of matrices]
   If SUM $\neq 0$, then set $t \leftarrow t + 1$, C[t] $\leftarrow$ SUM, and CCOL[t] $\leftarrow$ COLUMN.

9. [End of either row?]
    If j = AMAX, then set j ← 0.
    If k = BMAX, then set k ← 0.
10. [Adjust index to matrix C and increment row index]
    If t < CROW[i], then set CROW[i] ← 0.
    Set i ← i + 1.

For each pair of corresponding rows in matrices A and B, steps 3 to 10 are executed to add matrix elements from those rows. When j or k is zero, the nonzero elements in the row of matrix A or B, respectively, have all been accounted for. When both j and k are zero, the algorithm can proceed to add the next rows of the matrices. If j or k are not initially zero, they are set to zero when they reach the values AMAX or BMAX, respectively. AMAX and BMAX are the positions in the ACOL and A and BCOL and B vectors where the next row starts. However, if there is no next row, AMAX and BMAX have values r + 1 and s + 1, respectively (see steps 3 and 9).

Steps 5 to 7 inclusive perform the required additions of matrix elements. A number of different cases arise, depending on whether the row of one matrix has been completely scanned, the column indices are equal, or one column index is less than the other. Step 8 checks for an element having a value of zero before adding it to matrix C. If no elements are added to row i of matrix C, then CROW[i] is set to zero in step 10.

Sequential-allocation schemes for representing sparse matrices generally allow faster execution of matrix operations and are more storage efficient than linked-allocation schemes. Representing sparse matrices sequentially, however, has the shortcomings we have discussed earlier. The insertion and deletion of matrix elements necessitates the displacement of many other elements. In situations where insertions and deletions are common, a linked-allocation scheme such as described in the following discussion should be adopted.

To represent sparse matrices, a basic node structure called MATRIX_ELEMENT as depicted in Fig. 5-3.2 is required. The V, R, and C fields of one of these nodes contain the value, row, and column indices, respectively, of one matrix element. The fields LEFT and UP are pointers to the next element in a circular list containing matrix elements for a row or column, respectively. LEFT points to the node with the next smallest column subscript and UP points to the node with the next smallest row subscript. A multilinked structure that uses nodes of this type to represent the matrix A described previously in this section is given in Fig. 5-3.3.

A circular list represents each row and column. A column's list can share nodes with one or more of the rows' lists. Each row and column list has a head node so that more efficient insertion and deletion algorithms can be implemented. The head node of each row

LEFT	UP	
V	R	C

MATRIX_ELEMENT

FIGURE 5-3.2 Node structure for linked-allocation representation of a sparse matrix.

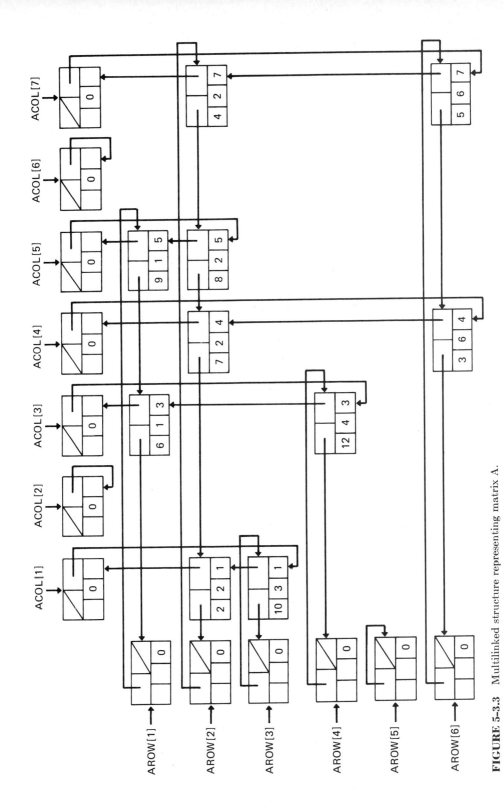

FIGURE 5-3.3 Multilinked structure representing matrix A.

list contains 0 in the C field; similarly, the head node of each column list has 0 in the R field. The row head nodes are pointed to by respective elements in the array of pointers AROW. Elements of ACOL point to the column head nodes. A row or column without nonzero elements is represented by a head node whose LEFT or UP field points to itself.

The pointers in this multilinked structure arouse suspicion because they point up and to the left. In scanning a circular list we therefore encounter matrix elements in order of decreasing row or column subscripts. This approach is used to simplify addition of new nodes to the structure. We assume that new nodes being added to a matrix are usually ordered by ascending-row subscript and ascending-column subscript. If this is the case, a new node is inserted following the head node all of the time and no searching of the list is necessary. This is illustrated by the matrix multiplication algorithm at the end of this section.

We now present an algorithm for constructing a multilinked structure representing a matrix, as represented in Fig. 5-3.3. It is assumed that input records for the algorithm consist of row, column, and nonzero matrix-element values in arbitrary order. No duplicate elements are input to the algorithm.

Algorithm CONSTRUCT_MATRIX.   It is required to form a multilinked representation of a matrix using the MATRIX_ELEMENT node structure previously described. The matrix dimensions m and n, representing the number of rows and number of columns, respectively, are known before execution of the algorithm. Arrays AROW and ACOL contain pointers to the head nodes of the circular lists. X and Y are used as auxiliary pointers. A row index, column index, and value of a matrix element are read into variables ROW, COLUMN, and VALUE, respectively.

1. [Initialize matrix structures]
    Repeat for i = 1, 2, ..., m:
        set AROW[i] ⇐ MATRIX_ELEMENT, C(AROW[i]) ← 0,
        and LEFT(AROW[i]) ← AROW[i].
    Repeat for i = 1, 2, ..., n:
        set ACOL[i] ⇐ MATRIX_ELEMENT, R(ACOL[i]) ← 0,
        and UP(ACOL[i]) ← ACOL[i].
2. [Obtain a matrix element and its row and column indices]
    Read ROW, COLUMN, and VALUE.
    If input records are exhausted, then Exit.
3. [Allocate and initialize a node]
    Set P ⇐ MATRIX_ELEMENT, R(P) ← ROW, C(P) ← COLUMN, and V(P) ← VALUE.
4. [Find new node's position in row list]
    Set Q ← AROW[R(P)].
    Repeat while C(P) < C(LEFT(Q)):   set Q ← LEFT(Q).
    Set LEFT(P) ← LEFT(Q) and LEFT(Q) ← P.
5. [Find new node's position in column list]
    Set Q ← ACOL[C(P)]
    Repeat while R(P) < R(UP(Q)):   set Q ← UP(Q).
    Set UP(P) ← UP(Q) and UP(Q) ← P.
    Go to step 2.

In step 1 of Algorithm CONSTRUCT_MATRIX, the required head nodes are allocated and initialized. For each ROW, COLUMN, and VALUE triplet subsequently read, a node is allocated and initialized. Steps 4 and 5 insert the new node in the appropriate row and column lists, respectively.

We now formulate an algorithm for multiplying two matrices, as represented in Fig. 5-3.3. When two matrices A and B are multiplied to form matrix C, that is, C = A × B, it is necessary that the number of columns in A equal the number of rows in B. If A has m rows and n columns, and B has n rows and t columns, then the product matrix C will have m rows and t columns. The elements of matrix C are

$$C[i, j] = \sum_{k=1}^{n} (A[i, k] \times B[k, j]) \qquad 1 \leq i \leq m, 1 \leq j \leq t$$

Algorithm MATRIX_MULTIPLICATION.   Given the pointer arrays AROW, ACOL, BROW, and BCOL pointing to multilinked representations of sparse matrices A and B with dimensions m × n and n × t, respectively, it is required to form the representation of the product matrix C = A × B. Pointer arrays CROW and CCOL are used to point to rows and columns of the matrix C, which has dimensions m × t. Variables i and j are used to count the rows of matrix A and the columns of matrix B, respectively. A and B are used as pointers for scanning the rows of matrix A and columns of matrix B. P is an auxiliary pointer.

1. [Set up head nodes for row lists]
    Repeat for i = 1, 2, . . ., m:
        set CROW[i] ⇐ MATRIX_ELEMENT, C(CROW[i]) ← 0,
        and LEFT(CROW[i]) ← CROW[i].
2. [Set up head nodes for column lists]
    Repeat for j = 1, 2, . . ., t:
        set CCOL[j] ⇐ MATRIX_ELEMENT, R(CCOL[j]) ← 0,
        and UP(CCOL[j]) ← CCOL[j].
3. [Use m rows of matrix A]
    Repeat steps 4 to 7 for i = 1, 2, . . ., m.
4. [Use t columns of matrix B]
    Repeat steps 5 to 7 for j = 1, 2, . . ., t.
5. [Initialize for scanning row i of matrix A and column j of matrix B]
    Set A ← LEFT(AROW[i]), B ← UP(BCOL[j]), and PRODUCT ← 0.
6. [Move pointers as necessary and multiply matching elements]
    Repeat while R(B) ≠ 0 and C(A) ≠ 0:
        if C(A) > R(B),
        then set A ← LEFT(A);
        otherwise,
            if R(B) > C(A)
            then set B ← UP(B);
            otherwise, set PRODUCT ← PRODUCT + V(A) * V(B),
                A ← LEFT(A), and B ← UP(B).

7. [If product is nonzero add it to matrix C]
    If PRODUCT $\neq$ 0,
    then set P $\Leftarrow$ MATRIX_ELEMENT, R(P) $\leftarrow$ i, C(P) $\leftarrow$ j, V(P) $\leftarrow$ PRODUCT,
        LEFT(P) $\leftarrow$ LEFT(CROW[i]), UP(P) $\leftarrow$ UP(CCOL[j]), LEFT(CROW[i]) $\leftarrow$ P,
        and UP(CCOL[j]) $\leftarrow$ P.
8. [Finished]   Exit.

Steps 1 and 2 initialize the head nodes for the product matrix C. Steps 3 and 4 provide the repetitions necessary to multiply each row of matrix A by each column of matrix B in steps 5 to 7, inclusively. Step 5 initializes pointers A and B to scan the circular lists of row i of matrix A and column j of matrix B, respectively. The variable PRODUCT is initialized in this step, and it will be used to total the products of corresponding row and column elements.

In step 6, note that row i and column j are being scanned in order of decreasing column and row subscripts, respectively. If the column subscript and row subscript of the nodes pointed to by A and B, respectively, are not equal, then one pointer is moved to the next node in the circular list. If those row and column subscripts are equal, however, then the variable PRODUCT is updated and both pointers A and B are changed to point to the next elements in each list. When the head node in either list is reached, the required product of row i and column j has been computed.

Step 7 allocates and initializes a new node if PRODUCT is nonzero. Because rows and columns are being scanned according to increasing subscript values, and because pointers in the nodes point left and up in the list structure, the new node can be inserted as successor to the head nodes of row i and column j.

A PL/I implementation of Algorithm MATRIX_MULTIPLICATION as a procedure is given in Fig. 5-3.4. Several extra statements are needed because subscripted pointers cannot be used as pointer qualifiers in PL/I. An intermediate assignment to an element variable pointer must first be made.

Exercises for Sec. 5-3.1

1. Write and test a computer program for Algorithm MATRIX_ADDITION. Trace this algorithm for matrix A given at the beginning of this section and the matrix

$$
B = \begin{bmatrix}
0 & 0 & 0 & 4 & 0 & 0 & 1 & 0 \\
9 & 0 & 0 & 0 & 0 & 0 & 0 & 3 \\
0 & 0 & 0 & 0 & 0 & 0 & 0 & 0 \\
0 & 6 & 7 & 8 & 0 & 0 & 0 & 0 \\
20 & 0 & 0 & 0 & 0 & 0 & 2 & 0 \\
0 & 0 & 0 & 0 & 1 & 0 & 0 & 0 \\
5 & 7 & 0 & 0 & 0 & 13 & 0 & 0
\end{bmatrix}
$$

with the last row and last column deleted.
2. Program Algorithm CONSTRUCT_MATRIX in PL/I.
3. Trace Algorithm MATRIX_MULTIPLICATION using matrix A and matrix B given in Exercise 1.

```
MATRIX_MULTIPLICATION:
    PROCEDURE(AROW, ACOL, BROW, BCOL, CROW, CCOL, M, N, T);
/*  THIS PROCEDURE MULTIPLIES TWO SPARSE MATRICES REPRESENTED BY
MULTILINKED STRUCTURES.  MATRICES A AND B WITH DIMENSIONS M X N AND
N X T RESPECTIVELY ARE MULTIPLIED TO FORM MATRIX C WITH DIMENSIONS
M X T. */
    DECLARE
        (M, N, T, I, J) BINARY FIXED,
        (AROW(*), ACOL(*), BROW(*), BCOL(*), CROW(*), CCOL(*),
         A, B, Q) POINTER;
    /* INITIALIZE MATRIX STRUCTURE */
    DO I = 1 TO M; /* ALLOCATE ROW HEAD NODES */
        ALLOCATE MATRIX_ELEMENT;
        P->C = 0;
        P->LEFT = P;
        CROW(I) = P;
    END;
    DO J = 1 TO T; /* ALLOCATE COLUMN HEAD NODES */
        ALLOCATE MATRIX_ELEMENT;
        P->R = 0;
        P->UP = P;
        CCOL(J) = P;
    END;
    DO I = 1 TO M;  /* SCAN ROWS OF MATRIX A */
        DO J = 1 TO T;  /* SCAN EACH COLUMN OF MATRIX B */
            /* INITIALIZE FOR SCANNING ROW I OF MATRIX A
               AND COLUMN J OF MATRIX B */
            Q = AROW(I);
            A = Q->LEFT;
            Q = BCOL(J);
            B = Q->UP;
            PRODUCT = 0;
            /* MOVE POINTERS AS NECESSARY
            AND MULTIPLY MATCHING ELEMENTS */
            DO WHILE(B->R ¬= 0 & A->C ¬= 0);
                IF A->C > B->R
                THEN A = A->LEFT;
                ELSE
                    IF B->R > A->C
                    THEN B = B->UP;
                    ELSE
                        DO;
                            PRODUCT = PRODUCT + A->V * B->V;
                            A = A->LEFT;    B = B->UP;
                        END;
            END;
            IF PRODUCT ¬= 0 /* THEN ADD IT TO MATRIX C */
            THEN
                DO;
                    ALLOCATE MATRIX_ELEMENT;
                    P->R = I;    P->C = J;
                    P->V = PRODUCT;
                    A = CROW(I);    B = CCOL(J);
                    P->LEFT = A->LEFT;    P->UP = B->UP;
                    A->LEFT = P;    B->UP = P;
                END;
        END;
    END;
END MATRIX_MULTIPLICATION;
```

FIGURE 5-3.4   Procedure for Algorithm MATRIX_MULTIPLICATION.

5-3.2   Index Generation

When writing a book we are confronted with the task of compiling an index. In the index, the major terms used throughout the book must be presented in lexical order. Several subterms may be associated with a major term and are written in lexical order immediately following that major term. Each major term and subterm is followed by a set of numbers that identifies the pages where the corresponding term is discussed. In this section, algorithms are presented that process a number of arbitrarily ordered major terms and subterms and their associated page numbers in a book, and subsequently print the required index.

The data to be processed must be presented to the algorithms in a standard format. It is convenient to adopt BNF notation, discussed in Sec. 2-2.2, for the description of this format. A <term> is a string of any characters, excluding # and @. In most cases <term> consists of alphabetic characters. Using <term> we can describe the input format as follows.

<page number> :: = 1 | 2 | 3 | ... | n − 2 | n − 1 | n
(We assume the book has n pages.)
<major term> :: = <term>
<major term string> :: = <major term> |
       <major term string> @ <page number>
<subterm string> :: = # <term> | <subterm string> @ <page number>
<major and subterm string> :: = <major term> <subterm string>

One <major term string>, <subterm string>, or <major and subterm string> is input to the index-generation algorithm at a time. A <subterm string> always corresponds to the <major term> most recently encountered in the input.

As an example, some input strings may be

OBJECT CODE @483 @478 @484
#OPTIMIZATION @531
OBJECT CODE #GENERATION @549 @539

Subterms OPTIMIZATION and GENERATION correspond to the major term OBJECT CODE.

In order to print the required index, the index must first be represented in computer memory. A multilinked structure with three types of nodes is used for this purpose. Such a structure is illustrated in Fig. 5-3.5.

To each major term there corresponds a node with four fields that we describe as MAJORNODE. The major term name is stored in the field TERM. The field MJLINK is a pointer to the node containing the next major term in a sequence of increasing major

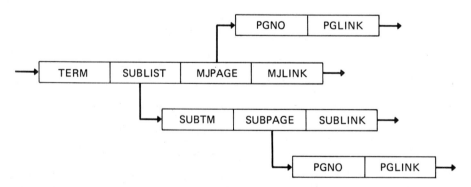

FIGURE 5-3.5   Multilinked structure for representation of an index.

terms (according to the computer's collating sequence). MJPAGE is a pointer to a linked linear list of page numbers where the major term is discussed. SUBLIST is a pointer to a linked linear list consisting of nodes, each of which is denoted as SUBNODE.

In each SUBNODE, the field SUBTM contains a term which is subsidiary to the major term in the MAJORNODE predecessor. SUBLINK points to the next SUBNODE. This linked linear list containing subterms is ordered according to the increasing lexical value of subterms. SUBPAGE is a pointer to a linked linear list of page numbers where the subterm is discussed.

The lists of page numbers consist of nodes, each of which is a PAGENODE. The field PGNO contains a page number for the predecessor major term or subterm. PGLINK is a pointer to the next PAGENODE. The nodes are ordered according to increasing page numbers.

Using these node structures, we can represent the major term OBJECT CODE and its subterms as in Fig. 5-3.6.

Algorithms are required for allocating and initializing the node structures MAJORNODE, SUBNODE, and PAGENODE.

Algorithm ALLOCATE_MJ.   Given a major term, MAJORTERM, it is required to allocate a MAJORNODE structure and initialize the TERM field to MAJORTERM and all pointer fields to NULL. P is a local pointer variable.

1. [Allocate a node]   Set P ⇐ MAJORNODE.
2. [Initialize new node]   Set TERM(P) ← MAJORTERM and
    SUBLIST(P) ← MJPAGE(P) ← MJLINK(P) ← NULL.
3. [Return pointer to new node]   Set ALLOCATE_MJ ← P, and Exit.

Algorithm ALLOCATE_SUB.   Given a subterm, SUBTERM, it is required to allocate a SUBNODE structure and initialize the SUBTM field to SUBTERM and the pointer fields to NULL. P is a local pointer variable.

1. [Allocate a node]   Set P ⇐ SUBNODE.

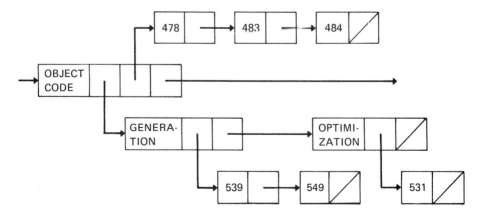

FIGURE 5-3.6   Representation of OBJECT CODE and its subterms.

2. [Initialize new node]   Set SUBTM(P) ← SUBTERM and
   SUBPAGE(P) ← SUBLINK(P) ← NULL.
3. [Return pointer to new node]   Set ALLOCATE_SUB ← P, and Exit.

Algorithm ALLOCATE_PG.   Given **PAGE**, a page number, it is required to allocate a
PAGENODE structure and to initialize its fields. P is a local pointer variable.

1. [Allocate a node]   Set P ⇐ PAGENODE.
2. [Initialize new node]   Set PGNO(P) ← PAGE and PGLINK(P) ← NULL.
3. [Return pointer to new node]   Set ALLOCATE_PG ← P, and Exit.

These three algorithms are invoked using the assignments

PTR ← ALLOCATE_MJ(MAJORTERM)
PTR ← ALLOCATE_SUB(SUBTERM)
PTR ← ALLOCATE_PG(PAGE)

In all cases, the address of the node allocated and initialized is assigned to **PTR**.
   When subterms and major terms are input to the algorithms for index generation,
it is possible that duplicate terms will be encountered. In these situations, an existing list
of page numbers must be updated. The following algorithm does this, and it also has the
capability to construct a new list of page numbers.

Algorithm PAGING.   Given **PAGEPTR**, a pointer to a linear list of page numbers that is
possibly empty, it is required to add to this list any page numbers from the string **PAGES**
that are not in the list. It is assumed that **PAGES** has the form

PAGES :: = <page number> | **PAGES** @ <page number> | "

P is an auxiliary variable used to index the '@' delimiters.

1. [All page numbers processed?]   If **PAGES** = ", then Exit.
2. [Obtain a page number]   Set P ← INDEX(PAGES, '@').
   If P = 0, then set PAGE ← PAGES and PAGES ← ";
   otherwise, set PAGE ← SUB(PAGES, 1, P − 1) and PAGES ← SUB(PAGES, P + 1).
3. [Empty linear list?]
   If PAGEPTR = NULL, then set PAGEPTR ← ALLOCATE_PG(PAGE) and go to step 1.
4. [Should PAGE be first in the list?]
   If PAGE < PGNO(PAGEPTR),
   then set SAVE ← ALLOCATE_PG(PAGE), PGLINK(SAVE) ← PAGEPTR,
   PAGEPTR ← SAVE, and go to step 1.
5. [Get first node]   Set SAVE ← PAGEPTR.
6. [Duplicate page number?]   If PAGE = PGNO(SAVE), then go to step 1.
7. [End of list?]
   If PGLINK(SAVE) = NULL,
   then set PGLINK(SAVE) ← ALLOCATE_PG(PAGE) and go to step 1.
8. [Get next node]   Set LAST ← SAVE and SAVE ← PGLINK(SAVE).

9. [Should a new node precede **SAVE** node?]
If PAGE < PGNO(SAVE),
then set PGLINK(LAST) ← ALLOCATE_PG(PAGE),
PGLINK(PGLINK(LAST)) ← SAVE, and go to step 1;
otherwise, go to step 6.

In Algorithm **PAGING**, " denotes the null string. In step 2, the first page number in the string **PAGES** is obtained and deleted from **PAGES**. Steps 3 to 9 scan the list referenced by **PAGEPTR** and insert a node containing **PAGE** in its proper position according to an ascending sequence of page numbers. If **PAGE** has previously been added to the list, however, it is ignored and the next page number is processed. This algorithm can be invoked using **PAGING(PAGEPTR, PAGES)**. Changes made to **PAGEPTR, PAGES**, and also the node structures designated **PAGENODE** are effective in the algorithm that invokes Algorithm **PAGING**, because **PAGEPTR** and **PAGES** are considered to be passed by name and the **PAGENODE** structures are global.

We require an algorithm that adds subterms to the subterm list of a major term. In the algorithm it is also necessary to invoke Algorithm **PAGING** to construct or update a list of page numbers for a subterm.

Algorithm INSERT. Given **SUBPTR**, a pointer to a possibly empty linear list of subterm nodes, this algorithm adds **SUBTERM** to that list if it was not added previously. Page numbers in the string **PAGES** are added to the list of page numbers for the subterm using Algorithm **PAGING**.

1. [Is subterm list empty?]
If SUBPTR = NULL,
then set SUBPTR ← ALLOCATE_SUB(SUBTERM), SAVE ← SUBPTR, and go to step 8.
2. [Should subterm be first in the list?]
If SUBTERM < SUBTM(SUBPTR),
then set SAVE ← ALLOCATE_SUB(SUBTERM), SUBLINK(SAVE) ← SUBPTR,
SUBPTR ← SAVE, and go to step 8.
3. [Get first node] Set SAVE ← SUBPTR.
4. [Duplicate subterm?] If SUBTERM = SUBTM(SAVE), then go to step 8.
5. [End of list?]
If SUBLINK(SAVE) = NULL,
then set SUBLINK(SAVE) ← ALLOCATE_SUB(SUBTERM),
SAVE ← SUBLINK(SAVE), and go to step 8.
6. [Get next node] Set LAST ← SAVE and SAVE ← SUBLINK(SAVE).
7. [Should a new node precede **SAVE** node?]
If SUBTERM < SUBTM(SAVE),
then set SUBLINK(LAST) ← ALLOCATE_SUB(SUBTERM),
LAST ← SUBLINK(LAST), SUBLINK(LAST) ← SAVE, and SAVE ← LAST;
otherwise, go to step 4.
8. [Update page number list]
Invoke Algorithm PAGING(SUBPAGE(SAVE), PAGES), and Exit.

This algorithm is invoked using INSERT(SUBPTR, SUBTERM, PAGES). Any changes made to SUBPTR, PAGES, and the node structures are valid in the invoking algorithm, because of call-by-reference argument passing and the globality of the structures.

The final algorithm necessary for the formation of the index structure can now be presented. It inputs data in the format previously described and determines the major term, subterm, and page number components. The list of major terms is constructed by the following algorithm, and Algorithms INSERT and PAGING are invoked to construct subterm and page number lists.

Algorithm CONSTRUCT_INDEX.   This algorithm reads one <major term string>, <subterm string>, or <major and subterm string> at a time into STRING. STRING is scanned to obtain the components MAJORTERM, SUBTERM, and PAGES. The multi-linked structure representing the index is constructed. FIRSTMJ is a pointer to the first MAJORNODE in the linear list of major terms; it is initially NULL, but eventually points to an existing index structure.

1. [Read the term strings]   Read STRING. If the data has been exhausted, then Exit.
2. [Locate special symbols]   Set A ← INDEX(STRING, '#') and B ← INDEX(STRING, '@').
3. [Obtain page numbers]
    If B ≠ 0,
    then set PAGES ← SUB(STRING, B + 1) and STRING ← SUB(STRING, 1, B − 1); otherwise, set PAGES ← ''.
4. [Obtain the subterm]
    If A ≠ 0,
    then set SUBTERM ← SUB(STRING, A + 1) and STRING ← SUB(STRING, 1, A − 1); otherwise, set SUBTERM ← ''.
5. [Obtain the major term]
    If STRING ≠ '', then set MAJORTERM ← STRING; otherwise, go to step 13.
6. [Empty list?]
    If FIRSTMJ = NULL,
    then set FIRSTMJ ← ALLOCATE_MJ(MAJORTERM), SAVE ← FIRSTMJ, and go to step 13.
7. [Should MAJORTERM be first in the list?]
    If MAJORTERM < TERM(FIRSTMJ),
    then set SAVE ← ALLOCATE_MJ(MAJORTERM),
    MJLINK(SAVE) ← FIRSTMJ, FIRSTMJ ← SAVE, and go to step 13.
8. [Get first node]   Set SAVE ← FIRSTMJ.
9. [Duplicate major term?]   If MAJORTERM = TERM(SAVE), then go to step 13.
10. [End of list?]
    If MJLINK(SAVE) = NULL,
    then set MJLINK(SAVE) ← ALLOCATE_MJ(MAJORTERM),
    SAVE ← MJLINK(SAVE), and go to step 13.
11. [Get next node]   Set LAST ← SAVE and SAVE ← MJLINK(SAVE).

12. [Should a new node precede **SAVE** node?]
    If MAJORTERM < TERM(SAVE),
    then set MJLINK(LAST) ← ALLOCATE _MJ(MAJORTERM),
    LAST ← MJLINK(LAST), MJLINK(LAST) ← SAVE, SAVE ← LAST,
    and go to step 13;
    otherwise, go to step 9.
13. [Update subterm and page number lists]
    If SUBTERM ≠ '',
    then call INSERT(SUBLIST(SAVE), SUBTERM, PAGES);
    otherwise, call PAGING(MJPAGE(SAVE), PAGES).
    Go to step 1.

In step 13 of this algorithm, **SAVE** is a pointer to a MAJORNODE whose subterm and page number lists are to be updated. **SAVE** is a local variable, so if control transfers from step 5 to step 13, **SAVE** will already have been set on an earlier iteration and will be pointing to the MAJORNODE for the major term recently input. It is assumed that the first input string must have a major term component.

Algorithms PAGING, INSERT, and CONSTRUCT_INDEX could be made more efficient with certain modifications. Also, different multilinked structures would enable more efficient index construction. Some modifications of these algorithms are suggested in the exercises of this section.

We now give the algorithms for scanning the multilinked representation of the index and printing the index terms. An example of the output produced by these algorithms for the terms in Figure 5-3.6 is as follows:

```
OBJECTCODE, 478, 483, 484
    GENERATION, 539, 549
    OPTIMIZATION, 531
```

The first algorithm is a subalgorithm for formatting page numbers.

Algorithm PAGE_STRING.   Given PAGEPTR, a pointer to a linked linear list of PAGENODE structures, it is required to form a string PAGES consisting of the page numbers in the list. The numbers are to appear in increasing order from left to right and each number is preceded by ', '.

1. [Initialize string and auxiliary pointer]   Set PAGES ← ''
   and SAVE ← PAGEPTR.
2. [Scan the linear list]   Repeat step 3 while SAVE ≠ NULL.
3. [Add page number to string]   Set PAGES ← PAGES ○ ', ' ○ PGNO(SAVE)
   and SAVE ← PGLINK(SAVE).
4. [Transfer string]   Set PAGE_STRING ← PAGES, and Exit.

This algorithm is invoked using PAGE_STRING(PAGEPTR) and a string of page numbers is returned. The following algorithm employs PAGE_STRING for printing the entire index.

Algorithm PRINT_INDEX. Given FIRSTMJ, a pointer to the multilinked structure representing an index, it is required to print the index.

1. [Initialize] Set SAVE ← FIRSTMJ.
2. [Scan the major terms] Repeat steps 3 to 5 while SAVE ≠ NULL.
   Exit.
3. [Print major term] Print TERM(SAVE) ○ PAGE_STRING(MJPAGE(SAVE)).
4. [Print subterms] Set SUBSAVE ← SUBLIST(SAVE).
   Repeat while SUBSAVE ≠ NULL:
       PRINT'   ' ○ SUBTM(SUBSAVE) ○ PAGE_STRING(SUBPAGE(SUBSAVE))
       and set SUBSAVE ← SUBLINK(SUBSAVE).
5. [Update pointer to MAJORNODE structures] Set SAVE ← MJLINK(SAVE).

The execution of this algorithm is simple. SAVE is used to scan each MAJORNODE and SUBSAVE is used to scan each SUBNODE of a subterm list.

Exercises for Sec. 5-3.2

1. Index terms are often referred to for a range of page numbers, for examples, 37–41, 29–70, 23–24, etc. Change algorithm PAGING so that it also accepts page numbers of the form

   $$<\text{page number list}> ::= <\text{page number}> - <\text{page number}>$$

   For a particular page number list, a page number is a duplicate if it lies in the specified range of numbers, for example, 40 is a duplicate page number if 37–41 is already in the index structure. Also, modify Algorithm PAGE_STRING so that two or more consecutive page numbers in a list are printed as a range of numbers.

2. Algorithm CONSTRUCT_INDEX is more efficient if major terms are organized as a binary tree. Modify the algorithm to accomplish this. Also, change Algorithm PRINT_ INDEX so that it can scan the binary tree of major terms.

3. Suggest and implement error-checking devices for the algorithms in this section. In particular, how can the input data be validated?

5-4 GRAPHS AND THEIR REPRESENTATIONS

A discussion of graph terminology was given in Sec. 5-1.1 where terms such as graph, node, edge, path, cycle, etc. were introduced. This section is concerned with a further discussion of graphs and their representations.

A diagrammatic representation of a graph may have a limited usefulness. However, such a representation is not feasible when the number of nodes and edges in a graph is large. The first subsection presents an alternative method of representing graphs by using matrices. This method of representation has several advantages. It is easy to store and manipulate matrices and hence the graphs represented by them in a computer. Certain well-known operations of matrix algebra can be used to obtain paths, cycles, and other characteristics of a graph.

The second subsection deals with the representation of a graph by a list structure. Several programming languages have been developed to allow easy processing of structures similar to those that will be described. The need for list processing arose from the high cost of main computer storage and the unpredictable nature of the storage requirements of computer programs and data. It is shown that a list structure can be used to represent a directed graph.

The remaining subsection gives a brief introduction to the representation of a general graph structure. Such representations are based, not only on the nature of the data, but also on the operations which are to be performed on this data.

A number of applications of graphs and their specific representations are discussed in Sec. 5-5.

5-4.1 Matrix Representation of Graphs

Given a simple digraph $G = (V, E)$, it is necessary to assume some kind of ordering of the nodes of the graph in the sense that a particular node is called a first node, another a second node, and so on. A matrix representation of G depends upon the ordering of the nodes.

Let $G = (V, E)$ be a simple digraph in which $V = \{v_1, v_2, \ldots, v_n\}$ and the nodes are assumed to be ordered from v_1 to v_n. An $n \times n$ matrix A whose elements a_{ij} are given by

$$a_{ij} = \begin{cases} 1 \text{ if } (v_i, v_j) \in E \\ 0 \text{ otherwise} \end{cases}$$

is called the *adjacency matrix* of the graph G.

Any element of the adjacency matrix is either 0 or 1. Any matrix whose elements are either 0 or 1 is called a *bit matrix* or a *Boolean matrix*. Note that the ith row in the adjacency matrix is determined by the edges which originate in the node v_i. The number of elements in the ith row whose value is 1 is equal to the outdegree of the node v_i. Similarly, the number of elements whose value is 1 in a column, say the jth column, is equal to the indegree of the node v_j. An adjacency matrix completely defines a simple digraph.

For a given digraph $G = (V, E)$, an adjacency matrix depends upon the ordering of the elements of V. For different orderings of the elements of V we get different adjacency matrices of the same graph G. However, any one of the adjacency matrices of G can be obtained from another adjacency matrix of the same graph by interchanging some of the rows and the corresponding columns of the matrix. We shall neglect the arbitrariness introduced in an adjacency matrix because of the ordering of the elements of V. Therefore, any adjacency matrix of the graph will satisfy a given purpose. In fact, if two digraphs are such that the adjacency matrix of one can be obtained from the adjacency matrix of the other by interchanging some of the rows and the corresponding columns, then the digraphs are equivalent.

As an example, consider the digraph given in Fig. 5-4.1a in which the order of the nodes is given as v_1, v_2, v_3, and v_4. The adjacency matrix for this digraph is given in Fig. 5-4.1b.

We can extend the idea of matrix representation to multigraphs and weighted graphs. For simple undirected graphs, such an extension simply gives a symmetric adjacency matrix. In the case of a multigraph or a weighted graph, we write $a_{ij} = w_{ij}$, where w_{ij} denotes either the multiplicity or the weight of the edge (v_i, v_j). If $(v_i, v_j) \notin E$, then we write $w_{ij} = 0$.

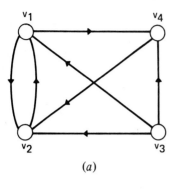

(a)

$$\begin{array}{c|cccc}
 & v_1 & v_2 & v_3 & v_4 \\
\hline
v_1 & 0 & 1 & 0 & 1 \\
v_2 & 1 & 0 & 0 & 0 \\
v_3 & 1 & 1 & 0 & 1 \\
v_4 & 0 & 1 & 0 & 0
\end{array}$$

(b)

FIGURE 5-4.1   A digraph and its adjacency matrix.

For a null graph which consists of only n nodes but no edges, the adjacency matrix has all its elements zero; i.e., the adjacency matrix is a null matrix. If there are loops at each node but no other edges in the graph, then the adjacency matrix is the identity or the unit matrix.

Let us now consider the powers of an adjacency matrix. Naturally, an entry of 1 in the ith row and jth column of A shows the existence of an edge (v_i, v_j), that is, a path of length 1 from v_i to v_j. Let us denote the elements of A^2 by $a_{ij}(2)$. Then

$$a_{ij}(2) = \sum_{k=1}^{n} a_{ik} a_{kj}$$

For any fixed k, $a_{ik}a_{kj} = 1$ if and only if both a_{ik} and a_{kj} equal 1; that is, (v_i, v_k) and (v_k, v_j) are the edges of the graph. For each such k we get a contribution of 1 in the sum. Now (v_i, v_k) and (v_k, v_j) imply that there is a path from v_i to v_j of length 2. Therefore, $a_{ij}(2)$ is equal to the number of different paths of exactly length 2 from v_i to v_j. Similarly, the diagonal element $a_{ii}(2)$ shows the number of cycles of length 2 at the node for v_i for $i = 1, 2, \ldots, n$.

By a similar argument, one can show that the element in the ith row and jth column of A^3 gives the number of paths of exactly length 3 from v_i to v_j. In general, the following statement can be shown:

Let A be the adjacency matrix of a digraph G. The element in the ith row and jth column of A^n $(n > 1)$ is equal to the number of paths of length n from the ith node to the jth node.

The matrices A^2, A^3, and A^4 for the graph given in Fig. 5-4.1 are given as follows:

$$A^2 = \begin{bmatrix} 1 & 1 & 0 & 0 \\ 0 & 1 & 0 & 1 \\ 1 & 2 & 0 & 1 \\ 1 & 0 & 0 & 0 \end{bmatrix} \qquad A^3 = \begin{bmatrix} 1 & 1 & 0 & 1 \\ 1 & 1 & 0 & 0 \\ 2 & 2 & 0 & 1 \\ 0 & 1 & 0 & 1 \end{bmatrix} \qquad A^4 = \begin{bmatrix} 1 & 2 & 0 & 1 \\ 1 & 1 & 0 & 1 \\ 2 & 3 & 0 & 2 \\ 1 & 1 & 0 & 0 \end{bmatrix}$$

For the graph given in Fig. 5-4.1, we see that there are two paths of length 2 from v_3 to v_2, hence the entry 2 in the third row and second column of A^2. Similarly, there are three paths of length 4 from v_3 to v_2, hence the corresponding entry in A^4.

Given a simple digraph $G = (V, E)$, let v_i and v_j be any two nodes of G. From the adjacency matrix of A we can immediately determine whether there exists an edge from v_i to v_j in G. Also from the matrix A^r, where r is some positive integer, we can establish the number of paths of length r from v_i to v_j. If we add the matrices A, A^2, A^3, ..., A^r to get B_r

$$B_r = A + A^2 + \cdots + A^r$$

then from the matrix B_r we can determine the number of paths of length less than or equal to r from v_i to v_j. If we wish to determine whether v_j is reachable from v_i, it would be necessary to investigate whether there exists a path of any length from v_i to v_j. In order to decide this, with the help of the adjacency matrix, we would have to consider all possible A^r for $r = 1, 2, \ldots$. This method is neither practical nor necessary, as we shall later show.

It is easily shown that in a simple digraph with n nodes, the length of an elementary path or cycle does not exceed n. Also, for a path between any two nodes, one can obtain an elementary path by deleting certain parts of the path which are cycles. Similarly (for cycles), we can always obtain an elementary cycle from a given cycle. If we are interested in determining whether there exists a path from v_i to v_j, all we need to examine are the elementary paths of length less than or equal to $n - 1$. In the case where $v_i = v_j$ and the path is a cycle, we need to examine all possible elementary cycles of length less than or equal to n. Such cycles or paths are easily determined from the matrix B_n where

$$B_n = A + A^2 + A^3 + \cdots + A^n$$

The element in the ith row and jth column of B_n shows the number of paths of length n or less which exist from v_i to v_j. If this element is nonzero, then it is clear that v_j is reachable from v_i. Of course, in order to determine reachability, we need to know the existence of a path, and not the number of paths between any two nodes. In any case, the matrix B_n furnishes the required information about the reachability of any node of the graph from any other node.

Let $G = (V, E)$ be a simple digraph which contains n nodes that are assumed to be ordered. An $n \times n$ matrix P whose elements are given by

$$p_{ij} = \begin{cases} 1 & \text{if there exists a path from } v_i \text{ to } v_j \\ 0 & \text{otherwise} \end{cases}$$

is called the *path matrix (reachability matrix)* of the graph G.

Note that the path matrix only shows the presence or absence of at least one path between a pair of points and also the presence or absence of a cycle at any node. It does not, however, show all the paths that may exist. In this sense a path matrix does not give as complete information about a graph as does the adjacency matrix. The path matrix is important in its own right.

The path matrix can be calculated from the matrix B_n by choosing $p_{ij} = 1$ if the element in the ith row and jth column of B_n is nonzero and $p_{ij} = 0$ otherwise. We shall apply this method of calculating the path matrix to our sample problem whose graph is given in Fig. 5-4.1. The adjacency matrix A and the powers A^2, A^3, A^4 have already been calculated. We thus have B_4 and the path matrix P given by

$$B_4 = \begin{bmatrix} 3 & 5 & 0 & 3 \\ 3 & 3 & 0 & 2 \\ 6 & 8 & 0 & 5 \\ 2 & 3 & 0 & 1 \end{bmatrix} \qquad P = \begin{bmatrix} 1 & 1 & 0 & 1 \\ 1 & 1 & 0 & 1 \\ 1 & 1 & 0 & 1 \\ 1 & 1 & 0 & 1 \end{bmatrix}$$

It may be remarked here that if we are interested in knowing the reachability of one node from another, it is sufficient to calculate B_{n-1}, because a path of length n cannot be elementary. The only difference between P calculated from B_{n-1} and P calculated from B_n is in the diagonal elements. For the purpose of reachability, every node is assumed to be reachable from itself. Some authors calculate the path matrix from B_{n-1}, while others do it from B_n.

The method of calculating the path matrix P of a graph by calculating first A, A^2, ..., A^n and then B_n is cumbersome. We shall now describe another method based upon a similar idea, but which is more efficient in practice. Observe that we are not interested in the number of paths of any particular length from a node, say v_i, to a node v_j. This information is obtained during the course of our calculation of the powers of A, and later it is suppressed because these numbers are not needed. To reduce the amount of calculation involved, this unwanted information is not generated. This is achieved by using Boolean matrix operations in our calculations, which will now be defined. The operators $\wedge$ and $\vee$ on B are given in Table 5-4.1. For any two $n \times n$ Boolean matrices A and B, the Boolean sum and Boolean product of A and B are written as $A \vee B$ and $A \wedge B$, which are also Boolean matrices, say C and D. The elements of C and D are given by

$$c_{ij} = a_{ij} \vee b_{ij} \qquad \text{and} \qquad d_{ij} = \bigvee_{k=1}^{n} (a_{ik} \wedge b_{kj}) \qquad \text{for all } i,j = 1, 2, ..., n$$

Note that the element d_{ij} is easily obtained by scanning the ith row of A from left to right and simultaneously the jth column of B from top to bottom. If, for any k, the kth element in the row for A and kth element in the column for B are both 1, then $d_{ij} = 1$; otherwise, $d_{ij} = 0$.

Table 5-4.1

$\wedge$	0	1		$\vee$	0	1
0	0	0		0	0	1
1	0	1		1	1	1

The adjacency matrix is a Boolean matrix, and so also is the path matrix. Let us write $A \wedge A = A^{(2)}$, $A \wedge A^{(r-1)} = A^{(r)}$ for any $r = 2, 3, \ldots$. The only difference between A^2 and $A^{(2)}$ is that $A^{(2)}$ is a Boolean matrix and the entry in the ith row and jth column of $A^{(2)}$ is 1 if there is at least one path of length 2 from v_i to v_j, while in A^2 the entry in the ith row and jth column shows the number of paths of length 2 from v_i to v_j. Similar remarks apply to A^3 and $A^{(3)}$ or in general A^r and $A^{(r)}$ for any positive integer r. From this description, it is clear that the path matrix P is given by

$$P = A \vee A^{(2)} \vee A^{(3)} \vee \cdots A^{(n)} = \bigvee_{k=1}^{n} A^{(k)}$$

If we take the sum from $k = 1$ to $k = n - 1$, we get a matrix which may differ (if at all) from P in the diagonal terms only.

For our sample example of the graph given in Fig. 5-4.1

$$A^{(2)} = \begin{bmatrix} 1 & 1 & 0 & 0 \\ 0 & 1 & 0 & 1 \\ 1 & 1 & 0 & 1 \\ 1 & 0 & 0 & 0 \end{bmatrix} \quad A^{(3)} = \begin{bmatrix} 1 & 1 & 0 & 1 \\ 1 & 1 & 0 & 0 \\ 1 & 1 & 0 & 1 \\ 0 & 1 & 0 & 1 \end{bmatrix} \quad A^{(4)} = \begin{bmatrix} 1 & 1 & 0 & 1 \\ 1 & 1 & 0 & 1 \\ 1 & 1 & 0 & 1 \\ 1 & 1 & 0 & 0 \end{bmatrix}$$

$$A \vee A^{(2)} \vee A^{(3)} = \begin{bmatrix} 1 & 1 & 0 & 1 \\ 1 & 1 & 0 & 1 \\ 1 & 1 & 0 & 1 \\ 1 & 1 & 0 & 1 \end{bmatrix} = A \vee A^{(2)} \vee A^{(3)} \vee A^{(4)} = P$$

This method of obtaining the path matrix of a simple digraph can easily be computed by using the following algorithm due to Warshall.

Algorithm WARSHALL. Given the adjacency matrix A, the following steps produce the path matrix P.

1. [Initialize] Set $P \leftarrow A$.
2. [Perform a pass] Repeat steps 3 and 4 for $k = 1, 2, \ldots, n$.
3. [Process rows] Repeat step 4 for $i = 1, 2, \ldots, n$.
4. [Process columns]
   Repeat for $j = 1, 2, \ldots, n$: set $p_{ij} \leftarrow p_{ij} \vee (p_{ik} \wedge p_{kj})$.
5. [Finished] Exit.

To show that this algorithm produces the required matrix, note that step 1 produces a matrix in which $p_{ij} = 1$ if there is a path of length 1 from v_i to v_j. Assume that for a fixed k, the intermediate matrix P produced by steps 3 and 4 of the algorithm is such that the element in the ith row and jth column in this matrix is 1 if and only if there is a path from v_i to v_j through the nodes $v_1, v_2, \ldots, v_k$, or an edge from v_i to v_j. Now with an updated value of k, we find that $p_{ij} = 1$ either if $p_{ij} = 1$ in an earlier step or if there is a path from p_i to p_j which traverses through v_{k+1}. This means that $p_{ij} = 1$ if and only if there is a path from v_i to v_j through the nodes $v_1, v_2, \ldots, v_{k+1}$ or an edge from v_i to v_j.

A PL/I program for this algorithm is given in Fig. 5-4.2. Notice that bit strings are used.

```
WARSHALL:
    PROCEDURE (A, P, N);
/* GIVEN THE ADJACENCY MATRIX A, PRODUCE THE PATH MATRIX P */
    DECLARE
        (A, P)(*,*) BIT(1),
        (N, K, I, J) BINARY FIXED;
    P = A;
    DO K = 1 TO N;
        DO I = 1 TO N;
            DO J = 1 TO N;
                P(I,J) = P(I,J) | (P(I,K) & P(K,J));
            END;
        END;
    END;
END WARSHALL;
```

FIGURE 5-4.2   PL/I procedure for Algorithm WARSHALL.

Algorithm WARSHALL can be modified further to obtain a matrix which gives the lengths of shortest paths between the nodes. For this purpose, let A be the adjacency matrix of the graph. Replace all those elements of A which are zero by ∞, which shows that there is no edge between the nodes in question. The following algorithm produces the required matrix which shows the lengths of minimum paths.

Algorithm MINIMAL.   Given the adjacency matrix in which the zero elements are replaced by infinity or by some very large number, let this matrix be denoted by B. The matrix C produced by the following steps shows the minimum lengths of paths between the nodes. MIN is a function which selects the algebraic minimum of its two arguments.

1. [Initialize]   Set C $\leftarrow$ B.
2. [Perform a pass]   Repeat steps 3 and 4 for k = 1, 2, ..., n.
3. [Process rows]   Repeat step 4 for i = 1, 2, ..., n.
4. [Process columns]
    Repeat for j = 1, 2, ..., n: set $c_{ij} \leftarrow$ MIN(c_{ij}, $c_{ik} + c_{kj}$).
5. [Finished]   Exit.

Here, + in step 4 means the ordinary adding of integers. In practice we are often interested not only in the length of the minimum path between any two nodes, but also in the actual path. It is a simple matter to modify the previous algorithm to obtain such a path, and therefore it is left as an exercise.

We shall end this subsection by showing how the path matrix of a digraph can be used in determining whether certain procedures in a program are recursive.

In some programming languages, a programmer must explicitly state that a procedure is recursive. For example, in PL/I the RECURSIVE option must be specified. In other languages which do not require any such specification, it is possible to use concepts from graph theory to determine which procedures are recursive. A recursive procedure is not necessarily one which invokes itself directly. If procedure p_1 invokes p_2, procedure p_2 invokes p_3, ..., procedure p_{n-1} invokes p_n, and procedure p_n invokes p_1, then procedure p_1 is recursive.

Let P = {p_1, p_2, ..., p_n} be the set of procedures in a program. In a directed graph consisting of nodes representing elements of P, there is an edge from p_i to p_j if procedure

p_i invokes p_j. Figure 5-4.3 shows a directed graph and its adjacency matrix representing the calls made by the set of procedures $P = \{p_1, p_2, \ldots, p_5\}$.

A procedure p_i is recursive if there exists a cycle involving p_i in the graph. Such cycles can be detected from the diagonal elements of the path matrix Q of the graph. Thus p_i is recursive iff $q_{ii} = 1$. The matrix Q can be obtained by using Warshall's algorithm. The matrix Q is given by

$$Q = \begin{bmatrix} 1 & 1 & 1 & 1 & 1 \\ 1 & 1 & 1 & 1 & 1 \\ 0 & 0 & 0 & 0 & 1 \\ 1 & 1 & 1 & 1 & 1 \\ 0 & 0 & 0 & 0 & 0 \end{bmatrix}$$

which shows that the procedures p_1, p_2, and p_4 are recursive.

Exercises for Sec. 5-4.1

1. Obtain the adjacency matrix A of the digraph given in Fig. 5-4.4. Find the elementary paths of lengths 1 and 2 from v_1 to v_4. Verify the results by calculating A^2.
2. For any $n \times n$ Boolean matrix A, show that

$$(I + A)^{(2)} = (I + A) \wedge (I + A) = I + A + A^{(2)}$$

where I is the $n \times n$ identity matrix and $A^{(2)} = A \wedge A$. Show also that for any positive integer r

$$(I + A)^{(r)} = I + A + A^{(2)} + \cdots + A^{(r)}$$

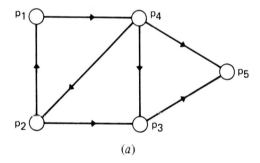

(a)

	p_1	p_2	p_3	p_4	p_5
p_1	0	0	0	1	0
p_2	1	0	1	0	0
p_3	0	0	0	0	1
p_4	0	1	1	0	1
p_5	0	0	0	0	0

(b)

FIGURE 5-4.3   Procedure calls among p_1, p_2, p_3, p_4, and p_5.

3. Using the result obtained in Prob. 2, show that the path matrix of a simple digraph is given by $P = (I + A)^{(n)}$, where A is the adjacency matrix of the digraph which has n nodes.

4. For a simple digraph $G = (V, E)$ whose adjacency matrix is denoted by A, its *distance matrix* is given by

$$d_{ij} = \infty \qquad \text{if } (v_i, v_j) \notin E$$

$$d_{ii} = 0 \qquad \text{for all } i = 1, 2, \ldots, n$$

$$d_{ij} = k \qquad \text{where k is the smallest integer for which } a_{ij}(k) \neq 0$$

Determine the distance matrix of the digraph given in Fig. 5-4.4. What does $d_{ij} = 1$ mean?

5. Modify Algorithm MINIMAL so that all minimum paths are computed.

6. Assume that a digraph has all of its edges labeled. Write a program which will display all minimum paths between all pairs of nodes.

5-4.2 List Structures

In this subsection we are concerned with the representation of a structure called a *list* structure. The manipulation of such structures is known as *list processing*. It will be shown that a list structure can be used to represent a directed graph.

The development of list processing structures, techniques, and programming languages was primarily a response to the requirements of a particular computer application field, namely, symbolic manipulation. Various problem areas such as artificial intelligence, algebraic manipulation, text processing, and graphics are included in this field. Recall that these all have in common the following characteristics:

1 Unpredictable storage requirements. The exact amount of data storage required by a program in these areas often depends on the particular data being processed and, consequently, this requirement cannot be easily determined at the time the program is written.

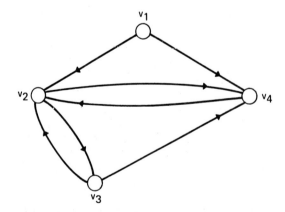

FIGURE 5-4.4.

2 Extensive manipulation of the stored data is required. Programs in these areas typically require that operations such as insertions and deletions be performed frequently on the data structures used.

Taking into consideration the high costs of fast computer storage and computing time, a data structure was required which would utilize the available storage space to provide maximum problem-solving capability and would support efficient (meaning time-wise efficient) manipulation algorithms. The list structure to be discussed satisfies both these criteria.

In the context of list processing, we define a *list* to be any finite sequence of zero or more *atoms* or *lists*, where an atom is taken to be any object (e.g., a string of symbols) which is distinguishable from a list by treating the atom as structurally indivisible. If we enclose lists within parentheses and separate elements of lists by commas, then the following can be considered to be lists:

(a, (b, c, d), e, (f, g))
( )
((a))

The first list contains four elements; namely, the atom a, the list (b, c, d) which contains the atoms b, c and d, the atom e, and the list (f, g) whose elements are the atoms f and g. The second list has no elements, but the null list is still a valid list according to our definition. The third list has one element, the list (a), which in turn contains the atom a. A graphical representation of these examples is given in Fig. 5-4.5.

Another notation which is often used to illustrate lists is similar to that used in the linked representation of trees. Each element of a list is indicated by a box; the arrows or pointers indicate whether the boxes are members of the same list or members of sublists. Each box is separated into two parts. The second part of an element contains a pointer to the next element in the same list or a slash (denoting a null pointer) to mark the end of a list. This "horizontal" pointer represents the relation of physical adjacency in a list. The first part of an element contains either the name of an atomic element or a pointer to the list representation for a list element. For a nonatomic element the pointer specifies the "vertical" or hierarchical relationship in a list.

The box and arrow representations of the previous lists are shown in Fig. 5-4.6. The symbol ⇒ indicates the root or first element of the list.

The following three properties are associated with list structures:

1 Order A transitive relation defined on the elements of the list and specified by the sequence in which the elements appear within the list. In the list (x, y, z), x precedes y and y precedes z implies that x precedes z. This list is not equal to the list (y, z, x).

In the box and arrow notation, order is defined by the horizontal arrows. Each horizontal arrow is interpreted to mean that the element from which the arrow originates precedes the element to which it points.

2 Depth The depth of a list is the maximum level attributed to any element within the list or within any sublist in the list. The level of an element is indicated by the nesting of lists within lists; i.e., by the number of pairs of parentheses surrounding the

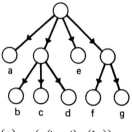

(*a*)   (a,(b,c,d),e,(f,g))

(*b*)   ()

(*c*)   ((a))

FIGURE 5-4.5   Graphic representation of list structures.

element. In the list of 5-4.5*a*, the elements *a* and *e* are at a level of 1, while the remaining elements b, c, d, f, and g have a level of 2. The depth of the entire list is 2.

In the box and arrow notation, the concepts of depth and level are easiest to understand if a number l is associated with each atomic and list element in the list. The value of l for an element x, denoted by $l(x)$, is the number of vertical arrows that must be followed in order to reach the element from the first element of the list. In Fig. 5-4.6*a*, $l(a) = 0$, $l(b) = 1$, etc. In general the level of any element x is given by $l(x) + 1$ and the depth of the list is the maximum value of this level over all the atoms in the list.

3 Length   The number of elements at level 1 in a list. For example, the length of list (a, (b, c), d) is 3.

As an example, let us consider a common occurrence of a list structure which is seldom recognized as such. An English sentence construction consists of a subject, verb, and object. Any such sentence can be interpreted as a three-element list whose elements can be atoms (single words) or lists (word phrases). The following sentences and their corresponding list representations are examples:

Man bites dog. = (Man, bites, dog)

The man bites the dog. = ((The, man), bites, (the, dog))

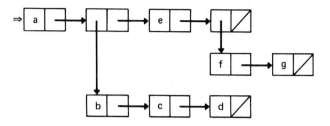

(a) (a,(b,c,d),e,(f,g))

⇒ (null pointer)

(b) ()

(c) ((a))

FIGURE 5-4.6 Storage representation of list structures.

The big man is biting the small dog. =

((The, big, man), (is, biting), (the, small, dog))

The subject and object of the last example can be further separated into nouns and qualifiers as in

(((The, big), (man)), (is, biting), ((the, small), (dog)))

The box and arrow representation of this sentence is given in Fig. 5-4.7.

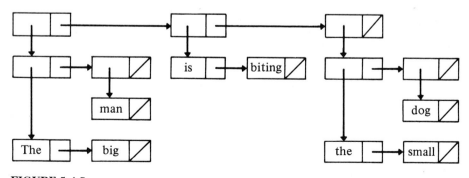

FIGURE 5-4.7.

The properties of this list are as follows:

the length is 3
the depth is 3
the level of 'man' is 3, the level of 'is' is 2, etc.

There is a distinct relationship between a list structure and a digraph. In particular, a list is a directed graph with one *source* node (a node whose indegree is 0) corresponding to the entire list and with every node immediately connected to the source node corresponding to an element of the list—either by being a node with outdegree 0 (for atoms) or by being a node that has branches (for elements which are lists) emanating from it. Every node except the source node has an indegree of 1. The edges leaving a node are considered to be ordered lists. This means that we distinguish the first edge, second edge, etc. which corresponds to the ordering of list elements by the first element, second element, etc. Furthermore, there are no cycles in the graph. The graphs of example lists are given in Fig. 5-4.5.

The preceding list definition could apply equally well to trees. However, lists are in fact extensions of trees in that a list can contain itself as an element and a tree cannot. Hence, there are some lists which cannot be represented as trees, but every tree can be represented as a list. Lists can have an essentially recursive nesting structure that no tree can have and, thus, there are some lists that have a finite representation in our parentheses-comma notation, but which correspond to infinite graphs. For example, the graph of the list structure M = (a, b, M) is shown in Fig. 5-4.8.

Next, we discuss the storage representation of list structures. Considering the criteria which such structures are designed to satisfy, a linked storage representation is certainly most effective. It provides dynamic allocation of nodes as needed, ease in manipulation, and the ability to share sublists. A list is generally represented by some variation of the binary tree representation of natural trees; i.e., by using two link fields—one to indicate membership within a list and one to indicate nesting.

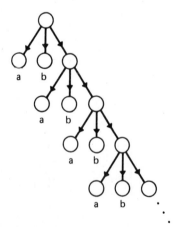

FIGURE 5-4.8.

DPTR	INFO	RPTR

FIGURE 5-4.9   Node representation of a list element.

DPTR	RPTR

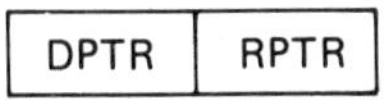

FIGURE 5-4.10   Alternate node representation of a list element.

A typical list node is shown in Fig. 5-4.9. DPTR is the link pointing to the first element of the sublist; RPTR points to the next element in the same list, and INFO contains information about the list (e.g., an alphabetic name). An atomic node is indicated by an empty RPTR, in which case INFO contains the atomic information.

This node format is sufficient for lists whose atomic information requires little storage space. In such a case, little storage space is wasted in the list nodes, which do not require a large INFO field.

A more typical situation is one in which the atomic information requires a relatively large amount of storage space. A more practical node format in this case is given in Fig. 5-4.10, where RPTR performs the same task as in the previous format. The DPTR field, however, points either to the first element of the sublist in a list node or to the information related to the atom in an atomic node. It is assumed that the atomic information contains some unique characteristic, such as a mark field, to enable atomic and list nodes to be distinguished.

This format allows all nodes within the list structure to be of one size, and yet avoids wasting the information space unnecessarily in the list nodes. It is for this reason, and for reasons of diagrammatic and algorithmic simplicity, that this second format is used in the remainder of this subsection. The figures will show atomic nodes in the same manner as Fig. 5-4.11, where the 'x' in the DPTR field denotes a pointer to the information related to atom x. As an example, the list (a, (b, c), d) is represented by Fig. 5-4.12.

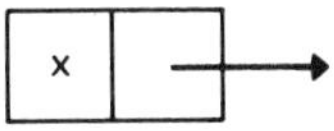

FIGURE 5-4.11   Atomic node representation.

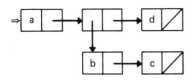

FIGURE 5-4.12   Storage representation of (a, (b, c), d).

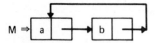

FIGURE 5-4.13 Storage representation of a recursive list.

Recall from Fig. 5-4.8 that the graphic representation of a recursive list contains an infinite repetition of the graph nodes. This practice is impractical for computer implementation. A more sensible method is to implement the list M = (a, b, M) shown in Fig. 5-4.13. This representation of a recursive list is obviously efficient; however, great care must be exercised in order to avoid infinite loops in programs which manipulate such structures.

The space-conserving attribute of lists is not restricted to only recursive structures. A more common situation involves duplicate lists, which occur frequently in practical applications. For example, the list (y, (z, w), (2, (z, w), a)) is represented by Fig. 5-4.14.

Let us consider what changes are required to delete the element z from the sublist (z, w) of Fig. 5-4.14 in order to create the list (y, (w), (2, (w), a)). It is necessary to locate and change both pointers to the element z. This is not a desirable feature since the backtracking necessary to locate the pointers is extremely time-consuming. Because the operation of removing the first element of a list is quite common, it is desirable to derive a storage structure on which such manipulations can be accomplished more efficiently.

In this revised representation, a *list header node* is associated with each list. Using the same node format as before, a list header node has RPTR pointing to the first element of the list and DPTR set to NULL to indicate that the node is a header. An empty list is indicated by DPTR = RPTR = NULL. In this representation each pointer to a list emanates from its list head rather than from its first element. Using this representation, the deletion of the first element of the list requires only changing the RPTR field of its header node. Using this header node representation, Fig. 5-4.14 would appear as in Fig. 5-4.15.

Although this representation requires slightly more storage, this drawback is more than compensated for by the manipulative efficiencies it allows.

The remainder of this subsection is concerned with certain list operations. The usual operations of creating a list and inserting or deleting an element of the list are very similar to the equivalent tree operations. The copying, traversal, and input-output operations are also similar to the corresponding tree operations. Examples of these list operations are given in Sec. 5-5.

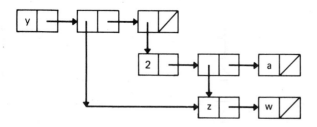

FIGURE 5-4.14.

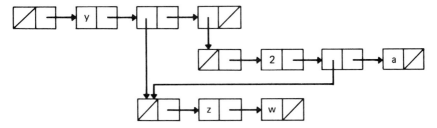

FIGURE 5-4.15 Storage representation of a list using a list head.

The destruction of a list is more complex than the destruction of a tree. A list cannot automatically be returned to the pool of available storage, since other lists may be referencing the list to be destroyed. This topic is discussed in detail in Sec. 5-6.

In the remaining pages we examine those operations that are generally unique to lists; namely, the list splitting and concatenating operations.

Typically, a list is considered to consist of two logical entities; a *head* and a *tail*. Consider the list ((a,b),c,(d,e)) shown in Fig. 5-4.16 in which the head is the list (a,b) and the tail is (c,(d,e)). The graphic representation of the head and tail is given in Fig. 5-4.17. Note the effect of the splitting operation on the level of the elements in the resultant lists. The elements of the head of the list have their level reduced by 1, while the level of the elements of the tail are unaltered.

Given a list structure which uses header nodes, the following algorithms return pointers to the head and tail of the list, respectively.

Algorithm HEAD. Given ROOT, a pointer to the list header node of a list structure, this algorithm returns a pointer to the head of the list. If the head is an atom, the pointer is to the description of the atom. P is a pointer variable.

1. [Check validity of list structure]
   If ROOT = NULL or DPTR(ROOT) ≠ NULL, then print 'invalid list', and Exit.
2. [Is the list null?] Set P ← RPTR(ROOT).
   If P = NULL, then print 'null list', and Exit.
3. [Return pointer to HEAD] Set HEAD ← DPTR(P), and Exit.

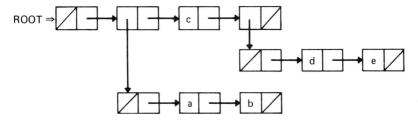

FIGURE 5-4.16.

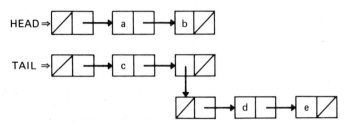

FIGURE 5-4.17   The head and tail representations of the list ((a, b), c, (d, e)).

Algorithm TAIL.   Given ROOT, a pointer to the list header node of a list structure, this algorithm creates a list header node and returns its address; the RPTR field of this header node points to the tail of the list. P is a temporary pointer variable. The name of the node structure is NODE.

1. [Check validity of list structure]
   If ROOT = NULL or DPTR(ROOT) ≠ NULL, then print 'invalid list', and Exit.
2. [Is the list null?]   Set P ← RPTR(ROOT).
   If P = NULL, then print 'null list', and Exit.
3. [Create a list head and return]   Set TAIL ⇐ NODE, DPTR(TAIL) ← NULL, RPTR(TAIL) ← RPTR(P), and Exit.

The operation which provides the opposite effect of HEAD and TAIL operations is the construct operation. Given two lists of an atom and a list, this operation creates a list which uses the first argument as the head of the created list and the second argument as its tail. For example, if A is the list (q) and B is the list (d,e), then the construct of A and B is the list ((q),d,e). As another example, if A is the atom s and B is the list (t,u) then the construct of A and B is the list (s,t,u).

Note that the level of each element in the first argument is increased by 1 as a result of the construct operation, while the level of all elements in the second argument is left unchanged. The construct operation is invalid if the second argument is not a list. The second argument, however, may be the null list. For example, if A is the atom x and B is the list ( ), then the construct of A and B is (x).

Algorithm CONSTRUCT.   Given A, the pointer to the list header node of a list structure or to an atom, and B a pointer to the list header node of a list structure, this algorithm creates a list header node and a node for the first element of the resultant list. The address of the header node is returned. The list L created is such that HEAD(L) = A and TAIL(L) = B. P is a pointer variable.

1. [Check validity of list structures]
   If A = NULL or B = NULL, then print 'invalid list', and Exit.
2. [Is B a list?]   If DPTR(B) ≠ NULL, then print 'invalid list B', and Exit.
3. [Create an element node for A]   Set P ⇐ NODE. If DPTR(A) = NULL, then DPTR(P) ←A; otherwise DPTR(P) ← value of atom A.
   RPTR(P) ← RPTR(B).
4. [Create list header node]   Set CONSTRUCT ⇐ NODE, DPTR(CONSTRUCT) ← NULL, RPTR(CONSTRUCT) ← P.   Exit.

Another familiar operation performed on list structures is the concatenation operation which we denote by APPEND. For example, if A is the list (a,(b,c)) and B is the list (d,f), then their concatenation is the list (a,(b,c),d,f). Note that the level of each element in both lists remains the same. This is shown graphically in Fig. 5-4.18.

Algorithm APPEND.   Given A and B, the pointers to the list header nodes of two list structures, this algorithm returns the address of the list header node of a list in which the elements at level 1 are the level 1 elements of both lists A and B. The elements of list A precede those of list B. The Algorithms CONSTRUCT, HEAD, and TAIL are used. An intermediate pointer stack Q with TOP denoting its top element is also required. The variable i is a counter.

1. [Check validity of list structures]
   If A = NULL or B = NULL, then print 'invalid list', and Exit.
   If DPTR(A) ≠ NULL or DPTR(B) ≠ NULL, then print 'invalid list', and Exit.
2. [Initialize stack and stack the successive heads of list A]
   Set TOP ← 0.
   Repeat while RPTR(A) ≠ NULL: (i.e., while A is not the null list)
       Set TOP ← TOP + 1, Q[TOP] ← HEAD(A), and A ← TAIL(A).
3. [Unstack the elements of A and add them to list B]
   Set APPEND ← B.
   Repeat for i = TOP, TOP − 1, ..., 1:
       Set APPEND ← CONSTRUCT(Q[i], APPEND).
   Exit.

As mentioned previously, several programming languages have been developed to allow easy processing of list structures. LISP 1.5 is one of the most powerful of these. In LISP 1.5 there are five basic or "pure" LISP functions; namely, CAR, CDR, CONS, EQ, and ATOM. The functions CAR, CDR, and CONS are equivalent to the list operations

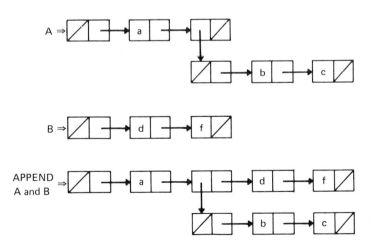

FIGURE 5-4.18.

HEAD, TAIL, and CONSTRUCT, as discussed previously in this subsection. EQ and ATOM
are logical functions (i.e., predicates). EQ tests for the equality of two atoms and ATOM
determines whether a list element is an atom or not. Any function provided in LISP 1.5
can be expressed in terms of the five "pure" LISP functions. For a thorough discussion of
LISP 1.5, the reader is invited to read McCarthy et al., [1969].

Exercises for Sec. 5-4.2

1. Give a storage representation for the following lists:

   (a, (b, (c, d)), e, f)
   ((x), y, A, z)   where A = (a, b, (c, d))

2. Represent the graph of Fig. 5-4.19 by a list structure. Draw its storage representation.
3. Give an algorithm for the function EQ which tests to see if two atomic arguments are
   equal.
4. Write an algorithm for the function ATOM which tests to see if an argument is atomic.
   (Note that an empty list is nonatomic.)
5. Using the Algorithms EQ and ATOM, plus HEAD, TAIL, and CONSTRUCT, derive
   algorithms for the UNION and INTERSECTION of two lists. For example, UNION((a, b,
   (c, d)), (a, (b))) is (a, b, (c, d), (b)), and INTERSECTION ((a, b, (c, d)), (a, (b))) is (a).
6. Construct an Algorithm REVERSE for reversing a given list. For example, REVERSE
   ((a, b, (c, d))) is ((c, d), b, a). Use the "pure" LISP functions in your algorithm.

5-4.3   Other Representations of Graphs

We will now discuss another storage method for graphs. The best storage representation
for some general graph depends on the nature of the data and on the operations which are
to be performed on these data. Furthermore, the choice of a suitable representation is
affected by other factors such as the number of nodes, the average number of edges
leaving a node, whether a graph is directed, the frequency of insertions and/or deletions
to be performed, etc.

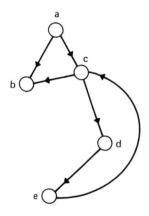

FIGURE 5-4.19.

Arrays can sometimes be used (when there is at most one edge between any pair of nodes and there are no *slings*) to represent graphs. In this case the nodes are numbered from 1 to n, and a two-dimensional array with n rows and n columns is used to represent the graph. Also, vectors could be required to store data on nodes in such a representation. This approach is not very suitable for a graph that has a large number of nodes or many nodes which are connected to only a few edges, nor when the graph must be continually altered.

If there are a number of branches between a pair of nodes and a considerable number of nodes that are connected to only a few other nodes, then a storage structure representation for such a graph could be the one shown in Fig. 5-4.20. Observe that the graph is weighted and that the storage representation consists of a node table directory and, associated with each entry in this directory, we can have an edge list. A typical node directory entry consists of a node number, the data associated with it, the number of edges emanating from it, and a pointer field which gives the address of the edge list associated with this node. Each edge list, in this case, is stored as a sequential table whose typical

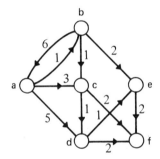

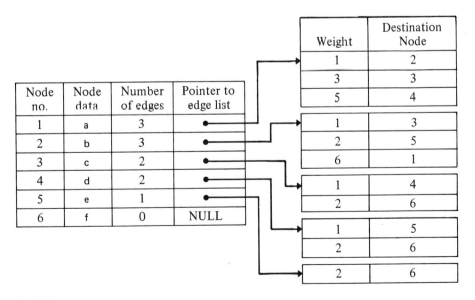

FIGURE 5-4.20.

entry consists of the weight of an edge and the node number at which that particular edge terminates. For a graph which is continually being changed, a representation which stores each edge list as a linked list is more desirable. In such a case it is not necessary to have the field which denotes the number of edges in the node table directory.

As another example, let us examine the storage representation of a grammar. Such a representation becomes important in applications where grammars must be examined and manipulated as in top-down parsing (see Sec. 5-2.3). In this application an efficient storage representation for the grammar is required, since various alternative rules must be tested for their applicability during each stage in the construction of a parse.

An example of an efficient representation uses a multilinked structure to represent the grammar. In this representation the node structure used is as follows:

NAME		
TYPE	ALTER	NEXT

Each node represents some symbol X in the right-hand side of some rule and consists of four fields NAME, TYPE, ALTER, and NEXT where:

1   NAME is the symbol X itself.
2   TYPE is a pointer variable which is NULL if X is a terminal symbol; otherwise, since in this case X is nonterminal, it points to the node which corresponds to the first symbol in the first right-hand side for X.
3   ALTER is a pointer variable which points to the first symbol of the next alternate right-hand side following the one in which the node is situated. This only applies for the first symbol in a right-hand side. Otherwise, the value is NULL.
4   NEXT is a pointer variable which denotes the next symbol in the right-hand side, or NULL.

Furthermore, each metavariable is represented by a pointer variable which points to the first symbol in its first right-hand side. Figure 5-4.21 represents the graph of the following grammar:

$$<e> ::= <e> \ <aop> \ <t> \ | \ <t>$$
$$<t> ::= <t> \ <mop> \ <f> \ | \ <f>$$
$$<f> ::= <f> \uparrow <p> \ | \ <p>$$
$$<p> ::= (<e>) \ | \ i$$
$$<aop> ::= + \ | \ -$$
$$<mop> ::= * \ | \ /$$

Exercises for Sec. 5-4.3

1.   Represent the graph of Fig. 5-1.5 by a list structure. Draw its storage representation.
2.   Draw a storage representation for the following grammar:

$$E ::= a \ | \ b \ | \ (E + E)$$
$$B ::= R \ | \ (B)$$
$$R ::= E = E$$

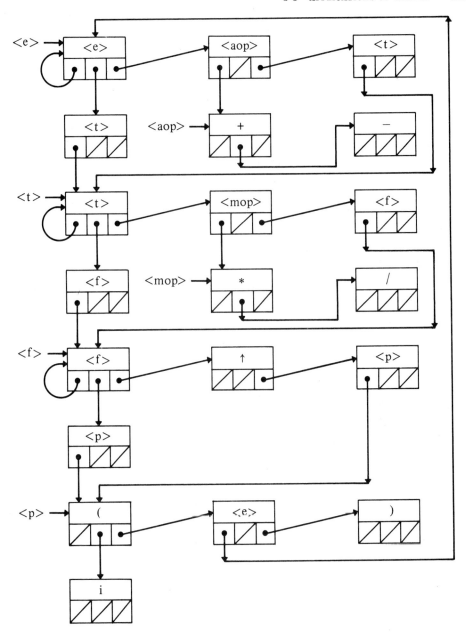

FIGURE 5-4.21   Multilinked representation of a grammar.

5-5   APPLICATIONS OF GRAPHS

The previous section discussed a number of possible storage structures for graphs. In this section we have selected four applications in which graph structures are extensively used. One of the first applications of graphs to be computerized was concerned with project scheduling, a technique which is often known as PERT or CPM. This topic is covered in the first subsection. Complex data structures are often used in computer graphics systems and, consequently, these are introduced in Sec. 5-5.2. One of the earliest symbol-manipulation applications to be computerized was symbolic differentiation. This application is discussed in the third subsection. The problem of topological sorting is described in Sec. 5-5.4.

5-5.1   PERT and Related Techniques

A directed graph is a natural way of describing, representing, and analyzing complex projects which consist of many interrelated activities. The project might be, for example, the design and construction of a power dam or the design and erection of an apartment building. In this section we are interested in determining the critical path of a digraph. Such a critical path is a very important management tool that can be applied to many situations. There are a number of management techniques such as PERT (Program Evaluation and Review Technique) and CPM (Critical Path Method) which employ a graph as the structure on which analysis is based. The problem of finding a minimal path between two nodes was discussed in Sec. 5-4.1. A critical path, however, involves finding the longest path between two nodes in a weighted digraph.

This section will introduce certain basic terminology associated with finding the critical path of a graph. An informal algorithm will be given for computing the critical path(s) of a weighted graph.

Formally, a PERT graph is a finite digraph, with no parallel edges or cycles, in which there is exactly one source (i.e., a node whose indegree is 0) and one sink (i.e., a node whose outdegree is 0). Furthermore, each edge in the graph is assigned a weight (time) value. The directed edges are meant to represent activities, with the directed edge joining nodes which represent the start time and finish time of the activity. The weight value of each edge is taken to be the time it takes to complete the activity.

Although there will be a number of independent activities in the graph, there will usually be certain essential dependencies, with respect to time, which have the form that activity a_i must be completed before activity a_j can begin. If all such time dependencies are available, then they can be conveniently displayed in a directed graph such as in Fig. 5-5.1. The project has eight activities, and the activities follow a particular order in the sense that certain activities must be completed before certain other activities can begin. Each node is called an *event* and represents a point in time. In particular, node v_1 denotes the start of the entire project (its source) and v_6 its completion (its sink). The numbers

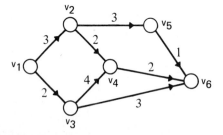

FIGURE 5-5.1   A PERT graph.

associated with the edges represent the number of days required to do that particular activity. From the graph we see that before activity $<v_3, v_4>$ can begin, activity $<v_1, v_3>$ must be completed. Similarly, before activity $<v_4, v_6>$ can begin, activities $<v_2, v_4>$ and $<v_3, v_4>$ must both be done, etc. Finally, in order to complete the project, activities $<v_5, v_6>$, $<v_3, v_6>$, and $<v_4, v_6>$ must all be completed.

We process the PERT graph by computing the earliest completion time for each activity under the restriction that, before an activity can begin, every activity upon which it depends must be completed. In terms of the graph, this corresponds to the assignment of time values to each node in such a manner that the value assigned to a node is the length of time to complete the activities along the longest path leading into that node. That is, we assign to a node the value which is the maximum, over all incoming edges, of the weight of an edge plus the time associated with that edge's source node. By definition, the value of 0 is assigned to the source node.

In summary, we can associate a time value with each event node in the following manner:

$$TE(v_1) = 0$$

$$TE(v_j) = \max \{t(P)\} \ j \neq 1$$

where $t(P)$ denotes the sum of time durations for a path P and where the maximum is taken over all paths from v_1 to v_j. When we finally assign a value to the sink node, this value is the earliest completion time for the entire project.

Referring to Fig. 5-5.1, node v_2 has only one incoming edge and, consequently, a value of $3 \ (= 0 + 3)$ is assigned to that node. Node v_4 has two incoming edges, so we must take the temporally longer path length $(v_1, v_3, v_4) \ (= 2 + 4)$ rather than the path $(v_1, v_2, v_4) \ (= 3 + 2)$ and assign 6 to node v_4. Node v_6 has four incoming paths (v_1, v_3, v_6), (v_1, v_3, v_4, v_6), (v_1, v_2, v_5, v_6), and (v_1, v_2, v_4, v_6). The value for the first path is 5, while that of the second is 8, and that of the third and fourth is 7; therefore, a value of 8 is assigned to v_6. Since v_6 is the sink node, assigning v_6 a value of 8 indicates that the project will require at least eight days to complete. The network with the earliest completion time, TE, assigned to each node is given in Fig. 5-5.2.

Having progressed this far, we can next calculate the latest completion time associated with each node. This is the latest time an activity can be completed without causing

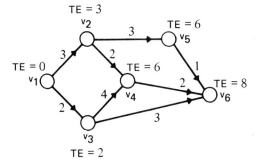

FIGURE 5-5.2.

a delay in the earliest completion date of the project (i.e., they are the latest completion times associated with the activities that do not cause the TE value of the sink node to be increased). These latest completion times, TL, are assigned to nodes in such a way that the assigned TL value is the largest value which will still allow every activity starting at that node to be completed without an overall time increase. In terms of the graph, we assign to a node the value which is the minimum, over all outgoing edges, of the edge's destination node TL value minus the edge weight. By definition, the TL value of the sink node equals its TE value.

In summary, we can associate a time value with each event node in the following manner:

$$TL(v_n) = TE(v_n)$$

$$TL(v_j) = TE(v_n) - \max \{t(P)\} \ j \neq n$$

where $t(P)$ denotes the sum of time durations for a path P from v_j to v_n and where the maximum is taken over all such paths and subtracted from $TE(v_n)$.

Returning to Fig. 5-5.2, since v_5 has only one outgoing edge, we assigned to v_5 a TL value of 7($=8 - 1$). Likewise, node v_4 has only one outgoing edge, so a TL value of 6($= 8 - 2$) is assigned to v_4. Node v_3 has two outgoing edges, $<v_3, v_4>$ and $<v_3, v_6>$. The minimum of 2 is assigned to that node. Continuing this process yields a TL value of 0 for the source node. The PERT graph of our example with its TE and TL values is given in Fig. 5-5.3.

After having computed the TE and TL values for each node in a graph, we can determine its critical path(s). A *critical path* is a path from the source node to the sink node such that if any activity on the path is delayed by an amount t, then the entire project is delayed by t. Each node on the critical path has its TL value equal to its TE value. This means that, if the project is to be completed by its earliest completion time, the nodes on the critical path must be reached at their earliest completion times. For our example graph, the nodes on the critical path are: v_1, v_3, v_4, v_6 and the critical path is (v_1, v_3, v_4, v_6). Nodes that are not on the critical path have slack time associated with them. *Slack time* of

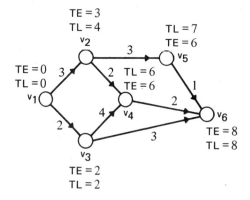

FIGURE 5-5.3.

a node is merely the difference between its TL and TE values, and it indicates the amount of spare time which is available in doing a particular activity. In our example, node v_2 has a slack time of one day. This means that the activities that must be completed at node v_2 can be delayed one day if necessary without causing a delay in the project.

In order to reduce the earliest completion time for the project, only those activities on the critical path must be speeded up. Since in practice the number of activities which lie on the critical path in large graphs is a small percentage of the total number of activities, say 10 percent, only those 10 percent need be improved.

We shall now consider the representation of a PERT graph according to the method suggested in Sec. 5-4.3 using arrays. For the node access directory, there will be four one-dimensional arrays, DATA, TE, TL, and POINTER. For node i, DATA[i] contains label data and information about i, TE[i] and TL[i] are the earliest and latest completion times for node i, and POINTER[i] is the index into the table of edges where the edges originating at node i are listed in successive array positions. For the table of edges, there will be two one-dimensional arrays, TIME and DEST, with TIME[j] being the weight of edge j in time units and DEST[j] being the destination node of edge j. The originating node for edge j is node i, where i is the largest number such that POINTER[i] $\leq$ j. Figure 5-5.4 illustrates the storage structures that we are now describing.

The following algorithm will create the desired storage structures by reading edge data from an input file. For convenience, this algorithm assumes that the input data has been sorted into ascending order by originating node number, with node 1 being the source node (the start of the project) and with the highest numbered node being the sink node, corresponding to the completion of the project. The edge data items are the following: ORIGIN, the node number of the originating node; INFO, data or information about the originating node; WEIGHT, the edge weight in time units; and END, the node number of the destination node. Note that INFO need be given only once for a particular originating node; it can be a null string other times. In order to input information and label data for the project sink node, an extra set of edge data items will have to be used since the sink node has outdegree 0. The destination node number will be zero in this case, and this input record will be functioning like a "trailer card," thus providing a second means of terminating data input.

NODE NO.	DATA	TE	TL	POINTER
1	v_1	0	∞	1
2	v_2	0	∞	3
3	v_3	0	∞	5
4	v_4	0	∞	7
5	v_5	0	∞	8
6	v_6	0	∞	9

EDGE NO.	TIME	DEST
1	3	2
2	2	3
3	2	4
4	3	5
5	4	4
6	3	6
7	2	6
8	1	6

FIGURE 5-5.4 The data arrays after Algorithm CREATE has read the input file.

Algorithm CREATE. Given the global array structures DATA, TE, TL, POINTER, TIME, and DEST, this algorithm reads edge data from an input file and assigns values to the elements of these arrays so as to reflect the relationships existing in a PERT graph. The variables NO_NODES and NO_EDGES are also considered to be global, and they give the number of different nodes and edges, respectively, that have been encountered in the graph.

1. [Initialize] Set TE ← POINTER ← 0, DATA ← ' ',NO_NODES ← NO_EDGES ← 0, TL ← ∞ (or some very large number).
2. [Read edge data items]
   If input file is exhausted, then Exit; otherwise, read ORIGIN, INFO, WEIGHT, and END.
3. [Assign to array elements]
   If ORIGIN < NO_NODES, then print 'data out of sequence', and Exit.
   If INFO ≠ ' ', then set DATA[ORIGIN] ← INFO.
   If ORIGIN > NO_NODES, (new originating node)
   then set NO_NODES ← NO_NODES + 1,
       POINTER[NO_NODES] ← NO_EDGES + 1,
       if END ≤ 0,
       then Exit;
       otherwise, set NO_EDGES ← NO_EDGES + 1, TIME[NO_EDGES] ← WEIGHT, and
           DEST[NO_EDGES] ← END;
   otherwise, (same originating node)
       if END ≤ 0,
       then print 'nonsink node has an edge with invalid destination', and Exit;
       otherwise, set NO_EDGES ← NO_EDGES + 1, TIME[NO_EDGES] ← WEIGHT, and
           DEST[NO_EDGES] ← END.
   Go to step 2.

Step 1 initializes the arrays and counters appropriately. In step 3, label information is stored if necessary. Then, if a new originating node has been encountered, the node counter is updated and the entry in the POINTER array is set. These actions are omitted if the node is a previously encountered one. At this time, the edge counter is updated if it is a valid edge, and the appropriate data is stored in the arrays.

In order to determine the critical path, the TE and TL values must be computed for each node. The following algorithm does this computation and then prints out the nodes on the critical path.

Algorithm PROCESS. Given the global arrays as previously described, along with NO_NODES and NO_EDGES, the number of different nodes and edges in the PERT graph, this algorithm computes and stores the TE and TL values for each node and then prints those nodes which lie on the critical path. NODE # and EDGE # indicate which node and which edge are currently being examined.

1. [Initialize to compute TE values] Set NODE # ← 1 and EDGE # ← POINTER[1].
2. [Compute TE value for each node]
   Repeat while NODE # < NO_NODES:

       repeat while EDGE # < POINTER[NODE # + 1]:
           set TE[DEST[EDGE #]] ← MAX(TE[DEST[EDGE #]], TE[NODE #] +
           TIME[EDGE #]) **and** EDGE # ← EDGE # + 1.
       Set NODE # ← NODE # + 1.
3. [Initialize to compute TL values]
    Set TL[NODE #] ← TE[NODE #], NODE # ← NO_NODES − 1,
    and EDGE # ← NO_EDGES.
4. [Compute TL values for each node]
    Repeat while NODE # ≥ 1:
       repeat while EDGE # ≥ POINTER[NODE #]:
           set TL[NODE #] ← MIN(TL[NODE #], TL[DEST[EDGE #]] −
           TIME[EDGE #]), **and** EDGE # ← EDGE # − 1.
       Set NODE # ← NODE # − 1.
5. [Output the nodes on the critical path]
    Repeat for NODE # = 1, 2, ..., NO_NODES:
       if TE[NODE #] = TL[NODE #], **then** print NODE # and DATA[NODE #].
    Exit.

    The operation of this algorithm is quite straightforward. In step 2 the elements $TE[v_j] = \max \{t(P)\}$ $j \neq 1$ are computed, thereby assigning to each node, v_j, the time taken along the longest path, P, from node v_1 to node v_j. In step 3 the latest completion time for the project finish node is defined to be the earliest completion time for the project, and the counters are reset. In step 4 the values $TL[v_j] = TE[v_n] - \max \{t(P)\}$ $j \neq n$ are computed, thereby assigning to each node v_j (other than the sink node v_n) the latest time value such that adding this time value to the time associated with the longest path from v_j to v_n does not exceed the project finish date. In step 5 the nodes on the critical path (those nodes whose TE and TL values are equal) are printed, along with appropriate labeling information.

    It is also possible to use linked lists as the method of representing a PERT graph. For example, each event node of the graph could be represented by a node structure of the form

OUT	DATA	TE	TL	IN	LINK

where OUT is a pointer to the first node in a list of the edges originating at this event node, IN is a pointer to the first node in a list of the edges whose destination is this event node, DATA is label information for this event node, TE and TL are the earliest and latest completion times for this event node, and LINK is a pointer to the next structural node in the list of event nodes. For the edges, a structure of the form

OUTL	SOURCE	TIME	DEST	INL

could be used. OUTL is a pointer to the next edge in the list of edges originating at the event node pointed to by SOURCE, INL is a pointer to the next edge in the list of edges whose destination is the event node pointed to by DEST, and TIME is the weight in time units of this edge which joins the nodes pointed to by SOURCE and DEST.

Algorithms to create such a representation of a PERT graph and determine the nodes on the critical path are relatively easy to construct. The computational logic is the same as that used in the array representation algorithms, but naturally the logic dealing with the manipulation of the storage structures will differ.

Exercises for Sec. 5-5.1

1. Trace Algorithms CREATE and PROCESS using as data the graph given in Fig. 5-5.4.
2. Given node structures for the event nodes and edges of a PERT graph as described at the end of Sec. 5-5.1, construct an algorithm that will create a linked-list representation of this graph. The algorithm should have input edge data in the form:

    ORIGIN, the label of the source node for some edge

    END, the label of the edge's destination node

    WEIGHT, the weight of the edge in time units

    The algorithm should create and insert nodes ORIGIN and END into the event node list, if they are not already there. It must then create an edge node and insert it into the proper incoming and outgoing edge lists and update all pointers correctly.
3. Given a linked representation of a PERT graph as constructed by the algorithm in Exercise 2, write an algorithm that will traverse this representation, computing the TE and TL values for the event node. The algorithm should then print out the nodes that are on the critical path.
4. Write PL/I procedures that implement Algorithms CREATE and PROCESS in Sec. 5-5.1 and the algorithms of Exercises 2 and 3. Evaluate the two representations, arrays and linked lists, in terms of storage use and processing speed for small and large PERT graphs.

5-5.2   Computer Graphics Applications

"*Computer graphics* is the general term applied herein to the use of a digital computer to form an internal model representation of an externally perceived graphical entity." (Abrams [1971].) Such modeling makes possible the modification, manipulation, or other such processing of the entity and the subsequent display of the entity in a visible format. Some typical applications of computer graphics include graph plotting, map drawing, cartoon drawing, as well as building, road, aircraft, and automobile design.

There are two extreme modes in computer graphics—interactive and passive. As an introduction to many facets of the subject, we will discuss a system typical of each mode. The reader should be aware that this distinction is primarily for pedagogic purposes; a typical practical system would be a hybrid of the two extremes.

Interactive computer graphics is that mode of graphics in which the user and computer interact or converse on-line. An on-line display device and manual input devices are used, providing very fast computer response to the user commands.

The most commonly used display is the cathode ray tube (CRT), a familiar device used in noncomputer equipment such as radar scopes and television screens. The method by which the CRT can display a computer-drawn picture is quite simple. Digital electrical signals generated by the computer are transformed, by a digital-to-analog converter, into a continuous signal. This signal controls the quantity and direction of electrons emitted by one portion of the CRT; these electrons create the visible spots on the phosphorescent surface of the tube.

The major drawback with the CRT is that the points produced by the electron bombardment are extremely temporary, i.e., they quickly fade. In order to maintain a picture, the process by which the picture was created must be constantly repeated. This process is called "refreshing" the display and must be repeated about 30 times a second to avoid a flickering picture.

Other output devices in which the picture does not vanish have been developed. These include the direct-view storage tube and the plasma panel. At present these devices have technical problems which make them less popular than the conventional CRT for most applications.

In an *interactive system*, the user must communicate quickly and effectively with the computer. The input device used must provide for issuing commands, positioning symbols on the screen, and specifying items to be deleted or changed. Devices created for this purpose include the keyboard, the light pen, and the tablet.

A typical interactive system is illustrated in Fig. 5-5.5. A tablet and keyboard are used as input devices; a CRT is the output device. Note the *display processor*. This processor interacts with the CPU and accesses main memory to obtain the instructions describing the picture to be generated. The display processor can interpret these instructions and pass the appropriate signals to the CRT. The display processor is also responsible for refreshing the CRT, thus relieving the CPU of this time-consuming task. Sophisticated display processors may have the capability to generate simple geometric shapes.

The second graphics mode is noninteractive, or passive. In this mode a system usually operates in a batch environment; the input devices are typically card, disk, or tape files, and the output devices are usually "hard copy," that is, they provide a permanent picture. Examples of such output devices are line printers, plotters, and drafting machines. The most common passive output device is the moving pen plotter. This device moves a pen in the xy plane, under computer control.

The hard-copy devices generate pictures very slowly and are thus seldom used in interactive systems. The only exception would be the case where a permanent record of the final product is desired.

A typical off-line system configuration is shown in Fig. 5-5.6. The processor generates the analog signals, which control the plotter, from the tape created by the main computer.

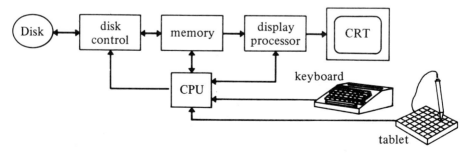

FIGURE 5-5.5 A typical interactive graphics system.

We will now discuss an aspect of computer graphics which is of greatest interest in this book—the data structures aspect. First consider some basic concepts.

All of the computer graphics output devices provide a two-dimensional surface on which the pictures are to be created. This surface is treated as a cartesian coordinate system; the only points which can be specified are those addressed by an x coordinate and y coordinate of the system. All the devices can display any point so addressed. Some of the more sophisticated devices have the capability to generate a continuous line between two addressable points; however, many create a line by displaying equally spaced points that lie along the line.

The earliest computer graphics systems were designed for graph plotting and data display. Simple data structures such as the one- and two-dimensional array were sufficient for this complexity of graphical display. The structure would either be a vector of the (x, y) coordinates of all points to be displayed, a vector of y coordinates corresponding to implicit x coordinates, or a two-dimensional array A in which A[i, j] would be set to indicate that the point (i, j) was to be displayed.

This type of structure is adequate for applications in which the displays are relatively static; however, much of the subsequent development of computer graphics has been in applications requiring more versatile displays. Some of the more promising areas are the design of buildings, aircraft, and automobiles, and this has led to the development of general graphics systems which can be used for any purpose.

Such applications require a versatile display that can be easily changed—deleting from, transforming, and adding to the display must be accommodated. The simple data structures previously discussed are not adequate for these operations. In order to provide the display capabilities desired, a more versatile data structure is necessary. An adequate data structure should satisfy the following criteria:

1 The structure must provide a conceptual model of the subject; that is, the ordering and relationships between the subject parts must be preserved.
2 The structure must support the displaying, manipulation, transformation, and analysis of the subject.
3 The structure must be satisfactory in terms of memory requirements and processing speeds.

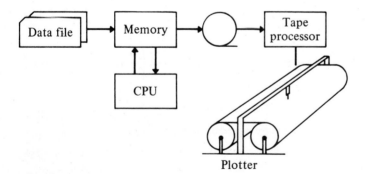

Plotter

FIGURE 5-5.6 A typical off-line system configuration.

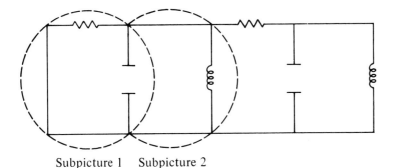

Subpicture 1   Subpicture 2

FIGURE 5-5.7.

The reader's knowledge of data structures at this point should indicate that some type of linked structure could satisfy these requirements.

Consider two instances of the simplest type of list structure, i.e., two linear lists, one with the coordinates of points to be displayed, and the other with the coordinates of end points of lines to be displayed.

Using a linked representation, the deletion or addition of a point or line is trivial, requiring only the changing of a few pointers rather than the shifting of many elements of an array. The concatenation of two pictures is also simple; the line and point lists of each need only be linked.

This structure would satisfy the three requirements for a simple system like interactive graph plotting. However, for more complex applications, a more complex data structure is necessary to satisfy the three criteria.

In order to satisfy the first criterion, the data structure must be capable of specifying relationships between entities within the picture. One important concept in graphics is the notion of a subpicture, that is, a segment of a picture. Consider Fig. 5-5.7, which is an electrical circuit composed of the combination of two simpler circuits. This hierarchical structure is illustrated by the tree diagram of Fig. 5-5.8.

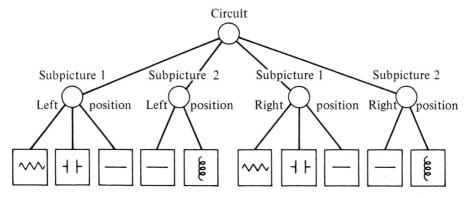

FIGURE 5-5.8.

Consider this structure with respect to the third criterion. Obviously, this data structure results in the inefficient use of storage because of the repetition of certain nodes. This inefficiency can be removed by using a directed graph. Such a structure, equivalent to Fig. 5-5.8, is shown in Fig. 5-5.9. This type of structure conserves memory space; by applying the subpicture concept, it also provides an implicit subroutine property. Each copy of a picture or subpicture is created by passing parameters to a subroutine which is responsible for generating all occurrences of an entity. For example, each node in Fig. 5-5.9 would contain scale and positional data characteristic of that particular occurrence of the subpicture.

A data structure similar to this is used by the Bell Telephone Laboratories GRAPHIC 2 system. Such a structure is sufficient for some limited on-line design, but is not as suitable for applications where frequent searching and updating are performed. As an example, consider the problem of finding all occurrences of a particular basic element, like the line element in Fig. 5-5.9. This would require that the entire graph be traversed, which would represent a significant amount of computing time.

The problem of providing for more efficient searching and updating can be solved by introducing a data structure that allows rapid access to graphical topology information. The hierarchical ring structure provides this facility to some extent. The hierarchical ring structure has levels, similar to the tree or directed graph discussed previously in this chapter, but the elements at any level are connected in a ring. Logically related elements are linked such that any data item can be accessed from any other item. Figure 5-5.10 shows a ring structure equivalent to the directed graph in Fig. 5-5.9.

Note that the occurrences of similar basic elements, i.e., the lowest-level elements, are linked together. It is this feature that improves the access efficiency of the structure. Insertion is relatively simple in such a structure; however, deletions must be executed with care to ensure that all relevant pointers are correctly changed.

Systems that use structures similar to this are the General Motors Graphics System

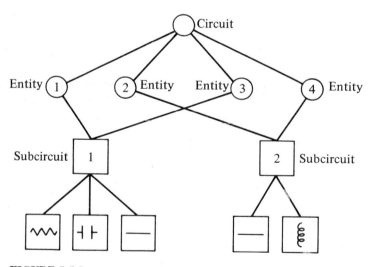

FIGURE 5-5.9.

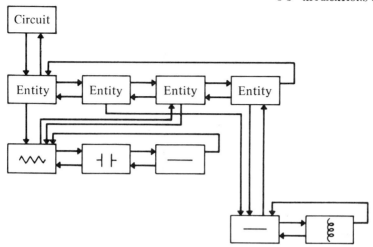

FIGURE 5-5.10.

(Williams [1971]), the 3DPDP system (van Dam [1971]), and the SKETCHPAD system (Sutherland [1963]).

The major drawback of the hierarchical ring structures is the amount of memory space required for the multitude of pointers. For many applications this problem is compensated for by the improved flexibility and accessibility of the structure.

As a detailed example of a possible data structure for an interactive graphics system, we will consider a structure similar to, but less complex and less general than, the structure used by the SKETCHPAD system. The basic elements of this system are points and lines, and it is assumed that we have an output device capable of displaying these two elements. The data structure is a variation of the hierarchical ring structure and uses double linkage to enable easy manipulation of the lists.

The data structure makes use of four types of nodes, which are illustrated in Fig. 5-5.11. For each picture or subpicture (entity), there is a MASTER node which has four fields. The PLINK, LLINK, and ELINK fields are the pointers to the rings of points, lines, and entities, respectively, which make up the picture. The TMATRIX field is the master transformation matrix, the purpose of which is explained later.

The POINT, LINE, and ENTITY nodes are ring nodes and, therefore, each has a LLINK and a RLINK field to point to the previous and next elements of the ring, respectively. The LINE node only has fields which are pointers to the nodes representing the end points of the line.

Each POINT node has X and Y fields which contain the x and y coordinates of the point. As well, there are three fields named LLINK1, LLINK2, and LLINK3 which are NULL or point to line nodes if the point is an end point. The LLINK4 field is used if the point is an endpoint to more than three lines; LLINK4 contains the address of a BUCKET node which consists of five fields, LLINK1, LLINK2, LLINK3, LLINK4, and BULINK, a pointer to the next bucket.

The MLINK field of the ENTITY node points to the MASTER node of the structure

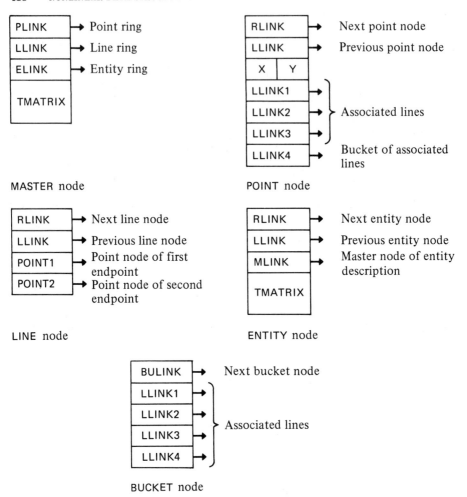

FIGURE 5-5.11.

representing the subpicture. The only field not discussed is the TMATRIX field. TMATRIX contains data pertinent to the particular occurrence of the subpicture that the ENTITY node represents.

To understand properly the use of the TMATRIX field, we must digress somewhat and present a brief discussion of the subject of picture transformations. The three most common picture transformations are rotation about a point, shifting or translation in the x and/or y direction, and scaling, which enlarges or decreases the picture in the x and/or y direction.

The shifting or translation of a point (x, y) can be expressed algebraically as

$$\left.\begin{aligned} x' &= x + T_x\\ y' &= y + T_y \end{aligned}\right\} \tag{1}$$

where T_x and T_y are the translation amounts in the x and y directions, respectively. The translation of the diagram in Fig. 5-5.12a by $T_x = 5$ and $T_y = 3$ is shown in Fig. 5-5.12b.

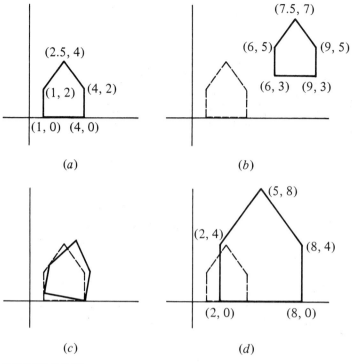

(7.5, 7)
(6, 5)   (9, 5)
(6, 3)   (9, 3)

(2.5, 4)
(1, 2) (4, 2)
(1, 0) (4, 0)

(a)

(b)

(5, 8)
(2, 4)
(8, 4)
(2, 0)   (8, 0)

(c)

(d)

FIGURE 5-5.12.

The rotation of a point (x, y) about the origin through a clockwise angle θ can be expressed as:

$$x' = x \cos \theta + y \sin \theta$$
$$y' = -x \sin \theta + y \cos \theta$$

$$(2)$$

The rotation of a point (x, y) about any other point (p, q) can be expressed as a combination of rotation and translation:

1   Shift the points such that (p, q) lies on the origin to give:

$$x' = x - p$$
$$y' = y - q$$

2   Rotate this point about the origin

$$x'' = x' \cos \theta + y' \sin \theta$$
$$y'' = -x' \sin \theta + y' \cos \theta$$

3   Shift the points such that (p, q) is returned to original position.

$$x''' = x'' + p$$
$$y''' = y'' + q$$

Figure 5-5.12c shows the original diagram rotated about the point (4, 0) by 10°.

The scaling of a point is the changing of the (x, y) coordinates by the factors S_x and S_y. This can be expressed:

$$\left. \begin{array}{l} x' = x \cdot S_x \\ y' = y \cdot S_y \end{array} \right\} \tag{3}$$

To double a picture choose $S_x = S_y = 2$. If $S_x \neq S_y$, the picture will appear distorted. Figure 5-5.12d shows the original diagram scaled with $S_x = S_y = 2$.

These two-dimensional transformations can be represented in a matrix format. The transformation of the point (x, y) to (x', y') can be represented as

$$[x'\ y'\ 1] = [x\ y\ 1] \begin{bmatrix} a & d & 0 \\ b & e & 0 \\ c & f & 1 \end{bmatrix}$$

The 3×3 matrix completely specifies any transformation consisting of any sequence of translations, rotations, and scalings. The matrix format of the transformations given by Eqs. (1), (2), and (3) is as follows:

$$\textit{Translation:}\quad [x'\ y'\ 1] = [x\ y\ 1] \begin{bmatrix} 1 & 0 & 0 \\ 0 & 1 & 0 \\ T_x & T_y & 1 \end{bmatrix}$$

$$\textit{Rotation:}\quad [x'\ y'\ 1] = [x\ y\ 1] \begin{bmatrix} \cos\theta & -\sin\theta & 0 \\ \sin\theta & \cos\theta & 0 \\ 0 & 0 & 1 \end{bmatrix}$$

$$\textit{Scaling:}\quad [x'\ y'\ 1] = [x\ y\ 1] \begin{bmatrix} S_x & 0 & 0 \\ 0 & S_y & 0 \\ 0 & 0 & 1 \end{bmatrix}$$

Note that a 3×3 matrix is required in order to specify point translations.

A sequence of transformations can be specified by multiplying together the independent matrices specifying each. If matrix A represents the first transformation and matrix B, the second, the matrix A·B will represent the first transformation followed by the second. The matrix B·A is not the same, as it represents the second transformation followed by the first. This multiplication can be repeated so that any sequence of transformations can be represented by one matrix.

As an example, consider the rotation of a point about any other point. The sequence of transformations necessary for this was discussed previously. This sequence can be represented as

$$[x'''\ y'''\ 1] = [x\ y\ 1] \begin{bmatrix} 1 & 0 & 0 \\ 0 & 1 & 0 \\ -T_x & -T_y & 1 \end{bmatrix} \begin{bmatrix} \cos\theta & -\sin\theta & 0 \\ \sin\theta & \cos\theta & 0 \\ 0 & 0 & 1 \end{bmatrix} \begin{bmatrix} 1 & 0 & 0 \\ 0 & 1 & 0 \\ T_x & T_y & 1 \end{bmatrix}$$

Now that we understand some of the operations necessary to effect picture transformation, we turn our attention to the data structure needed to accomplish these transformations.

The data structure corresponding to the picture in Fig. 5-5.13 is shown in Fig. 5-5.14. The node with the label PICTURE is the master node for the entire picture; note that the

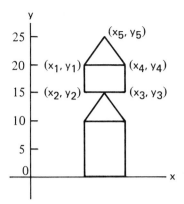

FIGURE 5-5.13.

PLINK and LLINK fields are NULL, indicating that there are no independent lines or points in the picture. The two subpictures from which the picture is composed are SQ and TRI. Each subpicture is composed of three lines. Note that neither subpicture has an independent point. The transformation matrices in the second and fourth nodes of the PIC-TURE entity ring contain the information necessary to shift and expand the top figure to the location and size of the bottom figure.

The basic manipulations to be performed on a graphic data structure are:

1 Insertion of elements
2 Deletion of elements
3 Transformation of structure or substructure
4 Display of elements

Algorithms to perform these manipulations are presented, but first some preliminary discussion is necessary. We assume the existence of an AVAIL function which, given a parameter description of nodes such as POINT_NODE, LINE_NODE, etc., returns the pointer to a node taken from the availability list. This node is the correct size, as derived from the parameter for the AVAIL function. We also assume that the statement 'set AVAIL ← X' returns the node to an appropriate location in the availability list.

We use three insertion algorithms: PINSERT, LINSERT, and ENTINSERT, which, along with the algorithm MASTER, can be used to create and make additions to picture displays.

Algorithm PINSERT. Given HEAD, a pointer to the master node of the structure into which the point is to be inserted, and X₁ and Y₁, the coordinates of the point to be inserted, Algorithm PINSERT creates a node to represent the point if a node does not exist already. A pointer to the point node is returned. P is a pointer.

1. [Start of point ring] Set P ← PLINK(HEAD).
2. [Check for node representing point]
    If P = HEAD,
    then go to step 3; (node not found)
    otherwise,

if X(P) = X$_1$ and Y(P) = Y$_1$,

then set PINSERT ← P, and Exit;

otherwise, set P ← RLINK(P) and repeat step 2.

3. [Create node]   Set P ← AVAIL(POINT_NODE), RLINK(P) ← PLINK(HEAD),
LLINK(P) ← HEAD, PLINK(HEAD) ← P, X(P) ← X$_1$, Y(P) ← Y$_1$,
LLINK1 ← LLINK2 ← LLINK3 ← LLINK4 ← NULL, LLINK(RLINK(P)) ← P,
PINSERT ← P, and Exit.

Algorithm LINSERT.   Given HEAD, a pointer to a master node and (X$_1$, Y$_1$), (X$_2$, Y$_2$), the endpoints of the line, Algorithm LINSERT inserts the line represented by the endpoints. New nodes are created if the points are not represented. The value returned is the pointer to the line node. P, Q, R, S, and T are pointer variables.

1.   [Create new nodes for endpoints using Algorithm PINSERT]
Set P ← PINSERT(HEAD, X$_1$, Y$_1$), Q ← PINSERT(HEAD, X$_2$, Y$_2$).

2.   [Check if line is already defined]   Set R ← LLINK(HEAD).

3.   [Match line node with points]   If R = HEAD, then go to step 4.   (no line)
If POINT1(R) = P and POINT2(R) = Q or POINT1(R) = Q and POINT2(R) = P,
then go to step 5;
otherwise, set R ← RLINK(R) and repeat step 3.

4.   [Create line node]   Set R ← AVAIL(LINE_NODE), RLINK(R) ← LLINK(HEAD),
LLINK(HEAD) ← R, LLINK(R) ← HEAD, LLINK(RLINK(R)) ← R, POINT1(R) ← P,
POINT2(R) ← Q.

5.   [Make sure the point nodes point to the line node]
Set T ← P, P ← Q, Q ← NULL.
If T = NULL, then set LINSERT ← R, and Exit.
If LLINK1(T) = R or LLINK2(T) = R or LLINK3(T) = R, then repeat step 5.
If LLINK1(T) = NULL, then set LLINK1(T) ← R and repeat step 5.
If LLINK2(T) = NULL, then set LLINK2(T) ← R and repeat step 5.
If LLINK3(T) = NULL, then set LLINK3(T) ← R and repeat step 5.
Set S ← LLINK4(T). (Check the buckets belonging to a point.)
Repeat while S ≠ NULL:
     if LLINK1(S) = R or LLINK2(S) = R or LLINK3(S) = R or LLINK4(S) = R,
     then repeat step 5;
     otherwise,
          if LLINK1(S) = NULL, then set LLINK1(S) ← R and repeat step 5,
          if LLINK2(S) = NULL, then set LLINK2(S) ← R and repeat step 5,
          if LLINK3(S) = NULL, then set LLINK3(S) ← R and repeat step 5,
          if LLINK4(S) = NULL, then set LLINK4(S) ← R and repeat step 5,
          set T ← S, S ← BULINK(S).

6.   [Create a new bucket]
Set S ← AVAIL(BUCKET_NODE), LLINK1(S) ← R, BULINK(S) ← NULL,
LLINK2(S) ← LLINK3(S) ← LLINK4(S) ← NULL.
If POINT1(R) = T or POINT2(R) = T,
then set LLINK4(T) ← S;
otherwise, set BULINK(T) ← S.
Go to step 5.

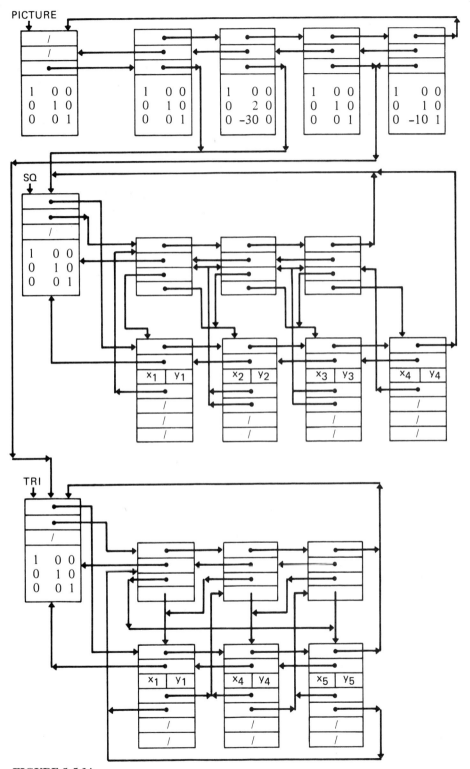

FIGURE 5-5.14.

Algorithm ENTINSERT.   Given HEAD, the pointer to the master node for the structure in which the entity is to be inserted; ENT, the pointer to the substructure representing the entity; and TRANS, the transformation matrix to be applied to the substructure, Algorithm ENTINSERT creates an entity node and links it to the entity ring. The value returned is the pointer to the entity node.

1. [Create node.]   Set P ← AVAIL(ENTITY_NODE), RLINK(P) ← ELINK(HEAD),
    LLINK(P) ← HEAD, MLINK(P) ← ENT, TMATRIX(P) ← TRANS,
    ELINK(HEAD) ← P, LLINK(RLINK(P)) ← P, ENTINSERT ← P, and Exit.

Algorithm MASTER.   This algorithm creates and returns a pointer to a master node which is initialized so that the TMATRIX is the identity matrix and the links point to the node itself.

1. [Create node.]   Set P ← AVAIL(MASTER_NODE),
    PLINK(P) ← LLINK(P) ← ELINK(P) ← P,

$$\text{TMATRIX}(P) \leftarrow \begin{bmatrix} 1 & 0 & 0 \\ 0 & 1 & 0 \\ 0 & 0 & 1 \end{bmatrix}, \text{MASTER} \leftarrow P.$$

As an example of the use of these algorithms, the structure shown in Fig. 5-5.14 could be created by the following sequence of algorithm steps:

1. [Create structure to represent triangle.]
    Set TRI ← MASTER,
    call LINSERT(TRI, X_1, Y_1, X_4, Y_4),
    call LINSERT(TRI, X_4, Y_4, X_5, Y_5),
    call LINSERT(TRI, X_1, Y_1, X_5, Y_5).
2. [Create structure to represent three-sided square.]
    Set SQ ← MASTER,
    call LINSERT(SQ, X_1, Y_1, X_2, Y_2),
    call LINSERT(SQ, X_2, Y_2, X_3, Y_3),
    call LINSERT(SQ, X_3, Y_3, X_4, Y_4).
3. [Create picture by combining the 4 occurrences of the entities.]
    Set PICTURE ← MASTER,

$$\text{call ENTINSERT(PICTURE, SQ, } \begin{bmatrix} 1 & 0 & 0 \\ 0 & 1 & 0 \\ 0 & 0 & 1 \end{bmatrix})$$

$$\text{call ENTINSERT(PICTURE, TRI, } \begin{bmatrix} 1 & 0 & 0 \\ 0 & 1 & 0 \\ 0 & 0 & 1 \end{bmatrix})$$

$$\text{call ENTINSERT(PICTURE, SQ, } \begin{bmatrix} 1 & 0 & 0 \\ 0 & 2 & 0 \\ 0 & -30 & 1 \end{bmatrix})$$

$$\text{call ENTINSERT(PICTURE, TRI, } \begin{bmatrix} 1 & 0 & 0 \\ 0 & 1 & 0 \\ 0 & -10 & 1 \end{bmatrix})$$

The deletion algorithms are based on the following assumptions:

1 The deletion of a point requires that all lines for which that point is an endpoint be deleted as well. (Note that the other endpoint is not deleted, though it must no longer refer to the deleted line node.)

2 The deletion of a line does not cause the deletion of the endpoint.

3 The deletion of an entity causes only one entity node to be deleted.

To accomplish these deletions we use four algorithms. LINEDELETE deletes a line node referenced by a pointer; LDELETE deletes a line referenced by its endpoints; PDELETE deletes a point referenced by coordinates; and ENTDELETE deletes an entity node referenced by a pointer to the entity substructure and the entity transformation matrix.

Note that the removal of a node from a ring requires special checks for the first and last nodes in order that the master node is correctly changed. These special checks could be eliminated by using a ring header node of the same type as the nodes in the ring. This would be a wise decision if adequate storage space were available.

Algorithm LINEDELETE. Given HEAD, the master node of the structure in question, and P, the pointer to the line node to be deleted, Algorithm LINEDELETE deletes the node referenced and removes the reference to the line from the associated line field. Q, R, S, T, and V are auxiliary pointer variables.

1. [Delete node]
   If RLINK(P) $\neq$ HEAD, then set LLINK(RLINK(P)) $\leftarrow$ LLINK(P).
   If LLINK(P) = HEAD,
   then set LLINK(HEAD) $\leftarrow$ RLINK(P);
   otherwise, set RLINK(LLINK(P)) $\leftarrow$ RLINK(P).
2. [Remove line reference from endpoints]
   Repeat steps 3 to 5 for Q = POINT1(P), POINT2(P).
3. [Find S, the node or bucket containing the line reference]   Set S $\leftarrow$ Q.
   If LLINK1(S) = P or LLINK2(S) = P or LLINK3(S) = P,
   then go to step 4;
   otherwise, set T $\leftarrow$ LLINK4(S).   (prepare to look in buckets)
   Repeat while T $\neq$ NULL:
       set S $\leftarrow$ T, T $\leftarrow$ BULINK(T),
       if LLINK1(S) = P or LLINK2(S) = P or LLINK3(S) = P or LLINK4(S) = P,
       then go to step 4.
   Go to step 7.   (error—no line reference found)
4. [Replace line reference in node S with last line reference]
   If S = Q,   (prepare to find last bucket, T)
   then set T $\leftarrow$ LLINK4(S);
   otherwise, set T $\leftarrow$ BULINK(S).
   If T = NULL
   then set T $\leftarrow$ S;
   otherwise, repeat while BULINK(T) $\neq$ NULL: set T $\leftarrow$ BULINK(T).   (look for last reference, R)
   If T $\neq$ Q and LLINK4(T) $\neq$ NULL,

then set R ← LLINK4(T), LLINK4(T) ← NULL and go to step 5.
If LLINK3(T) ≠ NULL,
then set R ← LLINK3(T), LLINK3(T) ← NULL and go to step 5.
If LLINK2(T) ≠ NULL,
then set R ← LLINK2(T), LLINK2(T) ← NULL and go to step 5.
If LLINK1(T) ≠ NULL,
then set R ← LLINK1(T), LLINK1(T) ← NULL,

    if S = Q and T = Q,
    then go to step 5;   (do not delete point node)
    otherwise,   (delete empty bucket)
    if LLINK4(Q) = T,
    then set LLINK4(Q) ← NULL, AVAIL ← T and go to step 5;
    otherwise,
        set V ← LLINK4(Q),
        repeat while BULINK(V) ≠ T: set V ← BULINK(V),
        set BULINK(V) ← NULL, AVAIL ← T and go to step 5.

   Go to step 7.   (error—no empty bucket should have been found)

5. [Make actual replacement if necessary]
   If R ≠ P,   (*note:* if R = P, we have already deleted it)
   then if LLINK1(S) = P, then LLINK1(S) ← R;
      otherwise, if LLINK2(S) = P, then LLINK2(S) ← R;
         otherwise, if LLINK3(S) = P, then LLINK3(S) ← R;
            otherwise, if S ≠ Q and LLINK4(S) = P,
               then LLINK4(S) = R;
  (error—no line reference in S)   otherwise, go to step 7.

6. [Return line node after deleting references to it]
   Set AVAIL ← P, and Exit.

7. [Error return—pointers or nodes were not found as anticipated]
   Print appropriate message and stop.

In step 1 of the algorithm, the line node to be deleted is removed from the chain of line nodes belonging to HEAD. Then, in steps 3 through 5 all references to this line node are removed from the two endpoint point nodes. In step 3, the pointer S is set to point to the node (point node or bucket node) in which a reference to the line is found. It is an error if no reference is found. In step 4, the pointer T is set to point to the last node (point node or bucket node) that contains any line references at all. Having determined T, the line reference fields in T are searched for the last non NULL reference. This reference is saved in R and the field is set to NULL. If this action happened to empty a bucket node, the bucket node is returned to available storage. If no reference was found in T, this is an error. In step 5, the line reference in node S is replaced by the last line reference, R, which we obtained from node T. Note that if the last reference in T was, in fact, the reference to the deleted line, then no replacement need take place. The reference has already been set to NULL. These steps are then repeated for the other endpoint. In step 6, the unchained line node is returned to available storage and control returns to the calling procedure. Step 7 is an error trap which halts the algorithm if the data structure is not set up as expected (possibly because a user neglected to update pointers correctly).

The method of line-reference deletion chosen, namely, overwriting by the last line reference in a point node's set of line references, has certain advantages. First, it avoids gaps in the list of line references still available for a point node, and secondly, it enables better storage management because empty bucket nodes can be returned when they are no longer needed.

Algorithm LDELETE. Given HEAD, the master node of the structure and X_1, Y_1, X_2, Y_2, the coordinates of the endpoints of a line, Algorithm LDELETE finds the node corresponding to the line and uses the LINEDELETE function to delete the node and references to it. P is a pointer variable.

1. [Find endpoints] Set P ← LLINK(HEAD).
2. [Test endpoints vs. arguments]
   If P = HEAD,
   then print 'error—no endpoint match' and stop;
   otherwise,
       if X(POINT1(P)) = X_1 and Y(POINT1(P)) = Y_1 and
           X(POINT2(P)) = X_2 and Y(POINT2(P)) = Y_2
       or X(POINT1(P)) = X_2 and Y(POINT1(P)) = Y_2 and
           X(POINT2(P)) = X_1 and Y(POINT2(P)) = Y_1
       then go to step 3;
       otherwise, set P ← RLINK(P) and repeat step 2.
3. [Delete node] Call LINEDELETE(P), and Exit.

Algorithms PDELETE and ENTDELETE are left as exercises.

The transformation of a picture or subpicture is relatively simple using this data structure. One need only multiply the TMATRIX of the appropriate master with the transformation matrix corresponding to the desired transformations and place this new value in the TMATRIX field. That is, you set TMATRIX ← TMATRIX * [new transformation].

In order to display the picture stored by this data structure, one multiplies each point vector in the point ring with the TMATRIX field of the picture master node and makes the proper line or point display requests. The entity subpictures are displayed recursively; the transformation matrix applicable to a point is the product of the TMATRIX field of the subpicture master node with the TMATRIX field of the master node.

Algorithm DISPLAY. Given PICTURE, the master node of the picture to be displayed, and MAT, the transformation matrix applicable at the present level, Algorithm DISPLAY recursively traverses the data structure in order to create the visual representation of the picture. The algorithm assumes the existence of two routines: LINEWRITE (X_1, Y_1, X_2, Y_2), which creates a line on the graphics device with endpoints (X_1, Y_1) and (X_2, Y_2); and POINTWRITE (U, V), which creates a point on the same device with coordinates (U, V). The main level reference to DISPLAY should have the identity matrix as the argument for the MAT parameter.

1. [Create corresponding transformation matrix]
   Set MAT ← TMATRIX(PICTURE) * MAT.
2. [Traverse line ring to display lines]
   Set P ← LLINK(PICTURE).

Repeat while P $\neq$ PICTURE:

    set [X$_1$, Y$_1$, n] $\leftarrow$ [X(POINT1(P)), Y(POINT1(P)), 1] * MAT;

    if n $\neq$ 1, then print 'invalid matrix' and stop;

    set [X$_2$, Y$_2$, n] $\leftarrow$ [X(POINT2(P)), Y(POINT2(P)), 1] * MAT;

    if n $\neq$ 1, then print 'invalid matrix' and stop;

    call LINEWRITE(X$_1$, Y$_1$, X$_2$, Y$_2$) and set P $\leftarrow$ RLINK(P).

3. [Traverse point ring to display points that are not endpoints]

    Set P $\leftarrow$ PLINK(PICTURE).

    Repeat while P $\neq$ PICTURE:

        if LLINK1(P) = NULL,

        then set [U, V, n] $\leftarrow$ [X(P), Y(P), 1] * MAT;

            if n $\neq$ 1, then print 'invalid matrix' and stop;

            call POINTWRITE (U, V);

        set P $\leftarrow$ RLINK(P).

4. [Traverse entity ring recursively displaying each]

    Set P $\leftarrow$ ELINK(PICTURE).

    Repeat while P $\neq$ PICTURE:

        call DISPLAY(MLINK(P), TMATRIX(P) * MAT);

        set P $\leftarrow$ RLINK(P).

5. Exit.

Exercises for Sec. 5-5.2

1. Construct an algorithm which, given HEAD, the pointer to the master node, and X$_1$ and Y$_1$, the coordinates of a point, deletes the node representing the point and deletes all lines of which the point is an endpoint.

2. Given ENT, the master node of a substructure, and TRANS, a transformation matrix, construct an algorithm which finds the entity node which references ENT and has TMATRIX = TRANS and deletes this node.

3. Formulate Algorithms PDELETE and ENTDELETE alluded to at the end of Sec. 5-5.2.

5-5.3 Symbolic Differentiation

Algebraic differentiation is one of the earliest symbolic manipulation applications to be computerized. Programs to obtain the derivative of an algebraic expression were written in the early 1950s. In this subsection we are concerned with the formulation of an algorithm for this application.

    The problem can be described briefly as follows. Given the rules for differentiation with respect to x,

$$D(x) = 1$$
$$D(a) = 0; a = \text{constant or variable other than x}$$
$$D(\ln u) = D(u)/u$$
$$D(-u) = -D(u)$$
$$D(u + v) = D(u) + D(v)$$
$$D(u - v) = D(u) - D(v)$$
$$D(u * v) = D(u) * v + D(v) * u$$
$$D(u/v) = D(u)/v - (u * D(v))/v^2$$

| DPTR | SYM | TYPE | RPTR |

FIGURE 5-5.15 Node structure
for symbolic differentiation.

create an algorithm which will accept an algebraic expression composed of valid operators
and operands and construct the derivative of this expression with respect to a given
variable.

For the purposes of this example, we assume that the valid operators are LN (natural logarithm), $\ominus$ (unary minus), $+$, $-$, $*$, and $/$; the valid operands are variables of 1 to
5 characters in length, the first of which must be a letter; constants are 1 to 5 digits in
length, which may include a decimal point and a minus sign.

The primary aspect of the solution to this problem is choosing an appropriate data
structure to represent the algebraic expressions. We shall use a list structure to represent
such expressions. The use of list structures avoids the need for the recopying of certain
elements of the expression, as would be necessary in the differentiation rules for multiplication and division, because these common elements can be shared.

In this example, we use a list structure with no header nodes. Header nodes are not
necessary, as no element deletion is involved in this problem. A typical node for such a
structure is given in Fig. 5-5.15, in which DPTR is the hierarchical pointer to indicate sublists, RPTR is a pointer which indicates the physical adjacency relation, SYM is the character representation of the element represented by the node (a list pointer node has this
field set to the empty string, which we will show in diagrams as '@', for convenience), and
TYPE is a code number which indicates the type of the element. The values of TYPE are as
follows:

Type	Meaning
0	list pointer node
1	constant
2	variable
3	$+$ (add)
4	$-$ (subtract)
5	$*$ (multiply)
6	$/$ (divide)
7	$\#$ (exponentiation operator)
8	$\ominus$ (unary minus)
9	LN (natural logarithm)

Note that the $\#$ symbol, which denotes exponentiation, is not allowed in the input expressions, but is used in the derivative and is therefore listed here.

Using this list representation, each list consists of two or three elements at level 1.
The first element represents the operator, the second element denotes the first operand,
and the third element, which exists only for binary operators, denotes the second operand.

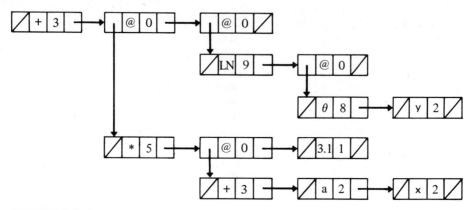

FIGURE 5-5.16.

A list-structure representation of the expression $(a + x) * 3.1 + \ln(\theta y)$ is shown in Fig. 5-5.16.

We will now develop a number of simple algorithms which will be used in the main differentiation routine. The first of these is a copy algorithm that copies a list structure which represents a single operand.

Algorithm COPY.   Given ROOT, a pointer to an element in a list structure, Algorithm COPY creates a new node whose fields are set equal to the corresponding field values of the node ROOT, except for the RPTR field, which is set to NULL. The value of COPY is the address of the newly created node. P is a pointer variable.

1. [Check for valid operand]   If ROOT = NULL, then set COPY ← NULL, and Exit.
2. [Create a new node]   Set P ⇐ NODE, SYM(P) ← SYM(ROOT), TYPE(P) ← TYPE(ROOT), DPTR(P) ← DPTR(ROOT), RPTR(P) ← NULL, and COPY ← P.

If the operand is a constant or a variable, i.e., a single node, then it is merely copied as is. If the operand is not an atom, however, the contents of the list header, except for its RPTR, are copied into the newly created node. The RPTR field of the new node is set to NULL. The result of executing this algorithm for the structure shown in Fig. 5-5.17 is in dotted form.

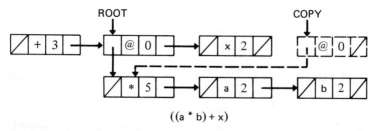

$$((a * b) + x)$$

FIGURE 5-5.17.

The next algorithm creates a list node and sets its TYPE field to a value which depends on the kind (i.e., constant, variable, etc.) of symbol which is passed to the algorithm.

Algorithm MAKE_NODE. Given VAL, a variable which contains the character representation of an algebraic element such as a constant or an operator, this algorithm creates a node whose DPTR and RPTR pointers are set to NULL. The TYPE field of this node is determined from VAL. The address of the new node is assigned to MAKE_NODE. X is a pointer variable, OPS is a string which represents the alphabet of valid operators, and DIGITS is a string which contains the alphabet of symbols for constants.

1. [Initialize] Set OPS ← '+ − */ #ΘLN', and DIGITS ← '−.0123456789'.
2. [Create a node] Set X ⇐ NODE, DPTR(X) ← RPTR(X) ← NULL, SYM(X) ← VAL,
   TYPE(X) ← 0.
3. [Determine node type]
   If VAL ≠ ' '
   then set TYPE(X) ← INDEX(OPS, VAL);
       if TYPE(X) ≠ 0,
       then set TYPE(X) ← TYPE(X) + 2;
       otherwise,
           if INDEX(DIGITS, SUBSTR(VAL, 1, 1)) ≠ 0,
           then TYPE(X) ← 1;
           otherwise, TYPE(X) ← 2.
4. [Finished] Set MAKE_NODE ← X, and Exit.

The following two algorithms are specialized list creation algorithms which are designed to create lists of two or three elements.

Algorithm MAKELIST2. Given N_1 and N_2, two pointers to list structures, this algorithm joins them such that N_1 precedes N_2 in the resultant list. A list pointer node which points to N_1 is also created. Algorithm MAKE_NODE is used in this algorithm.

1. [Join nodes] Set RPTR(N1) ← N2.
2. [Create header node] Set MAKELIST2 ← MAKE_NODE(' '), DPTR(MAKELIST2) ← N1,
   and Exit.

Algorithm MAKELIST3. Given N_1, N_2, and N_3, three pointers to list structures, this algorithm joins them such that N_1 precedes N_2 and N_2 precedes N_3. A list pointer node which points to N_1 is also created. Algorithm MAKE_NODE is used.

1. [Join nodes] Set RPTR(N1) ← N2, RPTR(N2) ← N3.
2. [Create header node] Set MAKELIST3 ← MAKE_NODE(' '), DPTR(MAKELIST3) ← N1,
   and Exit.

From the differentiation rules given earlier, it is easily seen that the derivative of the operand(s) must first be found before a rule corresponding to a particular operator can be applied. This process is readily described in a recursive manner within the list-processing framework. The general differentiation strategy is as follows:

    1 Find the operator.

    2 Differentiate the first operand.

    3 Differentiate the second operand, if it exists.

    4 Apply the proper rule.

Algorithm DIFFER. Given HEAD, the address of the root node of a list structure (like the one given in Fig. 5-5.16) representing an algebraic expression, and VAR, the variable with respect to which the expression is to be differentiated, this algorithm creates a list structure representing the derivative. The value returned via the algorithm name is the address of the derivative list structure. SAVE is a pointer variable to a single constant or variable node, or to an operator node in the expression. KEEP1 and KEEP2 are pointers to the derivatives of the first and second operands, if the operands exist. OP2 is a pointer to a copy of the second operand (if it exists). Algorithms COPY, MAKE_NODE, MAKELIST2, and MAKELIST3, which have been previously described, are used in this algorithm.

1. [Check for null expression] If HEAD = NULL, then set DIFFER ← NULL, and Exit.

2. [Is the current node a list pointer node?]
   If TYPE(HEAD) = 0, then set SAVE ← DPTR(HEAD); otherwise, set SAVE ← HEAD.

3. [Is current node a constant?]
   If TYPE(SAVE) = 1, then set DIFFER ← MAKE_NODE('0'), and Exit.

4. [Is current node a variable?]
   If TYPE(SAVE) = 2,
   then
       If SYM(SAVE) = VAR,
       then set DIFFER ← MAKE_NODE('1');
       otherwise, set DIFFER ← MAKE_NODE('0').
       Exit.

5. [Obtain operand(s) of operator] Set KEEP1 ← DIFFER(RPTR(SAVE), VAR).
   If RPTR(RPTR(SAVE)) ≠ NULL, then set KEEP2 ← DIFFER(RPTR(RPTR(SAVE)), VAR).

6. [Addition?]
   If TYPE(SAVE) = 3, then set DIFFER ← MAKELIST3(MAKE_NODE('+'), KEEP1, KEEP2), and Exit.

7. [Subtraction?]
   If TYPE(SAVE) = 4, then set DIFFER ← MAKELIST3(MAKE_NODE('−'), KEEP1, KEEP2), and Exit.

8. [Multiplication?]
   If TYPE(SAVE) = 5,
   then KEEP1 ← MAKELIST3(MAKE_NODE('*'), KEEP1, COPY(RPTR(RPTR(SAVE)))),
       KEEP2 ← MAKELIST3(MAKE_NODE('*'), KEEP2, COPY(RPTR(SAVE))),
       set DIFFER ← MAKELIST3(MAKE_NODE('+'), KEEP1, KEEP2), and Exit.

9. [Division?]
   If TYPE(SAVE) = 6,
   then set OP2 ← COPY(RPTR(RPTR(SAVE))),
       KEEP1 ← MAKELIST3(MAKE_NODE('/'), KEEP1, OP2),

> TEMP ← MAKELIST3(MAKE_NODE('*'), COPY(RPTR(SAVE)), KEEP2),
> TEMP2 ← MAKELIST3(MAKE_NODE(' #'), OP2, MAKE_NODE('2')),
> KEEP2 ← MAKELIST3(MAKE_NODE('/'), TEMP, TEMP2),
> DIFFER ← MAKELIST3(MAKE_NODE(' −'), KEEP1, KEEP2), and Exit.

10. [Unary minus?]
    If TYPE(SAVE) = 8,
    then set DIFFER ← MAKELIST2(MAKE_NODE('θ'), KEEP1), and Exit.

11. [Natural logarithm]
    If TYPE(SAVE) = 9,
    then set DIFFER ← MAKELIST3(MAKE_NODE('/'), KEEP1, COPY(RPTR(SAVE)))
    and Exit;
    otherwise, print 'error', and Exit.

The algorithm is straightforward and follows the rules of differentiation which were introduced earlier. Steps 3 and 4 correspond to the constant and variable cases, respectively. Step 5 obtains the operand(s) associated with a particular operator. In the case of a unary minus, only one operand is required. The differentiation for the four arithmetic operators is performed in steps 6 to 9. Step 10 handles the unary minus case and the last step corresponds to the case for the natural logarithm.

Exercises for Sec. 5-5.3

1. Modify Algorithm DIFFER to incorporate the exponentiation rule which is given as follows:

$$D(u \uparrow v) = D(u) \times (v \times (u \uparrow (v - 1))) + (\ln(u) \times D(v)) \times (u \uparrow v)$$

2. Modify the algorithm obtained in Exercise 1 so as to include the trigonometric functions, sin(u), cos(u), tan(u), etc.

3. Optimize the algorithm obtained in Exercise 2 such that expressions such as (x + 0), (x − 0), (0 − x), (1 × x), (x / 1), (x ↑ 1), (x ↑ 0), etc. are simplified.

5-5.4 Topological Sorting

The earliest use of topological sorting with computers was in conjunction with network analysis, for example, with techniques such as PERT (Program Evaluation and Review Technique). A PERT graph consists of directed edges corresponding to activities and nodes corresponding to events. A certain activity must be accomplished to move from one event to another. The PERT graph is used to analyze interrelated activities of complex projects. Activities may be taking place in parallel and one event may be the starting or ending point for a number of activities. The purpose of a topological sort is to order the events in a linear manner, i.e., first, second, third, and so on, with the restriction that an event cannot precede other events that must first take place.

In general, a topological sort defines a linear ordering on those nodes of a directed graph that have the following property: If node P is a predecessor of node Q, then Q cannot be the predecessor of node P. This property must hold even if P = Q, that is, P cannot be its own immediate predecessor and successor. In other words, a topological sort cannot order the nodes in a cycle.

As an example of the results of a topological sort, consider Fig. 5-5.18. Part (a) shows a graph containing no cycles and part (b) shows a linear ordering that could possibly result from a topological sort applied to this graph. The successors of each node P always appear to the right of P. (Note that other linear orderings of the nodes could be defined.)

Another application of topological sorting is the ordering of terms that must be defined in a book. Suppose we have a number of terms T_1, T_2, ..., T_n that are related by pairs (T_i, T_j) such that T_i is used in the definition of T_j. Then, we wish to order the terms so that each term T_i appears before each term T_j that uses T_i directly or indirectly in its definition. It is possible to have circular definitions, for example, (T_i, T_j), (T_j, T_k), and (T_k, T_i). In this case, a complete linear ordering of the terms cannot be made. Consider the examples in Fig. 5-5.19; the relationships between the definitions of record, file, field, key, and transaction (as found in two different books) are shown. An edge points from term T_i to T_j if T_i is used in the definition of T_j. In part (a) of Fig. 5-5.19, a linear ordering cannot be defined. For part (b), a topological sort could define the linear ordering

record – field – file – key – transaction

An alternative ordering is

record – file – field – key – transaction

In part (a), even though we cannot successfully apply a topological sort, the attempt to do so can be useful in detecting the circular definitions.

In general, with a topological sort we wish to specify a linear ordering for a set of nodes identified by descriptors, given a number of edges identified by ordered pairs of descriptors. The linear ordering must be such that all of a descriptor's successors appear

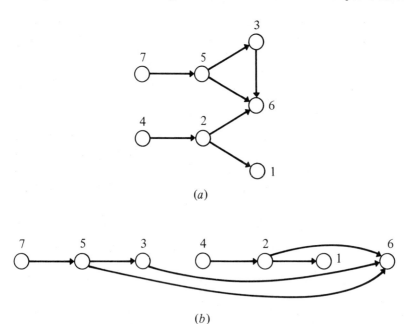

(a)

(b)

FIGURE 5-5.18   Example of a topological sort.

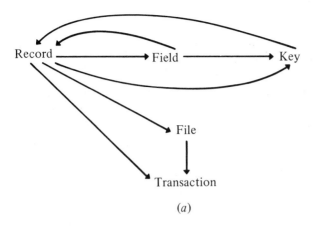

(a)

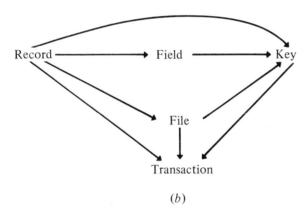

(b)

FIGURE 5-5.19   Relationships between definitions.

after that descriptor. If it is not possible to specify a complete linear ordering, then the loops that exist among the nodes or descriptors must be accounted for. In this section, we give an algorithm that performs a topological sort on nodes with any type of descriptors (character string or numeric). We also give an algorithm that detects one loop following an unsuccessful sort. Although we can only deal with small examples here, the number of descriptors or nodes in a typical application of topological sorting may be on the order of thousands.

The graph to which the topological sort is being applied can be represented using the structure shown in Fig. 5-5.20. In this figure, the graph shown in Fig. 5-5.19b is represented.

A value i between 1 and 9 is assigned to each descriptor in Fig. 5-5.19b. This assignment is done using a hashing which will be described shortly. The value i is used to reference the array elements DESPTR[i], PREDCOUNT[i], TAG[i], and SUCLIST[i]. DESPTR[i] is a pointer to a DESCRIPTOR node containing the descriptor corresponding to i. PREDCOUNT[i] is the number of immediate predecessors that the descriptor has.

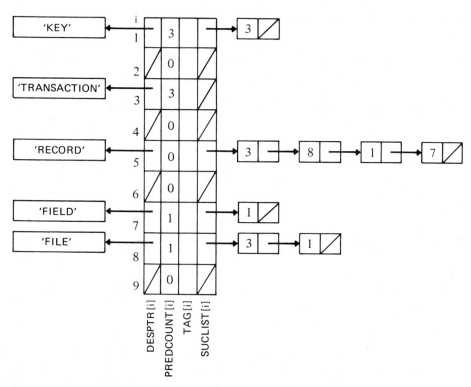

FIGURE 5-5.20   Data structure for representing a graph.

SUCLIST[i] is a pointer to a singly linked list of SUCCESSOR_NODE structures that contain the numbers corresponding to the immediate successors of the descriptor represented by i. The use of TAG[i] will be described later. Note that positions 2, 4, 6, and 9 in the arrays are not used. These empty locations are necessary so that an efficient searching algorithm based on a hashing function can be adopted in selecting an array position for each descriptor. This searching algorithm follows.

Algorithm STORE.   We are given a structure exemplified by Fig. 5-5.20 that contains m array elements and that currently has n descriptors. Given a descriptor STRING, it is required to find STRING in the structure and to return the array position corresponding to STRING. If STRING cannot be found, then it is allocated an unused array position, n is incremented, and the array position is returned. A hashing function HASH is used in the search process. The variables d and k are auxiliary indices.

1. [Initialize for search] Set d ← k ← HASH(STRING).
   (HASH returns a value between 1 and m inclusive.)
2. [Check descriptor pointer for indication of unused array location]
   If DESPTR[k] = NULL,
   then set P ⇐ DESCRIPTOR_NODE, DESCRIPTOR(P) ← STRING, DESPTR[k] ← P,
   n ← n + 1, STORE ← k, and Exit.
3. [Check descriptor to see if it matches STRING]
   If DESCRIPTOR(DESPTR[k]) = STRING, then set STORE ← k, and Exit.
4. [Update and test index] Set k ← k + 1. If k > m, then set k ← 1.
   If k = d,
   then print 'overflow of descriptor arrays – please specify a greater maximum limit
   for number of descriptors', and Exit;
   otherwise, go to step 2.

Hashing functions that could be used to map the descriptor STRING to a number between 1 and m are described in Sec. 4-3.2. The search mechanism used in this algorithm is termed linear probing. Consecutive array locations are scanned until STRING is found or an empty array location is encountered. If the array index k ever exceeds m, then it is reset to 1. In this manner, the entire array can be scanned if necessary. If all m array positions are scanned without finding STRING or an empty location, then an error message is printed and the algorithm halts. If the number of descriptors, n, is almost equal to m, linear probing is an inefficient search method. It is wise to choose an m at least 25 percent greater than the maximum value of n.

Algorithm STORE is used by the following algorithm that inputs a number of descriptor pairs and establishes the structure exemplified by Fig. 5-5.20. STORE is invoked by the assignment

   i ← STORE(STRING)

It is assumed that the structure in Fig. 5-5.20 and parameters m and n can be accessed by all algorithms discussed in this section.

Algorithm CONSTRUCT. Given a number of descriptor pairs (PRED, SUC) such that PRED is the immediate predecessor of SUC, it is required to construct the structure exemplified by Fig. 5-5.20. The number of unique descriptors n is counted. The user of this algorithm must ensure that m, the number of array locations, is greater than or equal to the maximum value of n.

1. [Initialize arrays] Set n ← 0.
   Repeat for k = 1, 2, . . ., m:
       set DESPTR[k] ← SUCLIST[k] ← NULL and PREDCOUNT[k] ← 0.
2. [Read next predecessor-successor pair of descriptors]
   Read PRED and SUC.   If there is no more input data, then Exit.
3. [Store or find descriptors and determine indices for them]
   Set i ← STORE(PRED) and j ← STORE(SUC).
4. [Update predecessor count of successor]
   Set PREDCOUNT[j] ← PREDCOUNT[j] + 1.

5. [Update successor list of predecessor]   Set Q ⇐ SUCCESSOR_NODE,
    SUCCESSOR(Q) ← j, NEXTSUC(Q) ← SUCLIST[i], and SUCLIST[i] ← Q.
    Go to step 2.

In order to construct the structure shown in Fig. 5-5.20, the following descriptor
pairs must be read by Algorithm CONSTRUCT. These pairs correspond to the edges of the
graph in Fig. 5-5.19b.

KEY	TRANSACTION
FIELD	KEY
RECORD	FIELD
RECORD	KEY
RECORD	FILE
FILE	KEY
RECORD	TRANSACTION
FILE	TRANSACTION

An algorithm for performing a topological sort is quite simple now that the structure
for representing a directed graph is available. The descriptors are to be printed in a linear
order by the sort. If a descriptor's predecessor count is zero, then it can be printed. After
this, the predecessor count of each of the descriptor's successors can be decremented by
one. Each time a descriptor's predecessor count reaches zero it is eligible to be printed.
Since more than one descriptor may have a zero predecessor count simultaneously, a
control mechanism is required to keep track of these descriptors. We use a linked queue,
and the following algorithm is required to add an element to the end of the queue.

Algorithm LQINSERT.   Given a number k corresponding to a descriptor as defined by
Algorithm CONSTRUCT, it is required to add k at the rear of a linked queue that has front
and rear pointers F and R, respectively. Each QUEUE_NODE has an information field, V,
and a link field, LINK.

1. [Allocate queue node]
    Set P ⇐ QUEUE_NODE, V(P) ← k, and LINK(P) ← NULL.
2. [Add node to rear of queue]
    If R = NULL,
    then set F ← R ← P;
    otherwise, set LINK(R) ← P and R ← P.
    Exit.

This algorithm can be called using LQINSERT(k). The deletion of the front element
of the queue is a simple task and will be included in the following algorithm.

Algorithm TOPOLOGICAL_SORT.   Given the structure for representing a directed
graph as previously described, it is required to print the descriptors of the nodes in a linear
order such that each descriptor is printed before its successors. A queue and Algorithm
LQINSERT are used to accomplish this. The variable n is global.

1. [Initialize queue pointers] Set F ← R ← NULL.
2. [Scan for descriptors without predecessors and add them to queue]
   Repeat for k = 1, 2, . . ., m:
     if DESPTR[k] $\neq$ NULL and PREDCOUNT[k] = 0,
     then call LQINSERT(k).
3. [Process each descriptor in queue]
   Repeat steps 4 and 5 while F $\neq$ NULL.
4. [Print and delete front descriptor in queue] Set k ← V(F),
   n ← n − 1, F ← LINK(F), and print DESCRIPTOR(DESPTR[k]).
   Set DESPTR[k] ← NULL.
   If F = NULL, then set R ← NULL.
5. [Scan successor list of descriptor printed]
   Set Q ← SUCLIST[k] and SUCLIST[k] ← NULL.
   Repeat while Q $\neq$ NULL:
     set PREDCOUNT[SUCCESSOR(Q)] ← PREDCOUNT[SUCCESSOR(Q)] − 1;
     if PREDCOUNT[SUCCESSOR(Q)] = 0,
     then call LQINSERT(SUCCESSOR(Q)).
     Set Q ← NEXTSUC(Q).
6. Exit.

In step 4, n is decremented by 1 every time that a descriptor is output. If n is not equal to zero on completion of the algorithm, then n descriptors are not included in the linear ordering and at least one cycle or loop exists among these descriptors. The next algorithm is used for determining the descriptors that are in a cycle.

Algorithm DETECT_CYCLE. Given a structure similar to that described in Fig. 5-5.20, with one or more descriptors among which one or more cycles exist, it is required to detect and print the descriptors in one cycle.

1. [Initialize arrays]
   Repeat for i = 1, 2, . . ., m: set PREDCOUNT[i] ← 0 and TAG[i] ← false.
2. [Check each descriptor and process those that were not printed]
   Repeat step 3 for i = 1, 2, . . ., m.
3. [Place subscript of predecessor in PREDCOUNT element of successor]
   If DESPTR[i] $\neq$ NULL,
   then set P ← SUCLIST[i], SUCLIST[i] ← NULL, and
   repeat while P $\neq$ NULL:
     if PREDCOUNT[SUCCESSOR(P)] = 0,
     then set PREDCOUNT[SUCCESSOR(P)] ← i.
     Set P ← NEXTSUC(P).
4. [Find the first i whose descriptor has not been printed]
   Repeat for i = 1, 2, . . ., m: if PREDCOUNT[i] $\neq$ 0, then go to step 5.
5. [Mark the predecessors with true TAG fields]
   Repeat while ⌐TAG[i]: set TAG[i] ← true and i ← PREDCOUNT[i].
6. [Reverse the list defined by the marked array elements starting at
   PREDCOUNT[i]]

Set j ← 0.
Repeat while PREDCOUNT[i] ≠ 0:
     set k ← j, j ← i, i ← PREDCOUNT[j], and PREDCOUNT[j] ← k.
Set PREDCOUNT[i] ← j.
7. [Print the descriptors in a cycle]
    Repeat while TAG[i]:
        print DESCRIPTOR(DESPTR[i]), set TAG[i] ← false, i ← PREDCOUNT[i].
8. [Output the first and last descriptor in the cycle]
    Print DESCRIPTOR(DESPTR[i]), and Exit.

This algorithm continues when Algorithm TOPOLOGICAL_SORT terminates, provided that a cycle exists among descriptors. If the pointer SUCLIST[i] is not null in step 3, then it points to a list of numbers of descriptors not printed. The array element PREDCOUNT of a successor descriptor is set to the predecessor number i in this step. This effectively constructs a linked list in which predecessors can be accessed via the PREDCOUNT values. In step 4 an array subscript is found that corresponds to a descriptor not yet printed. The list containing this subscript is scanned and each node is marked using the TAG elements which were shown in Fig. 5-5.20. When a TAG element with a value of true is encountered in step 5, the subscript i corresponds to the first descriptor in a completely marked cycle. Step 6 reverses the list corresponding to this cycle so that step 7 can print the descriptors with predecessors before successors. The first descriptor in the cycle or loop is printed in step 8.

In Fig. 5-5.21a, the data structure established by Algorithm CONSTRUCT as applied to the descriptor pairs

FIELD	KEY
RECORD	FIELD
RECORD	KEY
RECORD	FILE
RECORD	TRANSACTION
FILE	TRANSACTION
KEY	RECORD
FIELD	RECORD

is shown. These pairs correspond to the edges of the graph in Fig. 5-5.19a. This data structure is unchanged after Algorithm TOPOLOGICAL_SORT is executed because none of the predecessor counts are zero for the elements corresponding to descriptors.

Figure 5-5.21b shows the state of the arrays in the data structure following execution of step 3 in Algorithm DETECT_CYCLE. In the figure, we show the true and false values for the TAG fields as 1 and 0, respectively. The nonzero values in the PREDCOUNT array indicate the predecessors of the array locations' descriptors. Following step 5 of this algorithm, part (c) of the figure shows the state of the arrays. TAG[1] and TAG[5] have been set to 1 and indicate the elements in a cycle. After step 6 of Algorithm DETECT_CYCLE is executed, the arrays remain the same. Since the cycle detected consists of only two descriptors, it was not possible to reverse their order, as one item is always both the predecessor and the successor of the other item in a two-element cycle. Steps 7 and 8 print

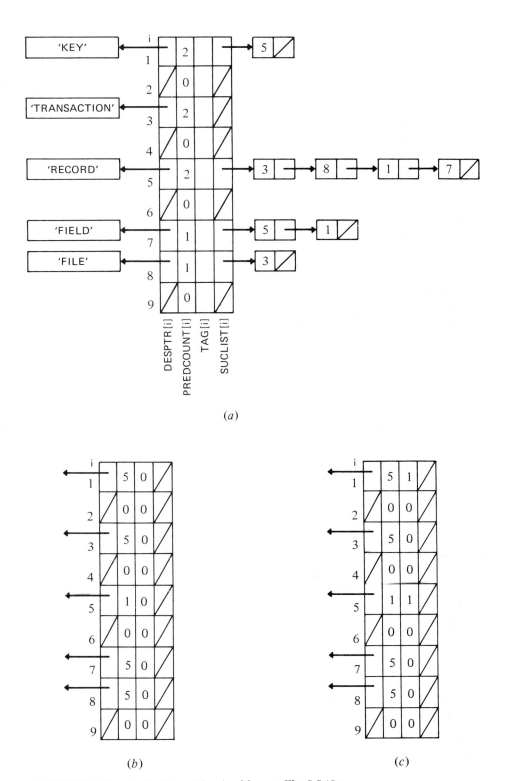

(a)

(b)　　　　　　　　*(c)*

FIGURE 5-5.21　Application of the algorithms to Fig. 5-5.19a.

KEY
RECORD
KEY

and reset the TAG fields to false as in Fig. 5-5.21*b*.

A final algorithm illustrates the implementation of the preceding algorithms for topological sorting with loop detection.

Algorithm TOPSORT.   Given the arrays DESPTR, PREDCOUNT, TAG, and SUCLIST and node structures DESCRIPTOR_NODE, QUEUE_NODE, and SUCCESSOR_NODE as previously defined, this algorithm attempts a topological sort, and if it fails to define a complete linear ordering, one cycle is then detected among the descriptors.

1.   [Initialize data structure]
     Read m and allocate m elements for each array.
     Call CONSTRUCT.
2.   [Attempt to sort the descriptors]
     Call TOPOLOGICAL_SORT.
3.   [Is detection of a cycle necessary?]
     If n > 0, then call DETECT_CYCLE.
     Exit.

We must restate that the arrays and node structures and the variables m and n are global to all algorithms in this section.

Exercises for Sec. 5-5.4

1.   List all of the valid linear orderings that could result if a topological sort is applied to the graph in Fig. 5-5.18*a*.
2.   Trace Algorithm TOPOLOGICAL_SORT using the directed graph from Fig. 5-5.18*a*. Assume that the edges are read by the algorithm in the order (7, 5), (5, 3), (3, 6), (5, 6), (2, 1), (2, 6), (4, 2).
3.   Eliminate the edge from KEY to RECORD in Fig. 5-5.19 and now trace Algorithms CONSTRUCT, TOPOLOGICAL_SORT, and DETECT_CYCLE as in Fig. 5-5.21.
4.   Could Algorithm TOPOLOGICAL_SORT completely order a set of descriptors if two pairs of descriptors read by Algorithm CONSTRUCT are duplicates? Explain. (Assume that the corresponding directed graph of descriptors has no cycles.)

5-6 DYNAMIC STORAGE MANAGEMENT

In many of the preceding sections we have made free use of structures that require a form of memory management in order to handle requests for storage and releases of storage. For example, for lists in Chap. 4 and trees in this chapter, we simply requested nodes whenever we needed them, and never bothered to indicate when or how these nodes were to be released when they were no longer needed. A similar approach was taken for strings in Chap. 2, except that there we never even asked for storage. We simply proceeded as if the creation of any new string was invariably accompanied by enough storage space to hold the string.

Such conveniences definitely make it easier for an applications programmer. In fact, it might be argued that these conveniences are almost a necessity now that certain applications have become so complex. As might be expected, a price must be paid. This price consists of the development cost of the requisite systems programs for such dynamic storage management and (in all likelihood) the slower execution of applications programs. Consequently, in this section we wish to examine some of the techniques and algorithms that could be used to provide various levels of storage management and control.

We begin by looking briefly at two of the simplest systems. In FORTRAN the problem is remarkably simple because all storage requirements are known explicitly at compile time. For example, a programmer cannot write a FORTRAN program in which the arrays' sizes are determined at run time. He must have dimensioned them already at compile time. Recursion is not permitted. There are no programmer-defined data structures whose creation could take place at data-determined times during execution, such as provided by SNOBOL's DATA statement together with an assignment or PL/I's structure declarations together with ALLOCATE statements. As well, there are no string operations provided, and hence string-handling capabilities are virtually nonexistent.

All these restrictions produce a situation in which the FORTRAN compiler, when translating a source program, is able to determine exactly how much storage will be required for the execution of that program. Storage management then ceases to be a problem because there is no dynamic storage management required by FORTRAN programs. The required amount of storage is allocated for each program and subprogram at loading time. Storage is freed only when the entire job has executed to completion and is being purged from the system.

In comparison to FORTRAN, in which there is no dynamic storage management, ALGOL 60 provides an example of a more sophisticated system that does provide storage management, though not really under the control of the programmer. A stack is used to hold the blocks of storage, each of which is an activation record of a program or block invocation. Because of the nested structure of program and block calls, their invocations follow a LIFO discipline, and hence a stack is ideally suited for the maintenance of the storage blocks in use at any particular time. Programs can be invoked recursively, but because a stack is being used, this presents no difficulties. This aspect was discussed in Sec. 3-7.1.

Storage for program code is allocated at loading time and remains until the entire job is purged. The stack is used for the data and the run-time control information associated with blocks and procedures as they are invoked during execution. Since ALGOL 60 requires that all data structures be declared upon block entry, all array declarations are processed immediately upon entering a subprogram or block for execution. Such an approach provides the information regarding array sizes, and this, together with the compile-time information about storage needs, serves to define exactly the storage requirements for a particular block. The appropriate amount of space is reserved on the run-time storage stack, and the block can be executed. When the block is finally exited, the stack is popped, and the storage allocated for this block is freed.

Use of a stack to provide the dynamic storage management capability is reasonably efficient, in that little computation is involved in determining the amounts of storage to allocate and in updating stack pointers. Such a stack mechanism is quite commonly used in cases, such as ALGOL programs, where the language exhibits a nested block structure, where subprogram invocations follow a LIFO discipline, and where exact storage requirements can be determined at the time of execution upon block entry.

There are, however, many applications which involve list, graph, or tree processing. With such processing the programmer is often made responsible for creating and removing nodes as the data require. In addition, many applications require a string-handling capability of a more powerful nature than that provided by FORTRAN or ALGOL. In particular, variable-length strings may be needed. As pointed out in Sec. 2-4, variable-length strings require some form of dynamic storage management. It is to this topic that we now turn.

In considering dynamic storage-management techniques, there are many factors which influence the selection of methods. For example, the statistical distribution of the sizes of storage areas requested, the distribution of the lengths of time that blocks of storage are required, and the frequency of requests and releases of storage are important factors. Furthermore, the features of the language which necessitate dynamic storage management, and the language implementor's philosophy regarding the degree to which a programmer is to be allowed to control storage, are important considerations. In this section we shall cover only some of the more basic techniques and algorithms. Most of the dynamic storage-management methods that are commonly used are variants of the techniques presented here.

The simplest case is that involving storage requests which are always for a fixed number of storage locations. Such a situation might arise in a language like LISP, which is devoted to the manipulation of list structures whose *blocks* are all of a single type and size. In this case, the total available dynamic storage can be subdivided into a series of blocks, each of the correct size. These blocks can be linked by LINK fields in the first word of each block to form a one-way linear list. A request for a storage block is then handled by a routine similar to Algorithm GET_BLOCK.

Algorithm GET_BLOCK.   Given HEAD, the pointer to the first block on the linked list of available storage blocks, GET_BLOCK returns the address, P, of an available block.

1. [Overflow?]   If HEAD = NULL, then exit to error routine.
2. [Allocate block]   Set P ← HEAD, HEAD ← LINK(P), and Exit.

In step 1, if we are out of storage (HEAD = NULL), then we can only terminate the job or attempt to recover some storage by techniques we will discuss later in this section.

The return of a block to the availability list is equally trivial. Simply attach it as the new first block in the list. We will temporarily defer the question of when blocks are to be returned, however, and simply note that to return a block in this present scheme, all that is needed is P, the block address, and HEAD, the pointer to the first block on the free list.

The situation becomes more complicated if the storage requests can be for blocks of varying sizes, as is common when strings are being handled or when programmer-defined data aggregates of varying sizes are being used. Now we can no longer treat the available storage as a linked list of blocks of the correct size, for there is no correct size. Instead, our linked list can contain blocks of various sizes, each being a potential candidate for allocation or for subdivision into two blocks of smaller size—one for immediate allocation and one for retention on the available list.

With variable-sized blocks, however, we encounter the problem of fragmentation, a problem which did not appear in the case of fixed-size requests. There are two types of memory fragmentation which can arise; namely, internal fragmentation and external fragmentation, both of which are explained as follows.

If a large number of storage blocks are requested and later returned, the linked list of available blocks can be reasonably lengthy (especially if returned contiguous blocks are not fused into one). This means that the average block size becomes small and that there are probably very few blocks which are large. If a request for a large block is received, it may have to be refused because there is no single block on the free list that is big enough, even though the total amount of free storage may be much greater than the requested amount. This phenomenon of decomposing the total available storage into a large number of relatively small blocks is called *external fragmentation*.

We can attempt to inhibit external fragmentation somewhat by occasionally allocating a block that is larger than the requested size (i.e., by refusing to split a block into pieces, one of which might be quite small). If we do this, it could happen that a request for storage must be refused because of the lack of blocks of the required size. This can take place even though the amount of storage that is "wasted" (i.e., allocated but unused) is more than sufficient to satisfy the request. This phenomenon of partitioning the total unused storage into available blocks and allocating these blocks with some portion of the blocks remaining unused, but not available, is called *internal fragmentation*.

Any algorithm for storage management in a context where variable-sized blocks will be used must seek, in some way or another, to minimize the inefficiencies due to fragmentation. Fragmentation is the major factor in making these algorithms more complicated than those for fixed-size blocks. In addition, because we cannot know in advance the sizes of blocks, each block generally contains a SIZE field to record its current size, as well as a LINK field to maintain the list structure. For convenience we assume that these fields are in the first word of each block or can be accessed directly once the address of the first word of the block is provided.

If we assume the free list has a list head of the form given in Fig. 5-6.1, with AVAIL being the address of this list head, LINK(AVAIL) being a pointer to the first block on the free list, and SIZE(AVAIL) being set to 0, then one method for servicing a request for a block of size n can be formulated as follows.

Algorithm ALLOCATE_FIRST.   Given AVAIL, the address of the list head and n, the size of block requested, this algorithm returns P, the address of a block of length $\geq$n, with SIZE(P) set to the actual length of the block. The variable MIN records the amount of storage we are willing to waste in order to reduce external fragmentation; no block of size MIN or smaller will be formed by splitting.

1. [Initialize]   Set Q ← AVAIL, P ← LINK(Q).
2. [Find block large enough for request]

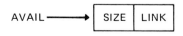

AVAIL ──────▶ | SIZE | LINK |

FIGURE 5-6.1.

Repeat while P $\neq$ NULL:
    if SIZE(P) $\geq$ n,
    then set k $\leftarrow$ SIZE(P) $-$ n;
        if k $\leq$ MIN,
        then set LINK(Q) $\leftarrow$ LINK(P), and Exit;
        otherwise, set SIZE(P) $\leftarrow$ k, P $\leftarrow$ P $+$ k, SIZE(P) $\leftarrow$ n, and Exit;
    otherwise, set Q $\leftarrow$ P, P $\leftarrow$ LINK(Q).
3. [No suitable block] Exit to error routine.

This algorithm assumes that arithmetic can be performed on addresses. If it is desired to eliminate internal fragmentation completely, simply set MIN to 0, though the utility of a block of size 1 is not very clear, especially since this single location (and perhaps, more) is taken up by the SIZE and LINK fields.

The algorithm just given is commonly called a "first-fit" algorithm because the block that is allocated is the first block (or a part) that is found to be larger than the requested amount. One might suspect that a "best-fit" method might be preferable, but, in fact, this is not necessarily the case. The "best-fit" method does not use the first suitable block found, but instead, continues searching the list until the smallest suitable block has been found. This tends to save the larger blocks for times when they are needed to service large requests. However, the best-fit method does have the unfortunate tendency to produce a larger number of very small free blocks, and these are often unusable by almost all requests. Furthermore, the best-fit method requires a search of the entire free list containing, say, N blocks, while the average length of search for first-fit would be N/2 or less, depending on the requested size, though tending to N/2 as the storage usage pattern becomes stable over time. (This latter result follows from a series of simulations carried out by Knuth [1973].)

The choice of methods, in any case, must be made in the context of some knowledge about the types of requests that will be encountered. Given a particular set of circumstances, best-fit might give better performance than first-fit, offsetting the potentially longer search time. It is interesting to note, however, that during the same series of simulations of storage-usage patterns performed in order to compare various management strategies, Knuth discovered that first-fit outperformed best-fit in all cases examined.

To this point, nothing has been said about any ordering imposed on the list of free blocks. This can have a significant effect on performance. If blocks on the free list are ordered by size, then the search time of the best-fit method could be reduced. An ascending-order sort has the effect of converting first-fit to best-fit. Descending order reduces the first-fit's search time to 1 because the first block found would be the largest. However, this can potentially convert first-fit into a method known as "worst-fit," in which the largest block is always used regardless of the size of the request. It may also cause unnecessary generation of many small blocks.

There is another ordering that might be imposed however. This is to have the blocks on the free list ordered by address (increasing, let us assume). This type of ordering does not necessarily improve search times for blocks of particular sizes, because there is no relation between block address and block size. However, it does make it possible to reduce external fragmentation and it would tend to reduce all search times because the free list can be shorter. Blocks sorted by address can be checked upon release and, if two consecutive blocks on the list are found to be contiguous, they are fused to form one larger block. This technique tends to keep block sizes larger, and hence to keep the number of blocks smaller. We shall see more of this fusing of blocks when we formulate algorithms for the release of allocated blocks. There is a lot of evidence, though, to suggest that, in the absence of special offsetting conditions, first-fit applied to a free list ordered by address, and hence a list that is essentially an unordered list when considering block size, is quite a good method to adopt.

Another addition that can be made to the first-fit algorithm than can reduce its search time quite noticeably is once again described by Knuth. The modification lies in starting a search for a suitable block at the point the previous search terminated, rather than always with the first block. This tends to distribute smaller blocks evenly over the entire list, rather than having them concentrated near the front of the list. Algorithm ALLOCATE_FIRST_M is the first-fit algorithm modified to make use of this varying search-start point.

Algorithm ALLOCATE_FIRST_M. Given AVAIL, n, and MIN as before, and M, a pointer to the last examined free node on the previous invocation of this routine, the algorithm returns P, the address of a suitable block and defines a new value for M. Prior to the first call to this routine, M is assumed to have been initialized to AVAIL. TIME is a flag associated with the traversal of the list. This flag is set to 1 when the end of the list is encountered.

1. [Initialize] Set Q ← M, P ← LINK(Q), and TIME ← 0.
2. [Find large enough block]
    Repeat while TIME = 0 or Q ≠ M :
        if P = NULL,
        then set Q ← AVAIL, P ← LINK(Q), and TIME ← 1;
        otherwise, if SIZE(P) ≥ n;
            then set k ← SIZE(P) − n;
            if k ≤ MIN,
            then set LINK(Q) ← LINK(P), M ← Q, and Exit;
            otherwise, set SIZE(P) ← k, M ← P, P ← P + k,
                SIZE(P) ← n, and Exit;
        otherwise, set Q ← P, and P ← LINK(Q).
3. [No suitable block] Exit to error routine.

In his simulation experiments on items, Knuth found, in one case at least, an improvement in the first-fit average length of search from 125 tests (which was N/2, as expected) to 2.8 tests—a significant enhancement. This modified first-fit algorithm operating on a free list ordered by address can serve as a storage-allocation mechanism for many applications.

Let us now consider the release of an allocated block of storage and its return to the free list. We still ignore the question of when and how the decision is made to free a block of storage and simply assume that a block of storage, starting at address RB, is now considered to be unused and a candidate for reallocation. The case of fixed-size blocks has already been covered, and so we confine our discussion to variable-sized blocks. In this case we assume that a size field, SIZE(RB), in the first word of the block contains the actual size of the block being freed.

The simplest solution is to insert every such freed block as a new first block on an unordered free list. This does, indeed, require a minimum of processing, but it has a serious drawback. After the storage allocation and freeing mechanism has been operating for a while, the free list is very likely to contain a large number of small blocks. The search time for the allocation routine will become longer and longer, and there will be an ever-increasing risk of being unable to meet certain requests because all the blocks are simply too small. The problem is, of course, that in this simple freeing method there is no mechanism running in opposition to the splitting mechanism in the allocation routine. In other words, we never reform big blocks.

The obvious solution is to form one block out of two contiguous free blocks. If every newly released block is checked for contiguity with its predecessor and successor blocks on the free list, and merged with them whenever contiguity occurs, then the free list will always contain the smallest number of blocks. Each block is as large as possible, given the current segments that are allocated. In order for this to work, however, the free list must be kept in order by block address, and this then requires a search of the free list in order to determine the position for insertion of a newly freed block.

The following algorithm can be used to insert a block on the free list, merging it as necessary with contiguous neighbors. Since we have available a second pointer into the free list—the variable search-start point—we can make use of it as a starting point rather than AVAIL on some occasions. It can be shown that this reduces the average length of search from $N/2$ to $N/3$. The algorithm incorporates this modification.

Algorithm FREE_BLOCK.   Given AVAIL, the address of the list head, M, the variable starting point for searching in the allocation routine, and RB, the address of the block to be inserted, this algorithm inserts block RB into the free list and merges contiguous blocks whenever possible. The algorithm assumes that AVAIL is less than the address of any block. This is guaranteed if the list head (with SIZE(AVAIL) set to 0) is the first word of the entire section of memory available for allocation. We also assume that the value NULL can be compared with valid addresses using any of the relational operators, with only $\neq$ yielding a 'true' result. Q is a pointer which denotes the predecessor of the node being freed.

1. [Initialize optimally]
   If RB > M then set Q ← M; otherwise, set Q ← AVAIL.   Set P ← LINK(Q).
2. [Find predecessor and successor in sorted list]
   Repeat while P $\neq$ NULL and RB > P: set Q ← P and P ← LINK(Q).
3. [Collapse with successor, P?]
   If P = NULL or RB + SIZE(RB) $\neq$ P,
   then set LINK(RB) ← P;
   otherwise, set LINK(RB) ← LINK(P) and SIZE(RB) ← SIZE(RB) + SIZE(P).
4. [Collapse with predecessor, Q?]
   If Q = AVAIL or Q + SIZE(Q) $\neq$ RB,
   then set LINK(Q) ← RB;
   otherwise, set LINK(Q) ← LINK(RB) and SIZE(Q) ← SIZE(Q) + SIZE(RB).
   Exit.

Note that it is the assumption that SIZE(AVAIL) is 0 that prevents the merging of block RB with the list head when Q is AVAIL, since with AVAIL < RB, we always have AVAIL + 0 ≠ RB.

To summarize, we now have a storage-allocation method with an average search time that can be very short, and we have a storage-freeing method with an average search time of about N/3. Our release technique tends to reduce external fragmentation because it maintains block sizes as large as possible. The degree of internal fragmentation is under our control through the variable MIN, though there is a trade-off between internal fragmentation and both external fragmentation and search times. Yet looking at these two storage-management mechanisms in terms of search times, we can see the possibility of the deallocation routine being a bottleneck because of the N/3 average length of search as compared with the enhanced search time due to the moving search pointer in the allocation routine. It might be appropriate to consider briefly a deallocation routine which does not require this length of searching time. The "boundary-tag" method of Knuth is the example chosen.

In the storage-release algorithm just given, it is the search through the blocks in the sorted list which allows the determination of the predecessor and successor blocks. Having these, it is simple to determine if they and the released block are contiguous. Without the search, all that one can do is examine the two words that are the immediate predecessor and successor of the released block. But unless they are specially marked with flags, there is no way of telling directly whether or not the blocks of which they are a part are on the free list. Consequently, in the boundary-tag method the first and last words of blocks are made to contain a flag field which indicates whether or not the block is allocated. It is also useful to have the last word of a block also contain a size field. From the last word of a block, the address of the first word can be determined directly. And finally, since searching is being avoided, the free list is maintained as a doubly linked list. The price paid for eliminating searching is, therefore, more storage being taken up for control fields. This may not be worthwhile if, because of some conditions of the application, the free list tends to be fairly short or the average block size is small. In other cases, it may be a very useful way of speeding up the deallocation of storage. The details can be found in Knuth's book.

The storage representation of the blocks are of the form given in Figs. 5-6.2a and b when the blocks are on the free list and allocated, respectively. If the block starting at address P is free, then the FLAG and FL fields are set to 0; otherwise, these fields are set to a positive value for a block which is allocated. The fields SIZE and SZ contain the length of block P. SUC(P) and PRED(P) are pointers to the successor and predecessor of block P on the free block list, respectively. We also assume a list head of the form given in Fig. 5-6.2c, with AVAIL being its address. The list head is considered to be the successor and the predecessor of the last and first blocks on the free list. For convenience, we assume that the list head is outside the segment of storage that is to be managed and that the first and last words of this segment have the correct flags set to show that these two words have been allocated. We now proceed to formulate a deallocation algorithm based on this representation.

Algorithm FREE_BLOCK_T. Given the block structure just described, this algorithm inserts a block with address RB onto the free list, merging it with contiguous blocks as

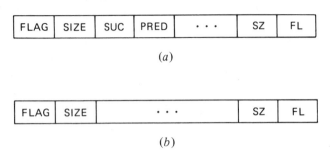

(a)

(b)

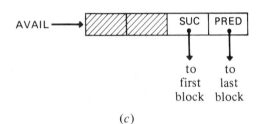

to   to
first   last
block   block

(c)

FIGURE 5-6.2 Boundary-tag block structure. (a) Free block;
(b) allocated block; (c) list head block.

necessary. It also redefines M, the variable search-start point, if required. It is assumed
that having the address of the first word of the block is sufficient to access immediately the
FLAG, SIZE, SUC, and PRED fields, and that the address of the last word of the block gives
direct access to the SZ and FL fields. The algorithm itself is little more than a basic insertion
in a two-way linked list.

1. [Remove predecessor Q and merge?]
    If FL(RB − 1) = 0,
    then set Q ← RB − SZ(RB − 1), PRED(SUC(Q)) ← PRED(Q),
        SUC(PRED(Q)) ← SUC(Q), SIZE(Q) ← SIZE(Q) + SIZE(RB), and RB ← Q.
2. [Remove successor Q and merge?]
    If FLAG(RB + SIZE(RB)) = 0,
    then set Q ← RB + SIZE(RB), PRED(SUC(Q)) ← PRED(Q),
        SUC(PRED(Q)) ← SUC(Q), SIZE(RB) ← SIZE(RB) + SIZE(Q),
        if M = Q, then set M ← RB.
3. [Add locations between RB and Q inclusive as new first block]
    Set Q ← RB + SIZE(RB) − 1, FLAG(RB) ← FL(Q) ← 0, SZ(Q) ← SIZE(RB),
    SUC(RB) ← SUC(AVAIL), SUC(AVAIL) ← RB, PRED(RB) ← AVAIL, and
    PRED(SUC(RB)) ← RB.   Exit.

Up to this point the sizes of blocks have either been fixed or completely arbitrary
(though larger than some minimum value). Another technique used in some storage-
management methods is to restrict the sizes of blocks to some fixed set of sizes. All the
blocks of each size can be linked together with the intent of speeding up the search for a

block of a suitable size. For a request for a block of size n, the number m, the smallest of the fixed sizes equal to or larger than n, is determined, and a block of size m is allocated. If no block of size m is available, then a larger block is split into two subblocks (known as "buddies"), each also of fixed size, and this process is repeated until a block of size m is produced.

Besides the improvement in search time, there is another advantage in using this technique. The collapsing of two smaller blocks into one larger block is relatively easy, since only the two buddies formed by splitting a larger block may be combined to form this larger block once again. Because the sizes are fixed relative to one another, the address of the buddy of a block is relatively easily determined.

There are, however, some potential disadvantages associated with this technique. Internal fragmentation will be increased generally because of the allocation of blocks which may be somewhat larger than the requested size. As well, there can be an increased amount of external fragmentation due to the fact that two blocks may be contiguous and yet not merged, because they are not buddies. Generally, though, this technique of storage management has proven to be quite efficient with performance comparable to the previous methods discussed.

The usual approach in implementing this method of storage management is to specify the fixed sizes, F_0, F_1, ..., F_{MAX}, for blocks according to some pattern such as the recurrence relation

$$\begin{cases} F_n = F_{n-1} + F_{n-k} & k \leq n \leq MAX \\ F_0 = a, F_1 = b, \ldots, F_{k-1} = c \end{cases}$$

where a, b, ..., c are minimum block sizes that are used, and k = 1 or 2 or 3 or .... For example, if k is 1 and F_0 is 1, then the block sizes, which are 1, 2, 4, 8, 16, ..., are the successive powers of 2 and the method is called the "buddy system." If k = 2 with $F_0 = F_1 = 1$, then the sizes are just the successive members of the Fibonacci sequence 1, 1, 2, 3, 5, 8, 13, ... In all likelihood, though, the F_0, F_1, etc. terms are not defined to be such small values. Blocks of size 1 are not of much use, especially if they must also carry control information so that the allocation and release mechanisms will work.

The feature that makes this system work is that the merges must correspond exactly to the splits. By this we mean that the only two blocks that can be merged are the precise two that were formed by splitting. Furthermore, before each block can be reformed, each of its subblocks must be reformed from their subblocks. Consequently, the storage-block pattern formed by the sequence of splits has the form of a binary tree. The problem we are faced with is the recording of the position of a particular block within this tree structure. A rather elegant solution has been provided by Hinds in a storage-management application.

His solution consists of a coding for each block by which we can reconstruct the splitting sequence that produced that block. Looking at the recurrence relation $F_n = F_{n-1} + F_{n-k}$, if we specify that the F_{n-1} term corresponds to the block that forms the left branch of a split (assumed to be at the lower address) and the F_{n-k} term is the right branch, then all we must record for each block is the size of the block, the number of splits it took to form the block, and whether it is a left block or a right block. Since one left block and one right block are formed in each split, we need only record the count of left blocks. In fact, this allows us to code the left-or-right factor together with the split count in one coded field. The left block has the relative split count (a number greater than 0), while the right block has a code of 0. The code for the parent block is thus determined in relation to the left block. The formulas to use are the following:

Initially: $CODE_{MAX}$ $= 0$ where F_{MAX} is the entire segment considered to be a right block

Splitting: $CODE_{LEFT}$ $= CODE_{PARENT} + 1$

$CODE_{RIGHT}$ $= 0$

Merging: $CODE_{PARENT} = CODE_{LEFT} - 1$

As an example, consider a storage block of 144 cells and the recurrence relation

$$F_n = F_{n-1} + F_{n-2} \qquad 2 \le n \le 6$$
$$F_0 = 8, \ F_1 = 13$$

The entire tree of possible splits is given in Fig. 5-6.3, where the vertex value is the block size and the superscript is the code value as computed by the above formulas. Consider the tree cross section which is the set of potential blocks of size 13. A block of size 13 with code of 0 is the right block formed by splitting a block of size 34. The left or right nature of this size 34 block is determined by the left buddy for the block of size 13. If its left buddy (of size 21) has a code of 1, then the size 34 block is a right block for some larger block of size 89, while if the left buddy has a code greater than 1, then the block of size 34 is a left block of some still larger block. A block of size 13 with a code value greater than 0 is the left block of a split block of size 21. The numeric value of the code for a left block of size 13 is the number of splits of some higher right block that had to be made to get this left block of size 13. Or, in other words, the value of the code for a left block is the

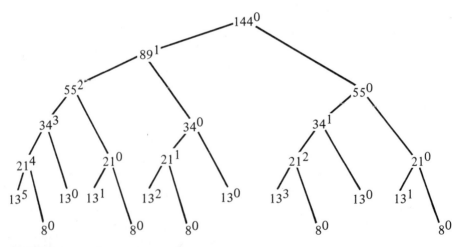

FIGURE 5-6.3   Storage-management tree.

number of merges that this left block must undergo to become the first 13 locations of some larger block which is finally a right block.

For the algorithms we will present, we assume blocks of the structure given in Figs. 5-6.4a and b, which correspond to free and allocated blocks, respectively. FREE(P) is 0 or greater than 0, depending on whether block P is free or not, SIZE(P) contains the value i for block P of size F_i, and SUC(P) and PRED(P) for a free block P are the forward and backward pointers to other free blocks of size F_i in a doubly linked list of all the free blocks of size F_i. The list head with address AVAIL[i] for this list is given in Fig. 5-6.4c. CODE(P) for block P is the code giving the left- or right-handedness of block P and the relative split count, if P is a left block. In addition to the array of list heads AVAIL[0:MAX], we also have the array F[0:MAX], which records the block sizes F_i, $0 \leq i \leq$ MAX, as determined by the recurrence relation. It is assumed that F_0 has a value large enough to allow the storage of all the control fields.

The following are two subalgorithms which take care of the insertion and deletion of blocks into and from the above linked lists.

Algorithm INSERT. Given the arrays and block structures as previously described, parameter i, and the address P of a block of size F_i, this algorithm inserts P into the list headed by AVAIL[i].

1. [Insert at the front of the list]
   Set FREE(P) ← 0, SIZE(P) ← i, SUC(P) ← SUC(AVAIL[i]),
   SUC(AVAIL[i]) ← P, PRED(P) ← AVAIL[i], PRED(SUC(P)) ← P, and Exit.

Algorithm DELETE. Given the arrays and block structures as previously described and the address P of a block, this algorithm deletes block P from the list in which it appears.

1. [Delete block P by unlinking it]
   Set SUC(PRED(P)) ← SUC(P), PRED(SUC(P)) ← PRED(P), and Exit.

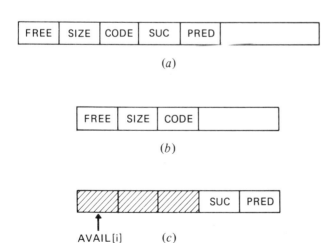

FREE	SIZE	CODE	SUC	PRED	

(a)

FREE	SIZE	CODE	

(b)

AVAIL[i]　　　　(c)

FIGURE 5-6.4 Block structure for storage management. (a) Free block; (b) allocated block; (c) list head block.

The following algorithms service the requests for storage blocks and the deallocation of blocks. Both presume that the value of k has been fixed so as to determine which recurrence relation is being used.

Algorithm ALLOCATE_BLOCK_REC.   Given the arrays and block structures as previously described, this algorithm receives a request for a block of size n and returns the pointer P set to the address of a block of size F_i, which is the smallest size larger than or equal to n.

1. [Determine size code]
    If n > F[MAX], then exit to error routine;
    otherwise, set i ← 0, repeat while n > F[i]:   set i ← i + 1.
2. [Find first available block]   Set j ← i.
    Repeat while SUC(AVAIL[j]) = AVAIL[j]:
        set j ← j + 1, if j > MAX, then exit to error routine.
    Set P ← SUC(AVAIL[j]) and call DELETE(P).
3. [Split as required until correct size is reached]
    Repeat while j > i:
        set Q ← P + F[j − 1], CODE(P) ← CODE(P) + 1, CODE(Q) ← 0,
        if i > j − k, then call INSERT(Q, j − k), and set j ← SIZE(P) ← j − 1;
        otherwise, call INSERT(P, j − 1), and set j ← SIZE(Q) ← j − k, P ← Q.
4. [Allocate block P of size F_i]   Set FREE(P) ← 1, and Exit.

Algorithm FREE_BLOCK_REC.   Given a block beginning at address P, this algorithm inserts it (or the mergers of it with appropriate buddies) onto the proper free list.

1. [Perform all possible merges]   Repeat step 2 while SIZE(P) < MAX:
2. [P is a left block?]
    If CODE(P) > 0,
    then set Q ← P + F[SIZE(P)];
        if FREE(Q) > 0 or SIZE(Q) ≠ SIZE(P) − k + 1,
        then call INSERT(P, SIZE(P)), and Exit;
        otherwise, set CODE(P) ← CODE(P) − 1, SIZE(P) ← SIZE(P) + 1,
            and call DELETE(Q);
    otherwise, (P is a right block)
        set Q ← P − F[SIZE(P) + k − 1];
        if FREE(Q) > 0 or SIZE(Q) ≠ SIZE(P) + k − 1,
        then call INSERT(P, SIZE(P)), and Exit;
        otherwise, set CODE(Q) ← CODE(Q) − 1, SIZE(Q) ← SIZE(Q) + 1,
            call DELETE(Q), and set P ← Q.
3. [We get here only if P is the maximal block]
    Call INSERT(P, MAX), and Exit.

It should be noted than when k = 1 (when the strategy is in effect the "buddy system"), then the addresses of buddies differ from each other by amounts that are integral powers of two. Since all addresses are in binary representation in a computer, the address calculation given above could be replaced by a method that makes use of this fact, thus possibly speeding up these algorithms.

With regard to the performance of these algorithms, Knuth's simulations showed that the buddy system performed quite well, comparable to his boundary-tag method, and, in fact, the buddy system has proven itself in practice. Statistical analysis has been performed on the Fibonacci system and the results appear to show it to be superior to the buddy system (quite possibly because of the wider range of block sizes available for a given segment of storage). The advantage of the Fibonacci system which makes it appear even more useful is that the average amount of wasted storage is less than for the buddy system. This is because there are at least as many Fibonacci numbers less than a given number than there are integral powers of two. In fact, for n > 4, there are always more Fibonacci numbers less than or equal to n than there are powers of two, while for n ≤ 4, there are at least as many Fibonacci numbers. Hence, the Fibonacci system has more sizes available and is more likely to get a better fit of allocated amount to requested amount. In summary, then, both of these methods appear to be suitable for use as part of a storage management system.

Now that we have looked at several methods of allocating and freeing storage, we still have to consider the question of when and how the decision to free storage is made.

Deciding when to allocate storage is simple. It is done when the programmer requests it by declaring a structure at program-block entry or by invoking a routine which creates a specific structure at run time. It is also done by the system when, at program-block entry, it processes the temporaries that were discovered at compile time, or when, during program execution, certain data-dependent temporaries are formed.

But to free storage is not as easy a matter. Obviously, at block exit, the storage allocated at entry for local variables can all be freed. The difficult storage to handle is that storage which is dynamically allocated, such as list structure nodes or programmer-created blocks, or strings in languages like SNOBOL.

One method is to make the responsibility for freeing storage the programmer's. But this, if applied universally, places too much of a burden on the programmer—it is too easy to forget about some temporaries, structures, etc. Some languages (for example, PL/I) do provide a **FREE** statement to allow the programmer some responsibility (if he chooses to accept it) for freeing at least some instances of his defined data structures. Most languages (and associated implementation systems), however, reserve to themselves the task of storage release, even if they do provide a **FREE** command by which the programmer can release certain blocks of storage.

Therefore, the problem now becomes one of determining by what means the system decides to free storage. There are several methods. One is to free no storage at all until there is almost none left. Then, all the allocated blocks are checked, and those that are no longer being used are freed. This method is called *garbage collection*. During the program execution, blocks of storage, which once were needed but which at some later time became unnecessary and unused, are called "garbage." A garbage collection simply goes through and recovers these garbage blocks. Another method is to free each block as soon as it becomes unused. This prevents the accumulation of garbage blocks, but requires more run-time checking during processing. This method is generally implemented by means of reference counters—counters which record how many pointers to this block are still in existence in the program.

Two problems arise in the context of storage release. One is the accumulation of garbage as mentioned before; this has the effect of decreasing the amount of free storage available and consequently increasing the chances of having to refuse a request for storage. The other problem is that of "dangling references." A dangling reference is a pointer existing in a program which still accesses a block that has been freed. If ever the block is reallocated and then this dangling pointer is used, the program once again has access to that block which is now being used for completely different purposes. Results can be catastrophic.

It is generally conceded that the dangling reference is potentially the more dangerous of the two problems, and so more effort is taken to minimize its likelihood of occurring. This, by the way, is another reason why not many systems allow the programmer much freedom to deallocate his own storage. It is too easy to do things like

```
ALLOCATE(P);
      .
      .
      .
Q = P;
FREE(P);
```

in which case Q has been created as a dangling reference. The system may well set P to NULL, when it does release the block, in order to break the association between the identifier P and the block, but it can do nothing about Q, which now records the address of a free block. There is no substitute for disciplined programming, but because many programmers like using "tricks," language implementors tend to try to protect them from their folly by means such as restricting the manner in which they may release storage.

In the reference-counter method, as mentioned earlier, a counter is kept which records how many different program elements have direct access (e.g., a pointer) to each block. When the block is first allocated its reference counter is set to 1. Each time another link is made pointing to this block, the reference counter is incremented; each time a link to it is broken, the reference counter is decremented. When the count reaches 0, then the block is inaccessible, and hence, unusable. At this point it is returned to the free list. Notice that this technique completely eliminates the dangling reference problem. The block is returned after there are no references to it in the program.

There are certain drawbacks in using this method, however. First, if the blocks that are allocated form a circular structure, then their reference counts will always remain set to at least 1, and none of the blocks will ever be freed, even if all pointers from outside the circular structure to blocks in the circular list are destroyed. We then have a circle of blocks, each of which is inaccessible from the program, and yet all the blocks will remain allocated—as permanent garbage. There are solutions for this, of course. One is simply to prohibit circular or recursive structures. In a number of applications, however, a circular structure is the most natural and reasonable one to use. Another solution is to flag circular structures as such, thereby signifying that they are to receive special treatment from the point of view of storage release. A third solution is to require that circular structures always use a special list head whose reference counter counts only references from outside the circle, and that all access to blocks in the circular structure are made through this list head. This is then a prohibition against direct accessing of any block in the circle. When the list head counter goes to 0, then the header block and all blocks in the circle can be freed.

Another drawback to the reference-counter method is the overhead involved in maintaining the reference counts. This is a more serious objection because it can increase the execution time of the program significantly. Every processing operation will have to be checked for effects on the reference counts, and these updated as necessary. For example, the simple statement P = SUC(PRED(Q)) can generate code to do the following, assuming that P and Q are known (perhaps by declarations) to be pointer variables:

1 Access block P and decrement its reference count. Let this new reference count be t.

2 Test t for zero. If so, free block P.

3 Evaluate SUC(PRED(Q)). Let the result be the address r.

4 Access block r and increment its reference count.

5 Assign the value r to the variable P.

Examination of even the simpler algorithms that may be used in a context where dynamic storage allocation and release are reasonable should indicate that the cost of this counter maintenance can easily become excessive.

The other method of determining when to free storage (aside from programmer-commanded release) is garbage collection. This method makes use of a special routine which is invoked whenever the available storage is almost exhausted, or whenever a particular request cannot be met, or, perhaps, whenever the amount of available storage has decreased beyond a certain predefined point. Normal program execution is interrupted while this routine frees garbage blocks and is resumed when the garbage collector has finished its work. The garbage-collection algorithm generally has two phases. The first phase consists of a tracing of all the access paths from all the program and system variables through the allocated blocks. Each block accessed in this way is marked. Phase two consists of moving through the entire segment of memory, resetting the marks of the marked blocks, and returning to the free list every allocated block that has not been marked.

Again, this method prevents the generation of dangling references because if there is any path of references leading to a block, this block is marked and is not freed in phase two. Because the garbage collector must trace paths of pointers from block to block, however, it is essential that, every time the garbage collector is invoked, all list and block structures are in their normal form with pointers pointing where they should. Otherwise, the garbage collector will not be able to make the proper tracing of all the reference paths, and either some garbage will remain uncollected or, more seriously, blocks still in use will be freed. Since the garbage collector can be invoked by the system at almost any point in program execution, it is required that the use of pointers be disciplined. There are certain algorithms, however, which, during their operation, temporarily distort structures—e.g., having pointers pointing up a tree instead of downwards to branches. If the garbage collector is invoked while the program is executing one of these algorithms, it is quite possible that the garbage collector will meet such a distorted tree. The marking phase can then no longer mark the correct blocks, and the situation when normal execution resumes can be horrendous.

A solution to this is, of course, to use pointers responsibly, avoiding the kind of algorithm that momentarily distorts structures. Certain applications, however, could well need that type of algorithm; it may be the only way to do the required task. In this case, the algorithm should begin by disabling the garbage collector so that it cannot be invoked while the algorithm is executing. If the algorithm should ever request storage and have the request refused, however, then a stalemate has developed. There is not necessarily any ready solution to this problem other than to terminate the job and rerun with more storage initially allocated to the job.

One of the drawbacks to the garbage collection technique is that its costs increase as the amount of free storage decreases, and yet, it is at this point that one would hope for efficient and cheap release of storage. When you have little free storage left, you expect the garbage collector to be called more often, and you want its use to cost as little as possible. The reason for the inverse relationship is, of course, that when there is little free storage, there is a lot of allocated storage and, hence, the marking process has to trace through many blocks. Because of this factor, and also perhaps to avoid the stalemate situation mentioned earlier, garbage-collection methods are sometimes implemented so that the collector is invoked well before memory gets close to full. For example, whenever the amount of free storage drops below half the total amount, the collector can be invoked intermittently. Also, to eliminate the intolerably repetitive calls to the collector that can result when memory is almost full, some systems consider the memory to be full whenever the garbage collector fails to restore the amount of free storage to a certain level. Such a condition causes the system to terminate when the next unsatisfiable request is encountered.

We now look at some of the algorithms that have been developed for garbage collection. We concentrate on the marking phase because the actual freeing phase, the sequential stepping through memory freeing unmarked blocks, is relatively simple. For fixed-size blocks of size n, with P being the address of the block with the lowest address in the total memory segment, the addresses of all the r blocks that were formed out of the total memory segment are given by $P + i*n$, $0 \leq i < r$. For variable-sized blocks, with P and Q being the addresses of the first and last words of the total memory segment, the addresses of all the blocks are given by the sequence of P values formed by:

$$P_1(=P), P_2(=P_1 + SIZE(P_1)), \ldots, P_m(=P_{m-1} + SIZE(P_{m-1})),$$

where $P_m + SIZE(P_m) = Q + 1$.

In the marking phase, the garbage collector must mark all blocks that are accessible by any path of references that begins with a program or system variable. Consequently, the collection algorithm must have access to a list of all the variables that currently contain references into the dynamic storage area. A scan through the symbol table or current identifier-association table will generally suffice. Once a variable has been found that points to a block of allocated storage, that block must be marked along with all the other blocks that are accessed by pointers within the first block, and all blocks accessed from these blocks, etc. Once all the blocks accessible from this variable have been marked, the next variable is processed in the same way. When all the variables have been processed, the total memory segment is stepped through and unmarked blocks are freed.

For the convenience of the marking algorithm, we assume that blocks which contain pointers to other blocks, thus forming a list-type structure, have these pointers located so that they are readily accessible given the block address. They can be located in the first words of the block following the block control fields. Therefore, we assume that block P, when allocated, has a structure of the form given in Fig. 5-6.5.

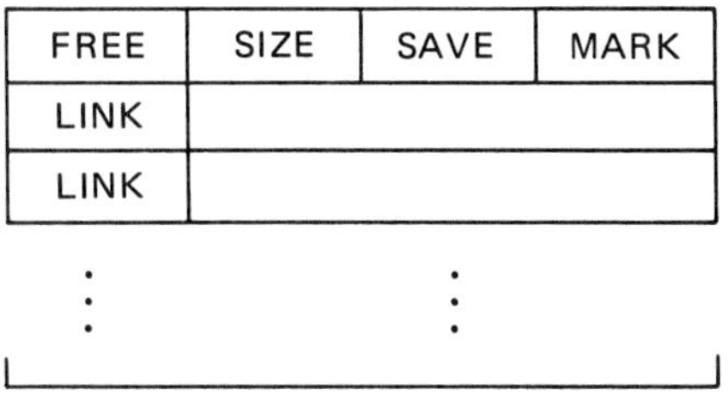

FREE	SIZE	SAVE	MARK
LINK			
LINK			

$$\vdots \qquad \vdots$$

FIGURE 5-6.5 Block structure for garbage collection.

FREE(P) contains a value equal to 1 + the number of LINK fields, SIZE(P) is the size of block P (or the coding for the size of block P as in the buddy or Fibonacci allocation system), SAVE(P) is a field to be used in the marking process by which a temporary distortion of the list structure needed for traversal can be eventually undone, MARK(P) is a field, initially set to 'false', which is set 'true' to denote that block P has been marked, and the LINK(P) fields are pointers to other blocks. Note that there need not be any such LINK fields. Note also that the SAVE field is not necessary for the first of the marking algorithms we shall give. In that case, simply assume that it is not there. Observe that the LINK fields can be accessed by the addresses Q, for P < Q < P + FREE(P). (Note that the allocation technique or release method may well require additional control fields. In such cases, simply assume that the correct fields are present.)

The first algorithm we give is very simple. It uses a stack S[1: MAX] to record unprocessed LINK fields encountered in the processing of a particular block. Upon the detection of an empty stack, all blocks on this chain have been marked.

Algorithm STACK_MARK.   Given P, the address of a block which is directly accessible via a program or system variable, the stack S, and blocks of the structure just described (without the SAVE field), this routine marks block P and all blocks accessible from block P.

1. [List structure?] If FREE(P) = 1, then set MARK(P) ← true, and Exit; otherwise, set TOP ← 1 and S[TOP] ← P.
2. [Process next block]
   Repeat while TOP > 0:
      set P ← S[TOP], TOP ← TOP − 1, MARK(P) ← true, and Q ← P + 1.
      Repeat while Q < P + FREE(P):   (stack LINK fields)
         if MARK(LINK(Q)) = false,
         then if FREE(LINK(Q)) = 1;
            then set MARK(LINK(Q)) ← true;
            otherwise, if TOP + 1 > MAX,
               then exit to an error routine;
               otherwise, set TOP ← TOP + 1 and S[TOP] ← LINK(Q).
      Set Q ← Q + 1.
3. [Finished] Exit.

It should be noted that, in order to save some unnecessary operations on the stack, only those unmarked blocks which actually have LINK fields ever get pushed onto the stack.

This algorithm will run in time that is proportional to the number of blocks marked, and this is quite good. But the drawback to this method is the use of the auxiliary stack. Presumably, garbage collection is invoked when available storage is getting to be in short supply. There may not be room for the stack, especially if the blocks form a fairly complicated list structure with much cross linking involved. Because of this problem, other algorithms have been proposed, including ones which do not require an auxiliary stack. The following is an algorithm modeled upon one devised by Schorr and Waite.

The algorithm that Schorr and Waite propose works in the following manner. One path of accesses is followed until it ends. In our case, this is the referencing of a block which has no more LINK fields to process or which is already marked because it is also on some other path. As this forward path is followed, the LINK fields which we traverse are set to point to the block from which we came. This temporary distortion of the structure is, however, the factor that enables the one-way path to be retraced. The SAVE field is used to record which of the several LINK fields in a block is currently reversed. When this path is retraced, as we enter a block on the return journey, we reset the altered LINK field to its correct value and then process all the other LINK fields of that block as if they initiated subpaths. That is, we follow one to its end, reversing LINK fields, and then trace it backwards, resetting LINK fields and following still further subpaths. It therefore follows that the logical structure of this algorithm involves a considerable degree of "nesting" of path fragments within path fragments. If it were not for the storage shortage, this would make an ideal candidate for a recursive treatment. The actual algorithm follows.

Algorithm LINK_MARK.   Given P, the address of a block which is directly accessible, and blocks with the structure described earlier, this algorithm marks block P and all blocks accessible from P. The pointers P and Q refer to the current block under process and the previous block, respectively.

1. [Initialize]   Set Q ← NULL.
2. [Mark a starting block]
    If MARK(P) = true, then go to step 4;
    otherwise, set MARK(P) ← true and SAVE(P) ← 0.
3. [Initiate a forward traversal?]   Set t ← SAVE(P) + 1.
    If t < FREE(P),   (reverse a LINK)
    then set SAVE(P) ← t, TEMP ← LINK(P + t), LINK(P + t) ← Q, Q ← P,
        P ← TEMP, and go to step 2.
4. [Reset a LINK and go backwards one step]
    If Q = NULL,
    then Exit;
    otherwise, set t ← SAVE(Q), TEMP ← LINK(Q + t), LINK(Q + t) ← P,
        P ← Q, and Q ← TEMP.
    Go to step 3.

It should be noted that this algorithm will run slower than the stack algorithm because each path must be traced twice. Such a price must be paid for being able to mark in very little space.

The better solution is, of course, to make use of a stack if one is available. If there is some amount of available space, then the stack algorithm should be used initially. If at some point, however, the stack becomes full and there is a block address which must be stacked, then the second algorithm can be used to mark the current block and all blocks accessible from it. When it returns from marking, the stack algorithm can continue because it no longer has to process that block. This blending of the two algorithms couples the speed of the stack algorithm with an additional capability of marking without a stack whenever the stack is full. To blend these two algorithms, all one has to do is alter the phrase "exit to an error routine" in Algorithm STACK_MARK to "call LINK_MARK(LINK(Q))".

As a final topic, we shall briefly discuss compaction as a technique for reclaiming storage. Compaction works by actually moving blocks of data, etc. from one location in memory to another so as to collect all the free blocks into one large block. The allocation problem then becomes completely simplified. Allocation now consists of merely moving a pointer which points to the top of this successively shortening block of storage. Once this single block gets too small again, the compaction mechanism is again invoked to reclaim what unused storage may now exist among allocated blocks. There is generally no storage release mechanism. Instead, a marking algorithm is used to mark blocks that are still in use. Then, instead of freeing each unmarked block by calling a release mechanism to put it on a free list, the compactor simply collects all unmarked blocks into one large block at one end of the memory segment. The only real problem in this method is the redefining of pointers. This is solved by making extra passes through memory. After blocks are marked, the entire memory is stepped through and the new address for each marked block is determined. This new address is stored in the block itself. Then another pass over memory is made. On this pass, pointers that point to marked blocks are reset to point to where the marked blocks will be after compaction. This is why the new address is stored right in the block—it is easily obtainable. After all pointers have been reset, then the marked blocks are moved to their new locations. An example of a compaction algorithm is the following one.

Algorithm COMPACT. Given blocks of the structure as described for garbage collection, this algorithm performs a compaction of unused storage into one large block whose starting address is TOP and which extends from TOP to STOP, the highest address in the entire memory segment. It is assumed that START is the address of the first word of the memory segment. The SAVE field in the marked blocks is used by the compaction routine to record the new address of each block.

1. [Mark blocks] Invoke garbage collection marking routine to mark blocks.
2. [Compute new addresses for marked blocks] Set LOC ← TOP ← START.
   Repeat while LOC ≤ STOP:
       if MARK(LOC) = true, then set SAVE(LOC) ← TOP, TOP ← TOP + SIZE(LOC).
       LOC ← LOC + SIZE(LOC).
3. [Redefine variable references for program and system pointer variables]
   Repeat for each variable: Set P ← value of variable, variable ← SAVE(P).
4. [Define new values for pointers in marked blocks] Set LOC ← START.
   Repeat while LOC ≤ STOP.
       If MARK(LOC) = true,
       then set P ← LOC + 1,

> repeat while P < LOC + FREE(LOC):
>   set LINK(P) ← SAVE(LINK(P)) and P ← P + 1.
> Set LOC ← LOC + SIZE(LOC).

5. [Move the marked blocks]   Set LOC ← TOP ← START.
   Repeat while LOC ≤ STOP:
      If MARK(LOC) = true,
      then set t ← SIZE(LOC) and k ← 0,
         repeat while k < t:
            Copy contents of LOC + k into location TOP + k, k ← k + 1,
         set MARK(TOP) ← false, TOP ← TOP + t, and LOC ← LOC + t;
      otherwise, set LOC ← LOC + SIZE(LOC).

6. [Finished]   Exit.

It should be noted that this compaction routine is a relatively costly process in terms of execution time because of its three passes through memory. However, the increased speed of allocation might well make it a reasonable option in certain circumstances. Many implementations of SNOBOL use this compaction algorithm (or a variant), so presumably, it cannot be too very inefficient.

We have now finished our survey of storage management and some of the problems involved in performing it. We have presented a number of different algorithms, ones which are reasonably typical of those that may be found in use. In practice, several of these techniques may be combined. This certainly is feasible; the methods are not necessarily incompatible with each other. In any case, the actual operating environment determines which methods should be used. The practical efficiency of these methods very often depends strongly on many parameters, among which are request frequency, size-of-request distribution, usage (e.g. batch vs. on-line), and the service philosophy of the computer center management.

BIBLIOGRAPHY

ABRAMS, M. D.: "Data Structures for Computer Graphics," *Proceedings of a Symposium on Data Structures in Programming Languages*, SIGPLAN Notices, Vol. 6, No. 2, February, 1971, pp. 268–286.

AHO, A. V. and J. D. ULLMAN: "The Theory of Parsing, Translation, and Compiling, Vol. 1: Parsing," Prentice-Hall, Inc., Englewood Cliffs, N.J., 1972.

BERZTISS, A. T.: "Data Structures: Theory and Practice," Academic Press, Inc., New York, 1971.

BRILLINGER, P. C. and D. J. COHEN: "Introduction to Data Structures and Nonnumeric Computations," Prentice-Hall, Inc., Englewood Cliffs, N.J., 1972.

DAVIDSON, C. H. and E. C. KOENIG: "Computers: Introduction to Computers and Applied Computing Concepts," John Wiley and Sons, Inc., New York, 1967.

DAVIS, S.: "Computer Data Displays," Prentice-Hall, Inc., Englewood Cliffs, N.J., 1969.

DIAL, R. B.: "Decision Table Translation," *Communications of the ACM*, Vol. 13, No. 9, September, 1970, pp. 571–572.

ELSON, M.: "Data Structures," Science Research Associates, Inc., Palo Alto, Calif., 1975.

GEAR, C. W.: "Introduction to Computer Science," Science Research Associates, Inc., Palo Alto, Calif., 1973.

GRAY, J. C.: "Compound Data Structures for Computer Aided Design; a Survey," *ACM Professional Development Seminar.*

GRIES, D. E.: "Compiler Construction for Digital Computers," John Wiley and Sons, Inc., New York, 1971.

HARRISON, M. C.: "Data Structures and Programming," Scott, Foresman and Company, Glenview, Ill., 1973.

HINDS, J. A.: "An Algorithm for Locating Adjacent Storage Blocks in the Buddy System," *Communications of the ACM*, Vol. 18, No. 4, 1975, pp. 221–222.

HIRSCHBERG, D. S.: "A Class of Dynamic Memory Allocation Algorithms," *Communications of the ACM*, Vol. 16, No. 10, 1973, pp. 615–618.

KAHN, A. B.: "Topological Sorting of Large Networks," *Communications of the ACM*, Vol. 5, No. 11, 1962, pp. 558–562.

KNUTH, D. E.: "The Art of Computer Programming, Vol. 1, Fundamental Algorithms," Second edition, Addison-Wesley Publishing Co., Inc., Reading, Mass., 1973.

LEVIN, RICHARD I. and CHARLES A. KIRKPATRICK: "Planning and Control with PERT/CPM," McGraw-Hill Book Company, New York, 1966.

LINDSTROM, G.: "Copying List Structures Using Bounded Workspace," *Communications of the ACM*, Vol. 17, No. 4, 1974, pp. 198–202.

MCCARTHY, J., et al.: "LISP 1.5 Programmer's Manual," 2nd edition, M.I.T. Press, Cambridge, Mass., 1969.

MONTALBANO, M.: "Decision Tables," Science Research Associates, Inc., Palo Alto, Calif., 1974.

NEWMAN, W. M. and R. F. SPROULL: "Principles of Interactive Computer Graphics," McGraw-Hill Book Company, New York, 1973.

POLLACK, S. L.: "Conversion of Limited-Entry Decision Tables to Computer Programs," Memorandum RM-4020PR, The Rand Corporation, Santa Monica, Calif., May, 1964.

PRATT, T. W.: "Programming Languages: Design and Implementation," Prentice-Hall, Inc., Englewood Cliffs, N.J., 1975.

REINWALD, L. T. and R. M. SOLAND: "Conversion of Limited-Entry Decision Tables to Optimal Computer Programs I: Minimum Average Processing Time," *Journal of the ACM*, July, 1966, pp. 339–358.

SCHORR, H. and W. M. WAITE: "An Efficient Machine-Independent Procedure for Garbage Collection in Various List Structures," *Communications of the ACM*, Vol. 10, No. 8, 1967, pp. 501–506.

SHEN, K. K. and J. L. PETERSON: "A Weighted Buddy Method for Dynamic Storage Allocation," *Communications of the ACM*, Vol. 17, No. 10, 1974, pp. 558–562.

SUTHERLAND, I. F.: "SKETCHPAD: A Man-Machine Graphical Communication System," Proceedings of the AFIPS 1963 SJCC, Vol. 23, Spartan Books, New York.

TREMBLAY, J. P. and R. M. MANOHAR: "Discrete Mathematical Structures and their Applications to Computer Science," McGraw-Hill Book Company, New York, 1975.

VAN DAM, A.: "Data and Storage Structures for Interactive Graphics," Proceedings of a Symposium on Data Structures in Programming Languages, SIGPLAN Notices, Vol. 6, No. 2, February, 1971, pp. 237–267.

VERHELST, M.: "The Conversion of Limited Entry Decision Tables to Optimal and Near-Optimal Flowcharts—Two New Algorithms," *Communications of the ACM*, Vol. 15, No. 11, November, 1972, pp. 974–980.

WILLIAMS, R.: "A Survey of Data Structures for Computer Graphics Systems," ACM Computing Surveys, Vol. 3, No. 1, March, 1971, pp. 1–21.

6

SORTING AND SEARCHING

In the previous chapters we have discussed many data structures and their storage representations. Algorithms for a number of operations such as insertion and deletion, which are commonly performed on these structures, were described in detail. This chapter is concerned with two additional operations that are frequently performed on data structures—namely, sorting and searching. We shall see that efficient algorithms for these operations can be realized when data are properly structured.

The algorithms to be discussed progress from the simple to the complex. A rough quantitative measure of each algorithm is given. The most comprehensive reference to this chapter is Knuth's book on Sorting and Searching. The methods that are described in this chapter assume that all data are stored in the main memory of the computer and are, therefore, called internal sorting and searching techniques.

6-1 SORTING

The operation of sorting is most often performed in business data-processing applications. This operation, however, has also become increasingly important in many scientific applications. The sorting methods which are discussed in this section give a representative sample of the most popular techniques used.

The methods that are described proceed from trivial (and inefficient) algorithms, such as the selection and bubble sorts, to the more complex (and efficient) algorithms such as quick sort, heap sort, and radix sort. Various data structures such as trees and queues are used to structure the data so as to achieve computational efficiency.

6-1.1 Notation and Concepts

Data can occur in many forms. In this section it is assumed that we are given a collection of elements. Each element is represented by a record which contains a number of information fields. The records are combined into a table which represents the information upon which the operation of sorting is to be performed. Each field in a record contains, in general, alphanumeric information. The organization of a record is application dependent and has no bearing on the basic algorithms which will be discussed.

A *table* is assumed to be an ordered sequence of n records $R_1, R_2, ..., R_n$. Each record in a table contains one or more keys. It is with respect to these keys that processing is carried out. For example, the key associated with a record could be an employee number or an employee name. Each record for our purpose will contain a single key field K_i and other additional information which is irrelevant to the present discussion.

Sorting is the operation of arranging the records of a table into some sequential order according to an ordering criterion. The sort is performed according to the key value of each record. Depending on the makeup of the key, records can be sorted either numerically or, more generally, alphanumerically. In numerical sorting, the records are arranged in ascending or descending order according to the numerical value of the key. An example of this type of sorting is the sorting of a symbol table according to the internal numeric value of the alphanumeric representation of each variable name. In general, a key can be any sequence of characters and the ordering imposed by sorting depends on the collating sequence associated with the particular character set which is being used (see Secs. 1-4.6 and 2-3.1). For convenience, it is assumed throughout this section that the key upon which the sorting is performed is numeric. This is not a restrictive assumption since all algorithms to be formulated also apply to any string of characters, given a particular collating sequence.

Most of the algorithms to be discussed involve the movement of records from one place to another in the table. Since records in certain applications can be quite long and consequently expensive to move, the records can be organized in such a manner as to minimize this moving cost while performing a sort.

One method of substantially reducing the cost of moving the records is to arrange the table as a simple linked list. Clearly, the movement of records is efficient when such a representation is used. The additional memory required for a pointer field becomes less significant as the record length increases.

Another method of reducing record movement is to use a pointer vector, each element of which contains the address of one record. As an illustration, Fig. 6-1.1 gives the representation of a small student-record table according to grades before and after sorting.

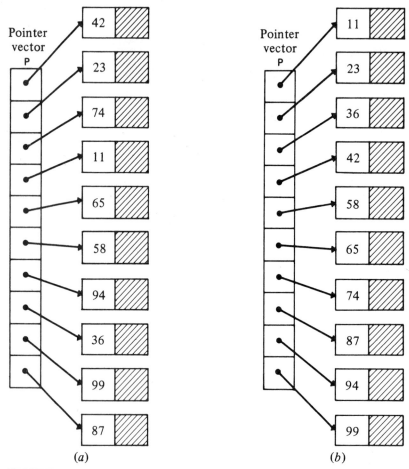

FIGURE 6-1.1 Representation of a table using a pointer vector. (*a*) Before sorting; (*b*) after sorting.

The hatched area in each record represents information such as name and course number, which can be ignored for our purpose.

All sorting methods to be discussed assume that the entire table can be sorted in the computer's main memory. A number of these methods, such as the merge sort and address-calculation sort, can easily be adapted to tables stored on auxiliary storage devices like disks and drums.

Each sorting method to be described will include an approximate quantitative description of the method as to number of comparisons and number of record movements required. Since, as previously mentioned, the expense of record movements can be reduced significantly, the more important factor is the number of comparisons which is required by a particular method.

The sorting methods that are described in the following pages proceed from the trivial to the complex. The suitable structuring of the table, such as in the heap sort, radix sort, and address-calculation sort, can lead to efficient sorting algorithms.

6-1.2 Selection Sort

One of the easiest ways to sort a table is by *selection*. Beginning with the first record in the table, a search is performed to locate the element which has the smallest key. When this element is found, it is interchanged with the first record in the table. This interchange places the record with the smallest key in the first position of the table. A search for the second smallest key is then carried out. This is accomplished by examining the keys of the records from the second element onwards. The element which has the second smallest key is interchanged with the element located in the second position of the table. The process of searching for the record with the next smallest key and placing it in its proper position (within the desired ordering) continues until all records have been sorted in ascending order. The following algorithm formalizes this process.

Algorithm SELECTION. Given a table of elements $R_1, R_2, \ldots, R_n$, this algorithm rearranges the table in ascending order; i.e., its keys will be in the order $K_1 \leq K_2 \leq \cdots \leq K_n$. The sorting process is based on the technique just described.

1. [Loop on pass index] **Repeat steps 2 to 4 for i = 1, 2, . . ., n − 1.**
2. [Initialize minimum index] **Set r ← i.**
3. [Make a pass and obtain smallest key]
   Repeat for j = i + 1, i + 2, . . ., n:
       If $K_j < K_r$, then set r ← j.
4. [Exchange records] **If r ≠ i, then $R_i \leftrightarrow R_r$.**
5. [Finished] **Exit.**

    In the algorithm, the search for the record with the next smallest key is called a *pass*. There are n − 1 such passes required in order to perform the sort. This is because each pass places one record into its proper location.

    An example of the selection sort is given in Fig. 6-1.2. Each encircled entry denotes

	Unsorted				Pass Number (i)					Sorted
j	K_j	1	2	3	4	5	6	7	8	9
1	42	11	11	11	11	11	11	11	11	11
2	23	(23)	23	23	23	23	23	23	23	23
3	74	74	74	36	36	36	36	36	36	36
4	(11)	42	42	(42)	42	42	42	42	42	42
5	65	65	65	65	65	58	58	58	58	58
6	58	58	58	58	(58)	(65)	65	65	65	65
7	94	94	94	94	94	94	94	74	74	74
8	36	36	(36)	74	74	74	(74)	94	87	87
9	99	99	99	99	99	99	99	99	99	94
10	87	87	87	87	87	87	87	(87)	(94)	99

FIGURE 6-1.2 Trace of a selection sort.

the record with the smallest key selected in a particular pass. The elements above the bar for a given pass are those elements that have been placed in order.

We now turn to the performance of this algorithm. During the first pass, in which the record with the smallest key is found, $n - 1$ records are compared. In general, for the ith pass of the sort, $n - i$ comparisons are required. The total number of comparisons is, therefore, the sum

$$\sum_{i=1}^{n-1} (n - i) = \tfrac{1}{2}n(n - 1)$$

Therefore, the number of comparisons is proportional to n^2, which is often denoted by $0(n^2)$ (i.e., order n^2). The number of record interchanges depends upon how unsorted the table is. Since, during each pass, no more than one interchange is required, the maximum number of interchanges for the sort is $n - 1$.

6-1.3 Bubble Sort

Another well-known sorting method is the *bubble sort*. It differs from the selection sort in that, instead of finding the smallest record and then performing an interchange, two records are interchanged immediately upon discovering that they are out of order.

Using this approach, at most $n - 1$ passes are required. During the first pass, K_1 and K_2 are compared and, if they are out of order, then records R_1 and R_2 are interchanged; this process is repeated for records R_2 and R_3, R_3 and R_4, and so on. This method will cause records with small keys to move or "bubble up." After the first pass, the record with the largest key will be in the nth position. On each successive pass, the records with the next largest key will be placed in position $n - 1, n - 2, \ldots, 2$, respectively, thereby resulting in a sorted table.

After each pass through the table, a check can be made to determine whether or not any interchanges were made during that pass. If no interchanges occurred, then the table must be sorted and no further passes are required. We now proceed to the formulation of this sorting process.

Algorithm BUBBLE. Given a table of records $R_1, R_2, \ldots, R_n$, this algorithm rearranges the table in ascending order; i.e., its keys will be in the order $K_1 \leq K_2 \leq \cdots \leq K_n$. The sorting technique is based on the method previously described.

1. [Loop on pass index]   Repeat steps 2 and 3 for $i = 1, 2, \ldots, n - 1$.
2. [Initialize interchange marker]   Set FLAG $\leftarrow 0$.
3. [Make a pass]
   Repeat for $j = 1, 2, \ldots, n - i$:
       If $K_{j+1} < K_j$, then set FLAG $\leftarrow 1$, $R_j \leftrightarrow R_{j+1}$.
   If FLAG $= 0$, then Exit.
4. [Finished]   Exit.

The algorithm is straightforward. Before each pass, the interchange marker FLAG is initialized to zero. This marker is checked at the end of every pass. If it has not been changed, then the sort is complete.

The worst case performance of the bubble sort is $\frac{1}{2}n(n-1)$ comparisons and $\frac{1}{2}n(n-1)$ exchanges. The average number of passes is approximately $n \times 1.25\sqrt{n}$ (see Stone). For $n = 10$ the average number of passes is 6, the number of passes required in Fig. 6-1.3. The average number of comparisons and exchanges are both $O(n^2)$.

A number of improvements can be made to the bubble sort. Some of these are considered in the exercises. These refinements, however, do not significantly improve the performance of the method. In summary, the bubble sort may be an acceptable method for sorting a table which contains a small number of records (less than 15), but it should not be used for larger-sized tables.

6-1.4 Partition-Exchange Sort

We now consider a sorting method which performs very well on larger tables. At each step in the method, the goal is to place a particular record in its final position within the table. In so doing, all records which precede this record have smaller keys, while all records that follow it have larger keys. This technique essentially partitions the table into two subtables. The same process can then be applied to each of these subtables and repeated until all records are placed in their final positions.

As an example, consider the following key set:

42   23   74   11   65   58   94   36   99   87

Two index variables i and j with initial values of 1 and 10, respectively, are used. Keys K_i and K_j are compared and, if no exchange is required, then j is decremented by 1 and the process is repeated. When $K_i \geq K_j$, the records R_i and R_j are interchanged. The process is now repeated with i being incremented and j fixed until another exchange occurs; at this time, j will again be decremented and i will be held fixed, etc.

	Unsorted			Pass Number (i)				Sorted
j	K_j	1	2	3	4	5	6	
1	42	23	23	11	11	11	11	
2	23	42	11	23	23	23	23	
3	74	11	42	42	42	36	36	
4	11	65	58	58	36	42	42	
5	65	58	65	36	58	58	58	
6	58	74	36	65	65	65	65	
7	94	36	74	74	74	74	74	
8	36	94	87	87	87	87	87	
9	99	87	94	94	94	94	94	
10	87	99	99	99	99	99	99	

FIGURE 6-1.3 Trace of a bubble sort.

The sequence of exchanges for placing 42 in its final position is given as follows, where the encircled entries on each line denote the keys being compared:

(42)	23	74	11	65	58	94	36	99	(87)
(42)	23	74	11	65	58	94	36	(99)	87
(42)	23	74	11	65	58	94	(36)	99	87
36	(23)	74	11	65	58	94	(42)	99	87
36	23	(74)	11	65	58	94	(42)	99	87
36	23	(42)	11	65	58	(94)	74	99	87
36	23	(42)	11	65	(58)	94	74	99	87
36	23	(42)	11	(65)	58	94	74	99	87
36	23	(42)	(11)	65	58	94	74	99	87
36	23	11	42	65	58	94	74	99	87

The original key set has been partitioned into the subtables, namely, the sets {36, 23, 11} and {65, 58, 94, 74, 99, 87}. The same process can be applied to each of these sets until the table is completely sorted. This partition-exchange method of sorting is also called *quick sort*.

Each time a table is subdivided into two subtables, one of these is processed while the boundaries of the other are stored so that it can be processed later. A stack can be used for this purpose. The boundaries of the largest subtable can be stacked while the other is processed. A stack entry describing an unprocessed subtable must consist of a left and a right boundary marker. This approach is incorporated in the following algorithm.

Algorithm QUICK_SORT.   Given a table of records $R_1, R_2, \ldots, R_n$, this algorithm sorts the table in ascending order. The sorting technique used is based on the partition-exchange method just described. A pair of dummy records R_0 and R_{n+1} are assumed where $K_0 \leq K_i \leq K_{n+1}$ for all $1 \leq i \leq n$. A stack which is used to store the lower and upper bounds of each unprocessed subtable is represented by vectors LOWER and UPPER, respectively. TOP denotes the top element on the stack. The variables LB and UB denote the lower and upper bounds of the current subtable being processed. The indices i and j are used during the processing of a subtable. TEMP contains the key which is to be placed in its final position within the sorted subtable.

1. [Initialize]   Set TOP ← 1, LOWER[TOP] ← 1, and UPPER[TOP] ← n.
2. [Perform sort]
     Repeat while(TOP ≠ 0):
          (Process new subfile)
          Set LB ← LOWER[TOP], UB ← UPPER[TOP], and TOP ← TOP − 1.
          Repeat steps 3 to 6 while(UB > LB).
     Exit.
3. [Initialize pass]   Set i ← LB, j ← UB, and TEMP ← K_i.
4. [Scan keys from right to left]

Repeat while(TEMP < K_j): set $j \leftarrow j - 1$.
If $j \leq i$, then set $K_i \leftarrow$ TEMP and go to step 6.
Set $K_i \leftarrow K_j$ and $i \leftarrow i + 1$.
5. [Scan keys from left to right]
Repeat while($K_i <$ TEMP): set $i \leftarrow i + 1$.
If $j > i$, then set $K_j \leftarrow K_i$, $j \leftarrow j - 1$, and go to step 4.
Set $K_j \leftarrow$ TEMP and $i \leftarrow j$.
6. [Push description of unprocessed subtable on stack]   Set TOP $\leftarrow$ TOP $+ 1$.
If $i - $ LB $<$ UB $- i$,
then set LOWER[TOP] $\leftarrow i + 1$, UPPER[TOP] $\leftarrow$ UB, and UB $\leftarrow i - 1$;
otherwise, set LOWER[TOP] $\leftarrow$ LB, UPPER[TOP] $\leftarrow i - 1$, and LB $\leftarrow i + 1$.

The algorithm begins by storing the boundaries of the entire table on the stack. Step 2 repeatedly unstacks the boundary information of each unprocessed subtable and then proceeds to partition it. Steps 3 to 6 partition a particular subtable. When a subtable is partitioned into two subsets, the description of the largest subset is stacked. The tracing of the algorithm for our example table is left as an exercise.

The average number of comparisons for this algorithm is $O(n \log_2 n)$. The worst case for this algorithm occurs when the table is already sorted where the number of comparisons is $O(n^2)$. In such a case Algorithm QUICK_SORT is no better than a selection sort.

6-1.5   Tree Sorts

In this subsection we examine two sorting techniques which are based on a tree representation of a given table. The first technique, which is straightforward, is a binary tree sort. The second method, however, although still involving binary trees is much more complex.

Since we have previously introduced all the concepts required to understand the binary tree sort, we merely outline the method here. The algorithm consists of two phases, namely, a construction phase and a traversal phase. The construction phase consists of successively inserting a new record in a tree structure in a manner similar to that taken in Sec. 5-2.2, which dealt with the construction of a symbol table. The tree obtained from this first phase can then be traversed in order (see Sec. 5-1.2), thus resulting in a sorted table. The average number of comparisons for this method is $O(n \log_2 n)$. In the worst case, however, the number of comparisons required is $O(n^2)$, a case which arises when the sort tree is severely "unbalanced." More will be said about unbalanced trees in Sec. 6-2.3.

The second sorting method can be explained in terms of a match-play golf tournament. Assume that this tournament consists of eight players and is to be played according to the schedule given in Fig. 6-1.4. The results of the tournament are also given in the diagram with Paul beating John, Bob beating Rick, etc., and finally Clarence beating Paul. Clarence is consequently declared the winner of the tournament. We now want to find the second best player. This player can be Paul or Bill or Harvey. The second best player can be determined by having Bill play Harvey and the winner of the match play Paul. The important point to note is that the complete tournament need not be replayed with Clarence absent.

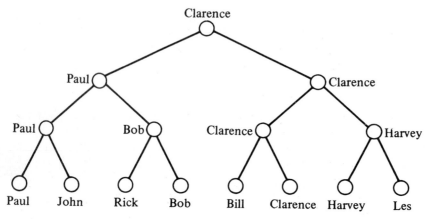

FIGURE 6-1.4   A match-play golf tournament.

The algorithm which we now formulate is a combination of algorithms due to Floyd and Williams. Figure 6-1.5 represents an example table by a particular kind of binary tree called a *heap*. In general, a heap which represents a table of n records satisfies the property

$K_j \le K_i$ for $2 \le j \le n$ and $i = \lfloor j/2 \rfloor$.

The binary tree is allocated sequentially such that the indices of the left and right sons (if they exist) of record i are 2i and 2i + 1, respectively. Conversely, the index of the parent of record j (if it exists) is $\lfloor j/2 \rfloor$. It is clear from Fig. 6-1.5 that the tree structure satisfies the definition of a heap.

Once we have a heap representation of a table, the record with the largest key is at the root of the tree (also called the top of the heap). We now formulate an algorithm which will have as input an unsorted sequentially allocated table and produce as output a heap.

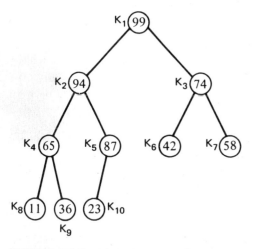

FIGURE 6-1.5   A heap representation of a sample key set.

The starting point is to have a heap initially (e.g., a one-record tree is a heap) and then insert a new record into the existing heap such that a new heap is formed after performing the insertion. Insertions are performed repeatedly until all records in the original table form a heap.

Algorithm CREATE_HEAP.   Given a table R containing records R_1, R_2, ..., R_n, this algorithm creates a heap as previously described. The index variable q controls the number of insertions which are to be performed. The variable j denotes the index of the parent of record R_i. NEW is a temporary record area and KEY contains the key of the record being inserted into an existing heap.

1. [Build heap]   **Repeat steps 2 to 6 for q = 2, 3, ..., n.**
2. [Initialize]   **Set i ← q, NEW ← R_q, and KEY ← K_q.**
3. [Place new record in existing heap]
   Repeat steps 4 and 5 while i > 1.
4. [Obtain parent of new record]   **Set j ← $\lfloor i/2 \rfloor$.**
5. [Interchange records?]
   If KEY > K_j, then set R_i ← R_j and i ← j; otherwise, go to step 6.
6. [Copy new record into its proper place]   **Set R_i ← NEW.**
7. [Finished]   **Exit.**

The first step of the algorithm is an iteration statement which controls the building of the desired heap by performing successive insertions. Step 2 selects the record to be inserted in an existing heap and copies this record into NEW. Steps 4 and 5 append the new record (as a leaf) to the existing heap (i.e., a binary tree) and move this record up the tree along the path between the new leaf and the top of the heap. This process continues until the new record reaches a position in the tree that satisfies the definition of a heap. The copying of the new record into its proper place in the tree is accomplished in step 6. A trace of the construction of the heap of Fig. 6-1.5 for the initial key set

$$42, 23, 74, 11, 65, 58, 94, 36, 99, 87$$

is given in Fig. 6-1.6. Each tree in the diagram represents its state after the insertion and reconstruction process is complete. Now that we have represented the initial table by a heap, we can use the notions of the match-play golf tournament to perform the sort. The record with the largest key is presently in R_1 and it can be written out directly. This is accomplished by interchanging R_1 and R_n and then reconstructing a new heap consisting of only n − 1 records. This is realized in a manner similar to that used in Algorithm CREATE_HEAP. The result of this reconstruction process is to place the record with second largest key in R_1. This record can now be exchanged with record R_{n-1}. A new heap is then constructed for n − 2 records. By repeating this exchange and reconstruction process, the initial table can be sorted. The sort algorithm follows.

Algorithm HEAP_SORT.   Given a table R consisting of n records R_1, R_2, ..., R_n and Algorithm CREATE_HEAP, which has been previously described, this algorithm sorts the table in ascending order. The variable q represents the pass index. Index variables i and j are used where the latter is the index of the left son of the former. SAVE is a temporary

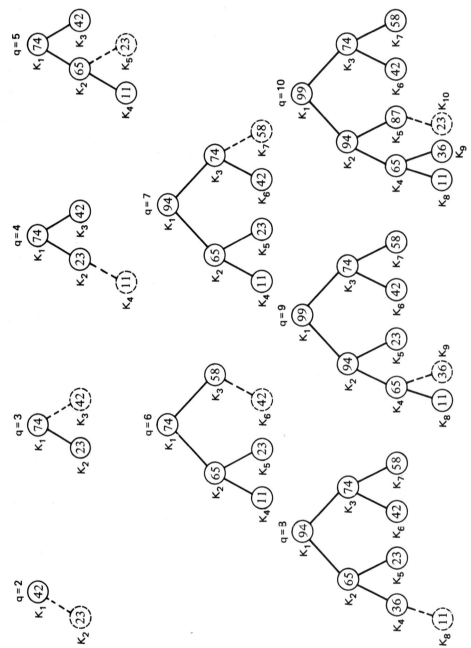

FIGURE 6-1.6 Trace of Algorithm CREATE_HEAP.

record area and KEY is a variable which contains the key of the record being swapped at each pass.

1. [Create heap]   Call CREATE_HEAP(R).
2. [Perform sort]   Repeat steps 2 to 8 for q = n, n − 1, . . ., 2.
3. [Output record]   Set $R_1 \leftrightarrow R_q$.
4. [Initialize]   Set i ← 1, SAVE ← R_1, KEY ← K_1 and j ← 2.
5. [Reconstruct the heap]   Repeat steps 6 and 7 while j ≤ q − 1.
6. [Obtain index of largest son]
   If j + 1 < q, then if K_{j+1} > K_j, then set j ← j + 1.
7. [Interchange records?]
   If K_j > KEY, then set R_i ← R_j, i ← j, and j ← 2 * i; otherwise, go to step 8.
8. [Copy record into its proper place]   Set R_i ← SAVE.
9. [Finished]   Exit.

The algorithm begins by constructing a heap for the entire table. Step 2 controls the n − 1 passes required to sort the table. The remaining steps of the algorithm are very similar to those used in Algorithm CREATE_HEAP to construct a new heap after the insertion of a new record. A trace of the sort for Fig. 6-1.5 is given in Fig. 6-1.7, where each tree represents the state of the sort at the end of each pass.

The worst case analysis of this algorithm (see Stone) shows that the number of comparisons is $0(n \log_2 n)$. Also, no extra working storage area, except for one record position, is required. Note that this algorithm, depending on the makeup of a particular key set, can outperform Algorithm QUICK_SORT, whose worst case is $0(n^2)$.

6-1.6 Merge Sorting

The operation of sorting is closely related to the process of *merging*. In the early days of data processing, merging was performed on cards with the aid of a machine called a *collator*. The collator had as input two separate decks of cards, each of which was sorted, and it proceeded to merge these two decks and to output a single sorted deck of cards. In this section we will formulate a sorting algorithm based on successive merges.

First, let us examine the merging of two ordered tables which can be combined to produce a single sorted table. This process can be accomplished easily by successively selecting the record with the smallest key occurring in either of the tables and placing this record in a new table, thereby creating an ordered list. For example, from the tables

Table 1	11	23	42
Table 2	9	25	

we obtain the following trace:

Table 1	11	23	42
Table 2	25		
New Table	9		
Table 1	23	42	
Table 2	25		

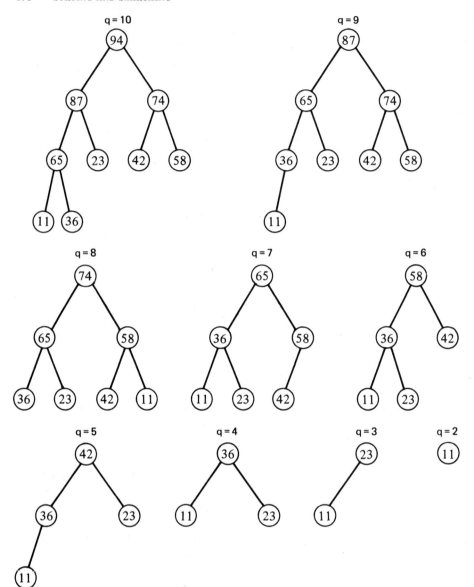

FIGURE 6-1.7   Trace of Algorithm HEAP_SORT.

New Table	9	11	
Table 1	42		
Table 2	25		
New Table	9	11	23
Table 1	42		
Table 2			

New Table	9	11	23	25	
Table 1					
Table 2					
New Table	9	11	23	25	42

This process is formalized in the following algorithm.

Algorithm SIMPLE_MERGE.   Given two ordered tables $a_1, a_2, \ldots, a_n$ and $b_1, b_2, \ldots, b_m$, this algorithm merges these tables and produces the ordered table $c_1, c_2, \ldots, c_{n+m}$. The variables i, j, and k are used as indices to the tables.

1. [Initialize]   Set $i \leftarrow j \leftarrow k \leftarrow 1$.
2. [Compare corresponding records and output the smallest]
   Repeat while ($i \leq n$ and $j \leq m$):
       if $a_i \leq b_j$,
       then set $c_k \leftarrow a_i$, $i \leftarrow i + 1$, and $k \leftarrow k + 1$;
       otherwise, set $c_k \leftarrow b_j$, $j \leftarrow j + 1$, and $k \leftarrow k + 1$.
3. [Copy the remaining unprocessed records into output area]
   If $i > n$,
   then repeat for $r = j, j + 1, \ldots, m$:   set $c_k \leftarrow b_r$ and $k \leftarrow k + 1$;
   otherwise, repeat for $r = i, i + 1, \ldots, n$:   set $c_k \leftarrow a_r$ and $k \leftarrow k + 1$.

The previous algorithm can be generalized to merge k sorted tables into a single sorted table. Such a merging operation is called *multiple merging* or *k-way merging*.

Multiple merging can also be accomplished by performing a simple merge repeatedly. For example, if we have 16 tables to merge, we can first merge them in pairs using Algorithm SIMPLE_MERGE. The result of this first step yields eight tables which are again merged in pairs to give four tables. This process is repeated until a single table is obtained. In this example, four separate passes are required to yield a single table. In general, k separate passes are required to merge 2^k separate tables into a single table. This strategy can easily be applied to sorting. Given a table containing n records, one merely considers this table to be a set of n tables, each of which contains a single record. Obviously, a table which contains a single record is sorted. The following algorithm performs one pass of the sort.

Algorithm MERGE_PASS.   Given a table R of n records which is considered to be partitioned into ordered subtables, each of which contains L records (or less), this algorithm merges these subtables by pairs. The records of R are denoted by $R_1, R_2, \ldots, R_n$. An auxiliary table C with records $C_1, C_2, \ldots, C_n$ is required in the merging process. The variables p and q keep track of which pair of subtables are currently being merged. Since n is not necessarily an integral power of 2, the sizes of the subtables being merged are not always the same (that is, L). The sizes of the tables are given by variables n_1 and n_2. The variables i and j are indices to the corresponding records of the subtables that are to be merged. The index variable k references a record in the output area and r is a temporary index variable.

1. [Initialize first pass]   Set $p \leftarrow 1$, $n_1 \leftarrow n_2 \leftarrow L$, and $q \leftarrow p + L$.
2. [Perform one pass]
    Repeat steps 3 to 7 while $q \leq n$.
3. [Initialize simple merge]   Set $i \leftarrow p$, $j \leftarrow q$, and $k \leftarrow p$.
4. [Compare corresponding records and output smallest]
    Repeat while $1 + i - p \leq n_1$ and $1 + j - q \leq n_2$:
        If $K_i \leq K_j$,
        then set $C_k \leftarrow R_i$, $i \leftarrow i + 1$, and $k \leftarrow k + 1$;
        otherwise, set $C_k \leftarrow R_j$, $j \leftarrow j + 1$, and $k \leftarrow k + 1$.
5. [Copy the remaining unprocessed records from a subtable into output area]
    If $1 + i - p > n_1$,
    then repeat for $r = j, j + 1, \ldots, q + n_2 - 1$:   set $C_k \leftarrow R_r$ and $k \leftarrow k + 1$;
    otherwise, repeat for $r = i, i + 1, \ldots, p + n_1 - 1$:   set $C_k \leftarrow R_r$ and $k \leftarrow k + 1$.
6. [Update and test direct subtable index]   Set $p \leftarrow q + n_2$.
    If $p > n$, then Exit.
7. [Update q and check bound of second subtable]   Set $q \leftarrow p + L$.
    If $q + L > n + 1$, then set $n_2 \leftarrow n - q + 1$.
8. [Copy unmatched subtable]
    Repeat for $r = p, p + 1, \ldots, n$:   set $C_r \leftarrow R_r$.
    Exit.

Steps 4 to 6 of the algorithm is a rewriting of Algorithm SIMPLE_MERGE, where the two ordered subfiles being merged are contained in table R. The resulting ordered table is written out in table C. Since n can be any positive integer, there may arise a case where a particular ordered subtable does not have another subtable with which it can be merged. In such a case, the unmatched subtable is merely copied into the output area, as shown in step 8. A sample trace is given in Fig. 6-1.8 for Algorithm MERGE_PASS.

Algorithm MERGE_PASS can now be invoked repeatedly to sort a given table. If $n = 2^k$ for some k, then k passes are required. For any n, however, $\lceil \log_2 n \rceil$ passes are required. The main algorithm for a two-way merge sort is as follows.

Algorithm TWO_WAY_MERGE_SORT.   Given a table R containing n records R_1, R_2, ..., R_n, this algorithm sorts the table in ascending order by successively invoking Algorithm MERGE_PASS. An auxiliary table C which has the same size as R is needed. L is a variable which specifies the number of elements in each subtable to be merged during a particular pass.

1. [Perform sort]
    Repeat for $L = 1, 2, 4, \ldots, 2^{\lceil \log_2 n \rceil - 1}$
        If $\log_2 L$ is even,
        then call MERGE_PASS(R, n, C, L);
        otherwise, call MERGE_PASS(C, n, R, L).
2. [Recopy, if required]
    If $\lceil \log_2 n \rceil$ is odd, then repeat for $i = 1, 2, \ldots, n$: set $R_i \leftarrow C_i$.
    Exit.

Assume L is 2, n is 7

After Step	p	q	n_1	n_2	R_1	R_2	R_3	R_4	R_5	R_6	R_7	C_1	C_2	C_3	C_4	C_5	C_6	C_7	i	j	k
1	1	3	2	2	11	13	2	15	14	17	6	–	–	–	–	–	–	–	–	–	–
2.1																					
3																			1	3	1
4.1												2								4	2
4.2													11						2		3
4.3														13					3		4
5															15						5
6		5																			
7		7	1																		
2.2																					
3																			5	7	5
4.1																6				8	6
5																	14	17			8
6		8																			

Exit without ever returning to step 2; repeat loop.

(step 4.i means "the ith iteration within step 4")

FIGURE 6-1.8   Trace of one pass of Algorithm MERGE_PASS.

In step 1, the logarithm of L is tested to determine which area, R or C, is the output area in a particular pass. The same technique is used to determine whether or not a final recopy operation is required after the table has been sorted. A trace of this algorithm for the sample table is given in Fig. 6-1.9.

This sorting method is quite efficient. Since $\lceil \log_2 n \rceil$ passes are required in the sort, the total number of comparisons needed is $O(n \log_2 n)$. Note that this quantity represents the worst case, as well as the average case. One obvious drawback in this method is the large auxiliary area required.

Another approach in performing a two-way merge sort is to take into consideration the degree of order which already exists in the initial table. A sort based on such an approach is given in Fig. 6-1.10. The formulation of the algorithm is left as an exercise.

6-1.7   Radix Sort

The radix sort is a method of sorting which predates any digital computer. This was performed and is still performed on a mechanical card sorter. Such a sorter usually processes a standard card of 80 columns, each of which may contain a character of some alphabet. When sorting cards on this type of sorter, only one column at a time is examined. A metal

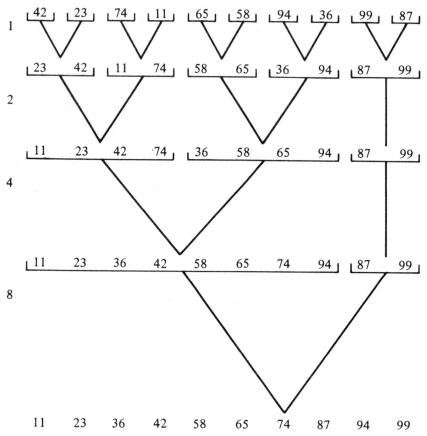

FIGURE 6-1.9   Two-way merge sorting.

pointer on the sorter is used to select any one of the 80 columns. For numerical data, the
sorter places all cards containing a given digit into an appropriate pocket. There are ten
pockets corresponding to the ten decimal digits. The operator of the sorter combines in
order the decks of cards from the ten pockets. The resulting deck has the cards of pocket 0
at the bottom and those of pocket 9 on top. In general, numbers consisting of more than
one digit are sorted. In such a case, an ascending-order sort can be accomplished by performing several individual digit sorts in order. That is, each column is sorted in turn starting with the lowest-order (rightmost) column first and proceeding through the other
columns from right to left. As an example, consider the following sequence of numbers
(one number on each card):

   42, 23, 74, 11, 65, 57, 94, 36, 99, 87, 70, 81, 61

After the first pass on the unit digit position of each number we have:

	61								
	81			94			87		
70	11	42	23	74	65	36	57		99
Pocket: 0	1	2	3	4	5	6	7	8	9

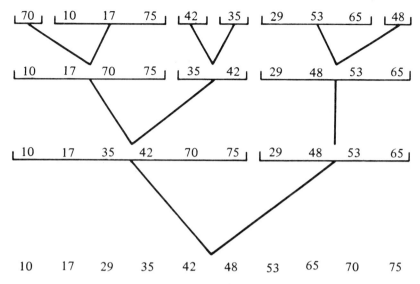

FIGURE 6-1.10   An alternate approach to a two-way merge sort.

Now by combining the contents of the pockets so that the contents of the "0" pocket are on the bottom and the contents of the "9" pocket are on the top, we obtain:

    70, 11, 81, 61, 42, 23, 74, 94, 65, 36, 57, 87, 99

On the second pass, we sort on the higher-order digit, thus yielding:

							65	74	87	99
		11	23	36	42	57	61	70	81	94
Pocket:	0	1	2	3	4	5	6	7	8	9

By combining the ten pockets in the same order as in the first pass, we complete the sort. This type of sort is called a *radix sort*.

    This mechanical method of sorting can be implemented on a computer. Sequential allocation techniques are not practical in representing the pockets, since we do not know how many records will occupy a particular pocket during a certain pass. Our inability to predict the number of records per pocket is solved by using linked allocation. Each pocket can be represented as a linked FIFO queue. At the end of each pass, these queues can be easily combined in the proper order. If the maximum number of digits in a key is m, then m successive passes, from the unit digit to the most significant digit, are required in order to sort the numbers. In the algorithm which follows, we assume that a key K contains m digits of the form $b_m b_{m-1} \ldots b_1$. It is also assumed that a selection mechanism is available for selecting each digit. The initial table is assumed to be arranged as a simple linked list.

Algorithm RADIX_SORT.   Given a table of n records arranged as a linked list, where each node in the list consists of a key field (K) and a pointer field (LINK), this algorithm performs a radix sort as previously described. The address of the first record in the linked table is given by the pointer variable FIRST. The vectors T and B are used to store the addresses of the rear and front records in each queue (pocket). In particular, the records T[i] and B[i] point to the top and bottom records in the ith pocket, respectively. The variable j is the pass index. The variable i is used as a pocket index, while r is a temporary index variable. The pointer variable R denotes the address of the current record being examined in the table and being directed to the appropriate pocket. PREV is a pointer variable which is used during the combining of the pockets at the end of each pass.

1. [Perform sort]   Repeat steps 2 to 4 for j = 1, 2, ..., m.
2. [Initialize pass]
   Repeat for i = 0, 1, ..., 9: set T[i] ← B[i] ← NULL.
   Set R ← FIRST.
3. [Distribute each record in the appropriate pocket]
   Repeat while R ≠ NULL:
       Set k ← b_j (Obtain jth digit of the key K(R)).
       Set NEXT ← LINK(R).
       If T[k] = NULL,
       then set T[k] ← B[k] ← R;
       otherwise, set LINK(T[k]) ← R and T[k] ← R.
       Set LINK(R) ← NULL and R ← NEXT.
4. [Combine the pockets]
   Set r ← 0.
   Repeat while B[r] = NULL: set r ← r + 1.
   Set FIRST ← B[r]
   Repeat for i = r + 1, r + 2, ..., 9:
       Set PREV ← T[i − 1].
       If T[i] ≠ NULL, then set LINK(PREV) ← B[i]; otherwise, set T[i] ← PREV.
5. [Finished] Exit.

The algorithm is straightforward. The first step controls the number of passes required to perform the sort. Step 2 initializes the arrays associated with the pockets so that all pockets are empty at the beginning of each pass. Also, the variable R is set to point to the first record in the table in this step. The third step of the algorithm processes each record in the table and directs each such record to the appropriate pocket. Step 4 combines the pockets into a new linked table which is used as input to the next pass. FIRST is set to point to the bottommost record in the first nonempty pocket (proceeding from pocket 0 through pocket 9). A trace of the algorithm for the previous table is given in Fig. 6-1.11.

This sorting method performs well, providing that the keys are relatively short. For a key of m digits, it requires m * n key accesses.

6-1.8   Address-Calculation Sort

As a final sorting method, we now look at the application of hashing functions to sorting. Recall from Sec. 4-3.2 the construction of a symbol table where each name was hashed into a number. Each set of names which were hashed into the same number was called an *equivalence class*. Each equivalence class was represented by a linked list. The same idea can be used to sort a table. The set of keys should, ideally, be uniformly distributed in the sense that the probability that a particular key will be hashed into any one of m equivalence class is 1/m. In applying the idea of a hashing function to the sorting process, a particular kind of hashing function is required. Let us assume that we have a hashing function H with the property

$$X_1 < X_2 \text{ implies that } H(X_1) \leq H(X_2).$$

A function which exhibits this property is called a nondecreasing function. Examples of such hashing functions are given in Sec. 6-2.4. When a particular key is hashed into a particular number (i.e., a linked list) to which some previous key has already been hashed

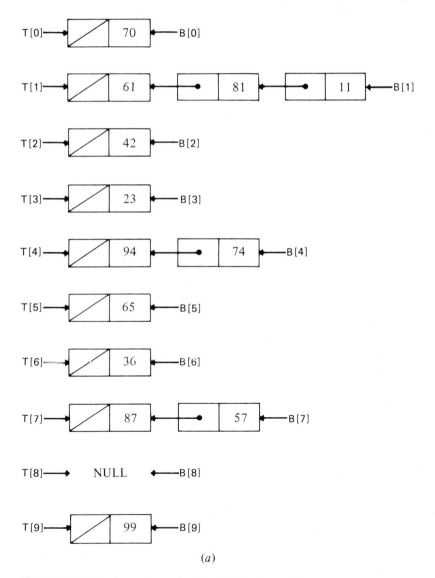

(a)

FIGURE 6-1.11 Trace of a radix sort. (a) First pass; (b) second pass.

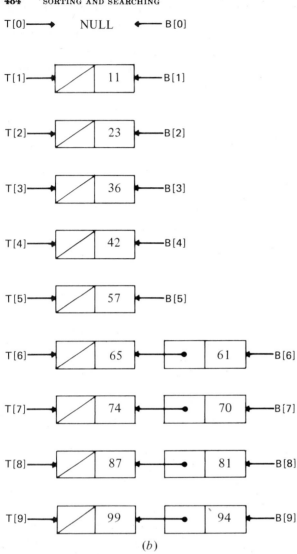

(b)

FIGURE 6-1.11 (Continued)

(i.e., a collision occurs), then the new key is inserted into that linked list so as to preserve the order of the keys. The result of hashing and inserting the sample key set

    42, 23, 74, 11, 65, 57, 94, 36, 99, 87, 70, 81, 61

using a nondecreasing hashing function in which all the keys in the ranges 1-20, 21-40, 41-60, 61-80, 81-100 are each hashed into a distinct equivalent class is shown in Fig. 6-1.12, where the element EQUIV[i] gives the address of the first record in the ith linked list. The m linked lists obtained during the hash and insert phase can now be merged trivially into a single linked list giving the desired sorted table. Knuth has shown that the average number of comparisons for this method is O(n)! This is the first sorting technique of order

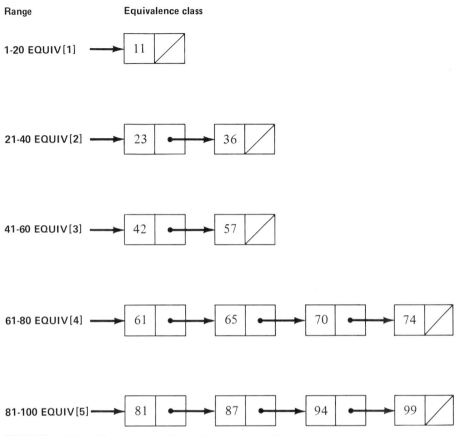

FIGURE 6-1.12 The representation of a table in address-calculation sorting.

n that we have discussed. Remember, however, that this result holds only if the probability of hashing any key to any number between 1 and m is 1/m. The worst case occurs when all keys are mapped into the same number. In this case the performance of the method degenerates to $O(n^2)$. Hashing functions can also be used in searching, and this idea will be pursued in Sec. 6-2.4.

In summary, the selection or bubble sorts can be used if the number of records in the table is small. If n is large and the keys are short, the radix sort can perform well. With a large n and long keys, quick sort, heap sort, or a merge sort can be used. If the table is, initially, almost sorted, then quick sort should be avoided. When the keys, after hashing, are uniformly distributed over the interval [1,m], then an address-calculation sort is a very good method to use.

Exercises for Sec. 6-1

1. Alter Algorithm **BUBBLE** to take advantage of the fact that all records below and including the last one to be exchanged must be in the correct order; consequently, these records do not have to be examined again.

2. Modify Algorithm **BUBBLE** such that alternate passes go in opposite directions. That is, during the first pass, the record with the largest key will be at the end of the table and during the second pass the record with the smallest key will be the first record in the table, etc.
3. Devise an algorithm for performing a selection sort when the table is represented as a linked list.
4. Trace Algorithm **QUICK_SORT** for the sample table given in that subsection.
5. Formulate an algorithm for a binary-tree sort.
6. Trace through Algorithm **HEAP_SORT** for the sample table given.
7. Devise an algorithm for a two-way merge so as to take into consideration the degree of order which already exists in the initial table as suggested at the end of Sec. 6-1.6.
8. Obtain an algorithm for a two-way merge sort using linked-allocation techniques.
9. Change Algorithm **RADIX_SORT** so that the queues are circular.
10. Formulate an algorithm for an address-calculation sort based on the discussion in the text.

6-2 SEARCHING

In this section we formulate a number of progressively more complex searching algorithms. The linear-search and binary-search methods are relatively straightforward, but they have serious shortcomings for certain operations. The balanced-tree search is efficient for many operations. A number of search techniques involving the use of hashing functions are also discussed.

6-2.1 Sequential Searching

The simplest technique for searching an unordered table for a particular record is to scan each entry in the table in a sequential manner until the desired record is found. An algorithm for such a search procedure is as follows.

Algorithm LINEAR_SEARCH.   Given an unordered table of records R_1, R_2, ..., R_n ($n \geq 1$) whose keys are K_1, K_2, ..., K_n, respectively, this algorithm searches for a record whose key is x. A sentinel record R_{n+1} is assumed.
1. [Initialize]   Set $K_{n+1} \leftarrow x$.
2. [Search Table]
   Set $i \leftarrow 1$.
   Repeat while $K_i \neq x$: set $i \leftarrow i + 1$.
   If $i = n + 1$, then print 'unsuccessful'; otherwise, print 'successful.'
       Exit.

The first step of the algorithm initializes the key value of the sentinel record to x. In the second step, a sequential search is then performed on the $n + 1$ records. If the index of the record found denotes record R_{n+1} then the search has failed; otherwise, the search is successful and i contains the index of the desired record.

The performance of a search method can be measured by counting the number of key comparisons taken to find a particular record. There are two cases which are important, namely, the average case and the worst case. The worst case for the previous algorithm consists of $n + 1$ key comparisons, while the average case takes $(n + 1)/2$ key comparisons. The average and worst search times for this method are both proportional to n, that is, of O(n). These estimates are based on the assumption that the probability of a request for a particular record is the same as for any other record.

Let P_i be the probability for the request of record R_i for $1 \leq i \leq n$. The average length of search (ALOS) for n records is given by

$$E[\text{ALOS}] = 1*P_1 + 2*P_2 + \ldots + n*P_n$$

where $P_1 + P_2 + \cdots + P_n = 1$.

Now suppose that the probabilities for requests for particular records are not equally likely, that is, $P_i \neq 1/n$ for $1 \leq i \leq n$. The question which naturally arises is: Can we rearrange the table so as to reduce the ALOS? The answer is yes, and the desired arrangement can be obtained by looking at the previous equation for the expected ALOS. This quantity will be minimized if the records are ordered such that

$$P_1 \geq P_2 \geq \ldots \geq P_n \tag{1}$$

For example, letting $n = 5$ and $P_i = 1/5$ for $1 \leq i \leq 5$ yields

$$E[\text{ALOS}] = 1*1/5 + 2*1/5 + 3*1/5 + 4*1/5 + 5*1/5 = 3$$

Now, assuming that $P_1 = 0.4$, $P_2 = 0.3$, $P_3 = 0.2$, $P_4 = 0.07$, and $P_5 = 0.03$, the average length of search in this case is

$$E[\text{ALOS}] = 1*0.4 + 2*0.3 + 3*0.2 + 4*0.07 + 5*0.03 = 2.03$$

A number which is substantially less than 3. The rearrangement of the initial table according to Eq. (1) is called *preloading*.

If the table is subjected to many deletions, then it should be represented as a linked list. The traversal of a linked table is almost as fast as the traversal of its sequential counterpart. Note that insertions can be performed very efficiently when the table is sequentially represented, assuming the table is not ordered.

If search time is to be improved further, then we must order the elements of the table. This approach is discussed in the next section.

6-2.2 Binary Searching

Another relatively simple method of accessing a table is the binary search method. The entries in the table are stored in alphabetically or numerically increasing order. An appropriate method discussed in the previous section can be used to achieve this ordering. A search for a particular item with a certain key value resembles the search for a name in a telephone directory. The approximate middle entry of the table is located and its key value is examined. If its value is too high, then the key value of the middle entry of the first half of the table is examined and the procedure is repeated on the first half until the required item is found. If the value is too low, then the key of the middle entry of the second half of the table is tried and the procedure is repeated on the second half. This process continues until the desired key is found or the search interval becomes empty. The following algorithm performs a binary search.

Algorithm BINARY_SEARCH.   Given a table of records $R_1, R_2, \ldots, R_n$ whose keys are in increasing order, this algorithm searches the structure for a given key x. The variables B and E denote the lower and upper limits of the search interval, respectively.

1. [Initialize]   Set B $\leftarrow$ 1 and E $\leftarrow$ n.
2. [Perform search]   Repeat steps 3 to 4 while B $\leq$ E.
3. [Obtain index of midpoint]   Set i $\leftarrow \lfloor$(B + E)/2$\rfloor$.
4. [Compare]
   If x < K_i,
   then set E $\leftarrow$ i $-$ 1;
   otherwise, if x > K_i,
       then set B $\leftarrow$ i $+$ 1;
       otherwise, print 'element found', and Exit.
5. [Unsuccessful search]   Print 'element not found', and Exit.

A trace of this algorithm for the sample table

75, 151, 203, 275, 318, 489, 524, 591, 647, and 727

is given for x = 275 and 727 in Table 6-2.1a and b, respectively.

An average of $\lfloor \log_2 n \rfloor - 1$ comparisons is required in order to locate an entry. The worst case will take at most $\lfloor \log_2 n \rfloor + 1$ comparisons. This is considerably better than the search time for the sequential search method.

The binary search technique has certain undesirable properties. An insertion of a new record requires that many records in the existing table be physically moved in order to preserve the sequential ordering. A similar situation prevails for deletions. The ratio of insertion time or deletion time to search time is quite high for this method. Binary search is suitable if few insertions and/or deletions are to be made to the table.

Table 6-2.1   Binary search trace.

Search for 275			*Search for 727*		
Iteration B	E	i	*Iteration* B	E	i
1 1	10	5	1 1	10	5
2 1	4	2	2 6	10	8
3 3	4	3	3 9	10	9
4 4	4	4	4 10	10	10

| (a) | (b) |

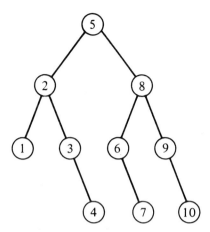

FIGURE 6-2.1 A binary tree which corresponds to a binary search for n = 10.

One way to improve this search method is to use linked binary trees to represent the table in order to improve the insertion and deletion problems. Such an avenue is discussed in the next subsection.

6-2.3 Search Trees

The binary search method given in the previous subsection can be explained easily in terms of binary trees. Figure 6-2.1 gives a binary-tree representation which corresponds to a binary search (according to Algorithm BINARY_SEARCH) with n = 10. In Sec. 5-2.2, linked binary trees were used in constructing a symbol table. The same structure can represent a table of records. The search algorithm for such a representation is very similar to Algorithm TABLE of Sec. 5-2.2 and is, therefore, omitted here.

The average length of search for this representation is also of $O(log_2 n)$. The worst case that can be encountered, however, has a search time of $O(n)$, a time which is no better than the worst case for a sequential search. Figure 6-2.2 shows some of the cases which can

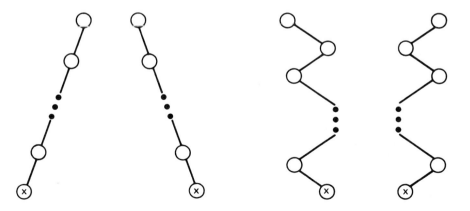

FIGURE 6-2.2 Worst search time cases for binary trees.

give this bad search performance. The first two cases involve trees which contain only nonnull left or right links. The remaining two cases represent zig-zag structures. Clearly, the search time for these structures takes n comparisons.

We have already considered the insertion of a leaf node in a binary tree. The operation of deleting an arbitrary node from a tree will now be examined. Note that any node can be deleted from a tree, even its root. Therefore, a number of cases arise. First, if a node with either an empty left or right subtree is marked for deletion, then the operation is trivial. Such a case is shown in Figure 6-2.3a, where node 6 is deleted. If, however, the node to be deleted has nonempty left and right subtrees, then the node's inorder successor is

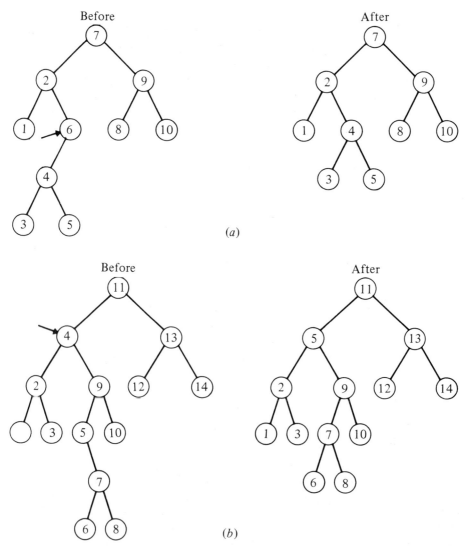

FIGURE 6-2.3   Deletion of a node from a binary tree.

deleted and then is used to replace the node initially marked for deletion. Note that this successor node always has an empty left subtree. An example of this second case is given in Fig. 6-2.3*b*, where node 4 has been marked for deletion.

The node structure that we assume contains four fields, namely LPTR, RPTR, K (the key), and DATA. The tree also contains a list head whose address is given by the pointer HEAD.

Algorithm TREE_DELETE.   Given an ordered linked binary tree with the node structure just described and a record key x, which denotes the record marked for deletion, this algorithm deletes the record whose key is x while still maintaining a binary-tree structure. PARENT denotes the address of the parent of the node marked for deletion. The variable P contains the address of the record whose key is x. PRED and SUC are pointer variables used to find the inorder successor of P. Q contains the address of the node to which either the left or right link of the parent of x must be assigned in order to complete the deletion. D contains the direction from the parent node to the node marked for deletion.

1. [Initialize]   If LPTR(HEAD) $\neq$ HEAD, then set P $\leftarrow$ LPTR(HEAD), PARENT $\leftarrow$ HEAD, D $\leftarrow$ 'L', otherwise, print 'tree is empty', and Exit.
2. [Compare]   If P = NULL, then print 'node not found', and Exit.
    If x < K(P), then set PARENT $\leftarrow$ P, P $\leftarrow$ LPTR(P), D $\leftarrow$ 'L', and go to step 2.
    If x > K(P), then set PARENT $\leftarrow$ P, P $\leftarrow$ RPTR(P), D $\leftarrow$ 'R', and go to step 2.
3. [Is LPTR NULL?]
    If LPTR(P) = NULL, then set Q $\leftarrow$ RPTR(P) and go to step 7.
4. [Is RPTR NULL?]
    If RPTR(P) = NULL, then set Q $\leftarrow$ LPTR(P) and go to step 7.
5. [Check right son]   Set PRED $\leftarrow$ RPTR(P),
    If LPTR(PRED) = NULL, then set LPTR(PRED) $\leftarrow$ LPTR(P), Q $\leftarrow$ PRED, and go to step 7.
6. [Search for successor]   Set SUC $\leftarrow$ LPTR(PRED),
    If LPTR(SUC) $\neq$ NULL,
    then set PRED $\leftarrow$ SUC and go to step 6;
    otherwise, set LPTR(PRED) $\leftarrow$ RPTR(SUC), LPTR(SUC) $\leftarrow$ LPTR(P),
        RPTR(SUC) $\leftarrow$ RPTR(P), Q $\leftarrow$ SUC.
7. [Change parent link]
    If D = 'L', then set LPTR(PARENT) $\leftarrow$ Q; otherwise, set RPTR(PARENT) $\leftarrow$ Q.
8. [Free record x]   Return node P to availability area, and Exit.

The first step of the algorithm checks for an empty tree. The initialization is performed when the tree is nonempty. Step 2 searches for the record which is to be deleted. If the desired record is not found, then the algorithm terminates. The variable D is used to record whether the record to be deleted is the root of the left or right subtree of PARENT. The simple case for deletion is checked in steps 3 and 4. Steps 5 and 6 handle the more complex second case. The appropriate link of the parent of record x is changed in step 7 to reflect the deletion, and in the last step the deleted node is returned to the availability area.

We now turn to the task of keeping a tree structure in such a way that the following operations can *all* be executed in a worst time of $O(\log_2 n)$:

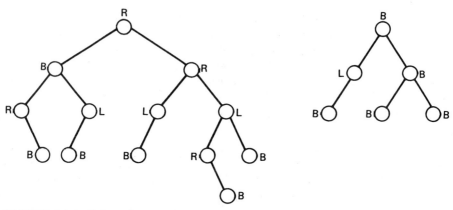

FIGURE 6-2.4   Balanced trees.

1   Enter a new element.
2   Delete a specified element.
3   Search for a specified element.

In order to prevent a tree unbalance such as the cases given in Fig. 6-2.2, we can associate a *balance indicator* with each node in the tree. This indicator will contain one of the three values which we denote as left (**L**), right (**R**), or balance (**B**), according to the following definitions:

Left: A node will be called *left heavy* if the longest path in its left subtree is one longer than the longest path of its right subtree.

Balance: A node will be called *balanced* if the longest paths in both of its subtrees are equal.

Right: A node will be called *right heavy* if the longest path in its right subtree is one longer than the longest path in its left subtree.

In a *balanced tree* each node must be in one of these three states. If there exists a node in a tree where this is not true, then such a tree is said to be *unbalanced*. Figure 6-2.4 gives examples of trees which are balanced, while Fig. 6-2.5 represents examples of unbalanced trees.

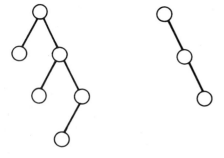

FIGURE 6-2.5   Unbalanced trees.

Let us now look at the operation of inserting a node into a balanced tree. In the following discussion, it is assumed that a new node is inserted at the leaf or terminal node level (either as a left or right subtree). The only nodes which can have their balance indicator changed by such an insertion are those which lie on a path between the root of the tree and the newly inserted leaf. The possible changes which can occur to a node on this path are as follows:

1 The node was either left or right heavy and has now become balanced.
2 The node was balanced and has now become left or right heavy.
3 The node was heavy and the new node has been inserted in the heavy subtree, thus creating an unbalanced subtree. Such a node is said to be a *critical node*.

If condition 1 applies to a current node, then the balance indicators of all ancestor nodes of this node remain unchanged, since the longest path in the subtree (in which the current node is its root) remains unchanged. When condition 2 applies to a current node, then the balance indicators of the ancestors of this node will change. If condition 3 applies to a current node, then the tree has become unbalanced and this node has become critical. Figure 6-2.6 contains examples of the three cases which can arise. The dotted branch and node denote the new element which is being inserted.

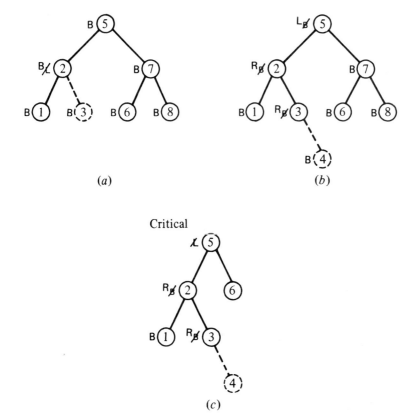

(a)   (b)

(c)

FIGURE 6-2.6 Examples of insertions into a balanced tree. (*a*) Condition 1; (*b*) condition 2; (*c*) condition 3.

We next turn to the rebalancing of a tree when a critical node has been encountered. There are two broad cases which can arise, each of which can be further subdivided into two essentially similar subcases. A general representation of case 1 is given in Fig. 6-2.7, where the rectangles labeled T_1, T_2, and T_3 represent trees and the node labeled **NEW** denotes the node being inserted. The expression at the bottom of each rectangle denotes the maximum path length in that tree after insertions. For example, in Fig. 6-2.7a, since node **X** is critical, then node **Y** must have been balanced prior to insertion. This case covers the situation when **Y** has become heavy in the same direction that **X** was heavy. A concrete example of the second possibility for case 1 is exemplified in Fig. 6-2.8. The **PATH** and

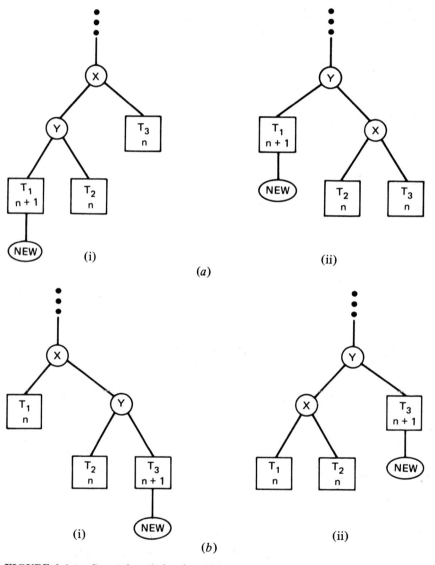

FIGURE 6-2.7   Case 1 for rebalancing a tree.

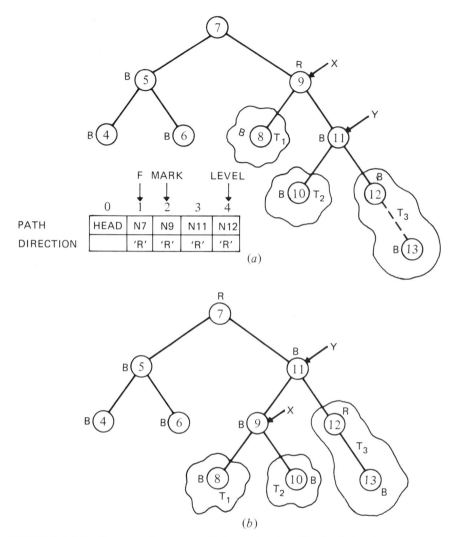

FIGURE 6-2.8   Example of case 1. (*a*) Before balancing; (*b*) after balancing.

DIRECTION vectors are defined in the next algorithm. Note that the basic steps involve the changing of three pointers.

The second case, which is given in Fig. 6-2.9, is much like the first, except that node **Y** becomes heavy in an opposite direction to that in which **X** was heavy. It is clear that node **Z** must have been balanced prior to insertion. Note that cases *a*(i) and *b*(i) are very similar. A specific example of case 2*b* is given in Fig. 6-2.10. Again **PATH** and **DIRECTION** refer to vectors that are associated with the next algorithm.

We now proceed to the formulation of an algorithm for the insertion of an element into a balanced tree. The node structure for the tree will consist of a left pointer (**LPTR**) and a right pointer (**RPTR**), a key field (**K**), a balance indicator (**BI**), and an information

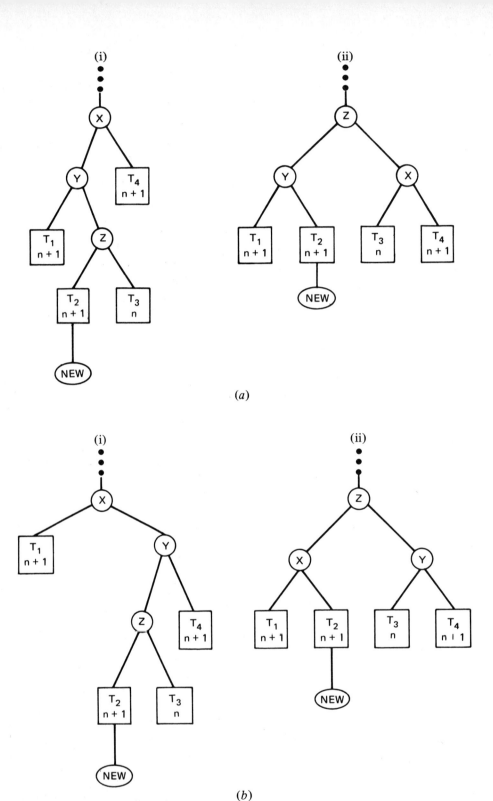

FIGURE 6-2.9 Case 2 for rebalancing a tree.

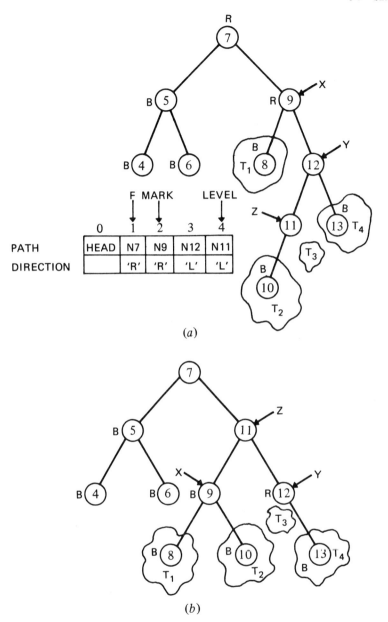

FIGURE 6-2.10   Example of case 2. (a) Before balancing; (b) after balancing.

field (DATA). The name of the node structure is NODE. A list head for the tree is assumed with its left pointer containing the address of the root of the actual tree.

Algorithm BALANCED_INSERT.   Given a linked representation of a balanced binary tree with a list head HEAD whose structure has just been described and the variables NAME and INFO, which contain the key value and information contents of the new element being inserted, this algorithm inserts the new element into the tree in such a manner as to maintain the balance property. NEW is the address of the new node created. The array PATH is used to store the address of the nodes between the list head and the point in the tree where the insertion is made. The corresponding vector DIRECTION is used to store the direction of each branch in this path. The values of 'L' and 'R' are used to denote a left and right branch, respectively. The variable MARK denotes the index of an array element in PATH which contains the address of the critical node (X). F points to the parent of the critical node before rebalancing takes place. The variables X, Y, and Z are pointer variables whose functions have been previously described. LEVEL is an index variable. T is a temporary pointer used in traversing the tree from the root to the node being inserted.

1. [Is this a first insertion?]   If LPTR(HEAD) = HEAD, then set NEW ⇐ NODE, LPTR(NEW) ← RPTR(NEW) ← NULL, BI(NEW) ← 'B', K(NEW) ← NAME, DATA(NEW) ← INFO, LPTR(HEAD) ← NEW, and Exit.
2. [Initialize]   Set LEVEL ← 0, PATH[LEVEL] ← HEAD, and T ← LPTR(HEAD).
3. [Compare and insert, if required]
    If NAME < K(T),
    then if LPTR(T) ≠ NULL,
        then set LEVEL ← LEVEL + 1, PATH[LEVEL] ← T, DIRECTION[LEVEL] ← 'L',
            T ← LPTR(T), and go to step 3;
        otherwise, set NEW ⇐ NODE, LPTR(NEW) ← RPTR(NEW) ← NULL,
            K(NEW) ← NAME, DATA(NEW) ← INFO, LPTR(T) ← NEW, BI(NEW) ← 'B',
            LEVEL ← LEVEL + 1, PATH[LEVEL] ← T,
            DIRECTION[LEVEL] ← 'L', and go to step 5.
    If NAME > K(T),
    then if RPTR(T) ≠ NULL,
        then set LEVEL ← LEVEL + 1, PATH[LEVEL] ← T, DIRECTION[LEVEL] ← 'R',
            T ← RPTR(T), and go to step 3;
        otherwise, set NEW ⇐ NODE, LPTR(NEW) ← RPTR(NEW) ← NULL,
            K(NEW) ← NAME, DATA(NEW) ← INFO, RPTR(T) ← NEW, BI(NEW) ← 'B',
            LEVEL ← LEVEL + 1, PATH[LEVEL] ← T,
            DIRECTION[LEVEL] ← 'R', and go to step 5.
4. [A match]   Print 'item already there', and Exit.
5. [Search for an unbalanced node]
    Repeat for i = LEVEL, LEVEL − 1, ..., 1:
        Set P ← PATH[i],
        If BI(P) ≠ 'B', then set MARK ← i, and go to step 6.
    Set MARK ← 0.
6. [Adjust balance indicators]
    Repeat for i = MARK + 1, MARK + 2, ..., LEVEL:
        If NAME < K(PATH[i]),
        then set BI(PATH[i]) ← 'L';
        otherwise, set BI(PATH[i]) ← 'R'.
7. [Is there a critical node?]
    If MARK = 0, then Exit.

Set D ← DIRECTION[MARK], X ← PATH[MARK], and Y ← PATH[MARK + 1].

(The node was balanced and now it becomes heavy.)

(*a*)   If BI(X) = 'B', then set BI(X) ← D, and Exit.

(The node was heavy and now becomes balanced.)

(*b*)   If BI(X) ≠ D, then set BI(X) ← 'B', and Exit.

(The node was heavy and now becomes critical.)

(*c*)   If BI(Y) ≠ D, then go to step 9.

8.   [Rebalance tree: case 1]

If D = 'L',

then set LPTR(X) ← RPTR(Y) and RPTR(Y) ← X;

otherwise, set RPTR(X) ← LPTR(Y) and LPTR(Y) ← X.

Set BI(X) ← BI(Y) ← 'B', F ← PATH[MARK − 1].

If X = LPTR(F), then set LPTR(F) ← Y; otherwise, set RPTR(F) ← Y.

Exit.

9.   [Rebalance tree: case 2]

(*a*)   (Change structure links.)

If D = 'L',

then set Z ← RPTR(Y), RPTR(Y) ← LPTR(Z), LPTR(Z) ← Y,

   LPTR(X) ← RPTR(Z), and RPTR(Z) ← X;

otherwise, set Z ← LPTR(Y), LPTR(Y) ← RPTR(Z), RPTR(Z) ← Y,

   RPTR(X) ← LPTR(Z), and LPTR(Z) ← X.

Set F ← PATH[MARK − 1],

If X = LPTR(F), then set LPTR(F) ← Z; otherwise, set RPTR(F) ← Z.

(*b*)   (Change balance indicators.)

If BI(Z) = D,

then set BI(Y) ← 'B', BI(Z) ← 'B';

   if D = 'L', then set BI(X) ← 'R'; otherwise, set BI(X) ← 'L', and

   Exit;

otherwise, set BI(X) ← 'B', BI(Z) ← 'B', BI(Y) ← D, and Exit.

The algorithm, although lengthy, is straightforward. Groups of steps, particularly in step 3, have been repeated. These could have been made into small modules and invoked as subalgorithms. Steps 1 through 4 are closely patterned after Algorithm **TABLE** of Sec. 5-2.2. Step 3 attaches the new node to the existing tree, if it is not there already, and stores into vectors **PATH** and **DIRECTION** the address of the nodes on the path between the list head and the leaf being inserted and the direction of the path at each node, respectively. Step 5 of the algorithm searches for an unbalanced node which is closest to the new node just inserted. In step 6 the balance indicators of the nodes between the unbalanced node found in the previous step and the new node are adjusted. Step 7 determines whether or not there is a critical node. If there is, control proceeds either to step 8 (case 1) or step 9 (case 2). When no critical node is found, the balance indicator of the unbalanced node found in step 5 is adjusted. The last two steps of the algorithm correspond to case 1 and case 2 in the previous discussion, and rebalancing of the tree is performed in each case. The reader should trace through the algorithm for the examples given in Figs. 6-2.8 and 6-2.10.

Let us now look at the performance of this balanced-tree algorithm. It can be shown that the maximum path length m in a balanced tree of n nodes is 1.5 $\log_2(n+1)$ (see Stone). The worst ALOS for performing an insertion with any necessary rebalancing is of $O(\log_2 n)$.

So far, all trees that we have discussed were of the binary type. This subsection concludes with a brief introduction to mary trees. Such tree structures are often used in the area of information organization and retrieval. The search method that follows is analogous to digital sorting discussed earlier. A *trie structure* is a complete mary tree in which each node consists of m components. Typically, the components are digits or letters. Table 6-2.2 gives an example of a trie structure for searching a set of records consisting of 29 English

Table 6-2.2   A trie structure for a list of words.

						Node Number						
	1	2	3	4	5	6	7	8	9	10	11	12
b	—	—	—	—	—	—	—	—	—	—	—	GO
A	ALLOCATE	—	CALL	—	—	—	—	—	—	—	—	—
B	2	—	—	—	—	—	—	—	—	—	—	—
C	3	—	—	DCL	—	—	—	—	—	—	—	—
D	4	—	—	—	—	—	—	—	—	—	END	—
E	5	BEGIN	—	—	—	—	GET	—	—	—	—	—
F	6	—	—	—	—	—	—	—	—	—	—	—
G	7	—	—	—	—	—	—	—	—	—	—	—
H	—	—	CHECK	—	—	—	—	—	THEN	WHILE	—	—
I	IF	—	—	—	—	—	—	—	—	—	—	—
J	—	—	—	—	—	—	—	—	—	—	—	—
K	—	—	—	—	—	—	—	—	—	—	—	—
L	—	—	CLOSE	—	ELSE	FLOW	—	—	—	—	—	—
M	—	—	—	—	—	—	—	—	—	—	—	—
N	NO	—	—	—	11	—	—	—	—	—	—	—
O	OPEN	—	—	DO	—	FORMAT	12	—	TO	—	—	—
P	8	—	—	—	—	—	—	—	—	—	—	—
Q	—	—	—	—	—	—	—	—	—	—	—	—
R	RETURN	—	—	—	—	FREE	—	PROC	—	WRITE	—	—
S	STOP	—	—	—	—	—	—	—	—	—	—	—
T	9	—	—	—	—	—	—	—	—	—	ENTRY	GOTO
U	—	—	—	—	—	—	—	PUT	—	—	—	—
V	—	—	—	—	—	—	—	—	—	—	—	—
W	10	—	—	—	—	—	—	—	—	—	—	—
X	—	—	—	—	EXIT	—	—	—	—	—	—	—
Y	—	BY	—	—	—	—	—	—	—	—	—	—
Z	—	—	—	—	—	—	—	—	—	—	—	—

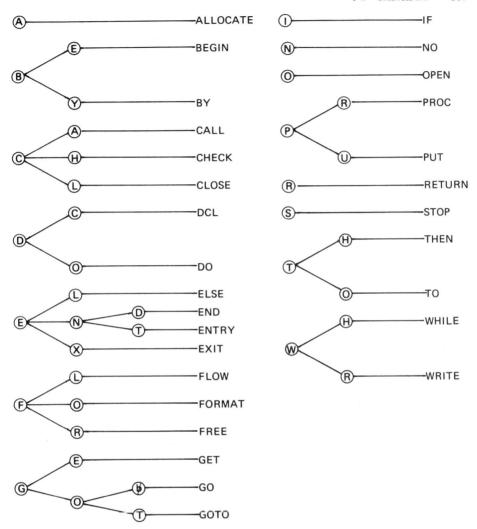

FIGURE 6-2.11 A forest representation of the trie given in Table 6-2.2.

words. It consists of 12 nodes, each of which is a vector of 27 elements. Each element contains either a dash, or the desired word, or a node number. A blank symbol (ƀ) is used to denote the end of a word during the scan of the key. Node 1 is the root of the tree.

As an example, we will trace through the search for the word END. The letter E tells us that we should go from node 1 to node 5. The second letter (N) is then used to select the appropriate element in node 5. The entry corresponding to label N transfers us to node 11. At this node, the letter D is finally used to find the desired word. An algorithm for such a search technique is easily formulated, and it is left as an exercise.

The trie of Table 6-2.2 is very wasteful of memory space. Memory can be saved at the expense of running time if each node is represented by a linked list. Figure 6-2.11 shows such a representation (a forest of trees) for the trie of Table 6-2.2.

The best situation, in terms of running time, occurs when only a few levels of a trie are used for the first few characters of the key and then some other structure, such as a linear list or binary tree, is used in the remainder of the search.

6-2.4 Hash-Table Methods

The best search methods introduced so far have a search time proportional to $\log_2 n$. In this subsection we investigate a class of search techniques whose search time can be independent of the number of records in a table. To achieve this goal, an entirely new approach to searching must be used. Using this approach, the position of a particular record in a table is determined by the value of the key for that record. The basic notions of this approach were briefly introduced in Sec. 4-3.2, and subsequently used in Sec. 5-5.4, where the relationship between the key value and its table position was specified by a hashing function. Unfortunately, more than one key can be mapped into the same address or position, so a collision-resolution technique is required.

We now proceed to discuss a number of hashing functions. These functions fall into two classes, namely, distribution-independent and distribution-dependent functions. A distribution-independent hashing function does not use the distribution of the keys of a table in computing the position of a record. A distribution-dependent hashing function, on the other hand, is obtained by examining the subset of keys corresponding to known records.

The second part of the subsection describes a number of collision-resolution techniques which can be used with a hashing function.

Let us first describe some terminology which will be used throughout this subsection.

A table is called *direct* when the key of each record is used to determine the position in which that record should be stored.

A hashing function is defined as a mapping $H: K \rightarrow A$, where K is the key space or set of keys, which may possibly identify records in a direct table, and A is the address space $\{c + 1, c + 2, \ldots, c + m\}$. In this subsection, the address space is considered to be $\{1, 2, \ldots, m\}$ so that certain discussions and formulas can be simplified. Note that if $H(x)$ gives addresses in this address space, then $H(x) + c$ can be used to address the former address space. A measure of space utilization in a direct table is the *load factor*, defined as the ratio of number of records to number of record locations. In this case the load factor α is n/m. Before describing a number of hashing functions, the key space K is investigated more closely.

Each element of K is an identifier which is numeric, alphabetic, or alphanumeric. Student numbers such as 692784, 712116, and 730786 are obviously numeric keys. Alphabetic keys may be names of authors, for example, DOE, JONES, and SMITH. In certain areas automobile license numbers consist of three letters followed by three digits, such as SAM097, VIC222, or RFD023. These could be used as alphanumeric keys in a table of automobile records. The hashing functions to be described perform arithmetic or logical operations on keys to produce addresses. They can still be applied to alphabetic or alphanumeric keys if the internal numeric representation of those keys is accessible. (Alphabetic and other special characters are numerically coded when represented internally by a computer.) As an alternative, the letters A, B, ..., Z can be encoded as decimal numbers 11, 12, ... , 36. For example, SMITH and SAM097 are coded as 2923193018 and 291123000907, respectively. This encoding preserves the uniqueness of alphabetic keys. It is always possible to convert keys to integers, so the key space is considered to be composed of integral values.

In many cases the numeric representation of a key is too large to be stored in one computer word; so, unless multiple precision operations are available, the keys must be compressed. Methods of key compression include some of the hashing functions which are described in the following paragraphs. It is common practice to use one hashing function to map keys to an intermediate space and then a second hashing function to map the values in that space to the address space.

Perhaps the most widely accepted hashing function is the *division method*, which is defined as

$$H(x) = x \bmod m + 1$$

for divisor m. It is one of the earliest and most popular hashing functions used.

In mapping keys to addresses, the division method preserves, to a certain extent, the uniformity that exists in a key set. Keys which are closely bunched together or clustered are mapped to unique addresses. For example, keys 2000, 2001, ..., and 2017 would be mapped to addresses 82, 83, ..., and 99 if the divisor for the division method is 101. Unfortunately, this preservation of uniformity is a disadvantage if two or more clusters of keys are mapped to the same addresses. For example, if another cluster of keys is 3310, 3311, 3313, 3314, ..., 3323, and 3324, then these keys are mapped to addresses 79, 80, 82, 83, ..., 92, and 93 by divisor 101, and there are many collisions with keys from the cluster starting at 2000. The reason for this is that keys in the two clusters are congruent modulo 101.

In general, if many keys are congruent modulo d, and m is not relatively prime to d, then using m as a divisor can result in poor performance of the division method. This is shown in the preceding example where m = d = 101. As another example, if all the keys in a table are congruent modulo 5 and the divisor is 65, then the keys are mapped to only **13** different positions. Since it is uncommon for a number of keys to be congruent modulo m, where m is a large prime number, a prime divisor should be used, although research has shown that odd divisors without factors less than 20 are also satisfactory. In particular, divisors which are even numbers are to be avoided, since even and odd keys would be mapped to odd and even addresses, respectively (assuming that the address space is {1, 2, ..., m}). This would be a problem in a table containing predominantly even or predominantly odd keys.

In the *midsquare hashing method*, a key is multiplied by itself and an address is obtained by truncating bits or digits at both ends of the product until the number of bits or digits left is equal to the desired address length. The same positions must be used from all products. As an example, consider a six-digit key, 113586. Squaring the key gives 12901779396. If a four-digit address is required, positions 5 to 8 could be chosen, giving address 1779. The midsquare method has been criticized, but it has given good results when applied to some key sets.

For the *folding method*, a key is partitioned into a number of parts, each of which has the same length as the required address (with the possible exception of the last part). The parts are then added together, ignoring the final carry, to form an address. If the keys are in binary form, then the exclusive-or operation may be substituted for addition. There are variations of this technique which can best be illustrated by an example involving the key 187249653. In the fold-shifting method, 187, 249, and 653 are added to yield 89. In the fold-boundary method, the digits of the outermost partitions are reversed, so that 781, 249, and 356 are added yielding 386. Folding is a hashing function useful for compressing multi-word keys so that other hashing functions can be used.

Radix transformation is a hashing method which attempts to produce a random distribution of keys over addresses of the address space. A key which is represented in radix q (q is usually 2 or 10) is considered to be a number expressed in radix p, where p is greater than q and p and q are relatively prime. The number in radix p is converted to radix q and an address is formed by choosing the rightmost digits or bits, or by applying the division method. For example, the key 530476_{10} may be viewed as 530476_{11} and is converted to radix 10 by the calculation

$$530476_{11} = (5)(11^5) + (3)(11^4) + (4)(11^2) + (7)(11) + 6 = 849745_{10}$$

Truncating three leftmost digits gives an address 745 in the address space $\{0, 1, \ldots, 999\}$.

A hashing method called *algebraic coding* is a cluster-separating hashing function based on algebraic coding theory. An r-bit key $(k_1 k_2 \cdots k_r)_2$ is considered as a polynomial

$$K(x) = \sum_{i=1}^{r} k_i x^{i-1}.$$

If an address in the range 0 to $m = 2^t - 1$ is required, then a polynomial

$$P(x) = x^t + \sum_{i=1}^{t} p_i x^{i-1}$$

is used to divide $K(x)$. The remainder

$$K(x) \bmod (P(x)) = \sum_{i=1}^{t} h_i x^{i-1}$$

obtained using polynomial arithmetic modulo 2 gives the address $(h_1 h_2 \ldots h_t)_2$.

Knuth (1973) states that for $r = 15$ and $t = 10$, the divisor polynomial

$$P(x) = x^{10} + x^8 + x^5 + x^4 + x^2 + x + 1$$

will result in a hashing function H such that $H(y_1)$ and $H(y_2)$ are unequal if y_1 and y_2 are distinct binary represented keys different in at most six bit positions. Algebraic coding was originally proposed for implementation in hardware rather than in software.

Knott (1975) and Knuth claim that another method, the multiplicative hashing function, is quite useful. For a nonnegative integral key x and constant c such that $0 < c < 1$, the function is

$$H(x) = \lfloor m(cx \bmod 1) \rfloor + 1$$

Here cx mod 1 is the fractional part of cx and $\lfloor \ \rfloor$ denotes the greatest integer less than or equal to its contents. This multiplicative hashing function should give good results if the constant c is properly chosen—a choice which is difficult to make.

All of the hashing functions considered so far are distribution-independent. We now turn to a discussion of distribution-dependent hashing functions.

Conventional hashing functions attempt to distribute keys uniformly over the address space, but are applied independently of the actual distribution of keys in the key space. This distribution-independence is often required if sets of keys are subject to frequent insertions and deletions. Distribution-dependent hashing functions are quite different from the hashing methods which have been extensively studied in the past. Knott (1971, 1975) and Deutscher (1975) have published discussions of such distribution-dependent functions and characterize them as follows.

Given a subset S of the key space K, we wish to find a hashing function H which maps the elements of S to the address space uniformly. That is, the keys are mapped to the addresses 1, 2, ..., m uniformly. The discrete cumulative distribution function $F_Z(x) = P(Z \le x)$ of the random variable Z, which assumes values of keys in S, can be used to form the required function. Assume that S contains n keys. Then the random variable $F_Z(Z)$ is such that

$$P\left(F_Z(Z) \le \frac{k}{n}\right) = \frac{k}{n}$$

for $0 \le k \le n$, if there are no duplicated elements in S. It follows that $F_Z(Z)$ has a discrete uniform distribution on

$$\left\{\frac{1}{n}, \ldots, \frac{n-1}{n}, 1\right\}$$

and so $mF_Z(Z)$ has a discrete uniform distribution on

$$\left\{\frac{m}{n}, \frac{2m}{n}, \ldots, m\right\}$$

Therefore $\lceil mF_Z(Z)\rceil$, where $\lceil\ \rceil$ denotes the least integer greater than or equal to its contents, is approximately uniform on $\{1, 2, \ldots, m\}$ (especially when $m \le n$).

Thus, given a key x, the distribution-dependent hashing function H is defined by:

$$H(x) = \lceil mF_Z(x)\rceil$$

In most cases, however, F_Z is not known and must be approximated. The distribution dependent hashing functions vary only in the approach used to estimate F_Z. All of the functions can only be defined following one or more scannings of the subset of keys corresponding to the known records. Since this subset may change drastically, due to frequent insertions into and deletions from the table, it may periodically be necessary to redefine the hashing function and reorganize the direct table.

A hashing transformation that is referred to as *digit analysis* is in a sense distribution-dependent. Addresses are formed by selecting and shifting digits or bits of the original key. For example, a key 1234567 might be transformed to an address 6543 by selecting digits in positions 3 through 6 and reversing their order. For a given key set, the same positions of the key and the same rearrangement pattern must be used consistently. An analysis is performed on a sample of the key set to determine which key positions should be used in forming an address. As an example, consider the digit analysis shown in Table 6-2.3. A total of 5,000 ten-digit keys are analyzed in order to determine which key positions should be used in forming elements of the address space $\{0, 1, \ldots, 9999\}$. Positions 1, 5, 6, and 8 have the most uniform distribution of digits, so they are selected.

Table 6-2.3   Digit analysis of a set of ten-digit part numbers.

					Key Position					
Digit	1	2	3	4	5	6	7	8	9	10
0	531	594	1565	5000	499	590	2540	562	1133	721
1	582	568	874	0	536	467	1581	612	759	905
2	571	620	657	0	531	563	557	542	606	553
3	546	565	555	0	511	512	332	522	482	277
4	518	529	284	0	495	461	0	546	521	0
5	503	503	276	0	500	463	0	472	469	673
6	488	456	263	0	469	510	0	426	296	629
7	449	411	212	0	500	459	0	425	365	0
8	422	431	159	0	470	457	0	455	310	501
9	390	323	155	0	489	518	0	438	59	741

A second distribution-dependent hashing function that can be used to approximate F_Z is a *piecewise-linear function*. The key space consists of integral values in the interval (a, d) and is divided into j equal subintervals of length L, that is, $L = (d - a)/j$. Given a key x, it can be determined in which of the j intervals it lies using the formula

$$i = 1 + \lfloor (x - a)/L \rfloor$$

where $\lfloor \ \rfloor$ denotes the greatest integer less than or equal to its contents. Using this equation, the numbers N_i and G_i for each interval

$$I_i = \begin{cases} (a, a + L) & i = 1 \\ [a + (i - 1)L, a + iL] & 2 \le i \le j \end{cases}$$

can be determined for a subset S containing n keys of the key space. N_i is defined as the number of keys from S contained in I_i, and G_i is the number of keys less than $a + iL$. Therefore, N_i and G_i are the frequency and cumulative frequency, respectively, of the interval I_i. Using N_i and G_i we can define

$$P_i(x) = (G_i + ((x - a)/L - i)N_i)/n$$

as a linear approximation of the cumulative frequency-distribution function F_Z for x in the interval I_i. The required hashing function for a key x on interval I_i is, therefore,

$$H_i(x) = \lceil mP_i(x) \rceil, \ 1 \le i \le j$$

Implementation of the piecewise-linear function for indirect addressing requires the following algorithm.

Algorithm PIECE_WISE (Piecewise-linear parameter calculation).   Given j, a, d, m, and n as previously defined and a key set $\{x_1, x_2, \ldots, x_n\}$, it is required to calculate interval length L and the frequencies and cumulative frequencies N_i and G_i, $1 \le i \le j$, for the piecewise-linear function.

1. [Initialize array N to zero]
   Repeat for i = 1, 2, ..., j:
      Set $N_i \leftarrow 0$.
2. [Determine interval length and interval frequencies]
   Set $L \leftarrow (d - a)/j$.
   Repeat for k = 1, 2, ..., n:
      Set $i \leftarrow 1 + \lfloor (x_k - a)/L \rfloor$ and $N_i \leftarrow N_i + 1$.
3. [Calculate interval cumulative frequencies]
   Set $G_1 \leftarrow N_1$.
   Repeat for i = 2, 3, ..., j:
      Set $G_i \leftarrow G_{i-1} + N_i$.
   Exit.

Algorithm PIECE_WISE is very simple and requires only one scan of the keys in the key set to determine the N and G elements. With the parameters it provides, an address is calculated from a key x in (a, d) using the following assignments:

$$\text{Set } i \leftarrow 1 + \lfloor (x - a)/L \rfloor \qquad \text{and} \qquad H(x) \leftarrow \lceil m(G_i + ((x - a)/L - i) N_i)/n \rceil.$$

$H(x)$ is the value of the hashing function.

As an example of the piecewise-linear method, consider the case where a = 0, d = 200, j = 10, n = 110, and L = 20 with the vectors N and G as given in Table 6-2.4. For a key value x = 105, with m = 100

$$i = 1 + \lfloor (105 - 0)/20 \rfloor = 6 \qquad \text{and}$$

$$H(x) = \lceil (100(53 + ((105 - 0)/20) - 6)13)/110 \rceil = 40$$

Another method devised for estimating the frequency distribution of a key set is again based on a piecewise-linear estimate. Starting with an arbitrary number of equally sized intervals dividing the key space, the storage of a subset S of keys is simulated. Those

Table 6-2.4

N	G
5	5
8	13
15	28
3	31
9	40
13	53
20	73
16	89
12	101
9	110

intervals which have an ALOS that is greater than a predetermined ALOS are divided so that a better estimate of the frequency distribution can be obtained for that interval. The process of splitting intervals is performed iteratively so that subintervals may also be split. The hashing function obtained using this method will be denoted as the *piecewise-linear function with interval splitting*. It requires the use of a fairly complex data structure that can be represented using an array. An example is given in Fig. 6-2.12.

Referring to Fig. 6-2.12, the range of the key space (a, d) is initially divided into $j = 10$ intervals of length $L = (d - a)/10$. The frequency N_i is given for each of these intervals. If the ith interval has not been split, then G_i will have a nonnegative value equal to the cumulative frequency for that interval. If G_i is negative, however, the absolute value of G_i is the index to the first of two consecutive pairs of array elements, $N_{|G_i|}$ and $G_{|G_i|}$, and $N_{|G_i|+1}$ and $G_{|G_i|+1}$. These elements correspond to the half-intervals of interval i, each half-interval having length $(d - a)/20$. $N_{|G_i|}$ and $N_{|G_i|+1}$ are the frequencies for the first and second half-intervals of interval i. Letting k be either $|G_i|$ or $|G_i| + 1$, if G_k is nonnegative, then it is the cumulative frequency of the corresponding half-interval. Otherwise, $|G_k|$ is the index to the first of two consecutive pairs of array elements which give information for the two quarter-intervals of the corresponding half-interval. This process is continued to obtain eighth-intervals.

Consider interval 8 with $N_8 = 10$ and $G_8 = -15$. This interval is split, so $|G_8| = 15$ references N_{15}, G_{15}, N_{16}, and G_{16} containing information for the half-intervals of interval 8. $N_{16} = 1$ and $G_{16} = 30$ implies that the second half-interval is not split. The first half-interval has $N_{15} = 9$ and $G_{15} = -19$, indicating that it is split and N_{19}, G_{19}, N_{20}, and G_{20} correspond to its quarter-intervals. The first quarter-interval is split, as indicated by $G_{19} = -23$, but the second quarter-interval, having no keys in it, is not split. N_{23}, G_{23}, N_{24}, and G_{24} give the frequencies and cumulative frequencies for the eighth-intervals of the first quarter-interval. It may be possible to split the eighth-intervals, but the process is stopped at this point.

The following algorithm calculates an address using this type of data structure for the piecewise-linear function with interval splitting. It is assumed that intervals may be split to no less than $(1/2)^{p-1}$ of their initial size. Thus, if $p = 1$, the algorithm is simply a calculation of the piecewise-linear function.

Algorithm ISAC (Interval splitting address calculation). Given L, a, m, n, and p as previously defined and arrays N and G, whose content is exemplified by Fig. 6-2.12, it is required to calculate an address H in {1, 2, ..., m} from the key x.

1. [Calculate initial interval number]
   Set $r \leftarrow i \leftarrow 1 + \lfloor (x - a)/L \rfloor$.
2. [Repetition clause]
   Repeat steps 3 and 4 for k = 1, 2, ..., p.
3. [Is the interval or subinterval split?]
   If $G_i \geq 0$, go to step 5.
4. [Calculate interval number and array index]
   Set $r \leftarrow 1 + \lfloor (x - a)/(L/2^k) \rfloor$ and $i \leftarrow -G_i - (r \bmod 2) + 1$.
5. [Calculate address]
   Set $H \leftarrow \lceil m (G_i + ((x - a)/(L/2^{k-1}) - r) N_i)/n \rceil$, and **Exit.**

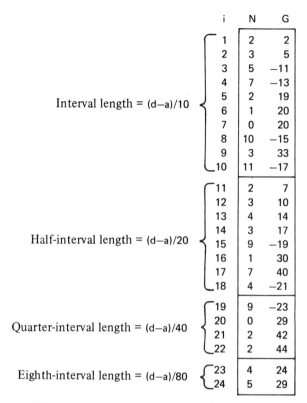

	i	N	G
Interval length = (d−a)/10	1	2	2
	2	3	5
	3	5	−11
	4	7	−13
	5	2	19
	6	1	20
	7	0	20
	8	10	−15
	9	3	33
	10	11	−17
Half-interval length = (d−a)/20	11	2	7
	12	3	10
	13	4	14
	14	3	17
	15	9	−19
	16	1	30
	17	7	40
	18	4	−21
Quarter-interval length = (d−a)/40	19	9	−23
	20	0	29
	21	2	42
	22	2	44
Eighth-interval length = (d−a)/80	23	4	24
	24	5	29

FIGURE 6-2.12 Representation of a data structure for the piecewise-linear function with internal splitting.

Note that r, calculated in step 4, is such that $1 \le r \le 2^k j$, where j is the initial number of subintervals. The value of r is used in the address calculation of step 5, and is also used to adjust $-G_i$ in step 4. If r is odd, then $-G_i$ is unchanged; but if it is even, then $-G_i$ is incremented by 1. This calculation determines i, the index to the array elements corresponding to the required half-interval. Since intervals are split to no more than $(1/2)^{p-1}$ of their initial size, step 1 is never executed when k = p. An algorithm for constructing the N and G arrays has a slow execution time. It requires that the key set be scanned 2p − 1 times.

Knott (1975), Lum et al. (1971), London (1973), Knuth (1973), Buchholz (1963), and Deutscher (1975) present studies of these hashing functions which have been briefly described. Although some of these methods often give a uniform distribution of keys over addresses, it is still necessary to experiment with hashing functions as applied to specific key sets. A performance measure is needed to compare different hashing functions, and the measure most widely adopted is the Average Length Of Search (ALOS). For a set of records in a direct file, it is the average number of accesses to the storage device required to retrieve a record. Usually, the best hashing function for use with a particular set of keys minimizes the ALOS. Note that there are other factors besides hashing functions to be considered in minimizing ALOS, as discussed in the remainder of this subsection.

A hashing function often maps a number of keys to the same address. In such a case, the colliding or overflow records must be stored and accessed at other storage locations as determined by a collision-resolution technique. There are basically two classes of such techniques, namely, *open addressing* and *chaining*. In the remaining pages of this subsection we present algorithms from both classes. Certain variations of the basic techniques are also mentioned.

With open addressing, if a key x is mapped to a storage location d, and this location is already occupied, then other locations in the table are scanned until a free record location is found for the overflow record to occupy. It is possible that the free record location contains a record that was previously deleted. When a record with key K_i is deleted, K_i is set to a special nonnegative value called MARK, which is not equal to the value of any key. The locations are scanned according to a sequence which could be defined in many ways. The simplest technique for handling collisions is to use the following sequence:

$$d, d + 1, \ldots, m - 1, m, 1, 2, \ldots, d - 1$$

A free record location is always found if at least one is available; otherwise, the search halts after scanning m locations. For retrieval of a record, the same sequence of locations is scanned until that record is located, or until an empty (never used) record position is found. In the latter case, the required record is not in the table and the search fails. This method of collision resolution is called *linear probing*.

The following algorithm inserts a record into a table using linear probing with the sequence d, d + 1, ..., m − 1, m, 1, 2, ..., d − 1. The table which contains m locations is represented by the table description given at the beginning of the chapter. It is assumed that if R_i has never contained a record, then K_i has a negative value.

Algorithm OPENLP.   Given a record REC identified by key x, it is required to insert REC into the table represented by structure R. The hashing function H is used to calculate an initial address.

1. [Calculate address]   Set i ← d ← H(x).
2. [Scan for available storage]
    If K_i < 0 or K_i = MARK, then set K_i ← x, and Exit.
3. [Increment and test index]   Set i ← i + 1.
    If i > m, then set i ← 1.
    If i = d, then print 'overflow', and Exit; otherwise, go to step 2.

The operation of Algorithm OPENLP is quite simple. In step 1 an initial address is calculated. Step 2 scans a position and, if it is a previously empty position or it belongs to a previously deleted key, the record is stored in this location and the algorithm is successful. Otherwise, step 3 is executed to increment index i and reset i to 1, if necessary. If i has become equal to d, its initial value, then no record locations are available and the algorithm terminates unsuccessfully.

A similar algorithm is used to retrieve a record and can be obtained from Algorithm OPENLP by replacing step 2 with the following:

2. [Scan for record with key x]

    If x = K$_i$,

    then set REC ← R$_i$, and Exit;

    otherwise,

    if K$_i$ < 0 then print 'unsuccessful search', and Exit.

As an example, let us assume the following:

the name NODE is mapped into 1

the name STORAGE is mapped into 2

the names AN and ADD are mapped into 3

the names FUNCTION, B, BRAND, and PARAMETER are mapped into 9

Assuming that the insertions are performed in the following order:

NODE, STORAGE, AN, ADD, FUNCTION, B, BRAND, and PARAMETER

Fig. 6-2.13 represents the resulting structure with m = 11. The first three keys are each placed in a single probe, but then ADD must go into position 4 instead of 3, which is already occupied. FUNCTION is placed in position 9 in one probe, but B and BRAND take two and three probes, respectively. Finally, PARAMETER ends up in position 5 after eight probes, since positions 9, 10, 11, 1, 2, 3, and 4 are all occupied. A search is completed successfully when the key x is found, or unsuccessfully if an empty record location is encountered. Steps 1 and 3 remain unchanged, so the same comments apply.

Each time that step 2 of Algorithm OPENLP is executed for either insertion or retrieval, one comparison is required. For a table of n records, if all records are stored or retrieved, then the number of times that step 2 is executed divided by n is the ALOS.

		Number of Probes
R$_1$	NODE	1
R$_2$	STORAGE	1
R$_3$	AN	1
R$_4$	ADD	2
R$_5$	PARAMETER	8
R$_6$	Empty	
R$_7$	Empty	
R$_8$	Empty	
R$_9$	FUNCTION	1
R$_{10}$	B	2
R$_{11}$	BRAND	3

FIGURE 6-2.13 Collision resolution by using open addressing.

Knuth gives a probabilistic model for analyzing collision-resolution techniques and develops formulas for the expected average length of a successful search (E[ALOS]) in the case of open addressing. The model assumes that each key has probability $1/m$ of being mapped to each of the m addresses in the table. Therefore, there are m^n ways of mapping keys to the address space.

E[ALOS] is dependent on the load factor. If $\alpha = n/m$ is the load factor for n and m as defined previously, then Knuth derives the following formulas:

$$E[ALOS] \simeq \begin{cases} \dfrac{1}{2}\left(1 + \dfrac{1}{1-\alpha}\right) & \text{for a successful search} \\[2ex] \dfrac{1}{2}\left(1 + \dfrac{1}{(1-\alpha)^2}\right) & \text{for an unsuccessful search} \end{cases}$$

Table 6-2.5 gives representative values for these formulas with a number of different load factors. E[ALOS] increases with increasing load factor, since a greater number of collisions is probable as more records are being stored in the table. Note that for $\alpha < 0.80$, the results are quite good as compared to the search methods discussed previously. The number of comparisons is proportional to the load factor This result, however, is based on the key set being uniformly mapped onto the address space.

The linear probing method of collision resolution has a number of shortcomings. Deletions are difficult to perform. The approach that was used consisted of having a special table entry with a value of **MARK**, which denoted the deletion of that entry. This strategy enabled us to search the table properly. For example, assume that the record whose key is **FUNCTION** in Fig. 6-2.13 is marked for deletion by assigning the value of **MARK** to K_9. Then, if it is desired to retrieve the record with a key value of **BRAND**, our previous algorithm will still work. The reader may wonder: Why bother to use a special value such as **MARK** to denote deleted entries? Why not just assign a negative value to the entry which is to be deleted? The reason is that if this were done in the previous example, the algorithm

Table 6-2.5   E[ALOS] for linear probing.

Load Factor	Number of Probes	
α	Successful	Unsuccessful
.10	1.056	1.118
.20	1.125	1.281
.30	1.214	1.520
.40	1.333	1.889
.50	1.500	2.500
.60	1.750	3.625
.70	2.167	6.060
.80	3.000	13.000
.90	5.500	50.500
.95	10.500	200.500

would find an empty position in position 9 and decide that **BRAND** was not in the table and proceed to insert it once more.

This solution to the deletion problem is tolerable if few deletions are made in a table. For the case of many deletions, however, the table will contain numerous entries that are marked for deletion and this may result in extensive search times. It is possible to devise an algorithm which will perform deletions by moving records, if necessary. Such an algorithm eliminates the necessity for having records with a value of **MARK**. In other words, record position can be either occupied or empty.

The approach that can be used is first to mark the deleted record as empty. An ordered search is then made for the next empty position. If a record, say y, is found whose hash value is not between the position of the record just marked for deletion and that of the present empty position, then record y can be moved to replace the deleted record. Then the position for record y is marked as empty and the entire process is repeated, starting at the position occupied by y. The precise formulation of this algorithm is left as an exercise.

Another shortcoming of the linear probing method is due to *clustering* effects which tend to become severe when the table becomes nearly full. This phenomenon can be explained by considering a trace of Fig. 6-2.13 which would show the state of the table after each insertion. Such a trace is given in Fig. 6-2.14. When the first insertion is made, the probability of a new element being inserted in a particular position is clearly 1/11. For the second insertion, however, the probability that position 2 will become occupied is twice as likely as any remaining available position; namely, the entry will be placed in position 2 if the key is mapped into either 1 or 2. Continuing in this manner, on the fifth insertion the probability that the new entry will be placed in position 5 is five times as likely as its being placed in any remaining unoccupied position. Thus, the trend is for long sequences of occupied positions to become longer. Such a phenomenon is called *primary clustering*.

The primary clustering problem can be improved if a different probing method is used. A method which accomplishes this is called *random probing*. This technique generates a random sequence of positions rather than an ordered sequence, as was the case in the linear probing method. The random sequence generated must contain every integer between 1 and m exactly once. The table is considered to be full when the first duplicate number is encountered. An example of a random-number generator which generates such a cyclic permutation of numbers consists of the statement

$$y \leftarrow (y + c) \bmod m$$

where y is the initial number of the sequence (the generator) and c and m are relatively prime, i.e., their greatest common divisor is 1. For example, assuming that m = 11 and c = 7, this statement starting with an initial value of 3 will generate the sequence 10, 6, 2, 9, 5, 1, 8, 4, 0, 7, and 3. Thus, adding 1 to each element transforms the sequence to a number in the desired interval [1, 11]. We can now formulate the following algorithm.

Algorithm OPENRP. Given a record **REC** identified by key x, it is required to insert **REC** into the table represented by the structure R. The hashing function H is used to calculate an initial address. **MARK** serves the same purpose as it did in Algorithm **OPENLP**.

514

After inserting record Contents of table after insertion

After inserting record							
NODE	NODE						
STORAGE	NODE	STORAGE					
AN	NODE	STORAGE	AN				
ADD	NODE	STORAGE	AN	ADD			
FUNCTION	NODE	STORAGE	AN	ADD	FUNCTION		
B	NODE	STORAGE	AN	ADD	FUNCTION	B	
BRAND	NODE	STORAGE	AN	ADD	FUNCTION	B	BRAND
PARAMETER	NODE	STORAGE	AN	ADD	PARAMETER	FUNCTION	B	BRAND

FIGURE 6-2.14.

1. [Initialize]   Set $d \leftarrow H(x)$.
2. [First probe]   If $K_d < 0$ or K_d = MARK, then set $K_d \leftarrow x$, and Exit.
3. [Initiate further search]   Set $y \leftarrow d - 1$.
4. [Scan next entry]   Set $y \leftarrow (y + c) \bmod m$ and $j \leftarrow y + 1$;
   If $j = d$, then print 'overflow', and Exit.
5. [Is this entry occupied?]
   If $K_j < 0$ or K_j = MARK, then set $K_j \leftarrow x$, and Exit; otherwise, go to step 4.

The deletion problem becomes more difficult with random probing than was the case for linear probing. Therefore, if the table is volatile, then some other method should be used to resolve collisions.

Although random probing has improved the problem of primary clustering, clustering can still occur. This situation arises when two keys are hashed into the same value. In such a case, the same sequence or path will be generated for both keys by the random-probe method just discussed. This phenomenon is called *secondary clustering*.

One way to alleviate this problem is to have a second hashing function, independent of the first, select a parameter (for example, c in Algorithm OPENRP) that will be used in random probing. For example, assume that H_1 is the first hashing function with $H_1(x_1) = H_1(x_2) = i$ where $x_1 \neq x_2$. Now, if we have a second hashing function, H_2, such that $H_2(x_1) \neq H_2(x_2)$ whenever $x_1 \neq x_2$, then we can use as the value of parameter c in Algorithm OPENRP a value of $H_2(x_1)$ or $H_2(x_2)$. The two random sequences generated by this scheme will be different if H_2 is independent of H_1. Therefore, secondary clustering has been curtailed. This variation of open addressing is called *double hashing*.

The average length of search for a double hashing technique where H_1 and H_2 are independent is given by the following pair of formulas:

$$E[\text{ALOS}] \simeq \begin{cases} -\dfrac{1}{\alpha} \ln(1 - \alpha) & \text{for a successful search} \\[2ex] \dfrac{1}{1 - \alpha} & \text{for an unsuccessful search} \end{cases}$$

Table 6-2.6 gives a summary of representative values for a double hashing method. Its performance is certainly better than that obtained for linear probing.

The open-addressing methods discussed thus far are impractical to apply to volatile tables because of the continual possibility of table overflow and the difficulty of physically deleting records from the table. We now turn to linked-allocation techniques to get around these problems.

Section 4-3.2 dealt with the construction of a linked dictionary or table where a hashing function was used to map names into equivalence classes. Two names were placed into the same class if they were hashed into the same number. Each equivalence class was kept as a separate linked list or chain. This technique of resolving collisions is called *separate chaining*. Figure 6-2.15 shows a separate-chaining representation of the sample keys used earlier in this subsection with $m = 11$ and $n = 8$. The keys are assumed to be inserted in the following order:

NODE, STORAGE, AN, ADD, FUNCTION, B, BRAND, and PARAMETER

Table 6-2.6   E[ALOS] for random probing with
double hashing.

| Load Factor | Number of Probes | |
α	Successful	Unsuccessful
.10	1.054	1.111
.20	1.116	1.250
.30	1.189	1.429
.40	1.277	1.667
.50	1.386	2.000
.60	1.527	2.500
.70	1.720	3.333
.80	2.012	5.000
.90	2.558	10.000
.95	3.153	20.000

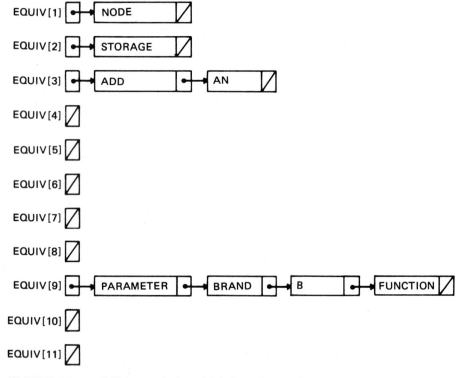

FIGURE 6-2.15   Collision resolution with independent chaining.

Note that each insertion is made at the front of the appropriate list. The average length of search for separate chaining is given as follows:

$$E[\text{ALOS}] \simeq \begin{cases} 1 + \dfrac{\alpha}{2} \text{ for a successful search} \\[2ex] \alpha + e^{-\alpha} \text{ for an unsuccessful search} \end{cases}$$

Representative values for this method are given in Table 6-2.7. Note that it is desirable to make the load factor as small as possible. This can be achieved by making m large. This will, however, make many of the lists empty and space will be wasted for their list heads. Although additional storage is required to store the links using this resolution technique, its performance and versatility make it far superior to open addressing when volatile tables are involved. Furthermore, the performance formulas given hold for $\alpha > 1$!

In an attempt to make m as large as possible, while at the same time avoiding the existence of many empty list heads, a different linking approach and organization can be adopted. The nodes in the linked lists can be overlapped with the list heads. This organization permits the storage of m records with only m links, rather than the m + n links required to store n records with separate chaining. Such a representation for our example set of keys is given in Fig. 6-2.16. The expected ALOS for this representation is slightly higher than that for separate chaining, but the saving of space realized with this alternate representation makes it attractive.

In summary, the linear-search method is acceptable, providing the number of entries in the table is small. The binary-search technique is ideally suited to static tables. If computational efficiency is required for a spectrum of operations, then a balanced tree search should be used for reasonably large n. Hashing functions can be used to great advantage if the key set can be uniformly distributed over the address space.

Table 6-2.7 E[ALOS] with separate chaining.

Load Factor	Number of Probes	
α	Successful	Unsuccessful
.10	1.050	1.005
.20	1.100	1.019
.30	1.150	1.041
.40	1.200	1.070
.50	1.250	1.107
.60	1.300	1.149
.70	1.350	1.197
.80	1.400	1.249
.90	1.450	1.307
.95	1.475	1.337

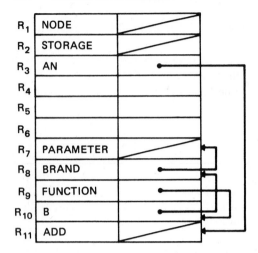

FIGURE 6-2.16   Collision resolution with internal chaining.

Exercises for Sec. 6-2

1. Formulate insertion and deletion algorithms for an ordered table.

2. Show the binary tree built from a sequence of insertions for the following sequence of keys:

    8, 17, 10, 15, 5, 2, 16, 19, 13, 1, 4, 11.

3. Using the tree obtained in Exercise 2 and Algorithm TREE_DELETE, show at each step the tree obtained for the sequence of deletions corresponding to the following keys:

    15, 2, 16, 13, 19.

4. Using Algorithm BALANCE_INSERT, show at each step the tree built from a sequence of insertions corresponding to the following keys:

    6, 7, 8, 12, 15, 17, 9, 10.

5. Formulate an algorithm which will delete a node from a balanced tree and leave the resulting tree balanced. (*Hint:* If the node is not a leaf, find its inorder predecessor to see if it can be deleted.)

6. Obtain an algorithm for performing a trie search based on the representation of a trie given in Table 6-2.2.

7. What happens in Algorithm OPENLP if step 3 is replaced by $i \leftarrow (i + c) \bmod m + 1$? Will this change improve the clustering problem?

8. Trace Algorithm OPENRP for the same sequence of names used in the text.

9. Design an algorithm for deleting a table item when the linear-probe method of resolution is used.

10. Obtain a searching algorithm based on double hashing.

11. Discuss the problems encountered in the formulation of a deletion algorithm when double hashing is used.

12. Formulate an algorithm for separate chaining where each equivalence class is to be represented as a tree structure, rather than as a one-way chain.

13. Formulate an insertion algorithm based on the discussion at the end of this section (see Fig. 6-2.16).

BIBLIOGRAPHY

ADEL'SON-VEL'SKII, G. M., and E. M. LANDIS: An Algorithm for the Organization of Information, *Dokl. Akad. Nauk SSSR, Mathemat.*, vol. 146, no. 2, pp. 263–266, 1962.

BERZTISS, A. T.: "Data Structures: Theory and Practice," 2d ed., Academic Press, Inc., New York, 1975.

BROOKS, F. P., and K. E. IVERSON: "Automatic Data Processing: System/360 Edition," John Wiley and Sons, Inc., New York, 1969.

BUCHHOLZ, WERNER: File Organization and Addressing, *IBM Systems Journal*, vol. 2, pp. 86–110, June, 1963.

DEUTSCHER, R. F., J. P. TREMBLAY, and P. G. SORENSON: A Comparative Study of Distribution-Dependent and Distribution-Independent Hashing Functions, *Proceedings of the ACM Pacific 75*, April 17 and 18, 1975, San Francisco, pp. 172–178.

DEUTSCHER, R. F., P. G. SORENSON, and J. P. TREMBLAY: Distribution-Dependent Hashing Functions and Their Characteristics, *Proceedings of the International Conference on the Management of Data, A.C.M./SIGMOD*, May 14–15, 1975, San Jose, pp. 224–236.

ELSON, MARK: "Data Structures," Science Research Associates, Inc., Palo Alto, California, 1975.

FLORES, IVAN: "Computer Sorting," Prentice-Hall, Inc., Englewood Cliffs, N.J., 1969.

FLOYD, R. W.: Algorithm 245, Treesort 3, *Communications of the ACM*, vol. 7, no. 12, p. 701, December, 1964.

HARRISON, M. C.: "Data Structures and Programming," Scott, Foresman and Company, Glenview, Illinois, 1973.

HOARE, C. A. R.: Algorithms 63 and 64, *Communications of the ACM*, vol. 4, no. 7, p. 321, July, 1961.

ISAAC, E. J., and R. C. SINGLETON: Sorting by Address Calculation, *Journal of the ACM*, vol. 3, pp. 169–174, July, 1956.

KNOTT, GARY D.: Expandable Open-Addressing Hash-Table Storage and Retrieval, *Proceedings of the SIGFIDET Workshop on Data Description, Access, and Control*, ACM, 1971, pp. 187–206.

KNOTT, GARY D.: Hashing Functions, to be published in *The Computer Journal*, 1975.

KNUTH, D. E.: "Sorting and Searching, The Art of Computer Programming," vol. 3, pp. 506–549, Addison-Wesley Publishing Company, Inc., Reading, Mass., 1973.

KRONMAL, R. A., and M. E. TARTER: Cumulative Polygon Address Calculation Sorting, *Proceedings of the 20th National Conference of the ACM*, 1965, pp. 376–385.

LONDON, K. R.: "Techniques for Direct Access," Auerbach Publishers, Inc., Philadelphia, 1973.

LUM, V. Y.: General Performance Analysis of Key-to-Address Transformation Methods

Using an Abstract File Concept, *Communications of the ACM*, vol. 16, no. 10, pp. 603–612, 1973.

LUM, V. Y., P. S. T. YUEN, and M. DODD: Key-to-Address Transform Techniques: A Fundamental Performance Study on Large Existing Formatted Files, *Communications of the ACM*, vol. 14, no. 4, pp. 228–239, 1971.

MAURER, W. D.: "Programming," Holden-Day, San Francisco, California, 1968.

MAURER, W. D., and T. G. LEWIS: Hash Table Methods, *ACM Computing Surveys*, vol. 7, no. 1, pp. 5–19, March, 1975.

MORRIS, ROBERT: Scatter Storage Techniques, *Communications of the ACM*, vol. 11, no. 1, pp. 38–44, 1968.

PETERSON, WILLIAM W.: Addressing for Random-Access Storage, *IBM Journal of Research and Development*, vol. 1, pp. 130–146, April, 1957.

PRICE, C. E.: Table Lookup Techniques, *ACM Computing Surveys*, vol. 3, no. 2, pp. 49–65, 1971.

STONE, H. S.: "Introduction to Computer Organization and Data Structures," McGraw-Hill Book Company, New York, 1972.

WILLIAMS, J. W. J.: Algorithm 232, Heapsort, *Communications of the ACM*, vol. 7, no. 6, pp. 347–348, June, 1964.

FILE STRUCTURES

To this point in the text, a major portion of the discussion has dealt with the representations of and operations on data structures. The storage representations and data manipulations described applied only to data entities which were assumed to reside in main memory. There are at least two reasons why not all information that is processed by a computer should reside in an immediately accessible form of memory. First, there are some programs and data for programs which are so large as not to fit conveniently into main memory, which is typically a scarce resource in a computer system. Second, it is often desirable or necessary to store information from one execution of a program to the next (e.g., in a payroll system). Therefore, large volumes of data and archival data are commonly stored in external memory as special data-holding entities called files.

In this chapter we concentrate on file structures (i.e., the storage representations of files) and operations on files. We begin with a description of external storage devices, the media on which files normally reside. Next, some important concepts and terminology are introduced and later used in the discussion of a number of file organizations—the sequential, indexed sequential, and direct organizations. Virtual memory is presented as an alternative method of handling large volumes of data. VSAM, a file organization used in conjunction with a virtual memory system, is described. Multikeyed access methods for files are examined, and finally the concepts and functions relevant to three types of data-base management systems are outlined.

7-1   EXTERNAL STORAGE DEVICES

The storage of information in the main or internal memory of a computer was discussed in Sec. 1-3. Any location in main memory can be accessed very quickly; a typical access time is less than 1 μsec ($= 10^{-6}$ sec). Main memory provides for the immediate storage requirements of the central processor for the execution of programs, including users' programs, assemblers, compilers, and supervisory routines of the operating system.

The storage capacity of main memory is limited by two major factors—the cost of main memory and the technical problems in developing a large-capacity main memory. The storage requirements for programs and the data on which they operate exceed the capacity of main memory in virtually all computer systems. Therefore, it is necessary to extend the storage capabilities of a computer by using devices external to main memory.

An *external storage device* may be loosely defined as a device, other than main memory, on which information or data can be stored and from which the information can be retrieved for processing at some subsequent point in time. The storage and retrieval operations are referred to as *writing* and *reading*, respectively. External storage devices have a larger capacity and are less expensive per bit of information stored than main memory. The time required to access information, however, is much greater with these devices.

The primary uses for external storage devices include:

1   Backup or overlay of programs during execution
2   Storage of programs and subprograms for future use
3   Storage of information in "files"

In this chapter we are concerned with the third use, although certain results may also be applied to the first and second uses.

A card reader/punch can be considered as a primitive external storage device. However, in this section we are concerned with devices that allow a more rapid transfer of data and a more convenient storage medium than punched cards. We discuss the most common external storage devices in the order of their initial development and use— magnetic-tape, drum, and disk devices. A brief description of physical characteristics as well as certain logical aspects of these devices is given. Some of the new technology relating to mass storage and intermediate storage devices is also described.

7-1.1   Magnetic Tapes

The first compact external storage medium to be widely used was magnetic tape. A tape is made of a plastic material coated with a ferrite substance which is easily magnetized. The physical appearance of the tape is similar to the tape used for sound recording, although computer magnetic tape is wider. Several thousand feet of tape are wound on one reel. Information is encoded on the tape character by character. A number of channels or tracks run the length of the tape, one channel being required for each bit position in the binary-coded representation of a character. An additional channel is usually used for parity check bits. It is possible to encode several hundred characters on one inch of magnetic tape; common encoding densities are 800 and 1,600 bytes per inch. On a 3,600-foot reel of tape which stores 1,600 bytes per inch, a maximum of 1,600 bytes/inch $\times$ 12 inches/foot $\times$ 3,600 feet = 69,120,000 bytes can be stored. (Assuming one byte is used to store a character, a tape can potentially store the text of 25 books the size of this one!) We will see that this maximum is virtually impossible to achieve.

Information is read from or written on magnetic tape through the use of a magnetic tape drive. The tape is fed past read/write heads at a typical speed of 125 inches per second. The data transfer rate for such a tape drive when information is encoded at a density of 1,600 bytes per inch is, therefore, 200,000 bytes per second.

When a tape drive is not reading or writing information, it is in a stopped position. When a command to read or write is issued by the processor, the tape must be accelerated to a constant high speed. Following the completion of a read or write command, the tape is decelerated to a stop position. During either an acceleration or deceleration phase, a certain length of tape is passed over. This section of tape is neither read nor written upon. It appears between successive records (groups of data) and is called an *interrecord gap* (see Fig. 7-1.1*a*). An interrecord gap varies from $\frac{1}{2}$ to $\frac{3}{4}$ inch, depending on the nature of the tape unit. The greater the number of interrecord gaps, the smaller is the storage capacity of the tape. For example, suppose records consisting of 800 bytes each are written one at a time on a tape having a density 1,600 bytes per inch. If $\frac{1}{2}$ inch interrecord gaps result, then only $\frac{1}{2}$ of that tape is used for storing data.

To circumvent this problem, records are often grouped in *blocks*. If records are blocked, one write command can transfer a number of consecutive records to the tape

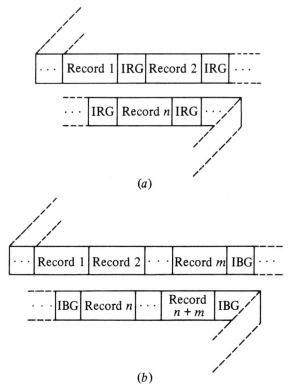

(*a*)

(*b*)

FIGURE 7-1.1 Record layout for a magnetic tape.

without requiring interrecord·gaps between them, as shown in Fig. 7-1.1*b*. Gaps appropriately called *interblock gaps* are placed between successive blocks. The utilization of a tape's storage capacity increases as the number of records in a block (often called the *blocking factor*) is made larger. If the blocking factor in the previous example is 10, then $800 \times 10 = 8{,}000$ bytes can be stored between gaps. Thus, the utilization increases to 10/11 from $\frac{1}{2}$.

The average time taken to read or write a record is inversely proportional to the blocking factor, since fewer gaps must be spanned and more records can be read or written per command. To utilize tape storage efficiently and to minimize read and write time, it appears that the blocking factor should be arbitrarily large. When a block of records is read or written, however, it is transferred to or from an area in main memory called a *buffer*. (More will be said about buffers in Sec. 7-4.1.) Since main memory is very often at a premium, the buffer size cannot be allowed to be arbitrarily large. Obviously, a trade-off exists between tape storage capacity and read/write time on the one hand and the amount of main memory available for buffering on the other.

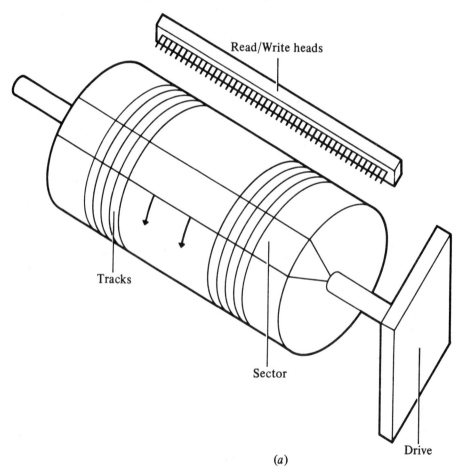

(*a*)

FIGURE 7-1.2   Magnetic drums. (*a*) With fixed read/write heads; (*b*) with movable read/write heads.

A limitation of magnetic-tape devices is that records must be processed in the order in which they reside on the tape. Therefore, accessing a record requires the scanning of all records that precede it. This form of access, called sequential access, will be discussed in detail in Sec. 7-4. Operations such as rewinding a tape or backspacing a certain number of records or blocks increase the performance and flexibility of a magnetic-tape device.

Magnetic tape is probably the cheapest form of external bulk storage; currently, the price of a reel of tape is around $25. In addition, a reel of tape can be easily placed on and removed from a tape drive, and hence it can be used for the off-line storage of data.

7-1.2 Magnetic Drums

A magnetic drum is a metal cylinder, from 10 to 36 inches in diameter, which has an outside surface coated with a magnetic recording material. The cylindrical surface of the drum is divided into a number of parallel bands called *tracks*, as illustrated in Fig. 7-1.2. The tracks are further subdivided into either *sectors* or *blocks*, depending on the nature of the drum. The sector or block is the smallest addressable unit of a drum. A particular

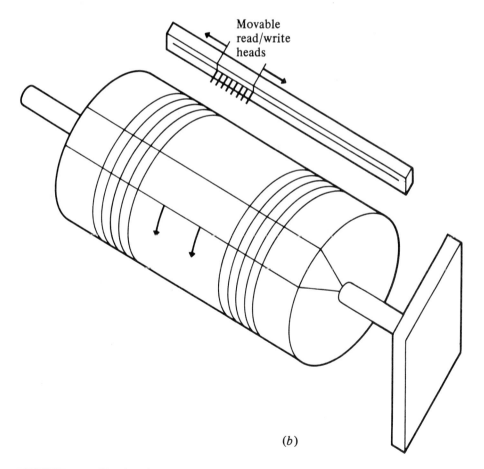

(*b*)

FIGURE 7-1.2 (Continued)

sector or block is directly addressable in the sense that to access a sector or block n of a drum, it is not necessary to access sectors or blocks 1 to $n - 1$, as would be the case when using a sequential type of device such as a magnetic tape. For this reason, a drum is referred to as a *direct-access storage device*.

Sectors are fixed-length arcs of a track, and an integral number of sectors make up a track. The size of a sector is the same for all tracks on a drum and is fixed either in the hardware of the drum unit or when the computer system is generated.

Block-addressable drums differ from sector-addressable drums in the sense that a block contains a programmer-defined number of records. (Note that this notion of block is the same as the notion presented in the previous discussion of tapes.) Therefore, the number of blocks which are stored on a track can differ from track to track, and even the size of the blocks stored on a given track can vary. In both sector-addressable and block-addressable drums, however, a complete sector or block, respectively, is read into or written from a buffer at one time.

Because all sectors are the same in size and there are an integral number of sectors per track, a specific sector can generally be located more quickly than a specific block. For a given application, however, the size of a record may not divide exactly into the size of a sector, and space in a sector may thus be wasted. In addition, a record may be larger than a sector, in which case more than one I/O command may be required to read or write the record.

In the discussion throughout this chapter, we will assume block-addressable devices unless stated otherwise. A sector addressable device can be thought of as a special case of a block-addressable device in which there are an integral number of blocks per track and all blocks are the same size.

Data is transferred to or from the drum as it rotates at a high speed past a number of read/write heads. Two schemes for arranging the read/write heads are used with magnetic drums. The most common scheme is to have *fixed* read/write heads, one for each track, as shown in Fig. 7-1.2a. A second architecture, shown in Fig. 7-1.2b, is to have a *movable* head in which a group of read/write heads are mounted on a rail and the heads are allowed to traverse the length of the drum. For example, a drum may have 100 tracks with a group of five read/write heads. Such a system permits the group of heads to be moved to any one of twenty positions. Five adjacent tracks can be accessed from one position.

For a fixed-head drum, the main component in the time to access a certain location is the *rotational delay* or *latency* (L), which is the time in waiting for the drum to rotate to the position where the requested data transfer can commence. Figure 7-1.3 illustrates the conditions of maximum, average, and minimum rotational delay. In movable-head drums, additional time is required to move a read/write head to the desired track. This additional component of the access time is often called the *seek time* (S). Therefore the *access time*, A(i), associated with a particular I/O operation, i, can be expressed as the sum of the latency time and the seek time for i. That is,

$$A(i) = L(i) + S(i)$$

An additional component, called the *transmission time* (T), is required to calculate the total time to complete a read or write operation. The transmission time, also called the *flow time*, is the time to read or write the record or series of records (so dictated by the I/O operation), given that the heads are positioned over the drum location of the first record to be read or written. The transmission time depends directly on how fast the drum rotates, as does the rotational delay. If we denote the total time to complete an operation i as $\tau(i)$, then

$$\tau(i) = L(i) + S(i) + T(i)$$

For a fixed-head drum, $S(i)$ is considered to be zero.

Note that $\tau(i)$ varies depending on where the heads are positioned, in the case of a movable-head drum, and at what location the first desired record is on the drum circumference associated with a track. Therefore, $\tau(i)$ will continually vary during the computer

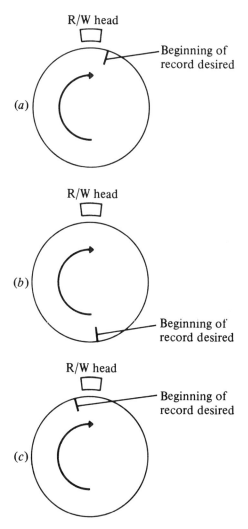

FIGURE 7-1.3 Conditions of (*a*) maximum, (*b*) average, and (*c*) minimum rotational delay.

system's operation. Consequently, a more useful statistic involves the average access time, which is the sum of the average seek time, and the average latency. That is,

$$\bar{A}(i) = \bar{L}(i) + \bar{S}(i)$$

Therefore, the average time to complete an I/O operation is

$$\bar{\tau}(i) = \bar{S}(i) + \bar{L}(i) + T(i) = \bar{A}(i) + T(i) \qquad (7\text{-}1.1)$$

Drums with fixed heads provide a very fast access time and data-transfer rate. They are expensive, however, and are most suitable as backup storage to main memory for programs which are being executed. A movable-head drum usually has a larger storage capacity and is more suitable for storing large volumes of data.

Examples of magnetic-drum devices are given in Table 7-1.1. The available storage capacity, sector capacity, access time, and data-transmission rate are given for each device. Note that IBM drums allow a variable format in storing data.

As mentioned previously, the addressable units (sectors or blocks) on drums are rapidly accessed for data transfers, and no scanning of extraneous data is required as with a magnetic tape. Also, unlike magnetic tape, a drum cannot be removed from its shaft or drive. Hence, the maximum storage capacity for a drum device is limited to the capacity of a single drum.

7-1.3 Magnetic Disks

The magnetic disk is a direct-access storage device which has become more widely used than the magnetic drum, mainly because of its lower cost. Disk devices provide relatively low access times and high-speed data transfer.

There are two types of disk devices, namely, fixed disks and exchangeable disks. For both types, the disk unit or pack consists of a number of metal platters which are stacked on top of each other on a spindle, as illustrated in Fig. 7-1.4. The upper and lower surfaces of each platter are coated with ferromagnetic particles that provide an informa-

Table 7-1.1 Magnetic drums.

System	IBM 360	UNIVAC 1108	UNIVAC FASTRAND	ICL 1900
Model	2301	FH 432	II	1964
Tracks/drum	200	128	6,144	512
Sector size (chars)	variable	6	168	4
Sectors/track	variable	2,048	64	1,024
Chars/track	20,483	12,288	10,752	4,048
Chars/drum	4,096,600	1,572,864	132,120,756	2,072,574
Avge. latency (ms)	8.6	4.25	35	20.5
Avge. seek time (ms)	0	0	58	0
Transmission rate (char/ms)	1,200	1,440	153.8	100

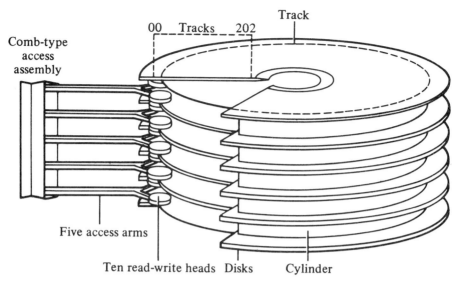

FIGURE 7-1.4 2311 disk-access mechanisms. (*Courtesy of IBM.*)

tion storage media. Often, the outermost surfaces of the top and bottom platters are not used for storing data, as they can be easily scratched or damaged.

The surfaces of each platter are divided into concentric bands called *tracks* (see Fig. 7-1.5). Just as in the case of the magnetic drum, each track is further subdivided into sectors (or blocks) which are the addressable storage units. Note that although the tracks vary in size, all tracks are capable of storing the same amount of information. Therefore, the recording density of the inner tracks is higher than the recording density of the outer tracks.

Information is transferred to or from a disk through read/write heads. Each read/write head floats just above or below the surface of a disk while the disk is rotating constantly at a high speed.

With a fixed-disk device, the disk unit is permanently mounted on the drive. Generally, each track of each disk recording surface has its own read/write head. This allows for fast access to data, since the seek time is essentially zero and a rotational delay is the only major component of access time.

An exchangeable-disk device has movable read/write heads. The heads are attached to a movable arm to form a comb-like access assembly, as shown in Fig. 7-1.4. When data on a particular track must be accessed, the whole assembly moves to position the read/write heads over the desired track. While many heads may be in position for a read/write transaction at a given point in time, data transmission can only take place through one head at one time. The complete head assembly can be moved free of the disk pack, thus allowing the pack to be removed and a new pack to be put in place.

The storage area on the disk to or from which data can be transferred without movement of the read/write heads is termed a *cylinder* or *seek area* (see Fig. 7-1.4). Hence, a cylinder is a set of vertically aligned tracks which reside on the platters of a disk. The cylinder concept applies to both fixed- and movable-head devices.

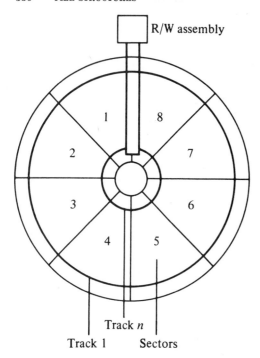

FIGURE 7-1.5   Disk surface of a sector-addressable disk.

Disk storage can be viewed as consisting of consecutively numbered cylinders. A *seek* is a movement of the read/write head to locate the cylinder in which a particular track resides. The time for a seek is the most significant delay when accessing data on a disk, just as it is when accessing data on a movable-head drum. Therefore, it is always desirable to minimize the total seek time. There is also rotational delay or latency in waiting for the disk surface to rotate to a sector or block where a data transfer can commence. Hence, the formula for the average time to complete an I/O operation given previously for magnetic drums applies to disks as well.

Characteristics of fixed- and exchangeable-disk units are summarized in Table 7-1.2 and 7-1.3, respectively. The IBM devices are block-oriented, and hence allow variable formats for data rather than the more rigid sector approach. It should also be noted that most of the disk devices have a number of drives, and hence a number of units or packs per device. The statistics given are for one unit or pack.

To provide a comparison of transaction times between comparable fixed and exchangeable disks, consider the problem of reading 4096 bytes of information from a track of a Burrough's B9370-2 fixed disk and a track of a CDC 853 exchangeable disk. Using formula 7-1.1, we have

$$\bar{\tau}_{B9870\text{-}2}(\text{read 4096 bytes}) = 17 \text{ ms} + \frac{4096 \text{ char}}{298.75 \text{ char/ms}}$$

$$= 17 \text{ ms} + 13.7 \text{ ms} = 30.7 \text{ ms}$$

Table 7-1.2 Fixed-disk units.

System	Burroughs B2500/3500	Digital PDP-11	IBM 360
Model	B9370-2	RS03	2305
Usable surfaces/unit	2	1	12
Tracks/surface	100	64	32
Sector size (chars)	100	64	variable
Sectors/track	100	64	variable
Chars/track	10,000	4,096	14,136
Chars/unit	2,000,000	262,144	5,428,224
Avge. latency (ms)	17	8.5	2.5
Transmission rate (char/ms)	298.75	250	3,000

$$\bar{\tau}_{853}(\text{read 4096 bytes}) = 85 \text{ ms} + 12.5 \text{ ms} + \frac{4096 \text{ char}}{288.3 \text{ char/ms}}$$

$$= 97.5 \text{ ms} + 14.2 \text{ ms} = 111.7 \text{ ms}$$

Observe that the total transaction time using the fixed disk is almost one-third of the average seek time for the exchangeable disk. This clearly illustrates the importance of minimizing seek time for disks with a movable arm.

Presently, disk storage devices are the most versatile storage device available. They can provide large capacity and fast access time, and hence satisfy the needs of most computer systems.

Table 7-1.3 Exchangeable-disk packs.

System	CDC 3100/3300	HP 2100	IBM 370		
Model	853	2315	2311	2314	3330
Usable surfaces/unit	10	4	10	20	19
Tracks/surface	100	200	203	200	404
Sector size (chars)	256	256	variable	variable	variable
Sectors/track	16	24	variable	variable	variable
Chars/track	4,096	6,144	3,650	7,294	13,030
Chars/unit	4,096,000	4,915,200	7,250,000	29,176,000	100,018,290
Avge. latency (ms)	12.5	12.5	12.5	12.5	8.3
Avge. seek time (ms)	85	30	75	60	30
Transmission rate (char/ms)	288.3	312.5	156	312	806

7-1.4   Mass Storage Devices

In the early 1960s, several computer manufacturers (NCR, IBM, ICL, and RCA) began marketing direct-access devices, called *card/strip devices*, that have storage capacities on the order of one-half billion characters. A card/strip device consists of groups (decks, magazines, cells, or arrays) of magnetic cards or strips on which data are encoded. The basic principle of operation for these devices involves the selection of a card from a group and the transportation of this card to a revolving cylinder, or *capstan*. The card is wrapped around the capstan and data are then transferred to or from the card via the read/write heads.

Because they are very mechanical in operation, these devices typically have an access time that is greater than one-half second. Their greatest advantage is their large storage capacity; however, magnetic-disk storage devices have been steadily increasing in capacity and decreasing in cost per bit, thus making magnetic card or strip devices obsolete.

While the card/strip devices have fallen into disuse, the principle by which they operate has been applied to the new IBM 3851 Mass Storage Facility (MSF). This mass storage device provides a third-level (tertiary) storage facility which contains the archival (permanent) information for the computer system. On-line, multibillion character database systems are now coming into existence, and with such systems, it becomes too expensive and impractical to store such large amounts of information on disk storage devices. Instead, it is more realistic to store copies of the "often-accessed" programs and data on disk, and to store all programs and data of the system on a cheaper, yet slower, mass storage unit. When a program and its data are required for on-line use, a copy is made on one of the direct-access secondary-memory devices and it is this copy that is used for as long as is necessary to complete the transactions associated with that particular program and its data. When these transactions are completed, the disk copy is returned to the mass storage device, replacing the old copy.

The IBM system which uses the 3851 Mass Storage Facility is called the 3850 Mass Storage System. IBM 3330 disk devices (as described in Table 7-1.3) are used as secondary storage. The 3851 MSF uses tape cartridges as its storage media. A tape cartridge is a spool of magnetic tape, 4 inches long and 2 inches in diameter, and has the capacity of one half of an IBM 3330 disk pack. Access to a particular cartridge is gained after the cartridge is located from a library of cartridges, and wrapped around a capstan so that it is properly positioned under a set of read/write heads. Data can be transferred cylinder by cylinder from the IBM 3330 to a tape cartridge and vice versa. The 3851 MSF can contain a maximum of 4,720 tape cartridges, creating a total capacity of 236 billion characters. It is not hard to envision that in the future mass storage devices such as the IBM 3851 will substantially reduce, if not eliminate, the need for storing large volumes of data off-line on reels of tape or removable disk packs.

7-1.5   Intermediate Storage Devices

A new development in the area of external storage devices is the electronic disk. The electronic disk is named "electronic" because it provides fast access times without mechanical movement. It is an intermediate form of storage because it is being developed to fill the gap between main memory and direct-access storage. This is achieved by having a lower cost than main memory and a lower access time than is currently available with external storage devices.

The devices that currently show the greatest potential for being an acceptable electronic disk are *charge-coupled devices*. They are based on semiconductor technology, but their cost per bit should be one-third that of main memory. The average access time they provide is 60 microseconds.

Other candidates for electronic disks include the domain tip propagation, electron beam, and magnetic bubbles technologies.

Exercises for Sec. 7-1

1. Calculate the number of 80-column punched card records that can be stored on a magnetic tape that is 3,600 feet in length assuming:
   (a) One record per block, 1,600 bytes-per-inch density, and ¾-inch interrecord gaps
   (b) Five records per block, 1,600 bytes-per-inch density, and ¾-inch interblock gaps
   (c) Twenty-five records per block, 3,200 bytes-per-inch density, and ½-inch interblock gaps
   (d) One record per block, 800 bytes-per-inch density, and ½-inch interrecord gaps

2. A number of standard tape densities, such as those given in Exercise 1, are used in the computer industry. Obviously, these are not effective tape density figures, since they are independent of the block size and the interblock gap size. Derive a formula for the effective tape density (expressed in effective bytes per inch) which is dependent upon three factors: standard density, block size, and gap size.

3. Calculate the effective density for (a), (b), (c), and (d) of Exercise 1.

4. Suppose average tape speeds of 125 inches per second and 30 inches per second are attained when reading recorded information and passing over gaps, respectively. Calculate the time required to read the tape configurations given in Exercise 1.

5. Direct-access devices are sometimes called *random-access devices*. What is the basis for this synonym-type of relationship?

6. How many tracks of a UNIVAC FASTRAND II drum are required to store a file of 10,000 records each 80 bytes in length, assuming records are not allowed to span sector boundaries? How long does it take to read the file if an initial average access time is included in the timing estimate?

7. Solve Exercise 6 assuming an IBM 2301 drum is available instead. Assume that 14 bytes of system information is stored per block and that a blocking factor of twenty is used. Records are not allowed to span track boundaries.

8. Compute the expected time to locate and read a particular 64-character record residing on the following disks: (a) Digital RS03, (b) IBM 3330, and (c) HP 2315. Suppose we are updating the record instead of reading it. In most systems, a read operation takes place immediately after a write operation. This additional read operation, which takes a time of one period of revolution, is needed to verify that the information placed in the direct-access device is correct.

9. Assume an average access time is required to commence reading two files of 64-byte records—one resides on a Digital RS03 and the other resides on an IBM 2314. How many records must be in each of the files in order that the total read time be equal (or approximately equal)? Make the same assumptions about the storage of records on the IBM 2314 that were made about the IBM 2301 in Exercise 7.

7-2   DEFINITIONS AND CONCEPTS

Many of the definitions and terminology used in the remainder of this chapter are introduced in this subsection. Because some of the concepts directly relate to external device characteristics, we have chosen to place this subsection after the discussion of external devices. Some of the terms that will be presented have been introduced previously. We reintroduce them here to provide a comprehensive and consistent overview of the hierarchy of information structures associated with file processing.

A *record* (sometimes called a *group* or *segment*) is a collection of information items about a particular entity. For example, a record may consist of information about a passenger on an airplane flight, or an article sold at a retail distribution store. An *item* (sometimes called a *field*) of a record is a unit of meaningful information about an entity. The different items of a passenger record may be the passenger's name, address, seat number, and menu restrictions. Generally, an item of a record is an integer, real, or character-string data element. However, items may themselves be composed of aggregates of items, such as an array of items or a subcollection of nonhomogeneous items. In PL/I, the notion of a record in its most general interpretation can be loosely equated to a structure. For example, a possible structure for a passenger record is declared as follows:

```
DECLARE 1 PASSENGER,
          2 NAME,
            3 INITIALS CHAR(2),
            3 SURNAME CHAR(20),
          2 ADDRESS CHAR(30),
          2 SEAT_NO CHAR(2),
          2 MENU CHAR(35);
```

A collection of records involving a set of entities with certain aspects in common and organized for some particular purpose is called a *file*. For example, the collection of all passenger records for the passengers on a particular flight constitutes a file.

A record item that uniquely identifies a record in a file is called a *key*. In the passenger file, individual passenger records can be uniquely identified by the passenger's name, assuming duplicate names do not occur for a particular flight. The seat-number item can also be used as a key, if desired, since seat numbers are uniquely assigned for a given flight.

It is a common practice to order the records in a file according to a key. Therefore, if the passenger name is selected as the key item, then the record for Adams appears before the record for Brown, which appears before the record for Camp in a lexical ordering by surname. Some files are ordered on a particular item, termed the *sequence item*, which may not be unique for each record. For example, in a file of monthly sales for a particular company, several records containing sales information may appear for one customer. The file can be ordered by customer account number with more than one occurrence of a record for a given account number.

Thus far we have observed a hierarchy of information structures in which items are composed to form records and records are composed to form files. Files can be composed to form a set of files. If the set of files is used by the application programs for some particular enterprise or application area, and if these files exhibit certain associations or relationships between the records of the files, then such a collection of files is referred to as a *data base*. Figure 7-2.1 shows the information-structure hierarchy as it applies to file-processing applications.

Items, records, files and data bases are logical terms in the sense that they have been introduced without any indication as to how they can be realized physically on an external device. A number of file structure concepts are associated with these logical terms. In the last subsection, we described how records are physically stored on several external storage devices. In particular, we pointed out that a logical record, as viewed by the programmer, can be grouped together with several other records to form a single physical entity called a *block* or *physical record*. This blocking of records does not affect the logical processing of those records. However, it does allow the processing to take place more efficiently because the number of read or write commands per logical record, as issued by the operating system, can be reduced significantly.

The term *file* has assumed both a logical and physical interpretation in the data-processing community. Physically, a file is considered to be a collection of physical records which almost always reside contiguously in external memory. To provide proper access to the physical records in the file, a number of tables are kept by the storage management routines in the operating system. These tables, along with other control information, which is stored in the physical record (such as the length of the record), are transparent to the user who is working with the file at a logical level.

In IBM systems, the physical file is often referred to as a *data set*. The physical makeup of the data set is described with a DD (Data Definition) statement in the JCL (Job Control Language) provided. A number of such statements will be described in the file-organization sections of this chapter.

A physical record is composed of fields made up of bytes and words of binary-encoded information. The term *physical field* can be associated with a binary-encoded information element that corresponds to an item or field of a logical record. For simplicity and consistency, we will use the term "field" when describing the field of a physical record, and "item" when referring to the field of a logical record. We will discover that there are some fields in a physical record, in particular, fields containing system maintained pointers, which have no counterpart items in the logical description of a record.

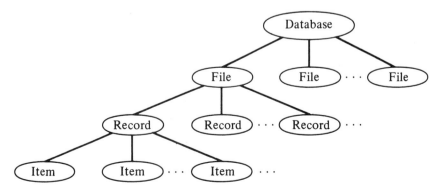

FIGURE 7-2.1   Information structure hierarchy for file processing.

Having introduced most of the terminology needed for our discussion of files, let us examine some of the factors which affect the organization of a file. The prime factor which determines the organization of a file is the nature of the operations that are to be performed on the file, as dictated by the application. The operations normally performed are the same as those discussed previously in the text; namely addition, deletion, and update. A particular operation involving a record or set of records is called a *transaction*. For example, "Delete Peter Hardy from the passenger list for Flight 279" is a transaction. Transactions are often processed against a file or set of files in the form of *transaction records*. These transaction records contain the keys of the records to be processed, along with the desired operation and any additional information required to complete the operation. In the sections to follow, we will see that the selection of a file organization not only depends on the operations or types of transactions, but also on the volume of transactions, the frequency with which transactions are submitted, and the response time required in the completion of a transaction or set of transactions.

The organization of a file is also dependent on the external storage media on which it is to reside. For example, we will discover that the file organization on a sequential device, such as a magnetic tape, differs appreciably from the file organizations that can be accommodated on a direct-access storage device such as a magnetic disk.

Other important concepts which we discuss and illustrate later in this chapter involve file generation and file reorganization.

7-3   RECORD ORGANIZATION

In the previous section, we described a record as an entity composed of items or fields. In this section, we concentrate on an important aspect of record organization, namely, the structure of record items.

Before discussing this aspect, the concept of the *range* of an item must be presented. The range of an item is simply those values which an item can assume. For example, if we are designing an application dealing with space allocation in a university, then one obvious item is the building location for a room in a record describing the attributes of a particular room. The range of values for such an item might typically represent the Administration, Agriculture, Arts, Chemistry, Commerce, Education, Engineering, General Purpose, Law, Medical, and Physics buildings. When all the range values for an item are known, such as in the last example, the item is said to have a *precoordinated range*. Some record items which contain textual information are not precoordinated. For example, in a record for a bibliography system, an item may be devoted to an abstract of a book. Obviously, not all book abstracts are known prior to the establishment of a file of bibliographic information.

We now present a spectrum of methods for representing both types of items and begin with techniques for precoordinated items.

Logically encoded items

For each possible value of a precoordinated item, a single logical value is reserved in a vector or string of logical values which constitute the item. In the item containing a building location of a room, we can allocate a bit value for each building on campus. We let the first value represent the Administration Building, the second value represent the Agriculture Building, and so on, finally letting the eleventh and final value represent the Physics Building. A record item with a value of '01000000000'B in PL/I bit-string notation represents the Agriculture Building if the logical values of 1 and 0 are used to denote the presence and absence of item values, respectively.

A logical-valued format has the tremendous advantage of being capable of representing a multifaceted item (i.e., an item which can take on more than one range value). For example, '10001000011'B indicates the Administration, Commerce, Medical, and Physics buildings. Of course, such a multifaceted item does not make sense in a record describing the properties of a room. However, if the item appears in the records of a file indicating the availability of certain facilities such as air conditioning, cafeteria services, libraries, etc., then a multifaceted item is needed. Note that a logically-encoded item is a fixed-length item which can represent a variable number of values from the range of an item. This is an important attribute, since variable-length items generate variable-length records and variable-length records cannot be processed as efficiently as fixed-length records. Further discussion on this subject takes place at the end of this section.

Binary-encoded items

A method involving binary encoding utilizes storage more efficiently than the logical-encoding method just discussed. If we assume an item has a range set of size n, then we can encode these item values using a binary scheme in which each element of the scheme is of length $\lceil \log_2 n \rceil$. An example of this type of encoding was given in Table 1-1.1 and discussed in Sec. 1-1. Basically, a binary-encoding scheme is established by assigning a unique binary number to each value of the item's range set. Table 7-3.1 illustrates a binary encoding represented in PL/I bit-string notation for the example set of campus buildings.

First it should be observed that, when using a binary-encoded scheme, an item value can be represented in 4 bits, whereas 11 bits are required for a logically-encoded item. However, multifaceted items cannot be represented unless they are incorporated in the encoding scheme (for example, '1111'B could represent the presence of both the Administration and Arts buildings).

Table 7-3.1

Building	Encoded Value	Building	Encoded Value
Administration	'0000'B	Engineering	'0110'B
Agriculture	'0001'B	General Purpose	'0111'B
Arts	'0010'B	Law	'1000'B
Chemistry	'0011'B	Medical	'1001'B
Commerce	'0100'B	Physics	'1010'B
Education	'0101'B		

Huffman encoded items

A Huffman encoding scheme makes use of an assumed set of item-value probabilities for items in the range set. Given these probabilities, a minimum average-length binary code can be constructed for each item in the precoordinated range. A Huffman encoding of the building location item is given in Table 7-3.2, assuming a priori knowledge of the listed probabilities. This a priori knowledge is essential in the derivation of Huffman-coded items.

In a Huffman coding scheme, a short code is associated with an item value which has a high probability of occurrence, and a long code is assigned to an item value with a low probability of occurrence. The expected or average length of a building-location item is found using the formula:

$$\text{Average length} = \sum_{i=1}^{n} l_i \times p_i,$$

where l_i and p_i are the length and probability associated with code i, respectively. Therefore, the average length of a building location item is

$$2 \times 1/4 + 2 \times 3/16 + 3 \times 1/8 + 3 \times 1/8 + 4 \times 1/16 + 5 \times 1/16 + 5 \times 1/16$$

$$+ 4 \times 1/16 + 5 \times 1/32 + 6 \times 1/64 + 6 \times 1/64 = 3\,3/32 \text{ bits} \simeq 3.09 \text{ bits}$$

Recall from Sec. 1-1, Eq. (1-1.1) for computing the average amount of information transmitted from a source, that is,

$$H = -\sum_{i=1}^{n} p_i \log_2 (p_i)$$

Applying this formula to the probabilities of the item values as given in Table 7-3.2, we have

$$H = -1/4 \times \log_2(1/4) - 3/16 \times \log_2(3/16) - \cdots - 1/64 \times \log_2 1/64 \simeq 3.04 \text{ bits}$$

Table 7-3.2

Location	Probability	Code
Arts	1/4	10
Engineering	3/16	00
Education	1/8	110
Medical	1/8	011
Commerce	1/16	1110
General Purpose	1/16	11111
Chemistry	1/16	11110
Law	1/16	0101
Agriculture	1/32	01001
Administration	1/64	010001
Physics	1/64	010000

Therefore the expected length of the building-location item is almost equal to the average amount of information transmitted for a given building-location item. Since H represents the minimum average amount of information needed to transmit a coded-item value, it is apparent that the Huffman coding scheme given in Table 7-3.2 is very efficient from a storage point of view. This efficiency is further supported by the realization that the same item, logically encoded and fixed-length binary encoded, requires 11 and 4 bits, respectively.

Let us briefly explain with the aid of Fig. 7-3.1 how a Huffman code is generated. It is assumed initially that each item value has as its code word an empty string. To produce a Huffman code, we order the item values according to their probabilities—from the item value with the largest probability to the item value with the smallest probability. Next, the item value with the smallest probability has a 0 concatenated at the front of its code word, and the item value with the second smallest probability has a 1 concatenated at the front of its code word. (Note that the second smallest can be equal to the smallest.) These item values are then grouped together to form a new item value with a probability equal to the sum of the two probabilities of the combined values. The table is then reordered, if necessary, and again the last two item values have each of their code words appended with a 0 or 1. These item values are then combined and the process is repeated. The entire procedure is terminated when the table is reduced to a size of two, and the final sets of item values have the appropriate binary values concatenated to the end of their code words. In Fig. 7-3.1, a trace of the derivation of the code word 010000, representing the Physics Building, is illustrated using bold arrows. The development of iterative and recursive algorithms for the derivation of a Huffman code is left as an exercise at the end of this section.

Huffman codes have two important properties. First, it can be proven (see Abramson [1963]) that a Huffman code is a minimum average-length binary code. Hence, Huffman-coded record items are minimum average-length items. It should also be noted that Huffman codes have the *prefix property*. That is, no other assigned code in a generated set of codes C is the prefix of another code. Or, for a given y ϵ C, there does not exist an x ϵ C such that x $\bigcirc$ z = y for some nonempty binary string z. Therefore, in a simple linear scan of a Huffman-encoded bit string, we can isolate the next coded-item value because of its unique prefix. For example, suppose we are scanning a record with the binary information '110100011 ... ' to isolate the next value for the building-location item. The Education Building as represented by '110'B is the item value and '100011...' is the remainder of the record. It can be seen that the prefix property is extremely important when decoding a variable-length record item.

Of course the main disadvantage with Huffman codes is that they are variable-length codes. Processing time is required in order to isolate an item value when it can assume any one of many different lengths.

Fixed items

When a record item has a fixed-length value and its range set is too large for an efficient bit encoding, a primitive data-structure (i.e., integer, real, string, etc.) format should be selected for the representation of the item. For example, it is unreasonable to bit encode an item representing the net sales for the month. Instead, we can declare a record containing

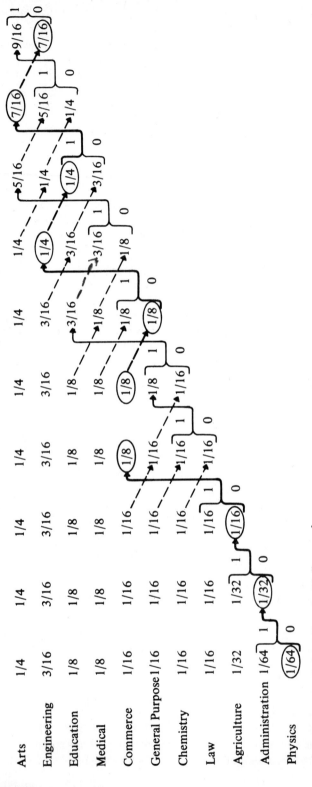

FIGURE 7-3.1 Construction of a Huffman code.

such an item in the programming language being used. In PL/I this declaration can be expressed as follows:

```
DECLARE 1 MONTHLY_REPORT,
        2 MONTH CHAR(9),
        2 NET_SALES FIXED(8,2),
        .
        .
        .
```

The net sales item can range in value from -999999.99 to 999999.99. It is unrealistic for the programmer to bit encode such a wide range of item values when the compiler provides an efficient encoding of an item value in binary with a fixed-decimal format. Note that the record item represented by MONTH can be significantly reduced in size if we use a fixed-length binary code of '0000'B for January, '0001'B for February, ..., '1011'B for December and declare the item to be of a type BIT(4). Other examples of record items which have range sets that are too large to be bit encoded are surnames and catalogue numbers.

Because both of these items may be considered as fixed-length items, they can technically be called precoordinated. That is, a fixed-length item can only have a finite set of values which can be a priori enumerated. However, we reserve the term precoordinated for those range sets which are completely established beforehand; in most systems dealing with surnames and catalogue numbers, such a priori knowledge is not available.

Thus far, we have examined record structures in which the items are fixed length, with the exception of Huffman-coded items. Let us now look at some record organizations involving items that often lead to variable-length records.

Repeating items

Many applications arise in which the value associated with a record item may be a list of entities. For example, "the degrees held" and "the programming languages used at a computer installation" are items which can assume multiple entities. In these instances, the item values may be "B.Sc., M.Sc., Ph.D." or "COBOL, FORTRAN, PL/I, BASIC," respectively.

The most popular method of handling repeating fields is to create an item which can accommodate up to some maximum number of replications. If we restrict this maximum number to *three*, then the example items can accommodate such information as "the three most recent degrees obtained" and "the three most often used programming languages."

Some computer systems allow the handling of a repeated item as a variable-length item, provided the item appears last in the record definition. This type of variable-length record is permitted in PL/I.

Tagged items

A tagged item is an item that contains not only information pertinent to a particular application, but also information concerning the structure of the item itself. For example, in a personnel system in which records are kept concerning the history of the employees

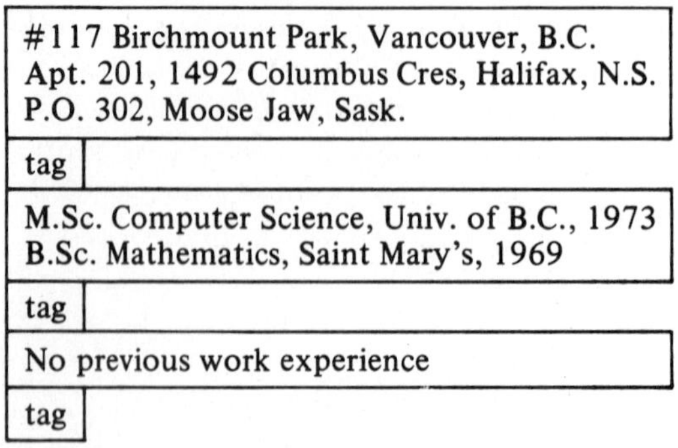

| #117 Birchmount Park, Vancouver, B.C. Apt. 201, 1492 Columbus Cres, Halifax, N.S. P.O. 302, Moose Jaw, Sask. |
| tag |
| M.Sc. Computer Science, Univ. of B.C., 1973 B.Sc. Mathematics, Saint Mary's, 1969 |
| tag |
| No previous work experience |
| tag |

FIGURE 7-3.2   Illustration of a preformatted personnel record with tagged items.

of a company, several data items may be recorded such as previous addresses, education, previous work experience, yearly achievement reports, etc. Instead of creating repeated items for each of these information fields, it can be more advantageous to store tags with each item. In general, a tag is used in one of two ways. One method assumes a fixed predetermined ordering of items in the record, and tag information is used to delimit items, as shown in Fig. 7-3.2. Item delimiting can be achieved by either a boundary-marker method or length descriptor method as described in Sec. 2-4.

The second approach to record organization using tagged items is to include, in the tag, a description or name of the item, as shown in Fig. 7-3.3. Using this technique, it is not required that item values for a record occur in any predetermined order. Of course, the added flexibility of a tag which dynamically describes the record syntax results in an increase in record length.

Textual items

There is a final type of record item which differs from the other item forms discussed thus far. Its difference is primarily due to the size of an item. By a textual item, we mean an item containing a large amount of textual information such as text for a manuscript, for

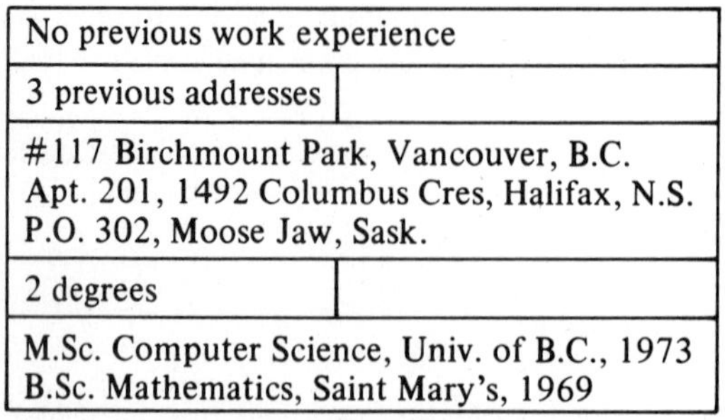

| No previous work experience |
| 3 previous addresses |
| #117 Birchmount Park, Vancouver, B.C. Apt. 201, 1492 Columbus Cres, Halifax, N.S. P.O. 302, Moose Jaw, Sask. |
| 2 degrees |
| M.Sc. Computer Science, Univ. of B.C., 1973 B.Sc. Mathematics, Saint Mary's, 1969 |

FIGURE 7-3.3   Illustration of self-descriptive tagged items in a personnel record.

the abstract of a book, for a company report, or for a newspaper's want ad. Typically, records for such items are single-item records. Because of the length of the textual-type record, it is not uncommon to decompose such a record and store it in several physical records or blocks. Data-compression techniques are often necessary to reduce the amount of storage required for textual items. One technique is to use a word-level *concordance* on the full text. In a concordance each unique word in the text is stored along with the various positions at which that word appears in the text. For example, a concordance of the previous sentence is given in Table 7-3.3. Usually, the word list for the concordance is arranged in alphabetical order. To restore the text to its "natural" form, it is necessary to concatenate the words together in an order dictated by the numbers in the position field of the concordance. The bit saving in terms of compression is in multiple occurrence of words such as "the" and "in," which are stored only once in the concordance.

The Huffman coding scheme discussed earlier might also be used in an attempt to reduce the length of the textual item.

In addition to restoring text to its uncompressed form, compressed information may require other types of processing. For example, can you imagine performing text-editing operations on text stored in a concordance form! In some applications, the additional processing time is the overriding factor.

Pointer items

In the remaining sections of this chapter, we will discover that a very important type of record item is an item which contains information that references another record in the file, and in some instances, a record in another file. The pointer information may be in the form of a key of another record, a relative record position in a file, or an absolute physical address based on a cylinder, track, segment (or block) address. In our discussion of direct files in Sec. 7-8, we will examine pointer items in detail and illustrate their use with some examples.

Before concluding this section, a final comment must be made concerning variable-length records. Variable-length records are used primarily in situations in which the

Table 7-3.3

Word	Position(s)	Word	Position(s)
a	2	stored	11
along	12	text	9, 24
appears	21	that	19
at	17	the	8, 14, 23
concordance	3	unique	5
each	4	various	15
in	1, 7, 22	which	18
is	10	with	13
positions	16	word	6, 20

record structure varies considerably from one record item to another in a file. They are used to save storage. Variable-length items such as Huffman-encoded items, repeated items, and tagged items are designed specifically to conserve storage. However, some additional processing time is required to encode and decode a record's format when such items are used. Usually, the development of programs to perform this encoding and decoding are left to the application programmer, since in many situations the format is application-dependent. Therefore, before adopting variable-length record formats, we should be aware of the problems which can arise. In the next section, a detailed description of a file structure used for variable-length records is given. After examining the format of a variable-length record, we can better appreciate the complexity involved in processing such a record.

In summary, we can say that items with a small precoordinated range can be efficiently represented using one of the binary-encoding schemes. Items with large range sets can best be represented in the data description facilities of the programming language in use. Multifaceted and replicated items generate variable-length records, unless they can be logically encoded, and textual information which is subject to very little text processing should be compressed. With a discussion of record organization completed, we can now consider how various types of items discussed in this section can be utilized to form the records which determine the organization of a file.

Exercises for Sec. 7-3

1. Give a practical example of a multifaceted record item for which a logical encoding would be appropriate.

2. A large multinational company manufactures its products in a number of cities. The value for an item in a record which describes a manufactured product contains one of the following city names: New York, Tokyo, Chicago, London, San Francisco, Paris, Montreal, Detroit, Düsseldorf, Mexico City, and St. Louis. Design a fixed-length binary code for the values of the item corresponding to a manufacturing location. How many more cities can be added to the list before the code length must be increased?

3. Develop an iterative algorithm for the derivation of a Huffman code given a set of probabilities $p_1, \ldots, p_n$ for n item values.

4. Design a recursive algorithm for the derivation of a Huffman code given a set of probabilities $p_1, \ldots, p_n$ for n item values.

5. The item values given in Exercise 2 are known to have the following approximate probabilities of occurrence, respectively, in a record describing a manufactured product: 1/4, 1/6, 1/8, 1/8, 1/12, 1/12, 1/16, 1/24, 1/48, 1/48, 1/48. Generate a Huffman code for these items. What is the expected length of an item using this code?

6. Compute the average amount of information transmitted (i.e., the information entropy) for the record item in Exercise 2 with the probabilities given in Exercise 5. What are the efficiencies of the codes derived in Exercise 2 and Exercise 5?

7. Describe how you would organize a record for a personnel file, which involves the following items: (a) name, (b) address, (c) number of years with company, (d) work classification (assume a fixed number of classifications are used), (e) degrees held, and (f) previous jobs held. Create a PL/I structure which is representative of the record.

8. Derive a word-level concordance for the first three sentences in this chapter, excluding the title.

9. What type of storage structures would you choose to represent the following record items:

  (a) The number of miles traveled by a salesman per month
  (b) The days of the week
  (c) Aunt Matilda's favorite recipes
  (d) The weather conditions for the day as best described by one of the following categories: clear, cloudy, overcast, raining, snowing, hurricane, or tornado
  (e) The same as number (d), but assume more than one category name can be used in the daily description
  (f) Former places of residence

7-4 SEQUENTIAL FILES

In Sec. 7-2, we noted that most operating systems provide a set of basic file organizations that are popular with the users of the system. The three most common types of organizations are sequential, indexed sequential, and direct, which are discussed in this section, Sec. 7-6, and Sec. 7-8, respectively. The presentation of each of these organizations begins with a description of its file structure. Next, the type of processing that can be accomplished with the file organization is examined and then exemplified by algorithms. Finally, each section contains a discussion of how files with that particular type of organization can be processed in PL/I. Applications illustrating each type of organization will be given in separate sections.

7-4.1 The Structure of Sequential Files

In a sequential file, records are stored one after the other on a storage device. Of course, a sequential type of storage representation is not new to us. Previously, we discussed the sequential representation of characters in a string, of arrays, and of certain linear and nonlinear lists. Because sequential allocation is conceptually simple, yet flexible enough to cope with many of the problems associated with handling large volumes of data, a sequential file has been the most popular basic file structure used in the data-processing industry.

All types of external storage devices support a sequential-file organization. Some devices, by their physical nature, can only support sequential files. For example, as described in Sec. 7-1, information is stored on a magnetic tape as a continuous series of records along the length of the tape. Accessing a particular record requires the accessing of all previous records in the file. Other devices which are strictly sequential in nature are paper tape readers, card readers, tape cassettes, and line printers.

Magnetic disks and drums provide both direct and sequential access to records, and hence support sequential files along with other types of files to be described later. A sequential file is physically placed on a drum or disk by storing the sequence of records in adjacent locations on a track. Of course, if the file is larger than the amount of space available on a track, then the records are stored on adjacent tracks. This notion of physical adjacency can be extended to cylinders and even to complete storage devices where more than one device is attached to a common control unit.

The operations that can be performed on a sequential file may differ slightly, depending on the storage device used. For example, a file on magnetic tape can be either an input file or output file, but not both at one time. A sequential file on disk can be used strictly for input, strictly for output, or for update. Update means that, as records are read, the record most recently read can be rewritten on the *same* file, if so desired. Some operating systems provide file-accessing facilities which allow a file to be extended by writing records after the current last record. Also, it is sometimes possible to move backwards and forwards a certain number of records in the file without reading or writing. This extension is beyond the scope of basic sequential-file processing and will not be elaborated upon.

Before discussing the type of processing that is normally applied to sequential files, it is important to examine how information on a file is transmitted to a user program and vice versa. In the previous sections in this chapter, we have defined a logical record and discussed the organization of such a record. In Sec. 7-1.1, it was suggested that it is often advantageous to group a number of logical records into a single physical record or block. Complete blocks and not individual records are transferred between main memory and the external storage.

Note, however, that the execution of a read or write instruction in a high-level programming language such as PL/I corresponds to the handling of only one logical record, as specified in the parameter list of an instruction. For example, consider the PL/I instruction

    READ FILE (MASTER) INTO (EMPLOYEE);

where EMPLOYEE is declared to be a PL/I structure as follows:

    DECLARE 1 EMPLOYEE,
              2 NAME,
                3 SURNAME CHAR(20),
                3 INITIALS CHAR(6),
              2 SOC_INS # FIXED(9),
              2 WAGE_PER_HR FIXED(5, 2),
              2 CLASSFCTN CHAR(3);

Each time the READ instruction is executed, the next record from the MASTER sequential file is moved into the program area and assigned to the structure EMPLOYEE. However, each time a read or write operation is executed for a particular storage device, a block of logical records is transferred. The apparent difference in a program's read and write statements and the read and write commands issued for a particular device is resolved by using a *buffer* between external storage and the data area of a program. A buffer is a section of main memory which is equal in size to the maximum size of a block of logical records used by a program. The data-management routines of the operating system use buffers for the "blocking" and "deblocking" of records.

To illustrate how the blocking and deblocking of records is accomplished using a buffer, consider the use of the MASTER sequential file as an input file. When the first READ statement is executed, a block of records is moved from external storage to a buffer. The first record in the block is then transferred to the program's data area, as illustrated in Fig. 7-4.1. For each subsequent execution of a READ statement, the next successive record in the buffer is transferred to the data area. Only after every record in the buffer has been moved to the data area, in response to READ statements, does the next READ statement cause another block to be transferred to the buffer from external storage. The new records in the buffer are moved to the data area, as described previously, and this entire process is repeated for each block that is read.

In a similar fashion, WRITE statements cause the transfer of program data to the buffer. When the buffer becomes full (corresponding to a block of logical records), then the block is written on the external storage device immediately after the preceding block of records.

The buffering technique just described is commonly called *single buffering*. *Multiple buffering* makes use of a queue of buffers which are normally controlled by the operating system. The need for more than one buffer arises because of the delay (which is in the order of milliseconds) necessary to read in or write out the next block of records. This delay in the execution of a program only occurs after every n executions of the READ or WRITE statement, when a blocking factor of n and a single buffer is used. However, if the program is executing in an environment where the desired response time is small and where processor and input/output activity need to be overlapped, then it is wise to eliminate this delay by using multiple buffers.

A circular queue of three buffers is shown in Fig. 7-4.2. When the first READ statement is executed, the three buffers, A, B, and C are filled with three consecutive blocks, one block per buffer. After all the records in buffer A have been processed, the execution of a subsequent READ instruction results in the transfer of the first record from buffer B to the program's data area. Concurrently, a read command is issued by the operating system and a block transfer from the sequential file on the external storage device to buffer A is initiated. Subsequent executions of READ instructions on the MASTER file cause records to

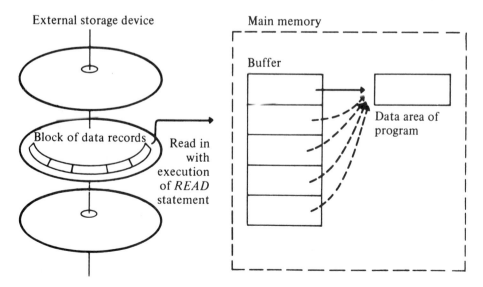

FIGURE 7-4.1 Illustration of the reading in of a block of records.

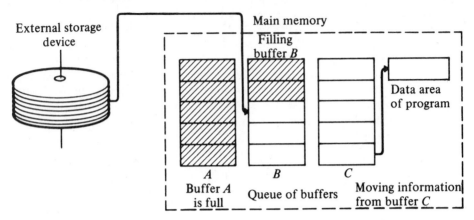

External storage device

Main memory

Filling buffer B

Data area of program

A
Buffer A is full

B
Queue of buffers

C
Moving information from buffer C

FIGURE 7-4.2   Three-buffer system.

be transferred in sequence from buffer B and then buffer C. By the time the records of buffer C are being processed, buffer A contains a new buffer full of records and buffer B is being refilled. If the process of filling one buffer with new records is generally balanced with the process of reading records from the remaining buffers, then the program should normally experience only one read or write delay, namely, when the buffers are initially being filled.

In some systems, such as an IBM 370 system, blocks of logical records which constitute a sequential file can be either fixed length (the case we have considered so far) or variable length. A variable-length block contains variable-length records. Therefore, it is not known how many records fit in a block, and hence a maximum length is defined for the block. This maximum length is used to estimate the size of a buffer needed to hold the block, and as many records as possible are grouped into the block by the data-management facilities. Figure 7-4.3 shows the record format for variable-length blocked and unblocked records. Note that a BL (block length) and an RL (record length) must be stored with each block and record, respectively. These lengths are needed when unblocking the records during a READ instruction.

The maximum length of a block depends on the storage device used for the file. With magnetic tape, the length depends on the maximum space available for the buffer in main memory. With disk storage, blocks are generally limited in size to the capacity of a track. Using a sector-addressable device, a block corresponds to some maximum number of sectors.

7-4.2   Processing Sequential Files

Having discussed the physical layout of a sequential file and how records are transferred to/from the program area from/to the file, let us examine the types of processing for which sequential files are most suitable. *Serial processing* is the accessing of records, one after the other, according to the physical order in which they appear in the file. Obviously, it is an easy matter to process a sequential file serially. *Sequential processing* is the accessing of records, one after the other, in ascending order by a key or index item of the record. If, for

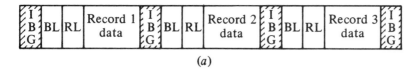

(a)

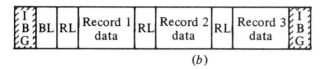

(b)

FIGURE 7-4.3 Record format for variable-length (a) unblocked, and (b) blocked records.

example, a MASTER file of employees' records is ordered by employee surname (e.g., the record for ADAMS is first, BAKER second, ..., ZURCHER last), then sequentially processing the file by surname is equivalent to serially processing the file. Most sequential files are ordered by a key or index item such as employee name, student identification number, or store catalogue number, when the file is created. The key or index item should be the item which is most often searched for when processing the file. To show the importance of key selection, assume the MASTER file of employees is ordered by social insurance number. Suppose we want to find the records of a number of employees given only their names. Finding the first employee's record, say ADAMS, is simply a matter of serially processing the file until a record with a name item of ADAMS appears (ignoring the possibility of name duplications). Consider the processing of a second record, say for BAKER. Since the position of BAKER's record bears no relationship with the position of ADAM's record, we have no alternative but to start once again serially processing at the beginning of the MASTER file.

On rare occasions, serial processing is all that is required on a file, irrespective of the key or item index upon which the file is ordered. For example, if we are to add a pay increase of \$2/hour to the wage item of all employees, it is irrelevant whether the file is sequenced by name or by social insurance number.

In sequential processing, transaction records are usually grouped together (i.e., batched) and are sorted according to the same index item as records in the file. Each successive record of the file is read, compared with an incoming transaction record, and then processed in a manner that is usually dependent upon whether the value of the record's index item is less than, equal to, or greater than the value of the index item of the transaction record.

Sequential and serial processing are most effective when a high percentage of the records in a file must be processed. Since every record in the file must be scanned, a relatively large number of transactions should be batched together for processing. If records are to be added to a file, it is necessary to create a new file unless the records are to be added to the end of the file. In many systems no facilities are provided which allow the direct extension of a sequential file. Records can be deleted from a sequential file by tagging them as "deleted" during a file update. However, this procedure leads to files with embedded "dummy" records, and storage is not efficiently used and processing time is increased. Usually, records to be deleted are physically removed by creating a new file. While creating a new file is sometimes necessary, it should be done as infrequently as possible.

To facilitate a description of file processing, it is necessary to extend our algorithmic notation so that the file-manipulation capabilities present in most programming languages can be expressed. A file is given an identifier name that is not subscripted or qualified by a pointer. We denote this identifier by the syntactic element <file name>. The first requirement before processing a file is to allocate storage for a buffer. It is also popular to identify the operations that can be performed on the file. Can the file be used for input, output, or both (update)? This serves as protection, particularly if we do not wish to write by accident on a file used for input. These functions can be expressed in our algorithmic notation as follows:

1 Open <file name> file for input
2 Open <file name> file for output
3 Open <file name> file for update

Input specifies that records may be read only; output specifies that records may be written only; and update specifies that records may be read and rewritten, or possibly written at the end of the file. Note that it is not possible to rewrite records in a sequential file stored on tape.

When the processing of a file is complete, the buffer space can be deallocated by writing

Close <file name> file

The open and close statements also prevent more than one user from accessing the file simultaneously in time-sharing and multiprogramming environments. A program cannot open a file that is currently open for writing by another program until that program closes the file. Some file systems allow several users to read from a file concurrently.

There are two basic operations that can be specified for a sequential file: read and write. The object of a read statement or the source of a write statement should be the identifier of a variable or structure that corresponds to the records in the file. We will denote this identifier by <record name>. A read statement has the form

Read from <file name> file into <record name>

and a write statement has the form

Write <record name> on <file name> file

A third operation that applies to sequential files stored on direct-access devices is

Rewrite <record name> on <file name> file

This operation can be used only when the file has been opened for update. It writes a record in the location of the record that is most recently read.

An algorithm is now presented in order to illustrate the basic operations that are performed when processing a file sequentially. Assume that we have a sequential file named MASTER to be processed. The records can be read into a structure MRECORD consisting of MKEY and MDATA. The records are sorted in an ascending sequence according to the value of MKEY. It is assumed that there are no duplicate keys.

The transaction records are stored in a sequential file named TRANSACTION. These records can be read into a structure TRECORD consisting of TKEY, TDATA, and CODE. The transaction records are sorted in ascending sequence by TKEY value, and again, no duplicates exist. CODE has one of three possible values, 1, 2, or 3, that have the following interpretation:

1 Update the record in the file MASTER with key TKEY using TDATA.
2 Add a record to the file MASTER with key TKEY and data TDATA.
3 Delete a record from the file MASTER that has key TKEY.

Algorithm SEQUENTIAL_PROCESSING.   Given the files MASTER and TRANSACTION, it is required to form a new file, NEW_MASTER, by performing the operations specified by the transaction records. NRECORD has format identical to MRECORD and consists of NKEY and NDATA.

1. [Open files]   Open MASTER file for input, TRANSACTION file for input, and NEW_MASTER file for output.
2. [Read next transaction]   Read from TRANSACTION file into TRECORD.
    If end of TRANSACTION file, then go to step 7.
3. [Read record from file being updated]
    Read from MASTER file into MRECORD.
    If end of MASTER file,
    then
            repeat while not end of TRANSACTION file:
                if CODE = 2 (add a record),
                then set NDATA ← TDATA and NKEY ← TKEY and
                write NRECORD on NEW_MASTER file;
                otherwise, print TRECORD and an error message.
                Read from TRANSACTION file into TRECORD.
            Go to step 8.
4. [Transfer old record]
    If MKEY < TKEY, then write MRECORD on NEW_MASTER file and go to step 3.
5. [Update a record or delete a record]
    If MKEY = TKEY,
    then
            if CODE = 1 (update a record),
            then set MDATA ← TDATA and write MRECORD on NEW_MASTER file;
            otherwise, (deletion or error)
                    if CODE ≠ 3,
                    then write MRECORD on NEW_MASTER file and print TRECORD
                    and an error message.
            Go to step 2.

6. [Add a new record]
    If CODE = 2 (add a record),
    then set NDATA ← TDATA, NKEY ← TKEY and
        and write NRECORD on NEW_MASTER file;
    otherwise, print TRECORD and an error message.
    Read from TRANSACTION file into TRECORD.
    If not end of TRANSACTION file, then go to step 4.
7. [Transfer remaining records from MASTER file]
    Repeat while not end of MASTER file:
        write MRECORD on NEW_MASTER file and read from MASTER file
        into MRECORD.
8. [Close files] Close MASTER, TRANSACTION, and NEW_MASTER files and Exit.

Algorithm SEQUENTIAL_PROCESSING demonstrates the complications that can arise in checking the TRANSACTION file against the MASTER file. Since either file may end first, the statements in steps 3 and 7 are needed to complete the scanning of TRANSACTION file and MASTER file, respectively. Two kinds of errors can be detected. In step 5, if TKEY and MKEY are equal, but neither an update or a deletion is specified, then either an illegal code or the addition of a record with a duplicate key is specified. If TKEY is ever less than MKEY (steps 3 and 6), but CODE is not 2, then the instruction to update or delete a non-existent record must be ignored.

The requirement that the records in a sequential file be ordered by their keys is not essential if the file is being scanned to perform the same operation on every record.

The important points concerning the sequential processing of sequential files can be summarized as follows:

1 Sequential processing is most advantageous if a large number of transactions can be batched to form a single "run" on the file.
2 A new file should be created if there are any additions and a significant number of deletions requested.
3 Quick response time should not be expected for a transaction or a batch of transactions.
4 The requirement that the records in a sequential file be ordered by a particular key is not essential if the file is being scanned to perform the same operation on every record (i.e., serial processing).

In the following sections we will see that certain other file organizations are more suitable if requirements such as quick response time and individual transaction handling exist. If the sequential file resides on a direct-access device (such as disk or drum), it is possible to improve the response time significantly. This can be achieved by performing an external binary search involving track locations within the file, and hence accessing records in a nonsequential manner. In some systems, however, the user is not always capable of acquiring specific knowledge concerning track addresses.

7-4.3 Sequential Files in PL/I

In the remainder of this section, we describe how sequential files can be created and accessed in PL/I. We do so with the explicit purpose of illustrating how sequential files are handled in a specific programming language. In addition, we heavily rely on this material in the discussion of file applications in Secs. 7-5, 7-7, and 7-9. By tradition, COBOL is the programming language which is used most often in file processing. We will use PL/I to preserve a continuity in the programs developed throughout the text. Almost all of the PL/I file-handling facilities discussed in this chapter have counterparts in COBOL.

There are two types of sequential files in PL/I, namely, **STREAM** files and **CONSECUTIVE RECORD** files. In this text, we are and have been assuming knowledge of the data-, list-, and edit-directed **STREAM** input/output facilities offered by PL/I, using the standard system files **SYSIN** and **SYSPRINT**. We plan to discuss some of the unfamiliar, yet important, properties of **STREAM** input/output. A comparison of **STREAM** input/output and **CONSECUTIVE RECORD** input/output is made. Since **RECORD** input/output is not assumed to be known by the reader, it will be covered in more detail.

A **STREAM**-oriented file, as the name suggests, can be considered as a continuous stream of information that flows into the program area via the execution of **GET** statements and out of the program area via the execution of **PUT** statements. This stream of information is stored externally on a file in *character form* (e.g., EBCDIC form). For convenience and efficiency, the information in the file is grouped into physical records or blocks; however, the contents of the blocks bear no relationship to the argument lists of the **GET** and **PUT** statements. This aspect will be illustrated presently.

A file is a data-holding entity just as any array or structure is in PL/I. Consequently, all files should be declared with the exception of the standard **STREAM** files, **SYSIN**, and **SYSPRINT**. Consider the following declaration

DECLARE TRIANGL FILE STREAM INPUT ENVIRONMENT(F(20));

The file **TRIANGL** is declared to be a **STREAM**-oriented file which can be used for input (i.e., only **GET** statements can be applied to this file). The **ENVIRONMENT** attribute, which can be abbreviated as **ENV**, contains a list of parameters which are needed by the data-management routines in the operating system. F(20) is interpreted as specifying a file with a blocksize of twenty characters or bytes which is fixed in length. In the remaining sections of this chapter, we will encounter other types of parameters for the ENV attribute.

In PL/I, files must be opened and closed in order to receive and release buffers from the operating system. This is accomplished with OPEN and CLOSE statements. For example,

OPEN FILE (TRIANGL);
.
.
.
CLOSE FILE (TRIANGL);

As an example of a simple program involving the nonstandard file **TRIANGL**, consider Fig. 7-4.4. The program reads in three values for A, B, and C, and tests if they form a set of dimensions for a triangle.

Information in the file **TRIANGL** is stored as illustrated in Fig. 7-4.5a. With the initial execution of the **GET** statement, the first two physical records are read into the two buffers that were allocated with the execution of the **OPEN** statement. Two buffers are

```
STREAM_EG: PROCEDURE OPTIONS (MAIN);

    DECLARE TRIANGL FILE STREAM INPUT ENV(F(20)),
            (A, B, C) FLOAT BINARY;

    ON ENDFILE (TRIANGL) STOP;
    OPEN FILE (TRIANGL);

    DO WHILE ('1'B);      /* DO UNTIL END OF FILE */

        GET FILE (TRIANGL) LIST (A, B, C);
        IF (A + B) < C  |  (A + C) < B  |  (B + C) < A

        THEN PUT SKIP FILE (SYSPRINT) LIST (A, B, C,
                'DOES NOT FORM A TRIANGLE');

        ELSE PUT SKIP FILE (SYSPRINT) LIST (A, B, C,
                'FORMS A TRIANGLE');

    END;

END STREAM_EG;
```

FIGURE 7-4.4   Example of STREAM-oriented file processing.

automatically supplied for STREAM-oriented input/output—the reason for this becomes obvious in the following discussion. The character information in the first buffer (see Fig. 7-4.5*b*) is interpreted by the PL/I subsystem for handling STREAM I/O. The information entities which correspond to items A, B, and C are isolated (i.e., intermediate blanks are treated as delimiters) and these entities (5.0, 3.0, and 4.0) are converted from their character formats to floating-point representations. The floating-point representations are assigned to the memory locations for A, B, and C that have been allocated in the program area. Hence, for STREAM input/output, a buffer assumes an additional purpose to that of smoothing out input/output transmission, namely, that of providing an intermediate area from which character conversion can take place.

After the initial execution of the GET statement, a system pointer references the point "a" in the buffer. During the interpretation of the information in the buffer, this pointer is moved along to record the position of the character which is to be scanned next. A second execution of the GET statement results in the interpretation of the next set of three entities in the information stream. The three entities fall across the block boundary, i.e., they reside in both buffers. However, with a two-buffer system this does not present a problem in either the interpretation or the conversion of data. The system pointer is simply moved from the end of one buffer to the front of the other. However, it does graphically illustrate that the amount of data stored in a block is not necessarily related to the argument list in the GET statement, and that a two-buffer system is needed for STREAM input/output. We will see that this is not the case in RECORD input/output.

The effects of the execution of a PUT statement are the opposite to those of a GET statement. With the execution of a PUT statement, the values of the list of arguments are converted to their character representation when moved from the program's data area to the buffers. After a buffer is full, its contents are written out to the specified file which resides on an external storage device. End-of-block characters (interblock gaps in the case of a tape) separate the different blocks. When the file is closed, an end of file (EOF) marker is placed at the end of the final block, along with some other information (often called *trailer information*). STREAM-oriented files should be exclusively used as files associated

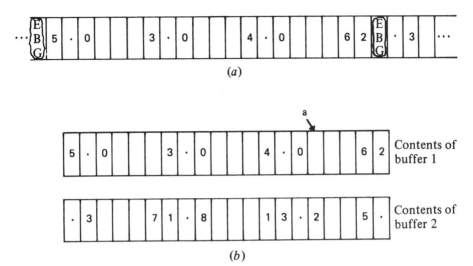

FIGURE 7-4.5 Representation of (*a*) a block in the file TRIANGL, and (*b*) the contents of two buffers after two blocks from the file have been read in. All information is stored in character format.

with off-line sequential devices such as card readers, line printers, and magnetic tapes since such devices are character-oriented. This does not imply that STREAM-oriented files should not reside on direct-access devices such as disks or drums; often they do. However, direct-access files are typically created as intermediate card files or line printer files by the operating system. Such files avoid the problem of slow program execution, which would arise if each program had to wait for individual cards to be read or lines to be printed. STREAM-oriented files are so commonly used as line printer files that a special type of STREAM file, called a PRINT file, is available in PL/I. A PRINT file allows the user to store in the first character of each block a special ANS character, which indicates line- and page-skipping control to the printer.

In PL/I there are many types of RECORD-oriented files (CONSECUTIVE, INDEXED, REGIONAL (1), REGIONAL (2), REGIONAL (3), and TRANSIENT). Only the CONSECUTIVE file is discussed in detail in this subsection. Before doing so, let us identify some properties of RECORD-oriented data transmission which are common to all RECORD files and which clearly distinguish RECORD files from STREAM files.

In record-oriented transmission, data in a file are considered to be a collection of records stored in any internal form (e.g., FLOAT or FIXED numbers, bit strings, character strings, etc.) acceptable by a PL/I program. Hence *no data conversion* need be performed during record-oriented input/output. On input, a READ statement such as

    READ FILE(MASTER) INTO (EMPLOYEE);

causes a single record to be transmitted to the program variable (EMPLOYEE) exactly as it is recorded in the file. On output, a WRITE statement such as

    WRITE FILE(MASTER) FROM (EMPLOYEE);

```
SEQPROC: PROCEDURE OPTIONS(MAIN);

/* A PROCEDURE WHICH READS IN TRANSACTION CARDS AND APPLIES THEM TO A
   MASTER EMPLOYEE FILE.  THE TRANSACTION CARDS ARE OF THE FORM
   <TYPE> <SURNAME> <INITIALS> <SOCIAL INS #> <WAGE/HR> <CLASSIFICATN>
   WHERE    CC 1   <TYPE>: 1=DELETE, 2=ADD, 3=UPDATE
            CC 2-22   <SURNAME>        CC 22-27   <INITIALS>
            CC 28-36  <SOCIAL INSURANCE NUMBER>
            CC 37-41  <WAGE PER HOUR>
            CC 42-44  <WORK CLASSIFICATION CODE>                    */

   DECLARE 1 EMPLOYEE,
             2 NAME,
               3 SURNAME CHAR(20),
               3 INITIALS CHAR(6),
             2 SOC_INS# FIXED(9),
             2 WAGE_PER_HR FIXED(5,2),
             2 CLASSIFICATION CHAR(3);

   DECLARE 1 TRAN_REC,
             2 NAME,
               3 SURNAME CHAR(20),
               3 INITIALS CHAR(6),
             2 SOC_INS# FIXED(9),
             2 WAGE_PER_HR FIXED(5,2),
             2 CLASSIFICATION CHAR(3);

   DECLARE MASTER FILE RECORD ENV (CONSECUTIVE F(370,37)),
           NEWMTR FILE RECORD ENV (CONSECUTIVE F(370,37)),
           CODE FIXED(1),
           L(3) LABEL,
           (MASTERDONE, SYSINDONE) BIT(1) INITIAL('0'B);

   ON ENDFILE(SYSIN) CALL COMPLETE;
   ON ENDFILE(MASTER) CALL EXTEND;
   OPEN FILE (MASTER) INPUT;   OPEN FILE (NEWMTR) OUTPUT;

   /* INITIAL READING OF MASTER AND TRANSACTION RECORDS */
   READ FILE(MASTER) INTO (EMPLOYEE);
   GET FILE(SYSIN) EDIT(CODE,TRAN_REC)(COL(1),F(1),A(20),A(6),F(9),
        F(5),A(3));

REPEAT:
   DO WHILE('1'B);   /* REPEAT UNTIL AN END OF FILE CONDITION */
      DO WHILE (EMPLOYEE.SOC_INS# < TRAN_REC.SOC_INS#);
         WRITE FILE (NEWMTR) FROM (EMPLOYEE);
         READ FILE(MASTER) INTO (EMPLOYEE);
      END;
      GO TO L(CODE);

   L(1):  /* DELETE */
      IF EMPLOYEE.SOC_INS# ¬= TRAN_REC.SOC_INS#
      THEN DO;
         PUT SKIP LIST('ERROR* RECORD TO BE DELETED DOES NOT EXIST');
         WRITE FILE (NEWMTR) FROM (EMPLOYEE);
      END;
      READ FILE(MASTER) INTO (EMPLOYEE);
      GO TO NEWCARD;

   L(2):  /* ADD */
      WRITE FILE (NEWMTR) FROM (TRAN_REC);
```

FIGURE 7-4.6 Processing a sequential file.

or a REWRITE statement (which is described later) causes a single record to be transmitted from the program variable (EMPLOYEE) to the file (MASTER) exactly as it is stored internally.

From the previous statements, it becomes obvious that a record is read into and written from a single program variable. A program variable may be a simple variable, an

```
        GO TO NEWCARD;

    L(3):   /* UPDATE */
        IF EMPLOYEE.SOC_INS# ¬= TRAN_REC.SOC_INS#
        THEN DO;
            PUT SKIP LIST('ERROR* RECORD TO BE UPDATED DOES NOT EXIST');
            WRITE FILE (NEWMTR) FROM (EMPLOYEE);
        END;
        ELSE WRITE FILE (NEWMTR) FROM (TRAN_REC);
        READ FILE(MASTER) INTO (EMPLOYEE);

NEWCARD: GET FILE(SYSIN) EDIT(CCDE,TRAN_REC)(COL(1),F(1),A(20),A(6),
            F(9),F(5),A(3));
    END REPEAT;


COMPLETE: PROCEDURE;
    IF MASTERDONE
    THEN DO; CLOSE FILE(MASTER), FILE(NEWMTR); STOP;  END;
    SYSINDONE = '1'B;
    DO WHILE('1'B); /* UNTIL END OF MASTER FILE */
        WRITE FILE (NEWMTR) FROM (EMPLOYEE);
        READ FILE(MASTER) INTO (EMPLOYEE);
    END;
END COMPLETE;


EXTEND: PROCEDURE;
    IF SYSINDONE
    THEN DO; CLOSE FILE(MASTER), FILE (NEWMTR); STOP;  END;
    MASTERDONE = '1'B;
    DO WHILE('1'B);    /* UNTIL END OF SYSIN FILE */
        IF CODE = 2 & EMPLOYEE.SOC_INS# < TRAN_REC.SOC_INS#
        THEN DO;
            WRITE FILE (NEWMTR) FROM (TRAN_REC);
            EMPLOYEE.SOC_INS# = TRAN_REC.SOC_INS# ;
            END;
        ELSE PUT SKIP LIST('ERROR - ILLEGAL ADDITION ATTEMPTED');
        GET FILE(SYSIN) EDIT(CCDE,TRAN_REC)(COL(1),F(1),A(20),A(6),F(9),
            F(5),A(3));
    END;
END EXTEND;

END SEQPROC;
```

FIGURE 7-4.6 (Continued)

array variable, or most commonly, a structure variable. Although the PL/I statements used in record-oriented input/output are concerned with records (as dictated by the contents of the program variable), data are actually transmitted to and from a file in blocks of records. Blocks can contain fixed-length or variable-length records in a form described in Sec. 7-1 (in particular, see Fig. 7-1.1). Consequently, for RECORD input/output, there is a definite relationship between a logical record, as derived from the contents of the program variable, and a block or physical record. There must be an integral number of logical records in a block—records are not allowed to cross block boundaries. The IBM System 370 does allow an exception to this rule in the case where a record is unusually large. If the record is so large as to be impossible or inconvenient to store in a single block, it is permissible to have the record span over several blocks. In practice, instances in which this might happen rarely occur.

To understand how sequential processing is performed in PL/I, let us examine the program in Fig. 7-4.6. The program basically follows the logic presented in Algorithm SEQUENTIAL_PROCESSING, in which a master file is updated according to a number of transaction records. The program is oriented towards a payroll application in which records from the MASTER file and transaction card file (SYSIN) are assumed to be ordered by the social insurance number.

In the program, both MASTER and NEWMTR (meaning "new master") are declared as RECORD-oriented files having the CONSECUTIVE property. The CONSECUTIVE property implies that the records in the file are stored in contiguous locations in external memory. RECORD CONSECUTIVE files are sequential files, since access to a particular record can be gained only by reading all previous records.

Some of the important programming aspects concerning the PL/I program are as follows. First, the standard input file SYSIN containing the transaction cards is opened and closed automatically by the operating system—no explicit OPEN or CLOSE statements are needed. Second, the ENV parameter F(370, 37) specifies that the MASTER and NEWMTR files are blocked with 10 records, each 37 bytes in length. Hence, the block size and buffer size are 370 bytes. Assuming a basic understanding of Algorithm SEQUENTIAL_PROCESS-ING, the remainder of the program should be straightforward.

One point that must be noted is that we have not provided enough information in the file declaration statement to identify fully the MASTER and NEWMTR files to the system. Besides the block size and logical record length, a complete description should include information such as the amount of space required by the file, the disposition of the file (e.g., whether it is already or just being created), and the type and volume of the device on which the file is to remain on the system. Such information is commonly described externally through statements in a system command language for the particular installation on which the program is executed. For example, in IBM systems, the system command language is called JCL (Job Control Language) and files are externally identified by the use of a DD (data definition) statement. The following DD statements coupled with the information in the ENV clauses describe the MASTER and NEWMTR files to the system:

```
//GO.MASTER DD DISP =(OLD,KEEP),UNIT =SYSDA,VOL =SER =USER01,
//     SPACE =(TRK,5)
//GO.NEWMTR DD DISP =(NEW,KEEP),UNIT =SYSDA,VOL =SER =USER01
//     SPACE =(TRK,5)
```

We are not going to provide the system command information (e.g., the DD statements) for all the programs in this chapter. Since such information can vary from computer installation to installation, it is suggested that a PL/I programmer's guide for a particular installation be consulted when writing programs involving file descriptions.

A final PL/I statement we must discuss before completing this subsection is the REWRITE command. If we want simply to update a file without creating or deleting records, we can do so by using the REWRITE statement if the file resides on a direct-access storage device. Figure 7-4.7 is a segment of a PL/I program which illustrates how the MASTER file can be updated without creating a new file, assuming only update transactions are handled. The declarations for MASTER, EMPLOYEE, and TRAN_REC are assumed to be given and are the same as described in Fig. 7-4.6. The REWRITE command is designed to overwrite the record that was last read. With this capability, it is easy to see how the program can update the MASTER file without creating a new file.

To reinforce our discussion on sequential files, we consider a small billing-system application which makes use of many of the concepts discussed in this section.

Exercises for Sec. 7-4

1. Suppose you are to create a sequential file which contains records describing potential new acquisitions for a library. A key which can be used to access information concerning a new book is the first author's surname. Are there any advantages to ordering the file by the first author's surname assuming (*a*) search requests are not batched, and (*b*) search requests are batched?

2. Suppose we are to create a sequential file which contains records describing in detail the descriptions of various course offerings at an educational institution. The class numbers can be used as a key for the file. Examples of class numbers are CMPT 181, MATH 222, and PHYS 111. Are there any advantages to ordering the file by the class number, assuming (*a*) search requests are not batched, and (*b*) search requests are batched? You are to assume that almost all requests concerning classes contain legitimate keys (i.e., a key for which a record exists). Can you propose a better type of ordering than by class number for the situation in which search requests are not batched?

3. Outline the major differences between STREAM input/output and CONSECUTIVE RECORD input/output in PL/I. For what types of applications should each be used?

4. You are placed in charge of the design and implementation of a small payroll system. The system contains the following employee information:
   (*a*) Employee number (5 digits)
   (*b*) Employee's salary (5 digits)
   (*c*) Social insurance number (9 digits)
   (*d*) Tax exemption (5 digits)
   (*e*) Group insurance premium (3 digits)
   (*f*) Parking (2 digits)
   (*g*) Association dues (3 digits)
   (*h*) Name (up to 37 characters)

   Changes to employee information are made via transactions which are applied to the system at the time pay checks are printed (i.e., once a month). Three types of transactions are required, and these are:
   (*a*) *Addition* transaction which must contain the information items for an employee, for example,

   ADD 67823 14400 708312694 01925 320 35 000 LISTOE, A.D.,

   (*b*) *Deletion* transaction which contains only an employee number, for example,

   DEL 67823

   (*c*) *Update* transaction which contains the employee number plus an explicit indication of the item to be changed, for example,

   UPD 67823 PARKING = 48 TAX_EMP = 02400

   On a month-end run, the system should print pay checks for each member on staff, including an initial pay check for an employee who is added and a final pay check for an employee who is deleted. Payments consist of two forms, as illustrated in Fig. 7-4.8, the check itself and the statement of net earnings.

```
/* EXAMPLE TO SHOW UPDATE OF A FILE WITHOUT CREATING A NEW FILE      */

/* UPDATES IS A SET OF NEW EMPLOYEE RECORDS TO REPLACE CORRESPONDING */
/*   RECORDS IN THE FILE 'MASTER'.  IN BOTH FILES,  RECORDS MUST BE  */
/*   ORDERED BY SOCIAL-INSURANCE-NUMBER.                             */

UPDATE: PROCEDURE OPTIONS (MAIN);


DECLARE MASTER FILE SEQUENTIAL RECORD ENV (CONSECUTIVE F(370,37));
DECLARE UPDATES FILE STREAM;

DECLARE 1 EMPLOYEE,
          2 NAME,
            3 SURNAME  CHAR(2C),
            3 INITIALS CHAR(6),
          2 SOC_INS# FIXED(9),
          2 WAGE_PER_HR FIXED(5,2),
          2 CLASSIFICATION CHAR(3);

DECLARE 1 TRAN_REC,
          2 NAME,
            3 SURNAME CHAR(20),
            3 INITIALS CHAR(6),
          2 SOC_INS# FIXED(9),
          2 WAGE_PER_HR FIXED(5,2),
          2 CLASSIFICATION CHAR(3);
DECLARE OLD_SOC_INS# FIXED(9) INIT(000000000);


ON ENDFILE (UPDATES) BEGIN;
                     CLOSE FILE (MASTER);
                     CLOSE FILE (UPDATES);
                     STOP;
                     END;

ON ENDFILE (MASTER) BEGIN;
                     PUT SKIP LIST ('END OF MASTER FILE');
                     CLOSE FILE (MASTER);
                     CLOSE FILE (UPDATES);
                     STOP;
                     END;
```

FIGURE 7-4.7   Updating a sequential file.

Income tax is calculated based on a graduated scale which may be approximated using the following formula (N is the taxable income, that is, N = regular pay − exemptions)

Income tax = $(N/25 + 16)\% \times N$

Therefore, the income tax paid by A. Listoe is

$((1200 − 200)/250 + 16)\% \times (\$1200 − \$200) = \$200$

Pension plan contributions are 8 percent of the income after taxes.

Design in detail and then implement the payroll system just outlined. The design phase should include a detailed discussion of transaction record, employee payroll record, and output record formats. The stylized printing on the payment forms should be printed as well, even though it would be preprinted on special forms in a production system.

```
OPEN FILE (UPDATES) INPUT;
OPEN FILE (MASTER) SEQUENTIAL UPDATE;

/* READ TO START UP */

READ FILE (MASTER) INTO (EMPLOYEE);

DO WHILE ('1'B); /* UNTIL END OF UPDATES FILE */

     GET FILE (UPDATES) EDIT (TRAN_REC)
               (COL(1),A(20),A(6),F(9),F(5,2),A(3));

     IF TRAN_REC.SOC_INS# < OLD_SOC_INS#
     THEN PUT SKIP EDIT ('ERROR* OUT OF ORDER CARD. NUMBER: ',
            TRAN_REC.SOC_INS#,'.  NAME: ',TRAN_REC.SURNAME)
              (A,F(9),A,A);

     ELSE DO;

        OLD_SOC_INS# = TRAN_REC.SOC_INS#;

        DO WHILE (EMPLOYEE.SOC_INS# < TRAN_REC.SOC_INS#);
           READ FILE (MASTER) INTO (EMPLOYEE);
        END;

        IF (EMPLOYEE.SOC_INS# = TRAN_REC.SOC_INS#)
        THEN REWRITE FILE (MASTER) FROM (TRAN_REC);
        ELSE PUT SKIP EDIT ('ERROR* NON-EXISTENT RECORD. NAME:',
              TRAN_REC.SURNAME,'.  NUMBER: ',TRAN_REC.SOC_INS#)
              (3 A,F(9));
     END;
END;

END UPDATE;
```

FIGURE 7-4.7 (Continued)

J. B. REGIONAL BANK
3972 — 9th AVE   August 1   19   75
MONTREAL, P. Q.

PAY TO THE
ORDER OF _____ A. D. Listoe _____ $ 889.34
EIGHT HUNDRED EIGHTY NINE.....................34 *DOLLAR*

DATE
08	01	75

TOT. EXEMP $2400
SALARY $14400

REGULAR PAY	1200.00
INCOME TAX	200.00—
GROUP INSURANCE	26.66—
PENSION	80.00—
PARKING	4.00—
DUES	.00
NET PAY	889.34

SOCIAL INSURANCE NO.	*EMP. NO.*
708-312-694	59138

FIGURE 7-4.8 Sample output for payroll system.

7-5 A SMALL BILLING SYSTEM

The format of this section, as well as the other application sections in this chapter, will consist of analyzing the problem, designing the system (in particular, deciding on the file structure needed in the system), and describing a possible implementation for the system. Each of these three phases of system development will be described in a separate subsection. It would be ideal if systems could be developed using a strict top-down approach that would initially involve a complete system analysis, then the design, and finally the implementation. In the discussion of the applications in this chapter, this ideal will appear at times to be easily achieved. In practice, however, it is almost never realized. As the system develops, we iterate between the analysis and the design phases, and between the design and implementation phases, until the system is complete. (During the development of some systems, there is even iteration between the analysis and implementation phases. This is disastrous and should be avoided at all cost!)

This particular section is concerned with the analysis, design, and implementation of a small billing system. While this example is included primarily as an application using sequential files, it is an interesting application in its own right since everyone, at some time, has interacted with such a system.

7-5.1 System Analysis

The Company of Canada, Ltd. operates a chain of small department stores. Recently, the company decided to offer a charge-account service to its customers by means of credit cards. A purchase form indicating the credit-card number, the items purchased, and their cost are filled out by the cashiers at the time of purchase. The form is also designed to show a customer credit in the case of returned articles. The credit card carries a six-digit customer-account number, and an imprinter at the point of sale indicates the date of the transaction.

The forms are sent on an almost daily basis to the head office for processing. The head office sends out monthly statements to all credit-card-carrying customers. All payments on charge accounts are also received at the head office. The company charges interest on these accounts at the rate of 1.5 percent of that part of last month's debit balance for which payments were not received this month.

The company has found it desirable to automate its billing system. The company is small. After some preliminary analysis, it is decided that the company could not afford the ongoing costs of its own computer, and arrangements have been made with another business to rent some magnetic-disk storage and purchase some CPU time once per month.

The company would like as output from each monthly run the following information:

 1 A listing of all credit-card-carrying customers. The listing should include for each given account number, the name, address, and current balance of account, and it should be ordered by account number.

 2 A monthly balance report which should include the total outstanding balance owed to the company, the total of purchases made for the month, the total of payment received, the interest charged, and the new total balance owed to the company.

3 A daily sales report which indicates, for each day, the total of the purchase receipts received at the head office.

4 Monthly statements for all customers which should include an initial balance forward figure, the date, name, and amount of any purchase, the date and amount of any payment on the account, the interest charged (if any), and a final current amount-owing figure. Also included is the customer's address, which is positioned on the statement so as to appear through a see-through window in the statement's envelope. The address must be no more than four lines and a line must be less than 30 characters in width.

The input to the billing system includes:

1 Credit-card receipts, each of which includes the customer identification number, date of purchase, description and amount of items purchased.

2 New customer credit-card applications, each of which includes the customer's name, address, and assigned identification number.

3 Payment receipts, each of which includes the customer identification number, the date of payment, and the amount paid.

4 Customer termination information, where each termination must provide the customer identification number and the date of termination.

There are some additional factors which can potentially affect the design of the system. First, all new credit cards must be issued by the head office. Second, as a service to the public customers are allowed to indicate the termination of their account by writing directly to the head office or by contacting the local business and having them send in a notice of termination.

7-5.2   System Design

We proceed with the system design first by deciding on how to format the input and output, and then by considering the problems of how best to generate the desired output. Inputs come from two sources: the point of sale (purchase and termination slips) and the customer (applications for credit cards, payments, and termination notices).

As purchases come in from point of sale locations, they are keypunched in preparation for data entry to the system. The following format is chosen:

PURCHASE card:

Card column 1–6:	Customer's identification number
7–12:	Date (two columns each for month, day, and year)
13–20:	Amount of purchase
21–40:	Item description

The card file that is formed by the encoding of these purchases will be called PURCHASE. Because terminations as well as purchases arrive from the points of sale, it is decided to indicate an account termination by placing the message 'DELETE THIS CUSTOMER' in the item description field of the PURCHASE record. Therefore, PURCHASE records must also be created for termination notices that are sent directly to the head office by the customer.

Two separate card files, PAYMENT and NEWACCT, are also created for customer payments and credit-card applications, respectively.

PAYMENT card:

Card column 1–6:	Customer's identification number
7–12:	Date (two columns each for month, day, and year)
13–20:	Amount of payment

NEWACCT card:

Card column 1–6:	Customer's identification number
7–26:	Customer's name
27–46:	Customer's street or P.O. box, etc.
47–65:	Customer's city, province, or state
66–72:	Customer's postal code
73–80:	Customer's initial balance (always set to zero)

An important part of any business system design is the design of output forms. In this application, the greatest effort must be expended on the design of the customer's statement. A format which does satisfy the company's needs is given in Fig. 7-5.1 Note that the boldface print identifies that part of the statement which is common to all statements. This common text should be preprinted on the statement by a printing shop before computer processing. This makes it necessary to print only the dates, purchases, balances, etc. for a specific customer. Such a procedure saves a tremendous amount of time and permits the generation of multicolored statements.

The customer listing as required by the company should be ordered by identification number, and all pertinent customer information should appear in a compact yet readable format. To achieve this, the information pertaining to a single customer is printed on one line in the form:

THE COMPANY OF CANADA, LTD.
4141 THE STREET
THE CITY, PROVINCE
A0A 1B1

CUSTOMER'S.NAME. . . .NUMBER
STREET.OR.BOX.NUMBER
CITY, PROVINCE.OR.STATE
POS COD

Date	TRANSACTION	DEBIT	CREDIT	BALANCE
	BALANCE FORWARD	$DD.DD		$BB.BB
MM/DD/YY	PURCHASE(ITEM)	$DD.DD		$BB.BB
MM/DD/YY	PAYMENT ON ACCOUNT		$CC.CC	$BB.BB
MM/DD/YY	INTEREST ON: $II.II	$DD.DD		$BB.BB
MM/DD/YY	CURRENT AMOUNT OWING			$BB.BB

FIGURE 7-5.1   General format of a customer's statement.

ID.NUM NAME... STREET.OR.P.O.BOX... CITY..., STATE... POST.CODE BALANCE

The monthly totals and daily payments received are printed on the same form in an easily readable format. Specific examples for all three of the forms will be illustrated in the next subsection.

We now turn to the design of the program which takes the specified input and creates the desired output properly formatted. Figure 7-5.2 shows a possible design for

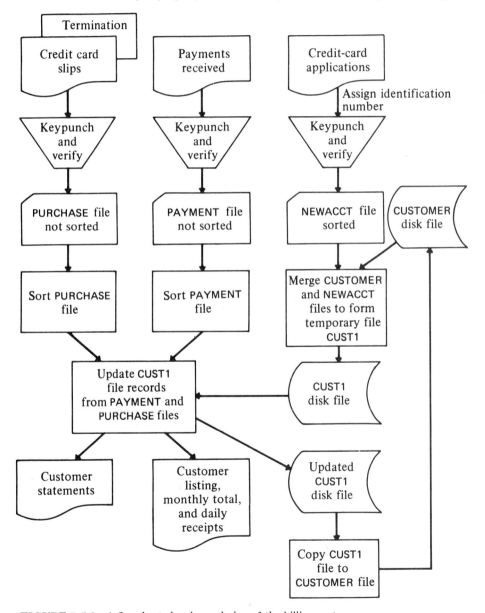

FIGURE 7-5.2 A flowchart showing a design of the billing system.

the system. It is not necessarily the best design, and some improvements will be considered later in this subsection.

An obvious, yet important, aspect of the system design is that each customer's current balance, along with his name, account number, and address, must be kept on a system file from one month's run to the next. We will call this file the CUSTOMER file and create it as a sequential file ordered by account number.

A conceptually simple way of handling new customers is to merge the set of new accounts with the CUSTOMER file and, by necessity, create a new sequential file which we call CUST1. On CUST1, a new account will have a "current-balance" field set to zero. Note that in the system we have designed, the assignment of a new account number is handled manually. While this may result in some extra bookkeeping, a sequential card file ordered by account number can be created quite easily during the month. This ordered sequential file, called NEWACCT, is the file that is merged with the CUSTOMER file to form CUST1.

To generate a customer's statement, it is necessary to combine the monthly purchases and payments for a customer with his previous month's balance. Grouping all receipts and payments with the previous month's balance would be an inefficient costly process if it were done using a separate run for each customer. However, by sorting the PURCHASE and PAYMENT files by account number and then merging the information in these two files with the information in the CUST1 file, we can produce all the customer statements in one run (i.e., in one pass over each of the three files). The PURCHASE and PAYMENT files each can be sorted by using a mechanical sorter, by using a system-sort routine, or by writing your own sort procedure, as is indicated in Fig. 7-5.2. The merging of the three files is quite simple and is outlined in the following six steps:

1   Read in a CUST1 record.
2   Read in and process all PURCHASE and PAYMENT records with the same account number as the CUST1 record. (Because the files are ordered by account number, any purchases or payments for the customer designated in the CUST1 record should appear as the "next" records during the sequential processing of the PURCHASE and PAYMENT files.)
3   Compute a new balance.
4   Calculate interest if necessary.
5   Print customer's statement and update CUST1 record.
6   Return to process the next CUST1 record.

The company reports can also be generated during the customer-file updating. A customer's account number, name, address, and balance can be printed immediately after calculating a new balance during the processing of the three files. However, customer statements are printed at the same time, so care must be taken to place the company's customer list and the customer statements on separate files for printing. In the discussion of the system implementation which follows, we will see how this can be accomplished.

The company report containing the monthly totals can be created by accumulating the totals as individual customer records are processed. The final report is output immediately after the updating of all customer records.

The daily sales report is generated by updating a vector of 31 elements, in which each element holds the accumulation of all purchases on a given day. Element n would hold the total of the purchase-slip amounts for the nth day of the month.

The final file processing to be completed in a monthly run is that of creating a new CUSTOMER file from the temporary CUST1 file. This involves nothing more than a simple record-by-record (i.e., serial) copying of the records in the CUST1 file into the CUSTOMER file.

In the previous discussion, we purposely neglected the problem of handling accounts which are terminated. One possibility is physically to delete terminating accounts after the processing of these accounts has taken place. The account number is set to 000000 during the merge-update on CUST1 and then all 000000 records are deleted when the new CUS-TOMER file is created. The disadvantage with this scheme is that tardy sales slips on terminated accounts may be received the next month, and the account number will have already been removed from the system. An alternative design is considered at the end of the next subsection.

7-5.3 Implementation

The PL/I program BILLS given in Fig. 7-5.3 follows the design decisions arrived at in the last section. BILLS consists of a mainline which is composed of file, record, and temporary-variable declarations, along with a series of five calls to the main modules of the system:

SORT_PURCHASES, SORT_PAYMENTS, MERGE_ACCTS, MERGE_UPDATE,
and COPY

Each module corresponds to a rectangular processing block in Fig. 7-5.2. Because the files CUSTOMER and CUST1 are not card or print oriented, they are declared as RECORD with the CONSECUTIVE property. CUSTOMER is retained from one run to the next; CUST1 is a temporary file. NEWACCT, PAYMENT, and PURCHASE are all INPUT STREAM files because of their card orientation. STATEMENT is an OUTPUT STREAM file (in particular, a PRINT file) which contains the customer's statements. The record structure CUST is used in the processing of the CUSTOMER and CUST1 files, PURCH is used in the processing of the PURCHASE file, and PAY is used in the processing of the PAYMENT file. PAY_DAY is the vector used for accumulating the daily receipts. The remaining variables are understandable through their context in the program and the program comments.

The procedures SORT_PURCHASES and SORT_PAYMENTS are not given. A sorting method, such as the merge sort given in Chap. 6, can be used to order the PURCHASE and PAYMENTS files. In addition, there exist several special-purpose external sorting methods such as the polyphase and oscillating sorts. These are described in Martin [1975] and Knuth [1973].

The procedure MERGE_ACCTS is also omitted because of the similarity between the type of processing required in the procedure and that given in the PL/I program in Fig. 7-4.6.

The procedure MERGE_UPDATE involves the sequential processing of the PUR-CHASE, PAYMENT, and CUST1 files, as was outlined in a six-step process given in the design subsection. The REWRITE statement is used in the updating of the CUST1 file. Of course, if CUST1 was a tape file instead of a disk file, rewriting would not be allowed and a new file would have to be created. Note also that we have used, to a significant extent, COBOL-like picture formats (i.e., format codes of the form P'$$9V.99') in the printing of the

```
// EXEC   PL1LFCLG,PARM='ATR,XREF'
//PL1L.SYSIN DD *


BILLS: PROCEDURE OPTIONS (MAIN);


/* THIS PROGRAM IS DESIGNED TO HANDLE THE BILLING REQUIREMENTS OF THE*/
/* COMPANY OF THE WORLD, LTD. AS FOLLOWS:                           */
/* THE PROGRAM IS COMPOSED OF FIVE LOGICALLY DISTINCT SEGMENTS.  THE */
/* FIRST TWO SORT THE CARD FILES, PURCHASE AND PAYMENT.  THE        */
/* THIRD OF THESE IS USED TO INSERT NEW CUSTOMERS INTO THE FILE OF  */
/* THE CURRENT CUSTOMERS OF THE COMPANY, AND TO DELETE THOSE OLD    */
/* CUSTOMERS WHICH ARE FLAGGED FOR DELETION.  THE FOURTH PART OF THIS*/
/* PROGRAM IS USED TO UPDATE THE CURRENT BALANCES OF EACH CUSTOMER  */
/* AND TO PRINT HIS MONTHLY STATEMENT.  THE PROGRAM ALSO PRINTS A   */
/* LIST OF TOTALS WHICH SERVE AS A CHECK ON THE BOOKKEEPING OF THE  */
/* COMPANY AND ON THIS PROGRAM.  THE FINAL PART CREATES A NEW       */
/* CUSTOMER FILE AFTER A MONTHLY RUN                                */

/* SOME OF THE KEY VARIABLES AND FILE NAMES USED IN THIS PROGRAM ARE */
/*       CUSTOMER   A DISK FILE OF SEQUENTIAL ORGANIZATION WHICH HOLDS */
/*                  THE OLD LIST OF CUSTOMERS AND THEIR OLD BALANCES  */
/*       NEWACCT    A CARD FILE WHICH CONTAINS A LIST OF NEW CUSTOMERS TO */
/*                  BE INSERTED INTO THE CUSTOMER FILE.              */
/*       PURCHASE   A CARD FILE USED TO CONTAIN A RECORD OF ALL PURCHASES */
/*                  MADE ON CREDIT IN THE LAST MONTH.               */
/*       PAYMENT    A CARD FILE USED TO CONTAIN A RECORD OF ALL PAYMENTS */
/*                  RECEIVED IN THE LAST MONTH.                     */
/*       CUST1      A DISK FILE, ALSO OF SEQUENTIAL ORGANIZATION, ON */
/*                  WHICH IS PLACED THE NEW LIST OF CUSTOMERS.      */
/*       STATMENT   A PRINT FILE ON WHICH ALL THE MONTHLY STATEMENTS ARE */
/*                  PRINTED.                                        */
/*       CUST       A STRUCTURE OF THE SAME FORMAT AS THE RECORDS ON */
/*                  THE CUSTOMER FILES                              */
/*       PURCH      A STRUCTURE USED TO INTERNALLY STORE THE RECORDS FROM */
/*                  THE PURCHASE CARD FILE                          */
/*       PAY        A STRUCTURE USED TO STORE INTERNALLY THE RECORDS FROM */
/*                  THE PAYMENT FILE.                               */
/*       OLD_BALANCE,PURCHASES,PAYMENTS,INTEREST,NEW_BALANCE,PAY_DAY: */
/*                  VARIABLES USED IN THE CALCULATION OF TOTALS.    */


      DECLARE (CUSTOMER, CUST1) FILE RECORD SEQUENTIAL
               ENV(CONSECUTIVE F(750,75)),
              (NEWACCT,PURCHASE,PAYMENT) FILE STREAM ENV(CONSECUTIVE),
              STATMENT FILE STREAM PRINT,

          1 CUST,
            2 ID FIXED DECIMAL (6,0),
            2 NAME CHARACTER (20),
            2 ADDRESS,
              3 LINE1 CHARACTER (20),
              3 LINE2 CHARACTER (19),
              3 POSTAL_CODE CHARACTER (7),
            2 BALANCE FIXED DECIMAL (8,2),

          1 PURCH,
            2 ID FIXED DECIMAL (6,0),
            2 PDATE,
              3 MONTH CHARACTER (2),
```

FIGURE 7-5.3 Small billing system.

forms required. Such formats allow the placement of '$' adjacent to the leftmost nonzero digit in a dollar figure. Also, they provide the ability to automatically place a 'CR' (for credit) or a 'DB' (for debit) following a number, depending on the sign of the number. The reader who is not familiar with COBOL picture formats should consult a PL/I reference manual to gain an understanding of this type of formatting.

```
              3 DAY   CHARACTER (2),
              3 YEAR  CHARACTER (2),
           2 AMOUNT FIXED DECIMAL (8,2),
           2 DESCRIPTION CHARACTER (20),

        1 PAY,
           2 ID FIXED DECIMAL (6,0),
           2 PDATE,
              3 MONTH CHARACTER (2),
              3 DAY   CHARACTER (2),
              3 YEAR  CHARACTER (2),
           2 AMOUNT FIXED DECIMAL (8,2),

        OLD_BALANCE FIXED DECIMAL (10,2) INITIAL (0),
        PURCHASES   FIXED DECIMAL (10,2) INITIAL (0),
        PAYMENTS    FIXED DECIMAL (10,2) INITIAL (0),
        INTEREST    FIXED DECIMAL (10,2) INITIAL (0),
        NEW_BALANCE FIXED DECIMAL (10,2) INITIAL (0),
        PAY_DAY(31) FIXED DECIMAL (10,2) INITIAL ( (31) 0 ),

        (CUR_BALANCE, INTEREST_AMT) FIXED DECIMAL (8,2),

        DELETE BIT(1) INITIAL ('0'B),

        (BDATE,TODAY) CHARACTER (8);

/* THIS STATEMENT DETERMINES THE DATE OF THIS RUN TO USE AS THE    */
/* CURRENT DATE ON THE STATEMENTS THAT ARE PRINTED.                */
       TODAY = SUBSTR(DATE,3,2) || '/' || SUBSTR (DATE,5,2) || '/' ||
               SUBSTR (DATE,1,2);

/*                    M A I N   L I N E                            */

       CALL SORT_PURCHASES;
       CALL SORT_PAYMENTS;
       CALL MERGE_ACCTS;
       CALL MERGE_UPDATE;
       CALL COPY;

/* A PROGRAM SEGMENT WHICH CONTAINS THE THREE INTERNAL PROCEDURES  */
/* SORT_PURCHASES, SORT_PAYMENTS AND MERGE_ACCTS WOULD NORMALLY FALL */
/* IN THIS SECTION.                                                */


MERGE_UPDATE: PROCEDURE;
/* THIS PROCEDURE READS A RECORD FROM THE CUST1 TEMPORARY FILE     */
/* AND THEN PROCESSES RECORDS FROM THE PURCHASE AND PAYMENTS FILES */
/* WHICH HAVE THE SAME ID NUMBER.  NOTE THAT THIS REQUIRES THAT THE */
/* PURCHASE AND PAYMENT FILES ARE ALSO SORTED IN ORDER OF ASCENDING */
/* ID NUMBERS.  (THIS IS ALSO A REQUIREMENT FOR THE NEWACCT FILE IN */
/* THE MERGE_ACCTS PROCEDURE).                                     */

       OPEN FILE(PURCHASE) INPUT,
            FILE (PAYMENT) INPUT,
            FILE (CUST1) UPDATE,
            FILE (STATMENT) OUTPUT;

       ON ENDFILE (CUST1) GO TO T;
       ON ENDFILE (PURCHASE) PURCH.ID = 0;
```

FIGURE 7-5.3 (Continued)

The final procedure, COPY, involves a simple loop which moves the records in CUST1 to the file CUSTOMER, overwriting the old CUSTOMER records in the process. Records marked with an account number of 000000 are excluded from the new CUSTOMER file.

The JLC for NEWACCTS, PURCHASE, and PAYMENT is given at the end of the pro-

```
        ON ENDFILE (PAYMENT) PAY.ID = 0;

        GET FILE (PURCHASE) EDIT (PURCH) (COLUMN(1),F(6),3 A(2),F(8,2),
                                          A(20));
        GET FILE (PAYMENT) EDIT (PAY) (COLUMN(1),F(6),3 A(2) ,F(8,2));
        DO WHILE ('1'B);
            READ FILE (CUST1) INTO (CUST);

/* PRINT STATEMENT HEADINGS AND PREVIOUS BALANCE                        */
            PUT FILE (STATMENT) EDIT ('THE COMPANY OF CANADA, LTD.',
                                      '4141 THE STREET',
                                      'THE CITY,  PROVINCE','AOA 1B1')
                (X(22),A,SKIP,X(28),A,SKIP,X(26),A,SKIP,X(32),A)
                (NAME,CUST.ID,ADDRESS)
                (SKIP(3),A(21),F(6),3 (SKIP, A))
                ('DATE','TRANSACTION','DEBIT','CREDIT','BALANCE')
                (SKIP(3),X(2),A(8),A(31),A(11),A(11),A(7))
                ('BALANCE FORWARD',BALANCE)
                (SKIP(2),X(10),A(49),P'$$$$,$$9V.99CR');

        IF BALANCE < 0
        THEN PUT FILE (STATMENT) EDIT (BALANCE)
                            (SKIP(0),X(47),P'$$$$,$$9V.99');
        ELSE IF BALANCE > 0
              THEN PUT FILE (STATMENT) EDIT (BALANCE)
                            (SKIP(0),X(35),P'$$$$,$$9V.99');

        OLD_BALANCE = OLD_BALANCE + BALANCE;
        CUR_BALANCE = BALANCE;

/************************************************************************/
/*                       P U R C H A S E S                            */
    /*  THIS SEGMENT IS SET UP TO HANDLE ALL PURCHASE RECORDS.        */
        DO WHILE (CUST.ID = PURCH.ID);

/* THIS IS WHERE AND HOW THE DELETE FLAG IS SET.                       */
            IF DESCRIPTION = 'DELETE THIS CUSTOMER'
            THEN DELETE = '1'B;

            ELSE DO;
                PURCHASES = PURCHASES + PURCH.AMOUNT;
                BDATE = PURCH.MONTH || '/' || PURCH.DAY || '/' ||
                        PURCH.YEAR;
                BALANCE = BALANCE + PURCH.AMOUNT;
                IF PURCH.AMOUNT >= 0
                THEN I = 5;
                ELSE I =17;

/* PUT OUT THE LINE INDICATING A PURCHASE.                             */
                PUT FILE (STATMENT) EDIT (BDATE,DESCRIPTION,
                         ABS(PURCH.AMOUNT),BALANCE)
                         (SKIP,A(10),A(20),X(I),P'$$$$,$$9V.99',
                         COLUMN(60),P'$$$$,$$9V.99CR');
            END;

            GET FILE (PURCHASE) EDIT (PURCH) (COLUMN(1),F(6),3 A(2),
                         F(8,2),A(20));
        END; /* OF PURCHASE SEGMENT */

/************************************************************************/
/*                       P A Y M E N T S                              */
```

FIGURE 7-5.3   (Continued)

gram. A set of sample reports for this data is shown in Fig. 7-5.4. Some information is assumed to reside in the CUSTOMER file initially.

To conclude this section, let us consider some changes in design of the system just implemented; remember, system development is an iterative process Two major changes can be accommodated quite easily. Instead of making a separate pass over the CUSTOMER

```
/* THIS SEGMENT IS SET UP TO HANDLE ALL PAYMENT RECORDS.        */
        DO WHILE (CUST.ID = PAY.ID);
             BALANCE = BALANCE - PAY.AMOUNT;
             CUR_BALANCE = CUR_BALANCE - PAY.AMOUNT;
             PAYMENTS = PAYMENTS + PAY.AMOUNT;
             PAY_DAY(PAY.DAY) = PAY_DAY(PAY.DAY) + PAY.AMOUNT;
             BDATE = PAY.MONTH || '/' || PAY.DAY || '/' || PAY.YEAR;
             IF PAY.AMOUNT > 0
             THEN I =17;
             ELSE I = 5;
/* PUT OUT THE LINE INDICATING A PAYMENT.                        */
             PUT FILE (STATMENT) EDIT ( BDATE,'PAYMENT ON ACCOUNT',
                        ABS(PAY.AMOUNT),BALANCE)
                        (SKIP,A(10),A(20),X(I),P'$$$$,$$9V.99',
                        COLUMN(60),P'$$$$,$$9V.99CR');
             GET FILE (PAYMENT) EDIT (PAY) (COLUMN(1),F(6),3 A(2),
                                     F(8,2));
        END;  /* OF PAYMENTS SEGMENT */

/* ************************************************************************* /
/*     I N T E R E S T   A N D   B A L A N C E   O W I N G         */
/* THIS SEGMENT CALCULATES THE AMOUNT OF INTEREST TO BE CHARGED.    */
/* INTEREST IS CHARGED ON THAT PORTION OF LAST MONTH'S DEFICIT BALANCE
/* FOR WHICH PAYMENTS WERE NOT RECEIVED THIS MONTH.                 */

        IF CUR_BALANCE > 0
        THEN DO;
             INTEREST_AMT = 0.015 * CUR_BALANCE;
             BALANCE = BALANCE + INTEREST_AMT;
             INTEREST = INTEREST + INTEREST_AMT;
             PUT FILE(STATMENT) EDIT (TODAY,'INTEREST ON ',
                  CUR_BALANCE,':',INTEREST_AMT,BALANCE)
                  (SKIP,A(10),A,P'$$$$,$$9V.99',A(3),P'$$$,$$9V.99',
                  COLUMN(60),P'$$$$,$$9V.99CR');
        END;

/* PRINT THE NEW BALANCE OWING (WHICH MAY BE A CREDIT BALANCE)      */

        PUT FILE (STATMENT) EDIT (TODAY,'CURRENT AMOUNT OWING',
                        BALANCE)
                        (SKIP(2),A(10),A(49),P'$$$$,$$9V.99CR');

        IF DELETE
        THEN DO;
             DELETE = '0'B;
             CUST.ID = 0;

/* IF THE CUSTOMER IS DELETED A MESSAGE IS PRINTED TO INDICATE THAT */
/* THIS IS HIS FINAL STATEMENT.                                    */

             PUT FILE (STATMENT) EDIT ('THIS IS YOUR FINAL STATEMENT',
                        '. THANKYOU FOR YOUR BUSINESS.')
                        (SKIP(3),A,A);
        END;

        NEW_BALANCE = NEW_BALANCE + BALANCE;
        PUT FILE (STATMENT) PAGE;
        REWRITE FILE (CUST1) FROM (CUST);
        PUT FILE (SYSPRINT) EDIT (CUST) (SKIP(1),F(6),X(1),3 A(20),
```

FIGURE 7-5.3 (Continued)

file to merge it with the NEWACCT file, we can simply include this merge in with the merge/update process, which involves the PURCHASE and PAYMENT files. Note that the temporary file CUST1 is still used. We could place the merged information from the four files immediately back into the file CUSTOMER, but this is risky. If the computer system fails in the middle of the merge/update procedure, the CUSTOMER file will contain both updated and old records. Such a situation would make a billing system restart impossible.

```
                                    A(7),F(9,2));
      END;  /* OF MAIN LOOP */


/*********************************************************************/
/*              M O N T H L Y    T O T A L S                         */
/* THIS SEGMENT IS USED TO PRINT OUT THE OVERALL TOTALS              */

T:    PUT FILE (SYSPRINT) PAGE EDIT('MONTHLY TOTALS') (A)
                          ('OLD BALANCE OWING', OLD_BALANCE,
                           'PURCHASES MADE', PURCHASES,
                           'PAYMENTS RECEIVED',PAYMENTS,
                           'INTEREST CHARGED',INTEREST,
                           'CURRENT BALANCE OWING',NEW_BALANCE)
               (SKIP(1), 5 (SKIP(1),A(23),P'$$$$,$$$,$$9V.99DB'));
      PUT FILE (SYSPRINT) EDIT ('DAILY PAYMENTS RECEIVED THIS MONTH')
                          (SKIP(5),A);
      DO I = 1 TO 31;
         IF (PAY_DAY(I) ¬= 0)
         THEN PUT FILE (SYSPRINT) EDIT (I,PAY_DAY(I))
                          (SKIP(2),F(2),X(2),P'$$$$,$$$,$$9V.99DB');
      END;
      CLOSE FILE (CUST1), FILE (STATMENT), FILE (PAYMENT),
           FILE(PURCHASE);
END MERGE_UPDATE;


COPY: PROCEDURE;
/* THIS PROCEDURE COPIES THE FINAL CUST1 RECORDS BACK INTO CUSTOMER, */
/* TO SET UP FOR NEXT MONTH'S RUN.  NOTE THAT THOSE CUSTOMERS WITH   */
/* AN ID OF 000000 ARE THOSE WHICH HAVE BEEN FLAGGED FOR DELETION.   */

      OPEN FILE (CUSTOMER) OUTPUT,
           FILE (CUST1) INPUT;
      ON ENDFILE (CUST1) STOP;
      DO WHILE ('1'B);
         READ FILE (CUST1) INTO (CUST);
         IF (CUST.ID ¬= 000000)
            THEN WRITE FILE (CUSTOMER) FROM (CUST);
      END;
END COPY;

END BILLS;
//GO.SYSPRINT DD SYSOUT=(J,,7316)
//GO.STATMENT DD SYSOUT=A
//GO.CUST1 DD DSN=&&CUSTOMER,DISP=(NEW,DELETE),UNIT=SYSDA,
//        VOL=SER=USER02,SPACE=(75,(25,5))
//GO.CUSTOMER DD DSN=&&CUSTOM,DISP=(OLD,KEEP),UNIT=SYSDA,
//        VOL=SER=USER02,SPACE=(75,(25,5))
//GO.NEWACCT DD *      (NEWACCT CARD FILE SHOULD FOLLOW IMMEDIATELY)
//GO.PURCHASE DD *     (PURCHASE CARD FILE SHOULD FOLLOW IMMEDIATELY)
//GO.PAYMENT DD *      (PAYMENT CARD FILE SHOULD FOLLOW HERE)
```

FIGURE 7-5.3   (Continued)

A second change accommodates the problem of tardy accounts—a problem which realistically cannot be ignored. Instead of replacing a terminating account number by 000000, we can copy the information for the account into a file called TERMINAL which is retained from month to month. The terminating account is removed from the CUSTOMER file. When purchases and payments are applied to an account which is not found in the CUSTOMER file, a search is made of the TERMINAL file. If applicable, the transactions are posted against this file and statements can be generated. Account closures can be completed based on the transactions applied to the TERMINAL file.

We have presented in this section a simplified view of a small customer-billing sys-

```
145203 JOHN Q. DRYDEN        BOX 400            JASPER,   AB          TOE 1E0       8.00
504858 PAMELA B. SCHULTZ     1356 OSLER ST.     SASKATOON,  SK        S7N 0V2      12.19
     0 PETER L. CLARKE       2337 WEST 10TH AVE. VANCOUVER,  BC       V2K 1H8      -1.43
529270 DAVID N. PARKER       4534 HIGHLAND ST.  EDMONTON,   AB        T2E 1K6    1353.03
532147 PATRICK L. WATSON     #123-1968 COMOX ST. VANCOUVER,  BC       V4R 3Z8      37.00
     0 RAYMOND M. JAMES      753 11TH ST. S.    CALGARY,   AB         T3B 2A0       0.00
538494 ALICE H. COCHRANE     2348 MAIN ST.      WINNIPEG,  MAN        R5K 7P1       0.00
542137 CINDY L. PARENT       4112 HIGH AVE.     CALGARY,   AB         T7C 5Y6     230.50
556090 DIANNE P. HOLMES      23 ASHTON CRES.    THUNDERBAY, ONT.      M9J 1T4     411.43
563619 PAUL E. JACKSON       1356 AVENUE ROAD   TORONTO, ONT.         M2D 0S9      -3.36
570144 RICHARD D WILLIAMSON  851 CACHE DRIVE    KAMLOOPS,   BC        U5X 3W9     443.30
587542 ROBERT C. SMYTHE      418 AVENUE S       SASKATOON,  SK        S7H 0K1     300.00
591146 LINDA T. GARDNER      2337 49TH ST. E.   CALGARY,   AB         TOM 2A0      25.37
609483 GEORGE H. ELSEY       #4-14015 77TH AVE. EDMONTON,   AB        T3K 0I0    3457.69
615966 JUDY R. JONES         315 SCARTH ST.     REGINA,   SK          S4N 303     -11.70
637263 SUSAN C. FROST        12 1ST ST. N.      KAMLOOPS,   BC        U30 1G5     653.21
643120 JOHN A. THOMPSON      8423 81ST ST.      EDMONTON,   AB        T3F 1S5      29.14
661301 ROY B. ANDERSON       2415 COLONY ST.    SASKATOON,  SK        S7N 0S7       0.10
678007 JAMES P. MACDONALD    4125 ARBUTUS ST.   VANCOUVER,  BC        V4G 1S2      39.22
686725 LARRY R. BROWN        4532 HIGHLAND BLVD. NORTH VANCOUVER, BC  V8D 2X3     145.46
693121 PATRICIA L. FOX       4105 36TH ST.      RED DEER,  AB         T5M 1U9     183.19
752145 DAVE BROADFOOT        7469 HILL CT.      KAMLOOPS,   BC        U8S 3E5     250.00
```

(a)

MONTHLY TOTALS   DAILY PAYMENTS RECEIVED THIS MONTH

OLD BALANCE OWING	$5,590.58	1	$5.00DB
PURCHASES MADE	$3,331.61		
PAYMENTS RECEIVED	$1,428.32	2	$9.00
INTEREST CHARGED	$68.47		
CURRENT BALANCE OWING	$7,562.34	3	$25.00
		4	$100.00

(b)

8	$50.00
9	$25.00
10	$30.00
11	$100.00
12	$5.00
13	$54.32
15	$115.00
18	$200.00
22	$100.00
25	$100.00
29	$50.00
30	$400.00
31	$70.00

(c)

FIGURE 7-5.4 Sample reports of (a) customer report, (b) monthly balance report, (c) daily sales report, and (d) a monthly statement.

```
                THE COMPANY OF CANADA, LTD.
                      4141 THE STREET
                    THE CITY,  PROVINCE
                         AOA 1B1


DIANNE P. HOLMES       556090
23 ASHTCN CRES.
THUNDERBAY, ONT.
M9J 1T4


   DATE     TRANSACTION              DEBIT       CREDIT     BALANCE

            BALANCE FORWARD         $300.24                 $300.24
 05/08/74   RECORD                    $5.00                 $305.24
 05/08/74   RECORD PLAYER           $253.94                 $559.18
 05/08/74   PAYMENT ON ACCOUNT                   $50.00     $509.18
 05/22/74   PAYMENT ON ACCOUNT                  $100.00     $409.18
 05/20/75   INTEREST ON    $150.24:   $2.25                 $411.43

 05/20/75   CURRENT AMOUNT OWING                            $411.43
```

(d)

FIGURE 7-5.4   (Continued)

tem. Nevertheless, the system illustrates the use and importance of sequential files and provides a glimpse of the type of processing necessary in a large billing system. We now turn our attention to a discussion of another basic file organization.

7-6 INDEXED SEQUENTIAL FILES

In the design of the billing system in the last section, we did not allow inquiries about the status of an account, except on a monthly basis. As the company expands its operation, it may become desirable or necessary to provide store clerks, at the point of sale, the facility to validate a customer account. Customers who exceed their credit limit and stolen credit cards are two facets of business the company must deal with. Validation at the store's counters must be instantaneous, for customers become irate if they are unnecessarily delayed.

A query on customer status can be handled, with slight modifications, using the system already implemented; however, the system's performance would undoubtedly be less than satisfactory. Since CUSTOMER (the main permanent file of the system) is a sequential file, it may be necessary to search almost the entire file before a desired record is located. The delay associated with such an activity can be prohibitively high. For example, suppose we have 5,000 records stored on the CUSTOMER file and we access the file sequentially at an average delay (including seek time, latency, and transmission time) of 30 milliseconds per record. The expected time taken to access the final record on the file is approximately 150,000 milliseconds, or 2.5 minutes!

To obtain a reasonable response time for an on-line query from a salesperson, the ability to go directly to the required record must be available. In this section, we will examine how a record can be directly accessed. In addition to a direct-access capability, it is also advantageous to retain in a small billing system the sequential ordering of the file.

This should be done to allow for the sequential processing of the CUSTOMER file when generating monthly reports and statements. We can process monthly reports by accessing customer records in a direct, yet nonsequential fashion. However, a tremendous amount of seek-time overhead is incurred due to the quasi-random movement of the disk heads as generated by the nonsequential processing of the records of the file. Therefore, the file structure that is required for such a billing system with on-line inquiry must support both a direct and sequential form of access. In this section, we examine a file organization which allows both types of access capabilities.

7-6.1 The Structure of Indexed Sequential Files

An important aspect affecting the file structure is the type of physical medium on which the file resides. The capability of directly accessing a record based on a key (or unique index) can only be achieved if the external storage device used supports this type of access. In particular, devices such as card readers and tape units allow the access of a particular record only after reading all the other records that physically appear before a desired record in the file. Hence, direct record access is impossible for these types of devices. The types of external storage devices that support both direct and sequential access are magnetic drums and fixed and exchangeable magnetic disks.

The file-structure concepts relating to indexed sequential files are best exemplified when considering an exchangeable disk as the storage medium. In addition, because of their low price/performance ratio and large total storage capacity, exchangeable head disks are generally chosen when using indexed sequential files. Hence, the discussion to follow assumes that the file structures are mapped onto such a device.

We will present two types of indexed sequential-file organizations—the first one is due to IBM, and the second is used by CDC. An IBM indexed sequential file consists of three separate areas: the prime area, the index area, and the overflow area. The *prime area* is an area into which data records are written when the file is first created. The file is created sequentially, that is, by writing records in the prime area in a sequence dictated by the lexical ordering of the keys of the records. The writing process starts at the second track of a particular cylinder, say the nth cylinder, of a disk. When this cylinder is filled, writing continues on the second track of the next ($n + 1$st) cylinder, and continues in this fashion until the file's creation is completed. If the newly created file is accessed sequentially according to the key item, the records are processed in the order they were written.

The second important area of an indexed sequential file, the *index area*, is created automatically by the data-management routines in the operating system. A number of index levels may be involved in an indexed sequential file. The lowest level of index is the *track index*, which is always written on the first track (named track 0) of the cylinders for the indexed sequential file. The track index contains two entries for each prime track of the cylinder—a *normal entry* and an *overflow entry*. The normal entry is composed of the address of the prime track to which the entry is associated and of the highest value of the keys for the records stored on that track. If there are no overflow records, the overflow entry is set equal to the normal entry. The significance of the overflow entry is described later in this subsection during a discussion of overflow records. Figure 7-6.1 illustrates the

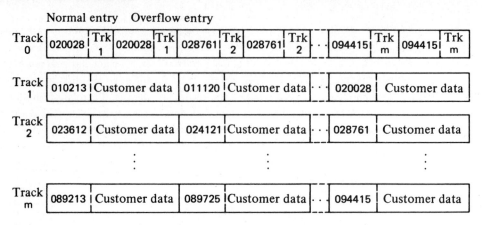

Normal entry   Overflow entry

Track 0	020028	Trk 1	020028	Trk 1	028761	Trk 2	028761	Trk 2	··	094415	Trk m	094415	Trk m

Track 1	010213	Customer data	011120	Customer data	··	020028	Customer data

Track 2	023612	Customer data	024121	Customer data	··	028761	Customer data

⋮   ⋮   ⋮

Track m	089213	Customer data	089725	Customer data	··	094415	Customer data

FIGURE 7-6.1   Track index and prime area of an indexed sequential file.

file structure for an indexed sequential file of customer records in which the key item is a six-digit account number. Only one cylinder is shown with a prime area of m tracks.

In the same manner as a track index describes the storage of records on the tracks of a cylinder, the *cylinder index* indicates how records are distributed over a number of cylinders. A cylinder index references a track index—one cylinder index entry per track index.

A final level of indexing exists in this hierarchical indexing structure. A *master index* is used for an extremely large file where a search of the cylinder index is too time consuming. This index forms the root node of the tree of indices used in an indexed sequential file. Figure 7-6.2 illustrates the relationships between the different levels of indices discussed.

Locating the record corresponding to the customer with account number 089631 involves a search of the master index to find the proper cylinder index with which the record is associated (i.e., cylinder index 1). Next, a search is made of the cylinder index to find the cylinder on which the record is located (i.e., cylinder 1). A search of the track index produces the track number on which the record resides (i.e., track m). Finally, a search of the track is required to locate the desired record. This searching process is more precisely described in Algorithm INDEXED_SEQ_ACCESS, which is given later in this section after we have discussed overflow records. It should be noted that a master index is not always necessary, and it should only be requested for large files. When it is used, it should reside in main memory during all processing of the indexed sequential file.

If records are added to a sequential file, a new sequential file must be created. We can use the same approach when handling additions for an indexed sequential file. However, because it is possible to access records directly in an indexed sequential file, this type of file is generally used in a more volatile and quick-response demanding environment, i.e., an environment in which many additions and deletions arise from on-line queries or small batches of queries. Such deletions and additions must be immediately reflected in the file; one cannot wait until the month's end.

The problems of adding records are handled by creating an overflow area or areas, usually on the same device on which the file resides. Two types of overflow areas are

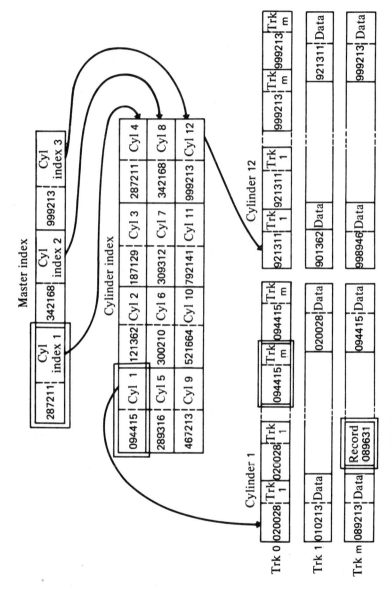

FIGURE 7-6.2 Relationships between the different levels of indices.

possible—a cylinder overflow area or an independent overflow area. A *cylinder overflow area* is a number of dedicated tracks on a cylinder that contains a number of prime-area tracks. If, through the addition of a record, an overflow is created in the prime-area tracks of the cylinder, then the overflow records are stored in the cylinder overflow area.

The effect that an overflow record has on the structure of the file is illustrated in Fig. 7-6.3. Note that we make the unrealistic yet simplifying assumption that one track contains only three records. Initially, a customer record with an account number of 026924 is added to the file, as depicted in Fig. 7-6.1. The record with account number 028761 must be moved to the cylinder overflow area at track $m + 1$ to preserve the sequential ordering of records in track 2 of the prime area. This change necessitates two other alterations to the file. First, the normal entry in the track index for track 2 must be changed from 028761 to 026924, since the latter number is now the highest key value for the track. Secondly, the overflow entry is adjusted so that its first subentry contains the largest key value of any overflow record for track 2 (i.e., the value 028761), and the second entry is set to the track/record address of the overflow record with the *smallest* key value for track 2.

An overflow record is identical to a prime record, except that a track/record address field is added to the end of the record. This track/record address field contains a pointer to the overflow record with the next largest key value in the list of overflow records for a particular track. Therefore, when the record with the key value 026924 becomes an overflow record with the addition of the record with a key value of 021008, the track/address field is set to point to the record with key value 028761. Figure 7-6.3, by necessity, presents a simplified view. In general, there may be a number of cylinder overflow tracks, and the overflow records for each track are grouped together in a linked list. The head of the link list is given by the track/record address in the track index. The final record in the linked list is specified by placing the number of the associated prime track in the track/record address field of the overflow record (e.g., track 2 is placed in the link field of overflow record 028761).

As more and more records are added to the indexed sequential file, the cylinder overflow area becomes full. When this happens, further overflow records are transferred to an *independent overflow area*, providing such an area is specified when the file is created. The independent overflow area resides on a cylinder or cylinders apart from any prime-area cylinder. Overflow records are linked together in the same manner as they are in the cylinder overflow area. Note, however, that for disks with movable heads, the use of independent overflow areas should be discouraged as a significant number of seeks are generated when the access arm is moved between the prime and independent overflow areas.

Thus far we have discussed the addition of records; let us now turn to the deletion of records. In IBM's indexed sequential organization, deleted records are not physically removed from a file, but are merely marked as deleted by placing '11111111' B in the first byte of the record. If a new record is added later which has the same key as a record previously deleted, then the space occupied by a deleted record is recovered.

Records which are placed in an overflow area are never moved back into the prime area due to a deletion. Only by reorganizing the file can an overflow record be placed in the prime area. Reorganization is achieved by sequentially copying the records of the file into a temporary file and then recreating the file by sequentially copying the records back into the original file. Because the retrieval of overflow records can carry a large overhead,

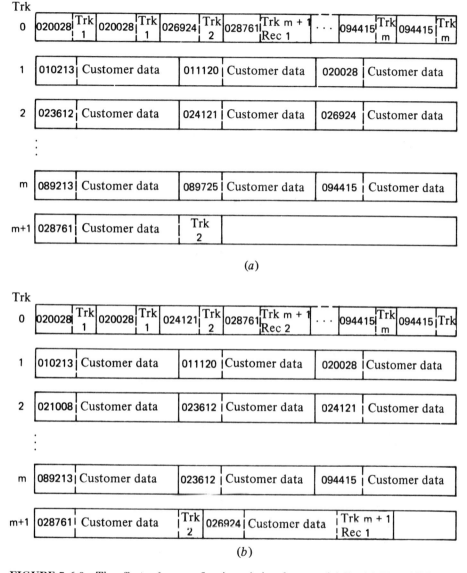

FIGURE 7-6.3 The effects of an overflow in an indexed sequential file. (*a*) The addition of a record with a key of 026924; (*b*) the addition of a record with a key of 021008.

the amount of disorganization in an indexed sequential file should be monitored closely. A good "rule of thumb" when using movable head disks is to reorganize when records must be placed in the independent overflow area.

We now leave the discussion of IBM's indexed sequential-file organization to consider briefly another file structure for an indexed sequential file. We return to the IBM organization when considering the processing of indexed sequential files in the next subsection.

The SCOPE monitor for the Control Data 6600 and CYBER series of machines provides an indexed sequential file that is structured very differently from the IBM system. A SCOPE Indexed Sequential (SIS) file is organized into *data blocks* and *index blocks*. Both blocks are handled as logical records which are allocated and transferred to and from main storage under the guidance of the SCOPE monitor. The user has no control over the physical placement of the blocks on the external storage device. This strict control is a necessary requirement because SCOPE allows the simultaneous sharing of disk files in a multiuser environment. The user does have control of the size of the data and index blocks.

A data block is composed of data records, keys with pointers to the data records within the data block, and padding space into which overflow records are placed. A set of data blocks is shown in Fig. 7-6.4. Note that the user may specify the size of the padding area as a factor of the size of the complete block (i.e., .5 means that half of the data block is assigned as padding).

The index blocks form a tree-structured hierarchy of keys and pointers much as the index areas do in the IBM system. An index block contains pairs of keys and addresses, and padding space for the addition of such pairs. A key/address pair is composed of the lowest key of a particular data block or a "lower level" index block, and the address of the data or index block in which this key resides. Figure 7-6.4 shows the relationship between index blocks and data blocks in a two-level index block file. Note that the user may select a padding factor for the index blocks and may specify the number of index levels for the file when it is created. In Fig. 7-6.4, the master index block (MB) references three subordinate index blocks (SIB1, SIB2, and SIB3). These index blocks point to data blocks (DB1, DB2, . . ., DBm).

Again we are presenting a somewhat unrealistic situation by allowing only three records in a data block. However, with the addition of two records with keys of 010943 and 010000, we can illustrate how overflow records are handled in the SCOPE system. Figure 7-6.5a shows the local effect the addition of record 010943 has on DB1. Figure 7-6.5b depicts the more global effects the addition of record 010000 has on DB1, SIB1, and MB. A byproduct of this addition is the creation of a new data block, DBm +1, which contains half of the records that would have resided in DB1 if there had been enough space.

As more data blocks are created, the index block becomes full. Overflows in an index block are handled in the same manner as for data blocks. A new block is created and half of the index records in the full index block are moved to the new index block. The reason for splitting an overflow block is to eliminate the problem of continually having to move overflow records from a full block into a separate overflow area, as is done with prime-area overflows in the IBM system. Of course, the "splitting" process requires more memory than a "record-at-a-time" overflow process, because of the padding space that must be reserved.

In the CDC SCOPE system, deleted records are "garbage collected." That is, the holes left by deleted records are replaced by the active records with higher key values in the block. Hence, both the active record area and the padding areas are always contiguous areas in a block.

Let us now examine the type of processing that is performed when using an indexed sequential file.

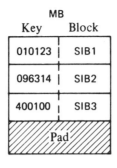

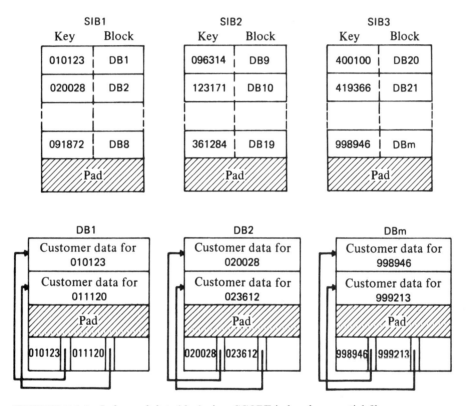

FIGURE 7-6.4 Index and data blocks in a SCOPE indexed sequential file.

7-6.2 Processing Indexed Sequential Files

By now it should be clear that the organization of an indexed sequential file is much more complex than that of a sequential file. Because of this complexity, most operating systems provide access facilities or methods which handle the file structure changes that can result from the insertion and deletion of records. In the discussion to follow, we point out those aspects of indexed sequential-file processing which are normally performed by system access methods and those that are left to the user.

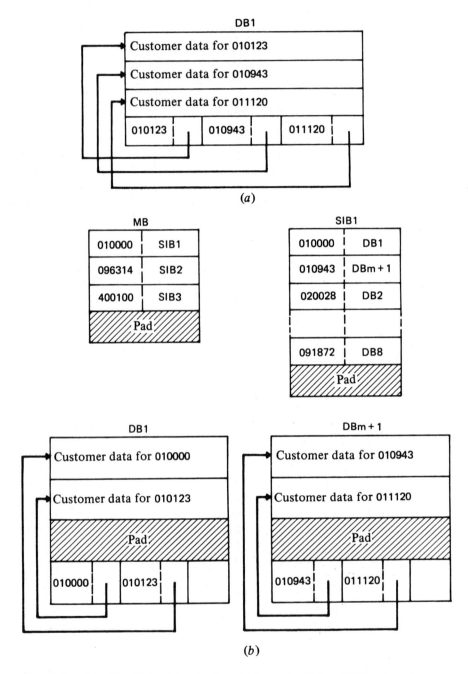

FIGURE 7-6.5 The effects of the addition of (a) record with key 010943 and (b) record with key 010000.

The main advantage of an indexed sequential file is that records can be processed either sequentially or directly. In this subsection, we describe both types of processing as they relate to IBM's indexed sequential file. The formulation of algorithms for sequential and direct processing of CDC's SCOPE indexed sequential file is left as an exercise at the end of this section.

The sequential processing of an indexed sequential file is logically identical to the sequential processing of a sequential file, i.e., records are processed in a sequence determined by the index item. The types of transactions that are performed are the reading, alteration, addition, and deletion of records. These are accomplished at a user level with **READ**, **WRITE**, and **REWRITE** statements, as described in Sec. 7-4. While the types of transactions and the operations used to effect these transaction types are usually the same for the sequential processing of sequential and indexed sequential files, the manner in which the records are accessed is substantially different, due to the differences in the file structures.

Algorithm **IS_SEQUENTIAL** outlines how records are processed sequentially in an indexed sequential file. In the algorithm, we purposely do not specify the type of transactions which are processed. Typically, a variety of transaction types would be handled, such as the addition, deletion, and alteration of records. The processing of these transaction types was described in detail in Algorithm **SEQUENTIAL_PROCESS** in Sec. 7-4 and, therefore, is not presented again here. Instead, in the algorithm the statement "process transaction" indicates that section in which transaction processing would take place. Algorithm **IS_SEQUENTIAL** simply shows how the sequential accessing of a particular record in a sequential file differs from the sequential accessing of a record in an indexed sequential file.

Algorithm IS_SEQUENTIAL. Given an indexed sequential file called **MASTER** which contains records that are each made up of a key and a set of information items, an algorithm is provided for accessing the records sequentially. During processing, the **MASTER** file records are read into a variable **MTR_REC** which contains **KEY** and **INFO** items. A prime-area record is denoted by the variable **PRIME_REC**, with subitems of **KEY** and **INFO**. The track index, **TRK_INDEX**, is considered to be a vector m in length in which each element contains four items: **NORMAL_KEY**, **NORMAL_ADDR**, **OVFLOW_KEY**, and **OVFLOW_ADDR**. An overflow record is referred to using the variable **OVFLOW_REC**, which consists of the three items: **KEY**, **INFO**, and **LINK**. For a given overflow record, **LINK** contains the track/record address of the overflow record with the next largest key value. The variables **CYL** and **TRK** denote the cylinder and track which is being accessed. **ADDR** is a special pointer variable which contains the track/record address of the next record to be processed. **ADDR** is implicitly initialized to point at the first record in the file when the file is opened.

1. [Initialize] Open MASTER for input.
2. [Process records from the first cylinder (represented by k) to the last cylinder (represented by n) as derived from the cylinder index]
   Repeat steps 3 to 5 for CYL = k, k+1, ..., n.
3. [Process prime-track records and their associated overflow records for a given cylinder]
   Repeat steps 4 and 5 for TRK = 1, 2, ..., m.

4. [Read records on a prime track and process]
   Set ADDR to point to the first record location in track TRK.
   Repeat while KEY of PRIME_REC(ADDR) ≠ NORMAL_KEY of TRK_INDEX[TRK]:
       read PRIME_REC at ADDR from MASTER file into MTR_REC;
       set ADDR to beginning of next track record;
       process transactions posted against MTR_REC.
   Read PRIME_REC at ADDR from MASTER file into MTR_REC.   (Process last record.)
5. [Read from linked list of overflow records and process]
   If NORMAL_KEY of TRK_INDEX[TRK] ≠ OVFLOW_KEY of TRK_INDEX[TRK],
   then
       set ADDR ← OVFLOW_ADDR of TRK_INDEX[TRK], initialize ADDR;
       repeat while ADDR ≠ TRK:
           read OVFLOW_REC at ADDR from MASTER file into MTR_REC;
           set ADDR ← LINK of OVFLOW_REC;
           process transactions posted against MTR_REC.
6. [Finished]   Exit.

Algorithm IS_SEQUENTIAL begins with the allocation of buffer space for processing of the MASTER file. The records for a particular prime track are processed in step 4. Note the use of the pointer variable ADDR when referencing a particular prime record [i.e., PRIME_REC(ADDR)]. In step 5, overflow records are read by following the overflow links for records in the cylinder overflow area and in the independent overflow area, if applicable. This processing continues for all tracks of all cylinders containing the indexed sequential file. The algorithm presupposes that the space allotted for an indexed sequential file is an integral number of cylinders. This supposition is true for IBM systems.

Algorithm IS_SEQUENTIAL illustrates the complex processing involved simply to read the next record in sequence. However, for the user, the sequential processing of an indexed sequential file is no different than the sequential processing of a sequential file which is ordered by a desired key. It involves the two steps:

1 Open MASTER file for input.
2 Repeat while not end of MASTER file:
     read the next record;
     process transactions posted against MTR_REC.

Therefore, the system access facilities automatically handle the incrementing of CYL and TRK and the updating of the variable ADDR in Algorithm IS_SEQUENTIAL.

The direct processing of an indexed sequential file differs substantially from the sequential processing just outlined. Algorithm IS_DIRECT shows how direct processing is accomplished given a transaction record which specifies the reading, alteration, or deletion of an existing record, or the addition of a new record. The algorithm assumes an input of just one transaction. This is realistic since, in practice, direct processing is used when a quick response time is needed for a number of individual requests, and yet there is not sufficient time to batch the requests and achieve a higher system throughput of requests. A transaction record is of the form

<transaction record> :: = <transaction type> <key> <info>

Table 7-6.1

\<transaction type\>	\<key\> \<info\>
READ	key of record only (no \<info\>)
UPDATE	key and new information items
DELETE	key of record only (no \<info\>)
ADD	key and information items of new record

where the \<transaction type\> and the corresponding \<info\> field are given in Table 7-6.1.

Algorithm IS_DIRECT. Given an indexed sequential file called MASTER which contains records each made up of a key and a set of information items, this algorithm accesses a record directly and performs the desired transaction on this record. The cylinder index, CYL_INDEX, is considered to be a vector p in length in which each element contains the two items CYLNO (meaning cylinder number) and KEY. The transaction record is referenced using the variable TRAN_REC which is composed of the items TRANS, KEY, and INFO. The remaining variables take on the roles described in Algorithm IS_SEQUENTIAL.

1. [Initialize]   Open MASTER file for update, and read TRAN_REC.
2. [Examine cylinder index]
    Repeat for i = 1, 2, ..., p − 1:
        if KEY of TRAN_REC ≤ KEY of CYL_INDEX[i],
        then set CYL ← CYLNO of CYL_INDEX[i], and go to step 3.
    Set CYL ← CYLNO of CYL_INDEX[p].
3. [Examine track index for CYL]
    Repeat for j = 1, 2, ..., m:
        if KEY of TRAN_REC ≤ OVFLOW_KEY of TRK_INDEX[j],
        then
            if KEY of TRAN_REC ≤ NORMAL_KEY of TRK_INDEX[j],
            then set ADDR ← NORMAL_ADDR of TRK_INDEX[j], and go to step 5,
            set ADDR ← OVFLOW_ADDR of TRK_INDEX[j], and go to step 6.
4. [Compare keys]
    If TRANS = 'ADD',
    then set KEY of CYL_INDEX[p] ← KEY of TRAN_REC, call IS_OF_INSERT,
    and Exit;
    otherwise, print 'ILLEGAL TRANSACTION', and Exit.
5. [Locate record in prime area]
    (ADDR is initially pointing at the first record on the prime track.)
    If TRANS = 'ADD', then call IS_PRIME_INSERT, and Exit.
    Repeat while KEY of PRIME_REC(ADDR) < KEY of TRAN_REC:
        set ADDR to beginning of the next prime-track record.
    If KEY of PRIME_REC(ADDR) = KEY of TRAN_REC, then go to step 7.
    Print 'TRANSACTION KEY DOES NOT MATCH A FILE KEY', and Exit.

6. [Locate record in overflow area]
   (ADDR is initially pointing at 1st record in list of overflow records.)
   If TRANS = 'ADD', then call IS_OF_INSERT, and Exit.
   Repeat while KEY of OVFLOW_REC(ADDR) < KEY of TRAN_REC:
       set ADDR ← LINK OF OVFLOW_REC(ADDR).
   If KEY of OVFLOW_REC(ADDR) ≠ KEY of TRAN_REC,
   then print 'TRANSACTION KEY DOES NOT MATCH A FILE KEY', and Exit.
7. [Process transaction]
   Read track record at ADDR from MASTER file into MTR_REC.
   If TRANS of TRAN_REC = 'DELETE',
   then delete track record at ADDR from MASTER file, and Exit.
   If TRANS of TRAN_REC = 'ALTER',
   then rewrite track record at ADDR in MASTER file with KEY and INFO of
   TRAN_REC, and Exit;
   Print 'ILLEGAL TRANSACTION SPECIFIED', and Exit.

Before describing Algorithm IS_DIRECT, it must be pointed out that a master index is not used in the algorithm. If it were considered, an extra step would be necessary to locate the proper cylinder index before executing step 2.

The algorithm begins by opening the MASTER file and reading in a transaction record. The track location of the MASTER file record corresponding to the key in the transaction record is found by searching the cylinder-index and track-index tables in steps 2 and 3. Step 4 handles the unusual, yet possible, situation of the addition of a record with a key that is greater than the keys of all other records in the file. When this occurs, the cylinder index must be updated and the record is added to the overflow area for the last cylinder. Steps 5 and 6 locate in the prime and overflow areas, respectively, the desired records for a read, deletion, or alteration transaction. Step 7 performs the requested transaction.

Two algorithms are invoked from Algorithm IS_DIRECT, namely, Algorithm IS_PRIME_INSERT, and Algorithm IS_OF_INSERT. Algorithm IS_PRIME_INSERT is responsible for establishing the record location for a given prime track at which the record from the transaction should be inserted. If a dummy or deleted record has the same key as the transaction key, then the new record is inserted at the dummy or deleted record location. A dummy record is simply a record that is written into a file, usually when the file is created. The record contains no meaningful information other than its key. This record is created in anticipation that it will store meaningful information later in the "life" of the file.

If no dummy or deleted record corresponds to the transaction key, then records with keys greater than the transaction key must be moved further along the prime track to leave room for the insertion of the record. Such a movement of records results in the transfer of the last record on the track to the overflow area. This new overflow record contains the lowest key of the overflow records for the prime track under consideration. Hence, the overflow track/record address field for the corresponding element of the track index table must be altered to point to the new overflow record. A formal, step-by-step description of Algorithm IS_PRIME_INSERT is left as an exercise. The second algorithm for record insertion, Algorithm IS_OF_INSERT, however, is described as follows.

Algorithm IS_OF_INSERT. Given the track/record address ADDR of the first overflow record of a particular prime track j, a new record, which is contained in the transaction record, is inserted at its proper location in the ordered list of overflow records for the given track. NEWLOC is a variable that is assigned the track/record location at which the new record is written. PREVADDR is a temporary address needed to insert the new record into the linked list of overflow records. OVFLOW_AVAIL is a pointer to the next available record location from a list of overflow record locations.

1. [Write the new record into next available overflow location]
    Set NEWLOC ← OVFLOW_AVAIL and update OVFLOW_AVAIL pointer.
    Write KEY and INFO of TRAN_REC on MASTER file at location NEWLOC.
2. [Initialize search for positioning of new record in overflow list]
    If KEY of OVFLOW_REC(ADDR) > KEY of TRAN_REC (add to head of list),
    then set OVFLOW_ADDR of TRK_INDEX[j] ← NEWLOC,
        set LINK of OVFLOW_REC(NEWLOC) ← ADDR, and Exit.
3. [Insert in middle of overflow list]
    Set PREVADDR ← ADDR and ADDR ← LINK of OVFLOW_REC(ADDR).
    Repeat while KEY of OVFLOW_REC(PREVADDR) ≠ OVFLOW_KEY of TRK_INDEX[j]:
    (continue until end of list)
        if KEY of OVFLOW_REC(ADDR) ≥ KEY of TRAN_REC,
        then
            set LINK of OVFLOW_REC(PREVADDR) ← NEWLOC,
            set LINK of OVFLOW_REC(NEWLOC) ← ADDR, and Exit;
        set PREVADDR ← ADDR, and ADDR ← LINK of OVFLOW_REC(ADDR).
4. [Insert at end of overflow list]
    Set LINK of OVFLOW_REC(ADDR) ← NEWLOC,
    Set LINK of OVFLOW_REC(NEWLOC) ← j. (Set link field to track ADDR.)
    Set OVFLOW_KEY of TRK_INDEX[j] ← KEY of TRANS_REC.

In the algorithm, it is assumed that a special pointer, OVFLOW_AVAIL, is used in managing available record space in the overflow area. The logic of Algorithm IS_OF_INSERT varies little from the logic of many of the algorithms presented in Sec. 4-2.1 and, therefore, should be comprehensible without a detailed explanation.

It should be evident from the discussion thus far that if the system access facilities for indexed sequential files are not provided, the file-management routines which the user would have to write would be very complex. However, if record searching and handling is accomplished by system facilities (as generally happens), we can express the user-level commands required for the direct processing of an indexed sequential file in the following six steps:

1. Open MASTER file for update, and read TRAN_REC.
2. If TRANS = 'ADD',
    then write INFO of TRAN_REC with key of TRAN_REC on MASTER file,
    and Exit.
3. Read from MASTER file into MTR_REC with key of TRAN_REC.
4. If TRANS = 'ALTER',

then rewrite INFO of TRAN_REC with key of TRAN_REC on MASTER file, and Exit.

5. If TRANS = 'DELETE',
    then delete from MASTER file the record with key KEY of TRAN_REC, and Exit.

6. If TRANS ≠ 'READ', then print 'ILLEGAL TRANSACTION'.   Exit.

Note that before a record is deleted or rewritten, it is read. This is done purposely to remain consistent with the access method used in IBM systems. The read statement is used to locate a record. If a desired record does not exist, a condition code is set by the system. The user can intercept this code and thus avoid executing a rewrite or delete command which can cause a system error. In our discussion of PL/I indexed sequential-file processing in the next subsection, we demonstrate how the condition code can be used.

To conclude this subsection, let us summarize the important properties relating to indexed sequential files:

1 Indexed sequential files provide reasonably fast access to records using either sequential or direct processing.

2 For relatively static files, the independent overflow area can be eliminated and the cylinder overflow area can be minimized, thus giving a high percentage of disk utilization.

3 For highly volatile files, the access time for a record becomes excessive as overflow areas become filled.

4 Indexed sequential access facilities are generally provided in most systems, thus relieving the programmer of a large amount of housekeeping detail in maintaining indexes and linked overflow areas. At the programmer level, the sequential processing of an indexed sequential file appears identical to the sequential processing of a sequential file.

7-6.3   Indexed Sequential Files in PL/I

An indexed sequential file is identified in a PL/I program through a declaration statement of the form

    DECLARE MASTER FILE RECORD KEYED ENV(INDEXED);

Two other sets of attributes are commonly associated with a declaration statement or are supplied in the OPEN statement for the file. These are the accessing-type attributes, namely, DIRECT or SEQUENTIAL, and the processing-mode attributes: INPUT, OUTPUT, or UPDATE. For example, to create an indexed sequential file, say MASTER, we use either

    OPEN FILE(MASTER) SEQUENTIAL OUTPUT;

or we add the attributes SEQUENTIAL and OUTPUT to the file declaration. Remember all indexed sequential files must be created sequentially and thereafter can be accessed directly or sequentially.

A number of different PL/I input/output statements are provided to perform operations on an indexed sequential file. Table 7-6.2 gives a list of these statements for the file CUSTOMER with the key of ACCT_NO. CUST is the record containing the specific information identified by the key ACCT_NO.

Table 7-6.2

Processing Mode	Access Type	Purpose	Sample I/O Statements
OUTPUT	SEQUENTIAL	To create a new indexed sequential file	WRITE FILE(CUSTOMER) FROM (CUST); /* OR */ WRITE FILE(CUSTOMER) FROM (CUST) KEYFROM(ACCT_NO);
INPUT	SEQUENTIAL	To process all the records in sequence	READ FILE(CUSTOMER) INTO (CUST); /* OR */ READ FILE(CUSTOMER) INTO (CUST) KEYTO(ACCT_NO);
INPUT	DIRECT	To process selected records	READ FILE(CUSTOMER) INTO (CUST) KEY(ACCT_NO);
UPDATE	SEQUENTIAL	To modify all records	REWRITE FILE(CUSTOMER); /* OR */ REWRITE FILE(CUSTOMER) FROM (CUST);
UPDATE	DIRECT	To modify selected records	REWRITE FILE(CUSTOMER) FROM (CUST) KEY(ACCT_NO);
UPDATE	DIRECT	To add new records to the file	WRITE FILE(CUSTOMER) FROM (CUST) KEYFROM (ACCT_NO);
UPDATE	DIRECT	To delete a specific record from the file	DELETE FILE(CUSTOMER) KEY (ACCT_NO);

Many of these I/O statements are illustrated in the PL/I program given in Fig. 7-6.6. The program is composed of three major segments. The first segment creates the file CUSTOMER sequentially. The second segment updates the CUSTOMER file directly in a similar manner to that described in Algorithm IS_DIRECT given in the last subsection. The single-letter transaction codes are: 'A' meaning 'ADD', 'C' meaning 'CHANGE', 'D' meaning 'DELETE', and 'R' meaning 'READ'. Note again, that we must read a record before it can be rewritten or deleted during a file update.

The third segment reads the file sequentially, printing the contents of each record while doing so. It should be observed that the KEYTO form of a SEQUENTIAL READ statement has been used. This form of READ statement is necessary if the key for a record is not embedded in the record. The clause KEYTO(ACCT_NO) causes the value of the nonembedded key to be assigned to ACCT_NO, and thus allows the printing of the account number along with the other pertinent customer information. If we omitted the KEYTO clause, we could not recover the account number, since it does not reside in the customer record.

The differences in record structure for records with embedded and nonembedded keys are illustrated in Figs. 7-6.7 and 7-6.8. To tell the file-management facilities of the location and length of a recorded key, the DCB parameters RKP (relative key position) and

```
//   EXEC PL1LFCLG
//PL1L.SYSIN DD *

 INDX_EG: PROCEDURE OPTIONS(MAIN);

 /*                    I N I T I A L I Z A T I O N                      */
        DECLARE CUSTOMER FILE RECORD KEYED ENV(INDEXED F(770,77)),
                TRANFILE FILE STREAM INPUT,
                1 CUST,
                  2 DELETE_FLAG BIT(8),
                  2 INFO,
                    3 NAME CHARACTER(20),
                    3 ADDRESS,
                      4 LINE1 CHARACTER(20),
                      4 LINE2 CHARACTER(19),
                      4 POSTAL_CODE CHARACTER(7),
                    3 BALANCE FIXED DECIMAL(7,2),
                  ACCT_NO CHAR (6),  /* USED AS A KEY ITEM FOR RECORDS */
                  CODE CHARACTER(1),
                  LAB(0:4) LABEL;
            DELETE_FLAG = (8)'0'B;

 /*                   C R E A T I N G   F I L E                        */
        ON ENDFILE(SYSIN) GO TO UPDTE;
        OPEN FILE(CUSTOMER) SEQUENTIAL OUTPUT;
        DO WHILE ('1'B);    /* UNTIL END OF FILE SYSIN */
          GET EDIT (ACCT_NO,CUST.INFO)
                   (COL(1),A(6),2 A(20),A(19),A(7),F(7,2));
          WRITE FILE(CUSTOMER) FROM(CUST) KEYFROM(ACCT_NO);
        END;

 UPDTE:
        CLOSE FILE(CUSTOMER);

 /*                   U P D A T I N G   F I L E                        */
        OPEN FILE(CUSTOMER) DIRECT UPDATE;
        OPEN FILE(TRANFILE);
        ON ENDFILE(TRANFILE) GO TO OTPT;
        ON KEY(CUSTOMER) BEGIN;
          IF ONCODE = 51 THEN PUT SKIP LIST(ACCT_NO,' NOT FOUND');
          IF ONCODE = 52 THEN PUT SKIP LIST('DUPLICATE ACCOUNT',ACCT_NO);
        END;

        DO WHILE('1'B);
          GET FILE(TRANFILE) EDIT(CODE)(COL(1),A(1));
          I = INDEX('ACDR',CODE);
          GO TO LAB(I);

 LAB(0): /* ILLEGAL TRANSACTION CODE */
          PUT SKIP LIST('ILLEGAL TRANSACTION CODE ',CODE);
          GO TO NEXT_TRAN;

 LAB(1): /* A - ADDITION TRANSACTION */
          GET FILE(TRANFILE) EDIT(ACCT_NO,CUST.INFO)
```

FIGURE 7-6.6   Example of a PL/I program using an indexed sequential file.

KEYLEN (key length) are used. For example, suppose that we wish to embed the key ACCT_NO in the CUST structure. Then CUST would be declared as indicated in the following statements:

```
        DECLARE 1 CUST,
                    2 DELETE_FLAG BIT(8),
```

```
                    (A(6),A(20),A(20),A(19),A(7),F(7,2));
        WRITE FILE(CUSTOMER) FROM(CUST) KEYFROM(ACCT_NO);
        GO TO NEXT_TRAN;

LAB(2): /* C - CHANGE OR ALTER TRANSACTION */
        GET FILE(TRANFILE) EDIT(ACCT_NO)(A(6));
        READ FILE(CUSTOMER) INTO(CUST) KEY(ACCT_NO);
        GET FILE(TRANFILE) EDIT(NAME,ADDRESS)(2 A(20),A(19),A(7));
        REWRITE FILE(CUSTOMER) FROM(CUST) KEY(ACCT_NO);
        GO TO NEXT_TRAN;

LAB(3): /* D - DELETE TRANSACTION */
        GET FILE(TRANFILE) EDIT(ACCT_NO)(A(6));
        READ FILE(CUSTOMER) INTO(CUST) KEY(ACCT_NO);
        DELETE FILE(CUSTOMER) KEY(ACCT_NO);
        GO TO NEXT_TRAN;

LAB(4): /* R - READ TRANSACTION */
        GET FILE(TRANFILE) EDIT(ACCT_NO)(A(6));
        READ FILE(CUSTOMER) INTO(CUST) KEY(ACCT_NO);

NEXT_TRAN: END; /* DO WHILE PROCESSING TRANFILE */

OTPT: CLOSE FILE(CUSTOMER);


    /*              O U T P U T   F I L E                        */

        OPEN FILE(CUSTOMER) INPUT SEQUENTIAL;
        ON ENDFILE(CUSTOMER) STOP;
        DO WHILE('1'B);   /* UNTIL END OF CUSTOMER FILE */
        READ FILE(CUSTOMER) INTO(CUST) KEYTO(ACCT_NO);
        PUT SKIP EDIT(ACCT_NO,CUST.INFO)(5 (A,X(1)), F(7,2));
        END;
END INDX_EG;
//GO.CUSTOMER DD DSNAME=BILLING(INDEX),DISP=(NEW,KEEP),UNIT=SYSDA,
//    VOL=SER=USER02,DCB=(DSORG=IS,RKP=0,KEYLEN=6,OPTCD=L),SPACE=(CYL,1)
//           DD DSNAME=BILLING(PRIME),DISP=(NEW,KEEP),UNIT=SYSDA,
//    VOL=SER=USER02,DCB=(DSORG=IS,RKP=0,KEYLEN=6,OPTCD=L),SPACE=(CYL,3)
//           DD DSNAME=BILLING(OVFLOW),DISP=(NEW,KEEP),UNIT=SYSDA,
//    VOL=SER=USER02,DCB=(DSORG=IS,RKP=0,KEYLEN=6,OPTCD=L),SPACE=(CYL,1)
//GO.SYSIN DD *
134679MR. JOHN Q. BROWN    445 5TH AVE. N.     SASKATOON, SASK.   S7K 2H6 123.45
654821MRS. ALICE W. SMITH 285 VANCOUVER AVE.   WINNIPEG, MAN.     R4T 5S5 512.34
753981MORE O THESAME       2 LITTLE DATUM RD.  ANYTOWN, ANYWHERE  A1A 1A1
987654MR GIGO DATA         12345 DATA AVE      DATA, DATA         D5A 4T1 123.56
//GO.TRANFILE DD *
A321548MR. JOHN W. SMITH   321 MONTREAL AVE.   CALGARY, ALTA.     R4T 2D9321.54
R134679
D987654
C654821MRS. ALICE W. SMITH 286 VANCOUVER AVE.   WINNIPEG, MAN.    R4T 5S5
```

FIGURE 7-6.6 (Continued)


```
        2 ACCT_NO CHARACTER (6),
        2 INFO,
            3 NAME CHARACTER(20),
                        .
                        .
                        .
            3 BALANCE FIXED DECIMAL(7,2);
```

In this case, RKP =1 and KEYLEN =6 would be used as DCB parameters. The RKP specifies the number of bytes from the first byte of a record at which the embedded key is found. An RKP of zero is the default value and it indicates that a nonembedded key is used.

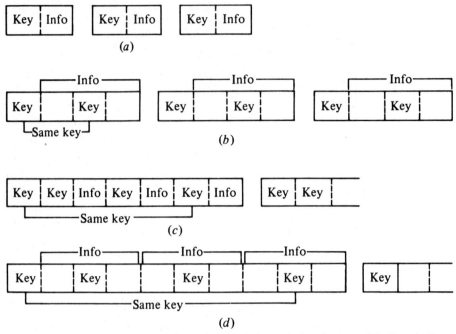

FIGURE 7-6.7 Structure of fixed-length records in an indexed sequential file. (*a*) Unblocked records—nonembedded keys; (*b*) unblocked records—embedded keys; (*c*) blocked records—nonembedded keys; (*d*) blocked records—embedded keys.

For variable-length records, the minimum RKP is 4 and implies a nonembedded key. The offset of four bytes is accounted for by the block- and record-length indicators that must accompany variable-length records. Therefore, the position of an embedded key is 4 plus the relative offset of the key from the beginning of the record.

The DD statements for the file CUSTOMER in Fig. 7-6.6 tell the system how to structure the indexed sequential file. The DSNAME parameters INDEX, PRIME, and OVFLOW specify the three different areas of the file. The DD statement with the INDEX parameter describes the file space needed for the cylinder index, the DD statement with the PRIME parameter describes the file space needed for the prime area, and the DD statement with the OVFLOW parameter describes the file space needed for the independent overflow area. No space has been allocated for a cylinder overflow area. If we wish to create a file with no cylinder index, no independent overflow area, and a cylinder overflow area of three tracks per cylinder, we would use the following DD statement:

```
//GO.CUSTOMER DD DSNAME = BILLING(PRIME),DISP = (NEW,KEEP),
//          UNIT = SYSDA,VOL = SER = USER02,DCB = (DSORG = IS,
//          RKP = 0,KEYLEN = 6,CYLOFL = 3),SPACE = (CYL,3)
```

The ON KEY type of ON condition is very important when processing files in PL/I. Its use is illustrated in Fig. 7-6.6. If an unusual condition occurs during an I/O statement, this condition is detected by the operating system and a condition code is assigned. A PL/I program can intercept this unusual condition using the ON KEY ON unit. The condition

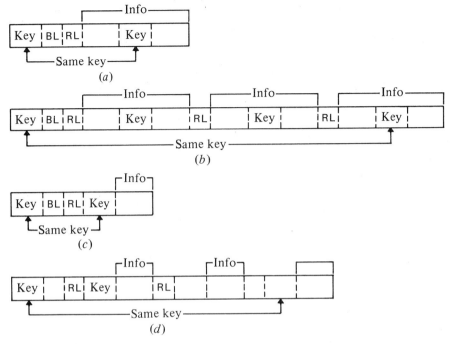

FIGURE 7-6.8 Structure of variable-length records in an indexed sequential file. (*a*) Unblocked variable-length records, RKP > 4; (*b*) blocked variable-length records, RKP > 4; (*c*) unblocked variable-length records, RKP = 4; (*d*) blocked variable-length records, RKP = 4.

code is assigned to a special PL/I pseudo variable, ONCODE, which can be used to warn the programmer of the I/O error and to allow alternate action to be taken. A list of ONCODE values that can be checked for are as follows:

ONCODE
- 50   KEY signal, used to test ON KEY conditions by setting the pseudo variable KEY to a legitimate ONCODE value
- 51   keyed record not found
- 52   attempt to add duplicate key
- 53   key sequence error, used when creating IS file
- 54   key conversion error, character string not used for key
- 55   key specification error
- 56   keyed region outside data set limit, used in REGIONAL files
- 57   no space available to add keyed record (or LMTCT reached)

As a final comment relating to the program in Fig. 7-6.6, it should be pointed out that the programmer is responsible for leaving a one-byte field for a delete flag indicator, if records are to be deleted from the file during UPDATE DIRECT processing. A DELETE statement marks a record as a dummy by putting (8)'1'B in the first byte of the record.

There are many other interesting file-processing features associated with indexed sequential files. For example, the GENKEY (generic key) ENVIRONMENT option allows the access of records according to their key class, as determined by a generic key. For example, the recorded keys '692138', '693112', '694761', and '698882' are all members of the class of keys identified by the generic key '69'.

To illustrate how the GENKEY option can be used, consider the following PL/I statements:

```
DECLARE CUSTOMER FILE RECORD SEQUENTIAL KEYED UPDATE
        ENV(INDEXED GENKEY);
        .
        .
        .

READ FILE(CUSTOMER) INTO(CUST) KEY('69');
        .
        .
        .

LOOP:   READ FILE(CUSTOMER) INTO(CUST);
        .
        .
        .

GO TO LOOP;
```

The first READ locates and reads the first record with key beginning '69'. The second READ reads the remaining records with keys which belong to the generic key class '69'.

To obtain a more comprehensive understanding of how to create and use indexed sequential files in PL/I, read the appropriate sections of the IBM PL/I(F) Programmer's Guide.

Let us now turn to an example application which helps illustrate many of the concepts presented in this section.

Exercises for Sec. 7-6

1. Formulate Algorithm IS_SEQ_SCOPE which depicts how records are processed sequentially in an indexed sequential file on the CDC Scope System.
2. Formulate Algorithm IS_DIR_SCOPE which depicts how records are processed directly in an indexed sequential file on the CDC Scope System.
3. Construct Algorithm IS_PRIME_INSERT which places a record which is to be added to an indexed sequential file (IBM variety) in its proper prime area location. Note that the placement of the new record may generate an overflow involving the last record on the prime track.
4. Assume that we always access a certain file sequentially. Under what conditions, if any, is it advantageous to have the file organized as an indexed sequential rather than a sequential file.
5. An important application area within many business systems is sales analysis. Sales analysis produces information giving management a review of sales data on customers, items, and salesmen. There are two basic methods of handling sales data—the

detail method and the *summary method.* Using the detail approach, detailed sales-transaction information is accumulated until the end of an established period (say, a month), at which time it is sorted and then analyzed to produce customer, item, and salesman information. Obviously, a sequential file can be used to store this accumulated information.

The summary method is based on sales values accumulated daily from sales information associated with order entry and invoicing, and inventory accounting. Individual inquiries return up-to-date information on customer, salesman, and item sales. To ensure immediate responses to such queries an indexed sequential organization should be considered.

Write a PL/I program which takes as input the following information as gathered from customer invoices: salesman's number, customer's account number, amounts sold (or returned) for each of article types A, B, C, and D and the total amount sold (or returned). Two files, a customer file and a salesman file, should be created and maintained for summary reports. The customer file is keyed on the customer's account number and contains an accumulated total of the purchases made to date by the customer. The salesman file is keyed on the salesman's number and it retains the total number of sales for each of the article types A, B, C, and D, and the total sales to date for the salesman. To thoroughly test your programs, intermix inquiries concerning the status of certain customer accounts or the performance of certain salesmen with the invoice information which is read in. Customer inquiries are keyed on account numbers and return the total purchases to date. Salesman inquiries are keyed on a salesman's name—a table relating salesman's name and number is required—and the sales to-date figures are returned for each article types A, B, C, and D, plus the total sales to-date figure.

7-7   CLASS-RECORDS RETRIEVAL SYSTEM

In this section, we describe a system for retrieving, maintaining, and processing students' marks on a class-by-class basis. When compared to most data-processing systems, the Class-Records Retrieval (CRR) System is small in size. Nevertheless, it is illustrative, comprehensible, and it involves an application area familiar to everyone. Again, the development of the system will be presented in three phases—the system analysis, system design, and the implementation phases.

7-7.1   System Analysis

A group of professors within the Department of Computer Science has decided to reduce the bookkeeping chores related to the recording of students' grades. A small computerized retrieval system is proposed as the tool to aid in the efficient and accurate handling of the class records. The desired system facilities the professors feel are necessary are the following:

   1   The ability to produce a complete listing of the students' names, numbers, and marks for all students in a particular class.

2 The ability to compute weighted averages for each student and a class average on any given assignment and final grades.

3 The ability to insert records for new students or to delete the records of students who cancel out.

4 The ability to insert or update marks.

It is desirable that the system be on-line to provide immediate access and to avoid an off-line form of input, such as punched cards or paper tape.

The form of input to the system should be in easy-to-learn English-like statements which allow the user to express requests such as

LIST OF STUDENTS WITH MARKS ON ASSIGNMENT 3 > 80

or   LIST OF STUDENTS, IDS, MARKS, GRADES

The term "grade" means the weighted final mark or weighted final mark to date if all term marks have not been recorded as yet.

The output should be in an easy-to-read format and printed in an order determined by the alphabetical ordering of the students' names. This ordering is the most convenient for transcribing marks to the official statements of standings for the University which list the students in alphabetical order.

7-7.2   System Design

We proceed with a top-down approach to the design of the system, beginning with the formulation of a query language and ending with the design of the file structures and file processing routines.

The design of the query language is one of the most important steps in the developments of systems, especially systems which can be used in an on-line environment. The user must be able to express his requests in a manner which fits the nature of the application. The CRR System is not the type of system which is used daily by a professor. Therefore, the language should not have a highly structured format with abbreviations for commands and command operands. In a system such as an airline reservation system, rigorous and abbreviated languages are acceptable, and even desirable, since the terminal operators are using their consoles hourly in a role which demands quick customer service.

The following BNF-like description defines a query language which is natural-language oriented, yet does not introduce the complexity of a full English query language. Grammatical expressions of the form {A} mean that the syntactic unit represented by A can appear 0, or 1, or 2, . . ., or n times for n equal to any nonnegative integer. Expressions of the form [A] mean that the syntactic unit represented by A appears once, or not at all.

<query>	:: = <proposition>
	| <maintenance function>
	| <marks weighting function>
<proposition>	:: = <subject1> <object1>
	| <subject2> <object2>
<subject1>	:: = LIST OF | NUMBER OF
<subject2>	:: = AVERAGE | MIN[IMUM] | MAX[IMUM]

<object1>   :: = <object head1> { <objective1> }
                     | { <objective2> } <object2>

<object2>   :: = <object head2> [<relational statement>]
                     { <objective1> } | { <objective2> }

<object head1>   :: = STUDENT[S] [<name list>]
                     | ID[S]
                     | <object head2>

<object head2>   :: = GRADE[S]
                     | MARK[S] [ON ASSIGNMENT <number>]

<objective1>   :: = <buzz word> <object head1>

<objective2>   :: = <buzz word> <object head2>
                     [<relational statements>]

<buzz word>   :: = WITH | FOR | ,

<relational statement>   :: = <relation> <number> [<connector>
                     <relation> <number>]

<relation>   :: = < | = | > | # | > = | < =

<connector>   :: = AND | OR

<number list>   :: = <number> | <number>, <number list>

<number>   :: = <digit> | <digit> <number>

<digit>   :: = 0|1|2|3|4|5|6|7|8|9

<name list>   :: = <name> | <name>, <name list>

<name>   :: = <letter> | <letter> <name>

<letter>   :: = A|B|C ... |X|Y|Z|&|.|-

<maintenance function>   :: = DELETE <name list>
                     | INSERT [MANY]
                     | <update head>

<update head>   :: = UPDATE ASSIGNMENT <number> [ALL]

<marks weighting function> :: = WEIGHTING <number list>

Example queries from this language are as follows:

```
LIST OF STUDENTS WITH MARKS ON ASSIGNMENT 3 > 80
LIST OF IDS, GRADES
LIST OF STUDENTS, IDS, MARKS, GRADES
AVERAGE MARKS, GRADES
MINIMUM GRADE
MAXIMUM MARK ON ASSIGNMENT 1
DELETE HARPER.B
INSERT MANY
UPDATE ASSIGNMENT 2
WEIGHTING 33, 34, 33
```

The first seven queries should be self-explanatory. The two system maintenance functions, INSERT and UPDATE, must be elaborated upon. When either of these requests is made, the system should be designed to prompt the user with the required input. For example, when a student is inserted into the system, initial information such as his/her name, student identification number, college, and year must be provided. A reliable way of ensuring that the necessary information is given is to lead the user with prompting *-commands such as

```
*ENTER THE STUDENT'S NAME . . .
 HARPER.B
*ENTER THE STUDENT'S IDENTIFICATION NUMBER . . .
 724115
*ENTER THE STUDENT'S COLLEGE . . .
 COMMERCE
*ENTER THE STUDENT'S YEAR . . .
 3
*HARPER.B HAS BEEN SUCCESSFULLY INSERTED.
```

The UPDATE command performs in a prompting mode also. The WEIGHTING command sets the relative weighting of the term assignments and exams. The list of numbers following the WEIGHTING keyword must total 100. Hence, a weighting of 34 in the second element of the list indicates that 34/100 of the final grade is based on the mark on assignment 2.

After adopting this query language, the next step in the design is to formulate the scanning and parsing (i.e., the syntactic analysis) strategies for the recognition of statements from the query language. The scanner, which is responsible for detecting the basic word-like units of the language, isolates the keywords such as LIST, NUMBER, OF, MIN, MINIMUM, GRADE, GRADES, AND, OR, DELETE, INSERT, etc., as well as the <name> and <number> syntactic units. (Refer to Sec. 2-5.2 for a more complete description of the function of a scanner.)

There are many different parsing techniques which can be employed in the recognition of query statements. We have described two general strategies, top-down and bottom-up parsing, in Chaps. 2 and 5 of the text. A description of most of the very powerful techniques is beyond the scope of this text (see Gries [1971]). However, one of the simplest parsing strategies to implement is recursive descent, which was discussed in Sec. 5-2.3. Since the query language is described with a relatively small grammar, the inefficiencies of this method can be tolerated and we have adopted this as the parsing strategy. Figure 7-7.1 illustrates the relationship of the query analysis phase with the complete system design. Notice that scanning errors (e.g., the input of a character like '?', which does not belong to the alphabet of the language) and parsing errors (e.g., an incorrect input like 'NUMB STUDENTS' instead of 'NUMBER OF STUDENTS') are identified and an error message is sent to the user.

If a query belongs to our previously defined query language, it must be acted upon. For the CRR System this action is either a correct response, as determined by the retrieval of an appropriate set of information, or the system data base (i.e., the set of student records) is manipulated correctly. Figure 7-7.1 depicts this logical breakdown of the query synthesis phase. The query-response generating section handles data-retrieval requests as expressed in the LIST OF, NUMBER OF, AVERAGE, MIN, and MAX commands. Most of these retrieval requests demand the sequential processing of a file of student records. For example, the query

NUMBER OF STUDENTS WITH GRADE > 80

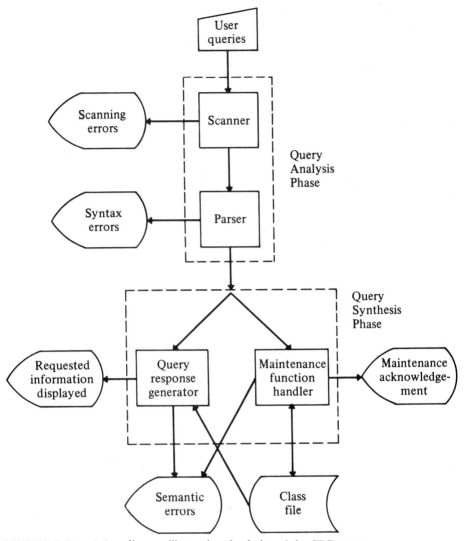

FIGURE 7-7.1   A flow diagram illustrating the design of the CRR system.

suggests the examination of each student record to determine if that student scored higher than 80. For each such score, a counter is incremented and the value of this counter is printed after all records have been examined. A similar form of processing is required to handle most of the other retrieval requests, except for those commands referring to specific students by name. For example,

LIST OF STUDENTS COOPER.R, RIDGWAY.W, NYLANDER.L
WITH MARKS ON ASSIGNMENT 1 > 90

requires the examination of only three specific student records. Hence, the ability to access directly student records by student name is a definite asset. Note that we could have designed the query language so as to insist that student identification numbers, rather than student names, be used to identify a student record in the system. However, such a design decision is not appealing from the user's point of view. Both professors and students communicate on a name, rather than number, basis. If we are designing a university-wide registration system, then student identification by number has many definite advantages, including record anonymity and a unique identification scheme for each student, which is not necessarily the case when names are the identification. Of course, student numbers were derived initially for registration systems.

The direct referencing of records is also needed when performing the system-maintenance function. We delete and update records by student name. When adding a new record, the student name along with other student information is requested. Hence, the file processing required in this application involves the examination of records in a sequential fashion, the printing of record information in alphabetical order of student name, and the direct processing of selected records based on a student name index. Clearly, the indexed sequential-file organization satisfies these processing needs, and an indexed sequential class-record file keyed on the student name item should be used. This file is referred to as the "class file" in Fig. 7-7.1.

To retain all the information required by the users of the system, a record in the class file must contain the student's name, I.D., college, year, marks for up to a reasonable number of assignments (say 12), and the student's final grade. Ideally, we should create a different file for each class. However, the minimum amount of space that can be allocated to an indexed sequential file for the IBM system is one cylinder. Assuming we are to implement the CRR System on an IBM system using an IBM 3330 disk pack, this minimum space is much too large for a file of records for only one class.

There are 13,030 bytes/track $\times$ 18 tracks/cylinder = 234,540 bytes/cylinder of prime and cylinder overflow area of an IBM 3330. Even assuming as much as $\frac{1}{2}$ of the bytes are devoted to overhead space, i.e., space for overflow chains, record-length descriptors, and other record-structure information, 117,270 bytes remain for storing record information. Approximately 40 bytes are needed to store the information for a student. (This figure will be confirmed in the next subsection when we discuss the implementation.) Therefore, one cylinder can hold 2,931 records (using an extremely conservative estimating procedure). It would be extremely wasteful of disk storage to devote a cylinder to each class.

A better approach is to place the records from all classes on a common cylinder and to make use of the GENKEY option when retrieving records for a particular class. The adoption of this strategy means that the key for the indexed sequential class file must be prefixed with a class number. For example, the key for D. Smith's record in class CMPT 316 is '316SMITH.D', and the key of D. Jones' record in class CMPT 441 is '441JONES.D'. All records in class CMPT 316 can be accessed in PL/I by first using the generic key '316', as described at the end of Sec. 7-6.3.

An initial class list is usually compiled when course lectures begin. The indexed sequential class file is created sequentially by writing the student records on file as ordered by the class number/student name key. From this initial file, updates, deletions, and alterations can be made without requiring a large overflow area.

There are three forms of output generated from the query synthesis phase. First, there is the information which is retrieved from the query-response commands such as

LIST and MAXIMUM. The output form should be clearly readable. Some example output is presented in the next subsection. Second, semantic errors can arise during the processing of requests. Attempts to delete a student who is not in the file or to add a student who is already in the file are examples of a semantic error. Third, an output response to the user by the system acknowledging the completion of a maintenance command, such as a deletion, is extremely helpful.

We have completed a description of the design phase and now turn to discussion of the implementation.

7-7.3 Implementation

The implementation of the CRR System involves the writing of programs for the four main modules in Fig. 7-7.1, namely, the scanner, the parser, the query-response generator, and the maintenance-function handler. The scanner is realized through a procedure called SCAN. The parser is composed of 19 procedures, many of which are recursive in nature because of the recursive-descent parsing strategy we have adopted. The parser is initially invoked by a call to the procedure QUERY, which invokes either directly or indirectly the other 18 parser procedures. Both the query-response generator and maintenance-function handler facilities reside in a procedure named RESPONSE.

These three procedures, SCAN, QUERY, and RESPONSE, are initially called in the CRR System mainline, as shown in Fig. 7-7.2. Also included in this figure is the declaration and initialization of many of the program variables. Specifically, we should note the entry statements for the different procedures, and the A_STUDENT structure declaration which is a description of the records which are stored in the indexed sequential file named CLASS. The procedure MSG is responsible for printing most of the user messages. The procedure SCAN is not given, except for a dummy heading. A discussion of the important aspects of the scanner, as they relate to data structures, was given in Sec. 2-5.2.

The mainline program begins by prompting the user with a 'HELLO' message and requesting a class number entry. After some initialization of system variables, the procedures SCAN, QUERY, and RESPONSE are invoked in order and repetitively until the user terminates the session.

The QUERY procedure and the recursive procedure for identifying the syntactic unit <OBJECT HEAD1> are shown in Fig. 7-7.3. Both procedures illustrate the direct relationship that exists between a given syntactic description and the set of procedure calls used to check the validity for that description. In the procedure OBJECT_HEAD1, the global-bit-string flags STUDENT and ID may be set, depending on the form of the query. These bit-string variables, as well as a number of other bit-string flags, are declared in Fig. 7-7.2 and are used in the response-generating section of the program. It is these variables which determine what system functions should be performed and what information should be retrieved.

Because our main emphasis in this section is on the application of indexed sequential files, we will present a more detailed discussion of the operations performed on the class file. These operations arise in the query synthesis phase, which is implemented as the procedure RESPONSE. A skeleton version of the RESPONSE procedure is given in Fig. 7-7.4.

A module for handling queries requesting the minimum or maximum mark for a specified list of students is given as an example from the response-generator section of the

```
CRR: PROCEDURE OPTIONS (MAIN);

/* THIS PROGRAM IS DESIGNED TC PERFORM A RETRIEVAL FUNCTION ON A DATA
SET THAT CONTAINS RECORDS WITH INFORMATION TO A CLASS.  FOR
THIS REASON IT IS KNOWN AS THE CLASS RECORDS RETRIEVAL SYSTEM (CRR).
A QUERY LANGUAGE IS USED TO EXTRACT THE DESIRED INFORMATION FROM THE
FILE.  THE PROGRAM IS COMPOSED OF TWO LOGICALLY DISTINCT PHASES.  THE
FIRST SCANS THE INPUT QUERY AND THEN TESTS IT FOR SEMANTIC VALIDITY.
THE SECOND PORTION OF THE PROGRAM PERFORMS THE ACTUAL RETRIEVAL OF IN-
FORMATION.                                                          */

         DECLARE SCAN          ENTRY RETURNS (CHARACTER (30) VARYING),
                 MSG           ENTRY (CHARACTER (*)),
                 QUERY         ENTRY,
                 RESPONSE      ENTRY;

/* THE FOLLOWING LIST OF PROCEDURES ARE USED IN THE  PARSING OF
THE INPUT QUERY.  A RECURSIVE DESCENT PARSE HAS BEEN IMPLEMENTED.    */

         DECLARE PROPOSITION          ENTRY RETURNS (BIT(1)),
                 MAINTENANCE          ENTRY RETURNS (BIT(1)),
                 WEIGHTING            ENTRY RETURNS (BIT(1)),
                 SUBJECT1             ENTRY RETURNS (BIT(1)),
                 SUBJECT2             ENTRY RETURNS (BIT(1)),
                 OBJECT1              ENTRY RETURNS (BIT(1)),
                 OBJECT2              ENTRY RETURNS (BIT(1)),
                 OBJECT_HEAD1         ENTRY RETURNS (BIT(1)),
                 OBJECT_HEAD2         ENTRY RETURNS (BIT(1)),
                 OBJECTIVE1           ENTRY RETURNS (BIT(1)),
                 OBJECTIVE2           ENTRY RETURNS (BIT(1)),
                 REL_STAT             ENTRY RETURNS (BIT(1)),
                 NAME                 ENTRY RETURNS (BIT(1)),
                 NAME_LIST            ENTRY RETURNS (BIT(1)),
                 RELATION             ENTRY RETURNS (BIT(1)),
                 NUMBER               ENTRY RETURNS (BIT(1)),
                 NUMBER_LIST          ENTRY RETURNS (BIT(1)),
                 UPDATE_HEAD          ENTRY RETURNS (BIT(1)),

/* FOLLOWING IS A LIST OF BIT STRING FLAGS WHICH ARE SET DURING THE
PARSING PROCEDURE AND THEN REFERENCED DURING THE RETRIEVAL OF INFOR-
MATION.  DECLARATIONS OF TEMPORARY VARIABLES ARE INCLUDED AS WELL.   */

         (NUM,LIST,MIN,MAX,AVERAGE,DUMMY,STUDENT,GRADE,ID,
          MARK,DELETE,INSERT,UPDTE,WEIGHT,ASNMT) BIT (1),
         ERROR BIT (1) INITIAL ('0'B),
         NEXTSYM CHARACTER (30) VARYING,
         RELATE (5) CHARACTER (2) VARYING,
         ST_NAMES (15) CHARACTER (20) VARYING,
         ASSIGN(16) CHARACTER (7) VARYING INITIAL ( (16) '-1'),
         LOOP BIT (1),
         COLUMN_SCAN FIXED,
         WORK CHARACTER (3),
         W(12) FIXED BINARY INITIAL ( (12) -1 ),
         NO_ST FIXED BINARY INITIAL (0),
         (STN, ASN) FIXEC;

/* THIS CLASS FILE IS THE FILE ASSOCIATED WITH THE DATA SET WHICH
CONTAINS THE CLASS RECORDS.  THE STRUCTURE:  'A_STUDENT' IS USED TO MA-
NIPULATE THE RECORDS INTERNALLY.  THE STRUCTURE SERVES TO INDICATE
```

FIGURE 7-7.2   Main-line program for the CRR system.

RESPONSE procedure. This program segment illustrates how the indexed sequential file
CLASS is accessed directly via the class number/student name key. Note that we have
used the **ON KEY** condition to detect inquiries involving students not in the file for a given
class.

The module for finding the minimum or maximum mark for a particular assignment
is not given. It should be clear, however, that such a module involves the sequential access

```
THE FORMAT AND CONTENTS OF EACH RECORD.                              */

        DECLARE CLASS FILE RECORD KEYED ENVIRONMENT (INDEXED GENKEY),
              1 A_STUDENT,
                2 FILLER CHARACTER (1),
                2 S_ID CHARACTER (6),
                2 S_CLASS CHARACTER(4),
                2 S_NAME CHARACTER (20),
                2 S_COLLEGE CHARACTER (14),
                2 S_YEAR CHARACTER (1),
                2 S_MARKS (12) FIXED DECIMAL (3),
                2 S_AVERAGE FIXED DECIMAL (5,2),


MSG: PROCEDURE (MESSAGE);
/* THE MSG PROCEDURE IS USED BY ALL PORTIONS OF THE PROGRAM TO PRINT
ANY KIND OF MESSAGE TO THE USER. . . .                               */
    DECLARE MESSAGE CHARACTER (*);
    PUT EDIT (MESSAGE) (SKIP (2), A);
    END MSG;

/******************         S C A N         ********************/
SCAN: PROCEDURE RETURNS (CHARACTER (30) VARYING);
/* THE 'SCAN' PROCEDURE SCANS THE INPUT MESSAGE RETURNING THE NEXT
LEXICAL UNIT TO BE USED BY THE PARSER. . . .                         */
END SCAN;

/********** Q U E R Y   P A R S I N G   P R O C E D U R E S **********/
/*** *******                      &                     *********/
/******** Q U E R Y   S Y N T H E S I S   P R O C E D U R E S ********/
/******                  F A L L   H E R E                *******/


/****************** M A I N   L I N E ********************/
/* THIS SECTION OF THE PROGRAM INTRODUCES THE USER TO THE SYSTEM AND
THEN INITIALIZES A NUMBER OF SYSTEM VARIABLES AND CALLS THE QUERY
PROCESSING ROUTINES.                                                 */

    ON ENDFILE(SYSIN) GO TC DONE;

    LOOP='1'B;

    DO WHILE(LOOP);
        PUT EDIT('HELLO ','PLEASE ENTER YOUR CLASS NUMBER (E.G. ',
                '313B,441A,102,ETC)','')
              ( (2) (COLUMN(1),A),A,COLUMN(1),A(0));
        GET EDIT (STRING) (COLUMN(1),A(72));
        I = 1;
        NEXTSYM = SCAN;
        IF (LENGTH(NEXTSYM) = 3) | (LENGTH(NEXTSYM) = 4)
        THEN DO;
            YOUR_CLASS = NEXTSYM;
            CALL MSG ('THANKYOU');
            LOOP = '0'B;
        END;
        ELSE CALL MSG ('CLASS NUMBER IS TOO LONG OR TOO SHORT');
    END; /* OF DO WHILE (LOOP); */

    LOOP = '1'B;
    ON ENDFILE (SYSIN) LOOP = '0'B;

    DO WHILE (LOOP);
```

FIGURE 7-7.2   (Continued)

of all student records for a class. The other modules which are devoted to retrieval-oriented commands such as LIST, NUMBER, and AVERAGE also require the reading of student records directly and sequentially. The records are accessed directly when a query relates to a particular list of students, and sequentially when all student records are involved.

To exhibit the file operations other than the read operation, we must examine the

```
      FILLER = LOW (1);
      NUM,LIST,MIN,MAX,AVERAGE,STUDENT,ID,GRADE,MARK,DELETE,
      INSERT,UPDTE,WEIGHT,ASNMT = '0'B;
      DO J = 1 TO 16;
          IF J <= 5 THEN RELATE (J) = '';
      END;
      COLUMN_SCAN = 81;
      NEXTSYM = SCAN;
      IF ¬ERROR
      THEN CALL QUERY;
      IF ¬ERROR
      THEN DO;
          CALL RESPONSE;
          CLOSE FILE(CLASS);
      END;
      ERROR = '0'B;
      PUT EDIT (' ') (COLUMN(1),A(0));
  END;
DONE: PUT SKIP LIST ('THIS RUN OF CRR IS NOW ENDED.');
END CRR;
```

FIGURE 7-7.2   (Continued)

maintenance functions of the system. The program modules for the DELETE, UPDATE, and INSERT functions are also exhibited in Fig. 7-7.4. Again the ON KEY feature is used to detect erroneous student-record specifications. The DELETE function is implemented with the aid of the PL/I DELETE instruction. The instruction marks the first byte of the specified student records with '11111111'B, thereby indicating that the record cannot be read.

The program section for the INSERT function is designed to prompt the user, and thereby help to ensure that all the information items for a student record are provided. The WRITE instruction is used to place the new record in the file based on the class number/student name key.

The UPDATE function can be used to update the marks on a specific assignment for the entire class or the mark for a specified student on a specific assignment. The program segment for the former update capability is given in Fig. 7-7.4. Of course, to update the indexed sequential class file, the REWRITE instruction is used. The value of ASSIGN(I) indicates which assignment is to be updated. The W array contains the relative weights of the assignments.

When performing an update, the user is again prompted by the system—this time a message containing the name of the next student to be updated is presented. In the case of an update for a specific student on a specific assignment, the user is prompted as follows:

```
  UPDATE ASSIGNMENT 4
  *ENTER THE STUDENT'S NAME
  THOMSON.C
  *ENTER THE STUDENT'S MARK
  91
  *MARK FOR THOMSON.C WAS UPDATED SUCCESSFULLY.
```

We have prefixed the system-generated commands with a * for clarity. In an interactive system, this would not be necessary, but is desirable for aiding in a review of the output from a terminal session.

The "skeleton" system presented is not provided with the capability of self-moni-

```
QUERY: PROCEDURE;
/* QUERY IS THE PROCEDURE CALLED INITIALLY IN THE RECURSIVE DESCENT
PARSER.  ALL OTHER PROCEDURES ARE CALLED EITHER DIRECTLY OR INDIRECTLY
FROM THIS PROCEDURE                                                   */

/* BNF NOTATION WILL BE USED WITH THE FOLLOWING ADDITIONS AND CHANGES:

        " WILL BE USED IN PLACE CF BRACES
        ( WILL BE USED IN PLACE OF THE LEFT SQUARE BRACKET
        ) WILL BE USED IN PLACE OF THE RIGHT SQUARE BRACKET          */


/* <QUERY> ::= <PROPOSITION>
          | <MAINTENANCE FUNCTION>
          | <MARKS WEIGHTING FUNCTION>                                */

     IF ¬PROPOSITION & ¬ERROR
     THEN IF ¬MAINTENANCE & ¬ERROR
          THEN IF ¬WEIGHTING & ¬ERROR
               THEN CALL MSG ('FIRST WORD OF COMMAND IS INVALID');
     COLUMN_SCAN = 81;
END QUERY;

/* A TYPICAL PROCEDURE IN THE RECURSIVE DESCENT PARSER IS SHOWN FCR THE
PRODUCTIONS INVOLVING THE NON-TERMINAL OBJECT_HEAD1.                  */

OBJECT_HEAD1: PROCEDURE RECURSIVE RETURNS (BIT(1));

/* <OBJECT HEAD1> ::= STUDENT(S)
                    | STUDENT(S) <NAME LIST>
                    | ID(S)
                    | <OBJECT HEAD2>                                  */

     IF NEXTSYM = 'STUDENT' | NEXTSYM = 'STUDENTS'
     THEN DO;
          NEXTSYM = SCAN;
          STUDENT = '1'B;
          IF (NEXTSYM¬='WITH' & NEXTSYM¬='FOR' & NEXTSYM¬=','
                              & NEXTSYM¬='*')
          THEN DO;
               IF ¬NAME_LIST
               THEN RETURN('0'B);
          END;
          RETURN ('1'B);
     END;

     IF NEXTSYM = 'ID' | NEXTSYM = 'IDS'
     THEN DO;
          NEXTSYM = SCAN;
          ID = '1'B;
          RETURN ('1'B);
     END;

     IF OBJECT_HEAD2
     THEN RETURN ('1'B);
     RETURN('0'B);
END OBJECT_HEAD1;
```

FIGURE 7-7.3   Examples of procedures for syntactically analyzing queries.

toring file activity. This is an important aspect in any system—especially systems using indexed sequential files. When the prime area of an indexed sequential file is full or nearly full, an overflow record can be generated with each insert. On the other hand, if a large number of deletion-type transactions are applied to the file, much of the file will contain "dummy" deleted records. Again, performance will be degraded. The number of insertions and deletions should be recorded, and after a certain level of insertion and deletion activity has been attained, the file should be reorganized by recreating it sequentially. There are

```
RESPONSE: PROCEDURE;

/* THE 'RESPONSE' PROCEDURE IS USED TO EVALUATE THE QUERY'S AND TO
PERFORM THE NECESSARY RETRIEVAL OF INFORMATION.  IT ALSO PERFORMS ALL
UPDATE FUNCTIONS WHICH ARE REQUIRED BY THE QUERY'S.                    */

/*************  M A I N T E N A N C E   F U N C T I O N S  ************/
       IF STN > 0        /* INDEX INTO ARRAY ST_NAMES */
          THEN DO;
             OPEN FILE(CLASS) DIRECT UPDATE;

/* THE DELETION OF A RECORD.  NOTE THAT THERE IS A CHECK TO SEE IF THE
.RECORD TO BE DELETED ACTUALLY EXISTS ON FILE.                        */

          IF DELETE
          THEN DO;
             ON KEY (CLASS)
             BEGIN;
                CALL MSG ('THE STUDENT YOU ARE TRYING TO DELETE -- '
                       || ST_NAMES(J) || ' -- IS NOT IN THE FILE');
                GO TO RET;
             END;

             DO J = 1 TO STN;
                IF ST_NAMES(J) ¬= '&&WEIGHTS&&'
                THEN DO;
                DELETE FILE (CLASS) KEY (YOUR_CLASS || ST_NAMES(J));
                NO_ST = NO_ST - 1;
                CALL MSG (ST_NAMES(J) || ' HAS BEEN SUCCESSFULLY ' ||
                       'DELETED ');
                END;
                ELSE CALL MSG ('&&WEIGHTS&& IS A PROTECTED NAME AND '
                       || 'MAY NOT BE DELETED FROM THE FILE.');

             ERROR = '0'B;
          END;
          RETURN;
       END;

/* INSERT A RECORD.  NOTE THAT THERE IS A CHECK TO MAKE SURE THAT THE
RECORD TO BE INSERTED IS NOT ALREADY ON FILE.                         */

          IF INSERT
          THEN DO;
             ON KEY (CLASS)
             BEGIN;
                CALL MSG ('THE STUDENT YOU ARE TRYING TO INSERT -- '
                       || S_NAME       || ' -- IS ALREADY IN THE FILE');
                GO TO RET;
             END;

             ST_NAMES(15) = NEXTSYM;

       P2:   PUT EDIT('ENTER THE STUDENT''S NAME',' ')
                    (COLUMN(1),A,COLUMN(1),A(0));
             STRING = S_NAME;
             GET EDIT(S_NAME   ) (SKIP(1),A(20));
             COLUMN_SCAN = 1;
             NEXTSYM,S_NAME = SCAN;
             IF S_NAME = 'END' THEN RETURN;
             IF ¬NAME
             THEN DO;
```

FIGURE 7-7.4   A procedure for handling query responses.

many other system enhancements that can be made to the CRR System; nevertheless, the
simple system presented adequately illustrates the important concepts related to indexed
sequential files.

In the last two sections, we have investigated a file organization which allows the
direct and sequential access of records. In order to permit both access capabilities, a sig-

```
            ERROR = '0'B;
            GO TO P2;
        END;


/* PROMPTING CYCLES TO ENSURE ENTRY OF STUDENT IDENTIFICATION NUMBER,
YEAR,  AND COLLEGE SHOULD APPEAR AT THIS POINT IN THE PROGRAM. . . . */


            S_AVERAGE = 0;
            S_CLASS = YOUR_CLASS;

            WRITE FILE (CLASS) FROM (A_STUDENT)
                             KEYFROM(S_CLASS || S_NAME);
            NO_ST = NO_ST + 1;
            PUT EDIT(S_NAME || ' HAS BEEN SUCCESSFULLY INSERTED ')
                    (COLUMN(1),A);
            IF ST_NAMES(15) = 'MANY' THEN GO TO P2;
            RETURN;
        END;

/* THIS SEGMENT HANDLES THE UPDATING OF MARKS ON A SPECIFIED
ASSIGNMENT FOR ALL STUDENTS IN THE CLASS.                        */

        IF UPDTE
        THEN DO;

          /* WORK IS USED AS A TEMPORARY CHARACTER STRING VARIABLE. */

            IF NEXTSYM = 'ALL'
            THEN DO;
                CLOSE FILE(CLASS);
                OPEN FILE (CLASS) SEQUENTIAL UPDATE;
                ON ENDFILE (CLASS)
                BEGIN;
                    STN = 0;          /* STUDENT INDEX SET TO ZERO */
                    S_NAME = 'I';     /* STUDENT NAME SET TO 'I' */
                END;
                READ FILE(CLASS) INTO (A_STUDENT) KEY(YOUR_CLASS);
                IF S_NAME = '&&WEIGHTS&&' THEN READ FILE(CLASS)
                                            INTO(A_STUDENT);
            DO WHILE(STN=1);
        P6:     PUT EDIT('ENTER THE MARK FOR ',S_NAME,' ')
                        (COLUMN(1),A,A,COLUMN(1),A(0));
                GET EDIT(WORK) (SKIP(1),A(3));
                STRING = WORK;
                SUBSTR(STRING,76,5) = ' * * ';
                COLUMN_SCAN = 1;
                NEXTSYM = SCAN;
                ERROR = '1'B;
                IF ¬NUMBER
                THEN DO;
                    ERROR = '0'B;
                    CALL MSG('THE VALUE ENTERED AS A MARK IS ' ||
                            'NON-NUMERIC');
                    GO TO P6;
                END;
                ERROR = '0'B;
                DO WHILE(SUBSTR(WORK,3,1) = ' ');
                    WORK = ' ' || SUBSTR(WORK,1,2);
                END;
                S_AVERAGE = 0;
```

FIGURE 7-7.4 (Continued)

nificant amount of overhead is incurred, particularly with respect to the movement of
records in the prime area and the creation and update of pointers in the index and overflow areas. In the next section, we examine a file organization which does not necessarily
provide the capability of sequentially accessing records, but does enable quicker direct
access and does not require as much file-management overhead.

```
                    S_MARKS(ASSIGN(1)) = WORK;
                    DO K = 1 TO 12;
                         S_AVERAGE = S_AVERAGE + ROUND(W(K) * 0.010000
                                                  * S_MARKS(K), 2);
                    END;
                    REWRITE FILE(CLASS) FROM(A_STUDENT);
                    PUT EDIT('THE MARK FOR ',S_NAME,' HAS BEEN ',
                              'UPDATED ') (COLUMN(1),4 (A));
          R6:       READ FILE(CLASS) INTO (A_STUDENT);
                    IF S_NAME = '&&WEIGHTS&&' THEN GO TO R6;
                    IF S_CLASS ¬= YOUR_CLASS THEN STN = 0;
               END;

          RETURN;
     END;

/* THE NEXT SECTION SHOULD HANDLE THE UPDATE OF THE MARKS FOR
A SPECIFIC STUDENT AND A SPECIFIC ASSIGNMENT. . . .              */


/* FOR ALL INFORMATION RETRIEVAL FUNCTIONS TO BE PERFORMED ON A SPECI-
FIED LIST OF STUDENTS, A CHECK IS MADE TO ENSURE THAT EACH STUDENT
IN THE LIST IS ON THE FILE.                                      */

     ON KEY (CLASS)
     BEGIN;
          CALL MSG('THIS STUDENT -- ' || ST_NAMES(J) || ' -- IS '
               || 'NOT IN THE FILE');
          GO TO RET;
     END;

/********* Q U E R Y   R E S P O N S E   F U N C T I O N S *********/
/* FINDING THE MINIMUM OR MAXIMUM MARK FOR SPECIFIED STUDENTS.   */

     IF MIN | MAX
     THEN IF ¬MARK | ASNMT
          THEN DO;
               CALL MSG('WHEN REFERRING TO SPECIFIC STUDENTS, THE '
                    || 'MIN(IMUM) OR MAX(IMUM) FUNCTIONS MUST ' ||
                    'REFER TO ALL MARKS OF THOSE STUDENTS');
               RETURN;
          END;

          ELSE DO;
               DO J = 1 TO STN;
                    READ FILE (CLASS) INTO (A_STUDENT)
                                   KEY(YOUR_CLASS || ST_NAMES(J));
                    IF MIN
                    THEN WORK = 101;
                    ELSE WORK = -1;
                    DO K = 1 TO 12;
                         IF MIN
                         THEN IF ((S_MARKS(K) < WORK) &
                                   (S_MARKS(K) ¬= -1))
                              THEN WORK = S_MARKS(K);
                              ELSE;
                         ELSE IF((S_MARKS(K) > WORK) &
                                   (S_MARKS(K) ¬= -1))
                              THEN WORK = S_MARKS(K);
                    END;
                    IF WORK = 101 | WORK = -1
                    THEN WORK = 0;
```

FIGURE 7-7.4   (Continued)

7-8   DIRECT FILES

To illustrate the type of file processing associated with a direct file, let us return momentarily to our small billing system example. We introduced the example as an application
of sequential files in Sec. 7-5, and reviewed it in the introduction to indexed sequential

```
                PUT EDIT (S_NAME,WORK) (COLUMN(1),A(21),A);
        END;
        RETURN;
    END;

/* THE REMAINING INFORMATION PROCESSING FUNCTIONS SUCH AS AVERAGE CAL-
CULATIONS, LISTING STUDENTS AND GRADES, ETC. APPEAR IN THIS SECTION
OF THE PROGRAM. . . .                                              */

    RET: RETURN;
  END RESPONSE;
```

FIGURE 7-7.4 (Continued)

files in Sec. 7-6. In Sec. 7-6, it was pointed out that in order to accommodate any form of on-line processing which concerns the status of an account, individual customer records must be accessed directly. It was also desirable to have the records ordered sequentially by account number. This is necessary to generate monthly customer bills based on receipts which are received in batches from points of sale.

It is relatively easy to hypothesize that in the near future our small company will want a billing system which does away with the process of filling out purchase slips at the point of sale and then of sending these to the main office for computer processing. A simpler, but more expensive, approach is to have a purchase or return posted against a customer account immediately via on-line terminals operated by point-of-sale clerks. On-line terminals would be remote from a computer, yet tied directly to it via telephone lines. If purchases and returns are handled at the point of sale, it would be unnecessary to batch all of the customer receipts and sequentially process them against the account via the merge procedure described in Sec. 7-5. With the need for sequential processing eliminated, we can design a system that requires only the capability of direct access. In this section, we consider a number of file structures which provide efficient direct access. This efficiency of access is gained because we remove the criterion that the file must be organized so that it can be accessed both sequentially and directly.

The section is again divided into three parts—file structures, direct file processing, and direct files in PL/I. In the next section, we examine an application which involves the processing of direct files in an on-line banking system.

7-8.1 The Structure of Direct Files

In a *direct* (also called *random*) file, a transformation or mapping is made from the key of a record to the address of the storage location at which that record is to reside in the file. One mechanism used for generating this transformation is called a *hashing algorithm*. In Sec. 6-2.4, we examined hashing algorithms as they applied to the placement of records in a hash table. It was pointed out that a hashing algorithm consists of two components—a hashing function, which defines a mapping from the key space to the address space, and a collision-resolution technique, which resolves conflicts that arise when more than one record key is mapped to the same table location.

The hashing algorithms used for direct files are very similar to those used for tables, and therefore it is necessary to have a complete understanding of Sec. 6-2.4 before reading this section. The main conceptual differences are due to the physical characteristics of external storage, which differ from the directly addressable storage characteristics assumed for tables in Chap. 6. In particular, the time to access a record in a table in main memory is in the order of microseconds, while the time to access a record in external memory is in the order of milliseconds. In addition, records in a file are stored in *buckets* in which each bucket contains b record locations, as opposed to just one location. The number of records in a bucket is called the *bucket capacity*. Basically, we can think of a bucket as a sector in a sector-addressable device, or a block in a block-addressable device. To isolate a particular record, the bucket in which the record resides must be located, the contents of the bucket are brought into a buffer in memory, and then the desired record is extracted from the buffer.

Let us define an *address space* A of size m such that $A = \{C + 1, C + 2, \ldots, C + m\}$, where C is an integer constant. Then, mb records can be accommodated by A, and the load factor for the direct file is $n/(mb)$, assuming a key set of size n is mapped into the address space.

A key set $S = \{X_1, X_2, \ldots, X_n\}$ is a subset of a set K of possible keys which is called the *key space*. If the size of K is equal to the number of record locations in A, and the key space is consecutive, then a transformation can be defined which assigns to each bucket of A exactly b keys from K. This type of one-to-one transformation is termed *direct addressing* and is an array-reference form of addressing.

In most situations, however, S is a small subset of K and direct addressing results in a ridiculously low utilization of direct-access storage. Instead, *indirect addressing* is implemented. That is, S is mapped into A with the distinct possibility that enough records will be assigned to the same bucket that a bucket *overflow* takes place. When this happens, a bucket-overflow handling technique must be used to store any overflow records. We will discover later in this subsection that the techniques for handling bucket overflow are very similar to those for collision resolution in a table.

Having reviewed some of the concepts related to hashing algorithms, let us examine in more detail the possible organizations for a direct file. We begin by reexamining the hashing functions which can be used for address translation. A more in-depth investigation of the overflow handling techniques is then considered.

In Sec. 6-2.4, hashing functions were divided into two general classes—distribution-independent and distribution-dependent hashing functions. The three most significant analyses of distribution-independent hashing functions were performed by Buchholz [1963], Lum et al. [1971], and Lum [1973]. The results from the three investigations indicated that the division method, using a prime divisor or a divisor that is relatively prime with the size of the address space, yielded the best performance on the average. This is not to say that, for certain key sets with certain load factors and bucket capacities, one of the other methods discussed in Sec. 6-2.4 cannot outperform the division method.

Deutscher et al. [1975] obtained results which indicate that certain distribution-dependent hashing functions (in particular, the piecewise-linear function with interval splitting, and the multiple-frequency function) can perform better than the division method. However, the computation of a hash value for these types of functions takes considerably more time than the computation of a value using the division method. Furthermore, a significant amount of storage is needed to record the distribution-dependent information. Because of these two factors and the fact that a priori knowledge of the distribution of keys in the key space is required, distribution-dependent functions are not viable hashing functions in many situations. When a direct file, and hence its key set, is rather static in nature, then distribution-dependent methods may be applied. The large amount of computation time required to generate a hash value remains insignificant when compared to the time to access a record in external memory.

The second aspect of a hashing algorithm is the collision-resolution technique. In a direct file, the smallest addressable unit is the bucket, which may contain many records that have been mapped to the same address. Hence, in a direct file with a given bucket capacity, a certain number of collisions are expected. When there are more colliding records for a given bucket than the bucket capacity, however, then some method must be found for handling these overflow records. The term *overflow handling technique* is used in place of collision-resolution technique, which is commonly adopted for hash-table methods.

In Sec. 6-2.4, two classes of collision-resolution techniques were given—open addressing and chaining. The same general classification can be applied to overflow handling techniques. When we use a bucket with a capacity greater than 1, we are in fact imposing a restricted linear-probe form of open addressing. When a record is added to a bucket which is not full, the new record is added at the next open location. Of course, the next open record location is in the bucket and is already reserved for records which are mapped to that bucket address.

In the discussion to follow, we refer to the bucket referenced by the address calculation of a record as the *primary bucket* for that record. If a record is not present in the primary bucket, it is located in an *overflow bucket*, or it is not in the file.

Since the complete contents of a bucket are brought into main memory with one request, it is extremely beneficial if the desired record is located somewhere in the primary bucket. If the record is not in the primary bucket, a request must be made to bring in an overflow bucket, as determined by the overflow handling method.

If a linear-probe open-address overflow handling method is used, then a successive search is made of the records in the remaining buckets in the file. The search is terminated successfully when the record is located. It is terminated unsuccessfully, however, if an empty (dummy) record is encountered, or if the search returns to the original bucket tested.

A random-probe form of open addressing or double hashing are not necessarily good overflow methods to use for direct files. In both methods the sequences of overflow buckets which are examined do not exhibit the property of physical adjacency. That is, two buckets which are adjacent in the overflow sequence are not necessarily physically adjacent. Physical adjacency can be important, since records which are not physically adjacent have a higher probability of requiring a seek in a movable-head storage device. The extra seek time may be prohibitive.

Overflow records can be chained from the primary to a separate overflow area. An overflow record should reside in an overflow bucket which is in the same seek area (e.g., the same cylinder) as the primary area for the overflow record. A particularly good strategy is to reserve the last few buckets of a seek area strictly for overflow records from the primary buckets in that area. That is the strategy adopted in using the cylinder overflow area in the indexed sequential organization. However, it may be difficult to adopt such a configuration strategy, since the overflow buckets would break up the linear-addressing scheme required for direct addressing (i.e., groups of prime area buckets and overflow buckets will be interspersed throughout the file space). Therefore, an independent overflow area which is totally separate from the prime area may be required.

A final overflow strategy also involves chaining. Knuth [1973] refers to the method as *chaining with coalescing lists*. With this method, overflow records are placed in available buckets in the prime area of the direct file, and overflows are located using pointers from one bucket to another. Therefore, when a key is hashed to a bucket, a search commences through a chain of buckets until the required record or an empty storage location is found. Keys may be mapped to buckets which are not the first in a chain, so it is necessary that lists be coalesced. In a chain of buckets, keys which are originally hashed to different addresses may be found.

A comparative analysis of the overflow handling methods is described in Knuth [1973]. It is shown that chaining with separate lists requires the smallest average length of search of the three overflow handling techniques discussed. However, this apparent advantage is gained due to two factors. First, the separate overflow area is not counted as part of the total file space. Hence, if n records are added to the file, all n records are placed in the primary area, using open addressing or chaining with coalescing lists. If there are m overflows, however, then only n − m records are placed in the primary area when using chaining with separate lists. Therefore, the effective load factor is less for chaining with separate lists.

The second factor contributes to the better performance of any chaining method over an open address method. For a chaining method, information concerning the location of the next overflow record is stored in the record itself. Hence, to access a particular overflow record, there is no need to examine a number of intermediate records which may not be overflow records. It must be noted, however, that the storage of overflow links enlarges the record size. This may be an important file-design consideration, especially if the file consists of many small records.

A final point that should be kept in mind is that access to an independent overflow area will most likely result in a seek request. Therefore, if moving-head external devices are being used, chaining to an independent overflow area may not be an efficient method. A possible compromise is to adopt chaining with coalescing lists. However, this method has not, as yet, been thoroughly investigated.

So far we have centered the discussion of file structures for direct files on hashing (or address-translation) techniques. There are other ways of organizing a direct file which are less popular, but nevertheless may be applicable in some situations.

If the number of records in the file is relatively small and the record size is relatively large (i.e., only a few records per bucket is achievable), then it may be worthwhile to consider a direct-addressing scheme. A number of methods for achieving direct-address translation involve the use of cross referencing or indexing. A *cross-reference table* is simply a table of keys and addresses in which a unique external storage address is assigned to each key. Figure 7-8.1 illustrates a cross-reference table of surnames and external storage addresses for a sector-addressable device. A cross-reference table is merely an associative list as discussed in Sec. 4-4. To locate a record given its key, it is simply a matter of retrieving the external address associated with the key and then issuing an I/O command which directly retrieves the desired record. In most programming languages, however, associative lists are not provided and the programmer must maintain the cross-reference

Surname	External Address (Cyl., Trk., Sector)
Ashcroft	1,07,04
Barnsley	1,07,05
Bernard	1,08,15
Duke	1,06,09
Edder	1,07,00
Groff	1,06,10
Katz	1,06,12
Murray	1,08,13
Paulsen	1,06,00
Smith	1,06,03
Thomas	1,06,04
Tollard	1,06,11
Yu	1,07,01

FIGURE 7-8.1   Cross-reference table.

table. The table can be kept as an unordered list and, therefore, can accommodate additions with ease. A linear search is then required to find an address, and record deletions create "holes" in the table. The table can be implemented as a list ordered by the key set. A binary search can be employed to locate an address more rapidly. Record additions and deletions, however, present problems because the table must be maintained in order.

Indexing methods involving binary trees, m-ary trees, and trie structures can also be chosen to achieve direct addressing in direct files. With tree-structured methods (which were discussed in Sec. 6-2.3), record additions and deletions can be handled more effectively. A binary-tree indexing scheme for the cross-reference table given in Fig. 7-8.1 is shown, in part, in Fig. 7-8.2.

In the discussion throughout this subsection, we have assumed that if a desired record is not located in its primary bucket, than a series of I/O commands is issued. Each command brings in an overflow bucket which is scanned in search of the required record. The search strategy just outlined is true for external memory units which are sector-addressable. Some record-addressable devices such as the IBM 3330, however, are capable of locating, via hardware, a particular record on a given track based on the key of the record. In the discussion of PL/I direct files in Sec. 7-8.3, we will discover that this hardware capability can help to eliminate much of the scanning of overflow buckets in main memory that must be done using sector-addressable devices.

Let us now turn our attention to the type of processing that is associated with direct files.

7-8.2 Processing Direct Files

The processing of a direct file is dependent on how the key set for the records is transformed into external device addresses. In the previous subsection, we reviewed a number

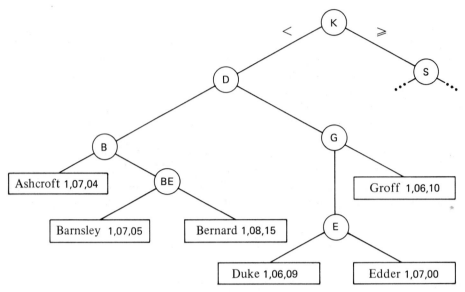

FIGURE 7-8.2   Binary-tree cross-reference indexing scheme.

of transformation methods. It is impractical to discuss direct-file processing for each method; therefore, we have chosen to present, as a representative example, the direct processing of a file which is accessed via a hashing algorithm using chaining with separate lists for overflow handling. Algorithms involving the processing of this form of organization are presented in this subsection.

Direct files are primarily processed directly. That is, a key is mapped to an address and, depending on the nature of the file transaction, a record is created, deleted, updated, or accessed at that address, or possibly at some subsequent address if a collision takes place. Of course, the subsequent address is determined by the overflow handling technique which is adopted.

When overflow handling is accommodated using chaining with separate lists, a pointer to a linked list of overflow records is included in each bucket. A representation of an overflow record in the separate list area is shown in Fig. 7-8.3. Each overflow location in the overflow area consists of two major parts—OR, containing an overflow record, and LINK, a pointer containing the address of the next location in a chain. KEY is the key of the record contained in OR.

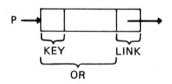

FIGURE 7-8.3   Representation of an overflow node.

A pointer to a chain of overflow records is included in each bucket, and for the ith bucket, this pointer is designated by PTR_i. If there are no overflow records for a bucket, then PTR_i has the value NULL; otherwise, it has the value of the address of the first record in the overflow chain for that bucket. The following algorithm inserts a record into a direct file which is organized according to the specifications given earlier.

Algorithm DIRECT_INSERT. Given a record R with key x, it is required to insert R into a direct file with n primary buckets $B_1, \ldots, B_n$, in which a particular bucket B_i contains m record locations $b_{i1}, b_{i2}, \ldots, b_{im}$. If a record is resident at location b_{ij}, then its key is denoted by k_{ij}. If no record is present, then the key field is represented with a negative number. [There are many other conventions that can be adopted to represent an empty record location. We will see in the next subsection that the placement of $(8)'1'B$ in the first record has been adopted by IBM.] If an overflow condition results, then R is stored in a location on a list of overflow locations for the primary bucket. The hashing function H is used to calculate an address.

1. [Apply hashing function] Set $i \leftarrow H(x)$.
2. [Scan the bucket indicated] If $PTR_i \neq$ NULL, then go to step 3.
   Repeat for $j = 1, 2, \ldots, m$:
       If $k_{ij} < 0$, then set $b_{ij} \leftarrow R$, and Exit.
3. [Put R in overflow storage at the head of overflow list]
   Obtain an overflow location and assign its address to P.
   Set $OR(P) \leftarrow R$, $LINK(P) \leftarrow PTR_i$, $PTR_i \leftarrow P$, and Exit.

In step 2, the record is placed in the bucket it is hashed to if a record location is available. Otherwise, an overflow node is obtained, its address is assigned to P, record R is placed at location P, and the pointers $LINK(P)$ and PTR_i are altered so that the new node is the first in the overflow chain for bucket i.

It should be noted that a check is not made to see if the key of the record being added matches the key of a record presently in the file. This checking should be done to prevent duplicate or inconsistent data. The necessary extensions to Algorithm DIRECT_INSERT to effect this checking are left as an exercise.

The algorithm for retrieving a record from a direct file using chaining with separate lists follows.

Algorithm DIRECT_RETRIEVE. Given a key x, it is required to retrieve the record identified by that key from the direct file with primary buckets $B_1, \ldots, B_n$ and the separate overflow storage.

1. [Apply hashing function] Set $i \leftarrow H(x)$.
2. [Search the bucket indicated]
   Repeat for $j = 1, 2, \ldots, m$:
       if $x = k_{ij}$,
       then set $R \leftarrow b_{ij}$, and Exit;
       otherwise, if $k_{ij} < 0$, then Exit unsuccessfully.
   Set $P \leftarrow PTR_i$.

3. [Search the overflow chain]
    If P = NULL, then Exit unsuccessfully.
    If KEY(P) = x, (if the key for the record referenced by P is x)
    then set R ← OR(P), and Exit;
    otherwise, set P ← LINK(P) and repeat this step.

In step 2, the required record is assigned to R if it is found in bucket B_i. If the bucket is not full and the record is not located, then the search ends unsuccessfully. Otherwise, in step 3 each successive node of the overflow chain is examined until the record is found or the end of the linked list is encountered.

If these algorithms are implemented using disk storage, overflow nodes should be located in a common seek area, and ideally, in the same area as their associated primary buckets. This is done so that extra seeks are not required to scan a linked list of overflow records.

Knuth [1973] has analytically derived formulae for the expected average length of search using a model which assumes chained overflow with bucket capacities of 1 or greater. Before using chained overflow, the reader is encouraged to examine these results.

In the last subsection, we reviewed open addressing as a popular method of handling overflows. Since several algorithms for direct access to a table using open addressing were given in Sec. 6-2.4, such algorithms are not repeated here. The reader is encouraged to review these algorithms. The extensions of these algorithms to make them applicable to direct files are left as an exercise.

Thus far, the only type of processing we have considered for direct files is direct processing. In some instances, it may be necessary to perform an identical transaction on all or nearly all records in the file. For example, in the small billing system, which we have often used to illustrate the material on file organization, it may be desirable to print monthly bills even though individual customer accounts can be accessed directly in an on-line mode. The generation of monthly bills can be accomplished by accessing the records in a physically sequential or serial manner.

Serial access of a direct file is not necessarily sequential access. That is, $x_1 \leq x_2$ for keys x_1 and x_2 does not imply $H(x_1) \leq H(x_2)$ for some hashing functions H. The fact is, we relinquished this ability of sequential access in favor of a quicker direct access when we proceeded from indexed sequential to direct files.

For most direct organizations, serial access presents no problems. Access commences at the physical beginning and terminates at the physical end of the file. If the file uses a separate overflow area, however, it may be difficult to access this area in a serial fashion independent of the prime area. Difficulties arise because the overflow area may be unblocked or blocked in a different manner than the prime area. A logically consistent, yet potentially time-consuming method, of serial access of a separate overflow area is to read all the records in the first prime area bucket, followed by all the overflow records for this bucket, and then return to read the next prime area bucket, followed by its overflow records, etc., until all records in the file have been accessed.

A final aspect of direct-file processing which we should consider is file maintenance. Many systems which support direct files simply mark deleted records and only recover the space occupied by these records when a new record can be added to the file at the marked location. The space occupied by a deleted record may require needless examination in search of a record in the prime bucket. In addition, deleted records affect performance when probing or chaining through a file in search of an overflow record. It is sometimes possible to remove deleted records logically, especially where chaining is involved; however, this is rarely done. Instead it is the programmer's responsibility to monitor the activity of the file and to reorganize it whenever performance degrades significantly. Reorganization can be accomplished by reading the file serially and creating a new direct file that involves only the active records of the old file.

We complete this subsection by summarizing the important properties related to direct files:

1 Direct access to records in a direct file is rapid, especially for files with low load factors and few overflow records.

2 Because a certain portion of the file remains unused in order to prevent an excessive number of overflow records, the space utilization for a direct file is poor when compared to the other file organizations we have discussed.

3 The performance attained using a direct file is very dependent upon the key-to-address transformation algorithm adopted. The transformation that is used is application-dependent and is generally implemented and maintained through users' programs.

4 Records can be accessed serially, but not sequentially unless a separate ordered list of keys is maintained.

7-8.3 Direct Files in PL/I

In PL/I, a direct file is called a *regional* file. There are three types of regional files available; namely, REGIONAL(1), REGIONAL(2), and REGIONAL(3). Each of these is examined in this subsection.

To appreciate fully the differences between these three direct file organizations, we must discuss in some detail the track formats for record-addressable storage devices as exemplified by IBM's 2311, 2314, 3330, and 3340 disks. While much of the discussion in this section is device-dependent, such emphasis is warranted because the PL/I instructions for regional files are heavily oriented towards, but not necessarily dependent upon, record-addressable direct-access devices.

There are two track formats on IBM direct-access storage devices. They are called *count-data* and *count-key-data formats*, and these are illustrated in Fig. 7-8.4.

For both formats, the count area is ten bytes in length and it contains the record's location in terms of the cylinder, head, and record number, the record's key length (which is 0 if no key is used), and the record's data field length. If a key is used, the key area holds a key that is between 1 and 255 bytes (characters) in length. The data area contains the user-provided data for the record. The maximum length of this field is determined by the device's track capacity. The data area can be thought of as a block (bucket or region) which may consist of several logical records. However, if more than one logical record is stored in a data area, blocking and unblocking is the responsibility of the user. This aspect is not discussed in this subsection. Note that record R0 is a special record maintained by the system. It contains information related to the status of a track, such as whether or not the track is defective and, if defective, the address of an alternate track.

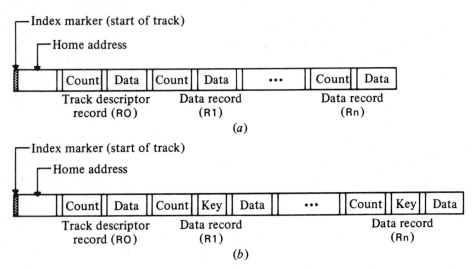

FIGURE 7-8.4   Track formats. (*a*) Count-data; (*b*) count-key-data.

All REGIONAL files are divided into *relative* regions, each of which is identified by a *region number*. The regions are numbered successively from zero to 16777215 ($2^{24} - 1$). A record is accessed by specifying its region number in a record-oriented I/O statement in one of two ways, namely, relative record or relative track.

A *relative record* is referenced by a number relative to the first record in the file. Figure 7-8.5*a* depicts the sectioning of a disk surface into relative records. In a relative record scheme, which is used in REGIONAL(1) and REGIONAL(2) files, only one record is allowed per region.

A *relative-track* specification refers to a particular track relative to the first track of the file. Figure 7-8.5*b* illustrates this type of organization. Each region is a track and more than one record can be stored in a region. REGIONAL(3) files provide this type of organization.

Before considering each of the three types of REGIONAL files, we must introduce and clearly distinguish between the notions of a source key and a recorded key. A *source key* is a character string specified in the record-oriented I/O statements following the KEY or KEYFROM options. For example, in

    READ FILE(INVEN) INTO (STORE_ITEM) KEY(CATLG#)

CATLG#, which typically may have a value such as 'A2E01101241', is the source key.

In a REGIONAL(1) file, the source key consists of a region number only, and it is this number which uniquely identifies a particular record. Hence, the source key for a REGIONAL(1) organization consists of an eight-position character string which is capable of representing the region numbers in the range of 0 to 16777215. Because there is no stored key in a REGIONAL(1) organization, a count-data track format is used.

The source key for REGIONAL(2) or REGIONAL(3) files has two logical parts—the *comparison key* and the *region number*. The region number is found in the rightmost eight characters of the source key, and the comparison key is generally formed from the re-

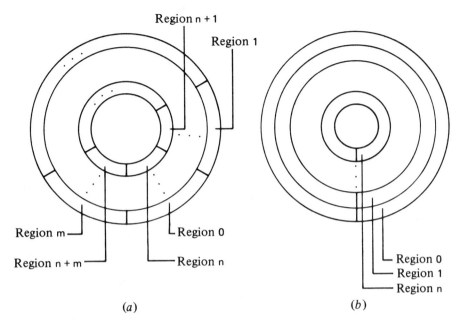

FIGURE 7-8.5 Regional specifications. (*a*) Relative record; (*b*) relative track.

mainder of the source key. Therefore, the source key with a value of 'A2E01101241' designates the region number '01101241' and comparison key of 'A2E'.

The portion of the source key that is stored in the key area of a record is called the *recorded key*. The recorded key may be from one to 255 characters in length. The length is specified through the KEYLENGTH option of the ENVIRONMENT clause or as a DCB parameter of the form KEYLEN =n in a DD job control statement.

The recorded key takes on the value of the comparison key. Therefore, to declare the file INVEN to be a REGIONAL(2) file with a recorded key equal to the comparison key based on the CATLG# source key, we write

DECLARE INVEN FILE RECORD KEYED ENV(REGIONAL(2) KEYLENGTH – 3);

Hence, the first three characters of the catalogue number form the recorded key. If we specify a KEYLENGTH of 1 or 4, then the comparison key and the recorded key for 'A2E01101241' become 'A' and 'A2E0', respectively. Therefore, part of the source key may be unused, and the comparison key and the recorded key can include part or all of the region number.

The distinction between the comparison key and the recorded key is a strictly functional one. On output, the comparison key is written as the recorded key, and on input, the comparison key is compared with the recorded key.

The format of the I/O statements for PL/I direct files is identical to the format for the I/O statement for indexed sequential files. An example READ statement for the file INVEN was given earlier in this section. A WRITE statement for directly writing into the INVEN file is as follows:

WRITE FILE(INVEN) FROM (STORE_ITEM) KEYFROM(CATLG#);

DELETE and REWRITE statements are available as well. All of these instructions will be illustrated in an example given later in this subsection.

Other similarities exist between direct and indexed sequential files in PL/I. Direct files can also be opened for INPUT, OUTPUT, or UPDATE. The DIRECT and SEQUENTIAL attributes can be used to specify the manner in which the records in the file are accessed. The DIRECT attribute designates that records are accessed by use of a key. SEQUENTIAL specifies that the records are accessed according to their physical sequence in the file. In other words, SEQUENTIAL implies serial access.

Let us now describe the three different REGIONAL organizations.

REGIONAL(1) files

REGIONAL(1) files are designed for applications involving direct-address translation (i.e., every key in the file corresponds to a unique external storage address). The source key for a REGIONAL(1) file is a region number, and it is this relative record address that is translated into a unique external storage address. It is a common occurrence in direct-address translation that not all record locations are filled. Those locations that are not filled with user information are identified as dummy records by placing the constant (8)'1'B in the first byte of the record (just as we did for indexed sequential files). Dummy records can be replaced by any valid data.

REGIONAL(1) files, and indeed any REGIONAL file, can be created sequentially or directly. However, when the SEQUENTIAL OUTPUT attribute is used to create a REGIONAL file, the records must be handled in ascending order by region number. An error in the sequence, or a duplicate key, will cause the KEY condition to be raised. Any region that is omitted during creation is filled with a dummy record. If the file is created directly, all of the space allocated to the file is filled with dummy records when the file is opened.

REGIONAL(1) files can be accessed serially (which is also sequentially by region number) and directly. The standard file operations of retrieval, addition, deletion, and alteration can be achieved using READ, WRITE, DELETE, and REWRITE statements. These operations are illustrated in the example program given in Fig. 7-8.6.

The program accepts transaction records of the form

<transaction type> <car license number> [detailed car information]

The <transaction type> can be 'REQUEST', 'ADD', 'UPDATE', and 'DELETE'. A <car license number> can be a six-digit or less license-plate number which conveniently is used as a region number. The detailed car information is described in the structure INFO.This information is not required and does not appear in the transaction records requesting or deleting information about a vehicle.

REGIONAL(2) files

Each record in a REGIONAL(2) data set is uniquely identified by a recorded key. However, the position of a record in the file relative to other records is determined by the region number as derived from the source key of the WRITE statement which created the record. When a record is added to the file, it is written with its recorded key in the first available space after the beginning of the track that contains the region specified. To read, rewrite,

```
// EXEC PL1LFCLG,PARM='ATR,XREF'
//PL1L.SYSIN DD *
 REG1_EG: PROCEDURE OPTIONS(MAIN);

      DECLARE CARS RECORD KEYED ENV(F(115) REGIONAL(1)),
               1 INFO,
                 2 DEL_CODE BIT(8),
                 2 NAME CHAR(30),
                 2 ADDR CHAR(80),
                 2 AGE FIXED(2),
                 2 OFF# FIXED(2),
               TRANSACTION CHAR(7),
               LICENSE# CHAR(6),
               I FIXED,
               TRAN(0:4) LABEL,
               TYPE_STR CHAR(28) INITIAL('REQUESTADD    UPDATE DELETE ');

      ON KEY(CARS) BEGIN;
          PUT SKIP LIST('RECORD REQUESTED IS NOT PRESENT OR ATTEMPTING'||
            ' TO ADD A DUPLICATE RECORD -- ONKEY IS: ', ONKEY);
          STOP;
      END;

      OPEN FILE(CARS) DIRECT UPDATE;
      ON ENDFILE(SYSIN) STOP;  /* SYSIN CONTAINS TRANSACTION RECORDS */

      DO WHILE('1'B);
          GET EDIT(TRANSACTION,LICENSE#)(COL(1),A(7),A(6));
          I = (INDEX(TYPE_STR,TRANSACTION) + 6) / 7;
          IF I ¬= 2 & I ¬= 0 /* NOT AN 'ADD' TRANSACTION */
          THEN READ FILE(CARS) INTO(INFO) KEY(LICENSE#);
          GO TO TRAN(I); /* I DETERMINES TRANSACTION TYPE */

      TRAN(0): /* ILLEGAL TRANSACTION */
          PUT SKIP LIST('ILLEGAL TRANSACTION'); GO TO CONTINUE;

      TRAN(1): /* 'REQUEST' TRANSACTION */
          PUT SKIP EDIT('THE INFORMATION CONCERNING LICENSE NUMBER ',
            LICENSE#, 'IS AS FOLLOWS:','NAME: ',NAME,'ADDRESS: ',ADDR,
            'AGE: ',AGE,'NUMBER OF PREVIOUS OFFENSES: ',OFF#)
            (3 A,SKIP,2 A,SKIP,2 A,SKIP,A,F(2),SKIP,A,F(2));
          GO TO CONTINUE;

      TRAN(2): /* 'ADD' TRANSACTION */
          GET EDIT(NAME,ADDR,AGE,OFF#)(COL(1),A(20),COL(1),A(80),2 F(2));
          WRITE FILE(CARS) FROM(INFO) KEYFROM(LICENSE#);
          GO TO CONTINUE;

      TRAN(3): /* 'UPDATE' TRANSACTION */
          GET EDIT(NAME,ADDR,AGE,OFF#)(COL(1),A(20),COL(1),A(80),2 F(2));
          REWRITE FILE(CARS) FROM(INFO) KEY(LICENSE#);
          GO TO CONTINUE;

      TRAN(4): /* 'DELETE' TRANSACTION */
          DELETE FILE(CARS) KEY(LICENSE#);

      CONTINUE: END; /* OF DO WHILE */
 END REG1_EG;
//GO.CARS DD DSN=LICENSE,DISP=(OLD,KEEP),UNIT=SYSDA
//GO.SYSIN DD *
(DATA GO HERE)
 /*
```

FIGURE 7-8.6 Example of a REGIONAL(1) file.

or delete a particular record, a search begins at the start of the track containing the specified region and continues until a record is found with the appropriate recorded key. This search continues across track boundaries and can progress to the end of the file. The search can be limited to a certain number of tracks by the LIMCT DCB parameter (i.e., LIMCT = n for some nonnegative integer n) of a job control language DD statement.

Let us look at an example of how records are placed in a REGIONAL(2) file. Assume we are using as a source key the CATLG# described earlier in this section. If we use the first three characters of the 11-character catalogue number as the recorded key, then 'A1E00000000' specifies a record with a region number of zero and a recorded key of 'A1E'. Let us assume that there are four regions (i.e., records) per track as illustrated in Fig. 7-8.7. The records with source keys of 'A1E00000000' and 'B2L00000002' are already created. If the instruction

> WRITE FILE(INVEN) FROM (SALES_ITEM) KEYFROM('Z6K00000003');

is executed, then this record is added to the file in region 1. It is placed at this location because region 1 is the first available space after the beginning of the track that contains the region specified.

When REGIONAL(2) files are created sequentially, the records must be presented in ascending order by region number. Any region that is omitted is assigned a dummy record, and if there is an error in the sequence or an attempt to place more than one record in the same region, the KEY condition is raised.

If a REGIONAL(2) file is created directly, the entire file space is filled with dummy records. Records can be presented in any order, and a KEY condition is *not* raised if there is a duplicate recorded key, duplicate region, or duplicate key and region. Hence, duplicate records are stored. To protect against such duplication, it is wise to execute a READ statement, using the source key of the record to be added, prior to the execution of the WRITE statement. If the READ statement fails and a KEY condition is invoked, then the record can be safely written.

When a REGIONAL(2) file is accessed sequentially, the KEYTO option can be used to extract the recorded key. For example, the execution of the statement

> READ FILE(INVEN) INTO (SALES_ITEM) KEYTO(CATLG#);

causes the next record, in order of ascending region number, to be read. The recorded key is concatenated with the region number and then is assigned to the variable CATLG#.

When records with duplicate recorded keys are accessed for retrieval, deletion, or update, the record closest to the beginning of the file is the record affected.

Figure 7-8.8 is an example program involving the generation and update of invoices in an order entry and invoicing system. A region number is equated to an invoice number, and the recorded key is the invoice number prefixed by one of four letters: 'O' meaning "on order"; 'S' meaning "shipped"; 'R' meaning "received and paid"; and 'D' meaning "some defective items returned." In most instances, there is a single invoice per region number (i.e., direct addressing is used). In some situations, however, the goods correspond-

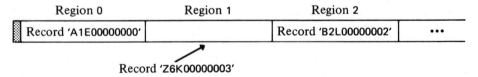

FIGURE 7-8.7 The insertion of a record in a REGIONAL(2) file.

ing to a particular invoice may be received, and then later some of them returned as defective. In this case, two records with the same region number are created for the invoice. To accommodate the spatial demands generated by allowing records with duplicate region numbers, invoice numbers ending with a zero are not used.

The program in Fig. 7-8.8 illustrates how REGIONAL(2) files can be used in a direct-addressing mode. Indirect addressing can be applied to REGIONAL(2) files as well. For example, in a parts-department application, many of the parts come from different manufacturers, each of whom has a different parts numbering scheme. Example part numbers are TC103, 176-232, and 6225AX. Assuming a direct file is a desirable type of file for the parts application, then a hashing function can be applied to a part number to generate a region number. If the actual part number is adopted as the recorded key, then records with duplicate region numbers are uniquely identified by the recorded key. Therefore, the region is used as a primary area and indicates the relative position of the record, and the recorded key is used to locate the desired record within this relative area.

REGIONAL(3) files

A REGIONAL(3) file differs from a REGIONAL(1) or REGIONAL(2) file in the following respects. Each region in a REGIONAL(3) file is a track on a direct-access device (see Fig. 7-8.5b) and the region number can be at most 32767. Probably the most significant differences are that a region can contain one or more records and records can be fixed or variable in length.

If the file is created sequentially, the records must be presented in ascending order of region numbers. Identical region numbers, however, can be specified for successive records. When a track is filled with records, the corresponding region number is automatically incremented. A further attempt to add a record with the previous region number will raise the KEY condition, as will any sequence error.

If the file is created directly with fixed-length records, the whole file space is initialized with dummy records when the file is opened. For variable-length records, only one dummy record is created per region, and this can occupy the entire track. As in the case of REGIONAL(2) records, no condition is raised by duplicate keys in the same region. When a record is added to a region, it is assigned to the first dummy record location encountered. For variable-length records, the record is located in the first available space on the track.

A record is accessed directly by scanning a particular track (as designated by the region number given in the source key) until a match is found between the comparison key and the recorded key. It should be noted that the space occupied by a fixed-length record can be reused. However, the space occupied by deleted variable-length records is not available. In addition, one cannot replace a variable-length record with a record that is larger. An attempt to do so can be detected using the ON RECORD condition.

An example program illustrating the processing of a REGIONAL(3) file is shown in Fig. 7-8.9. The file contains a number of abstracts of civil court case proceedings. The first ten characters of a record are a case-proceedings number which is used to obtain a detailed copy of the proceedings as compiled by the courtroom recorder. The remaining portion of a record contains a variable number of eighty-character lines of text which forms the abstract of the case proceedings.

```
// EXEC PL1LFCLG,PARM='SM=(2,80,1)'
//PL1L.SYSIN DO *
 REG2_EG: PROCEDURE OPTIONS (MAIN);

        DECLARE INVOICE RECORD KEYED ENV (REGIONAL(2) F(92)),
                1 RECORD,
                  2 DELETE_CODE BIT(8),
                  2 DATE FIXED (6),
                  2 ITEM_COUNT FIXED (1),
                  2 TOTAL_PRICE FIXED (10, 2),
                  2 ITEM (5),
                    3 PART# CHAR (6),
                    3 MANUF# CHAR (3),
                    3 QUANTITY FIXED (2),
                    3 UNIT_PRICE FIXED (8, 2),
                 (TYPE_CODE, NEW_TYPE_CODE) CHAR (1),
                  INVOICE# CHAR (8),
                  TRANSACTION CHAR (7),
                  TYPE_STR CHAR (28) INITIAL ('REQUESTADD   UPDATE DELETE '),
                  I FIXED,
                  LABEL (0:4) LABEL;

        ON KEY (INVOICE) BEGIN;
            PUT SKIP LIST ('ERROR -- KEY CONDITION RAISED','ONKEY=',ONKEY);
            END;

        OPEN FILE (INVOICE) DIRECT UPDATE;

        ON ENDFILE (SYSIN)  STOP;

LOOP:    DO WHILE ('1'B);

            GET FILE (SYSIN) EDIT (TRANSACTION, TYPE_CODE, INVOICE#)
                             (COL(1), A(7), A(1), A(8));
            I = (INDEX (TYPE_STR, TRANSACTION) + 6) / 7;
            IF I ¬= 2 & I ¬= 0  /* NOT AN 'ADD' */
            THEN  READ FILE (INVOICE) INTO (RECORD) KEY (TYPE_CODE || INVOICE#);
            GO TO LABEL(I);

        LABEL(0):  /* ILLEGAL TRANSACTION */
            PUT SKIP LIST ('ILLEGAL TRANSACTION :', TRANSACTION);
            GO TO CONTIN;

        LABEL(1):  /* 'REQUEST' TRANSACTION */
            PUT SKIP EDIT ('INVOICE #',INVOICE#,'DATE ',DATE,
                'PART','MANUFACTURER','QUANTITY','UNIT PRICE')
                (2 A,X(10),2 A,COL(1),A,COL(10),A,COL(30),A,COL(50),A);
            PUT SKIP EDIT ( (ITEM(I)  DO I=1 TO ITEM_COUNT) )
                ((ITEM_COUNT) (COL(1),A,COL(15),A,COL(33),F(2),COL(50),F(11,2)));
            PUT SKIP EDIT ('TOTAL PRICE', TOTAL_PRICE)
                            (COL(30),A,COL(48),F(13,2));
            GO TO CONTIN;

        LABEL(2):  /* 'ADD' TRANSACTION */
            GET EDIT (DATE, ITEM_COUNT, TOTAL_PRICE)
                     (COL(1), F(6), F(1), F(10,2));
            GET EDIT ( (ITEM (I)  DO I=1 TO ITEM_COUNT) )
                     ( (ITEM_COUNT) (COL(1),A(6),A(3),F(2),F(8,2)) );
            WRITE FILE (INVOICE) FROM (RECORD) KEYFROM (TYPE_CODE || INVOICE#);
            GO TO CONTIN;
```

FIGURE 7-8.8   Example of a REGIONAL(2) file.

The source key is made up of a twenty-five character comparison key which contains the names of the principal parties involved (e.g., HARTENGER – WILSON), and an eight-digit region number of which the first five characters are zeros and the last three characters are determined by a hashing function. The hashing function is based on the division method and uses the EBCDIC representation of the first three characters of the

```
LABEL(3):   /* 'UPDATE' TRANSACTION */
    GET EDIT (NEW_TYPE_CODE) (COL(1), A(1));
    GET EDIT (DATE, ITEM_COUNT, TOTAL_PRICE)
             (COL(1), F(6), F(1), F(10,2));
    GET EDIT ( (ITEM (I)  DO I=1 TO ITEM_COUNT) )
             ( (ITEM_COUNT) (COL(1),A(6),A(3),F(2),F(8,2)) );
    IF TYPE_CODE = NEW_TYPE_CODE
    THEN REWRITE FILE (INVOICE) FROM (RECORD) KEY (TYPE_CODE || INVOICE#);
    ELSE DO;
         WRITE FILE (INVOICE) FROM (RECORD)
               KEYFROM (NEW_TYPE_CODE || INVOICE#);
         GO TO LABEL(4);   /* TO DELETE OLD RECORD */
    END;
    GO TO CONTIN;

LABEL(4):   /* 'DELETE' TRANSACTION */
    DELETE FILE (INVOICE) KEY (TYPE_CODE || INVOICE#);

CONTIN:  END LOOP;

END REG2_EG;
//GO.INVOICE DD DSN=INVEN,DISP=(OLD,KEEP),UNIT=SYSDA,
//    DCB=(DSORG=DA,KEYLEN=9)
//GO.SYSIN DD *
(DATA GO HERE)
 /*
```

FIGURE 7-8.8   (Continued)

two names of the parties (e.g., for HAR and WIL we have $(C8C1D9)_{16}$ and $(E6C9D3)_{16}$ or 13,156,625 and 15,124,947, respectively). These numbers are added together and the result modulus 997 (the greatest prime less than 1000) is taken to be the region number (for the example, the region is 670).

Transaction records are composed, in part, of a command—either *RETRIEVE, *ADD, *DELETE, or *REPLACE—which together with the names of the principal parties involved form the first line of a transaction. For the *ADD and *REPLACE commands, the additional information items (i.e., the case-proceedings number and the case abstract) are required.

By now it should be evident that the REGIONAL file organizations differ from the organizations discussed earlier in the chapter with respect to the handling of collisions. With REGIONAL files there are no apparent collisions. There is an implicit assumption that the external device is capable of locating a particular record based on its key. An IBM 3330 (record-addressable) device has this capability, and it is not necessary to bring records into main memory for examination. In REGIONAL(2) and REGIONAL(3) files, records are added directly to the file without checking to see if there is another record with the same region number, i.e., there is no check for collisions. Instead, a record is placed at the first open location of the track associated with the record's region number. Of course, if this track is full, a search is made for an open record location on the succeeding tracks. Therefore, one can conceptually think of a track as being a bucket in which a REGIONAL(2) or RE-GIONAL(3) record resides. If a desired record is not located on the primary track (as dictated by the region number), then a progressive overflow-handling technique is followed.

In contrast, devices which are sector-addressable require more processing to locate an overflow record. First, the primary bucket (i.e., sector) is brought into memory and a scan of its contents is made to determine if the bucket holds the desired record. If it

```
// EXEC PL1LFCLG,PARM='SIZE=999999,SM=(2,80,1)'
//PL1L.SYSIN DD *
 REG3_EG: PROCEDURE OPTIONS (MAIN);
     DECLARE ABSTRACTS FILE RECORD KEYED ENV (REGIONAL(3) V(1618)),

 /* RECORD IS COMPOSED OF A TEN CHARACTER CASE NUMBER FOLLOWED BY
    A VARIABLE LENGTH CASE ABSTRACT */
             RECORD CHAR (1610) VARYING,
             CARD CHAR (80),
             EOF BIT (1) INIT ('0'B),
             REQUEST CHAR (8),
             REQUEST_STR CHAR (32) INIT ('RETRIEVEADD      DELETE  REPLACE '),
            (I, TYPE) FIXED,
             NAMES CHAR (17),
             HASH ENTRY (CHAR (*)) RETURNS (CHAR (8)),
             GETCARDS ENTRY,
             PROC (0:4) LABEL;

       ON ENDFILE (SYSIN)  EOF = '1'B;
       ON KEY (ABSTRACTS) BEGIN;
          PUT SKIP EDIT ('ERROR IN REQUEST: ', REQUEST, 'NAMES: ', NAMES)
                         (2 A,X(10),2 A);
          IF ONCODE = 51 THEN DO;
             PUT SKIP LIST ('RECORD NOT FOUND');
             CALL GETCARDS;
          END;
          GO TO CONTINUE;
       END;

       OPEN FILE (ABSTRACTS) DIRECT UPDATE;

       GET FILE (SYSIN) EDIT (CARD) (A (80));

 DO_LOOP: DO WHILE (¬EOF);

          REQUEST = SUBSTR (CARD, 2, 8);
          NAMES = SUBSTR (CARD, 10, 17);
          TYPE = (INDEX (REQUEST_STR, REQUEST) + 7) / 8;
          GO TO PROC (TYPE);

       PROC(0):  /* BAD REQUEST */
          PUT SKIP LIST ('UNKNOWN REQUEST :', REQUEST);
          CALL GETCARDS;
          GO TO CONTINUE;

       PROC(1):  /* 'RETRIEVE' REQUEST */
          READ FILE (ABSTRACTS) INTO (RECORD) KEY (NAMES || HASH (NAMES));
          PUT SKIP(2) EDIT ('CASE', NAMES, 'PROCEEDINGS #', SUBSTR (RECORD,1,10))
                         (A, X(4), A, COL(35),2 A);
          PUT SKIP(2) LIST ('ABSTRACT :');
          DO I = 11 BY 80 WHILE (I < LENGTH (RECORD));
              PUT SKIP LIST (SUBSTR (RECORD, I, 80));
          END;
          PUT SKIP;
          CALL GETCARDS;
          GO TO CONTINUE;

       PROC(2):  /* 'ADD' REQUEST */
          CALL GETCARDS;
          WRITE FILE (ABSTRACTS) FROM (RECORD)
                     KEYFROM (NAMES || HASH (NAMES));
```

FIGURE 7-8.9   Example of a REGIONAL(3) file.

does not, then an overflow bucket is brought into memory and examined. A progression of such overflow records may be considered before the correct record is located. Of course, the necessity to bring the contents of a bucket into memory and then to scan these contents for a particular record makes direct access on a sector-addressable device slower than on a record-addressable device.

```
              GO TO CONTINUE;

      PROC(3):   /* 'DELETE' REQUEST */
              DELETE FILE (ABSTRACTS) KEY (NAMES || HASH (NAMES));
              CALL GETCARDS;
              GO TO CONTINUE;

      PROC(4):   /* 'UPDATE' REQUEST */
              CALL GETCARDS;
              REWRITE FILE (ABSTRACTS) FROM (RECORD)
                            KEY (NAMES || HASH (NAMES));

      CONTINUE:  END DO_LOOP;

      GETCARDS: PROCEDURE;
/* READ PROCEEDINGS NO. AND ABSTRACT (IF NEEDED) AND GET NEXT REQUEST */

              GET FILE (SYSIN) EDIT (CARD) (A (80));
              IF SUBSTR (CARD, 1, 1) = '*'
              THEN RETURN;
              RECORD = SUBSTR (CARD, 1, 10);
              GET FILE (SYSIN) EDIT (CARD) (A (80));

              DO WHILE (¬EOF & SUBSTR (CARD, 1, 1) ¬= '*');
                  RECORD = RECORD || CARD;
                  GET FILE (SYSIN) EDIT (CARD) (A (80));
              END;
      END GETCARDS;

HASH: PROCEDURE (KEY) RETURNS (CHAR (8));

      DECLARE KEY CHAR (*),
              (I, HASHED) FIXED;

      I = INDEX (KEY, '-');

      HASHED = MOD (UNSPEC (SUBSTR (KEY, 1, 3)) +
                    UNSPEC (SUBSTR (KEY, I, 3)), 997);
      RETURN (HASHED);

END HASH;

END REG3_EG;
//GO.ABSTRACT DD DSNAME=CASES,DISP=(OLD,KEEP),UNIT=SYSDA,
//      DCB=(DSORG=DA,KEYLEN=17)
//GO.SYSIN DD *
(DATA GO HERE)
 /*
```

FIGURE 7-8.9 (Continued)

In the section to follow we discuss an on-line banking system as an application of direct files. Since a PL/I implementation is considered, much of the material presented in this subsection will be pertinent.

Exercises for Sec. 7-8

1. In what ways does the bucket capacity affect the performance of an information system in which direct files are used?

2. List the advantages and disadvantages of chained overflow with separate lists when compared to an open-addressing technique.

3. Formulate algorithms for inserting, deleting, and retrieving records from a direct file assuming chaining with coalescing lists is used as the overflow technique.

4. Formulate Algorithm DIRECT_SEQ for reading the records of a direct file in which chaining with separate lists is used as the overflow technique.

5. List the advantages and disadvantages of having a direct file on a record-addressable device (such as the IBM 3330) over having the file reside on a sector-addressable device.

6. Can you suggest why variable-length records are disallowed in REGIONAL(1) and REGIONAL(2) files?

7. A type of on-line information system which is familiar to all is an airline reservation system. One function the system must handle instantaneously is the reservation (and confirmation) of a passenger on a particular flight. In this question, you are to design and implement this part of the total system. Assume that two sets of information items are received when handling a flight reservation. The first item is in the form of a request made for a certain type of ticket (economy or first class) for a particular flight (for example, TW937) on a particular day. The system must immediately determine if such a request can be fulfilled. If it can, then a second set of information—the passenger's name and phone number—is received and used to complete the reservation.

Write a PL/I program in which a direct file (REGIONAL(3) file) is used in the reservation of a passenger. A flight name of the form <abbreviated airline name> <three digit number> is used as part of the key for the direct file. Example flight names are AM666, AC125, CP098, EA930, LU002, NW794, and TW365. The region number of a PL/I source key should be associated with each airline. Flight numbers and the date of the flight are used to distinguish flights within a given region of the file. Therefore, AM666 on January 5, 1975 is translated into the PL/I source key 666005197500000001 if the region number 00000001 is associated with American Airlines. The field 666 is the flight number, 005 is the fifth day of the year, and 1975 is the year.

The REGIONAL(3) file should contain an initial three records which hold the number of seats for each class which have not been reserved and the total number of seats available for the flight. The remaining records are source key values for a REGIONAL(1) file which contains records each holding a passenger's name and phone number. For example, when an economy-class passenger is added to a flight, he is assigned a number which serves as a source key in the REGIONAL(1) file. This number is placed in the REGIONAL(3) file and the second record in the file is decremented by 1. To complete the reservation, the name and phone number of the passenger are stored at the appropriate record locations in the REGIONAL(1) file. Cancellations of reservations are handled in a obvious manner. Be sure to place error-checking procedures into the system and test the system thoroughly.

8. What are the advantages and disadvantages of using two files instead of one file (i.e., only the REGIONAL(3) file) in Exercise 7?

7-9   AN ON-LINE BANKING SYSTEM

To demonstrate the use of direct files, we have chosen an application involving an on-line banking system which handles savings accounts. The PL/I implementation of the system illustrates the use of two types of direct files: REGIONAL(1) and REGIONAL(2). The system described is pedagogical and does not have many of the refinements that are now appearing in most modern banking systems. Nevertheless, an examination of its development is informative and interesting.

7-9.1   System Analysis

The system should permit bank customers to perform monetary transactions by interacting with a teller, who keys in the transactions, and to have these transactions registered instantaneously in his or her account. The current status of the account is available to the customer in a permanent form through the use of a passbook. If the customer presents a passbook to the teller, the teller can insert the passbook in a special recording slot in the terminal, and the current transaction plus all previously unrecorded transactions are printed in the passbook. There are a number of special banking terminals on the market, and a typical transaction-oriented keyboard is shown in Fig. 7-9.1.

It is important that the system be designed to handle monetary transactions without a customer's passbook; customers are notoriously forgetful or lazy. Interest is calculated monthly on the lowest balance of the past month. This calculation is performed automatically and is entered into the passbook the first time the book is presented in the month. Should the passbook not be presented during some month, the interest is accumulated until the passbook is brought in, at which time all necessary entries are made.

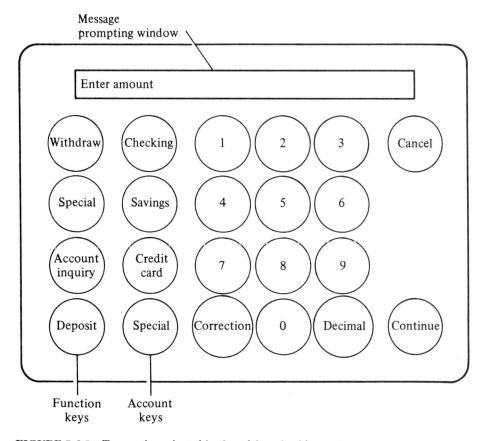

FIGURE 7-9.1   Transaction-oriented keyboard for a banking system.

The system will accommodate only one type of customer account—a savings account—for which the following transactions are permitted:

1 A new account may be opened.
2 Money may be deposited into an existing account.
3 Money may be withdrawn from an existing account (checking privileges are not allowed).
4 Passbooks may be updated.
5 An existing account may be closed.

The system should be designed to handle accounts from a number of different branches located in the same geographic area. Therefore, a customer need not be forced to go to the same branch for all transactions.

As a final requirement, the system should be reliable. If the computer responsible for updating customer accounts fails, then a backup mode of operation must be present. Ideally, a second computer should be simultaneously in operation and performing the same transactions as the first computer. If the first fails, the second can continue handling accounts without interruption of banking services. A less expensive form of backup is to employ a minicomputer to store on tape all monetary transactions which take place while the main system is down. When the system recovers, the transactions are sent in batch mode to the main computer. A final alternative is to revert to a manual method of recording in the event of a main-system failure. When the main system becomes operable again, delayed transactions are entered when time is available for the teller to do so. In the next subsection, however, we will only consider the design of the main system and will ignore the problem of system backup.

7-9.2 System Design

We begin by examining those aspects of the system's design that most directly affect the user—the transaction entry facility. In a fully automated banking system, tellers ideally key in customer transactions through a keyboard similar to that shown in Fig. 7-9.1. In our system, however, we will assume a standard input device (such as a CRT) is available. We make this assumption primarily to demonstrate clearly the interaction between a keyed request and the resulting file transaction in the PL/I implementation phase. In addition, specialized banking terminals are luxuries not all banks can afford.

It should be obvious that if a query language is used in an on-line banking system, it should be a terse language. Since tellers are constantly interacting with the system, an abbreviated command structure aids in efficiency and reduces keyboard errors, which are more likely to occur if long textual commands are required. Also, it is useful, wherever possible, to prompt the teller if prompting is requested. The inexperienced teller can be aided by such a facility. The experienced teller can turn this feature off.

The five customer transactions that normally occur in banking are account opening, withdrawal, deposit, inquiry, and account closing. Since the opening and closing of an account are relatively rare, yet very important events, special status is often given to these transactions. In some banking systems, only managers are allowed to complete these transactions and they do so by keying in special function codes of which they alone have access. Other banking systems do not handle deposits on-line for reasons of security.

The type of processing that is necessary in an on-line banking system is quite rudimentary. An input that is representative of a customer transaction is first examined. Once the nature of the transaction is determined, a system routine is activated. One such system routine is available for each customer transaction type. Figure 7-9.2 shows the general flow of system execution. A special module for scanning and identifying the basic lexical units of an input message is invoked several times per input by the input-evaluation routine. Such a module is not required in a function keyboard system such as that in Fig. 7-9.1.

Let us now turn to an examination of the file structures and file-level transactions required by the system.

In almost all modern-day banking systems, access to information concerning a bank account is gained through an account number. This is true in computerized or manual systems. An account number is the vehicle for providing a unique and a somewhat anonymous method for account identification.

The uniqueness property makes account numbers ideal primary keys for accessing

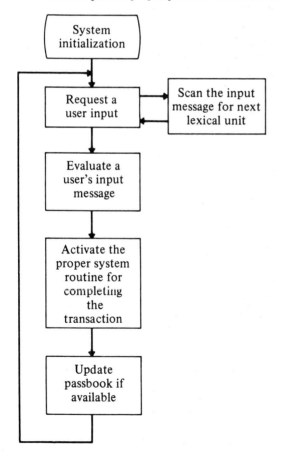

FIGURE 7-9.2 A flow diagram illustrating the handling of customer transactions in a banking system.

account information in a computerized system. If we assume we are designing an on-line system for a relatively small bank, then the following account-numbering scheme may be adopted. A five-digit account number is used, with the first two digits referring to a specific branch. If a branch is particularly large, several two-digit combinations can be assigned to the same branch. The final three digits are customer identifying digits.

Such an account-numbering scheme lends itself extremely well to a direct file in which the first two digits are used to locate the relative region in which a customer record resides, and the last three digits are used to isolate the desired record. In PL/I, a **REGIONAL(2)** organization models this form of access and is therefore adopted. Henceforth, we refer to this file as the account file.

To permit the deposit of money into and/or the withdrawal of money from an account without presenting a passbook, the on-line system needs a file which records those transactions not as yet printed in passbooks. For a given account, we must be able to determine if unrecorded entries exist. If they do, it is desirable that access to these records be achieved directly.

While there are various ways of handling the problem of unrecorded entries, we will examine one method which uses a direct file with direct addressing. For example, we can create a file containing 100 records numbered 0 through 99. The records are organized initially as a linear linked list with record n pointing to record $n + 1$ for $1 \leq n \leq 98$ and record 99 containing a link field value of -1 (indicating the end of the list). Record 0 is a special record in that it contains two pointers: one pointing to the current head of the list (initially set to 1), and the other pointing to the current tail of the list (initially set to 99). Record 0 is, in effect, a special list head.

A relationship exists between the account file and the unrecorded transaction file. Each record in the account file contains a pointer item which either references a linked list of records in the unrecorded-transaction file or contains a -1 (which is the initial value), indicating there are no unrecorded transactions for that account. Figure 7-9.3 depicts a relationship which can exist for an account file with just three accounts. In the figure, broken arrows represent the links of the list of available record locations and solid arrows represent the links containing unrecorded transactions.

A series of independent lists are formed in the unrecorded-transaction file, with one list for each account which has unrecorded transactions. When a passbook for one of these accounts is presented, it is updated by generating an entry for each node in the unrecorded-transaction list for that account. All nodes in the processed list are then available for other unrecorded transactions which later occur. Hence, an availability list with a list head of record 0 is used to manage free unrecorded-transaction file records. It should be clear that a **REGIONAL(1)** organization, with its direct-addressing capability, can be adopted for the unrecorded-transaction file.

There are many other design considerations that should be included in the design of a banking system. For example, it is desirable to be able to place an account on hold pending the settlement of a deceased customer's estate. System security features must be provided in a computerized system. Archival files are needed to record all transactions from the previous six months (or thereabouts) for auditing procedures and to provide a customer with an updated statement of his or her account if the passbook is lost or stolen. Provisions must be available to change erroneous transactions that have already been applied against an account. This aspect is very important in the design of a user-

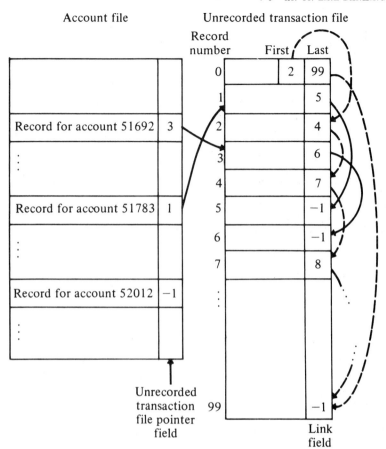

FIGURE 7-9.3 The relationship between the account file and the unrecorded transaction file.

oriented system. If errors cannot be easily and promptly corrected, users soon get frustrated and take their business elsewhere. Finally, the system we are examining only handles savings accounts. Checking, checking-savings, and loan accounts, along with credit-card accounting, are other facilities a banking system should accommodate.

7-9.3 Implementation

The implementation of the on-line banking system, as was the case with the implementations of the other system described in this chapter, involves the programming of a number of submodules which are called from a mainline module. The submodules, which are named EVALUATE, SCAN, ACTIVATE, and PASSWRITE, correspond to the processing boxes shown in Fig. 7-9.2.

The initialization section, the procedure SCAN, skeletons of the procedures EVALUATE and ACTIVATE, the procedure PASSWRITE, and the mainline section of the program

```
//  EXEC  PL1LFCG
//PL1L.SYSIN DD *
   /*                        ON-LINE BANKING SYSTEM                    */
   BANKS: PROCEDURE OPTIONS (MAIN);

   /* THIS PROGRAM IS DESIGNED TC SIMULATE AN ON-LINE BANKING SYSTEM.  */
   /*                                                                  */
   /* THIS IS A RATHER SIMPLIFIEC SYSTEM AS ONLY SAVINGS ACCOUNTS ARE  */
   /* DEALT WITH.  THE FOLLOWING TRANSACTIONS MAY BE PERFORMED ON THESE*/
   /* ACCOUNTS:  MONEY MAY BE WITHDRAWN OR DEPOSITED, NEW ACCOUNTS MAY  */
   /* BE OPENED AND OLD ONES MAY BE CLOSED.  ALSO, A SIMPLE PASSBOOK-UP-*/
   /* DATE FUNCTION MAY BE PERFORMED.  INTEREST IS CALCULATED AT THE    */
   /* GENEROUS RATE OF 1% PER MONTH, AND IS AUTOMATICALLY GIVEN TO      */
   /* THE CUSTOMER WHEN THE PASSBOOK IS PRESENTED.                      */
   /*                                                                  */
   /* SCME OF THE KEY VARIABLES USED IN THIS PROGRAM ARE:              */
   /*      INSTRUCTION:  A CHARACTER VARIABLE USED TO HOLD THE INCOMING */
   /*                    INSTRUCTION (OR PORTION THEREOF).             */
   /*      PART:  A CHARACTER VARIABLE USED TO HOLD THE PORTIONS OF THE */
   /*             INSTRUCTION AS THEY ARE RETURNED BY THE SCANNER.     */
   /*      SCAN:   A PROCEDURE USED TO SCAN THE INPUT INSTRUCTIONS AND  */
   /*             SEPARATE ITS INDIVIDUAL COMPONENTS.                  */
   /*      SOURCE_KEY:  A SOURCE KEY COMPOSED OF THE ACCOUNT NUMBER AND */
   /*                   THE FIRST TWO DIGITS OF IT -- IT IS USED TO     */
   /*                   REFERENCE THE RECORDS STORED ON THE ACCOUNT FILE*/
   /*                   WHICH HAVE RECORDED KEYS.                      */
   /*      ACCT_NO:  A VARIABLE USED TO TEMPORARILY HOLD THE ACCOUNT    */
   /*                NUMBER AS IT IS PICKED OFF BY THE SCANNER.        */
   /*      T_TYPE:  A VARIABLE USED TO TEMPORARILY STORE THE TRANSACTION*/
   /*               TYPE AS IT IS PICKED OFF BY THE SCANNER.          */
   /*      SAVE:  A VARIABLE USED TO HOLD THE AMOUNT OF THE TRANSACTION */
   /*             AS PICKED OFF BY THE SCANNER.                        */
   /*      PASSBK:  A PRINT FILE USED TO PRINT OUT RECORDS OF TRANS-    */
   /*               ACTIONS ONTO PASSBOOKS.                           */
   /*      TRANS:  A DISK FILE HAVING DIRECT ACCESS CAPABILITIES, USED  */
   /*              TO HOLD RECORCS OF ALL TRANSACTIONS MADE WHEN NO PASS*/
   /*              BOOK WAS PRESENTED.                                 */
   /*      ACCT:  A FILE HAVING DIRECT ACCESS CAPABILITIES WHICH HOLDS  */
   /*             ALL THE CUSTOMER ACCOUNTS INCLUDING THE CURRENT      */
   /*             BALANCE FOR EACH CUSTOMER'S ACCOUNT.                 */
   /*      ACCOUNT:  A STRUCTURE USED TO INTERNALLY HOLD RECORDS FROM   */
   /*                THE ACCT FILE.  IT GIVES THE READER A LOOK AT THE  */
   /*                INFORMATION STORED ON THAT FILE.                  */
   /*      TRANS_POINT:  A FIELD OF ACCOUNT WHICH POINTS INTO THE TRANS */
   /*                    FILE. TRANS_POINT POINTS TO A LIST OF          */
   /*                    UNRECORDED TRANSACTIONS INVOLVING THAT ACCOUNT.*/
   /*      TRANSACTION:  A STRUCTURE USED TO INTERNALLY HOLD RECORDS    */
   /*                    FROM THE TRANS FILE.  IT ALSO IS A DESCRIPTION */
   /*                    OF CONTENTS OF EACH RECORD ON THE FILE        */
   /*      LINK:  A FIELD OF TRANSACTION.  LINK IS USED TO FORM A       */
   /*             SINGLY-LINKED LIST OF THE UNRECORDED TRANSACTIONS FOR */
   /*             EACH CUSTOMER.  THE FIRST RECORD OF THIS FILE CONTAINS A*/
   /*             POINTER TO THE NEXT AVAILABLE NODE OF THIS LIST (THAT */
   /*             IS, THE NEXT FREE RECORD IN THE FILE) AND A POINTER TO*/
   /*             THE LAST NODE IN THE LIST.  THESE POINTERS ARE UPDATED*/
   /*             WHEN RECORDS ARE ADDED TO THE FILE OR WHEN LISTS ARE  */
   /*             DELETED FROM THE FILE.    THE DELETED SUBLISTS ARE    */
   /*             "TACKED" ON TO THE END OF THE LIST OF AVAILABLE NODES.*/
   /*             THUS, WE HAVE AN EXTERNAL LINEAR LINKED LIST.         */
```

FIGURE 7-9.4   Main-line and submodules for the on-line banking system.

are given in Fig. 7-9.4. The ACCT and TRANS file correspond to the account and unrecorded-transaction files as discussed in the previous subsections. ACCOUNT and TRANSACTION are the record descriptions which are associated with the ACCT and TRANS files, respectively. The procedure SCAN is called from the EVALUATE procedure whenever a new lexical unit from a user input must be isolated. The EVALUATE procedure will not be given, mainly because of its length and because it is not directly relevant to our discussion of file

```
DECLARE
    INSTRUCTION CHARACTER(74) VARYING,
    PART CHARACTER(10) VARYING,
    SCAN ENTRY RETURNS(CHARACTER(10) VARYING),
    (I,J,L) FIXED BINARY,
    SOURCE_KEY CHARACTER (13),
    ACCT_NO CHARACTER(5),
    (FIRST,LAST,TEMP) FIXED DEC(2,0),
    T_TYPE CHAR(1),
    SAVE FIXED DEC (9,2),
    PASSBK FILE STREAM PRINT,
    TRANS FILE RECORD KEYED ENVIRONMENT(F(20) REGIONAL(1)),
    ACCT FILE RECORD KEYED ENVIRONMENT(F(90) REGIONAL(2)),
    1 ACCOUNT,
        2 FILLER CHAR(1),
        2 TYPE CHAR(1),
        2 NUMBER CHAR(5),
        2 NAME CHAR(20),
        2 ADDRESS(3) CHAR(15),
        2 BALANCE FIXED DECIMAL(9,2),
        2 LAST_DATE CHAR(6),
        2 INT_BAL FIXED DECIMAL(9,2),
        2 TRANS_POINT FIXED DECIMAL(2,0),
    1 TRANSACTION,
        2 FILLER CHARACTER (1),
        2 TYPE CHARACTER(1),
        2 NUMBER FIXED DECIMAL (9,2),
        2 DAY CHARACTER (6),
        2 AMOUNT FIXED DECIMAL(9,2),
        2 LINK FIXED DECIMAL (2,0),
    PASSBOOK BIT(1);

SCAN: PROCEDURE RETURNS(CHARACTER(10) VARYING);

/* THE SCAN PROCEDURE IS USED TO PICK OFF THE INDIVIDUAL COMPONENTS */
/* OF THE INPUT INSTRUCTION.  NOTE THAT IT IS ASSUMED THAT THE      */
/* COMPONENTS ARE DELIMITED FROM ONE ANOTHER BY AT LEAST ONE BLANK. */

    DECLARE ELEMENT CHARACTER(10) VARYING;
    INSTRUCTION = SUBSTR(INSTRUCTION,VERIFY(INSTRUCTION,' '));
    /* TRIMS LEADING BLANKS.                                    */
    ELEMENT = '';
    IF SUBSTR(INSTRUCTION,1,1) = '*'
    THEN RETURN(ELEMENT);
    ELEMENT = SUBSTR(INSTRUCTION,1,(INDEX(INSTRUCTION,' ')-1));
    /* ELEMENT IS ASSIGNED THE VALUE OF THE FIRST WORD OF       */
    /* INSTRUCTION.                                             */
    INSTRUCTION = SUBSTR(INSTRUCTION,INDEX(INSTRUCTION,' '));
    /* FIRST WORD IS DELETED FROM INSTRUCTION.                  */
    RETURN(ELEMENT);
END SCAN;

EVALUATE: PROCEDURE;

/* EVALUATE IS A PROCEDURE USED TO EVALUATE THE INPUT TRANSACTION.   */
/* THIS PROCEDURE CALLS 'SCAN' TO ACCESS THE INDIVIDUAL PARTS OF THE */
/* INSTRUCTION AND THEN CHECKS THESE COMPONENTS FOR VALIDITY.  IT WILL */
/* REQUEST CORRECT INFORMATION IF ANY OF THAT WHICH IS SUPPLIED IS   */
/* FOUND TO BE INVALID.                                             */
```

FIGURE 7-9.4   (Continued)

structures. However, it should be capable of interacting with a user in a manner exemplified by the following session:

```
*ENTER TRANSACTION
 W 7812B 2150
*INVALID ACCOUNT NUMBER — REENTER TRANSACTION
 W 78127 21.500
```

```
                            •
                            •
                            •

    END EVALUATE;


    PASSWRITE: PROCEDURE;

/* THIS SHORT PROCEDURE IS USED TO OUTPUT THE LINES ONTO THE PASSBOOK*/
/* FILE.                                                             */
              PUT FILE(PASSBK) EDIT(SUBSTR(DAY,5,2),SUBSTR(DAY,3,2),
                           SUBSTR(DAY,1,2))
                           (COLUMN(1),3 (X(1),A(2)));
              IF TRANSACTION.TYPE = 'W'          /* WITHDRAWL */
              THEN PUT FILE(PASSBK) EDIT(AMOUNT,'') (F(11,2),X(20),A);
              ELSE DO;
                   PUT FILE(PASSBK) EDIT(AMOUNT) (X(12),F(10,2));
                   IF TRANSACTION.TYPE = 'I'     /* INTEREST */
                   THEN PUT FILE(PASSBK) EDIT('INTEREST') (X(1),A);
                   ELSE PUT FILE(PASSBK) EDIT('') (X(9),A(0));
              END;
              PUT FILE(PASSBK) EDIT(TRANSACTION.NUMBER) (F(11,2));
              RETURN;
        END PASSWRITE;

    ACTIVATE: PROCEDURE;

/* THE ACTIVATE PROCEDURE PROCESSES THE INSTRUCTIONS AND ALSO DOES   */
/* THE PRINTING OF THE TRANSACTION ONTO EITHER THE PASSBOOK FILE, OR */
/* THE TRANS FILE.                                                   */

                            •
                            •
                            •

    END ACTIVATE;


/* * * * * * * * * * * * *  M A I N L I N E  * * * * * * * * * * * * */
/* THE MAINLINE SECTION OF THE PROGRAM.                              */
        OPEN FILE(TRANS) DIRECT UPDATE,
             FILE(ACCT) DIRECT UPDATE,
             FILE(PASSBK) OUTPUT;

/* THE FIRST RECORD OF THE TRANSACTION FILE IS READ IN TO DETERMINE THE
/* AVAILABLE NODES OF THE TRANSACTION FILE.                          */
        READ FILE(TRANS) INTO(TRANSACTION) KEY('0');
        LAST=LINK;
        FIRST = TRANSACTION.NUMBER;
        ON ENDFILE(SYSIN) GO TO DONE;
        PUT FILE(PASSBK) EDIT('CATE','WITHDRAWAL','DEPOSIT','COMMENTS',
                         'BALANCE') (COLUMN(1),X(3),A(7),A(11),X(2),
                         A(9),A(9),X(3),A(7));

        DO WHILE('1'B);

            PUT FILE(PASSBK) EDIT(' ') (COLUMN(1),A(0));
            PASSBOOK = '1'B;
            CALL EVALUATE;
            CALL ACTIVATE;
        END;
```

FIGURE 7-9.4   (Continued)


```
    *INVALID AMOUNT — REENTER TRANSACTION
     V 78127 21.50
    *INVALID TRANSACTION TYPE — REENTER TRANSACTION
     W 78127 21.50
```

This session illustrates the type of syntactic errors that should be detected by the

```
DONE: TRANSACTION.NUMBER = FIRST;

      LINK = LAST;
      WRITE FILE(TRANS) FROM(TRANSACTION) KEYFROM('0');
      CLOSE FILE(TRANS),
            FILE(ACCT),
            FILE(PASSBK);

END BANKS;
//GO.TRANS DD UNIT=SYSDA,VOL=SER=USERO2,SPACE=(20,100),
//         DSN=TRNDATA,DISP=(OLD,KEEP)
//GO.ACCT DD UNIT=SYSDA,VOL=SER=USERO3,SPACE=(95,411),
//         DSN=ACTDATA,DCB=(KEYLEN=5,LMTCT=10),DISP=(OLD,KEEP)
//GO.SYSIN DD *
            (INCOMING TRANSACTIONS)
 /*
```

FIGURE 7-9.4 (Continued)

EVALUATE function. An '*' is placed before each system message to delineate it from a user input. Each message is of a prompting nature.

The processing of a customer transaction is performed by the **ACTIVATE** procedure, as shown in Fig. 7-9.5. The five types of transactions are handled by five different segments within the procedure. Account openings are processed first. They are unique from the other transactions in that no check is made for a valid existing account number, no writing is performed in a passbook, and a considerable amount of personal information about the customer is required. For each open transaction, a check is made to ensure that the assigned number is unique. The following is a sample session involving the opening of an account:

```
*ENTER TRANSACTION
 0 71444 .00
*ENTER CUSTOMER'S NAME
 GAIL W. WALKER
*ENTER THE FIRST LINE OF THE ADDRESS
 1002 LANDSDOWNE CRESCENT
*ENTER THE SECOND LINE OF THE ADDRESS
 WINNIPEG, MANITOBA
*ENTER THE THIRD LINE OF THE ADDRESS (IF THERE IS ONE), OR A NULL LINE
 S7K3J5 CANADA
```

Transaction types other than an account opening are handled after passbooks are updated and the interest is calculated for the previous months. The calculation of interest payments is left out—once again for brevity. The four modules corresponding to the customer transaction—**PASSBOOK, WITHDRAWAL, DEPOSIT,** and **CLOSE**—illustrate the use of each of the I/O commands which are available in PL/I for direct files. A number of semantic errors and special conditions can occur with a transaction, such as an attempt to take more money from an account than is currently in the account, a transaction-file full warning, and the closure of an account without a passbook. These conditions are detected in the **ACTIVATE** procedure. The procedure **PASSWRITE** is invoked from **ACTIVATE** and it is responsible for printing customer's transactions in the passbook.

This section concludes our discussion of direct files. The banking-system example

```
      ACTIVATE: PROCEDURE;

         DECLARE TRANS#(0:4) LABEL;

/* * * * * * * * * * * * * * *  O P E N  * * * * * * * * * * * * * * * */
/* WHEN AN ACCOUNT IS TO BE OPENED, A CHECK IS MADE TO SEE IF AN      */
/* ACCOUNT BY THAT NUMBER EXISTS.  IF SO, THE OPEN FUNCTION IS NOT    */
/* PERFORMED.                                                         */
            IF T_TYPE = 'O'
            THEN DO;
               ON KEY(ACCT) GO TO INITIALIZE;
               READ FILE(ACCT) INTO (ACCOUNT) KEY(SOURCE_KEY);
               PUT EDIT('THE ACCOUNT NUMBERED ',ACCT_NO,' HAS ALREADY ',
                        'BEEN OPENED.') (COLUMN(1),4 A);
               RETURN;
            INITIALIZE:
               ACCOUNT.FILLER = LOW(1);
               ACCOUNT.TYPE = 'S';
               ACCOUNT.NUMBER = ACCT_NO;
               BALANCE = AMOUNT;
               LAST_DATE = DATE;
               IF SUBSTR(DATE,5,2) = '01'
               THEN INT_BAL = AMOUNT;
               ELSE INT_BAL = 0;
               TRANS_POINT = -1;

/* WHEN OPENING AN ACCOUNT ADDITIONAL INFORMATION ABOUT THE CUSTOMER */
/* IS NEEDED.  THE PROGRAM REQUESTS THIS INFORMATION ONE LINE AT A   */
/* TIME.                                                            */

         P2:   PUT EDIT('ENTER THE CUSTOMER''S NAME','') (COLUMN(1),A);
               GET EDIT(NAME) (COLUMN(1),A(20));
               IF NAME = '' THEN GO TO P2;
         P3:   PUT EDIT('ENTER THE FIRST LINE OF THE ADDRESS','')
                        (COLUMN(1),A);
               GET EDIT(ADDRESS(1)) (COLUMN(1),A(15));
               IF ADDRESS(1) = '' THEN GO TO P3;
         P4:   PUT EDIT('ENTER THE SECOND LINE OF THE ADDRESS','')
                        (COLUMN(1),A);
               GET EDIT(ADDRESS(2)) (COLUMN(1),A(15));
               IF ADDRESS(2) = '' THEN GO TO P4;
               PUT EDIT('ENTER THE THIRD LINE OF THE ADDRESS (IF THERE '
                     || 'IS ONE), OR A NULL LINE','') (COLUMN(1),A);
               GET EDIT(ADDRESS(3)) (COLUMN(1),A(15));
               WRITE FILE(ACCT) FROM(ACCOUNT) KEYFROM(SOURCE_KEY);
               PUT FILE(PASSBK) EDIT(SUBSTR(DATE,5,2),SUBSTR(DATE,3,2),
                        SUBSTR(DATE,1,2),AMOUNT,'NEW',
                        AMOUNT) (COLUMN(1),3 (X(1),A(2)),
                                X(12),F(10,2),X(4),A(6),
                                F(10,2));
               RETURN;
            END;

            SAVE = AMOUNT;
/* FOR ALL OTHER CASES A CHECK IS MADE ON THE VALIDITY OF THE ACCOUNT*/
/* NUMBER BEING PROCESSED.  THAT IS, A CHECK IS MADE TO SEE WHETHER  */
/* OR NOT AN ACCOUNT BY THAT NUMBER EXISTS.                         */
            ON KEY(ACCT)
            BEGIN;
               PUT EDIT('THE FOLLOWING ACCOUNT NUMBER IS INVALID:',
                        SUBSTR(SOURCE_KEY,1,5),'') (COLUMN(1),A);
               GO TO RET1;
```

FIGURE 7-9.5   The procedure **ACTIVATE** for processing customer transactions.

helps to exhibit the most important property of a direct file—the ability to access a specific record quickly without the necessity of sequentially searching through a large number of records in the file.

In the following section, we look at alternative file organizations to the three most commonly used organizations we have discussed thus far.

```
        END;

        READ FILE(ACCT) INTO(ACCOUNT) KEY(SOURCE_KEY);

/* THIS SECTION UPDATES THE PASSBOOK IF THERE ARE TRANSACTIONS FOR   */
/* WHICH THE CUSTOMER DID NOT HAVE HIS PASSBOOK PRESENT.             */
        IF PASSBOOK & TRANS_POINT ¬= -1
        THEN DO;
            IF FIRST = -1
            THEN FIRST = TRANS_POINT;
            ELSE DO;
                READ FILE(TRANS) INTO(TRANSACTION) KEY(LAST);
                LINK = TRANS_POINT;
                WRITE FILE(TRANS) FROM(TRANSACTION) KEYFROM(LAST);
            END;
            LAST = TRANS_POINT;
            READ FILE(TRANS) INTO(TRANSACTION) KEY(TRANS_POINT);
            CALL PASSWRITE;
            DO WHILE(LINK¬=-1);
                LAST = LINK;
                READ FILE(TRANS) INTO(TRANSACTION) KEY(LINK);
                CALL PASSWRITE;
            END;
            TRANS_POINT = -1;
        END;

/* THIS SEGMENT CALCULATES THE INTEREST OWING THE CUSTOMER, IF THE   */
/* DATE OF HIS LAST VISIT TO THE BANK WAS NOT IN THE SAME MONTH AS   */
/* THE CURRENT VISIT.  INTEREST ENTRIES ARE CREATED FOR EACH MONTH   */

                          .
                          .
                          .

        LAST_DATE = DATE;
        GO TO TRANS#(INDEX('PWDC',T_TYPE));

/* * * * * * * * * * * * P A S S B O O K  * * * * * * * * * * * * */
/* IF THE ONLY PURPOSE OF THIS VISIT TO THE BANK WAS TO UPDATE A PASS*/
/* BOOK, THEN THE PROCESSING IS HALTED.                             */
        TRANS#(1):
            REWRITE FILE(ACCT) FROM(ACCOUNT) KEY(SOURCE_KEY);
            RETURN;

/* * * * * * * * * * * * W I T H D R A W L S  * * * * * * * * * * * */
/* THIS SEGMENT HANDLES 'WITHDRAWL' TYPE TRANSACTIONS.              */
        TRANS#(2):
            BALANCE = BALANCE - SAVE;
            IF INT_BAL > BALANCE
            THEN INT_BAL = BALANCE;
            IF PASSBOOK
            THEN PUT FILE(PASSBK) EDIT((SUBSTR(LAST_DATE,J,2) DO J
                        = 5 BY -2 TO 1),SAVE,BALANCE)
                        (COLUMN(1),3 (X(1),A(2)),F(11,2),
                        X(20),F(11,2));
            ELSE DO;
                IF FIRST = -1
                THEN DO;
                    PUT EDIT('*** WARNING *** THE TRANSACTION FILE IS FULL',
                            'THE FOLLOWING TRANSACTION CANNOT BE STORED:')
                            (COLUMN(1),A,COLUMN(1),X(17),A)
```

FIGURE 7-9.5 (Continued)

7-10 OTHER METHODS OF FILE ORGANIZATION

An important concept that is affecting the way data (and programs) are organized in many computer systems is virtual memory. We begin this section by describing what virtual memory is, by examining a number of schemes for implementing a virtual memory

```
                                ('WITHDRAW: ',SAVE,'; NEW BALANCE: ',BALANCE)
                                (COLUMN(1),A,F(10,2),A,F(10,2));
                RETURN;
            END;
            IF TRANS_POINT ¬= -1
            THEN DO;
                TEMP = TRANS_POINT;
                READ FILE(TRANS) INTO(TRANSACTION) KEY(TEMP);
                DO WHILE(LINK ¬= -1);
                    TEMP = LINK;
                    READ FILE(TRANS) INTO(TRANSACTION) KEY(LINK);
                END;
                LINK = FIRST;
                WRITE FILE(TRANS) FROM(TRANSACTION)
                                    KEYFROM(TEMP);
            END;
            ELSE TRANS_POINT = FIRST;

            READ FILE(TRANS) INTO(TRANSACTION) KEY(FIRST);
            TRANSACTION.FILLER = LOW(1);
            TRANSACTION.TYPE = 'W';
            TRANSACTION.NUMBER = BALANCE;
            AMOUNT = SAVE;
            DAY = DATE;
            TEMP = FIRST;
            FIRST = LINK;
            LINK = -1;
            WRITE FILE(TRANS) FROM(TRANSACTION) KEYFROM(TEMP);
        END;
        REWRITE FILE(ACCT) FROM(ACCOUNT) KEY(SOURCE_KEY);
        RETURN;

/* * * * * * * * * * * * * DEPOSITS * * * * * * * * * * * * * */
/* THIS SEGMENT HANDLES 'DEPOSIT' TYPE TRANSACTIONS.              */
        TRANS#(3):
            BALANCE = BALANCE + SAVE;
            IF INT_BAL> BALANCE
            THEN INT_BAL = BALANCE;
            IF PASSBOOK
            THEN PUT FILE(PASSBK) EDIT((SUBSTR(LAST_DATE,J,2) DO J
                        = 5 BY -2 TO 1),SAVE  ,BALANCE)
                        (COLUMN(1),3 (X(1),A(2)),X(11),F(11,2),
                        X(9),F(11,2));
            ELSE DO;
                IF FIRST = -1
                THEN DO;
                    PUT EDIT('*** WARNING *** THE TRANSACTION FILE IS FULL',
                        'THE FOLLOWING TRANSACTION CANNOT BE STORED:')
                        (COLUMN(1),A,COLUMN(1),X(17),A)
                        ('DEPOSIT: ',SAVE,'; NEW BALANCE: ',BALANCE)
                        (COLUMN(1),A,F(10,2),A,F(10,2));
                    RETURN;
                END;
                IF TRANS_POINT = -1
                THEN TRANS_POINT = FIRST;
                ELSE DO;
                    TEMP = TRANS_POINT;
                    READ FILE(TRANS) INTO(TRANSACTION) KEY(TEMP);
                    DO WHILE(LINK  ¬= -1);
                        TEMP = LINK;
                        READ FILE(TRANS) INTO(TRANSACTION) KEY(LINK);
                    END;
```

FIGURE 7-9.5   (Continued)

system, and by discussing the effects such systems have and will have on the development of file systems. Our investigation of virtual memory is by no means detailed, and the interested reader who is knowledgeable in operating systems is invited to delve into some of the references that are provided.

The second part of this subsection introduces a type of file organization, VSAM,

```
                    LINK = FIRST;
                    WRITE FILE(TRANS) FROM(TRANSACTION)
                                      KEYFROM(TEMP);
               END;

               READ FILE(TRANS) INTO(TRANSACTION) KEY(FIRST);
               TRANSACTION.FILLER = LOW(1);
               TRANSACTION.TYPE = 'D';
               TRANSACTION.NUMBER = BALANCE;
               AMOUNT = SAVE;
               DAY = DATE;
               TEMP = FIRST;
               FIRST = LINK;
               LINK = -1;
               WRITE FILE(TRANS) FROM(TRANSACTION) KEYFROM(TEMP);
          END;

          REWRITE FILE(ACCT) FROM(ACCOUNT) KEY(SOURCE_KEY);
          RETURN;

/* * * * * * * * * * * * * * *C L O S E * * * * * * * * * * * * * * */
/* THIS SEGMENT IS USED TO CLOSE OFF ANY FILES WHEN SUCH AN ACTION  */
/* HAS BEEN REQUESTED BY THE TELLER.                                */
          TRANS#(4):
               IF ¬PASSBOOK
               THEN DO;
                    PUT EDIT('PASSBOOK MUST BE PRESENTED WHEN CLOSING AN'
                             || ' ACCOUNT','') (COLUMN(1),A);
                    RETURN;
               END;

               AMOUNT = BALANCE;
               BALANCE = 0;
               IF AMOUNT > 0
               THEN PUT EDIT('THE FOLLOWING AMOUNT IS TO BE RETURNED TO'
                             || ' THE CUSTOMER:  ') (COLUMN(1),A);
               ELSE IF AMOUNT < 0
                    THEN PUT EDIT('THE CUSTOMER OWES THE BANK:  ')
                                 (COLUMN(1),A);
                    ELSE PUT EDIT('THE CUSTOMER''S ACCOUNT IS' ||
                                  ' "EMPTY".','') (COLUMN(1),A);
               IF AMOUNT ¬= 0
               THEN PUT EDIT(AMOUNT,'') (F(11,2),COLUMN(1),A(0));
               PUT FILE(PASSBK) EDIT((SUBSTR(DATE,J,2) DO J = 5 BY -2
                                TO 1),AMOUNT,'CLOSED',BALANCE)
                                (COLUMN(1),3 (X(1),A(2)),F(11,2),
                                X(13),A(8),F(10,2));
               DELETE FILE(ACCT) KEY(SOURCE_KEY);
     RET1: RETURN;

     END ACTIVATE;
```

FIGURE 7-9.5 (Continued)

that is designed to co-exist with a virtual memory system. It encompasses all three of the organizations described thus far in the chapter.

7-10.1 Virtual Memory

In the introduction to this chapter two reasons were given for storing information in files on an external medium. The first reason was to provide for the inexpensive storage of large amounts of data—amounts so large that the data could not fit into main memory at one time. The second reason related to the archival property of some data. For certain applications, it is desirable or necessary to store information from one execution of a program to the next (e.g., a payroll application). The information should be stored on a readily accessible medium (e.g., tape or disk) but not in main memory, which is a critical system resource shared by other programs on a continuous basis.

If main memory becomes extremely inexpensive, say 0.00001 cents per byte, and if billions and even trillions of bytes were directly adressable, then files, as they have been discussed thus far, would not be required. The data structures presented in Chaps. 1 through 5 would be sufficient to handle most programming problems.

While as yet main memory technology is not advanced to the degree just described, efforts have been made to extend main memory in a logical sense. One type of system which provides this logical extension is called a *virtual memory system*. A virtual memory system performs a dynamic mapping from a virtual address space (an address space which is many times larger than the main address space) to a main address space. In a virtual memory system, all currently active programs and data are allocated space (i.e., assigned virtual addresses) in virtual memory. The programs and data may not (in fact, usually do not) reside in main memory, but instead are located on fast auxiliary storage devices such as drums or fixed-head disks. When a program is executing and referencing data, all virtual addresses are translated automatically by the operating system into real main-memory addresses. If a program is called upon for execution and currently is not residing in main memory, then this fact will be detected during the virtual-to-real memory address translation. Automatically (i.e., without user initiation or knowledge), the program or a section of it which is scheduled for execution is brought into main memory so that execution on that program can continue. With this form of automatic address translation, we are able to enlarge our main memory to an effective size which is equivalent to that of a multimillion-byte virtual address space.

Before discussing how virtual memory systems help to solve some of the problems related to file processing, let us examine briefly three types of virtual memory systems—paging systems, segmentation systems, and segmented paging systems.

Paging systems

Paging is a memory-management technique in which the virtual address space is split into fixed-length blocks called *pages*. Main memory space is divided into physical sections of equal-size subsections called *page frames*. A page frame and a page are the same size. The transformation from a virtual address to a main (or real) address involves the mapping of a page to a page frame.

A virtual address in a paging system is made up of two components p and d, where p designates a page and d denotes the displacement within page p. The translation of this two-component address to a main memory address generally requires a page table and a paging algorithm.

A *page table* is associated with each user job (i.e., set of user programs and data). Each entry in the page table contains:

1 A presence bit (a flag indicating whether or not the page is in main memory)
2 The location of the page (in core or in auxiliary storage)
3 Protection bits that are used to check the type of access that is allowed for the page

To examine a particular example illustrating how paging is performed, let us refer to Fig. 7-10.1a. In this example, we assume a page size of 1,000 bytes (in most paging machines, page sizes are between 1,000 and 4,000 bytes in length), a virtual memory address space of 2,000,000 bytes, and a main memory of 50,000 bytes. An address such as 0630 can be expressed as a two-level address 0, 630 , where the first number is the page number and the second number is a displacement from the beginning of the page. For convenience, we have placed the programs and data for a sample job in the first six pages of virtual memory.

When an address such as 4444 (or 4, 444) is encountered during execution, the page table for that job is entered. The entry corresponding to page number p in the page table contains a pointer to the desired page which may or may not reside in main memory. Page 4 is located in main memory and may be found in page frame 3. By moving d locations down the page, the desired memory location can be reached. Therefore, the instruction LOAD 2110 is found 444 locations from the beginning of page 4 (i.e. page frame 3).

The execution of the machine-level instruction "LOAD 2110" requires that the data stored at the virtual address 2110 be loaded into a central-processing unit register. When a virtual-to-real memory address translation is initiated, it is discovered in the page table that page 2 does not reside in main memory currently. In order to continue executing the job, it is necessary that page 2 be brought in from external storage and placed in a page frame of main memory.

A *paging algorithm* (or page replacement strategy) is required to decide which of the pages that currently reside in main memory must be replaced by page 2. A variety of page replacement strategies have been analyzed and used in paging systems, and these are described in a number of advanced-level operating systems texts such as Madnick and Donovan [1974], Shaw [1974], and Tsichritzis and Bernstein [1974]. A detailed discussion of this topic is outside the scope of the text.

During the time period in which the selected page is removed and placed in auxiliary memory and then the required page is fetched from auxiliary memory, execution can begin on another user's job. At some later point in time, after the required page is brought into main memory, the job can commence execution with the instruction "LOAD 2110".

Some important advantages from a data-management point of view are gained by using a paging system. First, data is brought into main memory without any explicit user program specifications such as read instructions. The notions of a file and a system directory containing file names can be discarded. Secondly, since a complete page of information is brought into memory at one time, subsequent access of data on the same page may be achieved without having to read in or write out individual records. This is only possible if the page is not pulled from memory before such accesses take place. This property is particularly beneficial when data accesses are highly localized, as is the case for sequential processing. These first two advantages apply to all virtual memory systems discussed in this section.

In a paging system, all pages are of equal size and, therefore, a memory management problem does not exist. Any given page can be replaced by any other page. It should also be noted that in most paging systems, virtual-to-real address translation is performed by a special hardware unit. Therefore, the accessing of a data item which is in a page that is not in main memory can still be handled fairly efficiently.

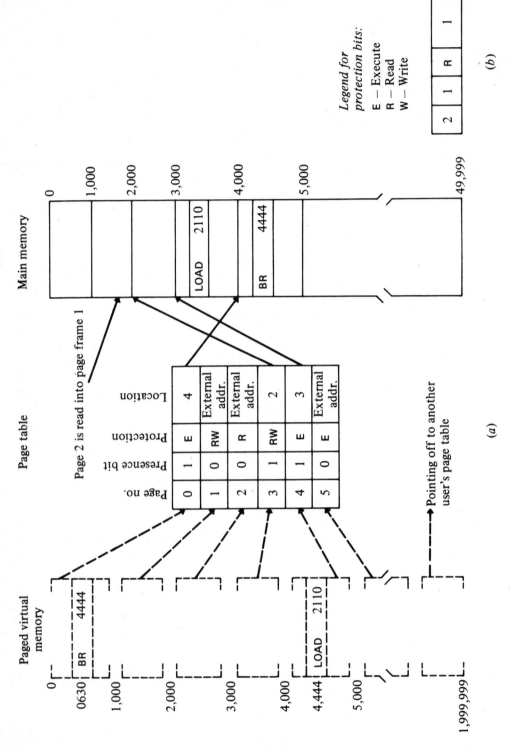

Main memory

Page table

Page 2 is read into page frame 1

Paged virtual memory

Page no.	Presence bit	Protection	Location
0	1	E	4
1	0	RW	External addr.
2	0	R	External addr.
3	1	RW	2
4	1	E	3
5	0	E	External addr.

Pointing off to another user's page table

(a)

Legend for
protection bits:

E – Execute
R – Read
W – Write

2	1	R	1

(b)

644

A major disadvantage with paging is the internal fragmentation that develops because the programs and data are placed in fixed-sized blocks (i.e., pages). The concepts of fragmentation are discussed in Sec. 5-6. Since the program and data for two different jobs are not allowed to reside in a common page, a large proportion of some pages may not be used.

Let us examine an alternative memory-management scheme which eliminates the problem of internal fragmentation.

Segmentation systems

Programs and their associated data are generally composed of a number of logical units such as procedures, program blocks, and data areas. *Segmentation* is a scheme in which the addressing structure of a program is based upon logical program divisions. In segmentation, each program's virtual memory address space is divided into variable-sized blocks, called *segments*, each of which contains one of these logical program divisions. To access a a word within a user's address space, we again use a two-part address as we did with paging. An address, s, d, specifies the location of a segment, s, and the displacement, d, within the segment.

The translation of a virtual memory address to a real address is a logically identical process for paging and segmentation. A segment table, as opposed to a page table, contains the actual address (i.e., the main memory or auxiliary memory address) for the beginning of a particular user segment. Each user job has its own segment table like the one illustrated in Fig. 7-10.2. To access a particular location such as " <DATA1>, 52" of the instruction "LOAD <DATA1>, 52", it is necessary first to locate the element in the segmentation table associated with " <DATA1>". (A discussion of how this is accomplished automatically is outside the scope of the text.) If the segment " <DATA1>" resides in main memory, which can be determined by the presence bit, then access can be achieved directly. If the segment is not in main memory, however, the external address is used to fetch the segment. The placement of the segment in main memory presents a problem, as did the placement of a page in a paging system. If there does not exist a contiguous unused area in main memory which can contain the segment, then a *segmentation replacement policy* must be called upon to remove a segment and place the required segment in the vacated area.

There are a number of possible segmentation replacement strategies that can be adopted, just as there are a wide variety of paging replacement schemes. It should be observed, however, that a segment replacement strategy is confronted with a memory-management problem which does not exist in paging systems. Because segments are variable-length blocks, *external fragmentation* arises. That is, a segment A may replace another segment, say B, in which the space occupied by B is slightly larger than the space required by A. A small unused section of main memory is created. After this type of replacement has happened thousands of times, memory becomes so fragmented with small sections as to become unusable. Therefore, a segmentation replacement strategy

---

FIGURE 7-10.1   An example illustrating the translation of a virtual memory address in a paging system.

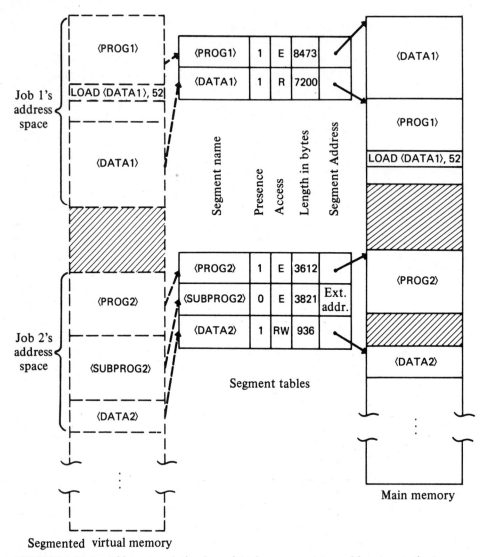

Segmented virtual memory

FIGURE 7-10.2 Address translation in a virtual memory system with segmentation.

must be chosen so as to reduce this type of fragmentation. Some of the memory management strategies such as first-fit, best-fit, and the buddy system (these were described in
Sec. 5-6) have been tried as segmentation replacement policies.

Regardless of which replacement rule is adopted, external fragmentation grows as
more jobs are executed. The free space fragments which are generated must, on occasion,
be collected and compacted into one contiguous area. Some of the garbage-collection
techniques discussed in Sec. 5-6 can be used for the compaction process.

Many of the advantages of segmentation are advantages of any virtual memory
system—in particular, the first two advantages listed for paging systems. Because seg-

mentation divides virtual memory into logical units, the notion of a file can still assume some meaning. It is possible to associate a name with a particular data area just as it is possible to associate a name with a file in some systems. The programmer can find this aspect, which is not available in paging systems, particularly appealing. In addition, there are other advantages to segmentation, such as ease of linking procedures and ease of sharing and protecting programs and data, which we will not discuss.

While the problem of internal fragmentation is overcome by using segmentation, the new and potentially more disturbing problem of external fragmentation arises. In an effort to minimize the effects of external fragmentation, and yet adopt some of the virtues of segmentation, many virtual memory systems have been developed which are hybrids of the two approaches.

Segmented paging systems

In unifying the two approaches, a virtual memory address has three components s, p, and d, where s is a segment name (or address into a segment table), p is an index into the page table for segment s, and d is the displacement within a page designated by the index p. Virtual memory space is now divided into a number of variable-length segments which are composed of smaller fixed-length pages.

Figure 7-10.3 illustrates the tables necessary to perform a virtual-to-real memory address translation for a segmented paging system. An address such as " $<$DATA1$>$, 3, 98" is translated into a real address by first finding the segment-table element corresponding to $<$DATA1$>$. The page table for this segment is then located. The element in the page table designates a page frame if the page resides in main memory. For our example address, a displacement of 98 is used to locate the desired word.

If, during the translation, the segment $<$DATA1$>$ is not marked as present in main memory, then all pages for this segment are fetched. Once a segment is brought in, its pages may be replaced on a demand basis. That is, if certain pages of the segment are seldom or never referenced, they may be pulled out of memory and replaced by more active pages from another segment. Therefore, during the translation process, it is possible that a page from a currently active segment may have to be retrieved because it was replaced due to its previous inactivity.

Segmented paging systems attempt to provide most of the advantages of paging and segmentation systems. External fragmentation is not present, since the basic unit of information handled by the system is the page. Data sharing, program linking, and protection are enhanced because the concept of a segment persists. Internal fragmentation is still present, and this can only be reduced by reducing the size of a page.

There are two disadvantages, namely, increased hardware costs and processor overhead which are incurred because of the three-level address translation that is necessary. In addition, more main memory is required to store the additional address translation tables (i.e., both segment and page tables).

Before describing the ramifications of virtual memory on file structures and file systems, it is important to point out that a number of commercially available systems provide a virtual memory capability. Paging was first used on the Atlas computer (Fotheringham [1961]) and later was adopted in the XDS 940 system. Segmentation is implemented in the Burroughs' B5000 series of computer (MacKenzie [1965]). The

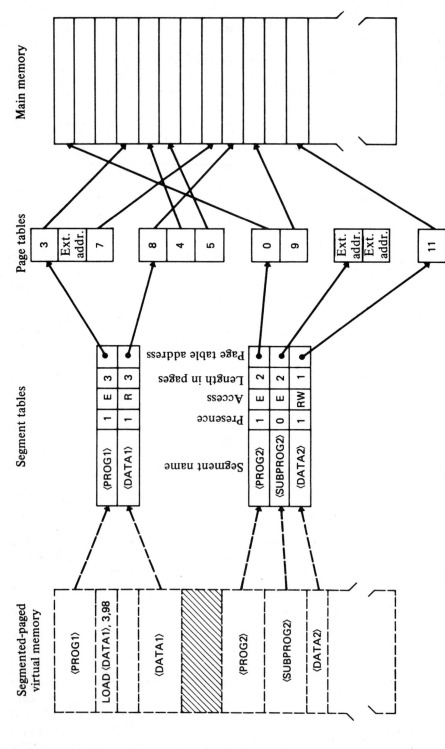

FIGURE 7-10.3 Address translation in a virtual memory system with segmented paging.

IBM/370 and the Honeywell 6180 (Bensoussan [1969]) systems use a segmented paging form of virtual memory management.

It is clear that virtual memory systems are here now and will be present in the future. Their effect on the management of data cannot be ignored. Currently, there are two schools of thought concerning the relationship between file-management systems and virtual memory systems. One is to integrate the file system and the segmentation and paging facilities, as exemplified in MULTICS (Madnick [1974]). This can easily be accomplished if the following similarities are recognized:

1 The notions of a file and a segment are similar notions both involving the logical organization of information.
2 Both files and segments require a two-dimensional form of addressing—a file name and a record address, and a segment name and word address, respectively.
3 Both files and segments may be variable in size—they grow and shrink dynamically.
4 Memory buffers can be considered to be functionally similar to page frames.

A main disadvantage of this approach is that a request for one record from a data segment (i.e., file) results in the fetching of a whole segment. This can lead to a tremendous amount of overhead when processing only a few records from each file for a large number of files. In addition, even if the entire segment is fetched, there is no guarantee that certain pages in the segment may not have to be re-retrieved later because of a certain pattern of record references.

The second school of thought suggests that the similarities between files and segments should be ignored and that separate mechanisms should be established for each. The OS/VS operating system follows this philosophy, and a discussion of the file mechanism provided by the system will be described in the next subsection. One of the advantages of this approach is that a file is an entity somewhat removed from the direct memory management of the system and, therefore, can be easily copied on a transportable device (i.e., a removable disk or tape) and used on another system. Of course, the disadvantage with this approach is that the user must be familiar with a special data-holding entity, a file, which must be explicitly referenced and treated in a manner different than the other data-holding entities in the program.

If the file system is incorporated within the virtual memory system, the two reasons for the existence of a file, as cited at the beginning of this subsection, disappear. If the two entities are separated, a file system is required only for archival and transportability purposes.

7-10.2   VSAM Files

In 1972, IBM announced a new access method called VSAM (Virtual Storage Access Method) for its series of 370 virtual storage machines. A discussion of a file organization for VSAM is important because of the capabilities this access method provides. VSAM was designed to replace all of the access methods (sequential, indexed sequential, and direct access methods) that IBM previously supported. In particular, we will see that the keyed access facility provided by VSAM is a significant departure from IBM's ISAM and resembles quite closely the indexed sequential facilities available in CDC's

SCOPE monitor discussed in Sec. 7-6.1. The reader is invited to reexamine the section of the text dealing with CDC's indexed sequential organization before continuing to read this subsection.

In this subsection, we begin by describing the possible file structures of a VSAM file. The types of processing that are associated with VSAM are then considered. Finally, the problem of accessing VSAM files in PL/I is briefly discussed.

Two types of file structures exist for a VSAM file—namely a *key-sequenced structure* and *entry-sequenced structure*. In a key-sequenced file, records are loaded in an ordered sequence defined by the collating sequence of the content of the key field in each record. Direct access to a record can be gained via the unique value in the key field. In an entry-sequenced file, records are loaded according to the order in which they are entered into the file. A record's position is independent of its contents. Direct access to a record is gained via a relative byte address (RBA) from the beginning of the file. Let us first discuss the concepts relevant to a key-sequenced VSAM file, and later determine how these notions relate to an entry-sequenced VSAM file.

A key-sequenced VSAM file is composed of continuous fixed-length areas of direct-access external storage called *control intervals*. A control interval is the unit of information that is transferred between virtual and auxiliary storage by the VSAM access facilities. The size of a control interval may vary from one file to another; however, for a given file the size of each control interval is fixed. The size may be chosen by the user or by VSAM, which attempts to select an optimal size for the type of direct-access storage device used.

Records in a control interval may be either fixed or variable in length—VSAM treats them identically. Control information describing the data records is placed at the end of the control interval. A *stored record* is the combination of a data record and its control information, even though they are not physically adjacent. Stored records may not span across control-interval boundaries, and when a file is defined, enough buffer space must be allocated to accommodate the largest stored record.

Parts of a control interval may be unused as is illustrated in Fig. 7-10.4. Later in this subsection, we describe how records can be added or deleted so as to keep this area contiguous. In general, free space can be initially distributed throughout a key-sequenced file in two ways—by leaving space at the end of all the used control intervals and by leaving some control intervals empty.

A data record is addressed by its displacement (in bytes) from the beginning of

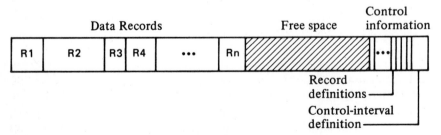

FIGURE 7-10.4   The relative placement of data, free space, and control information in a control interval.

the file (i.e., its relative byte address). VSAM considers the control intervals to be contiguous and treats a file as though it is stored in virtual storage beginning at address 0.

A set of control intervals can be logically grouped together to form a *control area*. This relationship is shown in Fig. 7-10.5. Relating these concepts to ISAM, it is best to think of a control interval as a logical track, and a control area as a logical cylinder. A set of indices is created for each control area and a particular set contains relative byte address pointers to the control intervals forming the control area. The indices for a control area form a *sequence-set element* and the sets of indices for all control areas in the file is called the *sequence set*.

Indices at higher levels can be constructed also. Each index is contained in a record, and the set of all such index records is called the *index set*. At the highest level of indices, only one index is allowed. An entry in an index-set record consists of the highest key that an index record in the next lower level contains, together with a pointer to the lower-level index record. For a sequence-set record, an entry consists of the highest key in a control interval and a pointer to that control interval.

In order to increase the number of entries in an index record, VSAM uses a technique called *key compression* in which it eliminates from the front and back of a key those characters that are not necessary to distinguish it from adjacent keys. Because the size of keys in index entries is reduced by compression, either a smaller index or an index with more entries is achievable.

Key-sequenced VSAM files can be processed in three ways—namely, *sequential*, *skip sequential*, and *direct*. In the sequential processing of a key-sequenced file, records are accessed in an order determined by the sequence of keys in the file. When the file is opened for sequential processing, the access facilities secure the RBA of the first record in the file and sequential processing continues from this address. Alternatively, a specific key or a generic key may be supplied with the first I/O statement which is executed. Sequential processing can then begin at the record with the given key or the first of the records having the generic key.

Skip-sequential processing involves the accessing in order of a subset of the records in a file. Assume we are given an ordered set of keys which forms a subset of the keys for the records in the file. When processing a next record based on the ordered set of keys, the horizontal links in the sequence set are used to locate the appropriate element from the sequence set records. The addressing information in this element is used to isolate the control interval for the desired data record. This control interval is brought into virtual memory and the requested record is processed.

As an example illustrating skip-sequential processing, let us examine the file as depicted in Fig. 7-10.5. Suppose the records we are interested in accessing are identified by the ordered set of keys {A3, E7, N6, Q3, Y5}. Processing begins by directly accessing the record identified by the key A3 (i.e., by searching through the index set and the sequence set to isolate the second control interval in the first control area). The next record to be accessed has the key E7. Instead of directly accessing the record by following the vertical pointers from the highest level of index down to the sequence set, we can proceed along the horizontal pointers at the sequence-set level. Therefore, in the example, we can move to the second sequence-set element, and thereby eventually find the record with key E7 without tracing through the higher index levels. Of course, the requirement that the set of search keys be ordered is crucial to the success of this method of access.

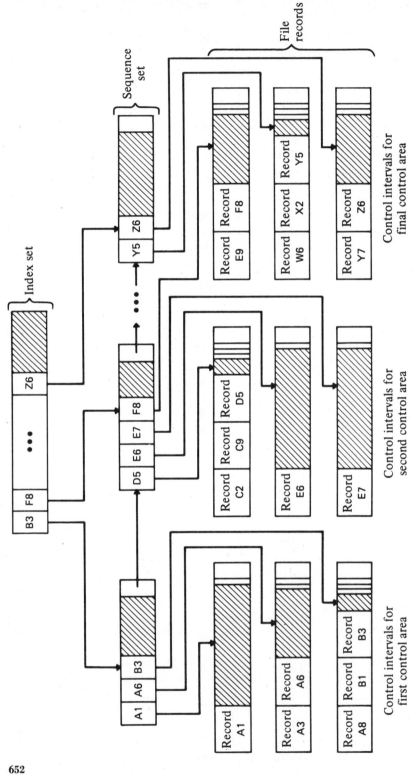

FIGURE 7-10.5 The structure of a VSAM file.

Record B1	Record B3	/////////////////////		

FIGURE 7-10.6   The third control interval after removing record **A8**.

Direct access to a record in a key-sequenced VSAM file is gained by traversing the tree of index records down to the sequence set. The appropriate control interval is then retrieved and the desired record is accessed in virtual memory. VSAM supports a very general and powerful form of record retrieval. A key can be used to specify the retrieval of:

1   A particular record (i.e., the key is an exact key).
2   A record with the next largest key (i.e., the key is an approximate key).
3   A record which is the first record to satisfy a generic key (i.e., the key is a generic key).

The most interesting features of VSAM are related to the management of data records when deletion, addition, and update operations are performed. When records are deleted from a key-sequenced file, the amount of space occupied by the record is recovered and added to the free-space section of a control interval. This recovery of available space is accomplished by moving data records in the control interval to ensure that the data-record sections and free-space section each remain contiguous areas. Figure 7-10.6 illustrates the effect of removing the record with a key of **A8** from the third control interval of the file shown in Fig. 7-10.5. Note that if record **B3** is removed from this interval, the third entry in the first sequence-set record and the first entry in the index-set record must be altered to indicate that **B1** is now the largest index in that particular control interval and control area, respectively.

When a record is added to a key-sequenced file, VSAM may move some of the existing records over to keep the records within a control interval physically in key sequence. For example, suppose a record with key **A9** is added to the third control interval in Fig. 7-10.5. The results of this insertion is shown in Fig. 7-10.7. The records **B1** and **B3** are moved, displacing some of the free-space area.

An obvious question arises: What if there is not enough room in a control interval to accommodate the insertion of a new record? VSAM handles this situation by performing a *control-interval split* which is almost identical to a data-block split in a CDC Scope indexed sequential file. In a control-interval split, stored records in the control interval are moved to an empty control interval in the same control area, and the new record is inserted in its proper key sequence. Just how the interval is split depends on the type of processing that is taking place. For a sequential insertion, the new record is placed in the original control interval, if possible, and all subsequent records are placed in the new control interval. Such a control-interval split is illustrated in Fig. 7-10.8a for the insertion of a small record with

Record A8	Record A9	Record B1	Record B3	////		

FIGURE 7-10.7   The third control interval after the addition of record **A9**.

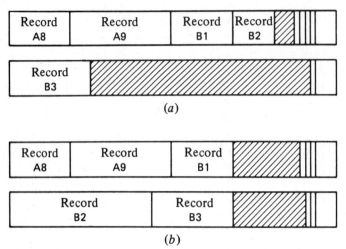

FIGURE 7-10.8   A control-interval split involving the insertion of
(*a*) a small record B2, and (*b*) a large record B2.

key B2 in the control interval shown in Fig. 7-10.7. If the new record is too large to be placed in the original control interval, it and all remaining records in the original control interval are placed in the new control interval. Figure 7-10.8*b* depicts such an insertion involving a large record with key B2. When VSAM detects that two or more records are to be inserted in sequence, a technique called *mass sequential insertion* is used to save I/O operations by buffering the records being inserted.

For direct insertion, approximately one-half of the records in a control interval are moved when a control-interval split occurs.

If there is not a free control interval in a control area when performing a control-interval split, a control-area split results. In such an operation, a new control area is established by making use of the space already allocated, or by extending the file if the initially allocated file space is full. Approximately half of the control intervals are moved from the full control area to an equal-sized new control area. The new record is placed in one of the control areas as dictated by the key value. Control-area splitting should be performed very infrequently, as it results in a major and expensive file reorganization.

The process of updating a record with a new record that is different in length precipitates the same type of file reorganization as a deletion or insertion. If the new record is shorter than the old record, then the extra space is returned to the free-space area in a similar manner as that used in returning space from a deleted record. If the new record is larger than the old record, then the extra space required is accommodated in the same manner as that adopted when acquiring space for the insertion of a record. Hence, control-interval splits and control-area splits can result from the expansion of an updated record. By now it should be evident that the file-processing facilities required to support key-sequenced VSAM files must be extremely sophisticated.

Now let us examine entry-sequenced VSAM files. The most noticeable difference between a key-sequenced and an entry-sequenced file is that no index is associated with the latter type of VSAM file. When a record is added sequentially to an entry-sequenced file, VSAM returns its RBA (Relative Byte Address). Using these RBAs, it is possible for us to create our own index or index set to aid in fast direct access.

If we wish to create and access the file directly, then we should preformat the file with blank records. To store a data record, it is necessary to transform the key item of the record to an RBA and retrieve the preformatted record at that RBA. If the record location as determined by the RBA is empty, the new record is stored at that location. If the record location already contains a data record, then a user-written collision-resolution procedure must be invoked which determines an alternate RBA for the record.

It can be concluded that entry-sequenced VSAM files provide very few file-processing facilities for the user. The development of file structures to enhance file access capabilities is entirely left to the user. A summary of the important differences between key-sequenced and entry-sequenced files is given in Table 7-10.1.

VSAM has not as yet received widespread acceptance in the data-processing community. The reason for this is partly due to the initial unsettled nature of the operating system, OS/VS, that is designed to support VSAM. Once these preliminary problems are overcome, VSAM will undoubtedly be heavily used. Currently, many of the compilers do not specifically support the access of VSAM files. VSAM files, however, can be accessed by using the language features which are provided for ISAM.

Exercises for Sec. 7-10

1. Formulate an algorithm representative of the steps necessary to locate a particular word in virtual memory, as described by the three-level address s, p, d, where s is a segment name, p is an index into the page table for segment s, and d is the displacement within page p. Assume segment tables and page tables are of the form illustrated in Fig. 7-10.3.

Table 7-10.1   A comparison of key-sequenced and entry-sequenced VSAM files.

Key-Sequenced File	Entry-Sequenced File
Records are ordered by key	Records are ordered by their sequence of entry
Access is by key, although RBA access is possible	Access is by RBA
A record's RBA can change with additions and deletions	A record's RBA cannot change
By distributing free space, it is possible to insert records and change the length of records relatively easily	Only space at the end of the file can be used to create new record locations
Within a control interval, the space available due to a deleted or shortened record is automatically reclaimed	Records cannot be physically deleted; however, the space can be reused for a record of the same length

2. Suppose you are converting a file-based information system from a machine with data-management facilities which support sequential, indexed sequential, and direct files to a virtual memory system with segmented paging. The file system is similar to that available in MULTICS in that the file system is integrated with the segmented paging system. Outline what you feel are potential advantages and disadvantages of such a conversion assuming sequential, indexed sequential, and direct files were used in the original information system.

3. In the virtual memory systems discussed in this section, it was pointed out that when a page or segment must be brought into main memory, a page or segment currently in main memory must be replaced. What is wrong with selecting the page or segment to be replaced on a strictly random basis? Can you suggest a better replacement strategy?

4. Derive algorithms for accessing a VSAM file in a skip sequential manner and in a direct manner. Use notation consistent with that given in this section.

5. List the advantages of key-sequenced VSAM file over an indexed sequential file (IBM variety). Are there any disadvantages?

7-11   MULTIPLE-KEY ACCESS

The file structures discussed thus far provide us with the ability to access a record based on a single key, often called the *primary key*. In many applications, however, it may be desirable or even necessary to access a record using any one of a number of keys. One such application, from which several examples will be drawn in this section, involves a hospital administration system designed to aid in the distribution of drugs to hospital patients. The users of such a system ask questions such as:

> List all patients in recovery rooms.
> Which patients of Dr. Novak require the drug XEN-02?
> How many patients are currently in the pediatric ward?
> Is John Brown a patient at the hospital?

Figure 7-11.1 depicts the records of a patient's file which is ordered by a state-wide hospitalization number. This number uniquely identifies each record of the file, and hence can be used as the primary key. The other given items of a patient's record are called *secondary index items* (also commonly called *secondary keys*, although this may be somewhat of a misnomer since they do not necessarily uniquely identify a record). A secondary index item is important in handling inquiries based on the value of the item, and it is used in a manner similar to or in conjunction with the primary key to access a record directly. For example, "List all patients in recovery rooms" can be answered by printing the names, plus any other information deemed to be important, of the patients with bed numbers beginning with R.

The nonindexed items in Fig. 7-11.1 may contain information such as the patient's address and a list of the different facilities and services used by the patient during his or her period of confinement (e.g., cobalt-treatment facilities and labor and delivery services). Some of the nonindexed items can also be considered as secondary index items if inquiries relevant to these items are in demand. For example, "List all patients requiring physiotherapy" is one such inquiry which may be handled most efficiently by

Primary Key	Secondary Indexed Items				Nonindexed Information
Hospitalization Number	Patient's Name	Bed Number	Patient's Doctor	Drug Prescribed	
0913628	Brown, J.H.	R67	Novak	XEN-02	
0931762	Copeck, J.A.	A02	Turtle	HYPOCH	
1013761	Rollie, R.K.	A04	Black	SULPH-3	
1029372	Cristie, L.H.	B21	Novak	CRYOL	
3056718	Jones, W.I.	R69	James	RESIN-A	
3084255	Watson, W.P.	B23	Turtle	CRYOL	
3931768	Andrews, A.K.	A09	Novak	NEOBEN	
4111234	McCord, G.A.	B24	James	HYPOCH	
4450902	Tash, R.R.	I33	King	SULPH-3	
6331313	Whyte, E.A.	A08	Black	LAX	
7614009	Dree, T.P.	R68	James	NEOBEN	
7729310	Bent, K.E.	A03	Novak	SULPH-3	

(*Bed number legend*: A = General Ward, B = Pediatric Ward,
I = Intensive Care, M = Maternity Ward, R = Recovery Room.)

FIGURE 7-11.1 Records for a hospital administration system.

adopting one of the secondary access methods to be described in this section for the facilities' item of a patient record.

In this section, we examine a number of file structures which aid in the retrieval of information for inquiries based on secondary index items. In particular, the *multilist* (multiple threaded list) and the *inverted-list* organizations are introduced. A structural continuum of these two methods is created simply by placing restrictions on the length of a multilist structure. Two file structures from this continuum—multilist with controlled list length and multilist with cellular partitions—are presented.

We will purposely emphasize secondary access methods, since these are the techniques which are used to effect multikey access given today's technology. Undoubtedly in the future, sophisticated hardware systems will be developed which will allow a record to be accessed directly by any one of a number of keys.

It should be noted that multikey access generally is not used in batch processing. The main reason for this is that in batch-processing systems all inquiries can be batched together, and all requests and updates can be handled on a record-by-record basis during a sequential scan of the entire file.

7-11.1 Multilist Organization

In a multilist organization, records which have equivalent values for a given secondary index item are linked together to form a list. Since a particular item usually assumes a number of values, say n, then n lists are created, one for each item value (hence the term multilist).

Figure 7-11.2 illustrates two multilists—one for the patient's doctor and one for the drug prescribed. Note that for brevity the name items, bed-number items, and the nonindexed items are omitted from the records. To provide a clear picture, lists for only three item values are shown, and a unique method is used for representing the links for each item in the diagram. An index is needed for each multilist, and each entry in the index contains three fields—the name of an item value, a link to the first record in a list of records containing that item value, and the length of the list. In effect, each index entry in the multilist structure is a list head with the addition of a length field.

The length field is extremely important when handling conjunctive queries such as: "Which patients of Dr. Novak require the drug CRYOL?". To service such a request, we

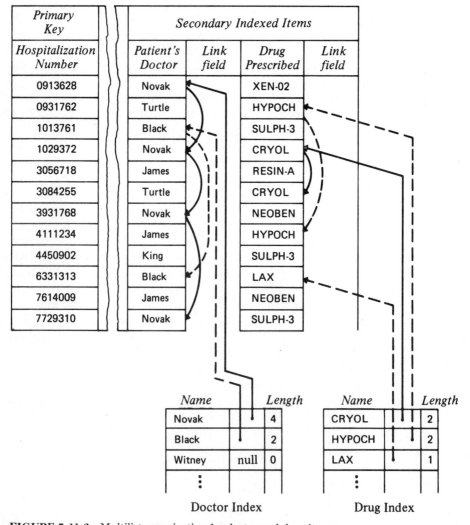

FIGURE 7-11.2   Multilist organization for doctor and drug items.

must locate the patient records with a doctor item of Novak and a drug item of CRYOL. The length field is used to detect which is the shorter list—the list of patients each of whom has a doctor named Novak, or the list of patients taking the drug CRYOL. Obviously, for this example, it is more efficient to retrieve the two records corresponding to patients taking CRYOL and examine the patient's doctor item for the value Novak, then to retrieve the four patient records corresponding to Novak and examine the drug item for the value CRYOL. Note that for some elements of the index, there may not exist any records with that item value. In such instances, conjunctive queries can be handled without accessing records from the main file, since no record contains information satisfying the query.

For some applications, a secondary index such as the doctor index or the drug index may be so large that it becomes necessary to store the index in a separate file. Access to a particular element in the file may be gained sequentially (using a sequential file), directly (using a direct file with the item value assuming the role of a key), or either sequentially or directly (using an indexed sequential file). It is often the case, however, that an index is small enough to reside as a table in main memory, and one of the search strategies discussed in Sec. 6-2 can be used to locate a particular element. To speed up the searching process, it is advantageous to have the index elements ordered as in the case for the drug index in Fig. 7-11.2.

The address field of an index element and the link field of the indexed item are depicted with arrows emanating from them in Fig. 7-11.2. In practice, these address fields contain either an absolute auxiliary memory address or a primary key value. An auxiliary memory address provides for quicker access; however, it is affected by the physical movement of records. For example, if the record corresponding to patient 3931768 is moved in a reorganization of the patient file, then all links pointing to this record must be updated. Such an update is nontrivial for a singly linked list. Primary key values, on the other hand, remain unaffected by the physical movement of records. Access to a record is slower, however, because a primary key must be transformed into an auxiliary address before the record can be located. Figure 7-11.3 depicts a primary-key type of linkage for the doctor index using only the first five records. Note also that if we are programming an information system using a high-level language such as PL/I or COBOL, we are responsible for creating tables for secondary indices. Since auxiliary memory addresses generally are not available at this level of programming, we are forced to use primary keys for record linkages.

Primary Key		Secondary Index Item			Name	Key	Length
Hospitalization Number		Patient's Doctor	Link Field				
0913628		Novak	1029372		Novak	0913628	4
0931762		Turtle	3084255		Black	1013761	2
1013761		Black	6331313		Witney	null	0
1029372		Novak	3931768				
3056718		James	4111234				

FIGURE 7-11.3 Multilist using primary-key link fields.

The greatest disadvantage of the multilist organization is that in order to respond to a query with a conjunctive term, all records corresponding to the term having the shortest list must be individually brought into main memory for examination. The principal advantages are the simplicity of programming and the flexibility in performing updates, which are described later in this section.

7-11.2   Inverted-List Organization

One way of overcoming the major disadvantage of the multilist approach (i.e., the necessity to access all records on the shortest list of the terms for a conjunctive query) is to remove all linkages from the file area and to place the list in the secondary index, that is, to create an inverted list. Figure 7-11.4 shows the inverted lists created for the patient's name and bed-number record items of the patient file. Figure 7-11.4a illustrates the inversion process associated with the formation of an inverted list. Normally, access to a particular patient name in the patient file is gained via the primary key, which is the hospitalization number. The inverted list (or table) in Fig. 7-11.4a provides an inverse relationship; that is, given a particular name, the corresponding hospitalization number can be located. The inverted list of patients' names allows for quick access in response to inquiries involving specific patients, such as: "Who is W.I. Jones' doctor?"

Figure 7-11.4b shows only a partial inversion of the bed-number record item. The list represents an inversion to the ward-level only, and hence is helpful in the handling of inquiries about a particular ward such as: "How many patients are in recovery?" If queries are required concerning individual beds (for example: "What drug is the patient in bed A04 receiving?"), then a complete inversion may be warranted.

Patient's Name	Primary Key
Andrews, A.K.	3931768
Bent, K.E.	7729310
Brown, J.H.	0913628
Copeck, J.A.	0931762
Cristie, L.H.	1029372
Dree, T.P.	7614009
Jones, W.I.	3056718
McCord, G.A.	4111234
Rollie, R.K.	1013761
Tash, R.R.	4450902
Watson, W.P.	3084255
Whyte, F.A.	6331313

Ward	Primary Key
General(A)	0931762
	1013761
	3931768
	6331313
	7729310
Pediatric(B)	1029372
	3084255
	4111234
Intensive(I)	4450902
Maternity(M)	null
Recovery(R)	0913628
	3056718
	7614009

(a)   (b)

FIGURE 7-11.4   Inverted lists for (a) patients' names, and for (b) patients' wards.

An inverted list can appear as a sequential, indexed sequential, or direct file, depending on how quickly we desire a response to a query. If a list is not extremely long, then it may be possible to retain it in main memory while processing user requests. Internal searching methods then can be applied. For many large applications, however, this may not be possible, especially with lists which have an entry for every record in the main file such as the patient's name list in Fig. 7-11.4a. Note that the patient's ward list in Fig. 7-11.4b is really composed of five sublists. It is possible to leave selected sublists in main memory for such an inverted structure.

For highly volatile files, it may be worthwhile to invert a secondary index item using a tree-type structure. Figure 7-8.2 illustrates such a structure for a primary index of a direct file. Additions and deletions can be handled very easily with this type of structure.

In Fig. 7-11.4, we have used the primary key as a pointer to the patient record(s) associated with a given inverted list element. We could also have used an external memory address. The advantages and disadvantages of the two types of linkage were discussed for the multilist structure. The arguments cited then apply when considering linkages in an inverted list or any of the other secondary processing methods discussed in this section.

One of the major advantages credited to the inverted list structure is its ability to handle queues with conjunctive terms. For example, the query: "Is R.K. Rollie in pediatrics?" can be answered by first locating Rollie's hospitalization number in the patient's name list (Fig. 7-11.4a). The hospitalization number of all patients in pediatrics can be found in the patient's ward list (Fig. 7-11.4b), and it is easy to determine if Rollie is in pediatrics by comparing Rollie's hospitalization number with those of the pediatrics ward. In fact, we can answer this question without accessing a record in the patient file! This is not true if a multilist structure is used for the name and bed-number items. In general, a query involving the conjunction of two terms which have associated inverted lists can be handled with the examination of only those records containing information satisfying the query statement. For example, the query: "Which patients of Dr. Novak require the drug CRYOL?", as discussed in the last subsection, requires only one patient-record retrieval, if the doctor and drug index items arc invertcd. Recall that two record retrievals were required using multilist structures.

Another advantagc of using an invertcd list is that statistics concerning the number of times a secondary index item has been used can be easily kept. An extra numeric field in the inverted list can be incremented each time a particular secondary index item is required. Such an entry can also be included in a multilist structure; however, the master file record must be rewritten each time the field is incremented.

One of the major disadvantages of the inverted list is that the item values being inverted generally have to be included in both the inverted list and the master file. For example, the patients' names are present in the inverted list (Fig. 7-11.4a) and the patient file (Fig. 7-11.1). If the only time a patient's name is used is in an inquiry function (for example: "Who is J.H. Brown's doctor?"), and it never appears as information in response to a query, then it is possible to remove the patient's name item from the patient record. Note that this same item can be removed if we use a multilist structure. However, in practice, this probably would not be the case. In a multilist structure, secondary index items are not duplicated and, therefore, it is storage-wise more efficient than an inverted list.

Later in this section we will discover that the maintenance of an inverted list is nontrivial.

7-11.3   The Controlled List Length Multilist Organization

In an effort to minimize the disadvantages of the multilist and inverted list structures, we now consider a compromise which involves controlling the length of a multilist. Figure 7-11.5 typifies this type of structure. The multilists for the bed-number item are restricted to a maximum length of three. As a consequence of this restriction, the patient records with general-ward bed numbers are placed on two lists. Of course, the example we are using is very limited in size; however, it is easy to visualize that for larger files, a given item value may have several lists associated with it.

The restriction on the length of a list provides two enhancements to the multilist. First, the breakdown of lists into sublists, each having their own list head entries in the secondary index, contributes to a faster average access time. For example, in Fig. 7-11.5, the accessing of information concerning bed A09 can be accomplished by first scanning and making comparisons with the "general-ward" entries in the index (that is, A02 and A08), and then proceeding down the "A08 list" until the record of the patient residing in bed A09

Primary Key		Secondary Indexed Item	
Hospitalization Number		Bed Number	Link field (primary key)
0913628		R67	7614009
0931762		A02	7729310
1013761		A04	null
1029372		B21	3084255
3056718		R69	null
3084255		B23	4111234
3931768		A09	null
4111234		B24	null
4450902		I33	null
6331313		A08	3931768
7614009		R68	3056718
7729310		A03	1013761

Ward	Bed	Link	Length
General	A02	0931762	3
General	A08	6331313	2
Pediatric	B21	1029372	3
Intensive	I33	4450902	1
Maternity	nil	null	0
Recovery	R67	0913628	3

FIGURE 7-11.5   Multilist with controlled list length.

is located. Therefore, only two records need to be retrieved, as opposed to as many as five records in the multilist case. It must be observed, however, that all records corresponding to the term of a conjunctive query with the shortest list must still be scanned for the controlled list length organization. For example, if we assume Dr. Novak had six patients and the patient's doctor item is considered as a secondary index item, then the inquiry "List all patients of Dr. Novak who are in the general ward" must involve the searching of the records on both of the general-ward lists, as given in Fig. 7-11.5. Nevertheless, there can be an advantage to having a long list split into several smaller sublists. If the individual lists reside on separate external-device modules (i.e., separate cylinders or units), it is sometimes possible to overlap the list accesses so that the processing of one list and the reading of another can take place in parallel.

By now, it should be evident that the multilist with a controlled list length of one is simply an inverted list structure, and that the multilist with a controlled list length of infinity is the multilist structure discussed earlier. As a hybrid structure, the multilist with a controlled list length carries some of the disadvantages of both "parent" structures. We have already discussed how the problems associated with conjunctive-term queries are not significantly reduced by controlling the list length of a multilist structure. The disadvantage of having to include indexed items redundantly in an inverted list and the records of the master file creeps into a controlled list length multilist structure. As more sublists are created, more entries appear in the secondary index. Each entry in the index contains a name field which is duplicated in the master file record.

We will look at some of the problems associated with maintaining a controlled list length multilist structure later in this section.

7-11.4 Cellular Partitioned Structures

To this point, we have almost completely ignored the physical placement of records in the secondary access methods which have been considered. An alternative is to take advantage of the cellular boundaries (i.e., the block or sector boundaries) of the direct-access storage medium being used. If possible, an attempt should be made to load records with a common attribute (e.g., records for patients with a common doctor) in the same cellular pattern. With this form of partitioning, all or many of the records with a common attribute can be accessed with only one read operation.

Most files, however, are organized based on their primary key, and the positioning of records with respect to a secondary key (or index item) often appears to be arbitrary. Even in this situation, it can be advantageous to organize secondary indices or inverted list structures based on the cellular partitioning of the file.

To illustrate what is meant by cellular partitioning, let us begin by considering a multilist structure such as the one in Fig. 7-11.6. An entry in the secondary index is created on each occasion an item value appears one or more times in a cellular partition. Therefore, the value "Novak" has three entries, since Novak appears in all three partitions, whereas "King" has but one entry, since it only appears in cell 3.

The relative position in the cell of the first record in a chain is included in the index to aid in the direct accessing of a record after it has been read into main memory. The length field is included as an informational aid when performing conjunctive query operations.

Primary Key	Secondary Index Item	
Hospitalization Number	Patient's Doctor	Link Field

Secondary Index Relative Record			
Name	Position	Cell #	Length
Novak	1	1	2
	3	2	1
	4	3	1
Turtle	2	1	1
	2	2	1
Black	3	1	1
	2	3	1
James	1	2	2
	3	3	1
King	1	3	1

Hospitalization Number	Patient's Doctor	Link Field
0913628	Novak	
0931761	Turtle	null
1013761	Black	null
1029372	Novak	null

3056718	James	
3084255	Turtle	null
3931768	Novak	null
4111234	James	null

4450902	King	null
6331313	Black	null
7614009	James	null
7729310	Novak	null

FIGURE 7-11.6   Multilist structure with cellular partitioning.

It should be noted that when handling queries which contain a conjunction of terms, some preprocessing can be carried out at the cellular level. For example, consider the query: "How many of Dr. James' patients receive HYPOCH?" Suppose the drug item is treated as a secondary index item accessible via a multilist list structure with cellular partitioning. Then "HYPOCH" appears in records in cells 1 and 2. Since "James" appears in records in cells 2 and 3, an intersection operation at the cell level indicates that all of James' patients (if any) taking HYPOCH can be found in cell 2.

A multilist structure with cellular partitioning is primarily useful when there is a large number of records residing in a cell. The additional space required by the link field is warranted if it significantly reduces the time to access a list of records in a cell. If there are relatively few records per cell, as in the case in Fig. 7-11.6, it is better to omit the link field and examine the record of a cell in a serial fashion. An index for this type of structure, as it relates to partitions of the patient file as shown in Fig. 7-11.6, is illustrated in Fig. 7-11.7a. Note that neither the relative record position or the length fields are included. Lefkovitz [1969] refers to this type of structure as a *cellular serial* structure. Martin [1975] presents a similar type of structure, which he terms a *cellular inverted list*. The index for such a structure is a binary matrix in which each element of the matrix indicates that a secondary index value is present (1 value) or absent (0 value) in a particular cellular partition. Figure 7-11.7b illustrates such a structure for both the patient's doctor and drug items. The latter type of organization can be used very efficiently in the processing of queries involving the logical "oring" (disjunction) and logical "anding" (conjunction) of query terms. For example, to determine the cells which contain information satisfying the query "List all

Name	Cell #
Novak	1
	2
	3
Turtle	1
	2
Black	1
	3
James	2
	3
King	3

(a)

	Secondary Index Item	Cellular Partitions		
		1	2	3
Doctor	Novak	1	1	1
	Turtle	1	1	0
	Black	1	0	1
	James	0	1	1
	King	0	0	1
Drug	XEN-02	1	0	0
	HYPOCH	1	1	0
	SULPH-3	1	0	1
	CRYOL	1	1	0
	NEOBEN	0	1	1
	LAX	0	0	1
	RESIN-A	0	1	0

(b)

FIGURE 7-11.7 Secondary index tables for the (a) cellular serial, and (b) cellular inverted-list structures.

those who are patients of Dr. Black or are receiving LAX" involves the logical operation $101 \lor 001 = 101$. Therefore, we need only serially search cells 1 and 3 to find all the information pertinent to the query.

A major advantage of cellular partitioning is the capability of being able to initiate simultaneously several read operations and to overlap these operations with the processing of a query and the generation of a response. Some search time can be reduced by first performing logical operations at the cellular partition level. If records with common item values are not clustered in a few cells (i.e., if item values are spread over a number of cells with only one or two records per cell containing common item values), then it is more advantageous to use an inverted list structure. The more spread out common item values are over the partitions of the file, the more entries are needed in the secondary index and the longer it takes to access a set of records having a common item value.

Thus far we have introduced a number of file structures which are used for secondary access, provided examples of each structure, and discussed the advantages and disadvantages of each in terms of the retrieval process (i.e., how easily each facilitates the handling of inquiries). Let us now examine how easy or difficult it is to maintain each of these structures. The types of maintenance operations we will be considering are the addition, deletion, and the updating of records in a file.

7-11.5   Maintenance of a Multilist

The addition of a record to a file can cause a substantial reorganization of the file due to the creation of overflow records and the changes in primary-key indexes that are necessitated. These effects were discussed in earlier sections of this chapter. If multikey access is provided, then the addition of a record can also alter the secondary index tables that are associated with each secondary key of the file. Additions can be handled relatively easily in a multilist structure. If the lists are not ordered, then an addition can be accommodated most easily by placing the new record at the logical head of the list. This simply involves a change in the address field of the index entry for each secondary index-item value present in the new record. Figure 7-11.8 shows the effect of such a change on the patients' doctor item. If the list must be ordered according to some criterion such as the primary key, then the new record may be inserted logically somewhere in the middle of a list. Finally, if the list is ordered by an activity count (i.e., a count of the number of times a particular record in the list is accessed), then the record should be inserted at the logical end of the list. In this case, it is helpful for faster insertion to keep the location of the last record of the list as an index entry. Note that the length field of the index entry must be incremented by 1 for each addition.

The deletion of a record involving a multilist structure can be treated as an inverse process of record insertion. The index entry corresponding to each secondary index-item value in the deleted record is located. Using the list head information provided by the index entry, we can chain through the list structure for the item value, locate the desired record, and delete it from the list by altering the link field. A process similar to Algorithm DELETE in Sec. 4-2.1 can be used to achieve the deletion. This process can be long and involved if there are a number of items in the deleted record which are in multilist structures.

We can reduce the time required to perform a deletion by simply marking the record as being deleted instead of logically removing the record from the multilist. The disadvantage with this approach is that we must consider deleted records as well as active records when accessing a particular list in a multilist structure. For volatile files, the overhead incurred by leaving deleted records in the multilist chains can be very costly. Performance can be improved by deleting the inactive records periodically using low-priority background processing.

If the system requires both on-line maintenance and retrieval, bidirectional links should be considered in the multilist structures. The deletion of an item from a doubly linked list was described in Algorithm DOUBDEL in Sec. 4-2.3. With this algorithm, a record can be deleted without having to chain through a linked structure starting from the list head. Hence, deletions can be performed more quickly with the additional storage overhead of a link field for every secondary item in the record.

For some applications, it is necessary to delete a secondary index item from a record and yet not delete the whole record. One of the following alternatives can be adopted

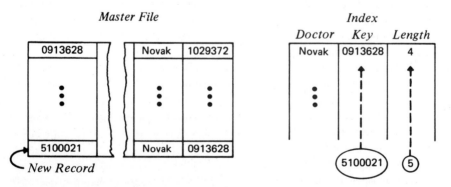

FIGURE 7-11.8   Addition of a new record to a multilist structure.

to achieve item deletion. First, a special value can be used to indicate that no meaningful item value is present (i.e., a "nil" value is used). Second, a bit accompanying the item can be used to denote if the item is deleted from the list or not. Lefkovitz [1969] suggests this method. Thirdly, the item can be logically deleted from a linked list using the techniques just discussed for record deletion, and then the record can be rewritten with the item removed. Let us now turn our attention to the problems related to record updates in a multilist structure.

Whenever records are rewritten some item is altered. If an item belonging to a multilist changes in value, then the record must be removed from one list and added to another list of the structure. The update involves the invocation of the deletion and addition algorithms for linked structures, which have already been discussed several times. Updates involving the addition of an item or the deletion of an item from a record are similarly straightforward to achieve. Depending on how the records are organized in the file, the addition of an item may involve the relocation of the record.

A final important consideration relevant to the maintenance of a multilist structure concerns system recovery in the event of a hardware failure (e.g., an external-device unit failure during a write operation) or a software failure (e.g., a programming error which erases a record). If the failure occurs while a pointer is being updated, then the result may be an erroneously written pointer. Recovery can be achieved relatively easily if the multilist structure is doubly linked (e.g., a backward link can be used to restore an erroneously written forward link). Recovery is difficult, if not impossible, using a singly linked structure.

7-11.6 Maintenance of an Inverted List

The addition of a record which contains one or more items that have been inverted can cause some substantial reorganizational problems. If the inverted list is maintained as a sequentially allocated table or sequential file, then the addition of a new record with an inverted item results in the movement of table entries or sequential file records to leave room for the new entry. As an example, consider what effects the addition of a patient record with a hospitalization number of 6293109, a name field of A.A. Atwood, and bed number of A07 would have on the inverted lists shown in Fig. 7-11.4. If the inverted list is maintained in a direct or indexed sequential file, then the new inverted item can create an overflow record. If the inverted structure is maintained as a tree or a linked list, an addition causes very few problems—simply the creation of a node in the list structure and the alteration of a few link fields. The addition of a new item value, such as the creation of a psychiatric (P) ward, to the ward list in Fig. 7-11.4 results in the formation of a completely new sublist within the current inverted list structure. In most applications, however, additions can be completed more quickly on an inverted list structure than a multilist structure, simply because the reading of master file records is avoided.

Deletion of records containing inverted items requires that the pointers to each such item be removed from the inverted list. For example, the removal of the patient record 3931768 results in the deletion of the element corresponding to Andrews in the patient's name list, and of an element from the general ward sublist in the patient's ward list for the inverted lists depicted in Fig. 7-11.4. Again, the difficulty of removing a pointer is dependent upon the storage (or file) structure associated with the list. Rather than physically removing the pointer, it may be more efficient to associate a deletion flag with each inverted list element, if a sequential storage structure is adopted. Periodically, such inverted lists can be reorganized and the deleted items can be removed physically. The removal of individual inverted items presents no additional problems from those already discussed concerning the removal of entire records. Similarly, the updating of records constitutes no new conceptual difficulties, and it can best be viewed as a process of removing an element from one inverted list and inserting a new element in another.

7-11.7   Maintenance of Constrained Multilist and Cellular Structures

The addition, deletion, or update of records with items which are designated as secondary keys increases or decreases the number of records on a particular list within a multilist structure. Therefore, maintaining a structure such as the controlled list-length multilist can involve some additional processing not required by the multilist with an indefinite list length. For example, the addition of a patient record with hospitalization number 6912488 and bed number A01 causes a major reorganization of the controlled list-length multilist structure exhibited in Fig. 7-11.5. The record with bed number A04 must be moved to the head of second sublist for the general ward and the new record with bed number A01 is placed at the head of the first sublist. Note that the addition of yet another patient to the general ward necessitates the creation of a new sublist and a new element in the secondary index.

The deletion of an element requires less processing since a new list cannot be generated. Nevertheless, index elements may have to be altered or removed completely if a list length drops to zero. A deletion bit can be used to speed up on-line deletions. Major reorganizations, which take into consideration maximum allowable list lengths, can be completed off-line. Updates to secondary keys constitute a deletion-insertion activity.

A cellular partitioned structure is more easily maintained than a controlled list-length multilist structure. Whenever possible, records should be placed so as to promote the clustering of common secondary index items in cellular partitions. This may be difficult or impossible to achieve due to the sequencing of records dictated by the primary key. For cellular multilist structures, index entries may have to be altered with the addition and deletion of records or individual secondary index items. Note that such changes are minimal when using a cellular serial or cellular inverted list structure.

7-11.8   Summary of Secondary Access Methods

Table 7-11.1 provides a summary of the advantages and disadvantages of the secondary access methods discussed in this section.

Unless we can take advantage of a certain degree of parallelism in read/write operations, the multilist and inverted list are the secondary access methods generally adopted. Multilist structures are ideal for systems which are constrained in terms of main memory, and/or are oriented towards single-term queries, and/or do not require fast response times. The simplicity of programming a system using multilist structures is an added benefit. For most large information systems, however, the inverted list structure is the best structure to use if fast response times is a system requirement.

Table 7-11.1 A summary of the results for secondary access methods.

Method	Advantages	Disadvantages
Multilist	Easily programmed. Easily updated especially if bidirectional links are used. Efficient use of storage, especially if secondary index item is not stored in master file record. Ordering lists by accession rate can improve speed of access. Good for queries involving a single secondary key, since all records in the list must be examined.	Slow access, since many master file records may have to be examined. Queries with conjunctive terms are not easily handled as they require a transfer to memory of all records from the shortest list.
Inverted list	Fastest access of all the methods and especially good for queries with conjunctive terms. Updating is relatively fast, especially if lists reside in main memory. Good for keeping track of file statistics for secondary access.	Deletions and additions can create problems if list is sequentially allocated. Inefficient storage use if secondary index item values appear in inverted list and master file records. No great advantage over multilist for single-term queries, unless records can be accessed in parallel.
Controlled list-length multilist	Parallel access may be possible. Lists are divided into sublists, and if it can be determined in which sublist a conjunctive term resides, then query handling is faster than for multilist. Can be altered relatively easily to take on the appearance of a multilist or an inverted list, depending on system demands.	All sublists of a list may have to be searched serially for certain conjunctive queries. Updating more difficult than for multilist. Many of disadvantages of the multilist or the inverted list as the sublist lengths are allowed to grow longer or are kept shorter, respectively.
Cellular multilist	Designed to take advantage of parallel access. Query handling can be enhanced by performing conjunctive operations at the cell level. Relatively easy to update when compared to controlled list-length multilist.	Scattering of secondary index terms yields poor performance. Many of the disadvantages of the multilist.

Table 7-11.1   A summary of the results for secondary access methods. (Continued)

Method	Advantages	Disadvantages
Cellular-serial and cellular-inverted list	Very little index maintenance. Better than cellular multilist if there are only a few records per cell. Bit-encoded index scheme provides fast logical operations on secondary index items at the cell level.	Scattering degrades performance. If there are many records per cell, then access time may be large.

In this section we have equated multikey access with secondary access. To a large degree, this association reflects the state of the art. Undoubtedly in the future, multikey access facilities will be as much a part of the data-management routines provided by the operating system as the primary access methods, such as ISAM and VSAM, are currently. In addition, the development of associative main memories and associative auxiliary memories is certain to play a major role in future multikey access systems.

Exercises for Sec. 7-11

1. Design an algorithm for answering a query of the form "List all items with properties x and y," where x and y are item values for two distinct items in a master file record. If a particular record in the file has these properties, then the value of a third item, say z, is returned. An example query is: "List the names of all patients in the general ward who are taking CRYOL." In this case, "the general ward" and "CRYOL" correspond to x and y, and "the names of all the patients" corresponds to an output z. The algorithm should be designed assuming that the items for x and y each provide secondary access through multilist structures. All assumptions concerning the forms of tables containing the secondary indices should be stated.

2. Answer Exercise 1 assuming inverted lists are used as secondary access methods for the x and y values.

3. Answer Exercise 1 assuming controlled list-length multilists are used as secondary access methods for the x and y values.

4. Answer Exercise 1 assuming cellular-serial access is used for the x and y values.

5. If two multilist structures are involved in a conjunctive query, then we should examine records from the shorter list. Suppose one term of the conjunctive query provides secondary access through an inverted list and a second term provides secondary access through a multilist. What criteria for record selection should we use in this situation?

6. An *involute structure* is a multilist structure in which all item values for secondary index items are removed from the master file and only link fields appear in their place. Figure 7-11.9 illustrates such a structure for the hospital-administration-system example. Discuss the advantages and disadvantages of such a structure.

7. Design a general algorithm for handling a conjunctive query involving n terms (e.g.: "How many items have properties x_1 and x_2 and x_3 and ... and x_n"), assuming all items provide secondary access through an inverted list structure.

Primary Key	Secondary Index Item Link Fields	
Hospitalization Number	Doctor Link	Drug Link
0931762	2066766	1010123
0955128	1967892	null
1010123	7936129	1967892
1967892	3077990	null
2066766	null	8813762
.	.	.
.	.	.
.	.	.

Doctor Index		
Doctor	Link	Length
Brown	0955128	3
Douglas	1010123	2
Hastings	0931762	2
.	.	.
.	.	.
.	.	.

Drug Index		
Drug	Link	Length
COBALT	2066766	2
CRYOL	0955128	1
DETRI	0931762	3
.	.	.
.	.	.
.	.	.

FIGURE 7-11.9   An involute structure.

8. Throughout this section we considered each patient record to have a drug item in which only one drug per patient was accommodated. This is unrealistic, since many patients often receive more than one drug. Discuss the problems associated with treating a repeated field item as a secondary index item. In particular, point out the advantages and disadvantages of using (*a*) a multilist, and (*b*) an inverted list for such an item.

7-12   AN INTRODUCTION TO DATA-BASE SYSTEMS

In Sec. 7-2, the notion of a data base was introduced. A data base was defined as a collection of files used by the application programs for some particular enterprise such that these files exhibit certain associations or relationships at the record level. In this section, we begin by elaborating on some general concepts relating to data base systems and then discuss three approaches which have been adopted in designing systems with large data bases. These are the hierarchical, network, and relational approaches.

7-12.1   General Concepts in Data-base Systems

The definition just given for a data base is sufficient from a structural point of view, but it omits an important property which ideally characterizes systems designed using the "data-base approach." This important property is termed *data independence*, and it can be described as a condition in which the data and the application programs are independent in the sense that either may be changed without changing the other. Hence, for example, application programs can be left unaffected by changes made to the data and the way they are organized.

To provide a clearer understanding of data independence, we can describe how such a term might relate to a manual filing system. Suppose we ask the secretary to retrieve information in the "Albert file." Any changes to the location of the file (i.e., changing the file from drawer A to drawer B), to the internal numbering of the file, or to the number of subfiles created from the main Albert file should not seriously affect the ability to retrieve the desired information. Therefore, the request for information is to a certain degree independent of how that information is stored or organized. However, if data independence is carried to an extreme (e.g., we remove Albert as an index in our filing system and subsume the file's information in a number of other files), then retrieval becomes difficult and time-consuming. We shall see that the degree of data independence which is achievable in a data-base system depends in part on the design approach adopted.

Besides providing some degree of data independence, integrated data-base systems should offer a centralized control operation. This form of operation aids in:

1   Reducing the amount of redundancy in the stored data
2   Promoting data integrity and avoiding problems of data inconsistency, i.e., changing one instance of a fact but leaving other instances of the same fact unchanged
3   Enhancing the sharing of data between users
4   Providing more uniform and effective controls for the security and privacy of user data

Martin [1975] describes in some detail how these goals can be achieved.

Figure 7-12.1 shows the general organization of a data-base system. This figure, as well as much of the terminology adopted in this section, follows that used by Date [1975]. The figure depicts the various levels at which we can view a data-base system. The top level is the user level. A user interacts with the system in a workspace using an application-dependent language. Several classes of users employing several different languages may coexist on one system while using the same data base. Statements in a user language are translated to *data sublanguage expressions*. Sublanguage expressions are then analyzed and retrievals are made from the data base, or modifications may be made on the data base. Examples of data sublanguages will be given later in this section.

To facilitate data independence, a *data model* is created and is administered by a person (or group of persons) called *data-base administrator(s)*. The data model provides a logical view of the stored information. This logical view should be significantly independent of the physical representation of the data. For example, access to a particular record may appear as an associative type of retrieval at the logical level, while the information is stored in a direct file which is really accessible using an address-transformation algorithm. Of course, changing this physical representation to one involving an indexed sequential file does not change the logical view.

Within the data-base system there may be data submodels (i.e., submodels of the data model) which are presented to special sectors of the data-base system community. These submodels provide restrictive views of the total data model, and such views may be necessary for security reasons.

We have already mentioned the very important mapping from the data model to the storage structure of the data base. Usually, this mapping involves the file-access

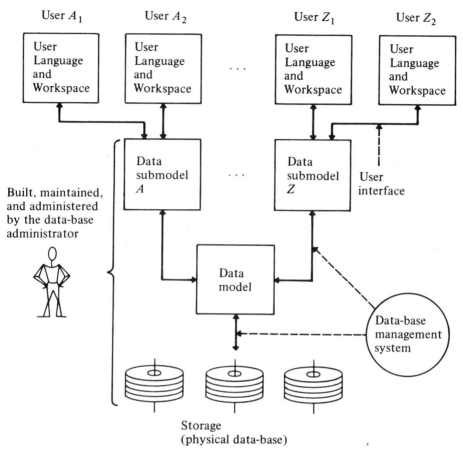

FIGURE 7-12.1 An architecture for a data-base system. Solid arrows refer to mappings which are realized in software.

methods provided by the data-management facilities of the operating system. The software necessary for this mapping, in addition to the software for performing the other mappings viewed in Fig. 7-12.1, constitutes the *data-base management system,* or DBMS.

It should be obvious that the role of data-base administrator is an important one and an elaboration of his or her duties is given in Date [1975]. They include deciding upon the information content of the data base, deciding upon the storage structure, providing liaison with users, defining authorization checks, defining backup and recovery strategies, and monitoring system performance and user behavior.

In the description of each of the three data-base management approaches which follows, we present a data model, describe how information can be accessed using a data sublanguage compatible with the data model, and discuss some of the advantages and disadvantages of the approach. Throughout the discussion, we will use an example based on an application involving the inventory control of parts. This example has been popularized by Codd [1970]. The information items relevant to the example application are:

1	Supplier name		*5*	Part name
2	Supplier number		*6*	Part number
3	Supplier location		*7*	Part size
4	Supplier delivery time		*8*	Supplier's quantity of a part

An instance of a data base which we will work with is shown in Fig. 7-12.2.

7-12.2   Hierarchical Approach

A hierarchical data-base system is a system in which the user views the data base as consisting of trees of segments. These segments may contain several sublevels of segments which culminate at the item level in the information hierarchy. A *segment* is a term due to IBM and it refers to a basic quantum of data which can be manipulated by the data-base management software. Roughly speaking, a segment can be a record or an aggregate of items.

For the data-processing industry has, by tradition, adopted the hierarchical structuring of data, as demonstrated by the acceptance of the COBOL record and PL/I structure. Consequently, most modern data-management systems are hierarchical in nature. IBM's Information Management System (IMS) exemplifies this type of approach.

For the suppliers-parts application, it is possible to structure the information using a hierarchical data model as exhibited in Figs. 7-12.3 and 7-12.4. Figure 7-12.3*a* shows an example data model in which a supplier segment is composed of a number of entities, including a parts segment, and Fig. 7-12.3*b* is an instance of the data model. Figure 7-12.4 depicts another model for the same data base. In this case, PART is the parent segment and SUPPLIER is a subservient segment.

SUPPLIER#	SNAME	DELVRY_TIME	CITY	PART#	PNAME	PSIZE	QTY
S1	Black	2	New York	P1	Nut	3/4	3
S1	Black	2	New York	P2	Bolt	3/4-2	1
S2	Lee	1	Toronto	P5	Spring	2	4
S2	Lee	1	Toronto	P6	Sprocket	4	2
S3	Waters	1	Chicago	P1	Nut	3/4	3
S3	Waters	1	Chicago	P2	Bolt	3/4-2	4
S3	Waters	2	Chicago	P3	Bolt	3/4-1	2
S3	Waters	1	Chicago	P6	Sprocket	4	2
S4	Dyck	3	St. Louis	P4	Screw	1/4-1	6
S5	Jones	1	Montreal	P4	Screw	1/4-1	2
S5	Jones	1	Montreal	P5	Spring	2	5
S5	Jones	1	Montreal	P6	Sprocket	4	4
S6	Whyte	2	Los Angeles	P1	Nut	3/4	3
S6	Whyte	2	Los Angeles	P2	Bolt	3/4-2	1
S6	Whyte	2	Los Angeles	P3	Bolt	3/4-1	2

FIGURE 7-12.2   Data for supplier-part application.

```
1  SUPPLIER,
     2 SUPPLIER#,
     2 SNAME,
     2 DELVRY,
     2 CITY,
     2 PART[N],
        3 PART#,
        3 PNAME,
        3 SIZE,
        3 QTY.
        (a)
```

S1	Black	2	New York	
P1	Nut	3/4	3
P2	Bolt	3/4-2	1

(b)

FIGURE 7-12.3 Data model with SUPPLIER as parent segment.

```
1  PART,
     2 PART#,
     2 PNAME,
     2 SIZE,
     2 SUPPLIER[N],
        3 SUPPLIER#,
        3 SNAME,
        3 DELVRY,
        3 CITY,
        3 QTY.
        (a)
```

P2	Bolt	3/4-2		
S1	Black	2	New York	1
S3	Waters	1	Chicago	4
S6	Whyte	2	Los Angeles	1

(b)

FIGURE 7-12.4 Data model with PART as parent segment.

We now discuss a data sublanguage for accessing information in a hierarchical data base. The language is functionally similar to DL/I, the data sublanguage used in IMS. Table 7-12.1 summarizes the important operations of this sublanguage.

Table 7-12.1 DL/I operations.

Operation	Semantics
GET UNIQUE	Direct retrieval
GET NEXT	Sequential retrieval
GET NEXT WITHIN PARENT	Sequential retrieval under current parent
GET HOLD UNIQUE, GET HOLD NEXT, GET HOLD NEXT WITHIN PARENT	Operations as above, but subsequent DELETE and REPLACE operations can be performed
INSERT	Add new segment
DELETE	Delete existing segment
REPLACE	Replace existing segment

Let us examine how we may answer two queries assuming the data model depicted in Fig. 7-12.4.

Question 1:   Find the supplier numbers for the suppliers who supply part P3:

```
PART_NOT_FOUND = '1'B; /*TRUE*/
GET UNIQUE PART (PART# = 'P3')
               SUPPLIER;
DO WHILE (PART_NOT_FOUND);
    print SUPPLIER# ;
    GET NEXT WITHIN PARENT SUPPLIER;
    IF end of parent segment
    THEN PART_NOT_FOUND = 'O'B; /*FALSE*/
END;
```

Question 2:   Find the part numbers for parts supplied by supplier S2:

```
ALL_PARTS_NOT_FOUND = '1'B; /*TRUE*/
DO WHILE (ALL_PARTS_NOT_FOUND);
    GET NEXT PART;
    IF end of file
    THEN ALL_PARTS_NOT_FOUND = 'O'B; /*FALSE*/
    ELSE DO;
        GET NEXT SUPPLIER (SUPPLIER# = 'S2');
        IF supplier S2 is present
        THEN print PART# ;
    END;
END;
```

Both of the queries are formulated in a high-level language (a "bastardized" PL/I) within which the data sublanguage operations are embedded. The practice of embedding a data sublanguage in a "host" language is not uncommon; for example, both PL/I and COBOL are host languages for DL/I.

It is obvious that the data model as given in Fig. 7-12.4 is much more conducive to the retrieval of the information necessary to answer Question 1 than Question 2. In answering Question 1, it is necessary only to locate the parent segment with a part number of P3 and then to search sequentially the subordinate SUPPLIER segment and print out the SUPPLIER#'s. To answer Question 2, however, it is necessary to access all PART segments, searching each for a supplier segment with a supplier number of S2, which is an extremely time-consuming task.

On the other hand, the data model given in Fig. 7-12.3 facilitates the answering of Question 2, but not Question 1. This illustrates a major problem with the hierarchical approach. Even though the two queries are symmetric, the data sublanguage procedures necessary to answer each question are not symmetric for a given data model. One of the procedures is unnecessarily complex. The user can reduce this complexity by requesting the data administrator to expand one of the data models to include both data models. Such a data model expansion, however, may require the duplicate storage of many data items.

There are additional disadvantages to the hierarchical approach which relate to maintaining the data base. For example, with the data model given in Fig. 7-12.3, we must introduce a dummy part before a new supplier can be introduced. This may not always be desirable. Similarly, in some hierarchical systems, deleting all occurrences of parts for a particular supplier may cause the supplier to be deleted as well. If we change the part size for a particular part, say P2, in the data model given in Fig. 7-12.3, then we must change the size item of every occurrence for that part.

In concluding our introduction to hierarchical data-base systems, we can say that the major advantage of the approach is that it reflects the hierarchical structuring of data that does exist in some "real world" applications. However, because of the strict hierarchical structure that is imposed with this approach, the user must spend time overcoming difficulties which are introduced by the model and are not intrinsic to the questions being posed.

7-12.3　Network Approach

A network data-base system is a system in which the user views the data base as a number of individual record occurrences in which a given node (i.e., item or item aggregate) may have any number of immediate superior or subordinate nodes. By superior node we mean a node which incorporates some given node. A network structure is equated to a graph structure, as discussed in Chap. 5, and differs from a hierarchical structure in that a node is not limited to a maximum of one superior.

With a network structure, it is possible to represent many-to-many relationships (e.g., many suppliers can supply many parts) instead of simply one-to-many relationships (e.g., one supplier supplying many parts, as shown in Fig. 7-12.3, or one part being supplied by many suppliers, as indicated in Fig. 7-12.4). This more general type of relationship is made possible by using link items within records. Figure 7-12.5a shows the general relationship that can exist in a hierarchical data model for the part-supplier application, and Fig. 7-12.5b depicts some instances of the data model as taken from the data in Fig. 7-12.2. The upper-level links on the supplier-part records link the parts and the associated quantity-on-hand for a given supplier. The lower-level links on the supplier-part records indicate the list of suppliers and their associated quantity-on-hand for a given part. The dotted-line segments illustrate that other supplier-part records reside in the chain, if the entire data base as given in Fig. 7-12.2 were to be shown.

Before considering the advantages and disadvantages of this approach, let us examine a data sublanguage which is feasible for retrieving and maintaining a network data base. The data sublanguage we introduce is based on the operations available in the COBOL DML (Data Manipulation Language) as described in CODASYL's DBLTG (Data Base Language Task Group) proposal [1971]. A summary of the important operations is given in Table 7-12.2.

Two important terms appearing in Table 7-12.2 must be elaborated upon. First, the *current occurrence of run-unit* refers to the most recently accessed record in the execution of a program involving the data sublanguage. A *set* is defined in the data model to have a certain record type as its owner and records of another record type (or types) as its members. For example, we can define S-SP to be a set in which the record type SUPPLIER is its owner and the record type SP (supplier part) is its member. A set is an information-carrying entity which defines the links between two record types. The data model as given in Fig. 7-12.5a is not complete, as it lacks any set definitions which describe the linkages

```
1  SUPPLIER,            1  SP,                 1  PART,
   2  SUPPLIER#,           2  SUPPLIER#,          2  PART#,
   2  SNAME,                2  PART#,              2  PNAME,
   2  DELVRY,               2  QTY.               2  SIZE.
   2  CITY.
```

(a)

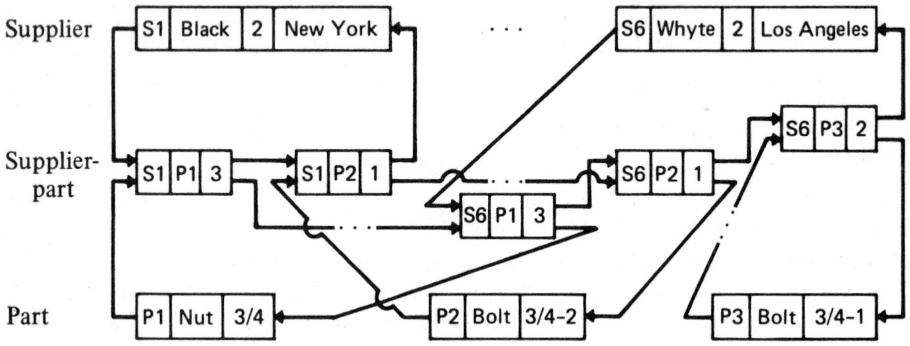

(b)

FIGURE 7-12.5   Network approach. (a) The general data model; (b) instances of the model.

between the record types as are shown in Fig. 7-12.5b. Therefore, to complete the data model we should include set definitions similar to those given in Fig. 7-12.6. The complete data model formed by combining Figs. 7-12.5a and 7-12.6 is sometimes called a *schema* (a term used by the DBLTG). Generically, a schema can be defined as any chart of all the data-item types and record types stored in a data base (Martin [1975]). It should be

Table 7-12.2   Data sublanguage commands for a network data-base system.

Operation	Semantics
FIND	Locates and establishes an existing record occurrence as the current active run-unit
GET	Retrieves the current occurrence of run-unit
STORE	Creates a new record occurrence and establishes it as the current occurrence of run-unit
MODIFY	Updates the current occurrence of run-unit
INSERT	Inserts the current occurrence of run-unit into one or more set occurrences
DELETE	Deletes the current occurrence of run-unit
REMOVE	Removes the current occurrence of run-unit from one or more set occurrences

```
SET   S-SP;
        MODE IS CHAINED;
        ORDER IS SORTED;
        OWNER IS SUPPLIER;
        MEMBER IS SP;
              ASCENDING KEY IS PART# IN SP
                    WITH DUPLICATES NOT ALLOWED;
SET   P-SP;
        MODE IS CHAINED;
        ORDER IS SORTED;
        OWNER IS PART;
        MEMBER IS SP;
              ASCENDING KEY IS SUPPLIER# IN SP
                    WITH DUPLICATES NOT ALLOWED;
```

FIGURE 7-12.6   Set definitions for S-SP and P-SP.

reiterated that the schema definition given only captures the flavor of what is a formally defined notion by the DBLTG, and for an accurate description the reader should check the references cited in the Bibliography.

Let us now return to answer the two questions which were entertained in the previous subsection given the data model (or schema) and the data sublanguage just described.

Question 1:   Find the supplier numbers for the suppliers who supply part P3.

```
          MOVE 'P3' TO PART# IN PART.
          FIND PART RECORD.
          FIND FIRST SP RECORD OF P-SP SET.
          IF ERROR-STATUS = 0307 (end of set occurrence) GO TO ENDING.
AGAIN.    GET SP.
          (add SUPPLIER# in SP to list of supplier numbers)
          FIND NEXT SP RECORD OF P-SP SET.
          IF ERROR-STATUS = 0307 (end of set occurrence) GO TO ENDING.
          GO TO AGAIN.
ENDING.   ...
```

Question 2:   Find the part numbers for parts supplied by supplier S2.

```
          MOVE 'S2' TO SUPPLIER# IN SUPPLIER.
          FIND SUPPLIER RECORD.
          FIND FIRST SP RECORD OF S-SP SET.
          IF ERROR-STATUS = 0307 (end of set occurrence) GO TO ENDING.
AGAIN.    GET SP.
          (add PART# in SP to list of part numbers)
          FIND NEXT SP RECORD OF S-SP SET.
          IF ERROR-STATUS = 0307 (end of set occurrence) GO TO ENDING.
          GO TO AGAIN.
ENDING.   ...
```

The answers to the questions are formulated in the data sublanguage which is embedded in a COBOL-like host language. For example, the MOVE instruction constitutes an assignment in COBOL.

It should be obvious that these programs are completely symmetric and therefore reflect the symmetry of the two questions. Hence, the major disadvantage with the hierarchical approach is avoided. This symmetry can be realized without duplicating large quantities of data (only SUPPLIER# and PART# are duplicated). Notice also that we can add a new supplier, say S7, without having to generate dummy part information. Initially, there are no links for the new supplier; its chain consists of a single pointer from the SUPPLIER record to itself. We can delete all parts for a supplier without deleting the supplier, and an update to the size of a particular part involves only one change—namely, to the SIZE item in the PART record.

Probably the major disadvantage with the network approach is the necessity to describe the relationships which exist between records using chains. As we have seen earlier in the text, a link is very much a storage-structure concept, and therefore it can be argued that the network model is partly a storage-structure model. There is thus a danger that the user will become locked into a particular storage structure (Date [1975]). This is contrary to the aim of data independence.

7-12.4   Relational Approach

The relational data-base system can best be described as a system in which the user views the data base as a number of interrelated "flat" files or tables. Figure 7-12.2, for example, depicts the data base as one large table in which the combined items of SUPPLIER# and PART# uniquely identify a row within the table.

The relational approach has its basis in a mathematical theory of relations. The term *relation* can be defined as follows. Given the sets $D_1, D_2, \ldots, D_n$ (not necessarily mutually distinct), R is a relation on these sets if it is a set of ordered n-tuples $<d_1, d_2, \ldots, d_n>$ such that d_1 belongs to D_1, d_2 belongs to D_2, ..., and d_n belongs to D_n, where the sets $D_1, D_2, \ldots, D_n$ are called the *domains* of R. R is said to be a relation of degree n.

Some important properties are associated with a table that represents a relation in the data base:

1 No two rows (i.e., n-tuples) can be identical.
2 The ordering of these rows is insignificant.
3 The ordering of the columns is insignificant.

Usually, the primary key of a relation is denoted by underlining it and placing it in the first column of the table. In some instances, however (such as in Fig. 7-12.2), the primary key may involve more than one domain and hence cannot appear in the first column.

A final important property of a relation is that each data item in its domain should be atomic (i.e., nondecomposable, such as an integer or character string). When this property along with the previous three holds, the relation is called *normalized*. A normalized relation is also said to be in the *first normal form* (1NF), which is a notation due to Codd [1972].

Two problems exist when using a first-normal-form relation. One is the apparent redundancy of data (e.g., how many times does 'S3' appear?). Of course, updating a particular nonkey item such as CITY constitutes a major search effort on a large data base in order to guarantee that all occurrences of CITY for a particular supplier are altered. The second, and potentially more serious problem, relates to certain nonfully functional dependencies which are allowed to exist in a 1NF relation.

We say that domain Y is *functionally dependent* on domain X, where X and Y are domains of a relation R, if and only if each X value has associated with it only one Y value at any one time. For example, SNAME is functionally dependent on SUPPLIER#. A domain Y is *fully functionally dependent* on domain X if it is functionally dependent on X and not functionally dependent on any subset of X (where X can be a composite domain). For example, QTY is fully functionally dependent on the combined domains PART#-SUPPLIER#; however, CITY is not fully functionally dependent on PART#-SUPPLIER# because it is functionally dependent on SUPPLIER#, but not PART#. Figure 7-12.7 illustrates these functional dependencies.

Because not all domains in the relation shown in Fig. 7-12.2 are fully functionally dependent upon the combined key domains of PART#-SUPPLIER#, some restrictions arise when maintaining our data base. First, we cannot add the fact that a particular supplier is located in a particular city with a particular delivery time, until that supplier is able to supply at least one part. The addition cannot be made because no appropriate primary key exists. Similarly, if we delete all occurrences of parts for a supplier, we must delete the supplier information, since no primary key with that supplier number will remain.

To alleviate these anomalies, Codd [1972] suggests the formulation of relations in *second normal form* (2NF). A normalized relation R is in 2NF if and only if the nonkey domains of R are fully functionally dependent on the primary key of R. A breakdown of our original data base, as given in Fig. 7-12.1, into three 2NF relations is shown in Fig. 7-12.8a and the functional dependencies which exist for these new relations are depicted in Fig. 7-12.8b.

An obvious question involving the definition of 2NF concerns the restriction that full functional dependency should exist between nonkey and primary key domains only. What about functional dependencies which exist between nonkey domains? Can problems arise if such functional dependencies exist? Let us alter in Fig. 7-12.8a the DELVRY_TIME item value for P3, as supplied by S3, to 1 in place of 2. Then, it may be argued that the nonkey item DELVRY_TIME is functionally dependent on the primary key item SUPPLIER# only and the SUPPLIER relation can be augmented to include the DELVRY_TIME item, as shown in Fig. 7-12.9a. Of course the DELVRY_TIME item should be removed from the SUPPLIER-PART relation. Also, note that DELVRY_TIME is now dependent on

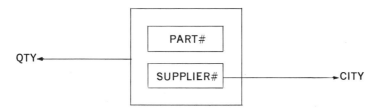

FIGURE 7-12.7 Functional dependencies in supplier-part application.

Supplier relation

SUPPLIER#	SNAME	CITY
S1	Black	New York
S2	Lee	Toronto
S3	Waters	Chicago
S4	Dyck	St. Louis
S5	Jones	Montreal
S6	Whyte	Los Angeles

SP relation

SUPPLIER#	PART#	QTY	DELVRY_TIME
S1	P1	3	2
S1	P2	1	2
S2	P5	4	1
S2	P6	2	1
S3	P1	3	1
S3	P2	4	1
S3	P3	2	2
S3	P6	2	1
S4	P4	6	3
S5	P4	2	1
S5	P5	5	1
S5	P6	4	1
S6	P1	3	2
S6	P2	1	2
S6	P3	2	2

Part Relation

PART#	PNAME	PSIZE
P1	Nut	3/4
P2	Bolt	3/4-2
P3	Bolt	3/4-1
P4	Screw	1/4-1
P5	Spring	2
P6	Sprocket	4

(a)

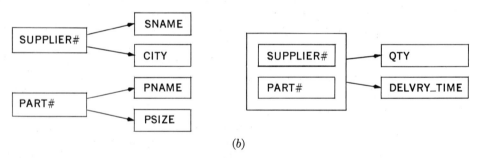

(b)

FIGURE 7-12.8   Formulation of supplier-part data base in 2NF. (a) The data base; (b) functional dependencies within the data base.

CITY and we have a functional dependency between two nonkey items. It may be desirable to express this new dependency apart from a **SUPPLIER#**. That is, if it is known that a new supplier is going to supply parts from **VANCOUVER** and the **DELVRY_TIME** for this city is 3, then we should be able to express this relationship in the system prior to knowing the new supplier's name or number. Figure 7-12.9b exhibits such a breakdown of the supplier relation shown in 7-12.9a.

Codd [1972] recognized the problems associated with recognizing nonkey dependencies and suggested a third normal form for a relation. A normalized relation R is said to be in *third normal form* (3NF) if and only if the nonkey domains of R are (1) mutually independent and (2) functionally dependent in the primary key of R. Nonkey items are *mutually independent* if no functional dependencies exist between them. Therefore, the relations in Figs. 7-12.8a and 7-12.9b are in 3NF, while the relation in Fig. 7-12.9a is in 2NF, but not in 3NF. Because of the manner in which we have defined the normal form, it can

Supplier relation

SUPPLIER#	SNAME	CITY	DELVRY_TIME
S1	Black	New York	2
S2	Lee	Toronto	1
S3	Waters	Chicago	1
S4	Dyck	St. Louis	3
S5	Jones	Montreal	1
S6	Whyte	Los Angeles	2

(a)

Supplier relation

SUPPLIER#	SNAME	CITY
S1	Black	New York
S2	Lee	Toronto
S3	Waters	Chicago
S4	Dyck	St. Louis
S5	Jones	Montreal
S6	Whyte	Los Angeles

Delivery relation

CITY	DELVRY_TIME
New York	2
Toronto	1
Chicago	2
St. Louis	3
Montreal	1
Los Angeles	2
Vancouver	3

(b)

FIGURE 7-12.9 New SUPPLIER relations generated by considering the DELVRY_TIME to be functionally dependent on the CITY.

be concluded that any relation that is in 3NF is in 2NF and 1NF, and any relation in 2NF is also in 1NF, and a hierarchy of normal forms is created.

Let us now look at a data sublanguage for the relational approach. Two types of languages have been formulated: the *relational algebra* (Codd [1972]) and the *relational calculus* (Codd [1972]). We examine only the relational calculus here. The relational calculus is a nonprocedural notation based on predicate calculus statements. (See Tremblay and Manohar [1975] for a discussion of the predicate calculus.) These statements involve the quantifiers "there exists" and "for all." Let us introduce the language by giving a number of examples assuming the 3NF relations in Fig. 7-12.8a. First, we answer the two questions posed earlier in the section.

Question 1:   Find the supplier numbers for the suppliers who supply part P3.

{SP.SUPPLIER#:   SP.PART# ='P3'}

Therefore, it is stated that we want to retrieve the SUPPLIER# values from the SP relation which are such that the associated PART# value is P3. The expression on the left of the colon indicates what is to be retrieved, the colon reads "such that," and the expression on the right is the predicate, which if satisfied returns the corresponding information as dictated by the left side.

Question 2:   Find the part numbers for parts supplied by supplier S2.

{SP.PART#:   SP.SUPPLIER# ='S2'}

This statement is symmetric with that given in answer to Question 1. Some other more complicated queries can be easily formulated in the relational calculus. For example,

Question 3:   For each supplier, find part numbers and supplier's cities from which the parts may be obtained.

{(SP.PART#,SUPPLIER.CITY):   SP.SUPPLIER# = SUPPLIER.SUPPLIER# }

Question 4:   Find the supplier numbers for suppliers who are from Toronto or Montreal and who supply a part of size 3/4.

{SP.SUPPLIER# :∃PART∃SUPPLIER(PART.SIZE ='3/4'∧PART.PART# =

SP.PART# ∧SP.SUPPLIER# = SUPPLIER.SUPPLIER# ∧(SUPPLIER.CITY =

'TORONTO'∨SUPPLIER.CITY ='MONTREAL'))}

Question 4 demonstrates that the queries can become quite complicated. Try formulating the same query in the hierarchical or network-system data sublanguages!

Because the relational calculus is nonprocedural (i.e., no step-by-step specification is given), we have not shown the underlying operations necessary for the manipulation and retrieval of information from the relations. Set algebraic operations such as joins, projections, and divisions are required and these are part of the relational algebraic approach. A detailed discussion of these operations is outside the scope of this text, but may be found in Date [1975].

7-12.5   Summary

One of the major points that can be made in this section is that a data-base system consists of data entities and a description of the relationships between these entities. In the hierarchical approach, these relationships are implicitly bound by the relative positions of the data entities or segments in the record definition. For example, a part may be a subordinate or superior entity to a supplier, depending on how the data model is defined.

In the network approach, relationships are exhibited explicitly by means of links. A data entity is subordinate, superior, or nonrelated to another entity, depending on the presence or absence of a pointer.

In the relational approach, relationships are also represented explicitly; however, the relationships and the data entities themselves both appear in relations (i.e., both are considered to be the same type of object). Hence, it is possible to provide a uniform look for the data base (i.e., both the entities and relationships) without considering storage and access details such as parent nodes or pointers.

Which approach is superior is not of significant importance in this text at this time—all approaches have been and will be used. What is important is that the wide variety of data structures and their associated storage representations that we have discussed in the text are very pertinent to the area of data-base systems. Even from this brief introduction to data-base systems, it is obvious how relevant the data structures such as trees, graphs, and associative structures (along with the many file structures) are to an understanding of data-base systems. Indeed, the text provides a sound basis for further study in this relatively new and expanding area.

BIBLIOGRAPHY

ABRAMSON, N.: "Information Theory and Coding," McGraw-Hill Book Company, New York, 1963.

BENSOUSSAN, A.: Overview of the Locking Strategy in the File System, "Multics Systems Programmers Manual," Section B.G. 19.00, November, 1969, pp. 1–10.

BUCHHOLZ, WERNER: File Organization and Addressing, *IBM Systems Journal*, vol. 2, June, 1963, pp. 86–110.

"CODASYL Data Description Language Committee," *Journal of Development*, June, 1973.

CODD, E. F.: A Relational Model of Data for Large Data Banks, *Communications of the ACM*, vol. 13, no. 6, 1970, pp. 377–387.

CODD, E. F.: Further Normalization of the Data Base Relational Model, *Data Base Systems*, Courant Computer Science Symposia Series, vol. 6, Prentice-Hall, Englewood Cliffs, N.J., 1972.

"Data Base Task Group of CODASYL Programming Language Committee Report," April, 1971. (Available from ACM.)

DATE, C. J.: "An Introduction to Database Systems," Addison Wesley Publishing Company, Reading, Mass., 1975.

DEUTSCHER, R. F., P. G. SORENSON, and J. P. TREMBLAY: Distribution Dependent Hashing Functions and Their Characteristics, *Proceedings of the International Conference of the Management of Data, ACM/SIGMOD*, May 14–15, 1975, San Jose, pp. 224–236.

FOTHERINGHAM, J.: Dynamic Storage Allocation in the Atlas Computer, Including an Automatic Use of Backing Store, *Communications of the ACM*, vol. 4, October, 1961, pp. 435–436.

GRIES, D. E.: "Compiler Construction for Digital Computers," John Wiley and Sons, Inc., New York, 1971.

HUGHES, J. K.: "PL/I Programming," John Wiley & Sons, New York, 1973.

"IBM System/360 Operating System PL/I(F) Language Reference Manual," IBM Form No. GC28-8201.

"IBM System/360 Operating System PL/I(F) Programmer's Guide," IBM Form No. GC28-6594.

"Information Management System/360 Version 2 General Information Manual," IBM Form No. GH20-0705.

"Information Management System/360 Version 2 Utilities Reference Manual," IBM Form No. SH20-0915

"Introducing the IBM 3600 Finance Communication System," IBM Form No. GA27-2764.

KINDRED, A. R.: "Data Systems and Management," Prentice-Hall, Englewood Cliffs, N.J., 1973.

KNUTH, D. E.: "The Art of Computer Programming, vol. 3, Searching and Sorting," Addison-Wesley Publishing Company, Reading, Mass., 1973.

LEFKOVITZ, D.: "File Structures for On-line Systems," Spartan Books, New York, 1969.

LONDON, K. R.: "Techniques for Direct Access," Auerbach Publishers, Philadelphia, 1973.

LUM, V. Y.: General Performance Analysis of Key-to-Address Transformation Methods Using an Abstract File Concept, *Communications of the ACM*, vol. 16, no. 10, 1973, pp. 603–612.

LUM, V. Y., P. S. T. YUEN, and M. DODD: Key-to-Address Transform Techniques: A Fundamental Performance Study on Large Existing Formatted Files, *Communications of the ACM*, vol. 14, no. 4, 1971, pp. 228–239.

MACKENZIE, F. B.: Automated Secondary Storage Management, *Datamation 11*, 1965, pp. 24–28.

MADNICK, S. E. and J. J. DONOVAN: "Operating Systems," McGraw-Hill Book Company, New York, 1974.

MARTIN, J.: "Computer Data-Base Organization," Prentice-Hall, Englewood Cliffs, N.J., 1975.

MEADOWS, C. T.: "The Analysis of Information Systems," 2d ed., Melville Publishing, Los Angeles, 1973.

MULLIN, J. K.: An Improved Indexed Sequential Access Method Using Hashed Overflow, *Communications of the ACM*, vol. 15, no. 5, May, 1972, pp. 301–307.

"OS/VS Virtual Storage Access Method (VSAM) Planning Guide," IBM Form No. GC26-3799.

"PDP-11 Peripherals Handbook," Digital Equipment Corporation, 1975.

PHILIPPAKIS, A. S. and L. J. KAZMIER: "Information Systems Through COBOL," McGraw-Hill Book Company, New York, 1974.

"Reference Manual for IBM 3330 Series Disk Storage," IBM Form No. GA26-1615.

"SCOPE Indexed Sequential System," Control Data Corporation, CDC-60305400A

SHAW, A. C.: "The Logical Design of Operating Systems," Prentice-Hall, Englewood Cliffs, N.J., 1974.

TREMBLAY, J. P., and R. P. MANOHAR: "Discrete Mathematical Structures with Applications to Computer Science," McGraw-Hill Book Company, New York, 1975.

TSICHRITZIS, D. C., and P. A. BERNSTEIN: "Operating Systems," Academic Press, New York, 1974.

WEINBERG, G. M.: "PL/I Programming: A Manual of Style," McGraw-Hill Book Company, New York, 1970.